Metaphysics
and the Future of Theology

Princeton Theological Monograph Series

K. C. Hanson, Charles M. Collier, and D. Christopher Spinks,
Series Editors

Recent volumes in the series:

Eliseo Pérez-Álvarez
A Vexing Gadfly: The Late Kierkegaard on Economic Matters

Gale Heide
System and Story: Narrative Critique and Construction in Theology

Todd B. Pokrifka
*Redescribing God: The Roles of Scripture, Tradition, and Reason
in Karl Barth's Doctrines of Divine Unity, Constancy, and Eternity*

Roger A. Johnson
*Peacemaking and Religious Violence: From Thomas Aquinas
to Thomas Jefferson*

Jeff B. Pool
*God's Wounds: Hermeneutic of the Christian Symbol
of Divine Suffering, Volume Two: Evil and Divine Suffering*

Joel Burnell
*Poetry, Providence, and Patriotism: Polish Messianism in Dialogue
with Dietrich Bonhoeffer*

Poul F. Guttesen
*Leaning Into the Future: The Kingdom of God in the Theology
of Jürgen Moltmann and the Book of Revelation*

Ilsup Ahn
*Position and Responsibility: Jürgen Habermas, Reinhold Niebuhr,
and the Co-Reconstruction of the Positional Imperative*

Metaphysics and the Future of Theology

The Voice of Theology in Public Life

WILLIAM J. MEYER

Foreword by Schubert M. Ogden

☙PICKWICK *Publications* • Eugene, Oregon

METAPHYSICS AND THE FUTURE OF THEOLOGY
The Voice of Theology in Public Life

Princeton Theological Monograph Series 126

Copyright © 2010 William J. Meyer. All rights reserved. Except for brief quotations in critical publications or reviews, no part of this book may be reproduced in any manner without prior written permission from the publisher. Write: Permissions, Wipf and Stock Publishers, 199 W. 8th Ave., Suite 3, Eugene, OR 97401.

Pickwick Publications
An Imprint of Wipf and Stock Publishers
199 W. 8th Ave., Suite 3
Eugene, OR 97401

www.wipfandstock.com

ISBN 13: 978-1-60608-322-2

Cataloging-in-Publication data

Meyer, William J.

Metaphysics and the future of theology : the voice of theology in public life / William J. Meyer ; with a foreword by Schubert M. Ogden.

xvi + 610 p. ; 23 cm. —Includes bibliographical references and index.

Princeton Theological Monograph Series 126

ISBN 13: 978-1-60608-322-2

1. Metaphysics. 2. Christianity and culture 3. Gustafson, James M. — Chriticism and interpretation. 4. Niebuhr, Reinhold, 1892–1971. 5. Hauerwas, Stanley, 1940–. 6. Milbank, John. I. Ogden, Schubert M. II. Title. III. Series.

BD215 .M44 2010

Manufactured in the U.S.A.

In loving memory of my father

N. A. "Bim" Meyer

and my mentor

Edmund F. Perry

with abiding gratitude
for all that they taught me
and contributed to my life

Contents

Foreword by Schubert M. Ogden / *ix*

Preface / *xi*

List of Abbreviations / *xv*

Introduction: Modernity and the Marginalization of Theology / 1

PART ONE: Defining the Problem: Diagnostic and Prescriptive Accounts

1. Diagnosing the Plight of Theology in the Modern World / 19

2. Reconsidering the Metaphysical Enterprise / 88

3. Intermediate Reflections / 152

PART TWO: A Typological Analysis: A Study of Six Theological Approaches

4. Defining the Terms of Analysis / 211

5. An Accountable Theology: The Approach of James Gustafson / 228

6. A Pragmatic Theology: The Approach of Reinhold Niebuhr / 255

7. A Witness Theology: The Approach of Stanley Hauerwas / 294

8. A Tradition-Engaged Theology: The Approach of Jean Porter / 341

9. A Radical-Orthodox Theology: The Approach of John Milbank / 407

10. A Transcendental-Process Theology: The Approach of Franklin Gamwell / 483

Conclusion: The Future of Theology and the Academy / 556

Bibliography / 597

Foreword

WILLIAM MEYER HAS WRITTEN AN IMPORTANT BOOK, AND I AM HONored by his invitation to introduce it to his readers. His book is important because, if the lessons it teaches, by example as well as precept, were to be learned and taken to heart by his fellow theologians generally, the future of theology would be a good deal brighter than it is.

Foremost among these lessons, as indicated by the book's title, is its thesis: that theology's future is dependent on metaphysics, and on it itself becoming forthrightly metaphysical, if only in a new, revisionary way. If theology, as Meyer holds, is "systematic reflection on and critical assessment of the meaning and truth of religious claims"; and if he is right that the foundational religious claim for the reality and necessity of God either is, logically, a metaphysical claim or necessarily implies such, then the only way theology can be itself is to argue metaphysically for the intelligibility and credibility of the foundational religious claim. Meyer allows, of course, that the claim to be meaningful and true is not the only claim to validity that religions characteristically make or imply, and that any theology of a specific religion such as Christian theology must be particularly concerned to validate its religion's claim to be appropriate to its own explicit authorizing source. But Meyer never wavers in his insistence that theology, like the religion on which it critically reflects, is ever concerned, finally, with the truth about things as they ultimately are and therefore cannot be itself—or, in terms of his own metaphor, cannot find its voice—unless it is straightforwardly metaphysical in making its case.

And this is all the more so, he reasons, in our situation today. Given the "formal commitments," as distinct from the "substantive conclusions," of modernity, no appeal to authority, whether religious or secular, can any longer suffice to determine what is ultimately true. But, then, the metaphysical claims expressed or implied by religion cannot be critically validated as meaningful and true by the merely consuetudinary criteria of special revelations, traditions, and institutions, but only by the ultimate criteria of common human experience and reason as they require to be differentiated in order to apply to claims of this logical type. And this means, in practice, only by developing an independent metaphysics that can withstand critical judgment by just such ultimate criteria. Meyer leaves no doubt, however, that the metaphysics indicated must be, in several respects, new and significantly different from any of the metaphysics of the philosophical and theological traditions. Not only will it have to dissociate itself from certain formal errors that have long since been rightly pointed out by critics of traditional metaphysical thinking, but it will also have to be "neoclassical," instead of "classical," in its material understanding of God and of ultimate reality generally.

But if Meyer's book is important, first and foremost, because of its thesis, it is also importantly instructive because of the masterful way in which he makes his case. His thesis is, in effect, his prescription for solving the problem of theology's future. But a large part of his book, significantly, is devoted to a painstaking diagnosis of the problem itself. And in it, as in his argument for a solution, he proceeds in the eminently rational way of trying to think effectively not only with his own mind but also with the minds of others—as well as of offering his thoughts to them and to all the rest of us in writing that is enviably clear and consistent and therefore facilitates return criticism. In other words, he proceeds throughout critically as well as constructively, learning as much as possible from those who have already thought and written on the same problem—as well as on different ways of possibly solving it. Neither conveniently ignoring views that challenge his own nor presuming to criticize them, negatively or positively, without having first carefully analyzed and interpreted their meaning, he builds an indefinitely stronger case, the while educating his readers on the larger discussion of the problem as well as on the strengths and weaknesses of a wide range of alternatives for analyzing and trying to solve it.

In sum: William Meyer has written an important book because he has written a good book—a book that in its *how* as in its *what* anticipates the future of theology for which some of us continue to hope. I congratulate him on his achievement and commend it to his readers accordingly.

Schubert M. Ogden

Preface

THIS BOOK SEEKS TO ADDRESS THREE OVERARCHING QUESTIONS: FIRST, why has theology lost its public voice in modern culture? Second, why do we have such difficulty addressing religious claims seriously in public? And, third, how can we be both fully modern and fully religious in an integrated way? Though I focus mainly on the first question, I seek to address the other two by implication if not always by explicit attention. For the answers to all three questions, I submit, relate at some level to the underlying issue of metaphysics. By "metaphysics," I mean the rational or philosophical attempt to understand and express the ultimate character of reality. The question of God, which lies at the heart of theology, is at root a metaphysical question. To speak of the reality of God is finally to make a metaphysical claim about the ultimate character of existence. Modern thought, however, including much of theology, has been decidedly anti- or postmetaphysical. That is, modern thought has widely held that metaphysical claims cannot be rationally validated or redeemed; thus it has tended to reject, dismiss, ignore, or privatize such claims. Given this postmetaphysical mindset, it is no wonder that theology has been marginalized in the modern academy and culture, that we have difficulty genuinely engaging the claims of religion in public life, and that we find it nearly impossible to be both fully modern and religious in an integrated fashion. I seek to show how the absence of metaphysics in modern thought has been a major cause of theology's marginalization by undercutting its ability to make a public case for the reality and necessity of God. What is needed is not a return to a medieval metaphysic, such as offered by Thomas Aquinas, but rather a fresh engagement with the metaphysical enterprise, such as offered by the modern process thought of Alfred North Whitehead and Charles Hartshorne. A process metaphysical theology, I argue, can make the needed case for the reality of God within the modern context and, thus, such a theology can help us to be both fully modern and religious in an integrated way.

To live with integrity requires that we live integrated lives; yet, that is what the absence of metaphysics ultimately inhibits us from doing. In a postmetaphysical setting, we cannot fully address or publicly engage our ultimate claims and convictions about the character, meaning, and value of existence. Instead, we tend either to privatize such claims or to publicly impose them through some appeal to authority and tradition. By advancing a modern metaphysical theology, I seek to affirm the way of integrity while affirming a pluralistic and democratic culture. We live, finally, in one world. Hence, the various truths that inform our lives must cohere in some integrated fashion. For too long we have assumed that the only viable options on the global stage are either to privatize religion or to impose it by appealing to the authority of tradition. The world of the twenty-first century demands fresh thinking on this critical matter; it demands reexamining long-held philosophical and theological assumptions that have defined our intellectual and cultural terrain. Based on such a critical reexamination, I contend that we must distinguish between modernity's formal commitments and its predominant substantive conclusions, for only such a distinction will enable us to seriously address and rationally redeem the metaphysical claims of religion within public discourse.

Speaking of his acclaimed work *The Invention of Autonomy*, the philosopher J. B. Schneewind jestingly remarked that he might not have undertaken it if he had known how long it would take to complete. At some point, he reflected, it just "seemed too late to stop" (xiii). I can identify with that sentiment; I began writing this book in the fall of 2000, when Bill Clinton was still the U.S. President. Given the events of September 11, 2001 and the intervening history of domestic and international affairs, the world has dramatically changed since I began typing away nearly a decade ago. Nine years in the writing, this book has been gestating even much longer. In many ways, the origin of this project goes back to my initial studies of Reinhold Niebuhr in the 1980s at the University of Edinburgh in Scotland. Given my abiding interests in religion, politics, ethics, and philosophy, I have long sought to conceive how we could genuinely address and civilly engage our deepest convictions and ultimate truth claims in public discourse. This work seeks to contribute to that important conversation.

Many people have generously helped me along the way. First, I am grateful to Jennifer Herdt, Timothy Beach-Verhey, Lois Malcolm, and Franklin Gamwell who read a complete earlier draft of the manuscript and who came to Maryville at the start of 2008 for a two-day working colloquium to offer me their feedback. I appreciate their time, effort, and insights. I also want to thank my former colleague and friend Stephen Soud who copyedited much of that draft and who gave me needed encouragement a decade ago to undertake this project. I am grateful to my former Dean, Robert Naylor, and to our Maryville College President, Gerald Gibson, for funding the aforementioned colloquium. I thank them also for my sabbatical leave during the winter and spring of 2008, which enabled me to revise the manuscript. I owe a debt of gratitude to my former Humanities Division Chair, Susan Schneibel, and to my new Chair, Peggy Cowan, for their ongoing support of my work. Without their cooperative assistance, I would not have been able to protect the time needed to pursue and complete this long-term endeavor. Among my colleagues, I want to offer special thanks to Sam Overstreet and Andrew Irvine for their timely assistance. I am grateful to my students in philosophy and religion who have helped me over the years to clarify significant questions, to glean insights from relevant texts, and to refine my understanding of important thinkers.

The first chapters of this manuscript were drafted in the main library at the Webb School of Knoxville. I want to thank Director Tena Litherland and her staff and Webb President Scott Hutchinson for providing me a quiet and conducive place to write while my son was beginning kindergarten there. On the other end of the process, I want to thank my editor Charlie Collier for guiding me through the final stages of publication and to express my profound appreciation to Schubert Ogden for his valuable feedback on the penultimate draft of the manuscript and for the honor and contribution of his foreword. In between, I am grateful for the unfailing support of family and friends, such as the Kuehls and especially Greg Good—whose logistical mind helped me to resolve a key issue regarding the book's organization. Most of all, I owe my deepest gratitude to my wife Cindy and to our son Robert Edmund, without whose abiding love, encouragement, patience, and good humor I would not have been able to bring this work to fruition. Finally,

I dedicate this book in memory of my father, Bim Meyer, and in memory of my undergraduate teacher and mentor at Northwestern University, Edmund Perry. I am forever grateful for all that they contributed to my life.

William J. Meyer
Maryville, Tennessee
April 2009

Abbreviations

James Gustafson
Ethics   *Ethics from a Theocentric Perspective* (2 volumes)

Immanuel Kant
TOPB   *The One Possible Basis for a Demonstration of the Existence of God*

Alasdair MacIntyre
DCB   *Difficulties in Christian Belief*
TRV   *Three Rival Versions of Moral Enquiry*
WJWR   *Whose Justice? Which Rationality?*

Introduction

Modernity and the Marginalization of Theology

> In this process there is no stopping; the greater the number of men to whom the treasures of knowledge become accessible, the more widespread is the falling-away from religious belief—at first only from its obsolete and objectionable trappings, but later from its fundamental postulates as well.
>
> —Sigmund Freud, *The Future of an Illusion*, 1927

> But the change in the social center of gravity of religion has gone on so steadily and is now so generally accomplished that it has faded from the thought of most persons.
>
> —John Dewey, *A Common Faith*, 1933

LOOKING BACK FROM THE PERSPECTIVE OF THE TWENTY-FIRST CENtury, the secularization thesis appears at best ambiguous. For in a world seemingly awash in religion, the assertion that religion would gradually fade from the stage of human affairs seems rather naive. Indeed, as one commentator observes, "Religion is no longer the opiate of the masses; we now have religion on speed!"[1] Yet if the secularization thesis was mistaken concerning the overall influence of religion, it appears to have been at least partly correct with regard to the marginalization of theology. By "theology" I mean systematic reflection on and critical assessment of the meaning and truth of religious claims. If theology was the queen of the sciences in the medieval context, it is at best a neglected stepchild in the modern framework; if it was then at the center of intellectual and university life, it is now at the periphery. Thus, at

---

1. Akbar Ahmed, a scholar of Islam, interviewed by Terry Gross, *Fresh Air*, NPR, October 10, 2006.

the same time that religion has increased its influence on and visible presence in the contemporary world, theology has remained a muted voice on the sidelines of the cultural conversation. What this combination translates into, one might say, is the increasing ascendancy of an uncritical and untutored religious voice in society. Or as one historian and cultural observer sharply puts it, this combination marks "the day the Enlightenment went out."[2]

This pointed description signals the tension between modernity and the role of religion in public life. Put simply, the modern world has never figured out how to address religious claims seriously in public. I will argue that the resolution of this deep-seated problem requires distinguishing between modernity's *formal commitments* and its predominant *substantive conclusions*. In order to begin to clarify and move toward this critical distinction, let us commence by examining an important related distinction.

In the modern public square, one tends to find religion on one side, a secularistic outlook on the other, and the notion of the secular or secularity in between. This middle set of terms is meant to indicate a modern commitment to reason and experience, rather than to authority and tradition, as the grounds for adjudicating truth claims and other claims to validity. What is significant here is that there is an important but often overlooked distinction between *secular* and *secularistic*, and between *secularity* and *secularism*. In each case, the former term (secular/secularity) is meant to indicate a *formal* commitment to how differing claims ought be assessed, namely, by appeal to human reason and common experience rather than by appeal to the authority of church, tradition, or political position. By contrast, the latter term (secularistic/secularism) indicates a *substantive* outlook that denies the validity of religious claims per se, such as claims about the reality of God. In short, secularism is a substantive worldview—a secularistic outlook is one that denies any source of transcendent meaning. By contrast, secularity is a formal approach for resolving disputed claims that is explicitly neutral between theism and secularism. Hence, the modern affirmation of a secular state need not mean an affirmation of a secularistic society;

---

2. Wills, "Day the Enlightenment Went Out." For his detailed account, see *Head and Heart*. For a discussion of the widespread religiosity and religious rhetoric in American culture coupled with the widespread lack of religious literacy, see Prothero, "Worshipping in Ignorance" and *Religious Literacy*.

in fact, one might have a fully secular state informed by a vital religious culture. In that event, the task is to be both fully modern and fully religious at the same time.³

Yet this is not how things have generally turned out. Instead, the modern world—and what some would now call the postmodern world—has often been defined by a polarity between an appeal to religious authority and tradition on one side, and a secularistic outlook on the other. Notably, both sides are inclined to assume that one cannot be both fully modern and fully religious in an integrated manner. Relatedly, both sides tend to blur the distinction between secular and secularistic, between secularity and secularism. For example, literary and social critic Stanley Fish equates the secular character of modern liberalism and secularism as being "one and the same." Similarly, another writer, who only needed to affirm the secularity of American politics to make her point, unhelpfully entitled her essay: "One Nation, Under Secularism."⁴

In the midst of this kind of blurring confusion, the common response of those who seek to affirm modern secularity is to insist on the privatization of religion, that is, on keeping religion out of public and political life. The unstated assumption here is that religious claims are intrinsically authoritarian or heteronomous and thus cannot abide by the canons of public reason or secularity. For instance, in the 2000 U.S. Presidential campaign, the Democratic Vice-Presidential nominee invoked George Washington's farewell admonition to "never indulge the supposition 'that morality can be maintained without religion.'" In sharp response, however, others quickly counseled that "religious belief, privately held, may well be good for democracy. . . . [But] its politicization [or public influence] is not." Likewise, after the events of September 11, 2001, novelist Salman Rushdie argued that "the restoration of re-

---

3. For this important distinction between "secular" and "secularistic," see Ogden, *Reality of God*, 6–12. Charles Taylor, in his massive and important book *A Secular Age*, does not clearly and consistently distinguish between secular and secularistic, secularity and secularism. However, at times he does assume this key distinction, such as when he says: "I also don't want to claim that modern secularity is somehow coterminous with exclusive humanism [i.e., secularism]. For one thing, . . . secularity is a condition in which our experience . . . occurs; and this is something we all share, believers and unbelievers alike" (19). Given this distinction, Taylor's guiding aim is to understand how and why secularism became a live option in the modern world (see 1–22).

4. Fish, "Liberalism and Secularism"; Susan Jacoby, "One Nation, Under Secularism."

ligion to the sphere of the personal, its depoliticization, is the nettle that all Muslim societies must grasp in order to become modern." He concluded that "the world of Islam must take on board the secularist-humanist principles on which the modern [world] is based." Rushdie assumes here that an affirmation of secularity requires the privatization of religion, whether in reference to Islam or to any other religious tradition. Similar assumptions have influenced debates in the academy. For example, given the increasing role of religion in the contemporary world, Harvard University proposed requiring a course under the rubric of "Reason & Faith" in its new College core curriculum. But this proposal met stiff resistance, especially from the science faculty, and was eventually abandoned in the face of opposition. As one faculty member retorted, "It's like having a requirement in 'Astronomy & Astrology.' They're not comparable topics."[5]

From the other side, from those who seek to reassert the voice of religion in society, one tends to see either a resistance to secularity or an outright rejection of it in the name of critiquing secularism. In Europe, for instance, there are those who resist the currents of secularism by advocating the inclusion of explicit God-language in the new European Union Constitution. In America, one sees the political power of the Christian Right and the cultural influence of Christian evangelicals. Such groups generally seek to reassert the authority of the Bible in public life, whether in regard to debates over evolution, abortion, or prayer in public schools. From a very different intellectual and political angle, there are important philosophers and theologians who directly challenge the assumptions of modernity and secularity altogether. Princeton philosopher of religion Jeffrey Stout describes these influential figures as the voices of "the new traditionalism."[6] These new traditionalists, most notably philosopher Alasdair MacIntyre and theologians Stanley Hauerwas and John Milbank, challenge the modern notions of common reason and experience and are generally suspicious of modern democracy. The voice of theology, they conclude, can only

---

5. "Mr. Lieberman's Religious Words," *New York Times*, editorial, August 31, 2000; McCarthy and Burris, "Singular Piety of Politics"; Rushdie, "Yes, This Is About Islam"; Miller, "BeliefWatch: Ivy League." For a good illustration of the polarized cultural debate over religion, see Jon Meacham, "God Debate," 58–63.

6. Fuller, "Europe Debates Whether to Admit God to Union." Stout, *Democracy and Tradition*, 2.

be reasserted by challenging and abandoning the basic architecture of modern thought.

Stepping back, we see here two widespread and opposing tendencies: one side affirms modern secularity but privatizes religion and comprehensive convictions; the other side reasserts substantive convictions but resists modern secularity. Over against each of these prevailing views, I argue that the persistent problem is and has been our inability to fully integrate religion and modernity, that is, to fully affirm and redeem comprehensive claims within the context of modern secularity. As one recent commentator astutely observes, "This struggle to embrace modernity without abandoning faith . . . is arguably the critical fault line" in the contemporary world. It is "the tectonic rift" that is fueling conflict in many places across the globe as well as advancing "the increasingly sectarian boundaries of American politics."[7] Our cultural inability to integrate religion and modernity, I submit, is directly related to the marginalization of theology. For if one understands why theology and theological ethics have been marginalized in the modern world, then one will largely understand why we have such difficulty integrating faith and reason, religion and secularity. Moreover, only by understanding why theology has been marginalized will we ever be in a position to begin to reverse this condition, and thus be able to integrate faith and reason, religion and public life.

With this cultural problematic in mind, the aim of this work is to take up this dual mantle of diagnosis and prescription. Focusing specifically on the Christian tradition, I will offer both an analysis for understanding why theology has been marginalized and a normative direction for theology to pursue in order to regain its voice in the wider culture. To accomplish these ends, I will critically engage a variety of philosophical and theological perspectives, and I will organize this work into two parts. Part One, which entails chapters 1–3, seeks to define and

---

7. Sullivan, "Goodbye to All That," 49. President Obama's visit to Turkey in April 2009 highlighted the importance of secular democracy and of finding a way to integrate faith and modernity, religion and secularity. See Sabrina Tavernise and Sebnem Arsu, "Obama Impresses Many on Both Sides of Turkey's Secular and Religious Divide," *New York Times*, April 7, 2009; and Asli Aydintasbas, "Turkey in Full," *New York Times*, op-ed., April 7, 2009. The media and cultural conversations, however, still lack sufficient clarity and precision; thus they fail to distinguish consistently between secular and secularistic, and between secularity and secularism. Obama's visit, nonetheless, offers a hopeful indicator that the aim of integrating faith and modernity, religion and secularity, might find a place on the global agenda.

respond to the overarching problem. I begin by examining three leading explanatory accounts and then proceed to offer and initially defend an alternative reading of the situation. In Part Two, which covers chapters 4–10, I seek to further explicate, illustrate, and defend my reading by offering a typological study of six different approaches in modern and contemporary theology.

Specifically, chapter 1 begins by setting forth and analyzing the influential diagnostic and prescriptive accounts offered by MacIntyre, Hauerwas, and Stout respectively. Beginning with MacIntyre, I examine his 1966 essay "The Fate of Theism" and then compare and contrast it with his later, better known neo-Aristotelian and neo-Thomistic thought. Next, I turn to Hauerwas's 1983 essay "On Keeping Theological Ethics Theological," where Hauerwas offers his explanation of what has gone wrong in modern Christian ethics. Third, I examine Stout's evolving analysis of the plight of theology as set forth in important sections of his three major books: *The Flight from Authority* (1981), *Ethics After Babel* (1988), and *Democracy and Tradition* (2004). In brief, according to the early views of MacIntyre and Stout, theology has been marginalized in modern culture due to a fateful dilemma imposed by modernity itself. In contrast, Hauerwas, as well as the more recent perspectives of MacIntyre and Stout, suggests that theology has been marginalized due to a fateful accommodation made by theology itself. I propose that both views are partly right—modernity has indeed thrown up a roadblock in front of theology and theology has in fact made a fateful accommodation to it. Yet, I submit that all three thinkers fail to recognize what the real roadblock is and what the fateful accommodation has been.

The primary roadblock confronting theology, I argue, has been the pervasive denial of metaphysics in modern thought, and theology's fateful accommodation has been its widespread acceptance of this denial. By "metaphysics," I mean the philosophical or rational attempt to understand and describe the nature of reality as such. Or, as the philosopher Charles Hartshorne puts it, metaphysics is "the search for 'universal and necessary truths of existence.'"[8] Going back as far as Aristotle

---

8. Hartshorne, *Insights and Oversights*, x. By "metaphysics," I do not mean the kind of mystical spiritualism or occultism that lines the shelves of contemporary bookstores under the moniker of "metaphysics." For a discussion of this more popular usage, especially in its historical dimensions, see Albanese, "Introduction: Awash in a Sea of Metaphysics."

and Plato, metaphysics has been that branch of philosophy that seeks to understand the ultimate character of reality. Modern thought, however, has been decidedly anti- or postmetaphysical. Whatever differences there are among diverse modern and contemporary thinkers, nearly all of them share the assumption that we live irreversibly in a postmetaphysical age. That is, since the Enlightenment philosophies of David Hume and Immanuel Kant, it has been widely held that it is impossible rationally to know anything about the ultimate character of reality.[9] But this metaphysical agnosticism, I contend, is the underlying reason why theology has been marginalized in the modern context; for theology's fundamental truth claims revolve around the central claim concerning the reality of God, which is itself ultimately a metaphysical claim about the nature of reality as such. Hence, if all metaphysical claims are beyond the scope of public knowledge and rationality, then so too are theology's central claims about God. Only by seeking to redeem such claims within the context of modern secularity will theology ever be able to regain its voice in the larger culture. As I will seek to show, MacIntyre, Hauerwas, and Stout all overlook or dismiss this diagnosis because they, too, share the modern aversion to metaphysics. Whereas they modify or reject modernity's commitment to secularity but agree with its aversion to metaphysics, I affirm the former but reject the latter. What is needed is a theistic metaphysics articulated and defended within modern rational terms. I recognize that MacIntyre, Stout, and Hauerwas all challenge the modern notion of a common or shared rationality; thus, I will respond to their critiques in subsequent chapters.

---

9. What is somewhat confusing is that Kant and some others have continued to use the term "metaphysics" but in a different and broader sense. What Kant subsequently meant by "metaphysics" was critical reflection that asks about the a priori characteristics of a concept (but without reference to reality as such) or asks about the a priori conditions of subjectivity as such, i.e., what are the necessary conditions to be a subject with understanding. So instead of metaphysics focusing specifically on the character of reality as such, which was its traditional meaning, Kant and others now use the term more broadly. To use a sports analogy, one might say that Kant's redefinition of metaphysics is akin to declaring that baseball is no longer possible, thus henceforth one will now call softball "baseball." But again, to be clear, I will use the term "metaphysics" only in the strict sense. To avoid confusion, Kant's broader definition will be described as "transcendental," which of course is a term that he also used. See Kant, *Critique of Pure Reason*, 68, 59, 659. See also Caygill, *Kant Dictionary*, "metaphysics," 291f. and "transcendental," 399–402.

To state my thesis in more precise terms, we must return to and explicitly develop the distinction between modernity's *formal commitments* and its *substantive conclusions*. By formal commitments, I refer to those practices that stem from and center around modernity's fundamental dedication to what I will call *formal autonomy*, that is, to an underlying affirmation that each person should think for him or herself. This commitment to formal autonomy is summed up memorably by Kant: "*Sapere aude!* 'Have courage to use your own reason!'—that is the motto of the Enlightenment."[10] By encouraging individuals to think for themselves, modernity gave final priority to appeals to reason and experience rather than to authority and tradition as the ultimate grounds for assessing and adjudicating claims for belief and practice. In order for human beings to "grow up" and mature, both individually and collectively, they must become self-governing, which, in turn, requires that they use their own critical faculties and judgment. This premise and commitment lie at the heart of modernity's affirmation of democracy, namely, that individuals should be citizens not subjects. What I mean by *secularity* is this notion of *formal autonomy*: a secular, democratic society is ideally one in which individuals think for themselves in the midst of community rather than simply defer to the authority and power of crown, church, tradition, or media. In essence, a secular society promotes formal autonomy.[11]

If the *formal commitments* of modernity refer to how we assess and adjudicate claims, then the *substantive conclusions* refer to the dominant intellectual assumptions and material propositions that have largely defined the modern age. At the center of these conclusions is the denial or absence of metaphysics; at least two important implications follow from this. First, the modern world has largely concluded that religion is nonrational because its metaphysical claims about ultimate reality are presumed to be beyond the limits of reason. Hence, given this assumption, modernity has tended to resist or at least privatize religious claims and beliefs. As Kant again famously remarks, "I have therefore found it

---

10. Kant, "What is Enlightenment?," 3; the Latin phrase is from Horace: literally "Dare to know," 3 n. 1.

11. To affirm formal autonomy does not require a monological view; to think for oneself does not mean that we should think alone or apart from community. But it does mean that the final appeal goes to reason and experience over authority and tradition; it does mean that we should be prepared to use our own faculties rather than simply always defer to the judgment of authorities or others.

necessary to deny *knowledge* [i.e., theoretical or metaphysical knowledge of reality as such,] in order to make room for faith."[12] Though Kant meant here to deny metaphysics in order to make room for practical reason and its postulates, such as that concerning the existence of God, what has in fact happened over time is that the denial of metaphysics has led to religious claims becoming a matter only of private belief and no longer a subject fit for public inquiry and knowledge. Second, because modernity has denied metaphysics and thus placed religious and theistic claims beyond the limits of reason, it has tended to affirm the autonomy of ethics. That is to say, it has sought to define and ground the moral good or right independently of religion or the question of God. I will describe this cluster of postmetaphysical conclusions as modernity's affirmation of *substantive autonomy*. By this, I mean that the modern world has presumed that coherent beliefs about the world and ourselves exclude metaphysics. Substantive autonomy assumes that one can make coherent sense of the world and our experience within it apart from any reference to or grounding in a divine or ultimate reality. It is modernity's affirmation of substantive autonomy (not formal autonomy) that has drawn it toward *secularism*. This secularism is explicit insofar as it openly denies the reality of God or any transcendent source of meaning; it is implicit insofar as it privatizes religious belief and thus, by implication, defines the world and our role within it in terms of substantive autonomy.

To be sure, it is widely assumed, among both modernity's supporters and detractors, that modernity's formal commitments necessarily lead to its substantive conclusions; that its embrace of formal autonomy necessarily leads to substantive autonomy; that secularity necessarily leads to secularism. Freud, for instance, takes this linkage for granted in the passage that I quoted at the outset. Likewise, Charles Taylor appears to assume it when describing the prevailing modern worldview: "[W]e can see," says Taylor, "how these two narrations, that of courageous coming to adulthood [formal autonomy], and that of subtraction of illusion [secularism], belong together. They are two sides of the same coin."[13] But this supposed inextricable bond is mistaken and lies

---

12. Kant, "Preface to Second Edition," *Critique of Pure Reason*, 29.

13. Taylor, *Secular Age*, 575. Though Taylor, unlike Freud, rejects the "subtraction" version of the secularization thesis (that science and reason have simply freed us by "subtracting" or eliminating the illusions and impediments of religion), it is

at the root of our inability to integrate faith and reason, religion and public life. What is needed is precisely an affirmation of modernity's formal commitments and a rejection of its substantive conclusions–an embrace of formal autonomy coupled with a rejection of substantive autonomy. MacIntyre, Hauerwas, and, to a lesser degree, Stout are inclined to think that modern theology has gone wrong insofar as it has embraced formal autonomy, that is, insofar as it has attempted to make theological claims publicly intelligible and credible through appeals to common reason and experience. But this attempt, I stress, is a virtue not a vice. On the contrary, the real problem is that theology has not directly challenged modernity's substantive or postmetaphysical character while, at the same time, fully embracing its formal commitments. In essence, theology has largely abandoned the critical effort to make a public case for the reality and necessity of God in a way that affirms the strengths of modernity while, at the same time, rejecting its errors.

Formulated in theological terms, my contention is that theology must affirm general revelation and not merely special revelation. By "general revelation," I denote that there must be some basic or inchoate intuition of God in all experience. "The experience of God," Reinhold Niebuhr aptly states, "is not so much a separate experience, as an overtone implied in all experience."[14] Based on this experiential overtone, some knowledge of God or ultimate reality must in theory be possible through some general means accessible to all human beings, such as through reason and common experience. Of course, in a postmetaphysical age, this is precisely what is denied. Instead, the presumption is that knowledge of God or ultimate reality is possible, if at all, only through some form of special revelation, which for Christians is the revelation of Jesus as the Christ. But in a world where religious claims are ultimately dependent on the authority of special revelation, one cannot finally avoid either the privatization of religion, insofar as modern secularity is affirmed, or the cultural heteronomy of religion, insofar as secularity is abandoned. For without the ability to critically engage

---

not explicitly clear whether Taylor accepts or rejects the supposed necessary bond between formal autonomy and secularism. From his formulation here, one gets the sense that he does in fact view them as "two sides of the same coin." However, at other places, Taylor explicitly distinguishes between the secular immanent frame, which we all share, and the question of ultimate explanation (theism vs. secularism): see, for example, 594, 637.

14. Niebuhr, *Nature and Destiny of Man*, 1:127.

the metaphysical truth claims of religion in a public way, one is forced either to privatize and marginalize such claims or else to impose them through various forms of cultural and political power. In their diverse ways, MacIntyre, Hauerwas, and Stout all think that these two alternatives can be avoided without metaphysics; but as I will seek to show, they are, I believe, mistaken.

Given the fact that my position "swims" against the strong postmetaphysical current of modernity, I outline in chapter 2 a case for why others should seriously reconsider the metaphysical enterprise. Metaphysics has largely been dismissed in contemporary thought because it has been closely identified with foundationalism. "Foundationalism," as I point out, is an ambiguous term. Broadly defined, it means any attempt to understand the whole or underlying character of reality. In this broad sense, metaphysics is indeed foundational; to dismiss it because it is foundational in this wide sense, however, is merely to beg the question. In a more narrow and commonly understood sense, foundationalism refers to an epistemological project, dating back to René Descartes, that seeks to identify true and certain knowledge about reality based on an architecture of indubitable and infallible first principles. Not only does one seek to know the nature of reality, one seeks to know it with certainty by proceeding deductively from secure first principles. It is foundationalism in this narrow, epistemological sense that has cast a long and troublesome shadow over metaphysics. Drawing on the modern process philosophy of Alfred North Whitehead and Charles Hartshorne, I argue that metaphysics should be freed from this shadow, for it should never have been tied to it in the first place. Put simply, the metaphysical enterprise needs to be distinguished from the prevailing way that metaphysics has long been done. To aid this disentanglement, I contend that metaphysics needs to be freed from four persistent errors, which I call respectively the *Existential Error*, the *Discursive Error*, the *Epistemological Error*, and the *Theological Error*. By seeking to identify and counter these four deep-seated errors in Western thought, I invite the reader to reconsider the metaphysical project by seeing it in a new light. Only such a revised endeavor, I maintain, can provide a public means for redeeming theology's metaphysical claims within the parameters of modern secularity, i.e., in accordance with modernity's formal commitments.

In chapter 3, I offer a further critical response to the views of MacIntyre, Hauerwas, and Stout. Since I will later devote an entire chapter to Hauerwas's theology, I focus here on what the three of them hold in common and on MacIntyre and Stout's specific proposals. All three thinkers are what I call "strong historicists." That is, they not only affirm that human thinking always occurs within and is influenced by some particular historical and cultural context (weak historicism), but they also implicitly make a stronger claim (strong historicism), one that denies that we can ever have any a priori knowledge–either in the form of transcendental reflection on the necessary conditions of human subjectivity or in the form of metaphysical reflection on the necessary characteristics of reality.[15] In brief, they posit that what we can know about reality is always merely logically and historically contingent. In reply, I argue that strong historicism is incoherent because either it must implicitly presuppose metaphysics or else it ends up succumbing to relativism. I then seek to support this claim by offering further detailed responses to the specific views of MacIntyre and Stout.

Whereas in Part One I introduce and initially defend my thesis, in Part Two I seek to support it further by demonstrating how the widespread aversion to metaphysics has affected modern and contemporary theology. In chapter 4, I launch this effort by defining terms for a typological analysis of the situation. My typology reflects the important distinction between modernity's formal commitments and its substantive conclusions. Beginning with the former, modernity's commitment to formal autonomy or secularity can be described as a two-fold commitment to making our claims publicly (1) intelligible and (2) credible. Alternatively, modernity's embrace of substantive autonomy, and thus its tendency to slide toward secularism and the privatization of religion, is reflected in its dominant material assumptions: (3) the denial or absence of metaphysics, and (4) the autonomy of ethics. Working with these four categories, I then seek to analyze how modern and contemporary theologians address each of them. Do they finally embrace or reject the modern commitments to intelligibility and credibility?

---

15. Strong historicism denies metaphysics in both a specific sense and in a broader "transcendental" sense. Since I will use the term "a priori" rather frequently (and to a lesser extent "a posteriori"), and since its common usage in modern philosophical writing has made it increasingly acceptable on stylistic grounds to no longer italicize it, I will forego the use of italics.

Do they ultimately accept or reject the absence of metaphysics and the autonomy of ethics? Based on responses to these four categories, I identify and examine six "live" options. For each of these alternatives, I select and analyze the works of a particular theologian, specifically, James Gustafson, Reinhold Niebuhr, Stanley Hauerwas, Jean Porter, John Milbank, and Franklin Gamwell. Though there are certainly other theologians that one could have used, I have chosen these six because they each clearly represent and express a distinct and important approach in modern theology and theological ethics. Moreover, since I am specifically interested in the voice of theology in public life, I have selected this group because they each, in their own way, address and develop the moral, social, and/or political implications of theology.

Accordingly, the bulk of Part Two (chapters 5–10) is devoted to a careful examination of and a critical conversation among these six thinkers. Briefly, what I call Gustafson's "accountable theology" and Niebuhr's "pragmatic theology" illustrate two distinct attempts to make theology intelligible and at least partly credible in the modern world. Gustafson's approach is in some ways the most typically modern insofar as he appears to accept, unlike Niebuhr, the autonomy of philosophical ethics. And though Niebuhr, more so than Gustafson, seeks to offer a theological apologetic to critique culture, what they finally have in common is an underlying acceptance of the modern denial of metaphysics. Hence, each of them leaves the metaphysical claim about the reality of God embedded in the background as a critical but unsubstantiated assumption, and thus they each abandon a commitment to credibility at some point. In sharp contrast, Hauerwas's "witness theology" alleges that Gustafson and Niebuhr's efforts represent much of what has gone wrong in modern Christian thought. Instead of seeking to make theology intelligible or credible to the wider culture, Hauerwas maintains that theology should focus on the radical distinctiveness of the Christian narrative and community. Yet for all of his differences with Gustafson and Niebuhr, Hauerwas also shares the modern aversion to metaphysics, and thus he, too, leaves the metaphysical claims of theology unsubstantiated. Porter's "tradition-engaged theology," which seeks to critically retrieve Aquinas's medieval thought for contemporary purposes, falls somewhere between Gustafson and Niebuhr, on one side, and Hauerwas, on the other. Following MacIntyre, Porter seeks to make theology intelligible and credible in an indirect way, through competition among different and incommensurable traditions. Yet, like the others, she shares the modern aversion to metaphysics—leaving the metaphysical claims of theology embedded in the background of the tradition.

Alternatively, one of the most refreshing things about Milbank's "radical-orthodox theology" is its attempt to reassert a medieval ontology or metaphysic to the fore of cultural conversation. But Milbank, who rejects not only modern secularism but also much of modern secularity, believes that such a metaphysic cannot be made rationally convincing; instead, it must simply rely on its illuminative quality and rhetorical persuasiveness. So Milbank not only critiques modernity's substantive conclusions, but he also rejects its commitment to rational public discourse and its political manifestation in liberal democracy. This is where Gamwell's "transcendental-process theology" offers an instructive contrast. Whereas Milbank criticizes modernity by retrieving a medieval ontology, Gamwell critiques and completes modernity by drawing upon Whitehead and Hartshorne's process metaphysics. Gamwell embraces secularity as he critiques secularism by arguing for the need for a public theistic metaphysics. Neither ethics nor politics, he adduces, can finally be properly understood apart from the reality of God. Yet, at the same time, he champions democracy, religious freedom, and the modern commitments to intelligibility and credibility as the proper and necessary social embodiments of this theistic vision. Based on my typological and comparative analysis, I argue that Gamwell's approach offers the most promising model for theology to regain its voice in the wider culture because only his theology fully embraces modernity's formal commitments while fundamentally critiquing its substantive conclusions.[16]

Given my interest in the public dimensions of theology, let me elaborate further on the notion of the "public." As others have helpfully observed, this term is multivalent in the sense that the theologian relates to at least three distinct publics: the academy, the church, and the wider society. The question of whether theologians should be concerned with

---

16. Though I am persuaded that process thought offers the most promising path forward, I recognize that there are some other contemporary voices also calling for the development of a public metaphysics. I welcome these other voices: see, for instance, Pannenberg, *Metaphysics and the Idea of God*; and Hösle, *Objective Idealism, Ethics, and Politics*, and "Idea of a Rationalistic Philosophy of Religion."

all three of these publics and, if so, how theology should be done are issues that have been significantly debated.[17] Hauerwas, for instance, gives unqualified priority to the church. As he sees it, theology should not be formulated in such a manner as to make its claims intelligible and credible to persons in the academy or wider society; instead, it should be geared to fostering a distinctive community called church. In contrast, I contend that theology needs to address the academy as much as the church. Yes, the theologian speaks to the church, but the theologian will influence the church and the wider society more effectively in the long run via the academy. If theology is going to be a vigorous voice arguing for the reality and centrality of God in relation to all aspects of life, and not just a narrow discipline speaking to a privatized faith, then it must do so in a manner that influences how all people think about the question of God in relation to reason and culture. Moreover, both the academy and the church, in their own ways, influence the life of the larger public. If theology, via the academy, can coherently and appropriately articulate how faith and modernity, religion and democracy can be fully integrated, then theology will have served the world in a valuable and transformative way. But to do this requires changing the social location of theology, which, in turn, requires changing what persons both inside and outside the church presuppose about these matters. Hence, it is critical for theology to speak to and through the academy.

With this endeavor in mind, I devote the conclusion of this work to focusing on the future of theology and the academy. More than a half-century ago, the theologian Bernard Loomer observed that "the failure of modern universities is in large part the failure of religion." This failure pertains to the lack of "intellectual integrity," suggests Loomer, for such integrity "involves the idea of wholeness, of unity, wherein the several disciplines that make up a university are synthesized." In my conclusion, I critically compare three different proposals for reclaiming intellectual integrity: first, I examine MacIntyre's call for a return to the medieval paradigm of competing authorities and traditions; then I analyze the neo-Calvinist vision of Christian scholarship as outlined by Nicholas Wolterstorff and Alvin Plantinga; finally, I offer what I call a "liberal-metaphysical" model as a way forward. In a postmetaphysical world, the

---

17. I believe David Tracy is the one who first explicitly defined the three publics of the theologian: see *Analogical Imagination*, chap. 1. For an excellent overview of the debates concerning public theology, see Breitenberg, "To Tell the Truth."

ideal of intellectual integrity is systematically abandoned; thus I call for the completion of modern universities by pursuing a new engagement with metaphysics within the parameters of modern secularity. Theology must champion this cause because, as Loomer notes, "the nature of religious faith is such that it must of necessity seek for intellectual integrity, for one intellectual world." Hence, Loomer insightfully concludes "that we shall not have better universities until we have better theology, and that we shall not have better theology until we have better universities." These better universities, I would add, are those that critically pursue and engage metaphysical questions within the context of modernity's formal commitments. An implied corollary, Loomer remarks, "is that we shall not have better universities until we have better churches, and that we shall not have better churches until we have better universities."[18] Loomer rightly recognizes the interrelationship between the three publics of the theologian: an adequate and authentic theology must speak to the academy, to the church, and to the wider culture, for, finally, only the pursuit of such holistic integrity is adequate to the ultimate integrity of the divine reality.

---

18. Loomer, "Religion and the Mind of the University," 167, 162, 166, 168.

PART ONE

Defining The Problem
Diagnostic and Prescriptive Accounts

1

Diagnosing the Plight of Theology in the Modern World

THOUGH MANY HAVE RECOGNIZED THAT THE VOICE OF THEOLOGY and theological ethics has been marginalized in modern public life, only some philosophers and theologians have sought systematically to identify the cause of this marginalization. From among this group, I will examine three prominent diagnoses, namely, those offered by Alasdair MacIntyre, Stanley Hauerwas, and Jeffrey Stout. Each of these eminent thinkers has his own intellectual approach, with its own distinctive characteristics and thematic emphases. Summarily put, MacIntyre is a neo-Aristotelian and neo-Thomistic philosopher, Hauerwas is a Methodist theologian who integrates both medieval Catholic and Anabaptist motifs into his theology, and Stout is a pragmatist philosopher of religion. Moreover, Stout has recently distanced himself from the anti-democratic tendencies of the "new traditionalism" of MacIntyre, Hauerwas, and Milbank. Nevertheless, MacIntyre, Hauerwas, and Stout all share an intellectual family resemblance, largely because MacIntyre has been like an influential, intellectual uncle to his two younger colleagues. For notwithstanding whatever real differences there are among them, it is quite clear that MacIntyre has had a profound effect on Hauerwas's thinking and a noteworthy influence on Stout's as well. For instance, at the same time that Stout distances himself from the new traditionalists, he also acknowledges his debt to MacIntyre and Hauerwas for helping him to launch his career.[1] As will become evident, this intellectual influence shows up in the way that each of them interprets the plight of modern theology. Along with this similarity, one also

---

1. Stout, *Democracy and Tradition*, 2, xi; see also, Stout, "Spirit of Democracy," 9f.

recognizes other thematic commonalities, such as an emphasis on social practices, narrative, virtue, community, tradition, and historicism.

By this last theme, I refer to the fact that MacIntyre, Hauerwas, and Stout all pursue and situate philosophy and theology within a historicist framework. By "historicist" or "historicism" they mean that "all thought is historically conditioned."[2] This claim can be interpreted in both a weak and strong sense. In a *weak* sense this means that all thinking occurs in some specific historical context such that all reasoning is influenced in some respects by the context itself. This influence occurs, for instance, in terms of the questions that are explicitly addressed, the conversation partners that are engaged, and the language and concepts that are employed. Thus, given that human reasoning is always situated, historical analysis can help us to understand how we got to where we are. Accordingly, MacIntyre, Hauerwas, and Stout all offer historical accounts of the plight of modern theology. Historicism in a *strong* sense, however, goes beyond merely mapping out an intellectual history. Rather, strong historicism makes an implicit philosophical claim that denies that there are any valid a priori conditions or reasons, at least when it comes to understanding the nature of reality or human existence. Strong historicism, in other words, implicitly denies that there are any substantive claims about reality or existence that are trans-historical in the sense of being rationally or logically necessary. According to this view, all such claims and forms of reasoning are logically and historically contingent and thus can be denied without contradiction. Hence, all forms of substantive reasoning, including those that are supposedly a priori, are in fact only historically specific. For MacIntyre and Hauerwas, this is expressed by saying that all rationality is tradition-dependent, i.e., takes place within and is constituted by a specific and well-integrated tradition. This tradition, and all the reasons that flow from it, is historically contingent; its claims can be denied without logical contradiction. For Stout, who affirms tradition but is less concerned with identifying and maintaining the singularity of traditions, this strong historicist view is expressed by seeking to humble all attempts at metaphysical or transcendental thought. As Stout declares, "Descartes's *Meditations*—and, for that matter, such works as Kant's first *Critique*—must be made to seem historically conditioned in ways that

---

2. Stout, *Flight from Authority*, 4.

belie the author's claims to transcendence."[3] The key point to recognize, therefore, is that MacIntyre, Hauerwas, and Stout are historicists in both a weak and a strong sense. By affirming strong historicism, they seek to avoid what they take to be "the bog of metaphysics."[4]

One of the valuable contributions made by these three thinkers is their insightful ability to recognize when a problem exists and to draw attention to it. Perhaps more than any other group of contemporary scholars, MacIntyre, Hauerwas, and Stout have helped us to recognize that modern theology has indeed been sidetracked somewhere along the path of history. Whether they have correctly diagnosed the problem, however, is a matter that I will take up at the end of this chapter. In the meantime, I will begin with an exposition of MacIntyre's view and then move on to a discussion of Hauerwas and Stout; along the way, I will seek to note their relevant similarities and differences.

Alasdair MacIntyre

MacIntyre's systematic diagnosis came in a 1966 Bampton Lecture at Columbia University entitled "The Fate of Theism." To the best of my knowledge, he has never returned to this analysis to update it in accordance with his more recent thought, with its emphasis on tradition-constituted rationality and Thomistic modes of inquiry. Hence, my discussion will consist of three parts: First, I will attend to his original, explicit diagnosis; then I will infer how his more recent thought contains its own implicit explanation; finally, I will compare how this latter account relates to his earlier view.

"The Fate of Theism"

In this important lecture, MacIntyre argues that the modern world has posed two related crises for theology. The first arose with the advent of modern science and became manifest in the seventeenth and eighteenth centuries. Echoing Karl Popper, MacIntyre contends that the hallmark of modern science has been its ongoing openness to questioning its

---

3. Ibid., 67.

4. This vivid expression is used by Charles Reynolds to describe what Stout's work seeks to avoid; I think it aptly applies to the views of MacIntyre and Hauerwas as well. See Reynolds, "Conversations with Jeffrey Stout on *Democracy and Tradition,*" 249. Stout himself uses the term "bog" with implicit reference to metaphysics in *Democracy and Tradition*, 255.

claims and theories in the light of counter-evidence. More precisely, one might say that modern science has largely been defined by two related characteristics, namely, revision and refutability. "Revision" refers to one's willingness to alter one's thinking in the light of new evidence. Of course if significant change is required, the original view may eventually have to be not only revised but abandoned altogether. Hence, "refutability" refers to one's willingness to abandon, at some point, a particular claim or theory in light of persuasive counter-evidence. The intuition here is that rationality requires a willingness to recognize some possible condition or state of affairs as a potential refutation of one's claim, for to insist that one's claim is true *no matter what* is to abandon rational conversation altogether.[5]

In sharp contrast to these modern characteristics, MacIntyre offers a very different portrait of the primitive mindset. Drawing on the anthropological work of Mary Douglas, MacIntyre alleges that the defining characteristic of the primitive mind was its resistance to change in the face of challenging events; it embraced neither revision nor refutability. He then proceeds to draw a parallel between the premodern roots of theism and the primitive perspective: both outlooks are strongly resistant to changing their beliefs in the face of counter-evidence. Indeed, MacIntyre contends that premodern theism had developed in such a manner that irrefutability was incorporated into the content of theistic belief itself. Hence, in a modern world that was being increasingly shaped by science and its principles of revision and refutability, theism found itself confronted with its first major crisis.[6]

In response to this crisis, theists faced two unpleasant options: either they could accommodate to modernity and be acclimatized, or they could resist and be marginalized. Those who chose the path of accommodation had to adapt to the scientific climate by declaring that theistic claims were hypotheses just like other hypotheses—revisable and refutable claims that seek to explain the facts of nature or experience based on the most probable reasoning. This alternative, however, inexorably pushed theism toward some form of deism and, consequently, left it open to rational critique. As scientific and other forms of inquiry

---

5. MacIntyre, "Fate of Theism," 9–10. To be unwilling to change one's view irrespective of the evidence is what C. S. Peirce calls the "method of tenacity." See Peirce, "Fixation of Belief," 102–3.

6. MacIntyre, "Fate of Theism," 9.

advanced, the God-hypothesis became increasingly vulnerable to the parsimonious arguments of those who claimed that the facts of nature could be adequately accounted for without reference to the divine. For instance, MacIntyre notes how Newton's hypothesis that God is required as the First Cause became vulnerable to counter-arguments offered by thinkers such as Pierre Simon Laplace and James Mill.[7]

Alternatively, those who chose the path of resistance were required to reject the modern scientific milieu by denying that public arguments could be offered to defend theistic truth claims at all. The consequence of this alternative was that it quarantined theology off from genuine conversation with other disciplines and currents in modern culture. Pascal is the chief exemplar of this option. According to MacIntyre,

> Pascal, unlike Aquinas or John Locke, is able to find no arguments in the character of the universe to address to [those who deny theism]. All he can confront [them] with is a choice, the choice elaborated in his doctrine of the wager. Pascal's notion that theistic belief is something to be chosen is quite new in the history of theism. His innovation makes him the precursor of both Kierkegaard and Karl Barth.[8]

In essence, this first crisis left modern theology with the choice between either some form of rationalistic deism or some early form of fideism or existentialism.[9]

The second crisis, which presupposed the first, arose in the nineteenth and twentieth centuries. Given the sharp rise and pervasive influence of science, the criteria of revisability and refutability became key standards for defining serious and critical thought in modern culture. MacIntyre identifies four responses to this cultural situation: two atheistic and two theistic. Beginning with the former, he suggests that modern atheism has taken two basic forms: one active and explicit, the other passive and implicit. "Active atheism" sought explicitly to deny the rational arguments of the deistic versions of theism. Thinkers ranging from James Mill to Bertrand Russell to Jean-Paul Sartre all sought, in various ways, to deny the theistic affirmation by explicitly addressing the theistic question. But as time passed, especially over the course of the twentieth century, an active denial of theism seemed to lose its

---

7 Ibid., 8–11.
8. Ibid., 13.
9. Ibid.

point. "The children of active free-thinkers often lapse into a merely passive atheism," MacIntyre observes. "The self-conscious ex-Christian atheist [should] thus be distinguished from the secularized unbeliever, who sees no point in actually denying the existence of God because he never saw any point in affirming it in the first place."[10] Along with this generational drift toward intellectual complacency, MacIntyre more importantly asserts that modern theology itself has been complicit in this trend toward passive atheism or secularism. To this I will return shortly.

Theistic forms of response took two general shapes, which he labels the "theistic enclave" and "Christian orthodoxy" respectively. The theistic enclave, unlike deistic versions, totally rejected "the attempt to adapt theism to the climate of secular thought." Instead, it emphasized the particularity and uniqueness of theistic beliefs, and by doing so, it sought to preserve the distinctive identity of religious life and convictions.[11] What seem both amusing and anachronistic, given the rise and influence of Hauerwas and other like-minded theologians in the late twentieth century, are the examples that MacIntyre uses in the 1960s

---

10. Ibid., 14–15. The cultural and existential implications of this passive secularism are poignantly illustrated in Douglas Coupland's late twentieth-century novel *Life After God*.

11. MacIntyre, "Fate of Theism," 15. MacIntyre's use of the term "secular" here reflects common usage but it also points to the ambiguity of that usage, which I discussed in my introduction. That is, to refer to "secular thought" or to secular thinkers, etc. does not clearly distinguish between secular and secularistic. I recognize that this ambiguity is latent in the common usage and, to that extent, difficult to avoid. Moreover, the term "secularistic" is perhaps not as felicitous as the more concise "secular." Thus, as I describe the views of various thinkers along the way, such as MacIntyre here, I will go with the flow of their own usage. However, whenever I am describing my own view or explicitly attempting to clarify other views, I will try to offer more precision in the use of these terms; for instance, whenever I use "secularistic" or "secularism," one can know that I am referring to a denial of theism. Furthermore, I trust that context will often clarify the intended meaning. For instance, in the passage above, where MacIntyre speaks of the "secularized unbeliever," the context seems to emphasize the notion of passive secularism. Of course, the underlying problem, as I indicated in my introduction, is that the prevailing view wrongly assumes that there is an inextricable link between secular (formal autonomy) and secularism (a denial of theism), which leads to the blurring ambiguity in our common uses of "secular," "secularized," and "secularization." On a separate note, it is not clear whether MacIntyre intends to imply any similarities here between the Pascalian resistance to culture in the seventeenth century and the resistance of the theistic enclave in the twentieth. Nevertheless, Pascal appears to have left at least two legacies to theology: one existential and the other counter-cultural.

to illustrate the theistic enclave. Specifically, he points to the Christian ecumenical movement and to the increasing openness of Christianity to other world religions as exemplifying an enclave approach. What he seems to have in mind is the fact that these movements and conversations were internal to religious communities and not directly challenging the secularistic currents of the wider culture. Hence, since the Christian ecumenical movement was focused on building internal and inter-religious rapprochement rather than on challenging the secularistic assumptions of culture, MacIntyre perceived its efforts as illustrating the enclave approach. Later in the essay, he offers a perhaps more expected example of the enclave mindset when he mentions Barth in such a manner as to suggest that he, too, illustrates this outlook.[12]

Christian orthodoxy offered a different response to culture. Unlike the theistic enclave, which either ignored secular culture or sought to keep it at bay, Christian orthodoxy attempted "to maintain a living relationship between [itself] and the culture of the world outside of the church, [yet without] the embarrassment of [direct] clashes and conflicts between [its] orthodox theism and contemporary secular culture." Like a boxer who dances in and out and throws occasional quick jabs rather than a fighter who engages in the direct give and take of body blows, Christian orthodoxy sought to carry out a strategy of one-way engagement by "renouncing and denouncing contemporary secular culture as a false culture." MacIntyre points to T. S. Eliot as an exemplar of this approach. Eliot's writings, he remarks, illustrate not only a self-conscious "plea for a lost [Christian] past," but especially "a plea for those elements in the past still embodied in the present, for an identity that we can now neither fully recover nor yet quite disown."[13]

Reading through "The Fate of Theism" one detects an undercurrent that laments the shift from a culture where active atheism had to confront theism, to a culture where an "impoverished," passive atheism reigns unchallenged. Accordingly, MacIntyre looks back wistfully upon a Victorian era in which

> the debate about God lay at the focal point of both culture and morality. The epistemological standards and methods built up in both [modern] science and history confronted a theism which was still intimately connected with moral life. The ques-

---

12. MacIntyre, "Fate of Theism," 15–16, 25.
13. Ibid., 16–17.

tion of whether theism was true could not be divorced from the question of what forms of morality were to be upheld.[14]

MacIntyre suggests here that there was a persistent but dwindling cultural presumption up through the Victorian era that presupposed some necessary connection between theism and ethics. Gradually, however, Enlightenment arguments that sought to ground ethics independently of theism eroded this cultural outlook. To be clear, MacIntyre himself is not claiming here that theism is necessary for ethics. Indeed, in his follow-up Bampton Lecture, entitled "Atheism and Morals," he explicitly denies that ethics requires theism. On the contrary, theism itself requires an independent, genuine evaluative language of ends and practices.[15] Rather, MacIntyre's point is simply to note that theology offered little or no substantive response to stem the secularistic tide; he laments the lost voice of theology in culture, especially the loss of its cognitive claims.

In one of the key passages in "The Fate of Theism," MacIntyre blames modern theology in part for its own marginalization. In response to the question of why there is not an active debate between theism and atheism, he replies:

> My answer is that the lack of confrontation is due not only to the directions in which secular knowledge is advancing but [also] to the directions in which theism is retreating. Theists are offering atheists less and less in which to disbelieve. Theism thereby deprives active atheism of much of its significance and power and encourages the more passive atheism of the indifferent. Thus the internal development of theism in response to the challenge of secular epistemological standards is an important factor in making the theism-versus-atheism dispute culturally marginal.[16]

To illustrate his charge, MacIntyre proceeds to identify and criticize three alternative paths pursued in mid-to late-twentieth-century theology. What all three have in common is their failure to adequately present the truth claims of theism.

The first alternative is the existentialist path, tracing its roots back to Pascal, with its defining existential choice or leap of faith. To suggest that one can "choose to believe," MacIntyre adduces, is to be confused

---

14. Ibid., 15, 17–18.
15. See MacIntyre, "Atheism and Morals."
16. MacIntyre, "Fate of Theism," 24.

about the nature of belief in general and to miss the point about the content of theistic belief in particular. For belief is a matter of the mind affirming or denying some proposition to be true, not a matter of choice or will. Neither does it help to say that one can choose to behave as if one does believe. Rather, one can wish that one did believe, but that is still not the same thing as genuinely believing something to be true.[17] More importantly, MacIntyre adds, this approach misses the point of Christian doctrine, namely, the assertion of its cognitive truth claims:

> For these dogmas are, or at least were, intended to be taken as factual truths in the same sense that it is a matter of fact whether or not tomorrow will bring rain. But if belief in truths of a factual kind cannot be chosen, then belief that can be chosen cannot have as its object truths of a factual kind. Therefore, if modern Christian theology treats Christian belief as belief that can be chosen, the truths of Christian orthodoxy must be regarded as something other than factual in kind.[18]

The second theological path is that which proclaims the therapeutic or pragmatic usefulness of theism. Such an approach, MacIntyre submits, logically confuses utility and validity: "It may of course be very useful to believe that certain statements are true; but this utility can never be a reason for 'believing' in them."[19] What I take him to mean here is that usefulness does not provide sufficient grounds for believing something to be objectively or validly the case. As Feuerbach, Freud, Jung, and others have pointed out, theism may implicitly carry out some anthropological or psychological function, but this does not validate its truth claims about the reality of God.

The third alternative might best be described as the path of translation, correlation, and demythologization. Citing figures such as Bultmann and Tillich, MacIntyre characterizes this approach as seeking to "restate Christian theology so that it will be a vital issue" again in culture. He views this path as a genuine but failed attempt to respond to the second crisis of theism without falling into the atheistic denial of theism (Russell), the self-enclosed formulas of the theistic enclave (Barth), or the "self-conscious archaism" of Christian orthodoxy (Eliot). What characterizes this third alternative is its attempt to distinguish

17. Ibid., 22–23.
18. Ibid., 23.
19. Ibid., 23–24.

between "the kernel of Christian theism" and its "outmoded husk." It does this in order to articulate the Christian message in such a way that it is "intelligible to contemporary educated, secular-minded men [and women]." In doing this, MacIntyre alleges that these theologians implicitly or explicitly accept "the substance of a modern secular standpoint in order to argue its compatibility with [theistic] faith."[20] Yet, he concludes that any theological attempt to be both authentically theistic and publicly intelligible is inherently doomed to failure. As he strongly puts it,

> I maintain . . . that these [two] aims are essentially incompatible with each other; that any presentation of theism which is able to secure a hearing from a secular audience has undergone a transformation that has evacuated it entirely of its theistic content. Conversely, any presentation which retains such theistic content will be unable to secure the place in contemporary culture which those theologians desire for it. I am thus advancing not merely the weaker contention that all their attempts so far have failed but the stronger contention that any attempt of this kind must inevitably fail.[21]

MacIntyre proceeds from here to offer brief assessments of theologians in this fold, including Bultmann and Tillich. "Bultmann's theology," he contends, "falls into two [dichotomous] categories: that which is made credible ceases to be theistic, and that which remains theistic is not made credible in any way." Less sharply but still problematically, Tillich oscillates between metaphysical and psychological language. Because Tillich's metaphysical characterization of God is stated in almost purely negative or apophatic terms, his positive description is reduced to merely human psychological categories: "'God' is [merely] a name given to human [ultimate] concern." But this reduction of a metaphysical claim to a psychological one was emblematic of Feuerbach's atheism in the nineteenth century. What has happened, MacIntyre proclaims, is that Feuerbach's famous prediction has been fulfilled: what was called atheism in the nineteenth century has become theism in the twentieth. Overall, MacIntyre is convinced that correlational theologies, with

---

20. Ibid., 25–26.
21. Ibid., 26.

their attempt to be publicly intelligible in modern terms, are themselves "symptoms of the very disease for which they profess to be the cure."[22]

Finishing "The Fate of Theism" one is struck by the strong chord of ambivalence running throughout. This ambivalence can be articulated in two related ways: First, MacIntyre blames modern theology for retreating from its cognitive claims. At the same time, nonetheless, he contends that a *de facto* cultural retreat was inevitable since any public attempt to maintain theistic content would end up on the cultural margins anyway. Thus, on the whole, does he place more blame on theism or on modernity? It appears that he is somewhat uncertain in his own mind; yet, in the end, it seems that his strong claim of inevitability places most of the blame in the lap of modernity itself. Second, MacIntyre desires a genuine public theological voice, one that clearly articulates and affirms its cognitive claims. Nevertheless, he is convinced that modernity has thrown up a roadblock that makes this goal impossible to achieve. He offers this account, all the while, from his then seemingly more secularistic outlook—an outlook that desires an active atheism, one that wrestles with theism rather than a passive atheism that slumbers into a complacent and unreflective secularism. Through this ambivalent mist, one can detect MacIntyre's mind searching for an alternative way, one that attempts to circumvent the roadblock of modernity without taking on its language and categories. MacIntyre, of course, believes that he has finally identified this alternative path in his more recent thought, to which I now turn.

MacIntyre's More Recent Thought

The cluster of neo-Aristotelian and neo-Thomistic themes that have defined MacIntyre's work over the past quarter-century or more, as set forth and developed in *After Virtue, Whose Justice? Which Rationality?* (hereafter *WJWR*), and *Three Rival Versions of Moral Enquiry* (hereafter *TRV*), is well known and does not need to be recounted here.[23] Instead,

---

22. Ibid., 27–28, 29.

23. Based on my reading of his later book, *Dependent Rational Animals*, I take it that MacIntyre largely presupposes there the methodological assumptions of tradition-constituted rationality that he has developed and articulated in his previous works. Hence, he speaks about human nature and human virtues from a neo-Thomistic tradition that is taken as a given. Indeed, Gordon Graham quotes MacIntyre to this effect. Based on private correspondence about *Dependent Rational Animals*, Graham quotes MacIntyre as saying: "We need to distinguish philosophical work within a tradition that

I will seek to discern from this cluster his implicit diagnosis of the condition of theism in modernity and see how this relates to his earlier, explicit analysis. In brief, I think he would largely stand by his earlier account as an accurate rendering of modern theism, whereas his recent view focuses more on theism over against modernity. That is to say, "The Fate of Theism" accurately captures the plight of theology when it allows the dominant assumptions of modernity to define its own agenda. One way or another, theology ends up losing its authentic voice—either by allowing itself to be marginalized from culture (theistic enclave) or by seeking to fit into culture (theological correlation). The only way to avoid this no-win situation, MacIntyre now suggests, is for theism to "fight from its own turf," that is, to speak from within its own language and tradition. Perhaps the best place from which to cull out MacIntyre's updated analysis of theism is in *TRV*.[24] Here, MacIntyre identifies three main competing modes of inquiry, which he calls "Encyclopedia" (modernity and Enlightenment), "Genealogy" (Nietzsche and Postmodernism), and "Tradition" (medieval Thomism). For our present purposes, we will focus only on his discussion of Encyclopedia and Tradition.

The encyclopaedists, as illustrated by Descartes and even more by Kant, tend to share five basic characteristics. First, they emphasize the autonomy of reason freed from the authority of tradition and religious communities. "The encyclopaedists had learned from Kant," MacIntyre remarks, "that to be rational is to think for oneself, to emancipate oneself from the tutelage of authority. Any notion that I can only think adequately by and for myself insofar as I do so in the company of others, to some of whom authority must be accorded, is quite alien to the encyclopaedist." Second, they tend to view reason as universal, impartial, and unifying. Third, they seek to employ reason as a means for reaching valid conclusions that "would be compelling to any fully rational person whatsoever." Fourth, for encyclopaedists, "Rationality,

---

takes the context supplied by that tradition more or less for granted from work that appeals explicitly to the narrative history in which it is embedded or work that defends one tradition and argues for its rational superiority to some rival." Graham, "MacIntyre on History and Philosophy," 36–37.

24. See especially chap. 3 in MacIntyre, *TRV*, 58–81. Moreover, since *TRV* is based on MacIntyre's 1988 Gifford Lectures, with the Gifford's historic focus on philosophical theology, it offers a promising source in which to find MacIntyre's updated account of theism.

like truth, is independent of time, place, and historical circumstances."[25] And fifth, they tend to assume, following Kant, that the objects of reality conform to the mind rather than that the mind needs to be trained in order to conform to reality. Echoing his earlier conclusions in "The Fate of Theism," MacIntyre states that modern theology, by going along with these underlying assumptions, "diminish[ed its] central Christian doctrine in a way that would make it acceptable to post-Enlightenment culture, the culture of the encyclopaedia."[26]

In contrast, *some* Thomists (whom I will call "traditionalists") began to recognize that a more appropriate strategy for theology is found in the alternative of Tradition.[27] Over against Encyclopedia, Tradition entails a philosophical outlook that emphasizes the historical situatedness of reason within a tradition, and the importance of authority as a necessary and proper form of tutelage for training the mind to see reality as it truly is. MacIntyre points to the nineteenth-century Jesuit Joseph Kleutgen as a key contributor to this approach. Instead of viewing the history of philosophy as a single cloth stretching from Socrates to the nineteenth century, Kleutgen argued that there had been a fundamental rupture in philosophy, dividing it into two different eras: a premodern strand running from Socrates to the Late Middle Ages, and a modern strand commencing with Descartes. Though MacIntyre thinks Kleutgen should have dated the rupture a bit earlier (right after Aquinas), his genuine insight, nevertheless, was to recognize the rupture itself, for it distinguishes two fundamentally different conceptions of rationality: a premodern conception, running from Socrates to Aquinas, and a modern conception, beginning with Descartes and the encyclopaedists. Unlike the modern approach, which attempts to reason in a disinterested manner independently of membership in any particular community, MacIntyre contends that the premodern approach was characterized by a dialectical method that required commitment to a

---

25. MacIntyre, *TRV*, 64, 59, 65.

26. Ibid., 69.

27. As far as I can tell, MacIntyre does not offer any specific name or helpful label for those who affirm Tradition. Hence, I will use the term "traditionalists" to refer to members of this group (over against encyclopaedists). To call them simply "Thomists" does not help because MacIntyre wants to differentiate between different types of Thomists, namely, those who wrongly read Thomas through the eyes of Enlightenment modernity and those who rightly read Thomas as an exemplar of a premodern dialectic. This distinction will become more clear as the discussion proceeds.

particular type of community, one that was devoted to the formation of requisite virtues and excluded fundamental dissent.[28]

The defining metaphor of this premodern approach is that of an apprentice learning a craft from a master—in this case the craft of philosophical or theological inquiry. The apprentice must initially accept on authority the standards of excellence or truth established by the master(s) and learn how to apply those standards appropriately. Only gradually, as the apprentice himself masters the tradition, does he earn the right and position to question and revise the best standards or conclusions achieved thus far. Suggestive of his strong historicist outlook, MacIntyre maintains that these standards can only be justified historically: "The standards of achievement within any craft are justified historically. They have emerged from the criticism of their predecessors and they are justified because and insofar as they have remedied defects and transcended the limitations of those predecessors as guides to excellent achievement within that particular craft." Given this historical and dialectical means of criticism, MacIntyre stresses that there is an open-ended character to this premodern method. This openness points to a second error in Kleutgen, namely, that he "treats Aquinas as presenting a finished system whose indebtedness to earlier writers is no more than an accidental feature of it." In other words, Kleutgen unwittingly attributes early modernist tendencies to Aquinas himself. In contrast to a static, ahistorical, closed system, which MacIntyre identifies with the early modernist tendencies of Descartes, MacIntyre portrays Aquinas as an exemplar of a fluid premodern dialectical tradition, one that acknowledges its indebtedness to the past and yet remains an ongoing, open-ended process.[29] In a helpful passage in *WJWR*, he summarizes the fluidity and revisability of this approach:

> Every article in [Aquinas'] *Summa* [*Theologiae*] poses a question whose answer depends upon the outcome of an essentially uncompleted debate. For the set of often disparate and heterogeneous arguments against whatever position Aquinas' enquiries so far have led him to accept is always open to addition by some as yet unforeseen argument. And there is no way, therefore, of ruling out in advance the possibility that what has so far

---

28. MacIntyre, *TRV*, 59, 73, 59–60. MacIntyre cites Joseph Kleutgen, *Die Philosophie der Vorzeit Verteidigt* (published in 4 vols. in Munich, 1853–1860).

29. MacIntyre, *TRV*, 61–62, 64, 74.

been accepted may yet have to be modified or even rejected. In this there is nothing peculiar to Aquinas' procedures. It is of the nature of all dialectic, understood as Aristotle understood it, to be essentially incomplete.[30]

In contrast to Encyclopedia, the key advantage of Tradition is that it can faithfully recapture and articulate theology's authentic cognitive voice, which is a voice of metaphysical realism. At the core of Christian theism, MacIntyre asserts, is "the view that the world is what it is independently of human thinking and judging and desiring and willing. There is a single true view of the world and its ordering, and for human judgments to be true and for human desiring and willing to be aimed at what is genuinely good they must be in conformity with that divinely created order."[31] To be sure, Kant's Copernican revolution denied that humans could have any theoretical knowledge of reality in itself. According to MacIntyre, "Kant himself had of course been completely in the right in understanding that there is no place for any true knowledge of God within the cognitive structures of the mind if the mind is characterized in terms of his three *Critiques*."[32] This statement suggests, as I will later argue, that MacIntyre accepts Kant's denial of metaphysics on its own terms. That is, he believes that any attempt to make cognitive claims about God within the parameters of modern secularity (formal autonomy) is bound to fail because of Kant's fundamental critique. Thus, instead of challenging this critique on modern grounds, MacIntyre seeks a return to premodern dialectic as a way to voice theism's cognitive claims. Such a premodern dialectic views the human mind as inadequate to understand the reality of God until it has been brought into conformity with that reality through the process of apprenticeship under authoritative tutelage. Premodern dialectic and metaphysical realism are, MacIntyre holds, deeply at odds with the modern turn to the subject and with modernity's insistence on subjecting all claims, including theological ones, to a common standard of rational assessment. A unitary standard of rationality, he submits, truncated theism to fit into the assumptions of modern epistemology: God was reduced to fit the categories of the human mind rather than asking the human mind to be trained to understand God. Whereas modern philosophy became

30. MacIntyre, *WJWR*, 171–72.
31. MacIntyre, *TRV*, 66–67.
32. Ibid., 70.

preoccupied with epistemological questions, premodern philosophy was concerned with metaphysical and teleological questions, pursued within its authoritative and ongoing dialectical tradition.[33]

Some Thomists insightfully recognized this difference; hence they sought to return to Aquinas and the medieval tradition in order to retrieve a form of metaphysical theism. Yet their response had, at best, ambiguous results. In his sketch of nineteenth- and twentieth-century Catholic thought, MacIntyre implies that there have basically been two types of Thomists in the modern era—those who have compromised the medieval tradition (especially the thought of Aquinas) and those who have remained more faithful to it. The "compromised" Thomists have been those who have sought to challenge modernity within modern terms. They have read the medieval tradition as offering some form of transcendental argument to counter Kant's own transcendentalism. MacIntyre points to figures such as Antonio Rosmini Serbati (1797–1855) and Karl Rahner as examples of this misguided approach. Rosmini believed that he was genuinely retrieving the premodern traditions of Augustine and Aquinas, but he was in fact heavily influenced and compromised by Kant. "[B]ecause [Rosmini's] central enterprise was to vindicate theology against its Kantian critics," remarks MacIntyre, "he absorbed into his own system a good deal of Kant and thereby, seemingly unwittingly, distorted those older positions by reworking them in Kantian terms."[34] Hence, Rosmini's error, and presumably Rahner's as well, was to go beyond Kant by claiming that humans have some implicit a priori awareness of the divine reality, which we can explicitly become aware of through transcendental reflection. Because MacIntyre accepts Kant's denial of metaphysics as a valid refutation of all modern metaphysical efforts, he believes that attempts such as Rosmini's—to move from transcendental awareness to a valid theistic metaphysics—fail on modern philosophical grounds. Furthermore, he thinks such efforts also fail on premodern theological grounds insofar as they suggest that the divine reality can be apprehended by the mind without the requisite authoritative training.[35]

In contrast to this misguided approach, the "faithful" Thomists (the traditionalists) have been those who have pursued a more histori-

33. Ibid., 68–69.
34. Ibid., 70.
35. Ibid., 70–71.

cal and exegetical path and, thus, have provided a more accurate picture of Aquinas's own view. As MacIntyre sees it, their exegetical efforts, by "retrieving . . . the historical understanding of what Aquinas himself said, wrote, and did, [have] recovered for us an understanding of what is distinctive about the [dialectical] mode of enquiry elaborated in its classical and most adequate form by Aquinas." Though MacIntyre believes that his own reading of Aquinas most fully uncovers and recaptures this dialectical form of inquiry, he notes helpful figures along the way, such as Grabmann, Gilson, and Weisheipl.[36]

What is rather ironic about MacIntyre's adulation of historical exegesis is precisely how modern it is; for the notion of empathetically seeking to recapture the author's original intent, to retrieve "what Aquinas himself said," is one of the defining characteristics of modern not medieval scholarship. As Jennifer Herdt observes,

> Aquinas could not even conceive of empathetic imagination as necessary, let alone advocate its use. . . . Despite an occasional glimmer of historical understanding, [Aquinas] did not see his task as that of trying to understand a view within its historical or cultural context. . . .
>
> . . . If I am right, then, MacIntyre's "empathetic imagination" is a [modern] liberal concept (in the broad sense in which MacIntyre uses the term), associated with liberal purposes and concerns. Despite all of his criticism of liberalism, a key element of MacIntyre's narrative rationality rests heavily on what can be regarded as one of the cardinal virtues of [modern] liberalism.[37]

Similarly, Jean Porter places MacIntyre within the modern liberal tradition insofar as he follows in the footsteps of those who emphasize historical analysis of particular communities.[38] Perhaps MacIntyre might respond by saying that these modernist elements are what make his view neo-Thomistic and not medieval as such. He might say, to borrow the words of one observer, that Aquinas's dialectical mode of inquiry "is supple and resilient enough to incorporate those genuine truths which modern philosophers [and scholarship] have brought to light but have either exaggerated or have failed to integrate into a larger and more

---

36. Ibid., 77.
37. Herdt, "Alasdair MacIntyre's 'Rationality of Traditions,'" 531–32.
38. Porter, "Openness and Constraint," 524–25.

adequate conceptual scheme."[39] Nevertheless, the presence of such modern methods buried deeply in MacIntyre's own work should not be overlooked. Moreover, it should put one on notice to be on the lookout for other modernist assumptions embedded in his thought.[40]

Conclusions

When one compares MacIntyre's earlier and more recent views of theism, one notices at least three things. First, he sharply reverses his characterizations of premodern and modern thought. In his earlier account, premodern theism was defined in terms of its inability to be open to any meaningful revision. "Theism," he claimed, "was elaborated in the light of that pre-scientific culture where the anomalous and the exceptional are not permitted to falsify existing beliefs."[41] By contrast, modern science was defined as the benchmark of ongoing openness to change. But when one turns to his more recent thought, the descriptions are nearly opposite: the premodern theism of Aquinas is described as a dialectical process of open-ended debate, where no answers are closed off from future revision. Alternatively, modern thought, especially in the Cartesian form of Encyclopedia, is characterized as more closed-off and less fluid than premodern dialectic. MacIntyre would presumably

---

39. Livingston, *Modern Christian Thought*, 1:344.

40. I recently reread, after a span of nearly twenty-five years, Kuhn's *The Structure of Scientific Revolutions*. I was particularly struck by the similarities between MacIntyre's notion of tradition-constituted inquiry and Kuhn's notion of science as a tradition- or paradigm-constituted form of inquiry. Likewise, one detects hints of similarity between MacIntyre's views and the 1934 preface to Popper's 1st edition of *Logic of Scientific Discovery*. Though this is not the time or place to develop it, I would venture to suggest (and others may well have already done so) that MacIntyre's notion of tradition-constituted inquiry is significantly influenced by modern philosophy of science, which MacIntyre then uses as a lens through which to read Aquinas and the medieval tradition. Though MacIntyre himself does not, to my knowledge, elaborate on this modern influence at length, he does point to it on multiple occasions in *TRV*. For instance, he writes: "It would of course be grossly anachronistic to portray Aquinas's understanding of his own early development, as he confronted two rival and incommensurable schemes of belief and enquiry, in the terms in which I have used. Aquinas was not responding to Bachelard, Kuhn, Feyerabend, and Davidson. But he was responding to a type of problem which we now understand much better, thanks to those and kindred writers" (*TRV*, 122). In sum, this influence from modern philosophy of science indicates again the extent to which MacIntyre's thought is shaped, implicitly or explicitly, by certain modern substantive assumptions.

41. MacIntyre, "Fate of Theism," 10.

now describe his earlier characterization of premodern theism as mistaken and overly simplistic. Instead of writing it off, he now espouses premodern theism, in the form of Aquinas's medieval dialectical mode of inquiry, as a fluid approach that combines a reverence for the past with an ongoing openness to revision.

Second, what is consistent between his earlier and more recent thought is the conclusion that if theology allows itself to stand under the umbrella of modern thought, with its Encyclopedic set of assumptions, it will inevitably end up either accommodating itself to modern culture or being marginalized by it. Accommodation occurs when theology seeks to speak in a manner that is intelligible to modern men and women and is consistent with modern standards of rationality. Such an effort necessarily results, he believes, in theology losing its authentic voice. Alternatively, marginalization occurs when theology stands under the modern umbrella but refuses to speak in a manner that is publicly accessible. In this case, in its efforts to remain faithful to its own voice, theology ends up failing to speak in a genuinely public way at all. In sum, both of these alternatives, accommodation and marginalization, result in a theology that fails to speak publicly in a genuinely cognitive voice that challenges the secularizing tendencies of modern culture.

Third, the only way for theology to speak its authentic voice is for it to stand under its own premodern umbrella (Tradition) and, at the same time, to challenge the modern framework (Encyclopedia) itself. In his earlier work, MacIntyre had not yet come to this conclusion, but he was implicitly searching for some way for theology to speak cognitively. He now believes that the only way for theology to avoid both accommodation and marginalization is for it to reclaim Aquinas's dialectical mode of inquiry as a way both to speak authentically and to challenge modernity and its secularizing effects. Such an approach claims that all reasoning is tradition-specific and holds that the truth claims set forth by different traditions can only be adjudicated through the dialectical process of inter-traditional rivalry and assessment. MacIntyre alleges that the rationally superior tradition is the one that can resolve the internal problems of other traditions better than they can themselves. For example, he argues that the medieval tradition of Aquinas, with its theistic teleology, is better able to resolve the difficulties of modern moral theory than can the Encyclopedic or Kantian tradition itself. In chapter 3, I will examine MacIntyre's tradition-constituted rationality in greater detail, but for now it is clear that he thinks theology must retrieve a neo-Thomistic stance within an understanding of Tradition.

Stanley Hauerwas

In 1983 Stanley Hauerwas co-edited a book of essays with MacIntyre setting forth some revised approaches in contemporary moral philosophy. In that collection, Hauerwas wrote a chapter called "On Keeping Theological Ethics Theological."[42] This essay is significant because it sets forth Hauerwas's most explicit and detailed assessment of what has gone wrong in modern theological ethics. Unlike the early MacIntyre, Hauerwas does not believe the problem is due to an inevitable and unsolvable modern dilemma. Rather, more akin to the later MacIntyre, Hauerwas argues that Christian ethics has lost its theological voice because it has made a fateful accommodation to the secular assumptions of modern philosophical ethics by mistakenly translating its insights into a non-theological idiom in order to try to remain publicly intelligible and relevant. Hauerwas's analysis consists of three main parts: He explains the plight of theological ethics; then he outlines the development of twentieth-century American Protestant ethics, which he believes illustrates the development and persistence of the basic problem.[43] Finally, he emphasizes the importance of the historical particularity of Christian claims. Only by reclaiming and proclaiming the uniqueness of the Christian story, he holds, can Christian ethics truly speak theologically.

The Basic Problem

Hauerwas begins by reflecting on the title of James Gustafson's 1981 Ryerson Lecture at the University of Chicago, "Say Something

---

42. Hauerwas, "On Keeping Theological Ethics Theological." This essay also appeared later in Hauerwas, *Against the Nations*. In citing this essay, I will quote only from *Against the Nations*.

43. In a footnote, Hauerwas indicates that he hopes to write a future book offering a more detailed account of twentieth-century Christian ethics in order to further illuminate his systematic diagnosis. Yet, in a later article, he states that he has now abandoned that project because he no longer sees the point of it given the strong shift in contemporary Christian ethics away from the church and seminary toward the secular university. See Hauerwas, "On Keeping Theological Ethics Theological," 45 n. 7; and then Hauerwas, "Christian Ethics in America." In spite of abandoning this project, his basic diagnosis remains the same.

Theological."⁴⁴ The request from secular-minded academic colleagues to "say something theological" represents a challenge, put to theologians, to offer a convincing case that theology has something essential to offer. At a popular level, many people still assume there is a necessary connection between religion and ethics, but such a conviction has certainly not been "compellingly evidenced on the philosophical level." What Hauerwas refers to here is the widespread view in modern philosophy that ethics is or can be autonomous from theology. The fact that popular opinion still assumes some close connection between religion and ethics, however, indicates that modern philosophy has failed to offer a widely persuasive alternative. In the midst of this cultural vacuum, theologians have been strongly tempted to fill the void by trying to show some continued public role for religion in relation to ethics. In spite of the fact that theologians "cannot [rationally] demonstrate the truth of theological claims," Hauerwas remarks, "they [believe they] can at least show the continued necessity of religious attitudes for the maintenance of our culture." Since the Enlightenment, it has been widely assumed that theologians must speak in such a way that makes theological insights intelligible to the wider public, which has meant dispensing with the historically particular claims of the Christian tradition in favor of more universal ones. This shift from the particular to the universal has forced theology to translate its claims into terms that are intelligible and potentially credible to persons outside the Christian tradition.⁴⁵

By giving up this historical particularity, however, Hauerwas contends that theologians have nothing distinctive left to say to culture. As he puts it,

> just to the extent this [translation] strategy has been successful, the more theologians have underwritten the assumption that anything said in a theological framework cannot be of much interest. For if what is said theologically is but a confirmation of what we can know on other grounds or can be said more clearly in nontheological language, then why bother saying it theologically at all?⁴⁶

---

44. I first discussed Hauerwas's diagnostic and prescriptive accounts in Meyer, "On Keeping Theological Ethics Theological: An Alternative to Hauerwas" 22–27. I will later address Gustafson's Ryerson Lecture in my chapter on Gustafson's theology.

45. Hauerwas, "On Keeping Theological Ethics Theological," 23, 24.

46. Ibid., 25.

To illustrate his point about the self-undermining nature of this translation strategy, Hauerwas turns to the field of medical ethics. In spite of the fact that much of the work done in medical ethics has been carried out by theologians, most of them have done it in such a way as to minimize the influence of theology. Indeed, their work is nearly indistinguishable from those who proceed without theological convictions. Precisely because it has tried to fit in and accommodate itself to the assumptions of modern philosophy and culture, theology has ended up undermining its credibility as well as its distinctiveness, thus reinforcing the notion that theologians have nothing valuable to say *qua* theologians and that theology itself "cannot be considered a serious intellectual endeavor."[47]

The failure of the translation strategy, Hauerwas concludes, indicates the persistent "inability of Christian theologians to find a sufficient medium to articulate their own best insights for those who do not share their [theological] convictions."[48] In other words, contrary to the sectarian label that he strongly rejects, Hauerwas believes that theology does have something important to say to modern philosophy and culture, but the problem has been that theology has not yet figured out how to communicate this alternative in an appropriate way.[49] In order to explain why theology has repeatedly failed to solve this problem, Hauerwas proceeds to sketch an historical narrative outlining some of the major figures and movements in the development of modern Christian ethics, particularly in the context of twentieth-century American Protestantism.

A Brief Historical Analysis of Modern Christian Ethics

The origin of Christian ethics as a discipline distinct from theology was a result of the Enlightenment assumption about the autonomy of ethics. Prior to the Enlightenment, Hauerwas recounts, Christian ethical reflection was always an activity within the scope of theology. But to the extent that Christian thought came to accept the widespread philosophical assumption that ethics can be coherently understood independently of theology, Christian ethics came into existence as a distinct discipline

---

47. Ibid.

48. Ibid., 26.

49. For an illustration of Hauerwas's rejection of the sectarian label, see "Will the Real Sectarian Stand Up?"

with the aim of trying to show some continued relevance of theology for "an independent realm called 'morality.'"[50] From its inception, modern theological ethics has been influenced by two different strands, one philosophical and the other pastoral. The philosophical strand traces its roots back through Protestant liberalism to Kant, for whom, of course, morality was finally the essence of religion. This priority of the ethical over the theological meant that theological convictions were ultimately secondary to ethical concerns.[51]

Hauerwas traces the pastoral strand back to the Social Gospel movement and its attempt to respond to the economic crises of modern industrialization. Drawing on the prophetic tradition, the social gospelers preached a message of social justice that appeared to reconnect theology and morality in a way that went against the secularizing currents of modernity. Nevertheless, they still took their theoretical bearings from Kantianism through the Protestant liberalism of Albrecht Ritschl. Thus, on the surface they proclaimed an ethical message that drew a connection between religion and ethics, yet underneath they still accepted Kantian philosophical assumptions that grounded morality independently of theology. And because they accepted the latter, they were never able to make a sustained and convincing case for the former. Instead, what they relied on were the receptive ears of a still dominant Protestant cultural ethos. "The social gospelers," Hauerwas observes, "were able to make direct appeals to their religious convictions to justify their social involvement, because in the late nineteenth century they could continue to presuppose that America was a 'religious' or even a 'Christian civilization and country.'"[52]

From the Social Gospel, Hauerwas moves on to brief discussions of Reinhold Niebuhr, H. Richard Niebuhr, Paul Ramsey, and James Gustafson. In spite of their respective differences, what all of them finally have in common with the Social Gospel is a persistent belief that Christian ethics should somehow be accessible and relevant to the wider public. This assumption led all of them to translate their theological convictions into non-theological terms. For example, Hauerwas notes that Reinhold Niebuhr

---

50. Hauerwas, "On Keeping Theological Ethics Theological," 27.
51. Ibid.
52. Ibid., 27–28, 32.

continued the liberal attempt to demonstrate the intelligibility of theological language through its power to illuminate the human condition. In spite of Niebuhr's personally profound theological convictions, many secular thinkers accepted his anthropology and social theory without accepting his theological presuppositions. And it is not clear that in doing so they were making a mistake, as the relationships between Niebuhr's theological and ethical positions were never clearly demonstrated.[53]

Hauerwas then points to Ramsey as a further illustration. Ramsey "claims that what makes ethics Christian is that theological convictions are necessary to sustain the deontological commitments of our culture. Therefore, in [his] work in such areas as medical ethics, most of the theology can be done in the 'Preface' of his books. As a result," even many of those who are sympathetic with his deontological commitments "see no reason why those . . . commitments require . . . theological views about the significance of covenant love to sustain that ethos."[54]

Hence, regardless of whether these various theologians were seeking to transform society or to undergird the status quo or to explain theological ethics to an increasingly secular public, their respective attempts to make theology intelligible to modern men and women all led, Hauerwas avers, to theological impoverishment. Instead of offering an alternative to the philosophical separation of ethics from theology, they accommodated themselves to this separation in their attempt to be publicly intelligible and relevant. "What they failed to see," Hauerwas declares, "was that the very philosophical sources from which they drew to clarify [or explicate] the nature of their normative claims made it difficult to suggest how religious convictions might challenge just those philosophical frameworks."[55] Thus, sounding the same critical note that he reached in the first part of his diagnosis, Hauerwas concludes his historical analysis by stating that

> just to the extent that the development of Christian ethics as a field was a success, it reinforced the assumption that more positive theological convictions had little purchase on the way things are or should be. It is no wonder, therefore, that the dominant modes of philosophical ethics received little challenge from the

---

53. Ibid., 31.
54. Ibid., 36.
55. Ibid.

theological community. Indeed, exactly to the contrary, theologians and religious thinkers have largely sought to show that the modes of argument and conclusions reached by philosophical ethicists are no different from those reached by ethicists with more explicit religious presuppositions. The task of Christian ethics, both socially and philosophically, was not revision but accommodation.[56]

An Argument for Particularity

If I have understood Hauerwas correctly, the fundamental error made by modern theological ethics has not been its goal of trying to say something theological to culture but, rather, its failed attempt to really do so. One might be tempted to say that Hauerwas's dispute with modern theological ethics is mainly over means rather than ends. However, I suspect he would allege that modern theological ethics even lost sight of its true end, of saying something theological, because it became too preoccupied with trying to be publicly relevant and intelligible in an increasingly secular public square. In short, the chosen means of communication (translation) ended up undermining the goal of saying something theological. If this reading is correct, it again reinforces Hauerwas's own stated position that he is not advocating a sectarian disengagement from society. On the contrary, he is trying to show modern philosophy and culture the insights of a theological alternative, but he thinks this cannot be done by trying to make such insights publicly intelligible and credible in modern terms. Such a move, he presumes, inevitably runs the theological ship aground on the philosophical sandbars of the Enlightenment. Any attempt to challenge the prejudices of modern philosophy and culture on their own terms, he proclaims, is "doomed to failure. The more theologians seek to find the means to translate theological convictions into terms acceptable to the nonbeliever, the more they substantiate the view that theology has little of importance to say in the area of ethics. It seems that the theologian is in a classical 'no win' situation."[57]

The only way out of this modern dilemma, Hauerwas believes, is for theological ethics to emphasize its own historical and cultural particularity. Following in the neo-Aristotelian tradition of MacIntyre,

56. Ibid., 39.
57. Ibid., 40.

Hauerwas advocates an empirical teleological approach to ethics to counter the a priori non-teleology of the dominant Kantian legacy.[58] That is to say, Hauerwas's approach is teleological insofar as it asserts the priority of the good over the right, and it is empirical insofar as it claims that the validity of the definition of the good must ultimately rest on the starting point of a given example, namely, a particular community and its tradition. This empirical emphasis is illustrated by Hauerwas when he holds that moral convictions are inherently historical and community-dependent in nature and cannot, therefore, be universally convincing. "The justification of our moral principles and assertions," he claims, "cannot be done from the point of view of [just] anyone, but rather requires a tradition of moral wisdom."[59] For Hauerwas, this tradition of moral wisdom is found in the church, which he defines as a community that calls people to a particular vision of the good and seeks to cultivate the virtues appropriate to that vision. Had modern Christian ethics rightly recognized the empirical and teleological character of ethics, it could have challenged the non-teleology of the Kantian legacy and its persistent attempt "to model the moral life ... on the analogy of the law." But precisely because modern theological ethics has so deeply accommodated itself to that legacy, it has wrongly believed that it has a stake in sustaining the status quo.[60]

Because Hauerwas thinks that ethics ultimately rests on the empirical basis of a particular community and its tradition, rather than on an a priori understanding of reason, he contends that theological claims should not focus directly on God but rather on the church. By focusing directly on God, Christian ethics ends up asserting beliefs and making claims that are rather metaphysical in character. As he sees it, such an approach looks like "some kind of primitive metaphysics that one must then try to analyze for their moral implications. To force Christian moral reflection into such a pattern is to make it appear but another philosophical account of the moral life." Instead, Hauerwas argues that such claims and beliefs about God are only intelligible against the background of the church, that is, within the context of a group of people who are called to live differently from the world because of their

---

58. This helpful distinction between "empirical teleology" and "a priori non-teleology" stems from Gamwell, *Divine Good*, chapters 2 and 3.

59. Hauerwas, "On Keeping Theological Ethics Theological," 41.

60. Ibid., 40, 41.

distinctive tradition and vision of the good, which trains them in the virtues that make them different. The validation of any claim about the reality of God, therefore, ultimately depends on the validating witness of a particular community and its distinctive form of life. I will examine Hauerwas's theology in detail in Part Two, but for now let me sum up by noting that he believes theologians do "have something significant to say about ethics, but they will not say it significantly if they try to disguise the fact that they think, write, and speak out of and to a distinctive community."[61]

Jeffrey Stout

As a non-theist, Jeffrey Stout has brought both an appreciative and a critical lens to his analysis of religion and its relation to ethics and culture. In terms of formative experiences, Stout was profoundly influenced by the Civil Rights movement of the 1960s. Though he himself has not been personally drawn to religious belief since at least his early adulthood, he nonetheless observed and took lasting note of the significant role that Christians played in the Civil Rights struggle. With this background in mind, one might say that Stout's intellectual enterprise has been guided by two overarching aims. As a non-theist, he has sought to articulate and defend a naturalistic piety that could galvanize political action in the way that Christianity did during the Civil Rights era. And, for these same social and political reasons, he has also sought to find a way for Christianity and other religious voices to again play a significant (preferably progressive) political role in American democracy. Hence, Stout's attentive and ongoing analysis of Christian theology is fundamentally instrumental and pragmatic. Christianity, he believes, will not be socially powerful unless Christians themselves can thoughtfully and faithfully express their underlying core convictions in some public manner.[62]

As noted earlier, Stout acknowledges his debt to MacIntyre and Hauerwas in helping him to launch his scholarly career, when, as co-editors, they invited him to write his first book and then published it in 1981 as part of a series they edited for the University of Notre Dame

---

61. Ibid., 42, 44.

62. I'm indebted to Jennifer Herdt for pointing out the value of Stout's biographical background as a helpful context for introducing his thought.

Press. That book, which includes Stout's initial exploration of what has gone wrong in modern theology, is entitled *The Flight from Authority: Religion, Morality, and the Quest for Autonomy*. Whereas MacIntyre offered a brief historical sketch in "The Fate of Theism," Stout offers here a more detailed account that seeks to show how modern thought itself "was born in a crisis of authority, took shape in flight from authority, and aspired from the start to autonomy from all traditional influence whatsoever."[63] Drawing on the work of Ian Hacking, Stout reports that, by the time of Descartes, medieval understandings of both rational knowledge (*scientia*, i.e., knowledge known with demonstrative certainty) and probable opinion (*opinio*, i.e., conclusions accepted without rational certainty based on the authority of those who espouse them) had deteriorated under the acids of late medieval nominalism and the multiplication of authorities during the Reformation. In response to this double erosion, Descartes sought to reclaim *scientia* and thus pursued his quest for rational certainty by rebuilding it from the ground up. But what was not historically available to him in the early seventeenth century was the modern notion of probability, which is based on judgments of internal evidence rather than on judgments of external authority. Modern probability was hinted at by Pascal's wager, but it was actually developed later in the century by Pascal's colleagues at Port Royal. The upshot of modern probability, as embodied in modern science, is that it eliminates the need for either rational certainty or medieval authority. Instead of seeking infallible reasons or deferring to the testimony of trusted authorities, it attempts to offer fallible but convincing reasons based on empirical evidence.[64] How this historic flight from authority affected modern theology is our first subject for discussion. We will then, in turn, look at Stout's assessments of theology in his second and third major books.

Theism and the Flight from Authority

Though he quibbles with some of the details of MacIntyre's account in "The Fate of Theism," Stout here generally agrees with MacIntyre's basic conclusion that modern theism has found itself in a cul-de-sac with an

---

63. Stout, *Flight from Authority*, 2–3.

64. Ibid., chap. 2, "Placing the Father," 37–61. Stout cites Ian Hacking, *Emergence of Probability* (Cambridge: Cambridge University Press, 1975).

irresolvable dilemma. Either it can conform to modern standards of rationality, and thus lose its theological distinctiveness, or it can resist, and thus become culturally marginalized.[65] In seeking to show how modern theology ended up in this dilemma, Stout situates his account of theism within the context of the emergence of modern probability.

Pointing to Aquinas, Stout observes how medieval theology relied on the authority of revelation to complete reason. Specifically, the authority of revelation consisted of the authority of Scripture and tradition as they were interpreted by the Church. This reliance on the testimony of external authorities (e.g., the Apostles and the Church) was central both to medieval theology and to the medieval notion of probability *(opinio)*. As Stout quotes Aquinas, "Argument from authority is the method most appropriate to this teaching in that its premises are held through revelation; consequently it has to accept the authority of those to whom revelation was made."[66] Hence, what did not make sense to reason in the medieval context could be reasonably accepted as a mystery of faith, based on testimony of respected external authorities, rather than jettisoned as an irrational paradox. However, with the rise of modern probability in the late seventeenth century, medieval mysteries gradually turned into problematic modern paradoxes. This shift from mystery to paradox, Stout proclaims, was the first crisis of modern theism. As modern probability turned away from the authority of external testimony and relied instead on the authority of internal evidence, it became possible to use internal evidence to make judgments about the reliability of external authorities themselves. Scriptural claims about miracles, for instance, came under increasing scrutiny and were judged by Hume and others to be rationally improbable.

Like MacIntyre, Stout views deism as a failed theological response to this first crisis. Deism sought to abide by the new standards of internal evidence and, thus, interpreted the "book of nature" as offering probable reasons for the existence of a divine creator. But such a move, on the one hand, shifted Christian theism away from orthodox beliefs and, on the other, made theistic claims mere hypotheses that were vulnerable to counter-argument. When the argument from design and other deistic arguments came under increasing attack by Hume and others, the deistic strategy of cultural compliance seemed to be losing on both fronts—

---

65. Stout, *Flight from Authority*, 102, 104.
66. Ibid., 107. Stout cites Aquinas, *Summa Theologiae*, I, 1.2.

losing both its claim to Christian authenticity and its claim to cultural credibility. In essence, the first crisis of theism meant that Christian claims went from medieval mysteries to modern paradoxes, which in turn were pushed to the margins of serious public conversation.[67]

The second crisis centered on theology's response to this fateful progression. The dominant response was a strategy of separation or bifurcation, which, in its radical form, eventually entailed an embrace of paradox. This bifurcation strategy, which stretches from Kant to Kierkegaard to Barth and beyond, sought to protect the orthodoxy of Christian faith, but did so at the cost of "altering significantly the social location of theology." This strategy took for granted Hume and Kant's denial of the possibility of theoretical or metaphysical knowledge of God. A posteriori arguments, such as the argument from design, were judged to be at best improbable, whereas a priori arguments were judged to be impossible—given that both Hume and Kant denied that a priori reasoning could know reality in itself. Though Kant agreed with Hume's rejection of metaphysical theism, he sought to overcome Hume's skeptical edge by means of his transcendental idealism. Referring to Kant, Stout remarks that "he declared Hume right about our ignorance of things-in-themselves but wrong about the structures of mind that make knowledge of the world of experience possible, and right about the inability of theoretical reason to achieve knowledge of things divine but wrong about the essence of religion."[68]

What Hume did not fully grasp about religion, according to Kant, is its non-cognitive essence. Noting Kant's Pietist upbringing, Stout suggests that Kant's "Pietist solution to the problem of faith and culture" was to claim that "religion is not essentially a theoretical matter at all," but instead a matter of morality. Stout proceeds to show how Schleiermacher, and his subsequent legacy for modern theology, accepted Kant's denial of metaphysical theism and sought to implement his own "Pietist solution" by redefining religion in terms of piety rather than morality. The implication of this trend is that it took for granted—and thus reinforced—Hume and Kant's denial of the cognitive claims of theism. As a result, "the attempt to refute Hume [and Kant] on [their] own terms, to revive natural theology by meeting the challenge head

---

67. Stout, *Flight from Authority*, chap. 6.
68. Ibid., 128, 130–31.

on, had retreated into obscure corners of the academy by the end of the Victorian period."[69]

Like MacIntyre, Stout recognizes that modern theology has lost its cognitive voice, and he is troubled by it. For instance, in regard to Schleiermacher's acceptance of Kant's denial of cognitive theism, Stout asks,

> But does not going this far with Kant threaten to reduce the interest of theology? What makes theology more interesting than [merely] so many *oohs* and *aahs* or descriptions of heartburn if it is essentially expressive or descriptive [only] of feelings? Even if we postpone the question of whether feeling and knowing can be distinguished as radically as Schleiermacher supposes, we shall need to ask how theology can retain interest without entering the cognitive sphere. It may be that Schleiermacher's theology *seems* interesting *only* because its essentially emotive character is masked by misleadingly propositional forms of expression. It is more likely, however, that Schleiermacher has simply smuggled extensive cognitive commitments past his own Kantian censor. Either way, his hopes for theology are jeopardized.[70]

Schleiermacher's hopes are jeopardized, Stout reasons, because if theology is non-cognitive, it loses its point; if it is cognitive, it succumbs to Kant's critique. As Stout sharply puts it, "either explanatory claims are being made here or not. If not, we remain in the realm of heartburn and tickles. But if such claims are being made, the Kantian criticisms can be brought to bear."[71] Thus, from Schleiermacher, Stout turns his attention to Hegel who, of course, sought to overcome Kant's criticisms in a cognitive way.

Hegel attempted to overcome Kant's bifurcation strategy and reassert the cognitive claims of theism by expressing them philosophically in his new metaphysical system. For instance, Hegel viewed the paradoxical Christian doctrine of incarnation as a symbolic expression of the metaphysical insight into the panentheistic nature of reality. Ordinary understanding found such doctrines to be unintelligible, but "Hegel took such responses as evidence of the limitations of ordinary understanding." Instead of eliminating these doctrines as irrational paradoxes,

69. Ibid., 131, 129.
70. Ibid., 132–33.
71. Ibid., 133.

Hegel argued that these cognitive truths could only be given adequate expression by stretching beyond ordinary language and understanding to a more adequate metaphysical scheme. As Stout reports, "far from reducing them to the categories of the understanding or mistaking their higher truths for ordinary falsehood, [Hegel's system] raises them up to the comprehensive intelligibility of reason."[72]

Though Stout acknowledges that he has long been influenced by Hegel, he has never warmed up to Hegel's metaphysics. Summarily speaking, he adopts Hegel's emphasis on history while discarding his metaphysical explanation of history. As Stout says in *Ethics After Babel*, Hegel's metaphysics "nowadays seems highly dubious. But what remains of his answer once the metaphysics has been filtered out, I submit, is simply [and desirably] . . . the immanent rationality of a tradition."[73] Here, of course, one again recognizes Stout's debt to MacIntyre. Putting aside the question of the relative merits of Hegel's own metaphysics, one detects that Stout finds all metaphysical efforts "highly dubious." In spite of this, Stout applauds Hegel's effort to overcome the bifurcation strategy and reassert the cognitive dimension of Christian theism. Only by taking its own cognitive claims seriously and expressing their distinctiveness in an adequate but intelligible manner could Christian theism hope to retain any central role in modern culture. Nevertheless, Stout concludes that Hegel's system was still "intrinsically unstable." By trying to affirm both the modern autonomy of reason and the distinctive claims of Christian theism, by trying to integrate Christian theism into modern culture without losing its distinctive cognitive claims, Stout surmises that Hegel was trying to do the impossible. "Religion could not be both distinguishable *and* thoroughly integrated," Stout purports. Thus, Hegel's legacy was left to be divided between those who gravitated to his metaphysical and theological-side, and those who gravitated to his historical and immanent worldliness.[74]

After the breakdown and fragmentation of Hegel's effort, Ritschl reasserted Kant's moral focus to the center of Christian liberal theology. But as is well known, theological liberalism was radically called into question in light of the battlefields and bloodshed of World War I. Stout

72. Ibid., 136–37.

73. Stout, *Ethics After Babel*, 143–44. For Stout's undergraduate interest in Hegel, see his preface to *Flight from Authority*, ix.

74. Stout, *Flight from Authority*, 139–40.

thus draws his historical narrative to a close by turning his attention to Barth.

Barth accepted Hume and Kant's denial of metaphysical theism and natural theology, but he also rejected all forms of what might be called the "anthropological" version of the bifurcation strategy. That is, Barth rejected all attempts to begin theology from human experience, such as exemplified in Kant's moral interpretation or in Schleiermacher's analysis of piety. All such efforts, Barth maintained, lead inexorably to Feuerbach's radical conclusion that religion and theology are ultimately merely human projections. Over against this, Barth proposed what might be called a "theological" version of the bifurcation strategy. Instead of drawing lines of demarcation between different perspectives of human reason or different spheres of human experience, Barth sharply separates theology itself from human experience or rationality as such. For Barth, as Stout recounts, "faith grounds itself in God's word. It does not need *grounding* from us. Attempts to place faith on firm grounding or to reach faith from a basis of human reason or experience are clearly an affront to God's otherness and bound to erode faith's essential content." Thus, Barth, especially the early Barth, like Kierkegaard before him, reasserted the paradoxical nature of Christian claims, which had either been eliminated by deism, softened by Schleiermacher, or rationally overcome by Hegel. Continuing his description of Barth, Stout states that "Christianity, if it is to be true to itself, will have to make ontological claims. But it cannot *defend* them in secular or philosophical terms. Theology cannot be apologetics. This is the conclusion that stands behind both Kierkegaard's indirect communication and Barth's *Dogmatics*."[75]

In the end, Stout holds up Barth as the great, heroic modern theologian. He does so because Barth tries to reassert the cognitive claims of theology without seeking to abide by the canons of modern rationality. Instead of going along with modernity, Barth "seeks to return theology to its 'proper basis' in the divine authority of God's word." At the same time, however, Stout acknowledges that Barth's approach has severely isolated theology from the rest of culture. But such isolation, he reasons, was inevitable anyway given the rise of modern probability and theol-

---

75. Ibid., 140, 141, 142, 143.

ogy's inherently paradoxical nature. In sum, the tide of history has "left theology unable to step meaningfully again into the public arena."[76]

"Theology since Barth," Stout concludes, "is a sad story." Reiterating MacIntyre's analysis of the correlational theologies of Bultmann and Tillich, Stout asserts that such alternatives end up sounding either like Feuerbach, insofar as they translate their claims into publicly intelligible speech, or like Barth, insofar as they remain distinctively Christian, i.e., paradoxical. "To leave the paradoxical features out, either by returning to Deism or by divorcing theology from the realm of ontological claims, is to make theistic vocabulary superfluous." This danger of superfluity has plagued theological efforts since Barth, as evidenced explicitly by the radical theologies of the 1960s and more implicitly by recent attempts at public theology in the academy. Such attempts, Stout contends, endlessly focus on method and thus lose both their church and academic audiences.[77]

Another Theological Voice: Ethics After Babel

A few years after the publication of *The Flight from Authority*, Stout returned his attention to the plight of theology in a published essay, which also appeared soon thereafter as a chapter in his second major book, *Ethics After Babel*.[78] In that chapter, entitled "The Voice of Theology," he once again notes how theology has lost its public influence, especially in the academy. In the public arena, Stout observes, "a hearing for theological ideas must be won, if they are to get a hearing at all." But this time, interestingly, Stout looks not to Barth or to a recent Barthian as the theological exemplar but rather to James Gustafson. To my knowledge, this shift from Barth to Gustafson has never been commented on either by Stout or others.[79] Whereas Barth rejected efforts to make Christian theology intelligible to a wider secular audience, Gustafson seeks to engage his academic colleagues in direct conversation. Considering

---

76. Ibid., 147, 144, 146, 241.

77. Ibid., 147, 146, 147.

78. The original essay is Stout, "Voice of Theology in Contemporary Culture." I will focus my attention on and quote only from the version in *Ethics After Babel*, "Voice of Theology," 163–88.

79. Stout, *Ethics After Babel*, 165. I briefly discussed Stout's shift from Barth to Gustafson in an extended footnote in my doctoral dissertation: Meyer, "The Relation of Theism to Ethics," 2 n. 1.

this shift, it appears that Stout, in his second book, believes that theology should at least try to be publicly conversant; however, to do so, he urges that it not try to identify philosophical grounds to guide public conversation or to validate public truth claims. As an example of such a misguided effort, Stout points to David Tracy's "fundamental theology," with its attempt to ground theological claims by appeal to a publicly valid metaphysics formulated in modern process terms. Unlike Tracy, who attempts to validate theological claims on "strictly public grounds that are open to all rational persons," Gustafson eschews philosophical foundations and seeks simply to interpret the ethical situation from the particularities of his theological stance, which is a stance that is also informed by the best lights of modern science.[80]

Stout outlines the roots of Gustafson's theology by tracing them back to the modern Reformed tradition of Schleiermacher, Troeltsch, and H. Richard Niebuhr. Following in this legacy, Gustafson defines theology as critical reflection on the experience of religious piety, and claims that theology presupposes religious piety for its persuasive power. What Stout likes about Gustafson's approach is the way that he tries to make theology publicly conversant; Gustafson seeks to earn the respect (if not the actual consent) of his secular-minded university colleagues, but he does so by means of selectively retrieving ideas and reasons from the theological tradition itself. Instead of attempting, like Tracy, to make theology philosophically credible, Gustafson seeks simply to speak from the theological tradition in a thoughtful and critical manner. For instance, Gustafson draws from the Reformed tradition a radical theocentric vision that challenges the anthropomorphic tendencies of much human and Christian religiosity. In putting forth this theocentric vision, Stout suggests that Gustafson avoids the straightforward bifurcation strategy of Schleiermacher, which undersells the cognitive claims of theology by strongly separating the affective and cognitive dimensions of life.[81]

These positive qualities notwithstanding, what Stout ultimately finds troubling about Gustafson's effort is that he, too, fails finally to offer any defense of the cognitive claims of theology. As Stout notes, "it remains unclear why, despite his stress on theocentricism, Gustafson

---

80. Stout, *Ethics After Babel*, 165, 167, 181. Stout cites Tracy, *Analogical Imagination*, 62, 64.

81. Stout, *Ethics After Babel*, 168–70, 170, 178–80, 178.

insists on speaking of God or divine purposes at all?" For example, he "does not make clear why we shouldn't view . . . secular piety . . . as the natural successor to theocentric piety." Furthermore, "he never explains clearly why one ought to speak of 'the powers that bear down upon us' as divine or . . . why [these] powers . . . should be construed *mono*theistically." In voicing these criticisms, Stout's concern is not that Gustafson has failed to offer knockdown compelling arguments, "arguments so powerful that any reasonable intellect would be forced to lay down its objections and submit." Stout doubts whether such arguments exist at all or "play a major role in any discipline." Rather, his concern is that Gustafson fails finally to offer any public reasons—even to explain "why he himself, 'even in piety,' might have reason to be convinced [by his own theocentric claims]."[82] Hence, in spite of his attraction to Gustafson's approach, Stout concludes that even Gustafson fails to defend the cognitive claims of theology in public discourse.

Thus, on one end, Stout here rejects Barth's refusal to make theology publicly conversant. On the other end, he rejects Tracy's attempt to make theology publicly conversant by seeking to make it philosophically credible. In between, he applauds Gustafson's attempt to make theology publicly conversant simply by critically selecting elements of the theological tradition. Nevertheless, Stout ultimately finds Gustafson's effort wanting as well insofar as he fails to offer a defense of the cognitive claims of theism. Therefore, Stout concludes by reaffirming what he takes to be the virtually unsolvable dilemma of modern theology, namely, that it is caught between the unbridgeable horns of public intelligibility and theological authenticity. It is this modern predicament, Stout reasons, that explains Gustafson's failure to offer a cognitive defense of a theocentric vision. As he describes it, Gustafson's

> theology illustrates with special clarity the difficulty posed by theology's current predicament. I think this predicament, not Gustafson's rigor as a theologian, explains his failure to make plain the distinctively theological content of his proposal and his reasons for accepting it.[83]

In sum, Stout strongly doubts whether Gustafson or anyone else can offer a genuinely theistic voice that is truly public: Barth opts for theo-

---

82. Ibid., 178, 182, 183.
83. Ibid., 184.

logical authenticity at the price of public conversation; Tracy opts for conversation at the price of authenticity; and Gustafson valiantly seeks both but fully achieves neither.

In the face of this modern dilemma, Stout proceeds to sketch a six-fold "map of the contemporary theological landscape." In the current context, theologians generally pursue one of the following options: (1) a selective and critical retrieval of Christian tradition that seeks to be publicly conversant without philosophical foundations; (2) a fundamental or metaphysical theology; (3) a separationist strategy bifurcating theology and science in a pact of nonagression; (4) a radical relativism that makes theological claims a matter of confession from within the Christian community but non-criticizable from without; (5) a form of Barthian dogmatics that unapologetically gives priority to biblical authority over public reason; or (6) a political attempt, from either the right or left, to overthrow the whole cultural and epistemic context of modern pluralism and autonomy.[84] On the whole, Stout is not particularly impressed with the first five options and he is mindful of the potential dangers of the sixth. Nonetheless, he suggests that at least the sixth option recognizes the type and scope of cultural change that is needed. For if theology is to regain any significant public voice, it will require some widespread religious revival and cultural shift, independent from and prior to theological articulation. As Stout sees it:

> [W]hether academic theologians can win a wide hearing even within the academy depends in part, it seems to me, on whether religious resurgence produces dramatic change, independently of theology, in what most people, including intellectuals, take for granted about the nature and existence of God when they speak to matters of moral importance in public settings. Such a change would shift the burden of proof in a way that might make some kind of theology central to the culture again. That, of course, is precisely the outcome sought by the champions of option (6).[85]

In setting forth this view, Stout apparently believes that the question concerning the "nature and existence of God" is ultimately beyond reason in some important sense; thus it requires the presence of religious piety for an affirmative answer. That is, much like Gustafson,

---

84. Ibid., 185.
85. Ibid., 186.

Stout assumes that the credibility of theism is relative to the religious piety it presupposes. Hence, only the cultural influence of something like another Great Awakening, with its resurgent spread of religious piety, could sufficiently shift the social location of theology to make it central once again to public moral discourse. Stout ends the chapter, however, by hedging his position. Even though he is not impressed with the current theological options, he insists that he cannot permanently rule out any of them:

> Nothing I have said shows that theologians of genius will never find a way through the dilemma as it now stands. Nor, my own skepticism notwithstanding, have I implied that certain theological claims are either false or at fault. For all I have said here, some version of theology could be true and the theologian's position at the margins of modern intellectual culture could be evidence of the decadence of that culture.[86]

A Return to Barth via Hunsinger: Democracy and Tradition

If Barth offered a distinctive theological voice but seemed to lack sufficient resources for public conversation, and if Gustafson tended toward conversation at the expense of theological articulation, Stout suggests in his third major book that he has now found the right combination—a more publicly conversant form of Barthianism as set forth by the theologian George Hunsinger. This return to Barth via Hunsinger occurs in Part Two of *Democracy and Tradition*, entitled "Religious Voices in a Secular Society." Here Stout once again takes up the issue of theology in public discourse, but does so this time within the context of a larger discussion of religion and democracy. Hence, my exposition in this section will require greater elaboration and analysis in order to understand the wider context in which Stout seeks to empower the public voice of theology. While his defining goal is to properly conceptualize democracy and religion's role within it, he sees two main impediments to achieving this aim: (1) various versions of liberalism (as illustrated by Rawls and Rorty) that wrongly seek to restrict religious voices in democratic political discourse, and (2) a misguided new traditionalism (MacIntyre, Hauerwas, and Milbank) that mistakenly accepts these "restrictive" conceptions as normative and thus wrongly advocates a blanket rejec-

---

86. Ibid., 187.

tion of democracy as such. Over against these two alternatives, Stout champions a vision of democracy that encourages all voices to speak, including theological ones.[87]

"What role, if any," Stout asks, "should religious premises play in the reasoning citizens engage in when they make and defend political decisions?" In addressing this central question, Stout argues that Rawls implicitly offers two distinct conceptions of public reasoning. In the weaker or less restrictive version,

> Each citizen may rightfully demand reasons why *he* or *she* should view the proposed policy as legitimate. It does not suffice in this context to be told why other people, on the basis of their idiosyncratic premises and collateral commitments, have reached this conclusion. It is not enough for a speaker to show that he or she is entitled to consider a proposal legitimate. The question on each concerned citizen's mind will rightly be, "Why should *I* accept this?" Fairness and respect require an honest effort, on the part of any citizen advocating a policy, to justify it to other reasonable citizens who may be approaching the issue from different points of view.[88]

In response to this conception, Stout declares his agreement. "So far, so good," he remarks. "Proper treatment of one's fellow citizens does seem to require an honest justificatory effort of this sort. When proposing a political policy one should do one's best to supply reasons for it that people occupying other points of view could reasonably accept."[89] At first blush, Stout's declaration here seems to put him in closer concert with Rawls and modern liberalism than is in fact the case, for Stout has a very different model in mind. But before getting to that, he describes what he takes to be Rawls's stronger or more stringent version of public reason.

The key provision of this stronger version, which Stout notes is "put forward in the original clothbound edition of *Political Liberalism*," is Rawls's insistence "that our reasoning in the public forum should appeal strictly to ideals and principles that no reasonable person could reasonably reject. By agreeing to abide by such principles and to rely

---

87. Stout, *Democracy and Tradition*, Part Two, "Religious Voices in a Secular Society," 61–179.

88. Ibid., 63, 65.

89. Ibid., 65.

solely on them when reasoning in the public forum, citizens enter a social contract." By using social contract language, Stout reckons, Rawls ratchets up the demand of public discourse to a point where one must give reasons "that no reasonable person could reasonably reject." But what counts as a "reasonable person?" Quoting Rawls, Stout says it describes those who "'are willing to govern their conduct by a principle from which they and others can reason in common.' ... And this means being willing to accept a common basis for reasoning that others, similarly motivated, could not reasonably reject." As suggested here, Rawls believes that public discourse should be governed by a principle that is based on common reasons, i.e., based on reasons that all participants could in theory agree to or share. And because Rawls follows in the postmetaphysical legacy of Kant, he does not believe that comprehensive doctrines can, even in theory, be addressed or adjudicated on the basis of common reasoning. Hence, Rawls implies here that public life and its social contract must be governed by a principle independent of any comprehensive doctrine. A "reasonable" person will therefore not appeal to any comprehensive doctrine to justify his or her claims in the public forum. But "this definition" of public reasoning, Stout retorts, "implicitly imputes *unreasonableness* to everyone who opts out of the contractarian project, regardless of the *reasons* they might have for doing so." This includes those, like Stout himself, who "consider the quest for a *common* justificatory basis morally unnecessary and epistemologically dubious."[90]

In putting together Stout's account of Rawls's two versions of public reasoning, it is essential to sort out the distinct elements involved. In the weaker version, what is required of all citizens making claims or policy proposals is *an honest effort* to offer reasons to others that others themselves might find convincing. In the stronger version, there are two key components, which Rawls equates, that are worth distinguishing for the sake of analytical clarity: *a commitment to reason in common* and *an exclusion of comprehensive doctrines from public reasoning.*

---

90. Ibid., 65–66, 67; Stout cites Rawls, *Political Liberalism*, (1993) 49 n. 1. In his later "wider view," Rawls downplays the notion of a single public principle in favor of simply "freestanding" reasoning—where participants may draw upon their comprehensive doctrines, but the principles of justice must still be able to be publicly justified independently of any such doctrine and, thus, are freestanding from any of them. See Rawls's "Introduction to the Paperback Edition," *Political Liberalism* (1996) li–lv.

Taken together, therefore, we have three distinct conceptions of public reasoning:

(A) an honest effort to offer reasons to others that they might find convincing
(B) a commitment to reason in common
(C) an exclusion of comprehensive doctrines from public reasoning

What both Stout and the new traditionalists most strongly object to here is Rawls's exclusion of comprehensive doctrines from public reasoning (C). This is the fatal error of modern liberalism, as they see it. But I would venture to say that both Stout and the new traditionalists also, to differing degrees, reject or at least have their doubts about a commitment to reasoning in common (B). For to reason in common means to be committed to offering reasons that *both* the speaker *and* the listener might find intelligible and convincing. Let me call this dialogical engagement the process of *common criticism*. Both Stout and the new traditionalists are doubtful that comprehensive doctrines can be publicly addressed and adjudicated on the basis of common criticism. This is because both are what I call strong historicists—thus they implicitly deny that any such common reasons exist when it comes to religious or metaphysical questions. Hence, on this single point, they agree with Rawls that comprehensive doctrines cannot be addressed and adjudicated on the basis of common criticism. But where Stout and the new traditionalists part company is in terms of where they go from here. The new traditionalists, who contend that all reasoning is tradition-specific, largely abandon the democratic project in favor of more tightly-bound communities of virtue. Alternatively, Stout argues that option (A) opens up a different conception of public reasoning, specifically one that can include comprehensive doctrines in democratic life and discourse. Thus, when Stout affirms that public reasoning requires an honest effort to offer reasons to others that they might find convincing (A), he does not have common criticism (B) in mind; instead, he envisions public conversation in terms of *immanent criticism*.

In Stout's model of immanent criticism, "citizens address one another qua citizens" but this does not stipulate how they should talk to each other. On the contrary, they are "free to frame their contributions to [public discourse] in whatever vocabulary they please." Most modern democracies are *"secularized,"* Stout contends, but not committed to *"secularism."* By this distinction, he means that democracy does not require persons "to relinquish their religious beliefs or to refrain from [publicly] employing them as reasons." By calling democracy secular rather than secularistic, Stout refers to "the fact that participants in [public discourse] are not in a position to take for granted that their interlocutors are making the same religious assumptions they are." Thus to call democracy secular is to offer a sociological observation that religious pluralism exists in our midst. In this empirical sense, he remarks, "it is true that modern democratic discourse tends not to be 'framed by a theological perspective,' but this does not prevent any of the individuals participating in it from adopting a theological perspective." Again, they are free to publicly employ "whatever vocabulary they please."[91]

"What they cannot reasonably do," Stout proclaims, "is expect a single theological perspective to be shared by all of their interlocutors." The crucial but ambiguous term here is "expect." In a weak sense, Stout simply has in mind his sociological observation that one cannot *presuppose* agreement where no current agreement exists. But in a stronger sense, he implies that one should not even *seek* agreement about a common theological perspective because, even if there is a shared underlying ultimate reality, no common knowledge of this ultimate reality is possible. Hence, he declares that "there is no point in pretending that [theologians] are articulating the implicit commitments and practices of their fellow citizens as a whole." In fact, it this misguided attempt to articulate the implicit dimensions of experience that explains why

> the recent debate over "public theology" is beset by confusion over what this phrase means. There is clearly little hope for public theology if this means the attempt to bring into expressive equilibrium the [implicit] theological commitments all members of our society share, for there are no such shared commitments.[92]

In this stronger sense, then, Stout not only denies that there is no explicit consensus in society about ultimate questions such as religion, but he

---

91. Stout, *Democracy and Tradition*, 93, 97. In addition to offering an empirical observation, one might say that Stout's notion of the secular character of democracy also offers a constitutional observation, namely, that the presuppositions of democratic discourse do not include explicit adherence to any comprehensive doctrine—religious or philosophical.

92. Stout, *Democracy and Tradition*, 97, 112–13.

also denies that there are any implicit theological or metaphysical commitments shared by humans as such. This double denial mirrors the two senses of historicism that I outlined at the beginning of the chapter. As a weak historicist, Stout notes the empirical conditions of our explicit situation; as a strong historicist, he subtly makes philosophical claims about what is or is not implicitly the case in regard to experience as such. So just as we earlier saw his criticism of Tracy's public theology, we again see his persistent criticism of any attempt to offer a common or public theology.[93]

Thankfully, "a theologian can give up this [misguided] ambition as unrealistic," Stout adds, "without giving up the hope of addressing a public audience—an audience that includes citizens who are outside of the church." It is at this juncture that he draws explicitly upon his notion of immanent criticism. A theologian or religious person can publicly engage and respect others by speaking first in his or her own theological vocabulary and then by trying to show others how they—within their own distinctive vocabulary—have their own internal reasons for agreeing with the proposed claim or policy. Stout describes this immanent criticism as "Socratic conversation":

> Suppose I tell you honestly why I favor a given policy, citing religious reasons. I then draw you into a Socratic conversation on the matter, take seriously the objections you raise against my premises, and make a concerted attempt to show you how *your* idiosyncratic premises give *you* reason to accept my conclusions.[94]

It is not immediately clear from this description why one ought initially to "take seriously the objections you raise against my premises." Put simply, are your objections formulated in your vocabulary, in a common vocabulary, or in my vocabulary? Stout might reply that it does not matter since he emphasizes "the importance of virtues in guiding a citizen through the process of discursive exchange and political decision making." These virtues include "the ability to listen with an open mind." But if citizens can understand and take with full seriousness all the reasons that others offer, then why is immanent criticism needed? Is this not what common criticism affirms, namely, that we are capable

---

93. By denying that there are any implicit shared theological or metaphysical commitments, Stout appears to be implicitly denying general revelation.

94. Stout, *Democracy and Tradition*, 113, 72.

of understanding and critically assessing reasons together? Indeed, at one point Stout even seems to downplay immanent criticism in favor of common criticism: "First, I would insist," he says, "that the ideal of respect for one's fellow citizens does not in every case require us to argue from a common justificatory basis of principles that no one properly motivated could reasonably reject." Here it sounds as though he accepts common criticism as the general norm and immanent criticism only as an occasional exception. But this seems to go against the general tenor of his overall discussion, especially when it comes to religion. For he goes on immediately to "recommend the mixed rhetorical strategy of expressing one's own (perhaps idiosyncratic) reasons for a political policy while also directing fair-minded . . . immanent criticism against one's opponent's reasons."[95] To answer my question, then, I presume that Stout would say that we take objections or criticisms most seriously when they are formulated in our own vocabulary. This points to the multivious conception of discourse he has in mind; everyone ought to be prepared to address everyone else in terms of everyone else's own distinctive or idiosyncratic vocabulary—this is his notion of public respect:

> Why would I be failing to show respect for X if I offered reasons to X that X ought to be moved by from X's [own] point of view? Why would it matter that there might be other people, Y and Z, who could reasonably reject those reasons? Suppose Y and Z are also part of my audience. . . . Does my immanent criticism of X then show disrespect to Y and Z? No, because I can [then] go on to show respect for them in the same way, by offering *different* reasons to them, reasons relevant *from their [own] point of view*.[96]

Having laid out this alternative vision of ongoing immanent criticism, Stout is exasperated by the new traditionalists' rejection of democracy. One does not need to buy into modern notions of common reason, common criticism, or social contract, he contends, to embrace democracy itself. Over against the rising tide of new traditionalists, who are increasingly influential in theological education and the church, Stout holds up George Hunsinger's interpretation of Barth as an exemplary model of a distinctly theological voice that still embraces

---

95. Ibid., 85.
96. Ibid., 73.

the secularity of democracy. Drawing on the historical example of the 1934 Barmen Declaration, written chiefly by Barth as an expression of the Confessing Church Movement's resistance to the Nazi takeover of German churches, Hunsinger shows how theology can be faithful to its own voice, challenge the reigning political powers, and still affirm secularity. "Hunsinger's appeal to Barth and to the politics of resistance that flowed from the Barmen Declaration," Stout declares, "illuminates . . . a theologically rich account of what it means for Christians to be involved in modern, secularized political communities."[97] In particular, the Barmen example illustrates that

> Christians must always be prepared to enter a broader discussion in which various words will be spoken. Their utterances in that domain should display the courage of their convictions. They must speak the truth as they see it, which means affirming Jesus Christ as the truth, and be ready to pay the price for saying what they believe. They should resist any form of pluralism or relativism that would be incompatible with the practice of making truth-claims or with their own commitment to this particular truth-claim. All parties involved in the discussion will have their own affirmations to offer. Without truth-claims, there would be no communication, no exchange of reasons. No one can make declarative statements without implying that those who deny the propositional content of those statements are committed to falsehoods. This, by itself, is not arrogant. But . . . [i]t would . . . be arrogant to assume that one knows in advance which human voices are speaking truly. This is what secularists assume when they rig the rules of discussion to exclude religious voices. And it is also what Christians assume when they treat the church as the only source of truths.[98]

In this summative passage, one sees all of Stout's central themes: theology should willingly enter the wider public and political conversation; and, in doing so, it must speak in its own voice and profess its own distinctive truth claims—including the Barthian proclamation "that Jesus Christ is *the* Truth and *the* Light and that all else stands under his authority."[99] Without strong substantive claims such as this, Stout avows,

---

97. Ibid., 109. Stout draws on two main works from Hunsinger: *How to Read Karl Barth*, and *Disruptive Grace*.

98. Stout, *Democracy and Tradition*, 111–12.

99. Ibid., 109.

both theology and public discourse become vacuous. Hence, theology should resist any version of democracy or pluralism "that would be incompatible with the practice of making truth-claims or with their own commitment to [the] particular truth-claim" that Jesus Christ is the defining truth. When one makes truth claims, like Barth's, one implies that those who reject those claims are mistaken and are thus implicitly "committed to falsehoods." But "this, by itself," Stout contends, "is not arrogant." Arrogance occurs only when one presumes that truth cannot be spoken by others—either by religious voices (the arrogance of modern liberalism) or by secular voices (the arrogance of new traditionalism).

As one reads Stout, it is not initially clear how his affirmation of immanent criticism and his recommendation of Barthian Christomonism can go together. By "Christomonism," I mean the all-encompassing and singular claim that Barth makes in regard to Christ. For example, speaking of Barth's view, Hunsinger states: "That there is only one theological truth, that it is exclusively the truth of Jesus Christ, and that all other truths must be conceived dialectically as distinctive forms, reflections, and reproductions of the one great truth."[100] But how is this claim compatible with immanent criticism? The key to immanent criticism is the ability to find *internal* reasons within the other person's distinctive vocabulary that can give *them* their *own reasons* to accept *your* claim. What *internal* reasons could a non-Christian, or perhaps even a non-Barthian, have for accepting this fundamental truth claim? The underlying assumption of immanent criticism is that one can find an indirect bridge between two different vocabularies—one that spans between my truth claim or policy proposal and the internal resources in your vocabulary that give you internal reasons for accepting my claim. Hence, there is an indirect link between my claim and your vocabulary, which leads to agreement between us without us ever reasoning in common—without us ever finding reasons that we each affirm. But what bridge could there be between Barth's Christomonistic claim and the vocabularies of others? Stout might answer by pointing out that this line of questioning overlooks an important distinction. Immanent criticism, he might say, is meant to be a discursive practice to convince others to accept our policy proposals (e.g., resist the Nazis, pay attention to global warming, raise taxes, etc.) but not to convince them to accept our premises or fundamental truth claims. Hence, it becomes

100. Hunsinger, *How to Read Karl Barth*, 272.

apparent that even though Stout encourages theology to make strong truth claims in public discourse, he qualifies or nuances this espousal in multiple ways.

First, he does so by the way that he paradigmatically defines public discourse. Drawing on the inferential pragmatism of Robert Brandom, Stout defines discourse as a pragmatic form of expressivism: the primary aim of discourse is to publicly express one's self-understanding and for other participants to then hold one accountable by making sure that one only draws inferences from that understanding to which one is entitled. One is entitled only to those inferences that follow logically from one's self-understanding and that are in general agreement with the reasons or "epistemic resources" available in one's historical and cultural context. As Stout notes elsewhere in a helpful explanatory essay, a key assumption behind this view is that "the notions of truth and justification swing free of each other." The question of entitlement pertains only to whether one is *justified* in what one believes, not to whether what one believes or claims is *true*. For instance, Stout suggests that Aquinas, in his epistemic context, was entitled to affirm a geocentric understanding of the universe, even if we later learned that it was a false understanding. Now if one's claim deals with empirical or practical matters, such as in the case of geocentricism, then there are constraints by which one can test the truth of the assertion, and not merely address the issue of justificatory entitlement.[101] But if, alternatively, one's claim pertains to metaphysical or theological matters, then there are few if any rational or logical measures by which to assess the question of truth. Instead, one can only address the issue of justification to see whether the person has drawn inferences to which he or she is entitled.

In regard to religion, therefore, Stout is more interested in finding a way for theological voices to publicly express their religious reasons than for those reasons to actually convince others of their own truth or validity. To deny religious voices this expressive freedom, he announces, would "deprive them of the central democratic good of expressing themselves to the rest of us on matters about which they care deeply." He goes on to add that such a denial would also deprive us of "the chance to learn from, and to critically examine what they say."[102] One can learn

---

101. Stout, "Radical Interpretation and Pragmatism," 28, 27, 28, 46, 47.

102. Stout, *Democracy and Tradition*, 80–83, 64. Stout draws principally upon Brandom's *Making it Explicit*, and *Articulating Reasons*.

from them their underlying religious rationale and how that rationale defines the context of their overall perspective. What one can critically examine are the inferences they draw from that rationale: specifically, one can see whether they are logically entitled to those inferences given their underlying commitments. Yet it is important to stress that one cannot rationally assess their underlying commitments or fundamental claims per se, such as illustrated by Barth's Christomonism. To explicate this key proviso we must introduce Stout's distinction between "faith-claims" and "religious claims," which he draws from Brandom, and which he introduces in response to Rorty's contention that religion is always a "conversation-stopper," and therefore should be kept out of public discourse.[103]

Compared to his customary clarity, Stout's articulation of this distinction is somewhat opaque. One source of this opacity stems from the uncertainty of whether he is referring to two different types of claims or whether he is referring to two different attitudes that a speaker might bring to a claim—an attitude willing to demonstrate entitlement to that claim versus an attitude unwilling to do so. The second source of opacity stems from the fact that Stout proceeds to make an implicit distinction between faith-claims in a strict sense and faith-claims in a broad sense. The puzzle all begins when he says: "There is one sort of religious premise that does have a tendency to stop a conversation, at least momentarily—namely, faith-claims." The focus of this statement is on religious premises, and the implication seems to be that there are in fact different kinds of premises or claims—each having its own distinct content or focus. The fact that "faith" is used here as an adjective to modify the word "claims" lends credence to this view. From this vantage point, then, faith-claims would appear to be one distinct type of claim, among others, with its own distinct content domain. However, Stout points in another direction when he refers to Brandom: "A faith-claim, according to Brandom, avows a cognitive commitment without claiming entitlement to that commitment." Here the focus seems to shift from premises to the implied speakers making claims. In this case, a faith-claim refers to a speaker who puts forth a cognitive claim without also being willing to demonstrate his or her entitlement to that claim. Thus the focus is not on different content domains, but rather on different attitudes or

---

103. Stout, *Democracy and Tradition*, 85–91. See Rorty, "Religion as Conversation-stopper."

Diagnosing the Plight of Theology in the Modern World 67

dispositions among speakers who make claims. In short, a faith-claim refers to speakers "who avow... premises [but who] are not prepared to argue for them." More precisely, Stout states:

> In the context of discursive exchange, if I make a faith-claim, I am authorizing others to attribute the commitment [or claim] to me and perhaps giving them a better understanding of why I have undertaken certain other cognitive or practical commitments. I am also making the claim available to others as a premise they might wish to employ in their reasoning. *But I am not accepting the responsibility of demonstrating my entitlement to it. If pressed for such a demonstration, I might say simply that it is a matter of faith.* In other words, "Don't ask me for reasons. I don't have any" [italics added].[104]

This suggests that faith-claims denote a failure of responsibility, namely, speakers who go "AWOL" from their duties when making claims. Brandom helps us to understand this: "[I]n making a claim," he writes, "one is implicitly endorsing a set of inferences, which articulate its conceptual content." And "giving reasons for a claim is producing other assertions [i.e., the set of logical inferences,] that *license* or *entitle* one to it, that *justify* it." So a faith-claim refers to a speaker unwilling to show that he is entitled to his claim by giving reasons for it, and these reasons are none other than the logical inferences that flow from it. "It should be clear," Stout observes, "how this [all too] common sort of discursive move tends to put a crimp in the exchange of reasons." But religious claims need not fall into this trap. "[A] claim can be religious," Stout adds, "without being a faith-claim. It is possible to assert a premise that is religious in content and stand ready to demonstrate one's entitlement to it. Many people are prepared to argue at great length in support of their religious claims."[105]

From this analysis, we can see that what Stout means by a faith-claim, strictly speaking, is an abdication of responsibility by a speaker, not a specific or unique content domain. Furthermore, both Stout and Brandom insist that faith-claims are not restricted to religion. "Everyone holds some beliefs on nonreligious topics," remarks Stout, "without claiming to know that they are true." To hold or affirm beliefs without

---

104. Stout, *Democracy and Tradition*, 86, 86, 87, 86–87.

105. Brandom, *Articulating Reasons*, 18, 19, 193; Stout, *Democracy and Tradition*, 87.

being able to demonstrate their truth, Stout implies, is what constitutes faith. Hence, whenever one makes a claim about such beliefs or offers them as a premise, one is making a faith-claim. What is significant here is that, as Stout broadens the scope and applicability of this notion to a broad range of persons, outlooks, and situations, the connotation of faith-claims begins to shift from a discursive failure to an unavoidable practice. "In fact, the phenomenon of nonreligious faith-claims is quite common in political discourse," says Stout, "because policy making often requires us to take some stand when we cannot honestly claim to know that our stand is correct. That is just the way politics is."[106] Since our ultimate values or convictions inevitably inform our political views, and since we cannot validate the truth of these ultimate convictions, Stout reasons, we therefore inevitably introduce faith-claims into public discourse.

As Stout continues this shift toward the inevitability of faith-claims, he begins to hint at an important distinction between faith-claims in a "strict" sense and faith-claims in a "broad" or inevitable sense. Note this revealing passage:

> It is important in this context to recall the distinction between being entitled to a belief and being able to justify that belief to someone else. Even in cases where individuals do plausibly claim to be epistemically entitled to religious premises, they might still be unable to produce an argument that would give their interlocutors reason to accept those premises. To assert such a premise would not qualify as a faith-claim in the strict sense that I have just defined, but it would create a potential impasse in conversation.[107]

He begins this illuminating paragraph by marking a distinction between "being entitled to a belief and being able to justify that belief to someone else." The implication here is that even if one seeks responsibly to show one's entitlement to a religious claim, one may still be unable to justify one's claim in the sense of being "unable to produce an argument that would give [others] reason to accept those premises." This distinction can also be cast in terms of the meaning of justification. That is, even if one is justified in the sense of having shown others that one is entitled to one's claim (having shown that one's claim is internally and

---

106. Stout, *Democracy and Tradition*, 87.
107. Ibid.

logically consistent with one's *chosen or given* convictions), one may still be unable to justify a claim in the sense of offering reasons why others should accept the truth or validity of that claim. Thus, even if one avoids faith-claims in a "strict sense," by seeking to show one's entitlement to a claim, one may not be able to avoid faith-claims in a "broad sense." Stout certainly hints at such a distinction in the final sentence above. Furthermore, he maintains that such broad or inevitable faith-claims are not restricted to persons making specifically religious assertions. Indeed, "the same sort of difficulty arises for all of us," he submits, "when we are asked to defend our most deeply engrained commitments." These deeply-held commitments, which Rorty calls our "final vocabularies," refer to our most basic existential and metaphysical convictions about life, the world, and ultimate reality. These claims or vocabularies are "final," according to Rorty and Stout, in the sense that there is no way to rationally justify or validate them as such. As Stout puts it, "What Rorty is describing here is the sort of discursive commitment one can be entitled to even though one would not know how to defend it. . . . Like Rorty [says], [persons] tend to be speechless when pressed for linear [or non-circular] reasons for adopting their final vocabularies."[108] This is what I meant earlier when I asserted that, from Stout's vantage point, one cannot rationally assess underlying commitments or fundamental claims per se, such as in the case of Barth's Christomonism.

In fact, Stout has this notion of final vocabularies (or faith-claims in a broad sense) in mind when describing Hunsinger's employment of Barthian Christomonism. "Like the rest of us," Stout declares, "[Hunsinger] is not in a position to argue for [his final] vocabulary in a noncircular way. Admitting this is part of the point of using Anselm's phrase, 'faith in search of understanding,' as a Barthian theological motto. It means that he is arguing from premises he does not know how to argue for in a straightforward, linear way." But what Hunsinger can and does do is to "take full responsibility for explaining and defending the inferential and practical commitments implicit in [and flowing from] his final vocabulary." So Hunsinger does not resort to faith-claims in the strict sense, but like the rest of us he inevitably make faith-claims in the broad sense, since he cannot rationally validate his Christomonistic starting point. Unlike Rorty, who takes this as a reason to banish religion and other final vocabularies from public discourse, Stout invites all final

108. Ibid., 87, 89.

vocabularies to speak in the public domain. To be sure, Stout would prefer that all voices demonstrate their entitlement to their claims, thus avoiding faith-claims in a strict sense, even as he simultaneously invites them to make faith-claims in a broad sense: "I can imagine no way of banning the use of final vocabularies . . . from political discussion, even if it were a desirable thing to do, which it plainly is not."[109] So Stout invites theological voices to publicly *express* their truth claims, such as those concerning the reality of God or the centrality of Christ, but the *truth* or *validity* of such claims can never be addressed or adjudicated in public discourse. Hence, the point of public discourse, for Stout, is to provide a context for expressing one's fundamental convictions or final vocabulary, but not for rationally testing those convictions per se. Rather, the give and take of reasons is reserved for the subsequent and more limited task of examining whether speakers are logically and practically entitled to the inferences they draw from their own final vocabulary. To epitomize, reason can test entitlement but not truth when it comes to religion or metaphysics.

Stout qualifies his endorsement of a public theological voice in another way as well. Having just affirmed religion's right to public self-expression, he immediately adds: "Of course, having a right does not necessarily mean that one would be justified in exercising it. Clearly, there are circumstances in which it would be imprudent or disrespectful for someone to reason solely from religious premises when defending a policy proposal." Relying on his practical instincts, Stout flashes here a cautionary light. Citing concerns about rhetorical effectiveness and moral respect for others, Stout urges theologians and others to be circumspect before appealing to religious reasons in public political discourse. Indeed, at another point he asserts even more strongly "that in most contexts it will simply be imprudent, rhetorically speaking, to introduce explicitly theological premises into an argument intended to persuade a religiously diverse public audience."[110] Hence, for both moral and prudential reasons, Stout counsels religious voices to exercise self-restraint.

Stout's cautionary stance here seems at odds with what he said earlier when championing Hunsinger's reading of Barth and Barmen.

---

109. Ibid., 116, 89.
110. Ibid., 64, 65, 98–99.

There, he insisted that Christians must speak in the public forum in a manner that displays

> the courage of their convictions. They must speak the truth as they see it, which means affirming Jesus Christ as the truth, and be ready to pay the price for saying what they believe. They should resist any form of pluralism or relativism that would be incompatible with the practice of making truth-claims or with their own commitment to this particular truth-claim.[111]

There is certainly no pragmatic calculation here about what is prudent or rhetorically effective. Neither is there self-restraint in proclaiming that Jesus Christ is the truth, for Christians must "be ready to pay the price for saying what they believe." So, on the one hand, Stout's democratic pragmatism leads him to encourage religious self-restraint in a pluralistic context, while, on the other hand, his attraction to Barthian theology—as the model of a distinctive theological voice—leads him to support strong Christomonistic claims in public. But how does he then reconcile these opposing tendencies?

The answer comes in his third and most important qualification. What Stout is most drawn to in Hunsinger's reading of Barth is the emphasis on listening to diverse others more than speaking to them. Even though Stout affirms that Christian theology ought to feel free to express Christomonistic claims in public, his real attraction to Hunsinger is found in Hunsinger's amplification of Barth's openness to listening for the Word of God in diverse voices. "The spirit of Hunsinger's political theology," Stout proclaims, "is most concisely expressed in Barth's dictum that 'God may speak to us through Russian Communism, a flute concerto, a blossoming shrub, or a dead dog.'" What Stout finds appealing about Barth's dictum is that it provides a theological rationale, over against the new traditionalists, for why theology should embrace rather than reject democratic discourse. "If God may speak through Godless Communism," Stout muses, "why not, then, through the words both Christians and non-Christians speak when holding one another responsible democratically for the justice and decency of their institutional arrangements?"[112] In essence, Stout begins his discussion of religion by defending the right of theology to speak and make claims

---

111. Ibid., 111.

112. Ibid., 109. Stout cites: Hunsinger, *Disruptive Grace*, 80; and Barth, *Church Dogmatics,* I/1, 60.

in public discourse, but his emphasis gradually shifts toward a focus on theology listening to other voices.

According to Hunsinger, this listening is encapsulated in Barth's notion of "secular parables," which Barth discusses in *Church Dogmatics* IV/3. For Barth, parables are "words which conform and agree materially with the Word, not as equals but as servants, and not by any capacity of their own but by grace." Put simply, they are "'secondary forms' of the one Word of God." Hence, secular parables are any words coming from non-Christian and non-theological voices that indirectly and unwittingly point to the Word of God itself. Quoting Barth, Hunsinger states that "'we may [thus] quietly listen to others. We may hear what is said by the whole story of religion, poetry, mythology, and philosophy. We shall certainly meet there many things which might be claimed as elements of the Word spoken by Jesus Christ.'" These secular parables are "incognito" forms of the Word at work in the world. Thus they "demand a real hearing from the [church], not deflecting it from 'its own mission to preach the one Word of God,' but assisting, comforting, and strengthening it on the way." Hunsinger strongly reiterates that there is no natural theology or general revelation at work here. On the contrary, these secular words are an incognito vehicle for the one true Word only because the Word itself has made use of them and placed them into the one true context. If they are "divorced and abstracted from the contextual whole established by the concrete life of Jesus Christ, these elements cannot help but say something else." Therefore, the claim "that Jesus Christ is the One Word of God . . . is axiomatic for dogmatic theology. [The Word of God] has and can have no other basis than the one it provides for itself."[113]

This notion of secular parables, and its openness to listening for the Word of God in diverse voices, illustrates what Hunsinger calls "*exclusivism without triumphalism.*" Barth's theology is exclusivist insofar as "it holds that one scheme of theological doctrines (Christianity), taken as a whole, is true in a way that no other such scheme, taken as a whole, can be. Indeed, when taken as a whole, any other such scheme . . . can only be regarded as false." But, at the same time, Barth's theology is non-triumphalist in that it is willing to listen to secular and diverse voices insofar as they may unwittingly be vehicles for the incognito

---

113. Hunsinger, *How to Read Karl Barth*, 254, 252, 255, 252. Hunsinger cites Barth, *Church Dogmatics*, IV/3, 108, 115.

Word of God. Stout is drawn to this theological view precisely because of its openness to the secular. For in describing Barth's view, Stout states that "there must not be any simple refusal of the secular, for this would be tantamount to denying Christ's freedom to fashion secular parables as he sees fit."[114]

At the same time that he affirms theology's openness to the secular, however, Stout does not endorse theological approaches that seek to formulate their claims within the parameters of modern secularity. Rather he posits that such approaches become "thinned out" in the sense that they fail to offer "a theologically inflected vocabulary." Borrowing a phrase from Van Harvey, Stout calls such efforts the work of an "alienated theologian." This alienation arises from the ways theologians respond to the tension posed, on the one side, by the demands of modern democracy, which require "the virtue of open-minded charity in listening well to others," and, on the other side, by the demands of "their calling as expounders of the [theological] commitments of their ecclesial community." With this situation in mind, Stout observes:

> Many are the academic theologians who have felt this tension acutely when, in dialogue with others, they have felt the force of reasons at odds with their confession of faith.... [In response to this tension,] [a]lienated theologians remain preoccupied with God-talk but abandon some or all of the basic commitments of their faith communities. As a result, their communities have trouble treating them as spokespersons.[115]

Following Barth, as well as perhaps the new traditionalists, Stout here defines the role of the theologian primarily in terms of the church rather than the academy. And even more importantly, he defines the theologian's role as that of expounding traditional orthodoxy rather than challenging it. Hence, the role of the theologian is not to prompt the church toward new understandings of the historic Christian faith, but rather to be a spokesperson for the theological status quo. What troubles Stout about alienated theologians is not their theological claims per se. Indeed, he says that "theologically, most of them are mov-

---

114. Hunsinger, *How to Read Karl Barth*, 278, 279; Stout, *Democracy and Tradition*, 111. For a helpful discussion of different types of exclusivism and their relation to Hunsinger's reading of Barth, see Greggs, "Bringing Barth's Critique of Religion to the Inter-faith Table," 79 n. 16.

115. Stout, *Democracy and Tradition*, 113, 115–16.

ing in the direction of heresies that I embrace." Rather, his concern is an instrumental and pragmatic one: "But democracy will suffer greatly, I fear, if orthodox Christians are unable to find a way to maintain their own [current] convictions while also taking up their responsibilities as citizens."[116]

Fortunately, Stout continues, Hunsinger's appropriation of Barth offers a way forward. "Hunsinger is hardly an alienated theologian. He is someone wholeheartedly committed to his ecclesial office as an expounder of a religious tradition's 'final vocabulary.'" As noted earlier, Stout claims that neither Hunsinger nor anyone else can argue directly for the underlying metaphysical or theological premises contained in their final vocabulary. "But this [limitation]," Stout submits, "does nothing to diminish the integrity of the message Hunsinger articulates." For Hunsinger does take adequate and appropriate "responsibility for explaining and defending the inferential and practical commitments implicit in his final vocabulary. He explicates and tests his premises in a self-critical spirit. And he puts himself in a position to converse with, and learn from, Christians and non-Christians who see things differently." In sum, therefore, "It is a good thing that Hunsinger is speaking his mind . . . in a distinctively theological idiom." For "democracy and orthodoxy will both be well served if this [Barthian] message gains as much attention from Christians in the next decade as the [new traditionalist] school of resentment has received in the last."[117]

Synoptic Conclusions

Before looking at MacIntyre, Hauerwas, and Stout together, let me offer some summative observations about the evolution of Stout's own view. He began by affirming Barth's paradoxical formulation of the cognitive claims of theology in the face of modernity. But such efforts, Stout then reasoned, "undermine the preconditions for genuine debate with secular thought."[118] Hence, he moved on to Gustafson, hoping that his open engagement with secular disciplines would offer a more promising alternative. Yet what Gustafson gained in public conversation, he lost in theological articulation. However, neither Barth nor Gustafson

---

116. Ibid., 116.
117. Ibid., 116, 117.
118. Stout, *Flight from Authority*, 146.

could ultimately be faulted because, like the early MacIntyre, Stout then believed that modernity had all but irreversibly marginalized theology into the shadows of cultural life. For academic theologians like Gustafson to ever win a hearing in the academy would require a religious resurgence across the culture that would fundamentally change "what most people, including intellectuals, take for granted about the nature and existence of God when they speak to matters of moral importance in public settings."[119] Without a third "Great Awakening," theology would remain a muted voice. But in his more recent work, Stout seems to believe that he has found a way forward. On the theological side, Hunsinger's reading of Barth offers a more open and conversant form of Barthianism. The cognitive claims of theology are asserted here along with an openness to listening to others for secular parables. On the philosophical side, Brandom's pragmatic expressivism and inferential reasoning give theology and other voices a way to offer reasons in public from a variety of different final vocabularies. The final vocabularies cannot themselves be rationally evaluated per se, but one can assess whether theology offers reasons and inferences to which it is entitled, given its underlying convictions. Thus, through immanent criticism of one's inferential reasoning, Stout believes that he has now found a way for theology both to assert its cognitive claims in public and to engage in conversation and debate with secular thought.

But two differences should be noted in Stout's shift from Gustafson to Hunsinger. First, the kind of public conversation modeled by Hunsinger is rather different from that exemplified by Gustafson. Gustafson pursues common criticism more fully than does Hunsinger's form of Barthianism. That is, Gustafson, at least to a point, seeks to offer reasons to others that are mutually intelligible and, likewise, he seeks to learn from secular disciplines on their own terms—not listening merely for the one Christomonistic truth incognito. Second, Stout might now describe Gustafson as an alienated theologian who does not represent or adequately speak for Christian orthodoxy. Rather, by seeking to engage secular colleagues in a conversation of common criticism, Gustafson's God-talk has become attenuated. Hence, he speaks more for himself than for the church community. Yet whereas Gustafson is intentionally seeking to challenge and prod the conventional orthodoxy in the pew, Stout is looking for a theological voice to represent traditional religion.

119. Stout, *Ethics After Babel*, 186.

Hunsinger, he believes, is the one to do so, for he offers a way to build a bridge between conventional orthodoxy and the wider responsibilities of democratic citizenship.

So the recent Stout, like Hauerwas and the later MacIntyre, now believes that theology need not inevitably lose its authentic voice in the modern world. But to avoid marginalization, Stout now appears to agree with them that theology ought not to translate its convictions into culturally accessible categories, as illustrated by Gustafson, for such efforts are part of the misguided modern endeavor of common criticism. Rather, theology must stay true to its own language and tradition. Likewise, all three of them concur that final vocabularies cannot be rationally assessed in a direct or straightforward way. Beyond this point, however, they part company. Stout resists MacIntyre and Hauerwas's wholesale rejection of modern democracy and culture. Though Stout views democracy itself as a particular tradition, he affirms the democratic tradition as a way to avoid the traditionalist tendencies of MacIntyre and Hauerwas. In other words, by affirming tradition, Stout does not seek to wall off theological voices from the fluid give-and-take of democratic life. Rather, Hunsinger's Barthianism, immanent criticism, and inferential reasoning offer theology a way to be true to its own voice while still directly listening to and conversing with others. In contrast, Hauerwas and MacIntyre contend that modern culture is an "acid" that erodes the underpinnings of tradition itself. Hence, theology must speak only from within the "walls" of its own tradition and only indirectly to a secular audience. For Hauerwas, this occurs through the collective witness of the church. The Christian final vocabulary can only be made intelligible and credible by showing the world truthful lives—lives informed by the distinctive virtues and practices of the Christian story. For MacIntyre, theistic claims can be validated only indirectly through the dialectical competition among rival traditions. For instance, if the Thomistic Christian tradition can successfully explain and overcome the internal problems of the encyclopaedic, secular approach to morality, namely by reasserting a theistic and teleological conception of human life, then it can demonstrate its superior rationality and offer convincing reasons to support its claims.

An Alternative Diagnosis: The Denial of Metaphysics

As stated earlier, one of the many valuable contributions made by MacIntyre, Hauerwas, and Stout is that each of them has, in his own way, issued a clarion call indicating that something has gone wrong in modern theology and theological ethics. One of their collective strengths is their ability to recognize when a problem exists and to draw attention to it. Clearly modern theology has "lost its voice, its ability to command attention as a distinctive contributor to public discourse in our culture."[120] Again, the early Stout, like the early MacIntyre, thinks this due to a fateful dilemma imposed by modernity, whereas Hauerwas, like the later MacIntyre and the recent Stout, thinks it due more to a fateful accommodation made by modern theology itself. Both views are partly right. On the one hand, modernity has indeed thrown up a roadblock in front of theology and, on the other hand, theology has in fact made a fateful accommodation to it. Yet I am persuaded that all three thinkers fail to recognize what the real roadblock is and what the fateful accommodation has been.

The real roadblock, I submit, has been the pervasive denial of metaphysics in modern thought, and the fateful accommodation has been theology's widespread acceptance of this denial. By "metaphysics," I again mean the rational attempt to understand and articulate the character of reality as such. I recognize that the notions of reason and rationality have been contested by MacIntyre and others, and I will take this into account in Part Two when analyzing different approaches in modern and contemporary theology. But for now, I will define metaphysics in what can arguably be described as the traditional sense, namely, as the rational or philosophical attempt to describe the ultimate nature of reality. The question of whether reality as such necessarily entails the existence of God is fundamentally a metaphysical question. "The question of God's reality," Schubert Ogden correctly notes,

> is in its logic a metaphysical question. This is amply confirmed by the concept of "God" itself.... Where God is conceived radically, as in monotheistic religions..., God is clearly understood as metaphysically real.... In fact, the God of theism in its most fully developed forms is the one metaphysical individual, the sole being whose individuality is constitutive of reality as such

---

120. Ibid., 163.

> and who, therefore, is the inclusive object of all our faith and understanding.
>
> ... Because "God" is the metaphysical concept par excellence, the question of how this concept is to be understood and whether it refers to anything real can be answered only as a metaphysical question.[121]

As Ogden's description implies, any wholesale denial of the metaphysical enterprise is also a wholesale denial of the distinctive theistic claim, namely, the central claim about the reality and necessity of God. Because the claim about the reality of God is at root metaphysical, the denial of metaphysics inevitably leads to the marginalization of the cognitive voice of theology. Hence, because modern thought, including nearly all of modern theology, has so widely accepted the absence of metaphysics, theology has lost its ability to be a distinctive contributor to public discourse. This denial is the real roadblock that has sent theology scurrying off on its various detours throughout the modern age. Instead of directly challenging this roadblock, theology has largely accepted it and sought to pursue back-road alternatives—hoping, without success, to reconnect with the main thoroughfare of public discourse.

The significance of this modern denial was perceptively anticipated by Hegel in the nineteenth century. "I have touched on a prominent question of the day," he writes, "the question, namely, whether it is possible to recognize God—or, since it has ceased to be a question, the doctrine, which has now become a prejudice, that it is impossible to know God." "It no longer gives our age any concern," he remarks elsewhere, "that it knows nothing of God; on the contrary, it is regarded as a mark of the highest intelligence to hold that such knowledge is not even possible." In these statements, Hegel points to three important elements: First, he recognizes the centrality of the metaphysical question, namely, whether theoretical knowledge of God is possible. Second, he detects that this question was already disappearing from the radar screen of public discourse, including theological discourse, due to the widespread view "that it is impossible to know God." And third, he realizes that such a view is at odds with the spirit of Christianity itself. As he puts it, "Following this doctrine we now contradict what the Holy Scripture commands as our highest duty, namely, not only to love but also to know God. . . . Thus, in placing the Divine Being beyond our cognition and the

---

121. Ogden, *On Theology*, 79, 80.

pale of all human things, we gain the convenient license of indulging in our own fancies. We are freed from the necessity of referring our knowledge to the True and Divine."[122] Hegel insightfully anticipates the consequences for theology when it accepts the denial of metaphysics and, hence, loses its cognitive voice. Similarly, the contemporary philosopher John Rist offers a parallel historical observation. Setting his sights somewhat earlier, Rist notes that

> one of the effects of the Reformation was to dethrone metaphysics, in the hope of replacing it by Biblical exegesis.... Hence, especially in lands where the effects of Protestantism were strong, we shall not be surprised to find an attempt to restate human nature [and theology] in non-metaphysical terms: if God is to be introduced, he is to be the God of the voluntarists and his nature beyond the reasoning of metaphysics. From an unknowable God we move fast to an irrelevant God, and eventually to his elimination as superfluous.[123]

In sum, unlike Stout, who seeks to appropriate a "metaphysically-lite" Hegel, I maintain that it is precisely the metaphysical instincts of philosophers like Hegel and Rist and theologians like Ogden that help us see what has gone wrong in modern theology.

The Metaphysical Key

When asked by a nonreligious colleague to say something theological, Gustafson answered exquisitely by simply saying "God." But to say little is also sometimes to say much, for whatever else theological speech entails, it fundamentally involves an affirmation of the divine reality. And when one affirms the reality of God, one inevitably makes metaphysical truth claims about the nature of reality as such. "It follows from the strictly metaphysical character of the question of God," Ogden notes, "that any argument for, or proof of, God's reality, as well as any counter-argument or disproof, can only be metaphysical." Theistic affirmation thereby entails a theistic metaphysics, which claims that reality cannot be properly understood without relation to the divine. As Wolfhart

---

122. Hegel, *Reason in History*, 16; Hegel, *On Art, Religion, Philosophy*, 160. The passages in these two texts reflect similar Hegelian assessments and observations—possibly they go back to a common written source or, perhaps more likely, Hegel said similar things in his lectures and written essays.

123. Rist, *Real Ethics*, 156–57.

Pannenberg helpfully adds, "If talk about God has any claim to truth, ... it must be possible to show that secular[istic] descriptions of reality are indeed abstracting from the fullness of its nature." Thus, if theology is to speak in its own authentic voice, then it must at some point make and defend metaphysical claims about the reality and necessity of God. Instead of avoiding the so-called "bog of metaphysics," as MacIntyre, Hauerwas, and Stout recommend, theologians must properly conceive and pursue the metaphysical enterprise. As we saw earlier, even Stout himself points in this direction in his early discussion of Barth when he says that "Christianity, if it is to be true to itself, will have to make ontological claims." The crucial difference, of course, is that he immediately proceeds to say that Christianity "cannot *defend* them in secular or philosophical terms. Theology cannot be apologetics."[124]

Undoubtedly, it was Hume and especially Kant who built or finished the roadblock that convinced Barth and others that they could not rationally defend the ontological or metaphysical claims of theology. One might argue that the footings for this roadblock were laid earlier, perhaps in the late medieval period (as we will see Milbank assert in Part Two) or in the Reformation (Rist), but Kant certainly put up what widely came to be identified as the insurmountable barrier. Hence, most subsequent philosophy and theology have tended to be located in what Milbank rightly calls "a post-Kantian intellectual space." Along these lines, Franklin Gamwell observes that

> few philosophical arguments have enjoyed an influence as pervasive and enduring as have Kant's treatments of the theistic proofs in the *Critique of Pure Reason*. Summarily stated, the dominant conclusion of subsequent Western philosophy asserts that Kant demonstrated once and for all the impossibility of [rationally] redeeming theistic claims ... and, therefore, gave preeminent expression to the conviction that theistic belief is, at least by implication, incurably heteronomous.[125]

So, on the one hand, the defining note of a theological voice is its truth claims about the reality of God—claims that are inescapably metaphysical in character. On the other hand, the defining roadblock of modernity has struck this note from the chorus of public discourse. Only by

---

124. Gustafson, "Say Something Theological," 86; Ogden, *On Theology*, 82; Pannenberg, *Introduction to Systematic Theology*, 9; Stout, *Flight from Authority*, 143.

125. Milbank, "Programme of Radical Orthodoxy," 38; Gamwell, *Divine Good*, 9.

recognizing this deep tension between the metaphysical nature of theism and the metaphysical agnosticism of modernity can one begin to understand how and why theology has lost its public voice. For in spite of whatever differences there have been among modern philosophers, nearly all of them have accepted Kant's conclusion that metaphysical claims cannot be rationally redeemed. The story in modern theology is parallel: in spite of whatever differences there have been among modern theologians, from Schleiermacher to Barth and beyond, nearly all of them have accepted the conclusion that metaphysics is a dead-end. To further illustrate the pervasive influence of this Kantian roadblock, let me return to MacIntyre.

An Analysis of MacIntyre's View in Regard to Metaphysics

Though one does not usually think of MacIntyre and Kant allied in any respect, I would venture to say that MacIntyre's thought about theology and metaphysics has been deeply and enduringly influenced by the Kantian legacy. As one commentator astutely observes, "In his distance from metaphysics, MacIntyre is typical of [modern and] contemporary philosophers, especially those committed to a revival of the primacy of practice."[126] To reveal this postmetaphysical Kantian influence, one must first go back to MacIntyre's 1959 book *Difficulties in Christian Belief* (hereafter *DCB*). There, in a chapter entitled "Proving God's Existence," MacIntyre addresses the standard theistic proofs (ontological, cosmological, and teleological) and concludes that "they are invalid, fallacious arguments." For example, in his discussion of the ontological argument, MacIntyre notes the distinction between logically contingent and logically necessary statements. Contingent statements are those that "can be denied without contradiction" whereas necessary ones are those "the denial of which produces a contradiction." Then, echoing Kant, MacIntyre proceeds to state that

> all factual statements are contingent and this includes all statements which assert that something exists. All statements the denial of which produces a contradiction are necessary. And clearly no statement could be both necessary and contingent. . . . On this distinction the Ontological argument founders. For it seeks to make a statement which asserts that something, i.e., God, exists, a statement the denial of which produces a

126. Thomas Hibbs, *Aquinas, Ethics, and Philosophy of Religion*, 7–8.

contradiction. It seeks to make "God exists" at once necessary and contingent. And therefore it cannot possibly succeed.[127]

It is evident here that MacIntyre agrees with Kant that all existential statements—all claims about existence—are logically contingent. Hence, there can be no valid arguments claiming a logically necessary existence, including the divine existence. Furthermore, MacIntyre joins ranks with Kant when he recites Kant's famous dictum that "'Existence is not a predicate.'"[128]

The cosmological argument, MacIntyre continues, seeks to push intelligibility to its limits by seeking to explain "why anything exists at all." To simply say that each event has a prior contingent cause, *ad infinitum*, without seeking to explain why there is anything at all, is, from the point of view of the argument, simply to beg the question. In contrast, modern thought holds that such questions cannot be intelligibly answered, for all such attempts are idle speculation. Modern science, for instance, seeks to identify only a prior contingent cause for each event and is willing to pursue this *ad infinitum* without seeking rationally to explain "why anything exists at all." With this distinction set forth, MacIntyre then concludes as follows:

> If the Cosmological argument is what I have taken it to be, it becomes clear that *it is not a proof in the rationalist metaphysician's sense. For one can reject it without being mistaken in any point of logic.* Where the difference lies between an adherent of the argument and a sceptic is in a willingness to adopt the whole vocabulary and set of concepts in terms of which the argument is phrased. . . . As a syllogism, [the argument] is beyond reproach. *Where the difficulty lies is in using the terms "contingent" and "necessary" at all. For* . . . to accept the use of "contingent" as a word applicable to the . . . objects of experience, is to accept already the thesis that these objects can only be explained by reference to a God. . . . *I hope it is now clear that the Cosmological argument is a valid, deductive proof, but only to those who will accept its way of talking—that is who will accept what is already implicitly a theistic way of talking* [italics added].[129]

---

127. MacIntyre, *DCB*, 65, 55.
128. Ibid., 56.
129. Ibid., 81, 81–82.

At least two themes present themselves here. First, it is again evident that MacIntyre accepts the modern denial of metaphysical or theistic proofs. There is no possibility of publicly validating theism's metaphysical claims about the reality and necessity of God, he reasons, for one can, as Kant maintained, always reject the theistic claim (both the subject and predicate) without logical contradiction. MacIntyre perhaps goes even a step further than Kant when he claims that acceptance of the modal distinction between "necessary" and "contingent" existence is itself already an implicit act of theistic affirmation. Hence, "To someone who rejects all the assumptions of belief in God," he asserts, "the Cosmological argument will be quite irrelevant."[130] Second, MacIntyre seems to anticipate here his later emphasis on narrative, tradition, and community. That is, within a communal framework of those who already hold theistic convictions and who are already shaped by a theistic vocabulary and understanding, the language of the argument makes sense and "is a valid deductive proof." What he apparently means is that if one already accepts the initial theistic premise—with its distinction between contingent and necessary existence—then and only then does the argument follow in tow. What the argument does is to help believers explicitly understand the logical implications of their beliefs, but it does not publicly validate the truth claims that those beliefs assert. Thus, the only proper use of the argument is for internal communal consumption rather than for public validation.

Bringing together MacIntyre's responses to the ontological and cosmological arguments, it is apparent that he thinks that the notion of "contingent existence" is redundant because he believes that all claims about existence are already inherently contingent. Hence, from his perspective, any public attempt to distinguish between "contingent" and "necessary" existence is at best misleading (it already presupposes theistic belief in the act of trying to prove it) because the concept of "necessary" existence is ultimately nonsensical. In order to respond to MacIntyre's position, therefore, and others like it, what is required is to show that the notion of "necessary existence" is not nonsense; in fact, what is needed is to make clear that the implication of his own position is itself nonsensical. In later sections of this book, I will seek to make that case. Drawing upon the insights of select thinkers, I will seek to

---

130. Ibid., 82.

demonstrate that "nothing exists" is nonsensical so that "something exists" is necessarily true and not merely contingently true.

Another relevant theme in *DCB* is found in MacIntyre's discussion of the nature of proof or validation. He suggests that all chains of reasoning eventually "fall back on certain first principles which determine for one what counts as a good reason." How does one evaluate or justify first principles? MacIntyre claims that rationalist metaphysics sought to justify first principles by trying to show that they are logically necessary or "self-evident." But all such efforts are misguided, he holds, because they all attempt to follow Descartes in pursuing "certain," "self-guaranteeing" principles, and such principles can only be achieved "at the cost of lack of content, of emptiness." In short, any genuine substantive first principle "cannot be [logically] self-evident." One's beliefs and reasoning, therefore, must always presuppose some set of fundamental principles, which are offered by some empirical community, but such principles themselves cannot ultimately be rationally justified or publicly validated. When it gets to that point, MacIntyre suggests, one must simply rest one's case.[131]

MacIntyre's recent thought is somewhat more sanguine insofar as he now believes that first principles can be indirectly justified through a comparative engagement of different traditions. His most detailed discussion of these matters is contained in his 1990 Aquinas Lectures at Marquette University, published as *First Principles, Final Ends and Contemporary Philosophical Issues*. Here he begins by observing "that nothing is more genuinely unacceptable in recent philosophy than any conception of a first principle." He then proceeds to claim that "we inhabit a time in the history of philosophy in which Thomism can only develop adequate responses to the rejections of its central positions in what must seem . . . to be unThomistic ways." These somewhat unThomistic ways involve an "indirect" rather than a direct defense of theistic, teleological, and metaphysical claims. Taking such an indirect approach, MacIntyre submits, "is not to suggest that Aquinas's central positions ought to be substantially . . . revised in . . . accommodation to the [modern] standpoints" that reject them. Rather, "it is necessary in our time to approach them indirectly through an internal critique of those [modern] theses and arguments which displaced them."[132]

131. Ibid., 84–85, 54–55.
132. MacIntyre, *First Principles*, 1, 2.

Such an internal critique seeks to reveal how Thomism offers more adequate conceptual resources than its modern counterparts to explain and resolve the internal difficulties of these modern positions themselves. For instance, MacIntyre argues that the modern rejection of teleology has left modern philosophy unable to understand or adequately explain the implicitly purposive and progressive assumptions of inquiry itself. If the modern rejection of Thomistic teleology was itself an advance or a progressive step, MacIntyre asks, then "towards what" was it or is it progressing? To offer an answer to this question is to affirm the Thomistic point about the need for teleology. By contrast, to deny that inquiry is seeking or moving toward any telos is to render inquiry senseless altogether; for if there is no aim to inquiry, then all inquiry, including philosophical inquiry, is merely a matter of relativistic opinions. Hence, MacIntyre claims that modern thought finds itself in a dilemma that only a Thomistic standpoint can satisfactorily resolve.[133]

MacIntyre's assertion that "we inhabit a time" in which Thomistic metaphysical and teleological claims can only be defended indirectly is evidence, I judge, of his implicit but nevertheless continued acceptance of the modern denial of metaphysics. That is to say, by denying the possibility of a direct or immediate defense, I take him to mean a denial of the possibility of rationally justifying any metaphysical, theistic, or teleological claim in a direct way. "It may be tempting," he says,

> to proceed by way of an immediate rejection of the [modern] rejection [of first principles], but this temptation must be resisted. For it will turn out that the [reasons offered against] . . . the possibility of there being either first principles or final ends are in fact theses which for the most part a Thomist should have no interest in denying. What he or she must have the strongest interest in denying are the implications which are commonly . . . supposed to follow from these.[134]

What MacIntyre implies here is that one should accept the modern denial of a direct validation of metaphysical, theistic, and teleological claims. These claims cannot be publicly validated in a direct manner, and Thomists should accept this view. To this extent, MacIntyre agrees with Kant that such claims are heteronomous in the specific sense that they require a framework of authority in order to validate their appeals.

133. Ibid., 66.
134. Ibid., 8.

However, MacIntyre rejects the modern elimination of these categories altogether. He contends that these types of claims are important, but he believes that they can only be addressed and made sense of when they are embedded within the communal context of a tradition and its practices of authoritative tutelage; only within such a tradition, with its master-apprentice relations, can the mind be adequately trained to move toward its proper telos.

According to the Thomistic tradition, that proper telos is ultimately God. When the various branches of knowledge are hierarchically organized, MacIntyre states,

> the most fundamental of sciences will specify that in terms of which everything that can be understood is to be understood. And this, as Aquinas remarks in a number of places, we call God.
>
> There is then an ineliminable theological dimension—theological, that is, in the sense that makes Aristotle's metaphysics a *theologia*—to enquiry conceived in an Aristotelian [or Thomistic] mode. For enquiry aspires to and is intelligible only in terms of its aspiration to finality, comprehensiveness and unity of explanation and understanding, not only in respect of the distinctive subject-matters . . . , but also in respect of those more pervasive and general features of contingent reality, which inform those wholes of which the [diverse] subject-matter of the subordinate sciences supply the constituent parts.[135]

In this passage, MacIntyre appears to affirm not only the importance of metaphysics as "the most fundamental of sciences," but also the theistic telos as the defining metaphysical principle "in terms of which everything that can be understood is to be understood." Yet, it is essential again to be clear that he thinks that such metaphysical and theistic claims cannot be rationally justified in any direct way. Rather, they can only be addressed indirectly, because they require a tradition-constituted and authoritative mode of inquiry, one that embeds and encapsulates these claims within a tradition. In sum, therefore, whatever changes may have occurred in MacIntyre's thought over the past half-century, he still denies the possibility of justifying metaphysical claims in a direct, rational, public way; whatever other substantive differences he may have with Kant, he continues to agree with him on this fundamental point.

---

135. Ibid., 29; see also p. 5.

Defining the Lines of Inquiry

My aim thus far has been to examine the influential diagnostic and prescriptive accounts offered by MacIntyre, Hauerwas, and Stout and then to offer an alternative reading of the situation. By asserting that the marginalization of theology stems largely from the modern denial of metaphysics, and particularly from theology's own acquiescence to this denial, I have set forth a claim that requires elaboration, investigation, and defense on multiple fronts. In advancing this claim, I realize that I am flying into a pervasive head-wind that presumes that metaphysics has rightly been put to rest once and for all. Therefore, in chapter 2, I will make an extended case for why the metaphysical enterprise, properly conceived and pursued, should be seriously reconsidered. If metaphysics has been in a bog, it is because of the way that it has long been pursued, not because of its inherent nature. In chapter 3, I will return to engage and critically assess the proposals of MacIntyre, Hauerwas, and Stout. Over against them, I will argue that only a metaphysical theology can give full voice to the cognitive claims of theology. In Part Two, I will offer a typological analysis of modern and contemporary theology that seeks to show how the question of metaphysics has largely been avoided or left in the background of most theological approaches. As noted at the outset, I will analyze six different theological approaches, namely, those exemplified by Gustafson, Niebuhr, Hauerwas, Porter, Milbank, and Gamwell.

2

Reconsidering the Metaphysical Enterprise

Referring to a criticism of Plato, Emerson is said to have once remarked: "When you strike at a king, you must *kill* him."[1] The "king" of modern thought, I have alleged, is the pervasive denial of metaphysics and only by "killing" this postmetaphysical mindset will theology ever be able to regain its public voice. I recognize that the ultimate success of this demanding endeavor is tied to the mission of offering a convincing metaphysics, and in regard to this important task I point especially to the modern efforts of Alfred North Whitehead and Charles Hartshorne. Within the scope and limits of this study, I will pursue the more modest aim of seeking to make a case for why others should reexamine the prevailing view and for why they should reconsider the possibility of metaphysics. Drawing on the work of Whitehead, Hartshorne, and others, I will argue that the metaphysical enterprise has wrongly been conflated with a specific approach to metaphysics.[2] Because of this conflation, the dominant view has tended to be based on at least four errors or confusions in its rejection of the metaphysical enterprise. In order to identify these errors, one must begin by reexamining the meanings of "foundationalism" and the far-reaching consequences of this project in its narrow sense.

1. Ralph Waldo Emerson quoted in Louis Menand, *Metaphysical Club*, 25. Menand indicates that Emerson was responding to a comment by the young Oliver Wendell Holmes. The quote comes from a letter that Holmes later wrote to someone else; see Menand 451 n. 5 for the original source from the Holmes papers in the Harvard Law School Library.

2. I recognize that there are some differences in the metaphysical formulations of Whitehead and Hartshorne, but I am inclined to agree with those who see their views as largely and constructively compatible. See Hartshorne, *Whitehead's Philosophy* (and Whitehead's letter to Hartshorne within it). For my purposes, I seek to draw on their combined insights to outline a more promising direction for the metaphysical project.

The Shadow of Foundationalism

There are few terms in contemporary philosophy or theology that have a more pejorative connotation than that of "foundationalism." Describing the views of others as "foundationalist" or "quasi-foundationalist" has come to be used as a license for immediate or reflexive dismissal and, conversely, the term "anti-foundationalist" has come to be seen as a badge of honor. Yet perhaps because of its connotation and widespread currency, there are few terms in the current lexicon that are as vague or slippery as "foundationalism." As Robert Audi remarks, the "term has been so widely [used and] misunderstood that there is some risk in using it [at all]." Nevertheless, in the midst of this lexical confusion, it is important to distinguish at least two general ways the term has been employed. In a broad sense, as David Ray Griffin observes, "foundationalism" has come to refer to "any position that affirms universally valid criteria," including, I would add, any position that seeks to provide a direct rational defense of metaphysical claims.[3] But to be anti-foundationalist in this broad sense simply presupposes the modern denial of metaphysics and thus dismisses the metaphysical enterprise out of hand. In short, it begs the question.

More narrowly, and as I will seek to show more problematically, "foundationalism" refers to an epistemological project that is rightly identified with Descartes and his legacy. As the "Father" of modern philosophy, Descartes has indeed cast a long shadow, a shadow which Richard J. Bernstein describes as "Cartesian Anxiety." What implicitly drove Descartes' project was his attempt to achieve existential certainty in the midst of a contingent and uncertain world. This "journey of the soul," as Bernstein calls it, sought to gain existential surety by seeking epistemological certainty. "Reading the *Meditations* as a journey of the soul," Bernstein writes, "helps us to appreciate that Descartes' search for a foundation or Archimedean point is more than a device to solve metaphysical and epistemological problems. It is the quest for some fixed point, some stable rock upon which we can secure our lives against the vicissitudes that constantly threaten us."[4]

---

3. Audi, *Architecture of Reason*, 29; Griffin, *Reenchantment without Supernaturalism*, 365.

4. Bernstein, *Beyond Objectivism and Relativism*, 18; see also 16–19.

Before Bernstein, John Dewey laid the groundwork for this type of analysis in his 1929 Gifford Lectures, published as *The Quest for Certainty*. Dewey argued that given our existential uncertainty and vulnerability, and given the inherent uncertainty of practical activity, philosophers have historically sought to escape the existential anxiety of the human condition by pursuing a quest for cognitive or theoretical certainty. Since at least the time of Aristotle, the dominant presumption in the West has been that theoretical certainty is to be found in knowledge of a Being whose perfection is defined in terms of a completely unchanging and self-sufficient nature. As Dewey notes, "the Being with which philosophy is occupied is . . . eternally perfect, that which is complete and self-sufficient." In other words, "True Being or Reality is complete; in being complete, it is perfect, divine, immutable, the 'unmoved mover.'" This classical conception of divine perfection led to a sharp epistemological distinction between knowledge and belief. Knowledge in its full sense was defined in terms of what is unchanging and immutable. Hence, knowledge came to be equated with what "is demonstrative, necessary—that is, sure. Belief on the contrary is only opinion; in its uncertainty and mere probability, it relates to the world of change as knowledge corresponds to the realm of true reality." In sum, as Dewey succinctly states, "The quest for certitude has determined our basic metaphysics."[5]

The combined insights of Dewey and Bernstein help us to discern an underlying nexus of assumptions that have shaped the predominant perception of and approach to metaphysics. This nexus involves existential, epistemological, discursive, and theological assumptions. These assumptions are not limited to metaphysical arguments; on the contrary, individually and collectively they are widespread in Western thought. But my contention is that this four-fold nexus has historically saddled the metaphysical enterprise with at least four mistaken assumptions, which I will call respectively:

The Existential Error

The Discursive Error

The Epistemological Error

The Theological Error

---

5. Dewey, *Quest for Certainty*, 15, 20, 18, 22.

What metaphysics needs is not to be dismissed, as modern thought has tended to do, but rather to be unsaddled from these four persistent errors so that it can be considered anew. Metaphysics must resist foundationalism in a narrow sense—with its quest for certainty and its fourfold baggage—and instead be formulated and pursued in a different manner. To be sure, metaphysics is foundationalist in the broad sense of seeking to understand the ultimate nature of reality. But it should not be foundationalist in the narrow sense as developed by Descartes and his legacy. In the remainder of this chapter I will attempt to elucidate these four errors and counterbalance them by sketching out an alternative conception of the metaphysical enterprise. I will begin by outlining the existential and discursive errors and then proceed to more in-depth analyses of the epistemological and theological errors.

The Existential Error: The Quest for Existential Certainty

As Bernstein and Dewey help us to recognize, the quest for certainty is not just about epistemology, rather, it is a two-part endeavor that stems from underlying existential roots and from there seeks to achieve visible epistemological aims. Dewey points to this two-part relation, for instance, when he observes that "the quest for certainty is a quest for a peace which is assured, an object which is unqualified by risk and the shadow of fear. . . . [This] [q]uest for complete certainty can be fulfilled in pure knowing alone. Such is the verdict of our most enduring philosophic tradition." It is this "felt need for assurance," Dewey adds, that is "the dominant emotion" driving the quest. "Perfect certainty is what [humans] want."[6] In essence, the quest for existential certainty involves the attempt to live in the world with a fundamental disposition that is free from all doubt, risk, and anxiety.

Yet, is this quest not an attempt to escape our basic human condition—with our fragmentary understandings of ourselves and of the world around us? As the modern existentialists have sought to teach us, are not anxiety and the possibility of doubt inherent aspects of our self-conscious or self-transcendent form of existence? Dewey rightly discerns that the quest for certainty involves a fundamentally misguided response to the very conditions of life, namely, it involves a "doctrine

6. Ibid., 8, 9, 21.

of escape from the vicissitudes of existence." It is one thing to seek and "achieve a reasonable degree of security in life," he correctly notes; it is another thing to seek existential certainty. Nevertheless, this existential error of seeking certainty has, as Dewey rightly observes, been influential in shaping the nature and course of much of Western metaphysics. But this error, I judge, can and ought to be eliminated from the metaphysical enterprise. Neither theology nor metaphysics should be about seeking existential escape via the path of certainty. Whereas Dewey responds to this misguided quest by pointing alternatively to the relative security of human activity and practice, I will outline here the way that theology can avoid this error, namely, by clarifying the meaning of faith.[7]

With Ogden, I will define "faith" in a basic sense to refer to one's fundamental trust in the meaningfulness and worth of existence. To have faith is to trust that our lives, actions, and relationships—to one another and to the world—have enduring value and significance. This basic faith is logically prior to religious expression. "Logically prior to every particular religious assertion," Ogden states, "is an original confidence in the meaning and worth of life, through which not simply all our religious answers, but even our religious questions first become possible or have any sense." Hence, "faith seeking understanding" is an accurate description of how human beings seek to make explicit sense of their basic trust in the meaning and worth of existence. As Ogden conveys, "*fides quaerens intellectum* [describes] that original faith itself in its search for a more fully conscious understanding of its own nature."[8] The key point I want to make is that faith involves trust not certitude; one can trust without seeking certainty and thus without seeking to escape from the vicissitudes of existence. The existential error occurs when, in the face of life's vulnerabilities, one seeks to transmute basic trust into a peace that is free from all risk, fear, and anxiety by "solidifying" that trust into a fixed point of certainty.

This act of "solidification," Ogden might suggest, occurs at the "religious" stage rather than at the underlying existential level. That is, as we consciously seek to understand our basic trust in the meaning and

---

7. Ibid., 17, 9. Dewey's recommendation of practice is developed throughout chapter 1, which is entitled "Escape from Peril," 1–25. Because human practice is activity with understanding, one might argue that the question of self-understanding, i.e., the question of faith, is itself logically prior to the question of practice.

8. Ogden, *Reality of God*, 34.

worth of life, we re-present that trust to ourselves and others through symbolic and conceptual means. "Because all religions are by their very nature re-presentative," says Ogden, "they never originate our faith in life's meaning, but rather provide us with particular symbolic forms through which that faith may be more or less adequately re-affirmed at the level of self-conscious belief."[9] It is important to stress that this act of representation can occur through either symbolic or conceptual means, for both religion and philosophy are implicit or explicit attempts to understand and express our basic trust in the meaning and worth of existence. The error occurs when we take our conceptual or symbolic expression to be an infallible or certain representation of what constitutes the legitimate ground of that existential trust. Ogden, therefore, might be inclined to define the error as "religious" or "expressive" rather than "existential." At the existential level, he might posit, we all have a basic confidence in the worth of existence; the problem occurs rather at the "higher" level of self-conscious expression and representation. Though I agree with Ogden that the error manifests itself in the act of representation, I am still persuaded that it originates at the deeper existential level. In the face of the vicissitudes of fragmentary existence, humans are tempted to change trust into something it is not, namely, certitude; in the midst of the flowing and uncertain waters of life, they are tempted to transmute the buoyancy of a life-jacket (trust) into the solidity and fixity of an anchor (certainty).[10] As we will later see in the work of Reinhold Niebuhr, to seek to deny or escape fully from the conditions of finitude and the vulnerability of life is one form of sin. To be sure, faith does seek peace and reassurance in the sense of seeking to gain subjective confidence that its trust is well placed. The Christian claim, for example, is that our existential faith is properly oriented by, grounded in, and understood in relation to the reality and love of

---

9. Ibid.

10. My use of a water metaphor in relation to faith is inspired by an analogy that Craig Dykstra offers for describing the life of Christian faith: he compares it with learning to swim. Before a child or an adult can learn to swim, he or she must first learn to trust the buoyancy of the water. Craig Dykstra, address given at the "Forum on Excellence in Ministry: Advancing Pastoral Excellence," sponsored by the Lilly Endowment and the Pulpit & Pew Project of the Duke Divinity School, Indianapolis, Indiana, May 3–5, 2006. Where one would need to clarify Dykstra's metaphor vis-à-vis Ogden's definition of faith is in the fact that existential faith, as Ogden notes, is not learned but is our basic disposition toward life. What is learned is how we consciously understand and represent that faith.

God, as represented in Jesus as the Christ, which, in turn, elicits from us practical embodiment and activity in the world. But this subjective confidence is always sought in the midst of, not in escape from, our finite and fragmentary conditions, conditions that entail the ever-present possibilities of risk, doubt, and uncertainty.[11]

In my judgment, no one has better understood or expressed the meaning of faith in the midst of finitude than Paul Tillich. "The doubt which is implicit in every act of faith," says Tillich,

> is aware of the element of insecurity in every existential truth. At the same time, the doubt which is implied in faith accepts this insecurity and takes it into itself in an act of courage. Faith includes courage. Therefore, it can include the doubt about itself....
>
> ... [D]oubt is not a permanent experience within the act of faith. But it is always present as an element in the structure of faith. This is the difference between faith and [the quest for certainty].... There is no faith without an intrinsic "in spite of" and the courageous affirmation of oneself in the state of ultimate concern.... If doubt appears, it should not be considered the negation of faith, but as an element which was always and will always be present in the act of faith. Existential doubt and faith are poles of the same reality, the state of ultimate concern.[12]

By noting that faith and doubt are not antithetical alternatives but rather two sides of the same existential coin, Tillich helps us to see what faith means under the fragmentary conditions of human finitude. Faith

---

11. Calvin's view of faith seems a bit ambiguous on this point. On the one hand, he writes: "Now we shall have a right definition of faith if we say that it is a steady and certain knowledge of the divine benevolence towards us, which is founded upon the truth of the gracious promise of God in Christ, and is both revealed to our minds and sealed in our hearts by the Holy Spirit." This statement clearly puts the emphasis on faith as a state of certainty. But he goes on to say: "When we stress that faith ought to be certain and secure, we do not have in mind a certainty without doubt or a security without any anxiety. Rather, we affirm that believers have a perpetual struggle with their own lack of faith, and are far from possessing a peaceful conscience, never interrupted by any disturbance." Here, Calvin seems to recognize that the state of faith is not free from doubt and anxiety. The key question is, is this state of doubt due only to the condition of sin, i.e., to the lack of true faith, or is it due to the inherent nature of faith within the fragmentary conditions of human existence? My point is the latter (faith is always a condition of trust in the midst of doubt and anxiety), whereas Calvin seems to imply the former. This passage from Calvin is quoted in McGrath, *Christian Theology Reader*, sect. 1.13, 26. McGrath cites Calvin, *Institutes* III.ii,7;17.

12. Tillich, *Dynamics of Faith*, 20, 21–22.

understood in this way expresses how one seeks relative security through trust without engaging in the misguided quest for certainty. This trust does not banish the possibility of doubt or questioning from one's life. Indeed, as illustrated by the recently revealed private letters of Mother Teresa, even the faith of a saint includes elements of profound doubt. At the same time, however, faith as trust grounds these doubts in a context of affirmation or ultimate concern in the midst of life's uncertainties and vulnerabilities. To borrow a felicitous phrase from Gustafson, one can live with "the grace of self-doubt" while still affirming the divine ground and end of all things. This affirmation and trust, I would add, is a rational faith as opposed to a "blind" faith insofar as one seeks to make and rationally defend truth claims about its central tenet, namely, the reality of God. Furthermore, such an effort will involve, at some point, formulating and offering metaphysical arguments. But before moving on to a discussion of these further steps, let us turn our attention to the second error.[13]

The Discursive Error: Misconstruing the Role of Arguments

An important connecting link between the existential and the epistemological aspects of the quest for certainty involves an underlying and interrelated set of assumptions about the function of arguments. These key assumptions are that a sound argument can (1) *compel* assent and (2) thus *directly* establish an existential outcome or condition. For instance, by seeking to acquire certain knowledge through rational argument based on clear and distinct reasons—reasons that compel assent, Descartes assumed that one could directly achieve existential certainty. This assumption is hinted at, for instance, when he writes: "I had always a most earnest desire to know how to distinguish the true from the false, *in order that* I might be able *clearly* to discriminate the right path in life, and proceed in it with *confidence*" (italics added). Descartes seeks here a sure way of being in the world existentially, which he presumes can be directly achieved by acquiring clear and distinct knowledge cognitively. This presumption, in part, was passed on to him in his youth:

---

13. See Van Biema, "Her Agony," *Time*, September 3, 2007. This article is prompted by the book: Mother Teresa, *Come Be My Light: The Private Writings of the Saint of Calcutta* (New York: Doubleday, 2007). The felicitous phrase comes from the sub-title of Gustafson's, *Examined Faith: The Grace of Self-Doubt*.

"From my childhood," he states, "I was given to believe that by [the help of learned letters and books] a clear and certain knowledge of all that is useful in life might be acquired."[14] In spite of his shift from relying on the authorities and traditions of the past to relying on his new method of radical doubt in pursuit of rational certainty, Descartes continues to presume at some level these two interrelated assumptions about the function of arguments. What he changes is the means by which he seeks to achieve his desired existential outcome. These underlying and persistent assumptions about arguments are the source of what I call the Discursive Error. Since these assumptions are interrelated, I will address them in a dialectical way, moving back and forth between them.[15]

To assume that sound arguments, including metaphysical ones, can compel assent and directly establish an existential outcome or create an existential commitment reflects a fundamental confusion about what rational arguments are capable of accomplishing, which, in turn, leads to exaggerated and misguided expectations. Yet, I would venture to say that there is a long-standing and widespread assumption in Western thought that sound arguments can achieve one or both of these aims. For instance, Philip Clayton states that "Descartes meant his theistic proofs to . . . compel assent from any reader with any starting point." Or as Descartes himself states in *Meditation V*, "the nature of my mind is such as to compel me to assent to what I clearly conceive while I so conceive it" and "I am of such a nature as to be unable, while I possess a very clear and distinct apprehension of a matter, to resist the conviction of its

---

14. Descartes, "A Discourse on Method," 45, 41. Philip Clayton quotes Aryeh Kosman to suggest that "the ultimate end of [Descartes'] *Meditations* is not the certainty which the narrator sets out to accomplish, but rather his discovery of faith in God's trustworthiness, which releases him from an undue desire for certainty." Though I'm clearly sympathetic to an existential outlook that focuses on trust rather than certainty, I'm not persuaded that this is an accurate reading of Descartes. Even Clayton himself goes on to say that Descartes, like Augustine, "begins with doubt and is searching for certitude." Clayton, *Problem of God in Modern Thought*, 78, 80–81. Clayton cites Aryeh Kosman, "The Naïve Narrator: Meditation in Descartes' *Meditations*," in *Essays in Descartes' Meditations*, ed. Amélie Oksenberg Rorty (Berkeley: University of California Press, 1986) 33.

15. Vincent Colapietro suggests that Peirce had a related observation about Descartes' continuity with medieval scholasticism: "Part of Peirce's critique of modernity is . . . that the shift from scholastic to Cartesian philosophy is too small: The traditional notion of infallible authority has not been jettisoned, [but rather] simply internalized." Colapietro, "Introduction to Charles Sanders Peirce," 46.

truth."[16] Similarly, Cleanthes, in Hume's *Dialogues Concerning Natural Religion*, states that "the declared profession of every reasonable sceptic is . . . to assent, [only whenever and] wherever any reasons strike him with so full a force, that he cannot, without the greatest violence, prevent it." Finally, Reinhold Niebuhr presumes that if a positive validation of Christian truth claims were possible, it would "compel conviction on purely rational grounds."[17] What these different thinkers have in common is that they all assume that sound arguments force one to assent to them; if one can resist at all, it is only with "the greatest of violence," as Cleanthes puts it. Moreover, what is further implied by this common view is that if an argument does not in fact compel assent from listeners, then that argument must somehow be flawed or inadequate. In regard to metaphysics, this means that if metaphysical arguments or theistic proofs do not compel the assent of listeners, then those arguments must be invalid.

But these discursive assumptions are, I think, deeply problematic. For on the contrary, in the insightful words of Stanley Cavell, arguments do not "work on people at random, like a ray." That is to say, not even sound arguments force people into submission and compel their cognitive assent, let alone lead directly to an existential change of life. For instance, the later Rawls rightly observes that "political philosophy cannot coerce our considered convictions any more than the principles of logic can."[18] No argument, I would add, metaphysical or otherwise, can force one's acceptance on either a cognitive or existential level. What a quality argument can do is offer good reasons as an invitation for acceptance on both levels. But like all invitations, it attracts or lures the listener by giving him or her grounds for accepting, but it does not force him or her to accept, no matter how good the invitation may be. Perhaps the most visible contemporary examples of this can be seen in discussions about global warming and smoking. The debate about global warming is an interesting illustration of how people can resist quality arguments and evidence. In spite of mounting scientific and environmental evidence of

---

16. See Clayton, *Problem of God in Modern Thought*, 77. Descartes, "Meditations on the First Philosophy," 154, 158.

17. Hume, *Dialogues Concerning Natural Religion*, 65; Niebuhr, *Faith and History*, 165.

18. Cavell, *Claim of Reason*, 326. I'm indebted to Stout for drawing my attention to Cavell's insight: see *Ethics After Babel*, 168. Rawls, *Political Liberalism*, 45.

the warming of the planet, and human and industrial complicity in this process, some persons, including some scientists, have withheld their cognitive or intellectual assent. In the case of smoking, we see an example of how persons can cognitively accept scientific arguments and, yet, such acceptance does not compel an existential or practical change of life. In other words, the validity of scientific arguments against smoking is now accepted by virtually everyone, yet such cognitive arguments by themselves do not compel a change of life in all those who accept their conclusions, as evidenced by the many persons who continue to smoke. Hence, over against the discursive error, I will contend that the proper role of arguments is neither to compel assent nor to directly establish an existential outcome or commitment; rather, the role of arguments is to offer reasons to others in the defense of truth and other validity claims—especially claims made in the context of public discourse. In brief, there is critical difference between, on the one hand, *creating* a commitment or *establishing* an outcome (on either the cognitive or existential level) and, on the other, *defending* a claim (offering reasons to others as an invitation and grounds for acceptance).[19] In order to clarify and develop this distinction, I will begin by pointing to traces of it in the philosophical and theological traditions.

In his discussion of St. Augustine, Frederick Copleston draws our attention to Augustine's distinction between "intellectual assent" and "real assent." Augustine, he reports,

> knew quite well that rational arguments can be adduced for God's existence, . . . , but it was not so much the intellectual assent to God's existence that interested him as the real assent, the positive adhesion of the will to God. . . . If there was question of convincing someone that God exists, Augustine would see the proof as a stage or as an instrument in the total process of man's conversion and salvation: he would recognize the proof as *in itself* rational, but he would be acutely conscious . . . of the moral [and existential] preparation necessary to give a real and living assent to the proof.[20]

---

19. This distinction between "establishing" and "defending" is adapted from Whitehead. He refers to the difference between establishing freedom and defending it. I think this distinction is useful even more broadly to identify the proper role of rational arguments as such. See Whitehead, *Adventures of Ideas*, 51.

20. Copleston, *History of Philosophy*, vol. 2, 48.

Augustine's distinction helpfully points to the difference between creating an existential outcome (real assent) and defending a claim (offering reasons and inviting intellectual assent). Put simply, an existential change of life requires much more than merely a sound rational argument; for the path from argument to existential assent is a long one, with no direct route or sure footing along the way. To understand why this is the case, one must recognize that "real assent" is ultimately informed by one's "constitutive choice."[21] By this I refer to one's fundamental choice of understanding in relation to one's existential trust in the meaningfulness of existence. That is, insofar as we presume the worth and value of existence, we do so implicitly in relation to some source of comprehensive meaning or center of value. Audi offers a similar description of the act of valuation: "[F]or valuations, a kind of axiological foundationalism holds: if one values anything at all, there is something or other one values intrinsically (for its own sake), and in that sense [one values it] non-inferentially; and any other valuations one holds are based on some intrinsic valuation."[22] Formulated in the terms above, the act or selection of intrinsic valuation is one's constitutive choice. And it is this constitutive choice or intrinsic valuation that implicitly informs all of our other understandings and activities, including our act of real or existential assent. Whether an argument or set of reasons seep down into the depths of our soul and truly inform our lives and actions will be significantly affected by our center of value—by our constitutive choice. Reasons and arguments, whether those about smoking, global warming, tax policy, or the reality of God, are filtered through the lens of our constitutive choice before we ever offer cognitive or existential assent.[23] In other words, our ultimate response to and judgment about

21. This apt phrase is taken from Gamwell, *Divine Good*, 37.
22. Audi, *Architecture of Reason*, 75.
23. To a limited extent, philosopher Daniel Garber makes a similar point when he says that "*mindsets [or constitutive outlooks] are the glasses through which people look at the world: they make certain facts and reasons more salient than others, and enable us to see some things and ignore others.*" The key difference, however, is that Garber, pointing to the work of Pascal, insists that these "mindsets" are not chosen. Garber, "Religion and Science, Faith and Reason," 8–9. As I will argue below, I recognize that one's "mind-set" or constitutive outlook remains mostly implicit and that one's constitutive choice is not consciously voluntary like other more explicit choices. Nevertheless, that one does choose, in some sense, one's fundamental understanding is essential if one is to avoid conceptual relativism and if one is to affirm human freedom and responsibility. Even Pascal's notion of the "wager" would suggest that there is an element of choice pertain-

the merits and worth of an argument is influenced by our underlying and prior constitutive choice. As Gamwell reflects: "An understanding or exercise of reason [is never] solely the product of prior or external causes [such as convincing reasons] but [rather] is always chosen."[24] This is why Cavell is so right to suggest that even strong arguments do not work on people like a ray that penetrates directly through to their "room of assent" and compels affirmation. Given this critical role played by our constitutive choice, two things should be noted.

First, given its comprehensive nature, our constitutive choice always remains at least partially implicit—hovering in the dim background of our explicit forms of awareness and our explicit choices of action. Descartes seemed to sense this, for example, when he perceived that many human beings "are not aware of what it is that they really believe; for as the act of mind by which a thing is [existentially] believed is different from that by which we [consciously or cognitively] know that we believe it, the one act is often found without the other." Here, Descartes not only points to a difference between cognitive and existential assent but he also notes that our underlying existential assent may be different from our conscious intellectual stance and vice versa.[25] Gamwell expresses the point even more directly: "The distinction between our explicit consciousness and our always implicit existential decision is absolutely fundamental to a proper account of distinctively human existence."[26] What is significant here is to recognize that our assessment of an argument, metaphysical or otherwise, is informed by our constitutive existential choice, which always remains partly hidden from our view. The influence of this background choice affects our

---

ing to life's most fundamental questions: one makes a constitutive choice about life and wager's one's life on that choice.

24. Gamwell, *Divine Good*, 35.

25. Descartes, "Discourse on Method," 56. This potential difference or tension reveals the complexity of Descartes' view regarding the relationship between the mind and the will. In short, he believes that arguments based on clear and distinct reasons compel assent but what is not compelled is the belief that some specific idea is in fact clear and distinct. Hence, one can be careful in checking out whether an idea is clear and distinct. I am indebted to J. B. Schneewind for this clarification (email correspondence, 5/19/06). For a discussion of Descartes on the relation between mind and will, see Schneewind, *Invention of Autonomy*, 187–89.

26. Gamwell, *Democracy on Purpose*, 56.

receptivity to arguments on both a cognitive and an existential level. Along these lines, Rist notes that

> we hold opinions not merely because they are logically well grounded, but as much because they are familiar to us and, like old friends, have been thus far part of "us," and we are similarly loath to abandon them.... In brief, to hold an opinion is not merely a matter of our rationality; it is also a matter of our emotions, our character, our loves. We do not usually want to change our ... opinions, and we cling the tighter to them if we sense ourselves becoming convinced on rational grounds that we should give them up. Hence we rationalize, procrastinate, change the subject.[27]

Rist points here to our resistance to arguments on a cognitive level fueled from below by our existential attachments and outlook. Or, as the case of smoking indicates, this resistance can also come in the form of cognitive acceptance coupled with existential and practical intransigence.

This notion of intransigence leads us to the second point, which is that our resistance to arguments on either a cognitive or existential level is due not only to the fact that our constitutive choice is partly hidden from our awareness, but also because it is susceptible to what Sartre calls "bad faith." "The [constitutive] decision to be in bad faith," Sartre observes, "does not dare to speak its name; it believes itself and does not believe itself in bad faith." Sartre correctly holds that this underlying choice is indeed a choice, though not one that is consciously voluntary or reflective. "One *puts oneself* in bad faith as one goes to sleep and one is in bad faith as one dreams. Once this mode of being has been realized, it is as difficult to get out of it as to wake oneself up; bad faith is a type of being in the world, like waking or dreaming, which by itself tends to perpetuate itself." This way of being in the world fundamentally influences our disposition toward and response to arguments. As Sartre adds:

> Bad faith does not hold the norms and criteria of truth as they are accepted by the critical thought of good faith. What it decides first, in fact, is the nature of truth.... [T]he ontological characteristic of the world of bad faith with which the subject suddenly surrounds himself is this: that here being is what it is not, and is not what it is. Consequently a peculiar type of

---

27. Rist, *Real Ethics*, 103.

evidence appears: *non-persuasive* evidence. Bad faith apprehends evidence but it is resigned in advance to not being fulfilled by this evidence, to not be being persuaded and transformed into good faith.[28]

Sartre's discussion of "non-persuasive evidence" is particularly illuminating. Our constitutive choice and existential disposition orient and filter our response to reasons and arguments. Hence, no matter how good the presented reasons or evidence might be, bad faith "is resigned in advance to not being fulfilled [or convinced] by this evidence." This applies not only to the question of existential assent but also to cognitive or intellectual assent. Not every rejected argument, of course, is due to bad faith rather than to a legitimate rejection on its merits, but Sartre does rightly point out that our prior existential disposition affects the way we receive and respond to evidence, reasons, and arguments—apart from their respective merits. Rist concurs in this assessment, arguing that we should be "more philosophically wary" of our response to reasons and arguments, not less. "Especially the last hundred years of psychology," he remarks, "have taught us to be more wary than were even the ancient Stoics of the likelihood of our own bad faith and associated inability to determine whether we are thinking about a problem honestly. In brief, we are more aware than the Greeks of . . . our need to know ourselves, and in particular to know how complicated (and hence potentially divisible [and conflictual]) we are."[29]

Given that our receptivity to reasons and arguments is affected by the background filter of our constitutive choice, and given the possibility of our being in bad faith, it seems even less plausible to assume that sound arguments compel assent on either a cognitive or existential level. The causative influence of arguments, one might say, is perhaps a necessary condition for rationally changing one's mind or behavior, but it is never a sufficient condition.[30] What is clear to this point is that the offering of arguments and reasons does not eliminate the role of choice or volition in human response. Even metaphysical arguments, which seek to identify and express the necessary characteristics of reality, do not eliminate or reduce the importance of human decision. Contrary

---

28. Sartre, *Being and Nothingness*, 68.

29. Rist, *Real Ethics*, 103, 103–4.

30. This distinction between necessary and sufficient aspects of a cause is informed by Hartshorne, *Zero Fallacy*, 162.

to Niebuhr and others, arguments, metaphysical or otherwise, do not compel conviction on purely rational grounds; the element of choice remains ever-present in our receptivity to reasons and arguments.

This point can be further amplified by turning to Stephen Toulmin's book *The Uses of Argument*. Suggesting that the study of logic has tended to focus too narrowly on theory rather than on practice, Toulmin sets out to investigate and reflect on the ways that arguments are actually used—what he calls "working logic" as opposed to logical theory. From this working perspective, "logic is concerned with the soundness of the claims we make—with the solidity of the grounds we produce to support them, ... [and] with the sort of *case* we present in defense of our claims." This reference to making a case is right on target, Toulmin argues, because jurisprudence is the proper model for understanding logic: "Logic ... is generalized jurisprudence. Arguments can be [rightly] compared with law-suits." Like legal cases, arguments generally follow three basic phases: the making of a claim, the setting out of evidence in support of that claim, and the offering of a response or verdict.[31]

Toulmin's analysis is helpful because it reminds us that the judgment about the merits of an argument is often made by someone other than the one making the case. Yet, perhaps even Toulmin does not state as clearly as he might have that phase two (offering reasons and evidence) cannot compel, control, or directly establish the judgment issued in phase three (offering a response or verdict). For instance, he writes:

> The rules of logic . . . apply to men and their arguments . . . as *standards of achievement* which a man, in arguing, can come up to or fall short of, and by which his arguments can be judged. A sound argument . . . is one which will stand up to criticism, one for which a case can be presented coming up to the standard required if it is to deserve a favourable verdict.[32]

The difference that Toulmin draws here between the logical standards and the judgment of others is both noteworthy and ambiguous. On the one hand, he asserts that sound arguments are those "for which a case *can be* presented coming up to the standard . . . if it is to deserve a favourable verdict" (emphasis added). On the other hand, he states that "a sound argument . . . is one which *will* stand up to criticism"

---

31. Toulmin, *Uses of Argument*, 9, 7, 16.
32. Ibid., 8.

(emphasis added). There is an important difference between the modal auxiliary "can be"—expressing possibility—and the periphrastic future "one which will"—indicating a statement of future fact. It is one thing to define sound arguments as those for which good reasons can be offered by an advocate, it is another to define them in terms of a positive or receptive verdict. To clarify, perhaps Toulmin means that a case can be made that an argument is sound or valid based on an analysis of its logic. Hence, to say that an argument will stand up to criticism is not to say that it will in fact receive the verdict it deserves. Rather, it is merely to say that the logic meets the standard and thus cannot be successfully criticized on logical grounds. If this is what he has in mind, then I would fully concur. But my point here is simply to emphasize that making a case, however strong, cannot compel or determine a verdict. For the reasons noted above, intellectual assent is not always forthcoming even in response to sound reasons and evidence. As C. S. Peirce aptly remarks, "Our perversity and that of others may indefinitely postpone the settlement of opinion; [in fact,] it might even conceivably cause an arbitrary proposition to be universally accepted as long as the human race should last."[33] Quality arguments do not always prevail in the court of law or in the court of public discourse.

This observation raises a cautionary flag about coming to premature conclusions based on the formation of a consensus or a lack thereof. To illustrate, let me offer two examples, one scientific, the other philosophical. First, there has been a long-standing consensus in human physiology that lactic acid is a negative byproduct that builds up in muscles when they are overused. The burning feeling in one's muscles is a sign of lactic acid buildup and, thus, an indicator that muscle fatigue has set in and peak muscle performance has been passed. Hence, highly trained athletes were taught "to work out at just below their 'lactic threshold'" in order to maximize their performance. But it turns out that the dominant consensus was wrong. Research and evidence now indicate that "lactic acid is actually a fuel, not a caustic waste product. Muscles make it deliberately, producing it from glucose, and they burn it to obtain energy." Highly trained athletes perform well because their bodies are more efficient at producing and absorbing lactic acid, not because they avoid it altogether. "The notion that lactic acid [is] bad [is] 'one of the classic mistakes in the history of science,'" remarks George A.

---

33. Peirce, "How to Make Our Ideas Clear," 133.

Brooks, professor of integrative biology at the University of California, Berkeley. The dominant consensus was based on research by a Nobel laureate, Otto Meyerhof, in the early twentieth century. From Meyerhof's research, "a theory was born. Lack of oxygen to muscles leads to lactic acid, leads to fatigue." For many decades, "few scientists questioned this view." Yet it was Brooks himself, beginning with his doctoral research, who persistently questioned this pervasive assumption. From his own research, Brooks concluded that "lactic acid . . . was a source of energy," not a negative byproduct. However, he had great difficulty getting his views published or taken seriously. And when he was able to get his views out, "other researchers challenged him at meetings and in print. . . . 'I had huge fights, I had terrible trouble getting my grants funded, I had my papers rejected,'" Brooks recalls. Nevertheless, he soldiered on and continued to make his case, laying out more evidence to support his claim. "Eventually, other researchers confirmed [his] work. And gradually, the thinking among exercise physiologists began to change."[34] Brooks' experience powerfully illustrates how sound arguments do not compel assent: in fact, they can be resisted indefinitely as Peirce emphatically notes.

My second example comes from philosophy, specifically MacIntyre's rejection of common or universal reason. In rejecting modern liberalism's claim that there are universally valid criteria for assessing arguments, such as a priori reasons, MacIntyre points to the historical shortcomings of liberalism as grounds for rejecting the universalist claim. What is clear, he states,

> is that liberalism is by far the strongest claimant to provide such a [universal] ground which has so far appeared in human history or which is likely to appear in the foreseeable future. *That liberalism fails in this respect, therefore, provides the strongest reason that we can actually have for asserting that there is no such neutral [or universal] ground, that there is no place for appeals to a practical [or theoretical]-rationality as such . . . to which all rational persons would by their very rationality be compelled to give their allegiance. There is instead only the practical [or theoretical]-rationality of this or that tradition and the justice-of-this-or-that-tradition* [italics added].[35]

---

34. Gina Kolata, "Lactic Acid is Not Muscles's Foe, It's Fuel."
35. MacIntyre, *WJWR*, 346.

Notice here MacIntyre's sweeping theoretical conclusion based on his assessment of the historical record of liberalism.[36] Liberalism, he alleges, offers the strongest case ever made for the notion of universal reason; but that case has failed, he concludes, and thus the notion of a universal standard of rationality is irredeemably false. My contention, however, is that modern liberalism has not in fact put forth the strongest case for understanding universal or a priori reason. As I am seeking to show in this chapter, modern thought, as evidenced by its rejection of the metaphysical enterprise, has been saddled with four persistent errors that have inhibited its case for properly thinking about these matters. Hence, whereas Brooks had a strong case but no one was listening, liberalism has put forth a less than strong case but MacIntyre is listening all too eagerly and thus drawing premature conclusions. The stronger case either still needs to be made, or it has already been calling out in the wilderness, like Brooks, waiting to be openly received and heard with new ears.

Up to this point I have sought to show that arguments do not compel conviction on either a cognitive or an existential level. Even sound arguments may not receive the verdict they deserve. At this juncture,

---

36. Notice also that MacIntyre here characterizes sound rational arguments as those that compel the allegiance of their listeners. Based on this passage alone, one might conclude that this reference merely reflects the views of liberalism and not MacIntyre himself. Yet on the previous page, MacIntyre unequivocally asserts that "liberalism can provide no compelling arguments in favor of its conception of the human good except by appeal to premises which collectively already presuppose that theory." And later, in describing his notion of the indirect comparative means of determining the superior rationality of one tradition over another, he states: "When [those within a tradition in crisis] have understood the beliefs of the alien tradition, they may find themselves compelled to recognize that within this other tradition it is possible to construct . . . a [more] cogent and illuminating explanation. . . ." In the next paragraph he continues: "In this kind of situation the rationality of tradition requires [i.e., compels] an acknowledgment by those [in the tradition in crisis that] the alien tradition is superior in rationality and in respect of its claims to truth [in comparison] to their own." In short, it appears that MacIntyre follows in the footsteps of those who presume that sound arguments compel assent, even though he goes on to acknowledge that this compelling nature may not in fact always be explicitly admitted. As he puts it, "From the fact that rationality, so understood [as being compelling in nature], requires this acknowledgment of defeat in respect of truth, it does not of course follow that there will be actual acknowledgment." This capacity to avoid or withhold acknowledgment, I would submit, should give MacIntyre and others reason to rethink their assumption that sound arguments compel at all; for sound arguments invite assent, they do not force it. MacIntyre, *WJWR*, 345, 364, 365.

therefore, it is worth recalling Kant's dictum: *ought implies can*. What we can control is the attempt to put forth quality reasons, reasons which we critically judge to measure up to the standards of logic and evidence; what we cannot control is how these reasons are received, assessed, and judged by others. For even in the case of a valid deductive argument, one can always give up one or more premises rather than accept the conclusion that logically follows from them.[37] Thus, the *raison d' être* of arguments, I contend, is rooted first and foremost in the act and responsibility of making a claim, not in the response of others. "[One] who makes an assertion," Toulmin notes, "puts forward a claim—a claim on our attention and to our belief." The merits of such a claim "depend on the merits of the argument which could be produced in its support." Whenever we make a claim, we may be asked, "'What have you got to go on?,' and if challenged it is up to us to produce whatever data, facts, or other backing *we consider to be relevant and sufficient* to make good the initial claim" (emphasis added).[38] Like Jürgen Habermas, Karl-Otto Apel, and others, Toulmin rightly discerns that the role of arguments arises out of the communicative act of making and defending claims, not out of the task of compelling assent or establishing conviction as such. That is, in making truth or validity claims, we implicitly promise others that, if asked, common reasons could be offered to justify or validate our claims.[39] To be sure, in making a claim or in offering an argument in support of a claim, we desire and seek the assent of others; we offer them an invitation in the form of reasons for acceptance—reasons that in theory they can understand and find convincing. Our implied promise and responsibility to validate our claims is related to this potential or actual influence on others. Because our claims and assertions may indeed influence their beliefs and actions, we have a responsibility to be prepared to offer them sound reasons for why those claims are valid. But again, *ought implies can* and all we can ultimately control is our own effort to justify our claims, not the response of others. In the case of making assertions about the reality and necessity of God, for

37. This point about deductive arguments is offered by Hartshorne, *Natural Theology for Our Time*, 29–30.

38. Toulmin, *Uses of Argument*, 11, 13.

39. See Habermas, *Theory of Communicative Action*, vol. 1 and Apel, "Communication Community." My use of "justify" and "validate" here is meant to be synonymous. That is, unlike Stout, who separates truth and justification, I mean "justification" here in terms of seeking to show the truth of one's claim, i.e., to seek to validate it.

instance, we are making metaphysical claims that need a rational defense as much as any other claims. The discursive task is not to compel assent or to establish theistic faith as such, but rather to follow through on our implied promise and responsibility to try to validate our claims.

To be clear, let me plainly state that even if we try our best to justify our claims, whatever those claims may be, our arguments may or may not in fact be sound. That is to say, our judgments about whether our own reasons and arguments are sound are themselves fallible judgments. The response of others is not simply shaped by their disposition and constitutive choice, but also by their own rational assessment of our proffered reasons. I have emphasized the former element because it has tended to be overlooked; the latter element, of course, is equally important, but it is commonly recognized, if not, in fact, taken for granted.

In setting forth this view, I am seeking to articulate a middle position between those who, like Descartes, assume that the role of sound arguments is to compel intellectual and existential assent, and those who, like Gustafson, say that "it is relatively meaningless to make a case for the existence or presence of God" to those who do not already have a religious disposition or outlook.[40] Both Descartes and Gustafson misconstrue the role of arguments: Descartes' error is to assume that quality arguments work on people like a ray that compels intellectual assent and directly establishes an existential outcome; by contrast, Gustafson's error is to assume that such arguments are relatively meaningless, since they cannot compel dramatic change. In spite of their differing conclusions, both Descartes and Gustafson assume that the *raison d' être* of arguments is to compel or directly establish conviction. This assumption has plagued the metaphysical enterprise throughout much of Western history by leading it down a false path (Descartes' quest for certainty), which, in turn, has resulted in its premature dismissal (as illustrated by Gustafson). Over against this legacy, I contend that we need to pursue metaphysical arguments precisely because we make implicit metaphysical claims whenever we speak of or affirm the reality of God and, thus, we have a responsibility to try to offer a sound defense of those claims. In short, metaphysical arguments are neither "expressways" that directly establish conviction nor "dead-ends" that are beside the point. Rather, they are necessary "service-roads" that stem from and seek to defend the claims that we assert to be true. Moreover, sound arguments work

---

40. Gustafson, *Ethics from a Theocentric Perspective*, 1:164.

more like lures that seek to draw our assent and gradually change our lives than like rays that compel direct and instant results. Hence, a reconsideration of the metaphysical enterprise points toward a more humble but no less important task than that which has come down to us through the centuries.[41]

The Epistemological Error: The Quest for Cognitive Certainty

In his quest to attain existential surety, Descartes pursued a rational metaphysics that: 1) sought epistemological certainty, 2) relied on a deductive method modeled on mathematics, and 3) appealed to what Kant would later call a priori modes of justification. The philosophical

---

41. I began by discussing Descartes' attempt to gain existential certainty by presenting arguments *to himself*. I then proceeded to discuss Toulmin and our attempt to offer convincing arguments *to others*. Are there any fundamental differences, one might ask, between the arguments that we present to ourselves and the arguments that we present to others? I do not think so. The difference, if any, seems to be one of degree rather than one of kind. One might be tempted to say that we have an easier time when we are seeking to convince ourselves rather than others, since "the attorney" defending the claim and "the jury" assessing the claim are one and the same person. What we find credible in defending a claim—what we judge to measure up to the standard—is presumably what we will find convincing in assessing a claim and reaching a conclusion. This may be true up to a point but the persistent background presence of our constitutive choice and the looming possibility of bad faith are always there. These elements continue to exercise influence over how we filter arguments and whether or not we find evidence persuasive. This is especially the case when it comes to existential assent. The task of truly convincing ourselves—of allowing our lives to be informed or changed—is not significantly easier in the monological case than in the dialogical one. For instance, I am intellectually persuaded that Descartes' metaphysical dualism of mind and body is too sharp and thus conceptually mistaken. Yet, at an existential level, I tend to continue to presume this sharp distinction in spite of my cognitive view. This presumption is reflected in the way that I continue to relate to and treat my own body—as a thing or "wagon" to carry out my purposes rather than as an integrated element of a holistic self. My existential and intellectual assents do not yet coincide and this is due, in part, to the hidden filter of my underlying constitutive choice. Only gradually as I seek to cultivate and habituate my response to the intellectual lure of an alternative view can such a view begin to take root in the cellar of my soul. MacIntyre and Hauerwas are right to suggest that tradition, community, and church have an important role to play in fostering this type of cultivation and habituation. Yet, this role does not negate the responsibility of trying to make our claims intelligible and credible to others, especially in the broader, diverse publics of the academy and intellectual marketplace. Again, the imperative of arguments stems directly from the act of making claims, and only indirectly from the desired outcome of bringing about intellectual assent or existential conversion.

tradition has tended to bundle these three elements together and has often conflated them. Yet, such a move overlooks the fact that they are distinct and that the metaphysical enterprise does not need all of them. Indeed, I would suggest that it is because of this tendency to bundle and conflate that the term foundationalism has come to be used broadly to disparage any attempt to offer a rational justification of universal or metaphysical claims. To begin to make my case, I will address the first two elements together (certainty and deductive method) and then later attend to the third item (a priori justification).

In his effort to attain existential surety, Descartes sought to achieve cognitive certitude. Our knowledge is certain when our claims or conclusions can be characterized as indubitable, incorrigible, and/or infallible. Briefly defined, a claim is "indubitable" when it is impossible to doubt, "incorrigible" when it cannot possibly be improved or corrected, and "infallible" when it is beyond the possibility of error. Again, what is desired here is a specific type of subjective condition, namely, one characterized by certainty about the nature of our knowledge based on the nature of our claims. In other words, the cash value sought in terms like "indubitable," "incorrigible" and "infallible" is an ultimate status for our knowledge-claims, which in turn is meant to confer an ultimate status on our subjective condition of knowing, which, in turn, is meant to quiet our existential anxiety. For instance, in describing his pursuit of cognitive certitude, Descartes says "my design was singly to find ground of assurance, and cast aside the loose earth and sand, that I might reach the rock of the clay." His quest for an Archimedean point is fueled by an existential aim and is navigated according to the lights of geometric demonstration. "The long chains of simple and easy reasonings," Descartes remarks, "by which geometers are accustomed to reach the conclusions of their most difficult demonstrations, had led me to imagine that all things . . . are mutually connected in the same way, and [are likewise knowable with certainty] . . . provided only we abstain from accepting the false for the true, and always preserve in our thoughts the order necessary for the deduction of one truth from another." The way to identify true propositions, he concludes, is to abide by the general principle "that all the things which we very clearly and distinctly conceive are true, only observing, however, that there is some difficulty in rightly determining the objects which we distinctly conceive."[42]

42. Descartes, "Discourse on Method," 59, 52, 63.

Just as Descartes' pursuit of existential certainty and his misconstrual of the role of arguments launched metaphysics down the wrong path, so too did his pursuit of cognitive certainty and his reliance on deductive method lead the metaphysical enterprise astray by saddling it with the wrong conceptual aims and navigational equipment. As Whitehead observes, "the chief error in philosophy is overstatement," and the quest for certainty has been one of its primary and most regrettable forms. "Philosophy has been haunted," Whitehead adds, "by the unfortunate notion that its method is dogmatically to indicate premises which are . . . clear, distinct, and certain; and to erect upon those premises a deductive system of thought." To be sure, as Dewey pointed out, this quest for certainty goes back to at least Aristotle. In agreement, Whitehead notes that "the methodology of rational thought from the Greeks to our own times has been vitiated by this fundamental misconception," namely, by "the doctrine of dogmatic finality" with its "emphasis [on] certainty."[43] Hence, though Descartes was by no means the original source of this pursuit, he certainly reinvigorated its presence in and its legacy for modernity by connecting it to the model of geometric demonstration. By seeking certainty and by defining deduction as the methodological benchmark, Descartes bequeathed to modern thought a persistently confused and "upside-down" approach to metaphysics. In attempting to remedy this misconception, Whitehead rightly asserts that

> the accurate expression of the final generalities is the goal of [metaphysical] discussion and not its origin. Philosophy has been misled by the example of mathematics; and even in mathematics the statement of the ultimate logical principles is beset with difficulties, as yet insuperable. The verification of a rationalistic [or metaphysical] scheme is to be sought in its general success, and not in the peculiar certainty, or initial clarity, of its first principles.[44]

There are at least four noteworthy points to garner from this passage and the above discussion. For the sake of clarity, I will enumerate them.

(1) Whitehead correctly denotes that reaching clarity or understanding about the most general aspects of reality is the ultimate *goal* of meta-

---

43. Whitehead, *Process and Reality*, 7, 8; Whitehead, *Adventures of Ideas*, 162.
44. Whitehead, *Process and Reality*, 8.

physical inquiry, *not* its starting point. This confusion is embedded in the ambiguity of the phrase "first principles." Metaphysics is indeed concerned with first principles, but "firstness" here properly refers to their ultimate generality—not to their chronological order in the pursuit of knowledge. Descartes, however, wanted both ultimate generality and chronological order because of his desire to achieve a subjective condition of cognitive certainty. Hence, he tried to model metaphysics on the deductive approach of mathematics: he wanted metaphysical and theistic proofs to compel assent in a manner analogous to geometrical proofs by starting with "a set of undeniable or axiomatic premises from which the desired conclusion could be deduced." But this aim and analogy were mistaken on multiple counts. To begin with, as noted earlier, even deductive arguments cannot compel cognitive assent because one can always choose to abandon one or more premises rather than to accept the conclusion that follows from them. Also, as Hartshorne states: "Today we realize that axiomatic status is a relative and more or less subjective matter. Scarcely anything of importance is axiomatic for everyone."[45] This is especially true when it comes to arguments about ultimate reality or the existence of God. Rist offers a similar assessment when he points out that matters are often less clear cut than they at first appear: "Over two thousand years of philosophy have taught us that conclusions on substantive matters are almost always less obvious than they seem: there is so often some complication in the argument which we missed at first and even at tenth glance." Hartshorne echoes this caution when he declares that "in philosophy no axioms have standing unless and until the possibility has been seriously considered that they are at best merely plausible, rather than genuinely self-evident and certain."[46] Finally (and relatedly), it is not always as clear as one might think as to what conclusion should be properly drawn when analyzing a deductive argument. This is particularly the case in regard to *ex absurdo* arguments. For instance, "when a contradiction issues from a train of reasoning," Whitehead observes, "the only logical conclusion to be drawn ... is that at least one of the premises involved in the inference is false. [Yet,] [i]t is rashly assumed ... that the peccant premise can at once be located. In mathematics this assumption is often justified," but this is where modern philosophy has been misled. "[For] in the absence

---

45. Hartshorne, *Natural Theology for Our Time*, 29–30.
46. Rist, *Real Ethics*, 103; Hartshorne, *Aquinas to Whitehead*, 4.

of a well-defined categoreal scheme of entities, issuing in a satisfactory metaphysical system, every premise in a philosophical argument is under suspicion."[47] In other words, in the absence of complete metaphysical knowledge, all premises remain open to the possibility of further questioning and revision, i.e., all remain fallible and revisable. In short, deductive arguments cannot carry the philosophical load that Descartes placed upon them.

Having indicated the limits of deductive arguments, and the error of basing the entire metaphysical enterprise upon them, one should also recognize their value as well. For instance, the *ex absurdo* argument, by pointing out contradiction, is helpful insofar as it alerts one to the presence of rational incoherence. Where the specific problem lies may not be self-evident, but that there is a problem is plain. Also, even though one can abandon a premise rather than accept a necessary conclusion, valid deductive arguments are useful insofar as they "establish a price for rejecting [their] conclusions. Suppose," Hartshorne remarks, that "P entails Q, then those who initially accept P must either accept Q also, or reconsider their acceptance of P." The argument is neutral between these options but it does at least clarify what is at stake in either accepting Q or in abandoning P. Similarly, Stout states that "logic can tell us what our beliefs imply, but not whether we should accept these implications while standing pat on premises." Clayton offers a useful example of this ineluctable element of decision when discussing the challenge of moving from the assertion of ideas, such as in the ontological argument, to the claim of existence for their objects: "Fine [says the skeptic], I will grant you your intuitions and their immediate [logical] implications as well. But if it were shown that the existence of an infinite being would follow directly from having these intuitive ideas, then I reserve the right to rescind my provisional acceptance and to reject the intuitions after all."[48] Hence, by clarifying the options among logical alternatives, deductive arguments point back to the underlying role of one's constitutive choice and how it affects the reasons that one will be open to receiving or find convincing. Just as it is a costly mistake to expect too much of deductive arguments, so too is it an error to overlook their contribution as well.

---

47. Whitehead, *Process and Reality*, 8.

48. Hartshorne, *Natural Theology for Our Time*, 30; Stout, *Flight from Authority*, 157; Clayton, *Problem of God in Modern Thought*, 130.

(2) Once one recognizes that the quest for certainty is entirely misplaced in the realm of metaphysics, the preoccupation with epistemological foundations should disappear. Why else would one be concerned with securing an epistemological foundation unless one wanted to achieve a particular kind of cognitive status for one's claims? Descartes wanted to reach existential certainty and to vanquish skepticism; in pursuit of these aims, he sought to achieve conclusions that could be deemed indubitable, incorrigible, and/or infallible. And to achieve this certainty, he sought to identify an Archimedean point as a cognitive foundation from which to build a structure of knowledge. But for the reasons outlined above, especially those pertaining to the limits of deductive arguments, no conclusion or premise can serve as an Archimedean rock upon which to build a system of knowledge. Given the fragmentary nature of human knowledge and existence, no claim can securely be deemed indubitable, incorrigible, or infallible. There is no epistemological "garden of Eden" from which to build a one-way structure of final and certain knowledge.

Some commentators like to make this point by suggesting that human knowledge is more like an interconnected "web" than a "building" with a secure foundation.[49] Stout, for instance, is thinking along these lines when he says "that the foundationalist's 'basic' knowledge itself presupposes at least enough other knowledge to make the interpretation of a proposition possible, which is a great deal of knowledge indeed."[50] This "web" metaphor is helpful insofar as it implies that no special or privileged epistemological genesis point exists. Rather, all claims are open to further questioning and require validation by appeal to common reason or experience. Yet what is potentially misleading about this metaphor is that some commentators, like Stout, take it to imply a denial of the metaphysical enterprise altogether. They equate the epistemological holism of the web metaphor with a strong historicist rendering or reduction of all claims, including metaphysical ones. For instance, Stout asserts that

> to deflate Descartes, we must also deflate ourselves. We must say that by virtue of being human we are all *situated* more radically than poets and philosophers typically pretend. Descartes *seemed* to transcend his situation in part because he thought

49. For instance see Griffin, *Reenchantment without Supernaturalism*, 363.
50. Stout, *Flight from Authority*, 20.

> he could. Historicism says he could not because no one can. That means that we cannot. The first step toward discontinuity with [Descartes] is to empty *oneself* of the hope for a perspective above history.
> ... [The strong historicist] may seem to cease to be a philosopher, though only because the search for absolute foundations, the perspective of eternity, has been taken for so long as the essence of the philosopher's task. To deny the possibility of transcendental perspective therefore seems antiphilosophical [but it is not].[51]

Stout is correct to want to deflate long-standing philosophical pretension, but the real source of pretension, I would argue, is rooted in the epistemological search for absolute foundations, not in the metaphysical enterprise as such. Stout unwittingly remains under the "spell" of Descartes insofar as he continues to link the metaphysical enterprise inextricably to the pretensions of epistemological foundationalism. This linkage is implied, for instance, by the ambiguity of what Stout means by "transcendental perspective," "the perspective of eternity," and "a perspective above history." Does he mean the epistemological attempt to attain a "God's-eye" view that is timeless by being indubitable, incorrigible, and infallible? Or does he mean the metaphysical attempt to identify those most general characteristics of reality that are omnipresent in all possible contexts? Like Descartes, Stout means both of these because, like the "Father," he too presumes that they inherently go together.

But Whitehead's whole point is that metaphysics should never have been tied to such a misguided epistemological quest. Metaphysical claims, like all claims, are fallible in nature and are always open to the possibility of revision. "Philosophers," Whitehead states, "can never hope finally [or exhaustively] to formulate ... metaphysical first principles." By this, he means that there is no finality or incorrigibility pertaining to human understanding or expression of the ultimate generalities. No human perspective is a God's-eye view from above history; rather, all claims are made from within a historical context and are subject to the conditions of finitude and fallibility. However, this situatedness does not preclude the possibility of gaining approximate or progressive understanding regarding the metaphysical generalities. Again, as Whitehead

---

51. Ibid., 66–67.

puts it, "There is no first principle which is in itself unknowable, not to be captured by a flash of insight." Similar to Peirce, Whitehead suggests that the nature of this progress is one "of an asymptotic approach to a scheme of [first] principles," that is, always approaching but never in a position to "close the book" on further discussion. To borrow an ecclesiastical phrase, one might say that metaphysics, like all disciplines, is "reformed and always reforming."[52]

Because Stout rightly wants to deflate Descartes' epistemological pretension, and yet wrongly presumes that such pretension is inherent to the metaphysical enterprise, he believes that the only way forward for philosophy is to jettison transcendental and metaphysical claims altogether and instead to be content with a "humbled" historicism. I would agree with Stout that modernity has for too long been plagued by the Cartesian link between epistemological certainty and metaphysics, and it is time to sever this Cartesian link once and for all. But instead of being left with Stout's strict alternatives of either metaphysical foundationalism or non-metaphysical historicism, I would contend that Whitehead points to a third alternative that has not been seriously or widely considered, namely, to a fallibilistic metaphysics. "Philosophy will not regain its proper status," Whitehead predicts, "until the gradual elaboration of [metaphysical] schemes . . . is recognized as its proper objective. There may be rival schemes, inconsistent among themselves; each with its own merits and its own failures. It will then be the purpose of research to conciliate the differences. Metaphysical categories are not dogmatic statements of the obvious; [rather] they are tentative formulations of the ultimate generalities."[53]

---

52. Whitehead, *Process and Reality*, 4. For Peirce's notion of an indefinite gradual progress toward knowledge, see "How to Make our Ideas Clear," 133–34. The ecclesiastical phrase is borrowed from the Presbyterian Church, USA. In his engaging reflections on the nature of historiography, John Lewis Gaddis draws attention to Caspar David Friedrich's nineteen-century painting *The Wanderer Above the Sea of Fog*. The painting portrays a man standing high up on the rocks overlooking a vast landscape set out before him. He is standing above the fog, looking out and seeing the general contours of the landscape, but not seeing the exact details below the fog. Gaddis uses this image to reflect on and explain how historians map the past. For my purposes, I would suggest that this image also nicely lends itself to thinking about metaphysics. That is, metaphysicians seek, from a situated point within history, to grasp and outline the most general characteristics of reality. It is not an omniscient God's-eye view, but it still partly transcends the situatedness of history. See Gaddis, *The Landscape of History*.

53. Whitehead, *Process and Reality*, 8.

(3) One of the most influential and unfortunate elements of Descartes' quest for certainty was his epistemological emphasis on "clear and distinct" ideas. In seeking to build his secure foundation, Descartes concluded that the way to identify true propositions is to abide by the general criterion "that all the things which we very clearly and distinctly conceive are true."[54] This fixation on what is clear and distinct has left an indelible mark on modern thought, even on those like Hume who sharply disagree with Descartes but who, nevertheless, still follow in his footsteps when they give epistemological priority to impressions that are vivid, lively, and forceful.[55] The significance of this legacy is that modern understandings of knowledge have tended to be defined narrowly and singularly in terms of what we perceive with clarity and distinctness. With the rise and dominance of empiricism, this emphasis has put a premium on sense perception and its clear and present sensations. What we perceive immediately, clearly, and distinctly through the five senses are the changing and "prominent facts" of our experience. Agreeing with Kant's basic insight, Whitehead recognizes that these "prominent facts" are not merely the result of a process of passive reception. Rather, the distinctive aspects of conscious sense perception contribute a constructive and formative influence as well; such perception, Whitehead remarks, "displays a world concealed under an adventitious show, a show of our own bodily production."[56] What results from this show are the prominent elements of our awareness and these "prominent facts are the variable facts,—[such as] the appearance of a tiger, of a clap of thunder, or a spasm of pain. They are the facts entering into our experience by the medium of our sense-organs."[57]

"But the prominent facts," Whitehead continues,

> are the superficial facts. They vary because they are superficial; and they enter into conscious discrimination because they vary. There are other elements in our experience, on the fringe of consciousness, and yet massively qualifying our experience. In regard to these other facts, it is our consciousness that flick-

---

54. Descartes, *Discourse on Method*, 63.
55. See, Hume's "An Enquiry Concerning Human Understanding," 316f.
56. Whitehead, *Symbolism*, 44.
57. Whitehead, *Adventures of Ideas*, 163.

ers, and not the facts themselves. They are always securely there, barely discriminated, and yet inescapable.[58]

In this important passage Whitehead points to two sets or aspects of facts that make up our experience. One set, consisting of those discernible to conscious sense perception, become the "prominent" and "superficial" aspects of our experience—literally those aspects that stand out on the surface, and hence are most readily apparent. What makes them conspicuous is that they are variable in our experience—sometimes they are present but other times they are not. The second set, by contrast, is inconspicuous because it consists of those ever-present aspects of existence. Due to their invariability, these facts are the powerful and persistent background of our experience, of which we are only vaguely aware. Their vagueness does not indicate their lack of reality or importance but, on the contrary, underscores their constant influence. Put simply, that which is omnipresent is that which is most difficult to discern. For this reason, our consciousness contains at best a flickering awareness of this massive base of experience. As Whitehead states elsewhere, "factors in our experience are 'clear and distinct' [only] in proportion to their variability, provided that they sustain themselves for that moderate period required for importance. The necessities [of experience however] are invariable, and for that reason remain in the background of thought, dimly and vaguely."[59] The challenging task of metaphysics, therefore, is to discern, express, and critically reflect on these ever-present aspects of existence, of which we are usually only dimly aware.

Given the modern epistemological emphasis on clarity and distinctness, philosophy has tended to deny, ignore, or redefine these omnipresent aspects of experience. For instance, because conscious sense perception does not discern the causal link between two events, Hume ascribes causation merely to the practice of habit or custom. Though Kant tries to give causation a more solid footing, he too never questions the singular emphasis on conscious awareness stemming from Descartes' legacy of clear and distinct ideas. Hence, even though Kant's transcendental idealism ascribes causation to the a priori conditions of human understanding rather than merely to the result of custom, he still concurs with Hume in denying our knowledge of the objective

---

58. Ibid.
59. Whitehead, *Modes of Thought*, vii.

or causative influence of the world upon us. Over against this legacy, Whitehead persuasively argues that modern thought has made a major mistake in defining perception in a singular way. "The weakness of the epistemology of the eighteenth and nineteenth centuries," he writes, "was that it based itself purely upon a narrow formulation of sense perception. . . . The result was to exclude all the really fundamental factors constituting our experience."[60]

To offer a way forward, Whitehead contends that perception of the world must be understood as consisting of two modes rather than just one. Full or complete perception, which he calls "symbolic reference," usually involves a mixing or integration of these two modes. In its pure or abstract form, he calls conscious sense perception "perception in the mode of presentational immediacy." This mode is found only in more complex organisms, such as human beings. It consists of the ability to consciously "experience [an] immediate world around us, a world decorated by sense-data." This "pure mode of presentational immediacy gives no information as to the past or the future. It merely presents . . . a cross-section of the universe" in a given moment. This is what Hume and Kant focus on, though they explain it differently, namely, conscious sense impressions in the present moment. These include the sense-data of color, shape, spatial relations, etc. The other mode of perception, which in its pure form Whitehead calls "perception in the mode of causal efficacy," involves the vectorial influence of the immediate past on the present. This conforming influence of the immediate past on the present points to the "primitive" elements of experience—elements common to both complex and simple things. This conformation to vectorial influence is more readily apparent in the simpler organisms than

---

60. Ibid., 162. Whitehead notes elsewhere that Francis Bacon at least partly glimpsed this insight at the advent of the modern era. Bacon distinguished between "perception" and "sense." All bodies or entities have perception, Bacon observed, whereas only conscious entities have sense or cognitive experience (Whitehead, *Science and the Modern World*, 41–42). Along with Bacon, Leibniz also recognized that modernity was headed down the wrong path with its narrow understanding of perception. Perception is much more inclusive, Leibniz argued, than merely consciousness or "apperception." "In this matter," he remarks, "the Cartesians [and their legacy] have fallen into a serious error, in that they treat as nonexistent those perceptions of which we are not conscious" (Leibniz, *Monadology*, #14: 456–57). The key difference between Whitehead and Leibniz is that Whitehead thinks that the monads—most basic elements of reality—have "open windows" to the world whereas Leibniz's notion of a divine pre-established harmony views them as "closed" (see Whitehead, *Process and Reality*, 47, 80).

in the complex ones. "A flower," for example, "turns to the light with much greater certainty than does a human being, and a stone conforms to the conditions set by its external environment with much greater certainty than does a flower." Nevertheless, this conformal influence is as much an ever-present aspect of human experience as it is for the stone or the flower. Because the complexities of human experience involve a greater degree of freedom of response, humans enjoy a greater ability to modify or qualify the influence of the past. But, again, the objective causative influence is still there—informing the parameters of present possible experience. For instance, when describing our conscious awareness of sense-data in the mode of presentational immediacy, Whitehead immediately adds that this conscious awareness is "dependent on the [causal influence of] immediate states of relevant parts of our own bodies." That is, we "see *with* our eyes, we taste *with* our palates, we touch *with* our hands." Our conscious sense perception is dependent on the *causal* influence of our body and its functions, which in turn are dependent on the causal influence of the world around us. Yet, we take this causal influence so for granted that we forget about it and pretend it is not there.[61]

To illustrate, Whitehead quotes two separate but telling passages from Hume's *A Treatise of Human Nature*. In the first, he quotes Hume as follows: "'Impressions may be divided into two kinds, those of *sensation* and those of *reflection*. The first kind arises in the soul originally, *from unknown causes*.'" In the second passage, he states: "'*If it be perceived by the eyes*, it must be a colour.'" Interpreting these two texts, Whitehead points out that, in the first quote, Hume attributes

> the visual sensations "in the soul" to "unknown causes." But in the second passage, the heat of the argument elicits his real conviction—everybody's real conviction—that visual sensation arises "*by* the eyes." The causes are not a bit "unknown," and among them is usually to be found the [causal] efficacy of the eyes. If Hume had stopped to investigate the alternative causes for the occurrence of visual sensations . . . he might have hesitated in his profession of ignorance. If the causes be indeed unknown, it is absurd to bother about eye-sight.[62]

61. In setting forth Whitehead's two modes of perception here, I draw upon and move back and forth with material from both *Symbolism*, 14, 42 and *Process and Reality*, 168, 170.

62. Whitehead, *Process and Reality*, 171. Whitehead cites Hume, *Treatise of Human Nature*, Bk. I, Part I, sects. II and VI.

To encapsulate, then, Whitehead argues against Hume and Kant that our commonsense assumption—regarding the objective and causative influence of the world upon us—is indeed accurate: the eye blinks *because of* the flash of light or *because of* the puff of air.[63] To be sure, such causative influence does not show up explicitly on the radar screen of perception in the mode of presentational immediacy. But by its very nature, perception in this mode abstracts from the concrete temporal influence of the immediate past and, instead, delineates simple sense-data, such as colors and shapes. But the primitive base of experience, Whitehead rightly holds, consists of this vectorial, causative influence with its affective tone.

By challenging the singular understanding of perception in modern thought, Whitehead seeks to enable philosophy to be attentive to the full dimensions of experience, and thus to enable it to understand both the prominent, superficial facts perceived by presentational immediacy, and the vague, omnipresent facts perceived by causal efficacy. Much like Freud, though stemming from very different suppositions and pursuing very different aims, Whitehead argues that the real base of experience lies below the surface of conscious awareness, in the vague omnipresent aspects of existence. Succinctly stated, experience is prior to consciousness, not the other way around. Due to the legacy of Descartes' emphasis on clear and distinct ideas, however, modern thought has tended to make consciousness the *sine qua non* of experience. In contrast, by making philosophy attentive to the full dimensions of experience, including especially the vague omnipresent background facts perceived by causal efficacy, Whitehead is opening the way for human experience to be a means for understanding the nature of reality as such. We are part of reality; thus the most generic or metaphysical characteristics of reality are also part of our experience. The key is to shift attention away from the prominent elements of experience, which we consciously perceive through the more unique capacities of human sense perception, toward

---

63. Whitehead, *Process and Reality*, 175. Recent research in neuroscience on human empathy seems to confirm something like Whitehead's notion of perception or receptivity in the mode of causal efficacy. "Empathy," says neuroscientist Jean Decety, "begins with the involuntary: shared emotion. 'This is something that is hard-wired into our brains—the capacity to automatically perceive and share others' feelings.'" In Gibson, "Mirrored Emotion," 35. Whitehead would say that this capacity is a metaphysical characteristic of all reality; hence, it is hard-wired, at some level, into all of reality, not just human experience.

the more vague background elements of experience, which are generic to all things. Whitehead's two-pronged understanding of perception opens the way for this type of reflection and analysis.

(4) In seeking to initiate a new understanding of and approach to metaphysics, Whitehead argues that the verification of a metaphysical scheme "is to be sought in its general success." By this he means that one ought to assess it using a combination of rational and empirical criteria. Specifically, he identifies four interrelated criteria by which to identify a valid scheme, namely, one that is *coherent, logical, applicable,* and *adequate*. By "coherence," he indicates that the fundamental ideas of a metaphysical view ought to "hang together" in such a manner that these basic ideas presuppose one another. Anything characterized by one of the ideas is also in some way characterized or implied by all of the others and vice versa. "The requirement of coherence," he remarks, "is the great preservative of rationalistic sanity." Conversely, "incoherence is the arbitrary disconnection of first principles." He points to Descartes' philosophy as an illustration:

> There is, in Descartes' philosophy, no reason why there should not be a one-substance world, only corporeal, or a one-substance world, only mental. According to Descartes, a substantial individual "requires nothing but itself in order to exist." Thus this system makes a virtue of its incoherence. But, on the other hand, the facts seem connected, while Descartes' system does not; for example, in the treatment of the body-mind problem.[64]

As part of this coherence, a metaphysical scheme should also be "logical" in the sense of being rationally consistent, i.e., without contradiction. Along with these rational criteria, the scheme must also be empirically successful in the sense that it enables one to interpret effectively some elements of experience ("applicable") and, even more importantly and stringently, in the sense that it is able to interpret effectively all elements of experience ("adequate"). To borrow a term from economics, there should be no "externalities" left outside the metaphysical framework. Hence, in an adequate metaphysical scheme, nothing, including God, can be conceived completely independently of or abstracted from the

---

64. Whitehead, *Process and Reality*, 3, 6. Audi offers a useful discussion of coherence that distinguishes between the positive claim of coherence as a ground for justification and the negative or "defeater" role of incoherence as grounds for a lack of justification. See Audi, *Architecture of Reason*, 24–29.

metaphysical categories that pertain to all of experience. This is not to say that all aspects of reality or experience are metaphysical. Rather, it is to say that nothing can be coherently conceived in a manner completely apart from these metaphysical characteristics. The business of metaphysics, Whitehead concludes, is to show "that no entity can be conceived in complete abstraction from the system of the universe."[65]

By insisting on the coherence (requiring logical consistency) and adequacy (requiring applicability) of a metaphysical scheme, Whitehead rightly points to the necessary aspect of metaphysical characteristics. Both the rational criterion of coherence and the empirical criterion of adequacy define a scheme that is necessary, so that a truly coherent scheme is adequate and vice-versa. For instance, in reference to adequacy he states:

> The adequacy of a scheme over every item does not mean adequacy over such items as happen to have been considered. It means that the texture of observed experience, as illustrating the philosophic scheme, is such that all related experience must exhibit the same texture. Thus the philosophic scheme should be "necessary," in the sense of bearing in itself its own warrant of universality throughout all experience.[66]

This necessity must draw upon logical necessity: in order for a metaphysical scheme to be adequate, it must apply to all conceivable states of affairs, not merely to those that have been explicitly considered. To identify one or more state of affairs that are logically conceivable apart from the philosophic scheme is to indicate that the scheme itself is inadequate and incoherent. In this case, one has identified externalities that can in fact be conceptualized and accounted for apart from the proposed scheme, and thus one has indicated the failure of the proposal itself. Through Whitehead's dual-procedure for examining metaphysical claims, one can test the putative coherence of a scheme by asking whether it is empirically adequate and, conversely, one can test the putative adequacy of a scheme by asking whether it is rationally coherent.

Given the fact that valid or successful metaphysical schemes must be logically necessary, it would seem to follow that such schemes must

---

65. Whitehead, *Process and Reality*, 3.

66. Ibid., 3–4. Again, given our earlier discussion of the objective, causative influence of the world on human experience, human experience is, for Whitehead, a point of access to the nature of reality as such.

be justified a priori. Whitehead himself seldom if ever uses this term in reference to his own view, perhaps because of its associations with Kant and other strands of modern thought from which he seeks to differ. But like the metaphysical enterprise as a whole, what the term "a priori" needs is to be carefully reexamined and not merely relegated to the dustbin of philosophical history. Such a careful reexamination is offered, for instance, by the contemporary philosopher Laurence Bonjour in his book *In Defense of Pure Reason*. I will draw on selected elements of Bonjour's work as I seek to outline a case for why a priori justification should be included as part of a fallibilistic metaphysics.

At the beginning of my discussion of the epistemological error, I suggested that Descartes himself appealed to something like a priori knowledge. For instance, he writes,

> I further concluded that it is almost impossible that our judgments can be so correct or solid as they would have been, had our reason been mature from the moment of our birth, and had we always been guided by it alone.[67]

This passage points to two or more distinct elements that have often been blurred in the history of philosophy. On the one hand, by raising the image of mature reason from birth, Descartes conjures up the traditional notion of "innate ideas"—ideas known from birth by reason alone. On the other hand, by raising the question of the validity of judgments, he draws attention to the issue of rational justification, specifically, to justification by appeal to reason alone. Now the notion of innate ideas itself harbors its own internal ambiguity. It is one thing to point to the ever-present elements of experience—those vague but significant and necessary aspects of all possible experience, which Whitehead just discussed, but it is another thing to express and articulate these aspects of experience in terms of specific ideas or concepts. The specific ideas or concepts that we use come to us through contingent historical and cultural means. Yet, it is still a third thing to validate claims about experience using these concepts by means of reason alone. Thus, there are at least three elements that need to be distinguished: those universal and necessary aspects of experience, our acquisition and use of ideas and concepts to express those aspects of reality, and the rational means we use to justify claims made by use of these concepts.

---

67. Descartes, "Discourse on Method," 47 (Part II).

Bonjour suggests that the tendency to blur these elements stems from a long-standing and mistaken habit of conflating the issues of "concept acquisition" and "justification." The former pertains to the question of how we acquire or come to understand a concept; the latter pertains to what kinds of reasons we offer to justify a claim that makes use of that concept. To illustrate, he puts forth the claim "that nothing can be red all over and green all over at the same time." How we acquire knowledge of red and green may indeed come through empirical experience, yet the proposed claim itself, which involves the logical relation between two distinct entities, is justified by reason alone. Bonjour appeals here to contingent elements of experience (to the experiences of red and green) to illustrate how the logical principle of non-contradiction is itself still necessarily true by reason alone: nothing can be X (red) and not-X (not red, i.e., green) at the same time in the same place in the same way. My discussion of the metaphysical aspects of experience obviously seeks to point to necessary rather than to merely contingent elements of experience. That is, I seek to draw attention to the omnipresent aspects of each and every experience, and not merely to passing elements, such as the experience of red or green. My basic point is that all experience contains both contingent and necessary elements. In spite of this different emphasis, Bonjour's distinction between justification and concept acquisition is still useful in that it enables us to recognize the distinct and complementary roles of reason and experience. As he puts it, "a proposition will count as being justified *a priori* as long as no appeal to experience is needed for the proposition to be justified *once it is [explicitly] understood*, where it is allowed that experience may have been needed to achieve such an understanding."[68] Bonjour points here to the error of the genetic fallacy and seeks to mark a sensible path around it. How we acquire or come to understand a concept or the content of a belief may indeed involve a contingent, historical, and cultural pathway; but once a concept or belief is understood, claims made employing it may still be justified a priori if no appeal to contingent experience is required for justifying the claim itself. Furthermore, though an empirical experience cannot provide a priori justification as such, it can sometimes invalidate a putative a priori claim. Whitehead recognized this in proposing his criterion of adequacy: an adequate metaphysical scheme is one that applies to all possible experience; if, however, one can appeal to one or

---

68. Bonjour, *In Defense of Pure Reason*, 9, 10.

more particular experiences for which the scheme cannot adequately account, then those experiences provide an empirical refutation of that proposed scheme.

Bonjour's distinction between justification and concept acquisition helps us to recognize that it is ultimately the justification of claims that is of primary relevance for the metaphysical enterprise. He offers further clarity by noting that there is a subtle but important difference between the "a priori—a posteriori" distinction and the "necessary—contingent" distinction. The former is "an *epistemological* distinction having to do with the way in which a claim or assertion is epistemically justified." The latter is "a *metaphysical* distinction having to do with the status of a proposition in relation to the ways the world might have been and having no immediate bearing on knowledge or justification." Significantly, Bonjour defines the epistemological distinction in terms of "claims" and the metaphysical distinction in terms of "propositions." He defines "propositions" as "assertive *contents* of belief, judgment, or thought, possessing truth values, which may . . . be linguistically expressed but which need not be and often are not thus expressed" (emphasis added).[69] Though he does not offer an explicit definition of "claims," I take it that he would define them as linguistic expressions or assertions in which some propositional content is said to be valid or true. Put simply, propositions pertain to content—to a potential or actual state of affairs in the world—whereas claims seek to give utterance to and make assertions about this content through language. Otherwise stated, propositions can be *valid* (can refer to an actual or normative state of affairs or to an aspect thereof) whereas claims require *validation* (the attempt to justify or redeem them). It is our claims about propositions that require justification, either in an a priori or a posteriori manner. Whitehead, perhaps even more than Bonjour, insists on this distinction between propositions and their linguistic expression: "Every proposition refers to a universe exhibiting some general systematic metaphysical character." But language, Whitehead observes, tends to break "down precisely at the task of expressing in explicit form the . . . very generalities which metaphysics seeks to express." Hence, language and verbal expression need to be stretched beyond their current or ordinary usage in order to press them toward more adequate articulation of the ultimate generalities.[70]

69. Ibid., 11, 26.
70. Whitehead, *Process and Reality*, 11, 4.

Distinctions such as these offered by Bonjour and Whitehead have tended to be overlooked in the modern dismissal of metaphysics. Their purchase, however, is that they enable us to see how and why it makes sense to think of metaphysics as a search for necessary propositions, as making use of a priori justification and, yet, as always making fallible claims. In order to build this case, I will begin by proposing the following table as a guide for gaining greater clarity about the metaphysical enterprise. The table identifies four distinct components and, within each component, it identifies the genuine alternatives:

Clarifying the Different Components Within Claims to Knowledge

	(A) Metaphysical Claims	(B) Empirical Claims
1) Focus of Content	Abstract or Universal elements of experience	Concrete or Particular elements of experience
2) Modal Status of Content	Necessary	Contingent
3) Form of Epistemic Justification	A Priori	A Posteriori
4) Subjective Form of Knowledge	Fallible	Fallible

By "focus of content," I refer to the fact that our claims and perception always entail some focus or center of attention. Perception discriminates among the raw data of experience, including ideas consciously entertained, and selectively attributes more concern to some aspects or elements than others. Metaphysical claims, therefore, focus on those aspects of experience that are the most general (1A). Philosopher Ivor Leclerc, commenting on the work of Whitehead, notes that facts "exhibit features which are 'general', in the sense of not being peculiar to those particular facts, but capable of exemplification in other facts. These 'general features' or 'principles' are capable of being 'conceived,' 'entertained in idea', [and] 'stated in abstraction.'" It is the chore of metaphysics to undertake these tasks. Science also, of course, seeks to understand things in terms of general features or principles; hence, one must clarify that metaphysics is concerned with those elements that are completely general, i.e., those that are most generic and thus pertain to all possible worlds, whereas science focuses on "features or principles of varying degrees of restricted generality, ones which thus characterize only some" facts of experience, such as those pertaining to biology, chemistry, or physics.[71]

This emphasis on the importance of complete generality raises the issue of the "modal status of the content." Metaphysics deals with necessary propositions (2A) rather than contingent ones because metaphysics seeks to identify those generic aspects of experience that are present in all possible worlds or situations, not merely some of them. As Bonjour states,

> A proposition is *necessary* (necessarily true) . . . [if] it is true in all possible worlds, that is, true in any possible situation that obtains or might have obtained, such that, in the strongest possible sense, it had to be true and could not have been false; it is *contingent* if it is true in some possible worlds or situations and false in others, so that its truth value, whatever it in fact may actually be, might have been different. . . . A necessary falsehood . . . is true in no possible world or situation.[72]

Kant and Kantians would presumably object to Bonjour's description of the necessary—contingent distinction as having to do "with the status of a proposition in relation to . . . the world." In contrast, they would maintain that this modal distinction is merely a rule or regulative ideal of human understanding and not a metaphysical characteristic of reality as such. This difference points to the fact that Bonjour in his own way, like Whitehead and Hartshorne, rejects Kant's denial of the possibility of knowing reality as such. For his part, Bonjour formulates his case by arguing against Kant's notion of the synthetic a priori. Whitehead, as we saw earlier, formulates his rejection in part by arguing against Kant's and modernity's narrow definition of perception. An adequate meta-

---

71. Leclerc, *Whitehead's Metaphysics*, 31, 32, 33.

72. Bonjour, *In Defense of Pure Reason*, 11–12. It is worth noting that Bonjour's equation of "necessary" with "all possible worlds" implies the necessity of *some* world, i.e., it implies that the complete absence of world is nonsense. Otherwise, what is true in all possible worlds would not be *logically* necessary. The logical necessity of some world will become more apparent in my discussion of the Theological Error.

physical scheme, Whitehead suggests, should be necessary "in the sense of bearing in itself its own warrant of universality throughout all experience, provided that we confine ourselves to that which communicates with immediate matter of fact. But what does not so communicate," Whitehead memorably adds, "is unknowable, and the unknowable is unknown." That is, unlike Kant, who thinks the unknowable (noumena) can be rationally identified and thought, Whitehead (like Hegel) thinks the unknowable is completely unknown. If we truly cannot know it, then we do not even know what the unknowable is, even in thought. Thus, the unknowable is itself unknowable, which means that the very concept "unknowable" cannot itself be known. Hence, talk about the unknowable is finally nonsensical.[73] For Whitehead, therefore, what is generic to experience as such is necessary for all possible reality and not merely for human understanding. As I will argue below in my discussion of the theological error, I think Kant's denial of the application of the modal distinction to reality itself stems in part from his classical understanding of God and, thus, from his inability to coherently affirm the idea of necessary existence. In the meantime, the point that I want to emphasize is that metaphysics seeks to identify necessary propositions, those that are true in any possible world.

In expressing and making claims about necessary propositions, metaphysics must at some point employ a priori (3A) and not merely a posteriori "forms of epistemic justification." Like many terms in the philosophical lexicon, "a priori" has acquired a range of meanings. By it, I mean arguments or forms of justification that attempt to demonstrate that a proposition is rationally necessary by seeking to show that its denial is self-contradictory. In sorting out the meaning and uses of "a priori," it helps to distinguish between at least two forms of contradiction: *performative* and *logical*. The notion of performative contradiction, outlined effectively by Apel, Habermas, and others, states that one falls into contradiction whenever the content of one's claim is directly at odds with the act of making the claim itself. Descartes' "Second Meditation," for instance, implicitly appeals to such a notion. Descartes comes to recognize that the explicit *content* of his doubting (doubting his own existence) is at odds with his performative *act* of doubting, since the latter necessarily affirms his existence, while the former explicitly calls it into question. Thus, positively stated, he concludes that the content

73. Bonjour, *In Defense of Pure Reason*, 20–26; Whitehead, *Process and Reality*, 4.

of the claim "I exist" is necessarily true every time the act of thinking it or claiming it is engaged. Now his own existence is not logically necessary—it is not a true or necessary feature of all possible worlds, but it is performatively necessary every time he makes a claim. Alternatively, a logical contradiction occurs whenever one denies a logically necessary proposition, i.e., denies a proposition that is true in all possible worlds. This form of contradiction is especially relevant to metaphysical claims, since they seek to identify precisely those aspects of reality that are generic to all possible experience and worlds. Hence, the denial of a valid metaphysical proposition involves a logical contradiction. For example, if "something exists" is a necessary proposition, as I will discuss in the next section, then its denial is self-contradictory. In fact, one should note that both forms of contradiction (logical and performative) are involved in the denial of valid metaphysical propositions, since the act of denial includes performative dimensions as well as strictly logical ones. For instance, the denial of "something exists" involves a performative contradiction insofar as the explicit act of denial is implicitly at odds with the performative existence of the one offering the denial.[74]

Thus far, I have argued that the metaphysical enterprise rightly entails a focus on the most general aspects of experience, involves propositions that are logically necessary, and requires a priori forms of justification. But the "subjective form of knowledge" always remains fallible (4A and 4B) and never certain. Metaphysics indeed seeks to make logically necessary claims and to justify these claims a priori, but this undertaking is always done within the parameters and limits of human understanding and language. And given these ever-present conditions, one can never meaningfully assert that one's metaphysical claims or conclusions are indubitable, incorrigible, or infallible. On the contrary, one's claims may be mistaken and are thus always subject to critical review and the possibility of correction. For example, if I claim that "something exists" is logically necessary and I seek to justify it a priori, I still do so within the horizon of fallible human understanding: *claims about necessary propositions* are always formulated within the fragmentary context of human understanding and are expressed through the communicative medium of language. As Hartshorne observes, "metaphysical blunders are due to the misuse of words." This misuse can stem from either our fallible understanding (we think something to be

---

74. My discussion here is informed by Gamwell, *Divine Good*, 159–63.

necessary but we are mistaken) or from the "baggage" or inadequacy of the words we choose (we use linguistic terms or concepts that fail to adequately express the metaphysical realities, e.g., tying metaphysics to the static language of "being" rather than "becoming"). "Verbal formulations in metaphysics," Hartshorne adds, "are simplest [and most dangerously misleading] when they state half-truths. For example, 'God is infinite, creatures are finite'" expresses a half-truth that is enticing in its simplicity but dangerously misleading in terms of metaphysical accuracy.[75] Given these ever-present possibilities of error, we must distinguish between the content or propositions that metaphysics seeks to understand, and our linguistically formulated claims about them; it is this latter element that ensures that metaphysics is and remains a fallible enterprise, just like any other human endeavor. In sum, therefore, one might say that metaphysics seeks logical certainty in the form of logical necessity, but never epistemological certainty.

The Theological Error: The Pervasive Influence of Classical Theism

As we learned from Dewey at the beginning of the chapter, metaphysics in the West has largely been determined by the quest for certitude. This quest, in turn, has been closely tied to a classical metaphysics in general, and to a classical understanding of God in particular. By "classical," I refer to the Greek tendency to emphasize and absolutize stasis, self-sufficiency, and completeness as marks of perfection. "True Being or Reality," as Dewey put it, "is complete; in being complete, it is perfect, divine, immutable, the 'unmoved mover.'"[76] The legacy of this conception stretches from Aristotle down through Western philosophy and theology to the present. To be sure, there has been internal diversity within both the Christian theological and Western philosophical traditions regarding the concept of God. For instance, when we later get to Milbank's theology, we will see some of the diverse strands within the premodern Christian tradition. Nonetheless, this diversity has remained to a significant extent within the wider orbit of classical theism. Key classical assumptions, such as the primacy of eternity over time and the notion that the world is fully dependent on God but God is not

---

75. Hartshorne, *Creative Synthesis and Philosophic Method*, 94, 95.
76. Dewey, *Quest for Certainty*, 20.

affected by the world, have largely been considered beyond dispute. As Hartshorne succinctly puts it, classical theism insists that "God may act, but cannot be acted upon." This classical outlook is further illustrated by Descartes: "I am assured . . . that he upon whom I am dependent possesses in himself all the good after which I aspire, and that not merely indefinitely and potentially, but infinitely and actually, and that he is thus God."[77] In keeping with the classical legacy, Descartes defines divine perfection here in terms of an infinite actualization of all good, thereby presuming that no additional value can be added to the divine experience.

This classical understanding is equally evident in Kant's writings, in both his pre-critical and critical thought (with 1770 traditionally considered as the transition between these two periods).[78] For instance, speaking of Kant's *Lectures on Philosophical Theology* from the 1780s, one commentator notes that "they show, perhaps surprisingly, that despite Kant's generally critical stance toward the transcendent metaphysics of the scholastics and rationalists, he remained quite sympathetic to traditional theology on many points."[79] This sympathy is evident in the *Lectures* when Kant describes God in traditional terms as "the *original being (ens originarium)*," "the *highest being (ens summum)*," "a being having every reality . . . *(ens realissmi)*," and as the maximum or greatest being "*(ente maximo)*." In describing God as the original being, Kant sounds much like Aristotle when Kant writes: "I represent God as completely isolated from everything, as existing for himself and from himself and as standing in community with no other being."[80] In the *Critique of Pure Reason*, which is also from the 1780s, Kant continues this trend by defining divinity in terms of *"ens realissimum,"* by which he means an "individual being" who "possesses all reality" in the sense of possessing all possible perfections and, hence, possesses an "unconditioned completeness." "The concept of such a being," says Kant, "is the

---

77. Hartshorne, *Natural Theology for Our Time*, 68; Descartes, "Meditations," 142.

78. Traditionally, 1770 is viewed as the pivotal year in the development and transition of Kant's thought with the publication of his *Inaugural Dissertation*. Yet, Schneewind argues that there are already important changes in Kant's moral philosophy by 1765. See Schneewind, *Invention of Autonomy*, 484–86.

79. Wood, "Translator's Introduction," 10.

80. Kant, *Lectures on Philosophical Theology*, 43.

concept of *God*."⁸¹ Here again we see the classical tendency to define perfection in terms of an unchanging completeness that actualizes all value.

Hartshorne suggests, however, that Kant at least partly recognized a potential problem with the notion of "unincreasable perfection," namely, that not all positive empirical predicates are mutually compatible. But rather than taking this problem as an indication of the need to revise the traditional conception of divine perfection, Kant instead took it only as an indication of "the need to renounce claims of supporting the idea by theoretical reason."⁸² Stephan Körner, in describing Kant's view, illustrates this dual response:

> God, [according to Kant], is . . . the bearer of all possible perfections. A "perfection" is . . . unlimited in the sense that it cannot be incompatible with any other positive predicate. No empirical predicate, therefore, can be a perfection. Any positive empirical predicate, e.g., "red" or "square," is incompatible with some other such predicate, say "green" or "triangular." The perfections of this most perfect being, or *ens realissimum* or God, can thus only be grasped "by analogy."⁸³

On the one hand, as Körner indicates, Kant recognized that experience teaches us that not all positive predicates are compatible with each other (red vs. green or square vs. triangular). Yet, on the other hand, instead of taking this as a signal to revise the traditional conception of divine perfection as an unchanging actualization of all value, Kant held on to this conception and concluded that it could only be grasped by analogy, and not literally by theoretical reason. Otherwise put, such a notion of divine perfection is not one that we can know through experience, since our experience applies to that which is definite, and definiteness entails limitation. But the whole point of the classical understanding of *ens realissimum* is to define perfection without limitation or change. In the *Lectures*, Kant addresses this tension directly. We must think of God, he states, as

> a maximum of all realities. . . . For fundamentally we can only think of God by ascribing to him without any limitation everything real which we meet with in ourselves. But . . . we ourselves

---

81. Kant, *Critique of Pure Reason*, 490 (A576/B604), 493 (A580/B608).
82. Hartshorne, *Aquinas to Whitehead*, 31.
83. Körner, *Kant*, 118–19.

> are limited creatures [whose experience shows us that we are] ... often unable to represent the real except under limitations. ... But we must nevertheless have [the concept of maximal unlimited reality] in our concept of God. ... So we ascribe it to God and admit the inability of our reason to think it in a wholly pure way.[84]

It is this conception of unchanging divine perfection, which is unknowable to experience, that shapes Kant's critical thought when he considers and rejects metaphysical arguments for the existence of God.

This conception is evident when one examines his discussion of necessary existence in the First Critique. In spite of his overall rejection of the various theistic arguments, Kant still finds something attractive about the notion of necessary existence. Nevertheless, he ultimately relegates it to the status of a heuristic or regulative ideal.[85] In order to understand this simultaneous combination of attraction and relegation, one must go back and distinguish among what might be called the traditional formulation of the ontological argument (as offered by Descartes), the cosmological argument, and Kant's own earlier version of an ontological argument, set forth in his 1763 pre-critical work *The One Possible Basis for a Demonstration of the Existence of God* (hereafter *TOPB*).

In the *Critique of Pure Reason*, Kant rejects the traditional formulation of the ontological argument as "a quite unnatural procedure and a mere innovation of scholastic subtlety." He finds this version unnatural because it seeks to argue *from* the idea of a perfect Being *(ens realissimum) to* the notion of necessary existence. Kant's criticism of this argument, including his assertion that existence is not a predicate, is well known; thus, I will not rehearse it here. Let me simply indicate that elements of this argument are partly anticipated in outline form in *TOPB*. In contrast to the misguided approach of the traditional ontological argument, Kant thinks a more "natural" and credible path begins by first establishing the notion of necessary existence and then connecting it to the idea of a perfect Being *(ens realissimum)*. This basic

---

84. Kant, *Lectures on Philosophical Theology*, 47.

85. Clayton notes how "Kant continued to give traditional metaphysical concepts a central place in his thought throughout all stages of his development." To be sure, his critical thought reinterprets these metaphysical concepts as merely regulative, but the centrality of these concepts is still present. See Clayton, *Problem of God in Modern Thought*, 304, 305.

strategy is followed in both the cosmological argument and in Kant's own version of an ontological argument in *TOPB*, which he himself describes as "ontological."[86]

Let us begin with Kant's own ontological argument. He contends that the very ground of possibility itself requires that something exists necessarily. This is the case, he submits, because every possibility entails *both* a *material* and a *formal* element. The former consists of some content or state of affairs whereas the latter involves the logical requirement that this or any state of affairs abide by the principle of non-contradiction. Kant offers the example of a "four-sided triangle," which is obviously self-contradictory in logical or formal terms. "Nevertheless," he notes, "a triangle as well as something four-sided is in itself something [i.e., there is still material content to be thought]." But in the case of "nothing exists," there is no material element at all. The problem stems, in other words, from a complete void or empty set, not from the formal element as such. "'Nothing exists,'" Kant observes, "means the same thing as 'There is absolutely nothing.'" And in that case, "nothing at all is given, no matter of anything conceivable; and [hence] all possibility is abolished." To claim "that there be some possibility and yet absolutely nothing actual," Kant argues, "contradicts itself." For to deny all actuality is to empty the material content of all possibility; to empty the material content of all possibility is to deny possibility itself; and that which denies possibility itself is literally impossible: "Consequently it is absolutely impossible that nothing at all exist."[87]

Having argued that the nature of possibility requires that something exist, Kant proceeds to a second phase by trying to show that this condition is actualized in one entity, not many. There are only two possible relations between possibility and existence: "Either the possible is conceivable only insofar as it is itself actual, [in which case] possibility is given as a determination in the actual; or it is possible because something else is actual; that is, its inner possibility is given as a consequence through another existence." This other existence, which serves as the source of possibilities, Kant calls "the ultimate real ground of . . . absolute possibility." Again, possibility requires both an ultimate logical ground (the principle of non-contradiction) and an ultimate material

---

86. See Kant, *Critique of Pure Reason*, 507 (A603/B631), 515 (A615/B643); and Kant, *TOPB*, 75, 233.

87. Kant, *TOPB*, 67, 69, 71.

ground, namely, "something actual in which and through which everything conceivable is given." This entity, "whose annulment or negation eradicates all possibility" as such, "exists in an absolutely necessary fashion." Having established the notion of necessary existence as integral to possibility itself, Kant defines contingent existence as referring to all entities whose denial does not annul possibility as such and, hence, whose non-being may be thought. In contrast, necessary existence refers to one actuality whose existence cannot be denied because it is the very source of all possibilities. As he states: "Because the necessary being contains the ultimate ground of the possibility of all other beings, every other thing is possible only insofar as it is given through it as a ground." In sum, if I understand Kant correctly, there cannot be multiple necessary actualities because, by definition, necessary existence means the ground of all possibilities, and multiple necessary actualities would mean multiple comprehensive grounds, which is contradictory.[88]

In the third and final phase, Kant defines this necessary actuality in classical theistic terms. To begin with, he defines it as simple or singular, which in effect absolutizes all attributes and thus leads to a static and one-dimensional conception of God. For instance, he writes:

> Because this existence presupposes both its own possibility and every other possibility, no other mode of existence is possible for it; that is, the necessary being cannot exist in multiple modes. . . . Thus it is not possible for it to be in any way other than it actually is, nor can it be determined in any other way or changed. Its non-existence is absolutely impossible, thus also its generation and decay; accordingly it is eternal.[89]

Put simply, this necessary Being or God is immutable, eternal, and unchanging in all respects. Kant proceeds then to define it in terms of *ens realissimum*:

> In the most real being, there can be no . . . positive conflict of its own determinations, since the consequence of that would be a privation or want, which would contradict its maximum reality. Real conflict would arise if all realities were to reside in it as determinations, so that they cannot be in it collectively as predi-

---

88. Ibid., 71, 79, 80.
89. Ibid., 83.

cates. Thus, since they are all given through it, they will belong either to its determinations or to its consequences.[90]

As Körner noted above, Kant recognizes here that empirical predicates cannot be part of the divine nature, since they are contingent and thus are often incompatible with each other—something may be red or green all over but cannot be both at the same time. Hence, following in true classical theistic fashion, Kant makes a sharp division between divine determinations (those positive values that are maximally and exhaustively achieved in God) and worldly consequences (those contingent values found in the world that are dependent on God as ground but do not affect the divine nature itself). Put simply, the relation between God and world is strictly one-way; the world is totally dependent on God as the ground of possibility, but God is not at all affected by the world. If a different set of contingent values or consequences had been actualized in the world, God would not be different in any way.[91]

At the end of *TOPB*, Kant partly anticipates a line of thought that will become central in his later critical perspective. "Experience of contingent things," he remarks,

> cannot give an adequate argument by which to comprehend the existence of something of which it is impossible that it not be. It is solely in that the denial of divine existence is absolutely nothing that the difference between this [divine] existence and that of other things lies. Internal possibility, the essence of things, is precisely that whose negation cancels all thought. This is what constitutes the unique characteristic of the existence of the essence [and possibility] of all being. Seek the proof here.[92]

In this passage, Kant asserts that human experience—experience of contingent things and values in the world—cannot "comprehend" the existence of an absolutely necessary Being. Yet reason convincingly shows that the denial of necessary existence leads to "absolutely nothing," which negates all possibility and "cancels all thought." In short, the pre-critical Kant is willing to live with this affirmation of a divine existence beyond experience, but the later Kant is not. For the Kant of the First Critique, things outside the bounds of experience can

---

90. Ibid., 85.

91. For a helpful brief discussion of classical theism, see Hartshorne, *Aquinas to Whitehead*, 5–7.

92. Kant, *TOPB*, 237, 239.

be thought but cannot be known to exist, for the scope of theoretical knowledge is now defined more narrowly in terms of what can be given to sense experience as it shaped by the conditions and categories of human understanding. Consequently, arguments such as the one in *TOPB* are now considered metaphysical illusions, not theistic proofs or demonstrations. Nevertheless, notwithstanding this major change, it is significant that the later Kant remains intrigued by the first phase of his earlier argument, by the notion that reason must conceive of possibility as related to necessity. As Milbank and his colleagues rightly observe, "Kant remained haunted by this question of ontological depth 'behind' finite phenomena." In his introduction to *TOPB*, Gordon Treash similarly describes this persistent element: "From *The One Possible Basis* to the *Critique of Pure Reason*, a time span of nearly twenty years, the notion persists that all determination of individual things presupposes a totality of possibility; if not an actuality which necessarily exists in order to ground possibility, then an idea of a presupposed completeness of possibility is a necessary condition of the knowledge of individual things."[93] This latter approach is nicely illustrated by Kant's discussion of the cosmological argument in the First Critique.

As earlier indicated, Kant is more favorably disposed toward the cosmological argument than the traditional ontological argument, because the former, like his own ontological argument, attempts to argue from necessary existence to a perfect Being, not the other way around. In its customary formulation, the cosmological argument seeks to argue from our experience of the nature of the world back to a necessary ground or First Cause. Though Kant's ontological argument does not take this precise path, it similarly seeks to identify the ground of all possibilities in a necessary existence. In fact, he observes that "although the cosmological proof presupposes an experience in general, it is not based on any particular property of this experience but on pure principles of reason, [and hence primarily] . . . relies on pure concepts alone." By analyzing the cosmological argument, Kant seeks to understand why humans are led into the "natural illusion" of connecting "the concepts of necessity and supreme reality *[ens realissimum]*."[94] I will quote him at length here because I believe this passage reveals how his underlying

---

93. Milbank, et al., "Suspending the Material," 5; Treash, in his Introduction to Kant's *TOPB*, 26.

94. Kant, *Critique of Pure Reason*, 514 (A615/B643).

classical theistic assumptions shape the way he responds to metaphysical arguments about necessary existence, arguments that he himself is still attracted to in some manner:

> There is something very strange in the fact, that once we assume something to exist we cannot avoid inferring that something exists necessarily. The cosmological argument rests on this quite natural ... inference. On the other hand, if I take the concept of anything, no matter what, I find that the existence of this thing can never be represented by me as absolutely necessary, ... [i.e.,] nothing prevents me from thinking its non-existence. Thus while I may indeed be obliged to assume something necessary as a condition of the existent in general, I cannot think any particular thing as in itself necessary. In other words, I can never *complete* the [cosmological] regress to the conditions of existence save by assuming a necessary being, and yet am never in a position to *begin* with [or to know] such a being.
>
> [Therefore,] [i]f I am constrained to think something necessary as a condition of existing things, but am unable to think any particular thing as in itself necessary, it inevitably follows that necessity and contingency do not concern the things themselves.... Consequently, neither of these two principles can be objective. They may, however, be regarded as subjective principles of reason. The one calls upon us to seek something necessary as a condition of all that is given as existent ... ; the other forbids us ... to treat anything empirical as unconditioned.... Viewed in this manner, the two principles [may be understood] as merely heuristic and *regulative*, and as concerning only the formal interest of reason.[95]

At least four key points should be noted about this critical passage. First, it is evident that Kant still finds the argument about necessary existence persuasive in some manner or form. If one recalls the first phase of his ontological argument, he maintained that "nothing exists" is an incoherent idea because it ultimately undermines possibility itself, which in turn is literally impossible; thus, something must exist necessarily. Here in the First Critique, he points in this same general direction when he says that "we cannot avoid inferring that something exists necessarily" or when he says "I may indeed be obliged to assume something necessary as a condition of the existent in general." The relevant point is that Kant still finds something persuasive about the fact that reason

95. Ibid., 515 (A615/B643–A617/B645).

must affirm necessary existence. How and why this rational necessity is differently construed here in the First Critique will become clear as we proceed.

Second, when Kant conceives of necessary existence, his thinking is still pervasively informed by classical metaphysical and theistic assumptions. He assumes that necessary existence means "absolutely necessary" or necessary in all respects. Hence, "we must regard the absolutely necessary as being *outside* the world."[96] This position is in keeping with his earlier theistic assumptions that God or *ens realissimum* must completely transcend the world.

Third, unlike his pre-critical period, Kant now holds that theoretical knowledge or knowledge of existence is limited to what can be given in and through sense experience. Therefore, nothing "outside the world" of experience can be known to exist. Anything "outside the world" must be completely negative, i.e., not accessible to experience and thus unknowable (noumena). But anything that is knowable, i.e., given in and through sense experience, is contingent and not necessary (phenomena). As he states, "I cannot think any particular thing as in itself necessary."

Fourth, having (1) affirmed that reason requires necessary existence, (2) assumed that necessary existence means necessary in all respects and, thus, outside the world of experience, and (3) insisted that knowledge of existence is limited to what can be known through sense experience, Kant finds himself in a dilemma that he seeks to solve by (4) concluding that "it inevitably follows that necessity and contingency do not concern the things themselves; otherwise there would be a contradiction. Consequently, neither of these two principles can be objective. [Rather,] [t]hey may, however, be regarded as subjective principles of reason." This conclusion, I would venture to say, has been one of the most influential in modern thought. The modal characteristics of necessity and contingency cannot apply to reality itself, Kant reasons, because there is no way to coherently reconcile steps (1)–(3).

Kant correctly recognizes that, taken together, steps (1)–(3) lead to a contradiction. Norman Kemp Smith, in his commentary on the First Critique, summarizes the problem and Kant's solution as follows:

---

96. Ibid., 516 (A617/B645).

> We are obliged to think something as necessary for all existence, and yet at the same time are unable to think anything as in itself necessary—God as little as anything else. The explanation of this strange fact must be that which follows as a corollary from the limitation of our knowledge to sense-experience, namely, that our concepts of necessity and contingency do not concern things in themselves, and cannot therefore be applied to them.[97]

But in drawing this far-reaching conclusion, Kant never considers that the real solution to the problem might be to reexamine one of his initial premises, namely (2), rather than to proceed to his conclusion (4). The Theological Error of modern thought is found in the unquestioned dominance of classical metaphysical and theistic assumptions, as illustrated by Kant's premise (2). Instead of reconsidering the notion of absolutely necessary existence (necessary in all respects) and recognizing that it is an incoherent and empty idea, Kant maintains this notion and postulates it as a noumenon—as that which is unknowable because it is beyond the world of experience. Hence, he thinks it makes sense to postulate a purely negative idea (noumenon = not phenomenon) as distinct from what is known in and through experience (phenomena). But this distinction between noumena and phenomena, as well as his distinction between a regulative ideal of reason and a representation of reality, is both unnecessary and misleading if one rightly abandons the classical assumptions of (2) and reconsiders what necessary existence might mean in relation to experience. This reconsideration is fruitfully offered by the process thought of Whitehead and, especially, by the neoclassical metaphysics of Hartshorne.

Hartshorne, like the early Kant, thinks that the statement "nothing exists" expresses an incoherent proposition and, thus, that "something exists" is necessary. "Nothing exists" is an example of what Hartshorne calls "a completely restrictive statement," one that "denies that any existential possibility is realized." Such statements, he argues, could never be validated or verified since verification requires someone or something to exist. Such statements, moreover, are constantly falsified insofar as we and other things do indeed exist. Furthermore, this falsification is not merely a contingent fact, but rather a necessary outcome, which is to say, Hartshorne argues that "nothing exists" is necessarily false. Akin to Kant's ontological argument, Hartshorne asks, "If nothing were

---

97. Smith, *Commentary to Kant's "Critique of Pure Reason,"* 534–35.

to exist, what would make this true? Bare nothing? And what would 'existence' mean if it were wholly unexemplified? Would the idea or possibility of 'existence' still remain in some Platonic heaven of forms?" Here, Hartshorne suggests that the very *possibility* of "existence" is annulled if it is not exemplified in some manner. Likewise, Kant argued that possibility as such is annulled if some possibility is not actualized in some way. Hence, Hartshorne concludes "that a completely restrictive or wholly negative statement [such as "nothing exists"] expresses an impossibility, not a conceivable but [simply] unrealized fact."[98]

For his part, Kant appears never to have fully appreciated the implications of his own ontological argument, namely, that wholly negative statements express an impossibility. If he had, then he would have recognized that his later supposition of noumena (as purely negative, i.e., not phenomena) was mistaken. Kant never recognized this, I would venture to say, due at least in part to his persistent adherence to classical theistic assumptions. The early Kant held two convictions: (1) "that something exists necessarily," and (2) "this necessary existence is a God who is completely outside the world of experience." The later Kant, who makes sense experience the *sine qua non* of any possible knowledge of existence, reduces conviction (1) from an objective metaphysical claim to a subjective principle of reason because he never questions his own classical theistic assumptions in the latter part of (2). Put simply, the later Kant thinks of God in the same *ens realissimum* terms as did the early Kant; the only difference is that he now claims that the existence of such an entity is unknowable while, at the same time, he postulates the notion of noumena—the supposition of something that purports to be free from any specifiable or positive implications. But is not such a wholly negative notion—one free from all positive content—just like the completely restrictive existential statement "nothing exists" that both the early Kant and Hartshorne reject? I submit that it is and that the later Kant should have taken this as cue to rethink his assumptions about the nature of divinity.

In contrast, Hartshorne offers an alternative conception of divinity, one that opens up possibilities for the metaphysical enterprise that Kant never seriously considered, let alone refuted. To get at this alternative conception, it is helpful to begin with Hartshorne's understanding of necessary existence. The opposite of "completely restrictive" statements

98. Hartshorne, *Creative Synthesis and Philosophic Method*, 159.

are "completely non-restrictive" ones, such as illustrated by the statement "something exists." Over against these two poles, most everyday statements are "partially restrictive." "Ordinary factual statements," he observes, "are partially restrictive of existential possibilities: for, if they are affirmative, they also implicitly deny something; and if they are negative, they also implicitly affirm something."[99] For instance, to say "the book cover is totally blue" is to implicitly deny that it is some other color. Conversely, to deny that it is blue is to implicitly affirm that it is some other color (assuming that black and white can be considered colors). Hartshorne's point is that empirical states of affairs are definite and, in their definiteness, they are restrictive in the sense that they affirm some existential states of affairs as they simultaneously deny others, and vice versa.

"Completely non-restrictive" statements, on the other hand, do not entail such restrictions. For instance, the statement "something exists" excludes no possible state of affairs—once it has been shown that its contradictory, "nothing exists," is impossible. Hence, "something exists" entails not only the empirical implication that some state of affairs does exist, but also the deeper metaphysical implication that some state of affairs *must* exist. Thus, over against the modern consensus, which asserts that all existential statements are contingent, Hartshorne adduces that the correct formulation is to say that *"all partially restrictive statements are contingent,* that is, all those which, affirming or denying the existence of something, also by implication deny or affirm the existence of something else likewise conceivable."[100]

With these distinctions in place, one can begin to contrast Hartshorne's "dipolar" conception of divinity with the singular or "monopolar" understanding of classical theism, such as found in Kant. By "dipolar," Hartshorne means that the divine nature is defined by contrasting pairs of characteristics that are each true of God in differing respects—in differing respects, God is both changing and unchanging, temporal and eternal, immanent and transcendent, relative and absolute, necessary and contingent, etc. One of the key claims behind this view is the insistence that God is not an exception to the metaphysical

---

99. Ibid.

100. Ibid., 161, 163. If metaphysical claims about God are completely non-restrictive, then the refutability of theism must ultimately take the form of showing that the notion of God is impossible or incoherent.

categories but rather is their supreme exemplification. This means that what metaphysically applies to the world also literally applies to God in some way, and vice versa. In contrast, classical theism tends to define God's greatness in terms of how God is an exception to the metaphysical characteristics of the world—"as being *outside* the world," as Kant has it. So in these classical terms, God is defined in sharp contrast to the world and therefore "as deny[ing] any and every limitation or form of dependence. We thus produce [from this conception]," remarks Hartshorne, "the idea of 'the absolute,' or 'the infinite,' or . . . the 'absolutely infinite,' [i.e.,] infinite in every respect." Hence, God is defined as not changing, as not temporal, as not immanent, as not relative, as not contingent, etc. But if God is defined in merely negative terms, how does God "differ from bare nothing?"[101] Differently stated, if God is defined in terms completely outside the world of experience, then one is back to the problem of a wholly negative notion like "noumena." Now some might posit that one can use analogical (but not literal or univocal) language to speak of God in positive terms, while still adhering to classical characteristics. Hence, according to this perspective, one can affirm God's transcendence while also affirming (though not literally) God's immanent relation to the world. But as I will later argue in my assessment of Milbank's theology, analogical language must be grounded at some point in literal terms, otherwise the analogies end up either begging the question or equivocating. In sum, God must be defined in some literal and positive terms, and only a dipolar conception can coherently do so.

In order to make sense of Hartshorne's dipolar view, it is essential to understand his seminal distinction between "existence" and "actuality." Following Whitehead, Hartshorne advances a metaphysics of dynamic process not enduring substance—one of becoming, not being. Given the fact that process is the defining characteristic of reality, it is misleading to define "existence" in terms of an unchanging substance. Existence is indeed embodied in enduring individuals, but in what manner? Hartshorne answers as follows:

> Species or properties exist in individuals, *individuals exist in concrete events* or states [of affairs]. That a property [or characteristic] exists means that there is at least one event constituting a state of the individual. The state is the actuality. *To exist is to*

101. Hartshorne, *Creative Synthesis and Philosophic Method*, 228.

be somehow actualized, in some individual and state [of affairs]. By "actuality" is meant the how, the state, of actualization [italics added].[102]

What is most fully real, according to Hartshorne and Whitehead, are the concrete events or actualities, the concrete states of affairs that make up the world. Whitehead calls these events "actual entities" or "actual occasions" or, to use a more vivid phrase, "drops of experience."[103] Process consists of the coming to be of actual occasions and the immediate passing on of those occasions as data for all future occasions. Thus, "to exist," as Hartshorne describes it, "is to be somehow actualized, in some individual and state [of affairs]." There is no existence without actuality; the former is dependent on the latter. Put another way, existence is an abstraction from the concrete actualities; or perhaps more precisely, ongoing existence is an abstraction—is a "connecting of the dots"—between distinct events or actualities. My existence as an individual is the ongoing trajectory of inherited events or actualities. As long as I exist, my existence is continually actualized in some new "drop of experience," in some new concrete state of affairs. Hence, my persisting existence consists of the ongoing trajectory of this stream of inherited actual occasions; but, to repeat, a trajectory is an abstraction from the concrete particularities or actualities themselves. This critical distinction between "existence" and "actuality" pertains to our overall discussion in at least three ways.

First, it applies to all things: to humans, to desks, to molecules, and to God. Again, God is not an exception to the metaphysical categories but rather their supreme exemplification. For God to exist or for a molecule to exist means that each of them must be concretely actualized in some way. This concreteness involves limitation and definiteness. Hence, existence must be actualized and actuality requires limitation. "Dread of limitation," Feuerbach incisively remarks, "is dread of existence." Or, as Whitehead puts it, "To be an actual thing is to be limited."[104]

102. Ibid., 254. For a concise discussion of Hartshorne's distinction between "existence" and "actuality," see Hartshorne, *Anselm's Discovery*, x–xi.
103. Whitehead, *Process and Reality*, 18.
104. Feuerbach, *Essence of Christianity*, 15. On that same page, Feuerbach is also correct to critique the classical theistic tendency of insisting that the divine existence can be known but that the divine nature can only be defined in negative terms, i.e., precluding any articulation of positive predicates. Whitehead, *Religion in the Making*, 150.

Second, it gives a whole new look to the discussion of necessary existence. Kant could only envision either absolutely necessary existence outside of the world or contingent existence within it. Given this tension, the later Kant sided with the priority of experience and relegated his persisting rational intuition about necessary existence to merely heuristic status. In contrast, Hartshorne's insightful distinction eliminates the tension by changing our fundamental understanding of "existence" and its relationship to the contingency of the world. As we said above, existence is an abstraction from the stream of concrete actualities. Hence, existence (abstract element) and actuality (concrete element) are a dipolar pair of metaphysical characteristics. In reference to God this means that "the necessity of God . . . does not . . . apply to his entire reality, but only to his [abstract] identity as God and no other."[105] The divine uniqueness, as the ontological argument suggests, is embodied in the fact that God is the one individual whose existence is necessary because it is completely non-restrictive and, therefore, not incompatible or competitive with any possible state of affairs. In basic agreement with the first two phases of the early Kant's ontological argument, Hartshorne contends that "something exits" is necessary and that this necessary existence is embodied in a comprehensive or universal individual, namely, God. Sounding much like the early Kant, Hartshorne states:

> Possibility requires a ground if anything does. By contrast, absolute impossibility is a mere privation and needs no cause. The necessity of God is the absence of an alternative possibility. Nothing makes or could make his non-existence possible; so there is no such possibility. God himself is conceived as the ground of all possibility, presupposed by any affirmation, any possibly legitimate negation, any state of affairs, [or by] any truth. Either that, or an absurdity.[106]

Unlike the third phase of Kant's ontological argument, however, Hartshorne holds that God's existence can only be actualized in some contingent manner: "With all individuals, even God, in what actual state the individual exists is contingent. *Actuality can in no case be necessary.* This is the truth misstated in the dogma, 'existence is never a property.' Existence, being somehow actualized, can be a property; but never

---

105. Hartshorne, *Creative Synthesis and Philosophic Method*, 246.
106. Ibid., 258.

actuality, the precise how of actualization [can never be necessary]." If the necessary individual's existence must be actualized in some contingent way, then some world or concrete state of affairs must also be necessary. That is, the dipolar pair of *God*—and—*some world* are both necessary. As Hartshorne parses it, "The necessarily existent abstraction 'something [exists]' divides *a priori* into two correlative abstractions, divine . . . something and non-divine [worldly] something. Both sides are equally abstract. If, then, abstraction implies necessity, 'God' and 'not God' [world] must both be necessary. However, the necessity applies only to these abstractions as somehow actualized." The concrete how of actualization is always contingent for both God and world because concreteness implies definiteness, and definiteness implies limitation. As Hartshorne succinctly remarks: "The definite cannot be necessary for a simple reason; there are mutually contradictory forms of definiteness. Red just here now excludes green just here now. [Yet,] both are equally positive [states of affairs]."[107] Spinoza and Leibniz sought in their own distinct ways to make the world's concrete actualities necessary. But Hartshorne agrees with Kant, Hume, and the empiricists that any actual or concrete world is contingent. Where Hartshorne (and Whitehead) stands apart from the rest, however, is by arguing for the dipolar combination of abstract necessity and concrete and contingent actuality. God's necessary existence must be actualized in some contingent divine actuality, which in turn includes some world of contingent non-divine actualities, all of which are in God. Thus Hartshorne's view is rightly described as *panentheism*, literally all-in-God, i.e., all concrete-contingent states of affairs are part of the divine experience.

By reconceiving necessary existence in terms of a dipolar combination of abstract necessity and contingent actuality, Hartshorne asserts that God must indeed be knowable within human experience. Drawing on the modal logic of C. I. Lewis, Hartshorne notes that "a necessary proposition is one 'implied by any and every proposition.'" Since God's existence is completely non-restrictive, and non-restrictive statements refer to necessary propositions, God's existence "is included in the meaning of any restrictive existential statement." That is, any contingent statement, such as "elephants exist," implicitly includes the background proposition "God exists." This point about propositions is also true of experience. As Hartshorne writes:

107. Ibid., 254, 250–51.

> [E]very intuition has God as object, whatever other objects it may have, and however incapable conscious introspection may be of disclosing this universal object. It is [plain] that the universally experienced is not the most obviously experienced. Kant assumes, [but] he does not prove, that there is no intuition of God; the theistic proofs, if they prove anything, prove that there is such an intuition. They do so by a *reductio ad absurdum* of the denial. This, at least, is their implied claim.[108]

The upshot of this passage is that Hartshorne agrees with the later Kant that whatever is knowable must be accessible to experience; but the crucial difference lies in how one defines experience. This difference arose earlier in our discussion of the epistemological error. Hartshorne and Whitehead concur that the metaphysical aspects of experience, such as the intuition of God, are the most omnipresent or generic. And what is omnipresent cannot be detected by noticing changes or differences in our experience, which are precisely what the senses heed. This again is why Whitehead argues, against Kant, that one must distinguish between two modes of perception, with the more basic or primitive one being that by which we intuit or experience the metaphysical realities, such as God and causality. Conscious sense perception is a highly developed form of experience, but precisely because of its complexity, it cannot detect the most generic or universal aspects of experience. In sum, it is important to see that the modern denial of metaphysics emanates from both Kant's theological error and his epistemological error: From one end, he denies the possibility of metaphysical knowledge because he conceives of necessary existence in classical theistic terms, and thus concludes that necessary existence can never be known within experience. From the other end, he defines perception singularly in terms of conscious sense experience and thus excludes the possibility of perceiving the most generic aspects of experience, namely, the metaphysical characteristics, which "fly below the radar screen" of conscious sense perception.

The third and final consequence to be drawn from Hartshorne's distinction between existence and actuality is to show how it leads to a different understanding of divine perfection. Unlike the classical assumption of *ens realissimum*, which defines God's perfection in terms of a static, "most real Being," a dipolar conception maintains that God is

---

108. Ibid., 162, 247–48.

a universal individual who is supremely related to all things, and thus is continually enriched by the values and experiences of the world's concrete actualities. As noted above, all actualities are definite, which means that all values are not compatible or compossible with each other—to actualize some requires leaving others as merely potential. Hence, the notion of maximum possible value, Hartshorne rightly argues, is as nonsensical as the notion of highest possible number, since in both cases one can always add to the present sum. Consequently, there must be potential in God, which means that God must be open to growth and enrichment in order to fully and continually enjoy the values that come to be actualized in the world. God's perfection should thus be defined in terms of God's unsurpassable relatedness to and enjoyment of all actualized values, not in terms of some putative "otherworldly" pure actuality removed from the concrete values of experience. As we saw in Körner's description of Kant, this latter definition seeks to step around the fact that empirical values or predicates involve definiteness, limitation, and the potential for incompatibility. Such a move, however, does not work: Either God knows the concrete values of the world or not. If not, then God lacks the value of knowing what we know, which is our experience and enjoyment of concrete actualities, such as the beauty of a sunset or a piece of music by Bach. Alternatively, if God does know these concrete values and actualities, then God cannot know *as actual* what other concrete values might have occurred. The pieces of music that Bach did not write must forever remain unrealized possibilities, even for God. In sum, "From Aristotle to Kant," Hartshorne observes, classical theism "played a central role" in shaping assumptions about theism and metaphysics. Only by letting go of this mistaken conception, I submit, can theism and metaphysics be properly conceived and pursued.[109]

Summary: The Need for a Different Approach to Metaphysics

Western metaphysics, as we learned from Dewey, has been largely defined by the quest for certainty. I have argued that this quest has burdened the metaphysical enterprise with at least four misguided assumptions, which I have called respectively the existential, discursive,

---

109. Ibid., 229–30, 229.

epistemological, and theological errors. These deep-rooted assumptions have significantly contributed to the anti-metaphysical proclivities of modern thought. Only by rejecting these underlying assumptions and by reconsidering metaphysics anew will theology be able to regain its authentic public voice. In order to discard these problematic assumptions, one must begin by abandoning the presumption that metaphysics or theology is guided by the aim of achieving existential certainty. A constructive response to the vicissitudes of existence, I have suggested, is found not in an existential quest for certainty but, rather, in a proper understanding of faith—one that is defined by trust, not certitude. One can trust without seeking certainty and, hence, without seeking to escape from the fallible and fragmentary conditions of human existence. Second, one must abandon the presumption that sound arguments are coercive in nature and thus lead directly to cognitive assent or to an existential change of life. On the contrary, sound arguments, including metaphysical and theistic ones, compel neither intellectual nor existential assent. Rather, they work more like persuasive lures that rationally invite our agreement and the reorientation of our lives than like irresistible rays that force us into submission. Our obligation to offer sound arguments stems first and foremost from the implied responsibilities of making and defending truth or validity claims, not from the possible effects our claims may have on our hearers and respondents. Of course, we make claims in the hope of influencing others; thus our responsibility to justify our claims issues in part from this potential or actual influence. The metaphysical claim about the reality of God is a central and inescapable element of Christian theology, and this claim, like all others, requires that we offer reasons to others as invitations for their consideration and possible assent. Third, one must free metaphysics completely and irrevocably from the epistemological quest for certainty. Metaphysical claims, like all claims, are always fallible in nature and open to the possibility of correction or revision. The subjective form of our knowledge is always fallible, but this does not preclude the fact that metaphysics rightly seeks to express necessary propositions and requires a priori justification. One must distinguish, not conflate, the different components within claims to knowledge. And, finally, one must free metaphysics once and for all from classical theistic assumptions. The modern presumption against metaphysics is correct to deny that reason can know an absolutely necessary Being or *ens realissimum*. What is needed, therefore, is a more adequate metaphysical conception, such as found in the dipolar panentheism of Whitehead and Hartshorne. Only such an alternative, I submit, can offer a promising path for a public theology and metaphysics.

3

Intermediate Reflections

As we learned in chapter 1, MacIntyre, Hauerwas, and Stout all believe that theology has lost its authentic voice somewhere along the path of history. At first, MacIntyre and Stout concluded that this was inevitable. But in their more recent modes of thought, they concur with Hauerwas that theology made a fateful accommodation—one that could have been avoided or at least one that can now be avoided. According to MacIntyre, this accommodation is rooted in modernity's mistaken notion of a common reason or rationality. There are no universal or common rational standards, he alleges, at least no substantive ones by which one can evaluate philosophical, religious, or ethical claims; rather, all rationality is tradition-dependent. Hence, theology makes a fateful mistake whenever it seeks to articulate and defend its claims in terms of a common reason. Theology can only reclaim its authentic voice when it recognizes that it can speak solely from within the context of its own tradition. This means that the truth of its claims can be made publicly credible only in an indirect way through the comparative engagement of different traditions. For Hauerwas, who concurs with MacIntyre that all rationality is tradition-dependent, theology can speak authentically only when it recognizes that it speaks out of its own particularity, specifically as a distinct community called the church. For Stout, who likewise affirms the centrality of traditions, though more broadly construed, theology can only reclaim its cognitive voice by speaking out of its own distinct vocabulary and by taking up its public responsibility to demonstrate its entitlement to its claims.

Along with these three thinkers, I too have asserted that theology has lost its authentic voice. But over against them, I have alleged that the fateful mistake made by theology stems from its acceptance of the modern denial of metaphysics. Theology's fundamental claims are at root metaphysical claims about the reality and necessity of God; these are the underlying cognitive claims that theology makes. Stout himself implicitly points in this direction when he incisively articulates that theology must be cognitive, and not merely expressive. "What makes theology more interesting than [merely] so many *oohs* and *aahs* or descriptions of heartburn," asks Stout, "if it is essentially expressive or descriptive [only] of feelings? [At some point,] ... we shall need to ask how theology can retain interest without entering the cognitive sphere." Even when speaking of Barth, Stout says that "Christianity, if it is to be true to itself, will have to make ontological claims."[1] Some might hold that the central cognitive claims of Christianity are first and foremost christological. But even if one asserts this, such claims are meaningful finally only in relation to claims about the reality of God. The former without the latter ultimately results in some variation of Feuerbach, i.e., in the affirmation of desirable predicates or virtues without affirming the divine reality as the ontological ground of such characteristics. Theology, therefore, cannot avoid its metaphysical implications; it can only regain its authentic voice when it explicitly articulates and defends its underlying metaphysical claims. With this aim in mind, I argued in chapter 2 that a reconsideration of the metaphysical enterprise is in order. This reconsideration requires not only an open-minded reexamination of metaphysics, but also a fresh understanding of what it ought to entail. In Part Two, I will seek to analyze how modern and contemporary theologians address or fail to address the metaphysical claims of theology. But at this juncture, I would like to return to, in order to further engage, the views of my three interlocutors, especially the views of MacIntyre and Stout. Since I will later devote an entire chapter to Hauerwas's theology, I will only attend to his view here by implication. Along this line, let me begin by offering a critical assessment of the strong historicism that all three of these thinkers share, and, from there, I will then offer specific further responses to MacIntyre and Stout.

A Critique of Strong Historicism

What MacIntyre, Hauerwas, and Stout share with Kant and the prevailing currents of modernity is an underlying assumption that all existential claims are logically or rationally contingent. MacIntyre, for instance,

---

1. Stout, *Flight from Authority*, 132-33, 143.

states this unequivocally in his early work when he declares that "all factual statements are contingent and this includes all statements which assert that something exists." This assumption about existence goes hand in hand with their ongoing affirmation of strong historicism. Hauerwas, for example, implies this when he asserts that the valuable and distinctive content of theology can only be found in its historical particularity. Likewise, Stout intimates this when he denies that there are any implicit religious, existential, or metaphysical commitments shared by human beings as such. Or, more explicitly, he points in this direction when he denies the possibility of any transcendental claims.[2] For these three thinkers, in other words, all existential conditions or characteristics are contingent—they are only empirical, historical, and/or cultural particularities, not metaphysical necessities or commonalities. Hence, Stout, MacIntyre, and Hauerwas all contend that reality can only be understood historically, through the particularity and givenness of traditions—either traditions construed more narrowly (MacIntyre and Hauerwas) or more broadly (Stout). Relatedly, these traditions are recognized precisely as traditions, as self-conscious or self-aware phenomena. Only when we recognize and accept this, only when we give up our metaphysical pretensions, they conclude, will we be on the right track. But the problem with strong historicism, I contend, is that it either tacitly introduces metaphysical commitments or else it finally succumbs to relativism. To make this case, let me begin by drawing on the work of William James.

In characterizing the basic difference between empiricists and rationalists, James suggests that empiricists emphasize "parts" rather than the "whole" whereas rationalists explain parts in terms of the whole. Both of these camps, says James, are nonetheless "loyal to the world that bears them; . . . neither wishes to regard it as an insane incoherence; both want to keep it as a universe of some kind. . . . [W]hether we be empiricists or rationalists," he concludes, "we are, ourselves, parts of the universe and share the same one deep concern in its destinies."[3] James's formulation here rightly implies that each of these alternatives runs the potential danger of losing one side of the equation—of either losing sight of the whole altogether (the empiricist danger) or of losing the

---

2. MacIntyre, *DCB*, 55. See Hauerwas, "On Keeping Theological Ethics Theological," 40–44. Stout, *Democracy and Tradition*, 112, and Stout, *Flight from Authority*, 66–67.

3. James, "Types of Philosophic Thinking," 153, 153–54.

particularity of the parts in the whole itself (the rationalist danger). It is the empiricist danger that I want to focus on for the moment. The empiricist position, such as found in the case of strong historicism, cannot coherently affirm the notion of a meaningful universe, and thus ward off incoherence, without implicitly affirming some genuine knowledge of the whole.

Now, to be clear, the concept of the "whole" is ambiguous insofar as it can have at least two distinct meanings. On one account, it can refer to the generic qualities or characteristics that are necessary to and thus partly constitutive of each and every part—whatever other unique characteristics each part may also embody. In this sense, the "whole" refers to generic commonality—to the essential conditions that underlie each and every part. Metaphorically speaking, these conditions are the constitutive threads that provide the backing for a tapestry. Each part of the tapestry may indeed have its own distinctive particularity, but undergirding all parts are the generic conditions that permeate the whole. Alternatively, the "whole" can refer to the all-inclusive totality of all things in both their generic commonality and their unique detail. If the first meaning refers to the underlying constitutive backing, then this second refers to the complete tapestry in all of its particularity and generality. To add a geographical analogy, the first meaning refers to the necessary and generic characteristics found in each and every part of the United States (to be a state dedicated to and accepted into statehood within the union), and the second refers to a detailed satellite view of the United States in minute and exhaustive detail. It is this second meaning of the "whole," as all-inclusive, that is aptly called a "God's-eye" view—one that sees all detail and generality.

It is important to distinguish these two different meanings because the metaphysical enterprise, properly understood, is not about seeking this "God's-eye" view; it is not about seeking all-inclusive knowledge. In fact, from the perspective of the fallibilistic, process metaphysics that I outlined in the previous chapter, such all-inclusive knowledge is only available to the divine reality and, even for God, such knowledge is not exhaustive in a static sense because reality is an ongoing processive endeavor—as new possibilities become actualized, even God's knowledge increases. Since we are fragmentarily and fallibly situated within this ongoing process, our knowledge of the whole relates to the generic characteristics present in each and every part. To be sure, insofar as metaphysics identifies an all-inclusive individual or divine reality as a generic element present to each and every part, it does properly affirm *that* there is an all-inclusive whole, that there is a God's-eye view, even if at the same time metaphysics does not claim to see, speak, or know *from* this all-inclusive perspective. In other words, the distinction between the two meanings of the whole is affirmed and maintained even if, at the same time, metaphysics seeks to know in the one sense and not in the other.[4] To further illustrate the metaphysical endeavor, let me return to James's discussion of a coherent universe.

What does the notion of "universe" mean? It means the whole of reality taken together in such a manner that all become one in an integrated totality. Now the potential danger of the rationalist view is to lose the particularity of the parts in this oneness; a monism that either diminishes or swallows up the particularities of the world is indeed a mistake. In contrast, however, an empiricism that fails to affirm the integrity of the whole is unable to affirm a coherent universe at all. Put simply, the universe is not merely an aggregate of unrelated parts. A mere aggregate of twenty thousand soldiers, for instance, does not constitute an army; an army requires coordination and integration throughout its multiple components. The same is true for the notion of a meaningful universe. It requires some orderly integration of the parts, and this integrative quality permeates all of the parts themselves. Hence, each part necessarily exemplifies this generic integrative quality in some manner. Any perspective that emphasizes particularity without universality, that emphasizes parts without any articulation of the character of the whole, is a perspective that finally cannot ward off incoherence. Empiricism,

---

4. To state this point even more precisely, one might say that the necessary character of an actuality is self-differentiating, in the sense that it implies two metaphysically distinct kinds of exemplification: exemplification in actualities that relate *fragmentarily* to other things, and exemplification in actualities that relate *completely* to all other things; and the latter type of exemplification are actualities of a necessary or metaphysical individual (divinity). Thus, *that* there is an all-inclusive whole (or more precisely all-inclusive wholes, since all things contribute to the ongoing and additive process of the divine experience; one complete actualized whole is succeeded by another in each new moment of the divine experience) is itself metaphysical or implied by "whole" in the first sense (as generic characteristics). Hence, metaphysics can be defined as reflection on the whole in the first sense without thereby denying the reality of the whole(s) in the second sense. To be sure, someone might affirm metaphysics in the first sense while denying the reality of the whole(s) in the second sense; but this would mean that they deny metaphysical theism, even while they affirm metaphysics. In brief, process metaphysics holds that their denial is inconsistent with their affirmation.

therefore, must finally either presuppose some knowledge of the whole, when it focuses on the parts, or else it falls into relativistic and incoherent fragments.[5]

As a form of empiricism, strong historicism cannot escape this dilemma. If one starts from the particularity and contingency of a given tradition, one can make claims about one's own tradition, about other traditions, or about reality as a whole—including all traditions. But the key point is that one cannot understand any of these alternatives unless one already has some implicit knowledge of the whole itself, for the very delineation of each and every part already presupposes some background knowledge of and relation to the whole itself. You mark off a tradition in relation to and against the backdrop of the whole. Strong historicists might be willing to concede this point; that is, they might be willing to say that each tradition presupposes and offers some vision of the whole of reality—offers some universe of meaning. But if they are willing to affirm this, they are unwilling to affirm that each and every part contains necessary characteristics that are generic to the whole itself, because they deny that reason can identify such generic or necessary qualities of existence. Hence, any claims that they are willing to make about the whole itself are either simply asserted or are justified by appealing back to the particularity of a tradition. It makes no sense, however, to justify or ground claims about the whole by appealing back to the particularity of the parts, for such an appeal merely begs the question. How can that which is uniquely particular justify that which is generically common? Stated otherwise, it makes no sense to say that the distinction between the whole and any one of its parts is determined by that part, because this implies that there might be a different distinction and thus a different whole for two or more parts. So whatever claims strong historicists might be willing to make about the whole, the

---

5. I am not persuaded that James's own pluralistic version of "radical empiricism" can coherently affirm a meaningful universe. He is so intent on warding off a monism that swallows up the particularity of the parts that he is finally unwilling to affirm that all parts contribute to a universal whole. "[T]he pluralistic view which I prefer to adopt," says James, "is willing to believe that there may ultimately never be an all-form at all, that the substance of reality may never get totally collected, that some of it may remain outside of the largest combination of it ever made. . . ." James, "Types of Philosophic Thinking," 159. By leaving parts outside of the whole, James undermines the notion of a coherent universe itself. What is needed is a conception of the whole that maintains the particularity of the parts without either swallowing them up or leaving them outside the universe of meaning altogether.

problem remains that their identification of the whole is dependent on the particularity of a tradition, i.e., the distinction between the whole and the part is determined by that part. What is required, instead, are grounds or reasons that are necessary, that are characteristic of any and every possible part of the whole and, thus, cannot fail to be exemplified in each part—not grounds that are unique or contingent to the particularity of any one or more parts.

To be sure, as I sought to make clear in the previous chapter, our knowledge of the whole is always fallible. We may be mistaken in what we explicitly judge to be necessary characteristics of the whole. To make claims about necessity is one thing, to claim that our knowledge of this necessity is infallible is quite another. The former does not and should not presuppose the latter; indeed, it has been the mistaken and problematical legacy of Western metaphysics to presume that it does. As I argued earlier, the modal status of the content of our claims (as being either necessary or contingent) is distinct from the subjective form of our knowledge (as fallible). The point of ongoing discourse is to test all claims, including claims about necessity. Likewise, and relatedly, our knowledge of the whole is always fragmentary, incomplete, or non-exhaustive. As suggested in chapter 2, our relation to the whole is part of the dim, implicit background knowledge of our everyday experience. The task of the metaphysical enterprise is to explicate the necessary features of the whole. But to say that we know some characteristics of the whole is not to say that we know all of them. Insofar as such characteristics are necessary, and insofar as a metaphysical scheme should be coherent, it is true that all metaphysical characteristics should mutually cohere and imply one another. Thus, for instance, if "something exists" is indeed a valid metaphysical assertion, then one should in theory be able to infer all other metaphysical characteristics from it, and vice versa. But such a task, given our fallible and fragmentary understanding, is an endlessly ongoing endeavor. Again, as Whitehead observes, "in the absence of a well-defined categoreal scheme of entities, issuing in a satisfactory [and complete] metaphysical system, every premise in a philosophical argument is under suspicion."[6] This is why metaphysics is an ongoing, progressive endeavor—an asymptotic approach—that is always open to revising its claims or abandoning its formulations for the sake of gaining more adequate expression and understanding.

6. Whitehead, *Process and Reality*, 8.

Finally, and again relatedly, our knowledge of the whole always occurs in a context. We know the whole from the vantage point of our particular part. But the key is that we still glimpse the character of the whole and not merely our own part. Leibniz vividly expresses this point in the *Monadology:*

> And as the same city regarded from different sides appears entirely different, and is, as it were multiplied respectively, so [likewise], because of the infinite number of simple substances, there are a similar infinite number of universes which are, nevertheless, only the aspects of a single [universe] as seen from the point of view of each monad.[7]

Just as we view the same city from the particularity of our diverse locations, and thus create a multiplicity of perspectives, we nevertheless still see the same city. There is unity in the midst of diversity. In fact, it is precisely the backdrop of the common city (the whole) that enables each angle of vision to be delineated in the first place. Intelligible differences arise in relation to an underlying common reality. Likewise, even though our metaphysical knowledge of the whole is situated—it occurs from a particular historical and cultural angle of vision—it still includes knowledge of the character of the whole. To epitomize, all knowledge is situated, but that does not mean that the content of our knowledge is restricted merely to our own situation; we know more than our situation, even though we know it from the vantage point of our situation. When it comes to knowledge of the whole, therefore, the task of metaphysics is precisely to articulate the necessary or generic characteristics of reality. This conception of metaphysics accepts and endorses historicism in a weak sense by recognizing our situatedness and the role of history in understanding our context. But the problem with strong historicism is that it either denies that we see the same city, i.e., denies that we have any knowledge of the whole, which leads to relativism, or else it seeks to justify claims about the whole by appealing back to the particularity of our location, which seems problematical indeed. The first horn of this problem arises insofar as strong historicism implies that *differing perspectives* on the whole are in fact perspectives on *differing wholes*. The second horn emerges insofar as strong historicism seeks to redeem

---

7. This quote comes from Leibniz's *Monadology*, #57, 464. Leibniz also offers a preliminary formulation of this point in his earlier *Discourse on Metaphysics*, section IX, 417–18.

claims about the whole by appealing to what is tradition-specific, by appealing to that which is unique or contingent to one or more parts. The only way to avoid these twin pitfalls is by pursuing a rational metaphysics—by discerning the necessary characteristics of the whole as manifest in each and every part.

Reflecting on the relationship between history and metaphysics, Whitehead offers the following observation. "It is a curious delusion," he notes, to think

> that the rock upon which our beliefs can be founded is an historical investigation. You can only interpret the past in terms of the present. The present is all that you have; and unless in this present you can find general principles which interpret the present as including a representation of the whole community of existents, you cannot move a step beyond your little patch of immediacy.

Thus, history presupposes a metaphysic.[8]

When Whitehead concludes that "history presupposes a metaphysic," he appears to have two distinct but related meanings in mind. First, one cannot avoid relativism unless one ultimately grounds one's assertions or beliefs about any part of experience in a metaphysical understanding of the whole. Second, this is the case because the past is actual only in the present, and the present itself necessarily contains some implicit or explicit relation to and understanding of totality. Let me unpack these two points by taking them up in reverse order. The past, or a tradition, is always interpreted from the vantage point of the present, Whitehead suggests, since "the present is all that you have." In other words, what is actual is always only the present; the present includes the past, but the past is always only a constituent of the present. Yesterday is actual only as an inherited part of today. Yet, in addition to containing the past as a key constituent, the present must also contain some implicit or explicit understanding of totality—some understanding "of the whole community of existents." It "is certainly the case," Whitehead acknowledges, "that we believe in the past and talk about it without settling our metaphysical principles."[9] But the deeper point is that our beliefs always

---

8. Whitehead, *Religion in the Making*, 84. Or as Whitehead puts it elsewhere, "You cannot have a rational justification for your appeal to history till your metaphysics has assured you that there *is* a history to appeal to" (*Science and the Modern World*, 44).

9. Whitehead, *Religion in the Making*, 84. Another way to express Whitehead's point might be as follows: Since the present is all that you have, there is no past unless you

presuppose some present comprehensive understanding. Previously, I spoke of our inescapable constitutive choice—our unavoidable choice of some underlying source of meaning and value that orients our lives in relation to the world. But this choice also includes some "constitutive understanding" of the nature of reality as such. To employ the language of Clifford Geertz, we live and act in the world with a comprehensive vision that includes both a metaphysical "model of" reality and a related ethical "model for" our lives in relation to reality.[10] Thus our present experience contains some implicit or explicit "model of" reality—some "representation of the whole." The delusion, Whitehead argues, is to think that one can form coherent beliefs about the world without relation to this comprehensive conception. To appeal simply to the particularity of tradition or history as the ultimate ground of one's beliefs about the world is once again either to try to understand the parts without reference to the whole or, alternatively, to attempt to understand the whole based on an appeal to the particularity of the parts. But in either case, as Whitehead pointedly observes, "you cannot move a step beyond your little patch of immediacy." You cannot, in short, avoid relativism.

In response to this logical critique of strong historicism, MacIntyre, Hauerwas, and Stout might insist that their historicism is not as "strong" as I portray it to be. Historicists, they might say, do not categorically rule out anything, including the possibility of some universal rational standard for assessing metaphysical claims or the possibility of some a priori metaphysical knowledge. In fact, they would acknowledge that such a categorical denial would put them in a strange position as self-proclaimed historicists. As MacIntyre remarks, "From the fact that liberalism does not provide a neutral tradition-independent ground from which a verdict may be passed upon the rival claims of conflicting traditions . . . , it does not of course follow that there is no such neutral ground. [Moreover] it is clear that there can be no sound *a priori*

---

can interpret the present as including the past. But this can only be an interpretation of the "whole community of existents," i.e., all of the past, because one cannot interpret the present as including only a part of the past without implicitly referring to all of the past in distinguishing that part (the tradition). For again to demarcate a part presupposes the whole; to identify a strand of the past is to presuppose the whole of the past in relation to which one distinguishes that strand or tradition. Thus the present must contain some implicit or explicit understanding "of the whole community of existents."

10. The phrase "constitutive understanding" comes from Gamwell, *Divine Good*, 37; Geertz, *Interpretation of Cultures*, 93–94.

argument to demonstrate that such [a neutral ground] is impossible."[11] To offer such a categorical denial, as Herdt rightly points out, would land MacIntyre and the other strong historicists in a performative self-contradiction. The act of asserting a categorical claim, such as, "there can be no universal rational grounds for assessing claims, since all rationality can only be tradition-specific," would imply either (a) that such a claim is itself valid on tradition-independent grounds, thereby contradicting the stated content of the claim, or (b) that such a claim is valid only within the context of its own tradition, thereby undermining the point of making the assertion altogether. As Herdt sees it, "Either the statement puts itself forward as just such a tradition-independent ground, which in being stated cancels itself, or, alternatively, the statement has validity only within a given tradition" and, thus, ends up asserting merely a weak, relativistic, and self-defeating claim.[12]

In seeking to avoid this trap, MacIntyre and his fellow historicists allege that they are putting forth a more modest historical claim, namely, that all such efforts have thus far failed, including and especially modern liberalism. Based on this historical failure, they submit that there are no good reasons to expect that any independent grounds will be found in the future to validate universal moral, religious, or metaphysical assertions. "That liberalism fails in this respect," MacIntyre states, "provides the strongest reason that we can actually have for *asserting that there is no such neutral ground, that there is no place for appeals to a [theoretical or] practical-rationality-as-such . . . to which all rational persons would by their very rationality be compelled to give their allegiance. There is instead only the [theoretical or] practical-rationality-of-this-or-that-tradition*" [italics added].[13]

In spite of his recognition of the pitfalls of a categorical stance, and in spite of his appeal to more modest, historical claims, notice here (as indicated by the italics) what MacIntyre still asserts: he still claims that there is no neutral or universal ground; on the contrary, he maintains that there is only tradition-specific rationality. But this formulation still

11. MacIntyre, *WJWR*, 346.

12. Herdt, "MacIntyre's 'Rationality of Traditions,'" 527.

13. MacIntyre, *WJWR*, 346. MacIntyre appears to assume here that to affirm a universal rational standard requires one to affirm that valid arguments compel assent. But as I argued at length in the last chapter, such is not the case. Stout himself concurs with me on this point insofar as he dispels the notion that any argument, in any discipline, compels or forces assent. See Stout, *Ethics After Babel*, 183.

stumbles into the dilemma of performative contradiction. For if strong historicists are to avoid this dilemma, it is performatively necessary that they continually grant the logical possibility that there *can be* a neutral or universal ground—that there *can be* a common rationality as such. And given this necessity, the most that MacIntyre can consistently say is that "we have not found a neutral ground," which is certainly more circumspect than saying that "there is no such neutral ground." In other words, appeals to the failures of history, such as the failures of liberalism, can never provide adequate grounds for making claims about the nature of rationality as such. Historically, I agree that modern liberalism has failed, but I would contend that MacIntyre and company have overlooked the real source of this failure, namely, the failure to develop a coherent metaphysics. To further defend this claim, I will now offer specific responses to MacIntyre and Stout respectively, since they proceed from here in their own distinct directions.

A Further Response to MacIntyre

Since MacIntyre points to the failure of modern liberalism as his primary argument against a common rational standard, let me summarize his description of it and his response to it in the following terms. Modern liberalism, as exemplified by Kant, offered a convincing critique of traditional metaphysics, as illustrated by Aquinas. As we saw earlier, MacIntyre himself implicitly endorses this critique in *DCB* and also partially endorses it more recently in *TRV* insofar as he states that "Kant himself had of course been completely in the right in understanding that there is no place for any true knowledge of God within the cognitive structures of the mind if the mind is characterized in [modern or Kantian] terms." But along with partially accepting this critique in its own terms, MacIntyre argues that modern liberalism lacks a teleology and thus lacks an adequate means for understanding life and the world. "What I am going to suggest," he declares, "is that the predicaments of contemporary philosophy . . . are best understood as arising as a long-term consequence of the rejection of Aristotelian and Thomistic teleology at the threshold of the modern world." This trajectory, which began with "the widespread rejection of Aristotelian teleology and of a whole family of cognate notions in the sixteenth and seventeenth centuries resulted in . . . a deprivation. In consequence," he concludes, "conceptions of truth and rationality became, as it were, free floating."[14] MacIntyre assumes here that an affirmation of teleology requires an affirmation of tradition-dependent rationality; but why does he assume this? He assumes it, in part, because he accepts Kant's notion that there cannot be a direct rational validation of any metaphysical or teleological claim. Consequently, the affirmation of a telos or metaphysical vision can only come from the affirmation of a particular tradition and its sources of authority.[15]

To this point, I have spoken repeatedly of MacIntyre's emphasis on tradition and tradition-constituted rationality; at this juncture, let me outline more explicitly what he means by these respective notions. At least two factors lie behind and fuel his emphasis. The subtler one, which I have tried to bring to light, is the fact that, from his earliest works, MacIntyre has accepted, on some level, the modern critique of metaphysics. He agrees with the prevailing modern view that human reason cannot identify a common rational standard by which to evaluate claims about the nature or purpose of reality as such. Kant, of course, went on to claim that human reason could identify a common

14. MacIntyre, *TRV*, 70; MacIntyre, *First Principles*, 58, 61.

15. In contrast to MacIntyre, Whitehead rejects both the modern denial of metaphysics and the modern denial of teleology. Whitehead agrees with MacIntyre that modern thought has been impoverished because it has banished teleology. "The rejection of purpose [or teleology] dates from Francis Bacon at the beginning of the seventeenth century," observes Whitehead. But this "radical extrusion of final causation from our cosmological theory" has made it impossible to understand the function of reason itself. Like MacIntyre, who argues that one cannot make sense of inquiry without presupposing some telos, Whitehead argues that one cannot comprehend why reason is part of the evolutionary process without affirming some notion of purpose or teleology. Only if "we admit the category of final causation," he says, can we "consistently define the primary function of Reason. This function is to constitute, emphasize, and criticize the final causes and strength of aims" that are embedded in the activities of the world. (Whitehead, *Function of Reason*, 26). Yet, unlike MacIntyre, Whitehead seeks to make his case for a dynamic teleology by arguing for the need for a rational metaphysics, one that rejects classical theism in favor of a process or neoclassical view. Whitehead agrees with Kant insofar as Kant offers a critique of *classical* metaphysics. But Whitehead rejects Kant's presumption that this critique is sound against any possible metaphysic. By contrast, MacIntyre seeks to retrieve Aquinas's classical metaphysical and teleological vision and to defend it in rather "unThomistic ways." That is to say, since MacIntyre believes that Kant has already offered a convincing critique of any direct or universal way of defending metaphysical claims, MacIntyre now seeks to defend a Thomistic view by arguing that all rational standards are tradition-dependent. Hence, he turns to genealogy and history rather than to Aquinas's own theistic proofs to defend his retrieval of a Thomistic metaphysical vision (see MacIntyre, *First Principles*, 57–58).

rational standard by which to evaluate moral claims, but this standard was defined apart from any moral telos. MacIntyre, accepting Kant's denial of metaphysics but rejecting his notion of a common morality independent of teleology, proceeds to go beyond Kant by claiming that there is no such thing as a common reason or common rationality at all. The second and more explicit factor contributing to MacIntyre's focus on the language of traditions is his belief that distinct worldviews or cultural-philosophical schemes are ultimately "incommensurable." By this, he means that there is no common measure or standard by which to evaluate their respective metaphysical, moral, existential, or religious claims. Contributing to this view is his related belief that not all human languages, concepts, or texts are translatable into one another. Contrary to the Enlightenment belief that we could, in theory, ultimately come to understand one another through translation, travel, and mutual openness, MacIntyre alleges that different conceptual schemes are fundamentally alien to one another. We understand those within our own scheme, within our own tradition, but we cannot truly understand those without. Texts, concepts, and rational standards can only be understood within their own context; thus the only way to truly understand others, MacIntyre argues, is to immerse oneself in their tradition and thus become native speakers in their language and worldview. In short, one must learn "a second-first language."[16] By becoming linguistically and conceptually bilingual, a person can jump back and forth between two worldviews, but one can never directly bring them into conversation or assess their claims by a common rational standard. Whereas Kant's bifurcation held that we could look at the world theoretically or practically, but we could never integrate these two perspectives into a single worldview, MacIntyre's bifurcation holds that we can look at the world through the prism of our own tradition, or we can look at the world through the lens of another tradition by becoming fluent in its language and scheme, but we can never integrate these two perspectives into a direct conversation or assess their claims in relation to a common or universal rational standard. MacIntyre recognizes that the specter of relativism hovers over and around his affirmation of incommensurabil-

---

16. For MacIntyre's discussion of incommensurability, tradition, and translation, see chapter 19, "Tradition and Translation," in *WJWR*, 370–88. For his notion of a "second-first language," see 384.

ity; he believes, nonetheless, that his understanding of tradition, and how traditions relate to one another, wards off this looming threat.

MacIntyre's conception of a tradition, as Porter describes it, consists of two basic elements: "an institutionally embodied framework of shared commitments" and "ongoing problematics through which ongoing inquiry and debate are rendered possible." Most of the time, a tradition can solve the questions and problems it faces by drawing upon its own intellectual resources. But sometimes, MacIntyre contends, the problems confronted by a tradition pose an epistemological crisis for that tradition precisely because its intellectual resources are not up to the task. "In this situation," notes commentator Micah Lott, "the adherents of the tradition in crisis might turn to a rival tradition for help." In order to garner this help, three things must occur. First, adherents of the tradition in crisis must learn the conceptual language of the rival tradition—from the rival's own internal perspective—in order to understand the rival's conceptual scheme. Second, having done this, members of the crisis-tradition "might discover that the rival tradition provides the conceptual resources lacking in their own tradition to solve, by their own standards of rationality, the problems of their own tradition which had led to [the] crisis." If they find this help, then the rival tradition will also enable them "to explain why those problems were unsolvable" from the perspective of their own tradition. In other words, the rival tradition will be able to offer resources to formulate a superior narrative history of what went wrong within the crisis-tradition itself. Third, "recognizing [now] the superiority of the rival tradition in this [comparative] way, members of the tradition in crisis may choose to abandon their tradition in favor of [the rival]." This "account of crisis and competition," remarks Lott, "shows . . . how a tradition may rationally compete with another on the basis of its ability to solve its rival's problems better than the rival tradition can solve them itself."[17] This notion of competition among traditions, MacIntyre believes, avoids relativism by providing an indirect form of rational validation. The claims put forth by various traditions are never tested or validated in any direct manner; rather, such claims are always left embedded within the context of their own tradition and its own set of practices and authorities. It is only the problem-solving capacity of the tradition as a whole that is tested, and this is done by bilingual speakers who jump back and forth between

---

17. Porter, "Openness and Constraint," 518; Lott, "Reasonably Traditional," 320, 321.

their own tradition and that of the other. With this outline now in place, let me offer some further criticisms of MacIntyre's view.

First, MacIntyre claims that the rational superiority of one tradition over another can be demonstrated insofar as the superior tradition has resources to solve internal problems within the defeated tradition—solved and shown in terms of the defeated tradition's own standard of rationality—and that the superior tradition does not have analogous internal problems of its own. But this supposed idea of rational superiority becomes problematic when the Enlightenment project itself is taken as a tradition. Its philosophical standard, as developed and illustrated by Kant, is a priori status. To show that the Enlightenment tradition is inferior, therefore, is to make clear that it has a problem that cannot be solved by appeal to a priori argument. But how will MacIntyre demonstrate this without assuming that there are no valid a priori arguments, that is, without assuming his notion of tradition-constituted rationality? In other words, the Enlightenment project denies his notion of tradition-constituted rationality and his notion of rational superiority. How can he then demonstrate that this project has problems it cannot solve within a priori terms without assuming that a priori standards are impossible? If he is to avoid performative self-contradiction, MacIntyre can never rule out the possibility of valid a priori standards. So how can he then, by appealing to historical or empirical reasons, show that the Enlightenment has problems that *cannot* be solved in an a priori manner? As far as I can judge, he cannot. The most he can say is that it has *thus far* not adequately resolved these matters in an a priori fashion; but he cannot, without mere assumption, say that the Enlightenment has problems that *cannot* be solved by a priori means. Moreover, on the flip side, how could he ever show the superiority of a rival tradition—measured in terms of the Enlightenment's own internal a priori standard—without employing a priori arguments? The whole point of his indirect comparative model is that members of the defeated tradition will be able to recognize the superiority of the rival's resources measured within the defeated tradition's own standard of rationality. But if that standard is a priori status, then no non-a priori arguments will ever measure up.

Second, what it means to be committed to reason, according to MacIntyre, is to be willing to adopt the best theory or alternative offered so far. That is, as a strong historicist, he contends that rational superiority is only measured in terms of historical and comparative success among traditions; the successful tradition is the one that is able to outnarrate its rivals through indirect comparative engagement. MacIntyre's theory of tradition-constituted rationality is an overarching account of how the best theory or tradition so far is determined; he is providing the metanarrative and outlining the meta-standards for this process. But his overarching account cannot itself be merely the best theory offered so far, because, absent his account, one cannot know what "best theory so far" even means. In other words, standards cannot be merely a product of a process of which they themselves are the defining measure, for they are always already presupposed by the process itself. Otherwise, it would be like saying that the *nature* of empirical accounts can only be defined through an empirical account. But any such definition would already presuppose what an empirical account consists in and thus the definition could not itself be discovered merely empirically. So, in spite of his intentions, it appears that MacIntyre is implicitly presupposing a universal character of rationality in his act of outlining the nature of rational superiority, and thus he is back in the dilemma of performative self-contradiction. MacIntyre, of course, denies this; but as a closer examination of his theory of competition among traditions reveals, he cannot finally escape it.

As we have seen, one of MacIntyre's key propositions is the claim that there is no universal rational standard by which competing traditions can be evaluated; rather, each tradition has its own rational and evaluative standards. However, I would argue that a competition in which each competitor has his or her own independent measure of success is not a coherent competition at all. How can one meaningfully talk about a competition among different competitors or traditions if there is no common standard or goal that defines the overarching contest? If MacIntyre acknowledges that there is a common standard or goal, then he contradicts his stated position. Conversely, if he maintains that there is no common goal or standard, then it makes little sense to say that they are each participants in a shared or coherent competition. For instance, if one person is seeking to hit a little white ball into a distant hole, then she is playing golf. Alternatively, if another person is seeking to throw a ball through a hoop, then she is playing basketball. These different activities may share some similarities, such as an athletic motion, but they have different aims and evaluative standards. The aim of the former is to minimize the number of strokes whereas the aim of the latter is to maximize the number of baskets made. They are not engaged in the same competition. Likewise, how can one talk about a coherent competition among different traditions, each with its own standard of rationality and success, if there is no common standard overall? As far as I can see, one cannot. To speak of a competition in a coherent or meaningful sense requires the presence of some common aim or shared evaluative standard. Therefore, either MacIntyre is unwittingly smuggling in some implicit common standard by using the language of competition or else his position ends up succumbing to relativism.

Herdt persuasively argues that he does in fact operate with an implicit universal standard, which she calls MacIntyre's "tradition-transcendental" standard of rationality. That is, in spite of his assertion that all reasoning is tradition-dependent, Herdt convincingly demonstrates that his theory presupposes a transcendental standard of rationality for adjudicating claims among rival traditions. As we have seen, MacIntyre puts forth his model of indirect comparative engagement as a way to try to avoid relativism. But within this model, Herdt points out, he presupposes certain trans-traditional competencies and a trans-traditional standard of rationality. The competencies are implied by his assumption that members of different traditions share a common capacity for "empathetic imagination," which enables them to understand rival viewpoints from within the rival tradition's own set of assumptions. The apparent tension here is evident: on the one hand, MacIntyre insists on the particularity and boundedness of human life within traditions, yet on the other, he presupposes a widespread human capacity for becoming bilingual and for understanding others in their own terms. Across traditions, he implies, humans have this common potential for becoming cognitively ambidextrous. Herdt, however, draws us back to the tension:

> Given MacIntyre's claim that there are no tradition-independent resources adequate to settling intertraditional debates, it seems worth asking in which tradition this empathetic conceptual imagination originates. Despite his insistence that traditions establish their claim to truth by means of the adequacy and explanatory power of the histories they write, MacIntyre does not provide us with a historical account of this particularly valuable of resources. At one point, he does imply that

empathetic imagination can be traced back to Saint Thomas Aquinas and, therefore, to the tradition that he champions.[18]

Herdt proceeds to note that, at times, MacIntyre "talks as though empathetic conceptual imagination is something that each of us [is capable of and] has an intellectual responsibility to strive for," while at other times, "he treats it . . . as a rare gift" exemplified only by those outstanding figures, like Aquinas, who become authorities within their own traditions. Her most salient point here, however, is that, for MacIntyre's theory to work, empathy cannot be a tradition-dependent capacity or virtue. To explain this, she "invoke[s] the distinction between origin and validity; any concept that is articulated within a specific tradition or specific language is tradition dependent in the weak sense of origin." This goes along with my affirmation of historicism in a weak sense. All thinking takes place somewhere at some time and thus is influenced by the linguistic and intellectual stock available in that context. "But it does not follow [from this] that [the] ideas [expressed through this cultural stock] have validity only within the tradition or language in which they originated." Thus, "empathetic imagination cannot be tradition dependent in this stronger sense," argues Herdt, "since MacIntyre proposes that it be used to resolve conflicts" among all traditions. That is, "in order legitimately to resolve any conflict between two traditions, empathetic imagination must be a valid approach for both, not just for the one from which it may have originated."[19] Herdt makes a strong case here that MacIntyre's theory of tradition-constituted rationality does in fact implicitly presuppose some universal or trans-traditional human capacities. If dialectical understanding and competition among traditions is possible at all, then it presupposes some common human capacities that transcend traditions. This universal element becomes even more apparent when Herdt shines her light on MacIntyre's implicit transcendental standard of rationality.

MacIntyre's theory of adjudication among traditions, Herdt argues, presupposes a transcendental criterion in the form of a procedural rationality. Given the fact that an appeal to procedural rationality is a recurring motif in modern liberalism, Herdt underscores the irony of such a principle operating implicitly within MacIntyre's own theory.

---

18. Herdt, "MacIntyre's 'Rationality of Traditions,'" 529, 530.
19. Ibid., 530, 531, 534.

Her point here is similar to the one I made above, namely, that in order to speak of a coherent competition among different traditions, one must appeal to some common standard for adjudicating the competition itself. Each team does not make up its own rules or definitions of victory; rather, all the different teams play under a common rule or procedure for deciding the contest. Herdt sets forth her case as follows:

> MacIntyre's procedure can be stated as a universal standard or principle of rationality: When a tradition B can provide a cogent and illuminating explanation of an epistemological crisis faced by rival tradition A according to tradition A's own standards, and B does not face a similar crisis, then rationality requires members of A to acknowledge the superior rationality of B. I will call this principle Rt. [But] [t]here are difficulties here: According to MacIntyre, members of A are to draw on *concepts* and *theories* peculiar to B in constructing an explanation of A's epistemological crisis, but they are to employ their own [A] *standards* of judging cogency and illumination. It is important to note, first, that although MacIntyre insists that traditions will have different such standards, he also indicates that they will always be standards of cogency and illumination. This implies a degree of universality, however, minimal, among such standards. Second, what is to happen when the members of A transfer their allegiance to B? Presumably at that point they must shift from their own standards of cogency and illumination to those of B. In what light can this shift in standards of cogency be reasonable, however? Not simply because of the power of B's theories and concepts but [more fundamentally] because of Rt, the general standard of rationality of traditions, which dictates when a shift in more specific standards is required. Without this [overarching] standard, which transcends the conflicting traditions, the shift of loyalty would be irrational.[20]

Herdt offers here two critical observations about how MacIntyre's theory plays out. First, even though he holds that each tradition supplies the content for its own ultimate evaluative standard, he conveniently assumes that such standards will always pertain to measures of cogency and illumination. But why should one assume that different tradition-specific standards will always be seeking to evaluate the same thing? Presumably, if they were as incommensurable as MacIntyre alleges, then they would likely be looking for and measuring different things

20. Ibid., 535–36.

altogether. However, by asserting that all traditions offer standards pertaining to illumination and cogency, MacIntyre is trying to insure that all traditions are in fact playing the same game—and thus can be meaningfully said to be contestants in the same competition. But this implies, as Herdt indicates, a degree of commonality and universality across traditions that seems to pull against MacIntyre's insistence on incommensurability.

Second, and even more importantly, she notes that MacIntyre's competition must have some common procedural standard, to which all contestants subscribe, to decide the outcome of the contest: Herdt calls this standard Rt. The need for such a standard comes to light when one considers what evaluative grounds one tradition could possibly have for abandoning its own ultimate evaluative standards and adopting those of another tradition. As Herdt implies, MacIntyre's theory operates on two levels. At a micro-level, tradition A, which is in crisis, draws upon the theories and concepts of B in order to explain A's own internal problems. But A still uses its own overarching standard to judge that these new micro-resources contribute to greater illumination and cogency. In short, A is supposed to see the value of B's concepts in terms of A's own standard of illumination. But for the contest to be decided at the macro-level, A must recognize the superiority of B overall—including especially the superiority of B's overarching standard—and A must be willing to abandon its own tradition and its own overarching standard in favor of B. The problem, Herdt points out, is by what standard does A now rationally evaluate and decide this comprehensive decision, this macro-leap? It measured value at the micro-level in terms of its own standard. Now, at the macro-level, by what standard should it abandon its own standard? It is not yet a member of B, so it would not measure the inadequacy of A in terms of B. Alternatively, A cannot use its own evaluative yardstick to measure the inadequacy of its own evaluative yardstick—A cannot concomitantly affirm and employ its own evaluative standard as a means of repudiating and abandoning that standard altogether; such an act would involve a performative self-contradiction. Likewise, one cannot measure the superiority of B's yardstick in terms of A's yardstick, since such a conclusion would implicitly endorse A insofar as A's yardstick is the basis of this evaluation. So in order for the macro-contest to be decided, all contestants must subscribe to some common rule or yardstick, which Herdt calls Rt. All contestants must subscribe to the formal overarching rule that they will abandon their own tradition at the macro-level when they have judged, by their own standards, the explanatory value of the concepts of another tradition at the micro-level. This macro-rule is implied in the practices of each tradition.

In seeking to demonstrate this implicit tradition-transcendental criterion, Herdt deftly quotes MacIntyre himself. In particular, she points to a passage in *WJWR* in which he writes: "Notice that grounds for an answer to relativism and perspectivism are to be found, not in any theory of rationality as yet explicitly articulated and advanced within one or more of the traditions with which we have been concerned, but rather with a theory embodied in and presupposed by their practices of enquiry, yet never fully spelled out [by any one of them]."[21] Significantly, what MacIntyre does here is move away from his stated focus on explicit historical traditions toward a focus on what is implicit in all traditions; he shifts attention away from explicit theories of rationality, as spelled out by the different competing traditions themselves, and focuses instead on an implicit theory of rationality embedded in the practices of all traditions. I must emphasize that such an implicit theory cannot be limited to any one or more specific traditions. Rather, it must be presupposed by all possible traditions if it is to fulfill the adjudicatory role that MacIntyre envisions for it. Otherwise, he would be stuck with the relativistic conclusion that his theory seeks to avoid, viz., that there are some incommensurable traditions beyond the bounds of indirect comparative rational assessment. Instead, by shifting attention to the embedded assumptions in inquiry itself, assumptions logically prior to the traditions themselves, Herdt notes how MacIntyre subtly but unmistakably moves onto transcendental grounds.

The significance of this transcendental shift toward inescapable implicit assumptions is further amplified when MacIntyre states in *First Principles* that "all knowledge . . . points beyond itself to a more final achievement in ways that we may not as yet have grasped. Hence, *we can know without as yet knowing that we know*" (italics added). What we know implicitly are the first principles. MacIntyre contrasts this implicit knowing with Descartes' insistence that all knowing must involve explicit knowing—"knowing that we know that we know." This Cartesian insistence emanates from Descartes' quest for epistemologi-

---

21. MacIntyre, *WJWR*, 354; Herdt "MacIntyre's 'Rationality of Traditions,'" 538.

cal certainty—from his assumption that all knowledge must proceed explicitly from self-evident first principles, thereby guaranteeing all knowledge deduced from them. Over against this, MacIntyre argues that "our present knowledge involves reference forward to that knowledge of the *archê/principium* which will, if we achieve it, give us subsequent knowledge of the knowledge that we now have."[22]

MacIntyre's statements here are both illuminating and ambiguous. On the one hand, he seems to suggest that all genuine knowing, irrespective of the particular matter at hand, already implicitly entails knowledge of the first principles that ultimately validate that particular knowledge. Hence, "we can know [the first principles implicitly] without as yet knowing [explicitly] that we know [them]." Such a view is similar to what Whitehead had in mind when he suggested that our understanding of the present must contain some implicit understanding of the whole. MacIntyre's emphasis here on our implicit knowledge of first principles is suggestive of an a priori dialectical method rather than merely an empirical one.[23] That is to say, the first principles are always already known vaguely and implicitly (a priori) in the dim background of our experience and not only explicitly at some empirical or historical moment. Yet, on the other hand, when MacIntyre uses language such as "reference forward" and "subsequent knowledge," one gets the sense that he is trying to avoid speaking of implicit knowledge altogether, and instead is trying to speak only proleptically of some kind of future historical achievement. This attempt at avoidance, and the ambiguity it produces, is illustrated in the following long and cumbersome sentence from MacIntyre: "If . . . one genuinely knows at all, then one knows as one would know if one knew in light of the relevant set of first principles, but one may, nonetheless, genuinely know, without as yet possessing that further knowledge of first principles and of their relationship to this particular piece of knowledge which would finally vindicate one's claim."[24] This cloudy statement seems to be trying to back away from the position that we implicitly know the first principles without explicitly knowing that we know them. Instead, MacIntyre appears to suggest here that all knowledge is related to and justified

22. MacIntyre, *First Principles*, 13–14.

23. For a discussion of a priori vs. empirical dialectical method, see Gamwell, *Divine Good*, 82–84.

24. MacIntyre, *First Principles*, 13.

by first principles, but we do not currently know these first principles either implicitly or explicitly. Rather, we proleptically anticipate them and presently know by inference that knowledge of such first principles is precisely what we need ultimately to justify our current claims. But how does one anticipate something that one knows nothing about, either implicitly or explicitly? I would contend that anticipation itself presupposes some vague implicit awareness or knowledge, which one is seeking to understand more explicitly and fully. Indeed, one of the defined meanings of "prolepsis" is "a presupposed or a priori principle."[25] Hence, I would argue that MacIntyre is closer to getting it right when he states above that "if . . . one genuinely knows at all, then one knows . . . in light of the relevant set of first principles." This knowledge of the first principles may remain implicit—indefinitely or until some future historical occasion—but, nevertheless, that knowledge is still implicitly there all the while.

Herdt rightly suggests that this type of avoidance and ambiguity in MacIntyre's position stems in part from the fact that he does not adequately distinguish between the "validity" of a claim and the "vindication" of that claim.[26] The process of vindicating a claim—of seeking to convince others in a particular time and place—is indeed historically situated; one can only marshal those arguments of which one is explicitly aware at that point in history. Hence, if one does not yet explicitly recognize the metaphysical first principles, or recognize that they are always implicitly in place, then one cannot vindicate one's claims by appeal to them. However, becoming aware of and drawing upon such principles in a historical context, and actually validating those first principles are two distinct matters. Since valid first principles describe those fundamental conditions that are always implicitly present, no matter what possible state of affairs may be, the only proper way to validate them is to demonstrate that they are rationally necessary, i.e., to show that they cannot be denied without contradiction. It is indeed the case that explicit awareness of and appeal to metaphysical principles originates at some historical point in time, just as awareness of the conditions of general relativity arose at the time of Einstein. But what makes either of these views valid is not the historical timing of awareness or the historical process itself. Rather, in each case, one must provide appropriate

25. *New Shorter Oxford English Dictionary* (1973; reprint 1993) s.v. "prolepsis."
26. Herdt, "MacIntyre's 'Rationality of Traditions,'" 540. See also 534.

arguments to validate the type of claim being made. In short, the distinction between "vindication" and "validity" is crucial. This means that explicit awareness of transcendental and metaphysical conditions does indeed arise at specific points in history, but it does not mean that these conditions were not present or valid before this awareness occurred. Thus an argument for the importance of theistic metaphysics or for an a priori dialectical method does not need to deny the importance of history. Rather, it must simply recognize that the conditions under which an explicit idea or claim originates are not the same conditions that will validate or invalidate its claim to truth.

As should be evident by now, my overall argument asserts that only a universal, substantive, metaphysical standard could ultimately provide sufficient grounds for adjudicating among competing macro-claims. Herdt herself, of course, is offering the more limited claim here that MacIntyre's theory presupposes a universal formal principle, which she calls Rt. My primary purpose in using her analysis has been to point out that MacIntyre's position does in fact implicitly presuppose some universal standard. By contrast, Lott seeks to come to MacIntyre's defense by offering a counter-critique of Herdt. The bulk of his criticism is aimed at resisting Herdt's allegation that MacIntyre's position gets entangled in contradiction. Herdt offers, I judge, at least two distinct claims: first, the inner logic of MacIntyre's own theory implicitly presupposes a universal formal principle of adjudication (Rt); second, MacIntyre's position gets entangled in contradiction because it asserts that all standards of evaluation are tradition-dependent while implicitly presupposing this universal standard (Rt). Another way to formulate this possible contradiction is to raise the following questions. When MacIntyre alleges that all rationality is tradition-dependent, is this claim itself tradition-specific or is it universally valid, i.e., is it true of all traditions? If it is indeed universally valid, then does its validity depend upon or appeal to something shared, some universal ground, or does it appeal to something unique to a specific tradition? Lott answers the first question by saying that MacIntyre's theory is universally valid in the sense of being universal in scope or application; it applies to all, not just to the Thomistic tradition from which it emerges. But in regard to the second question, Lott returns to an emphasis on particularity by saying that the grounds for this universal validity are not themselves universal, but rather are tradition-specific. Hence, according to Lott,

MacIntyre does not contradict himself: he is making a claim universal in scope but tradition-dependent in terms of the grounds of its validity. To explain this juxtaposition, Lott, quoting MacIntyre, offers the following response to Herdt:

> As [MacIntyre] says: "But I am irremediably anti-Hegelian in rejecting the notion of an absolute standpoint, independent of the particularity of all traditions. I have therefore to assert that the concept of a tradition, together with the criteria for its use and application, is itself one developed from within one particular tradition-based standpoint. This does not preclude its application to the very tradition within which it was developed." Thus, MacIntyre's position is not susceptible to inconsistency involved in the "point of view problem." And what Herdt calls Rt, then, is [merely] a theory about the rational vindication of a tradition against its rivals that is itself vindicated against its rivals according to the process spelled out in the theory itself.[27]

In Lott's quote from MacIntyre, one can again see that MacIntyre is anti-metaphysical in the sense of rejecting any universal grounds for validating metaphysical first-principles. In this regard, he is strongly anti-Hegelian. From here, Lott then asserts that Rt is simply "a theory about the rational vindication of a tradition . . . that is itself vindicated . . . according to the process spelled out in the theory itself." By this, he seems to mean that Rt is not a transcendental presupposition of all dialectic or competition. Rather, Rt is merely a contingent claim or theory put forth by one of the historical competitors in the competition, namely, a claim that purports to be universal in scope but tradition-dependent in terms of its grounds of validity. But Herdt's whole point is that the competition among different traditions collapses without an independent or universal principle for adjudicating among traditions at the macro-level. In other words, if the game itself presupposes Rt, then there is no game at all without Rt. Hence, for Lott to assert that Rt is merely a theory proposed by one of the competitors in the game, to be validated by the game itself, is to beg the question. In sum, as I noted earlier, standards cannot be merely a product of a process of which they themselves are the defining measure.

27. Lott, "Reasonably Traditional," 337. Lott cites MacIntyre, "A Partial Response to My Critics," in *After MacIntyre: Critical Perspectives on the Work of Alasdair MacIntyre*, ed. John Horton and Susan Mendus (Notre Dame, IN: University of Notre Dame Press, 1994) 295.

Lott, however, might insist that this interpretation misunderstands his position. At one point, he acknowledges that MacIntyre has some general or universal principles at work in his theory. Yet, Lott contends that these principles are too thin or insubstantial to adjudicate among the conflicting claims of traditions. "MacIntyre," he states, "can acknowledge a limited role for general [or weak] standards of rationality, while still maintaining that these [general] standards are not adequate, in themselves, to settle debates between rival traditions, and that the strong standards of rationality may [indeed] differ between rival traditions."[28] This suggests that MacIntyre affirms general standards insofar as all traditions abide, for instance, by the rules of logic, but such rules, by themselves, are too thin to adjudicate among traditions. Hence, Lott might also say that MacIntyre can accept the idea of Rt as a universal procedural standard, but this standard is too thin or formal to validate or adjudicate substantive claims among traditions. But Herdt's insight, again, is that the "thick" tradition-dependent rationalities and evaluative standards of the different competitors cannot themselves be used as the standard by which the macro-competition is itself decided. So if, on the one hand, Lott is correct that Rt is too thin or formal to resolve matters and if, on the other hand, Herdt is correct that the competition among traditions requires a universal principle of adjudication, then I would argue that a third alternative is needed, namely, a universal substantive or metaphysical principle. A purely procedural notion like Rt is indeed too thin to serve as an adequate principle of adjudication. For what reason could one have for committing oneself to such a universal rule without some corresponding universal reason? There must be some substantive universal ground for binding oneself to a universal procedure. Hence, I would again assert that MacIntyre comes closest to getting it right when he suggests that "we can know [the metaphysical first principles implicitly] without [explicitly] knowing that we know [them]."

Finally, Lott is certainly right to hold that any claim or theory, including Rt, is explicitly validated in a community of inquiry, for the act of validating a claim involves inquirers making and defending claims to one another. But like MacIntyre, Lott appears to confuse validity and vindication (in spite of the fact that he accuses Herdt of confusing

---

28. Lott, "Reasonably Traditional," 329.

validity as scope vs. validity as justification).²⁹ It is one thing to say that all claims are validated by participating in the game of competing views, and that this game is always situated within history; this is what it means to be part of the broad community of inquiry. But it is another thing to say that, in seeking to validate one's claims within this process, one can and should appeal only to reasons that are historically or tradition-specific. If one is making a universal claim, such as Rt is the inescapable adjudicatory principle among all traditions, then one cannot appeal to the particularity of one or more traditions as the ground upon which this assertion is itself validated; to do so would again make the mistake of appealing to the particularity of a part in order to ground claims generic to the whole. If Rt or some other such principle is the universally valid adjudicatory principle, then that principle must be inescapably presupposed by all participants already. It may be that one participant (tradition) explicitly recognizes it, asserts it, and seeks to justify it, but the basis of its validity must be found in transcendental and metaphysical grounds shared by all, not in tradition-specific grounds unique to one or more.³⁰

---

29. See Lott, "Reasonably Traditional," 333–36 for his criticism of Herdt on this point.

30. One will have noticed by now that both MacIntyre and Whitehead affirm some notion of progress in regard to inquiry. For MacIntyre, as we have seen, this progress is defined in terms of an empirical dialectic, that is, in terms of one tradition outstripping its rivals by outnarrating them via indirect comparative rational means. He purports that one gets closer to the truth about reality through this indirect comparative engagement of rationally and historically contingent claims, which are grounded upon tradition-specific reasons. For Whitehead, alternatively, this progress is defined in terms of an a priori dialectic, that is, in terms of seeking to identify and defend claims about characteristics that are necessary to any possible experience or reality. Metaphysical inquiry, Whitehead suggests, is a progressive endeavor in at least two ways. First, since all valid metaphysical characteristics mutually cohere and imply one another, one seeks progress by bringing to light this mutual implication, i.e., by moving from what is explicitly known to what is implied by that knowledge. One constantly seeks to articulate a progressively more complete metaphysical scheme. But this is never an easy endeavor: "Apart from a complete metaphysical understanding of the universe," says Whitehead, "it is very difficult to understand any proposition clearly and distinctly." Thus, the second way that metaphysical inquiry endeavors to progress is by improving, clarifying, and refining its understanding and articulation of the first principles or final generalities. Given our fallible and fragmentary understanding, and given our historical and linguistic situatedness, our ability to express these final generalities is always an ongoing progressive enterprise. "Every construction of human intelligence," he observes, "is more . . . limited than was its original aim." We know more vaguely and implicitly than we are able to articulate precisely and explicitly. "[W]e know more than can be

MacIntyre might contend that I have thus far inadequately addressed his account of the incommensurability thesis because I have not yet attended to his claim that some languages and traditions are untranslatable. In the penultimate chapter of *WJWR*, entitled "Tradition and Translation," he sets forth and develops this position in opposition to the views of Donald Davidson. On the one hand, in at least a partial nod to Davidson, MacIntyre acknowledges that in order for two or more traditions to be genuinely different, and thus potential or actual rivals, they must understand each other to some significant degree. For his part, Davidson argues: "Different points of view make sense, but only if there is a common co-ordinate system on which to plot them; yet the existence of a common system belies the claim of dramatic incomparability." Hence, Davidson asserts that there are "limits to conceptual contrast."[31] Against Davidson, MacIntyre maintains that there is no common coordinate system; rather there are fundamental differences between some languages and schemes that are basically untranslatable. As one would expect, MacIntyre stresses the tight interconnection between language, culture, beliefs, and authority. In fact, his criticism of modern international languages, like English, is that they lack these strong linguistic ties of shared communal belief. They reflect, in essence, the impersonal thinness of modern *Gesellschaft* (lacking substantive communal ties) in contrast to the interpersonal thickness of premodern *Gemeinschaft*. Given this impersonal thinness, modern languages encourage the assumption that all linguistic expressions are always intertranslatable in

---

formulated in one finite systematized scheme of abstractions, however important that scheme may be in the elucidation of some aspect of the order of things." Hence, metaphysics is an ongoing, progressive endeavor—an asymptotic approach—that is always open to revising its claims or formulations for the sake of gaining more adequate expression and understanding. "Progress in truth," concludes Whitehead, "is mainly a progress in the framing of concepts, in discarding artificial abstractions or partial metaphors, and in evolving notions which strike more deeply into the root of reality." Such a progressive endeavor, I judge, is more adequate for striking deeper into the root of reality than is MacIntyre's indirect comparative engagement. For the reasons cited above, I do not see how MacIntyre's insistence on merely contingent, tradition-specific reasons can get us one step closer to understanding the necessary first principles that are characteristic of reality as such. (Whitehead, *Function of Reason*, 68, 87; Whitehead, *Religion in the Making*, 143, 131). I'm indebted to Lisa Bellantoni for drawing my attention to these passages in relation to Whitehead's understanding of the progressive nature of inquiry; see her *Moral Progress*, 37–43.

31. MacIntyre, *WJWR*, 370; Davidson, "On the Very Idea of a Conceptual Scheme," 184.

some manner, if not by "same-saying" then at least by direct "linguistic innovation," such as by directly incorporating some new word or phrase into one's language (e.g., the absorption of the German "Gemeinschaft" and "Gesellschaft" into academic English usage or the absorption of English terms like "internet" across the contemporary world). But this assumption, MacIntyre believes, is mistaken. Languages are always situated in a historical and social context—in "a particular time and place with particular shared beliefs, institutions, and practices." In a modern context, where shared beliefs are more loosely held, we tend to view language as a neutral medium through which thoughts and feelings can be conveyed and understood without sharing fundamental convictions. In contrast, MacIntyre points to premodern (high medieval Latin and Arabic) and clannish societies (Irish) as examples of where language-use presupposes a shared web of beliefs and authorities. In such cases, "the language will provide standard uses for a necessary range of expressions and idioms, the use of which will presuppose commitment to [an underlying set of] beliefs, institutions and practices. . . . Limits to the possibilities of speaking otherwise than in accordance with the dominant beliefs of such communities are set by the language-in-use of those communities."[32] In a tightly bound linguistic community and tradition, MacIntyre suggests, language-use presupposes adherence to certain underlying beliefs and authorities. Hence, one cannot fully translate such a language into other languages, because outsiders will not share those same underlying commitments—the thick-meaning of its linguistic terms will either be lost or found offensive.

To illustrate, MacIntyre points to the Irish name "Doire Columcille" for the city in Northern Ireland that the English call "Londonderry." The Irish name refers to St. Columba's historic role in the Catholic tradition of Ireland dating back to 564 CE; literally rendered as "St. Columba's oak grave." The English name loses this thick description altogether and is thus not a translation. In fact, it offers a rival Protestant name and tradition dating from the seventeenth century, one that emphasizes commercial and colonial ties to London. Hence, "to use either name," concludes MacIntyre, "is to deny the legitimacy of the other. Consequently, there is no way to translate 'Doire Columcille' into English, except by using 'Doire Columcille' and appending an explanation." As another example, MacIntyre cites the attempt to translate from Latin

32. MacIntyre, *WJWR*, 384, 372, 373.

the fifth ode in Horace's third book of Odes into the Hebrew of the contemporary first-century BCE Jewish community in Palestine: . . . ("We have believed that Juppiter thundering reigns in the sky; Augustus will be held a present divinity . . ."). What Horace said could only have emerged in Hebrew as at once false and blasphemous; the Hebrew explanation of the Roman conception of a god could only have been in terms of an idolatrous regard for evil spirits. It is in the course of just this type of explanation that "daimon" is transformed into "demon."[33]

Since the attempt to translate and explain such incommensurable texts gravely distorts meaning, MacIntyre holds, only a bilingual speaker, who attains a second first-language, can understand the text in a sympathetic and undistorted way within its own thick web of cultural meanings.

MacIntyre is certainly correct that language-use always takes place within a historical and cultural context. He is also right to note that there can be contested names over places and other particularities. However, I am not persuaded that his examples make a sufficient case for his strong overarching claim of untranslatability and incommensurability. It is indeed true that translation cannot always occur simply by same-saying, since one language might lack the linguistic terms needed to directly or easily render a foreign concept. But this is why direct linguistic innovation and/or explanation are valuable creative endeavors. Even when translation by same-saying is possible, linguistic adoption might be preferable. For instance, the German term *Zeitgeist* crisply refers to the feel and texture of a given historical ethos, which is rendered less crisply in English as "the spirit of the age." Nevertheless, the concept is still understandable in English—even though the German term is richer. Thus, when MacIntyre says that "there is no way to translate 'Doire Columcille' into English, except by using 'Doire Columcille' and appending an explanation," I do not see why this alternative is to be so quickly dismissed. I do not speak Irish Gaelic, but MacIntyre's own English explanation of "Doire Columcille" makes perfectly good sense to me. This does not make me an Irish-insider, but it does allow me to understand, appreciate, and respect their historic ties to that place.[34] In fact, if MacIntyre could not explain the meaning of such distinctive terms and names to his English readers, then his readers would

33. Ibid., 378, 380.

34. I'm indebted to the scholar Karl Jost for offering me a brief overview of Gaelic in the context of Ireland.

not recognize any differences at all, and his case would never get off the ground. This is an important point. In seeking to make his case, MacIntyre implicitly presupposes that there is some common ground that enables readers to recognize and understand each side of the supposed untranslatable divide, whether in the case of Ireland or ancient Latin and Hebrew. Again, were there no such common ground for understanding, his case would simply fall on deaf ears. This is why Davidson's position makes good sense, namely, that the recognition of difference presupposes an underlying commonality, which, in turn, belies the claim to incommensurability.

Perhaps MacIntyre would say that his second example shows why explanation is an inadequate method for seeking to understand difference. The Hebrew attempt to translate and explain Horace's Latin verse distorts the meaning, MacIntyre insists. I grant that the polytheism of Horace's ode would ultimately be rejected from a monotheistic Jewish standpoint. But in order to reject the position, they would first have to understand it, at least insofar as it is polytheistic. Evaluation requires some understanding. To be sure, a quick and unsympathetic translation would certainly lead to distorted meanings—such as the Greek "daimon" (Latin *daemon*) becoming "demon." Though MacIntyre offers this latter point as an add-on to his second example, let me use it for a moment to assess his Hebrew illustration. It seems to me that a sympathetic Hebrew rendering of "daimon" could have rendered it, at least in part, along the lines of the "spirit of Yahweh" coming upon an anointed figure like David (1 Sam 16:13), or in terms of affirming the accessibility and indwelling of divine wisdom (Proverbs 8), or along the lines of inspiration in the prophetic literature—"the spirit of the Lord has come upon me" (Isaiah 61:1). These explanations would have emphasized and made clear some of the positive connotations of "daimon," of divinity being manifest in special individuals.[35] Now if, and insofar as, the term also requires calling such individuals divinities per se, rather than being merely inspired by divinity, then Hebrew monotheism begins to cast the term in a more negative light (demon). My point is that a Hebrew translation of "daimon" need not preclude substantive understanding even if it also leads eventually to disagreement. Furthermore, would not

---

35. I'm grateful to my colleagues Peggy Cowan and Phillip Sherman for sharing their expertise in Hebrew Bible with me, in order to help me think about ancient Hebrew literature in relation to MacIntyre's claim.

MacIntyre's bilingual speaker have the same troubles that he ascribes to direct translation? The native Hebrew speaker who learns Latin or Greek as a second first-language is still going to reject the polytheism, and is still going to have to try to explain the Latin or Greek terms and ideas to his fellow Jews if he is going to persuade them that the other tradition offers intellectual and linguistic resources lacking in Hebrew. In other words, he is still going to have to explain the positive connotations of "daimon" in terms of relative equivalents in the Hebrew Bible.

Returning to the larger discussion with Davidson, MacIntyre too quickly dismisses the significance of his initial concession to him. For instance, he declares that Davidson's position "can be interpreted as saying no more than what would be conceded, I take it, by anyone: that there will always be something in common between any two languages or any two sets of thoughts." Notice the way that MacIntyre formulates this—as a confident declaration of future fact rather than as a rational necessity. He does not want to grant Davidson's fundamental insight that recognition of difference rationally requires an underlying commonality ("a common co-ordinate system" on which to identify and map out all differences), for such an admission would undercut his position. Instead, MacIntyre suggests that commonality between languages and traditions is merely an empirical and happy coincidence, in the form of a partial overlap—one that will always conveniently occur and thus will enable us to get to the point where we run into incommensurable differences. For Davidson, linguistic and conceptual differences are relative to the one reality. "Since there is at most one world," he reflects, differences must be relative, not absolute. In contrast, MacIntyre's assertion of incommensurability implies that reality is relative to different linguistic and conceptual schemes. And, yet, at the same time, MacIntyre does not want to travel fully down this road; he, too, wants to say that finally there is one reality that can be approached and known through an indirect comparison of different traditions. I would venture to say that this tension reflects the fact that MacIntyre's affirmation of incommensurability stems from his "post-Kantian intellectual space" whereas his affirmation of the one reality stems from his reclamation of medieval Thomism.[36]

---

36. MacIntyre, *WJWR*, 371; Davidson, "On the Very Idea of a Conceptual Scheme," 184, 187; Milbank, "Programme of Radical Orthodoxy," 38.

In an illuminating article, Kevin Schilbrack argues that Davidson's famous essay "On the Very Idea of a Conceptual Scheme" is at root "an attack on the [Kantian] idea of noumena." That is, a scheme-content dualism posits that there is some reality-in-itself that cannot be known. This unknowable reality provides the content to be organized and interpreted by different and incommensurable cultural schemes. So just as Kant contends that we can and must presuppose unknowable "noumena," so also do MacIntyre and the incommensurability thesis contend that we can and must presuppose untranslatable and incommensurable differences. The scheme-content dualism of the incommensurability thesis, Schilbrack observes, "has been employed precisely to block metaphysical inquiry into the nature of things, on the grounds, that the things in themselves are on the far side of our conceptual scheme and so forever inaccessible to our knowledge. By rejecting scheme/content dualism," Schilbrack concludes, Davidson "shows how the modern and postmodern antipathy to metaphysics . . . depends on a dualism that is no longer tenable."[37] The post-Kantian side of MacIntyre reveals this antipathy. Hence, his Thomistic side must again always seek to defend its Thomism in rather "unThomistic" ways. In sum, it appears that the two sources fueling MacIntyre's insistence on the particularity of traditions, namely, his implicit acceptance of the modern Kantian denial of metaphysics and his explicit endorsement of the incommensurability thesis, are more interrelated than they at first seemed.

MacIntyre might agree that he does accept the Kantian denial of metaphysics in some form, but he might maintain, rather, that his point is to direct criticism against what I have called the modern commitment to formal autonomy. The false assumption behind this commitment, he might say, is found in the opening words of Descartes' "Discourse on Method" when Descartes claims that "the power of . . . distinguishing truth from error, which is properly what is called good sense or reason, is by nature equal in all men." This assumption is further exemplified in Kant's essay on enlightenment when Kant calls for all persons to throw off their "self-incurred tutelage" and have courage to make use of their own reason—to dare to make public use of their own capacity to

---

37. Schilbrack, "Study of Religion After Davidson," 338, 347. Though he offers a more critical view of Davidson's overall position than does Schilbrack, John Allan Knight appears to find Schilbrack's reading of Davidson generally persuasive; see his "Why Not Davidson," 170–71 n. 44.

discern truth from error.[38] In opposition, MacIntyre might contend that learning to distinguish truth from error is not something constitutively or equally available to all, but instead requires serving apprenticeship in a bounded community of inquiry under the tutelage of an authoritative master. In such a community, he asserts, "fundamental dissent has to be excluded." By this, I take him to mean in part that there cannot be dissent over the ultimate metaphysical presuppositions—that the "umbrella" of first principles must be accepted on authority in order for learning and tradition-constituted reasoning to occur. In MacIntyre's words, "A prior commitment [to the community and its authorities] is required and the conclusions which emerge as enquiry progresses will of course have been partially and crucially predetermined by the nature of this initial commitment."[39] Yet, to affirm formal autonomy, I would urge, does not require one to affirm equality *de facto*, but rather only *de jure*. There is an ambiguity in Descartes' affirmation of a common power to reason, a common power to discern truth from error. Surely he means (or ought to mean) that all persons by nature have a basic common potential, not that all persons in fact have an equally developed capacity. Hence, there is indeed an educational role for communities to play in fostering and cultivating rational judgment; but this role neither bars fundamental dissent over substantive matters nor substitutes authority for rational validation.

To formulate my point another way, can MacIntyre or anyone else seek to offer a convincing case against the commitment to formal autonomy without implicitly affirming and presupposing that commitment? Can he successfully present his case without attempting to make his position intelligible to others and without attempting to offer at least some credible reasons for why they should abandon the modern commitment to formal autonomy altogether? Must he not assume, in other words, Descartes' egalitarian point when he seeks to argue against it? Notice that within the internal structure of his own writings, MacIntyre himself does not appeal to some specific authority, such as his own philosophical mastery, or to the Catholic Church, or to scripture, as if that provided sufficient grounds for justifying his stated claims about the need for tradition-constituted rationality. Indeed, he goes to admirable lengths to try to make his position intelligible to others who do not

---

38. Descartes, "Discourse on Method," 39; Kant, "What is Enlightenment?," 3.
39. MacIntyre, *TRV*, 60.

share his views. Moreover, he seeks to offer them at least some convincing reasons for why they should judge his claims to be true rather than false. There is, therefore, an underlying tension between MacIntyre's stated position, which claims the need for appeals to authority within bounded traditions, and the implicit assumptions of his own philosophical arguments, which presuppose the modern commitment itself. In short, MacIntyre's explicit rejection of the modern commitment to formal autonomy is self-refuting because, in trying to make his case, he must implicitly presuppose that commitment. To respond, MacIntyre might declare that the choice between a tradition-constituted approach and a modern-commitment approach is properly decided by which alternative offers a more adequate genealogical account of Western intellectual developments and problems. Yet, such an argument presupposes some common procedure for assessing the merits of alternative historical accounts and what is at issue between the two approaches themselves is precisely the question of what appeals should count in deciding such questions. As we saw earlier, Whitehead argues that history presupposes metaphysics, whereas MacIntyre contends that metaphysics presupposes history. To say that appeals to authority or tradition are sufficient grounds for deciding such fundamental questions would simply beg the question.[40]

A Further Response to Stout

If MacIntyre thinks that the future of theology is to be found in a tightly bound neo-Thomistic tradition, one which philosophically presupposes tradition-constituted rationality and the incommensurability thesis, then Stout thinks the future of theology is to be found in a neo-Barthianism that embraces democracy and the secular sphere in the form of an exclusivism without triumphalism. Stout wants substantive theological voices to speak in public and he wants them to feel at home in a democratic society. This combination, he believes, is possible in the context of a public sphere that operates along the lines of pragmatic expressivism and immanent criticism. But before addressing this position directly, let me back up momentarily to widen the context. As we saw earlier, Stout declares in *Ethics After Babel* that serious theological

---

40. My argument here against MacIntyre, concerning the modern commitment, is informed by Gamwell's argument against Reinhold Niebuhr on this same general point. See Gamwell, *Divine Good*, 12–13.

ideas will not gain any real traction in the contemporary world until there is a "dramatic change . . . in what most people, including intellectuals, take for granted about the nature and existence of God when they speak to matters of moral importance in public settings." As this statement stands, I think Stout is exactly right. A dramatic change is needed in what people presuppose about the nature and existence of God. What I intentionally left out here for the moment, for the sake of clarity, is Stout's assertion that this change must come "independently of theology." Theology cannot initiate or foster such change, he presumes; only a widespread "religious resurgence" could produce such a dramatic transformation. One can argue that we have indeed witnessed a widespread religious resurgence in American culture in recent decades, as well as in many places and forms across the globe. Yet, this resurgence has not led to any dramatic change in theological assumptions. If anything, traditional assumptions have become more recalcitrant and ossified. My contention is that theology must be a catalyst for changing the way people think about God, metaphysics, and the rationality of religion in the public sphere. It is noteworthy that in *Democracy and Tradition* Stout appears to have abandoned any hope or call for a dramatic change in what people presuppose about the nature and existence of God. Instead, he declares that Hunsinger's reading of Barth, coupled with an expressive pragmatist view of public discourse, offers a way for traditional theological voices to speak and be heard in a democratic society. As he sees it, such a way enables "orthodox Christians . . . to maintain their own convictions . . . while also taking up their responsibilities as citizens."[41] What is apparent throughout Stout's various writings, and perhaps especially in his recent work, is the fact that he does not believe that any rational public consensus can be achieved, even in theory, when it comes to fundamental religious and metaphysical convictions. This outlook stems from his underlying dismissal of metaphysics, and shapes his views of what it means to defend theological claims and to listen to others in public discourse. I will take up these points in reverse order.

One will recall that Stout is drawn to Hunsinger's reading of Barth in large part because of its theological emphasis on listening to diverse voices in the wider public. The Barthian rationale for this centers on listening for "secular parables"—diverse words and cultural forms that

---

41. Stout, *Ethics After Babel*, 186; Stout, *Democracy and Tradition*, 116.

reveal incognito the one exclusive truth of Jesus Christ. Stout's willingness to endorse Barthian exclusivism for the sake of purchasing some partial openness to the secular is both revealing and problematic. The underlying attitude of this exclusivist position is: *I will listen to you, but not because your views may be true as such and, therefore, that I might have something to learn from your position per se. Rather, I will listen to you because your words and ideas may unwittingly serve as vehicles of the one Christian truth (Jesus Christ) that I proclaim. Hence, they may offer incognito words to me that challenge and benefit me from my own comprehensive perspective.*[42] Given Stout's commitment to democracy, one wonders whether this attitude sufficiently embodies the democratic virtue of listening to others with a genuinely open mind. At face value, it does not appear to do so. For a more promising alternative, one might look to Ogden's theology. In contrast to Barth and Hunsinger's position, Ogden advocates a form of critical engagement that takes Christian theological convictions seriously but also affirms that other voices may speak truly in their own terms. That is, whereas Barth and Hunsinger's monistic exclusivism maintains that there *can be only one* true religion, Ogden argues that there *can be more than one*. In asserting this, he does

---

42. Hunsinger might suggest that this characterization misses the mark—that it exaggerates the Barthian position. "The confession of Jesus Christ as the one Word of God," says Hunsinger, "has nothing to do with an arbitrary self-glorification of Christianity, the church, or the Christian. It is strictly 'a christological statement'. As such, it does not entail any exaltation of the Christian over the non-Christian, but rather an important bond between them. . . . Barth thus sets the superiority of the Word over against all human words as such, whether they arise from the Bible, the church, or the world. All human words as such are relativized by the Word and thus joined in a certain solidarity." But my point is that, according to Barth's own view, the Word that stands above and relativizes all human words can only be known through the revelation of Jesus Christ, and *this* revelation can only be *explicitly* articulated and conceptualized in terms of the Christian witness of faith and in and through the Christian canonical scriptures. Put simply, it is only Christians who express ultimate reality in terms of *christological statements*. Indeed, as Hunsinger himself proceeds to note, "The concrete content of this [overarching] Word is, *in nuce*, the life of Jesus Christ." And since this comprehensive Word is constitutively and exclusively defined in terms of the "particular existence" and "narratable history" of Jesus Christ, the only explicit expression of truth within history must proclaim this particular existence and narrate this particular history (i.e., the Christian tradition at its best). Other voices can, at most, be incognito vehicles of this one exclusive truth. This is why Hunsinger himself describes the world as Christ's "unwitting witness." In sum, the Barthian position may have some degree of humility, it may be *"exclusivism without triumphalism,"* but it is still *"exclusivism"*: there can be only one true religion or comprehensive doctrine and that doctrine can only be christological (Hunsinger, *How to Read Karl Barth*, 244–45, 251, 247, 278).

not jump to the pluralist conclusion that *there are many* true religions. Rather, he seeks an intermediate stance that leaves open the possibility that ultimate reality might validly be expressed in and by different religious traditions. Hence, this intermediate position affirms genuine and critical inter-religious dialogue. For instance, speaking of Christianity and Buddhism, Ogden contends that "provided the self-understandings made explicit in the two explanations are substantially the same, both explanations can be true even though only Christians have reason to offer the one [explanation] and only Buddhists have reason to offer the other." In seeking to assess these different views, Ogden advocates the difficult constructive task of understanding and critically engaging the existential, metaphysical, and ethical implications of each religious perspective. What is required, he states, "is a mutual recognition of one another's . . . *claims* to validity that are equally in need and equally deserving of critical validation in terms of our common human experience and reason."[43] Of course, it is at this is point that Ogden and Stout would quickly part company. Whereas Ogden thinks that the implicit and explicit metaphysical claims of the two traditions can be compared and assessed in terms of common human reason and experience, Stout denies that any such common reason or experience exists, at least when it comes to religious or metaphysical claims. Stated otherwise, Ogden seeks to identify the implicit dimensions of experience as such and to test all religious claims in light of them. Conversely, as we saw in his critique of public theology, Stout denies that there are any such implicitly shared dimensions or commitments. Hence, in contrast to Ogden's model of listening to others in pursuit of identifying a common reality or truth expressed in different terms, Stout affirms a Barthian model that listens to others to discern secular parables that are true only by virtue of a Christian paradigm. Summarily put, whereas Ogden seeks a meeting of diverse minds, Stout seeks a pragmatic *modus vivendi* that enables idiosyncratic views to get along.

One of the key differences between Ogden's model of critical engagement and Barth's model of secular parables stems from an underlying difference in their respective christologies. Barth, in keeping with

---

43. Ogden, *Is There Only One True Religion*, 102–3, 56. For an example of a pluralist theology, see Reat and Perry, *World Theology*. I analyzed Ogden's view in relation to that of Reat and Perry in a combined review of these two books: see Meyer, review in *Religion* 29 (April 1999) 188–91.

traditional theology, offers what Ogden calls a "constitutive" christology. By this, he means that Barth and others believe that Christ originates or constitutes the possibility of God's redemptive work in the world. But this widespread and long-standing assumption, Ogden holds, harbors a fundamental mistake. As he notes,

> the New Testament does *not* affirm that in Christ our salvation "becomes possible." It affirms, rather, that in him what has always been possible now "becomes manifest," in the sense of being decisively presented in a human word of witness. Its message is not that God "is the one who must be reconciled," which, as Tillich has rightly argued, is the unavoidable implication of the [constitutive view], but that "God, who is eternally reconciled, wants us to be reconciled to him."[44]

Because God's essential nature is love, the eternal divine love constitutes or makes possible our salvation. Hence, "The only cause of our salvation," Ogden declares,

> is the primordial and everlasting love of God.... Because of this love, which is ... God's very essence, ... no event in time and history, including the event of Jesus Christ, can be the cause of salvation in the sense of the necessary condition of its possibility. On the contrary, any event, including the Christ event, can be at most a consequence of the salvation, ... which [issues from] God's own essential being as all-embracing love.[45]

Barth's Christomonism stems largely from his version of a constitutive christology. If Christ constitutes the fundamental truth about human life and its relation to ultimate reality, then no substantive truth can be found in other religions or positions as such. At most, they may contain incognito forms of the one Christian truth. In contrast, Ogden advocates a "representative" christology: Christ manifests or re-presents to the world what has always been the case, namely, the character of God, which is God's all-embracing love.[46] A representative christology, however, unlike a constitutive one, leaves open the possibility that the truth about ultimate reality and its relation to human existence might also be validly expressed in other religious or philosophical forms—in other

---

44. Ogden, *Christ Without Myth*, 143. Ogden cites Tillich, *Systematic Theology*, vol. 2, 169f. and 175f.

45. Ogden, *Is There Only One True Religion*, 92.

46. Ibid., 84f.

representations. In fact, other representations might offer the Christian perspective some instructive insight. On this point, Ogden would agree with Whitehead in noting that "perhaps our [own religious] dogmas require correction."[47] A representative christology, therefore, fuels an attitude of genuine openness and respect for diverse voices, since those voices may teach the Christian and others in important ways. I would contend that Ogden's christology offers Stout a more adequate model for democratic discourse and citizenship than does Barth's; a genuine openness to pluralist understandings is more respectful of diverse voices than is an exclusivism without triumphalism. Stout certainly wants theological voices to listen attentively to diverse others, yet he seeks to achieve this by simply accommodating traditional theological viewpoints. I would again maintain that Stout came closer to getting it right when he at least hoped for a dramatic change in theological understandings, such as illustrated here by a change in christology. Such a theological change can contribute to a public discourse where religious claims are listened to in their own right and not just as incognito vehicles of a hegemonic outlook.

Stout might reply that he himself is drawn to Ogden's representative christology. But such a nontraditional view, he might add, indicates that Ogden is an "alienated" theologian—speaking from the academy but not for the mainstream church. In contrast, Hunsinger and Barth's constitutive christology and exclusivism without triumphalism are closer to the average person in the pew. Hence, given Stout's pragmatic concerns about democracy, he might submit that the Barthian position is a safer, more minimalist bet for the near-term health of democracy; it is sufficiently open to the views of others to get Christian buy-in to democratic citizenship, which is all that Stout pragmatically wants. I grant that the language of secular parables is more open to diverse voices than many conservative theological positions in contemporary culture. Yet, given Stout's own progressivist tendencies, I find his dismissal of so-called "alienated" theologians itself a surprisingly conservative move. What contemporary democracy needs are progressive religious and theological voices that model how the church can take theistic convictions seriously and, at the same time, fully embrace the democratic virtue of openly listening to the claims that others make. Ogden would argue, rightly I judge, that a representative christology and all the

---

47. Whitehead, *Religion in the Making*, 128.

implications that follow from it are more authentically Christian than a constitutive view. Likewise, he would assert that he speaks this word to the church as well as to the academy and the wider public. Instead of the new traditionalists taking the church away from democracy, or Barthian exclusivism taking the church part way into democratic engagement, I would contend that the church needs a model of full-fledged democratic participation, which in turn requires a model that illustrates how faith and reason can go fully hand in hand. But Stout of course thinks that faith and reason cannot go fully hand in hand, since faith claims in a broad sense, i.e., final vocabularies of metaphysical and existential convictions, cannot themselves be rationally justified. Hence, he cannot go beyond the Barthian position.

This last point serves as a segue from the issue of listening to diverse others to justifying theological claims to others. Given his dismissal of metaphysics, Stout endorses the Barthian version of "faith seeking understanding" to mean that one cannot ultimately or directly justify one's most basic convictions. Rather, one can only seek to show entitlement to them. The key provision of inferential pragmatism is the assertion that truth and justification are independent of each other. This means that rational justification of theological claims extends only as far as showing others that one is logically entitled to making claims that emanate from one's basic convictions. It does not include seeking to show others that one's basic claims or convictions are true. This is why Stout ultimately abandons any attempt to validate the truth claims of theology, or any other metaphysical or existential conviction for that matter. From his vantage point, the fundamental truth claim about the reality and necessity of God can never be rationally validated. Instead, all others can do is assess whether one is making logical inferences from this initial starting point to which one is entitled. "Faith" means acceptance of an initial starting point beyond rational assessment, as in the case of theistic conviction. "Seeking understanding" means rational explication and testing of inferences that flow from this initial starting point. This is why when it comes to addressing the truth claims of theology, Stout must agree with Rorty that religion is a conversation stopper, at least in this specific sense, and this is why Stout makes a "distinction between being entitled to a belief and being able to justify [the truth-claim of] that belief to someone else." Even when one is "epistemically entitled to religious premises," Stout admits, one may indeed "still be unable to produce an argument that would give [others] reason to accept those premises."[48]

Throughout his career, Stout has insightfully observed that theology has lost its cognitive voice. But what does it mean to have a cognitive voice? It means making and defending truth claims. "Without truth-claims," Stout says approvingly in describing Barth's position, "there would be no communication, no exchange of reasons." This is exactly right. But Stout's own position ultimately fails to address the truth claims of theology in any direct or substantive manner. In his discussion of Gustafson, Stout noted that a public "hearing for theological ideas must be won, if they are to get a hearing at all." This, too, is correct. But the only way for theology to win a hearing for its ideas is for it to directly defend its fundamental truth claims. And these claims, such as those about the reality of God, are metaphysical or ontological at root, which in turn requires at some point offering and defending metaphysical claims. To divorce "theology from the realm of ontological claims," Stout concluded in *The Flight from Authority*, "is to make theistic vocabulary superfluous."[49] Again, right on the mark. So why then does Stout zero in on the proper cognitive questions but, at the same time, offer what appear to be anemic answers to those questions? I would submit that his own underlying aversion to metaphysics leaves him unable to adequately support the cognitive dimension to which he rightly draws attention. He wants the benefit of ontological claims (to ward off relativism), but he is unwilling to pay the metaphysical freight for them. Of course, he thinks there is no such freight to pay, since he believes that the metaphysical enterprise is both unnecessary and harmful.

This view is evident in a central chapter in *Democracy and Tradition*, entitled "Ethics Without Metaphysics," where Stout describes his "metaphysically austere treatment" of these matters. He seeks to endorse a view of truth that is neither merely relativistic (truth as justified belief) nor fully realistic (truth as a correspondence to reality). As he sees it, the former is "narcissistic" and the latter "has no explanatory value." Instead, he endeavors to offer a middle alternative, which he calls "modest pragmatism." Though this modest pragmatism is reluctant to offer its own definition of truth, it can be deemed a "minimal realism," Stout holds, insofar as it affirms the objective notion "that whether a belief is true or

---

48. Stout, *Democracy and Tradition*, 87.
49. Stout, Ibid., 111; *Ethics After Babel*, 165; *Flight from Authority*, 147.

false depends in part on the objects, events, properties, relations, values, and proprieties to which reference is made." Central to this minimal realism is the "equivalence use" of truth, namely, that "it is true that *P* if and only if *P*." For instance, the assertion that "'courageous acts deserve praise' is true if and only if courageous acts deserve praise." Stout acknowledges that this equivalence use might "be trivial in the logician's sense," but he maintains that it has the virtue of reminding one that an inquiry "into the truth or falsity of *P* involves directing one's attention to what *P refers to* and holding one's beliefs and claims answerable to that." Drawing on the work of Arthur Fine, he also suggests that this modest pragmatism affirms "the natural ontological attitude" toward truth. By this, I take Stout and Fine to mean that in everyday usage, we presuppose that our claims to truth are claims about what we take to be objectively true in the realm of being or existence, i.e., in the real state of affairs of the world. But this natural ontological attitude, Stout contends, is non-metaphysical: "Truth-talk is not an implicitly metaphysical affair, standing in need of metaphysical articulation and defense. It is an aspect of ordinary language use, to be made sense of in terms of an empirically oriented linguistic theory." In fact, modest pragmatism is not merely non-metaphysical but also "antimetaphysical." Drawing on the work of Mark Johnston, Stout offers a critique of what he and Johnston call "metaphysics in the pejorative sense." In a footnote, Stout approvingly quotes Johnston as follows: "'Let us say that metaphysics in the pejorative sense is a confused conception of what legitimates our practices; confused because metaphysics in this sense is a series of pictures of the world containing various independent demands for our practices, when [in fact] the only real legitimation of those practices consists in showing their worthiness to survive on the testing ground of daily life.'" Metaphysics in the "pejorative" sense includes all attempts to describe or make claims about the nature of being as such, and thereby to offer independent standards inherent in the nature of reality itself by which to evaluate all human practices. In contradistinction to this common or traditional understanding of the metaphysical enterprise, Johnston and Stout assert that there could be a more modest, practical or pragmatic use of the term "metaphysics." "'So defined,'" Johnston continues, "'metaphysics is the proper object of that practical criticism which asks whether the apparently legitimating stories which help sustain our practices really do legitimate, and whether the real explanations of our practices allow us to justify them.'"[50] Thus, it appears that Stout is willing to abide the term "metaphysics" as long as it refers to nothing more than an empirically and linguistically oriented criticism of moral and social practices. From this perspective, he is willing to describe his own version of pragmatism as a form of non-pejorative metaphysics.

Before proceeding further, let me take stock. Stout affirms that: (1) theology makes truth claims, (2) these claims cannot be divorced from ontological claims, (3) normal, everyday practice implies a natural ontological attitude toward truth, (4) there is a difference between truth and justified belief, because whether some claim is true or not depends in part on objects, events, values, relations, etc. that are objective or independent of one's beliefs or claims about them, yet (5) none of these four points implies or entails pursuing metaphysics in the traditional or "pejorative" sense of seeking to understand the nature of being or reality as such. But what is an ontological claim, I ask, if not a claim about the nature of being as such? What is the natural ontological attitude toward a theological truth claim about the reality of God, if not the presumption that such a claim asserts the existence of a divine reality? Clearly, as suggested in (4), the truth of such a claim depends in some important sense on a reality independent of our beliefs. I would therefore hold that the equivalence use of truth remains merely an unredeemed conditional assertion (it is true that P if and only if P) unless one can offer some independent grounds for thinking that P is indeed true. Let P refer to the claim "God exists." Thus, "it is true that God exists if and only if God exists." Yes, but now one must offer some other reasons for thinking that God exists, otherwise this claim remains merely a tautology or, at best, an ongoing hypothetical. It is for this reason, among others, that full-fledged realists tend to construe the equivalence use of truth in terms of some "relation of correspondence." I am not wedded to the term "corre-

---

50. Stout, "Ethics Without Metaphysics," chap. 11 in *Democracy and Tradition*, 246–69. In my summary discussion here, I have drawn on material from 246, 250, 248, 251, 255, 253, 249, 253, 249, 253, 251, 255, 256, 268, 331–32 n. 1. Stout cites Arthur Fine, *The Shaky Game* (Chicago: University of Chicago Press, 1986) chaps. 7 & 8; and Mark Johnston, "Objectivity Refigured: Pragmatism without Verificationism," in *Reality, Representation, and Projection*, ed. John Haldane and Crispin Wright (Oxford: Oxford University Press, 1993) 85. It should be noted that Stout's notion of metaphysics in the "pejorative" sense also rejects Kant's revised, broad, transcendental understanding of metaphysics. So Stout rejects—as metaphysics in the pejorative sense—any attempt to articulate the rationally necessary characteristics of understanding (Kant) or of reality as such.

spondence" for its own sake, but I would contend that it is the nature of reality that makes theological claims true or valid, if they are indeed so. As Davidson remarks, "the truth of an utterance depends on ... how the world is arranged."[51] Hence, if one is to move theological claims about God beyond the realm of mere hypothetical or idle assertion, then one must offer some reasons and arguments pertaining to the metaphysical arrangement or structure of the world.

In fact, for these reasons, I would argue that Stout's anti-metaphysical stance makes his position implicitly anti-theological, in spite of his expressed interest in theology. Stout himself acknowledges this charge: "It might be objected that pragmatism, pursued as a general antimetaphysical strategy within philosophy, is inherently antitheological." In response, he thinks he is innocent because "there are numerous theologians and theologically committed philosophers who hope to free themselves and the culture as a whole from the compulsion of pursuing metaphysics in the pejorative sense. Their work is ... an apt reminder that theological commitments need not be seen as a subset of metaphysical commitments." I would certainly agree that there are numerous theologians (and theologically committed philosophers) who seek to affirm claims about God apart from metaphysics; but as I will attempt to show in Part Two, I think they are as mistaken on this count as Stout. "My opposition to metaphysics," Stout adds, "is not intended to rule out a class of claims simply because they refer to something *beyond* or *above* the ontological framework assumed in the natural sciences."[52] Yet, given his anti-metaphysical proclivities, Stout never seeks to redeem such claims. At most, he grants that a theist might be permitted or entitled to such claims, but, as he himself admits, such entitlement does not itself offer others any reasons for accepting such claims to be true. In effect, what he gives with the right hand, he takes away with the left.

Stout's approach is exemplified in his discussion of the views of Timothy Jackson and Robert Merrihew Adams, whom he offers as examples of metaphysical theologians in a pejorative sense. Both Jackson and Adams claim that moral obligations must be metaphysi-

51. Stout, *Democracy and Tradition*, 260, 249; Davidson, "Coherence Theory of Truth and Knowledge," 309. I'm indebted to Schilbrack for drawing my attention to this quote, but unfortunately he accidentally cites the wrong source with the correct page number: Schilbrack, "Study of Religious Belief After Donald Davidson," 339; both the Davidson source and page that I have cited here are correct.

52. Stout, *Democracy and Tradition*, 256.

cally grounded in the divine reality in some manner. Alternatively, Stout contends that modest pragmatism can provide moral standards and still make room for theistic claims without resorting to metaphysics. To illustrate, he describes Adams's view as follows: "If a personal God exists and chooses to interact with us, then our relationship with God, according to [Adams's theory], should be capable of giving rise to [moral] obligations." Stout adds that these moral obligations, stemming from divine commands, are social, that they pertain to "social bonds," and they are "recognized as good—as excellent—by the human beings involved in" them. The consequence of a divine command theory, Stout reasons, is that it "would transform all morally valid obligations into religious obligations." But most if not all of this can still be accommodated, Stout purports, "if we begin [instead] with a social-pragmatic theory of obligation and then factor in a theistic view of what the relevant relationships are like and who are involved in them. Nontheistic pragmatists will not accept the additions, but that goes without saying. Still, the controversial additions need not involve metaphysics in the pejorative sense, just some questionable ontological claims." This revealing passage says it all. Notice first that Stout seeks to define valid moral obligations in a free-standing way, independently of theistic convictions. It is only then that these "controversial [theistic] additions" can be added on or accommodated. Adams's point, I presume, is that God is the ultimate measure of good or excellence and thus the ground of all valid moral claims, not some superfluous add-on to be accommodated. As Stout later admits in a partial concession to Jackson: "If God created the earth and immediately declared it excellent, and only then proceeded to create human beings, it makes little sense to insist that excellence, as a normative status, is a creature of *human* practices."[53] But of course the theistic ground of moral claims can be dismissed or compartmentalized as long as the fundamental claim about the reality of God remains merely a hypothetical assertion, a truth claim beyond rational validation. This leads to a second important observation. Notice how Stout claims that Adams's theistic affirmations can be added in a nonmetaphysical way, but observe, at the same time, how easily these affirmations are then dismissed by Stout (and other nontheists) because

---

53. Ibid., 260, 268. In an endnote, Stout acknowledges his partial concession to Jackson: see 336 n. 44. My discussion of the anti-theological implications of Stout's position is informed by Gamwell, "Comment on Jeffrey Stout," 5–6.

they offer what he calls "questionable ontological claims." The ontological truth claims are indeed at the heart of the matter. Yet, as long as the metaphysical enterprise is dismissed, such claims will remain merely hypothetical niceties to be accommodated, not truth claims to be seriously or publicly engaged.

But such truth claims need never be publicly engaged, Stout retorts, because a pragmatic moral theory can "make clear that a society divided over the nature and existence of God is not thereby condemned to view its ethical discourse as an unconstrained endeavor." Pragmatism's criticism is directed only at "metaphysics in a pejorative sense," he maintains, only at "the God of Descartes and the God of analytic metaphysics." By contrast, pragmatism is quite compatible with religious belief "taken simply as a story faithfully believed. Its quarrel is not with the God of Amos and Dorothy Day, or even with the God of Barthian theology." Rather, conflict arises between theology and pragmatism only when someone asserts that the validity of any moral claim depends "for its *objectivity* on positing a transcendent and perfect being." Now Stout's formulation here is suggestive of the classical theism and metaphysics that I critiqued in the last chapter. In this specific sense, I agree with him. But it is readily apparent that his real concern here is with any theistic metaphysics that rationally claims that the objectivity or ground of ethics depends on the divine reality. This is why Stout finds Barth's theology more suitable than Adams's. Barth, to be sure, thinks that ethics is a subset of dogmatics and that "all finite forms of excellence [are] pale reflections of God's excellence." Yet, Barth's grounding of ethics in the divine is based strictly on an analogy of faith, whereas Adams's account is based on a Platonic or metaphysical analogy of being. Whereas Adams claims that one can and must move rationally and directly from our experience of excellence in the world toward the conclusion that all such excellence depends on the divine excellence, Barth denies any such direct rational or experiential move. Instead, he holds that the recognition of the divine ground of ethics requires the intervention of divine grace. Hence, the "Barthian affirmation of God as the [ground and] archetype of excellence," says Stout, presupposes the givenness and particularity of "faith as its absolute presupposition. Theology properly conceived, according to Barth, shatters all attempts to argue on strictly philosophical grounds from the experience of finite things to a God posited as a metaphysical *explanans*." In sum, as evident here, Stout thinks that theology can be socially accommodated as long as it does not publicly and rationally insist on the metaphysical and moral implications of its fundamental claim about the reality of God. Theology can voice its claims to special revelation and divine grace because such claims are particular rather than general—they presuppose a given outlook and do not claim rational public validity as such. Put simply, they have no grounds for seeking to define a public ethic. Rather, they are "taken merely as a story faithfully believed" by some—not a claim that must be engaged by all. Hence, such claims are compatible with pragmatism's nonmetaphysical understanding of moral obligation and excellence. And as long as one does not try to make public metaphysical claims, Stout concludes, then modest pragmatism "can accommodate whatever persons, social relationships and practices there happen to be," including theological ones.[54] But such accommodation, I would contend, marginalizes theology's truth claims by neutering them.

In a somewhat surprising move, reminiscent of the various empirical approaches of Aristotle, J. S. Mill, and MacIntyre, Stout argues that the objectivity of moral standards, such as excellence, is measured by and in terms of qualified and authoritative persons. Given his overall emphasis on democratic equality, this appeal to authority is rather unexpected. Given his rejection of the metaphysical enterprise, however, his pragmatic moral theory ultimately has nowhere else to turn except to an appeal to authority. "Excellence of a given kind," he states, "normally manifests itself to competent judges of the relevant sort. What such judges steadily love or admire, when given full information and ample opportunity to reflect critically, is our best guide to excellence." On the one hand, Stout appears here to suggest that the standard of excellence is an objective measure embedded in the particular practices themselves; it reveals or "manifests itself" to the competent judges in each endeavor. Each practice, whether it is baseball or child rearing, has an "overall point" or telos, and excellence is measured in terms of approaching this aim. In Stout's words, "Our grasp of excellence—of what it is—consists in our ability to reflect meaningfully on our experience of normative ascent within a number of particular practices." Thus, "one can get a reasonably clear sense of what ideally competent judges would have to know. . . . So there is no reason to suppose that we are dealing here with a merely subjective [or authoritative] matter." Yet, in spite of

---

54. Stout, *Democracy and Tradition*, 268, 267, 268.

this assertion, Stout on the other hand has great difficulty defining these standards independently of the judgments of the competent authorities themselves. As we have seen, he resists any attempt to define good or excellence in a comprehensive or metaphysical manner, instead he emphasizes that excellence is always defined narrowly only in terms of a specific practice, like baseball or jazz. But if moral virtue deals with human character and life across the board, then one must ask what is the "overall point" of human life as a whole? What is the aim or goal by which we measure "normative ascent" in the comprehensive practice known as human life? At this juncture, Stout has little to say. In fact, he resorts to conceptual silence: "To understand excellence," he declares, "is thus to possess a kind of wisdom that is difficult or impossible to state propositionally." It is impossible to state, from his vantage point, precisely because he rejects any general or universal measure of value. "The metaphysical temptation," he adds, "is to think that an explicit, highly general propositional formulation would represent an advance on the practical understanding gained through experience of particular excellent things." He is correct; metaphysics thinks that such a formulation "would represent an advance," because one ought not to beg the question by appealing merely to the authority of the judge or to the particularity of the practice as the measure of value. For instance, Stout says that "a competent judge is someone who has mastered a repertoire of appropriate noninferential responses (ranging from revulsion to admiration) and the inferential habits involved in reflecting critically on such responses." But what defines "appropriate" responses other than the judges themselves? For Stout, it appears that appropriateness for each practice is defined ultimately in terms of what a competent judge would do, and whatever a competent judge does is considered appropriate because it is he or she that does it. To put the point somewhat differently, one might ask what these different manifestations of excellence, embedded in these various particular practices, share in common that merits all of them being called forms of excellence? Again, Stout can offer no answer because he rejects any attempt to define excellence in a comprehensive or metaphysical way. When Adams seeks to answer by saying that the excellence of any finite thing or practice consists in its resemblance to "God as the transcendent Good," Stout rejects this claim as "unwarranted reification."[55] In the end, however, Stout himself can

55. Ibid., 262, 264, 266, 264, 263, 266.

identify no measure of value beyond the authority of the judges themselves; he has no noncircular way to measure excellence: the judges are considered excellent because of their responses, and their responses are considered excellent because the judges are the ones making them.

This circularity becomes even more evident when Stout seeks to explain how one resolves an impasse between "conflicting communities of competent judges." Since he has no recourse to any universal evaluative standard, he can only appeal to the hope that "over time a [higher] class of competent judges" will emerge and establish its greater authority to decide such matters. What he has in mind is the formation of some critical "metapractice" by "which various human ethical practices can be judged comparatively." But by what common critical standard, I ask, will these meta-judges evaluate these different practices and community-specific evaluations? If there is no common or universal measure of value, the judges will simply have to fall back on their own authority or on the particularity of their own community-specific standard, which of course will simply perpetuate the conflict. Notice that Stout has nowhere to go from here except to keep hoping for and appealing to authority:

> The hope once again is that the claim to be a competent judge of such matters can at some point honestly be presented as an earned entitlement. Without the construction and development of such a practice, all we have are various communities making ill-informed, biased judgments of each other's valuations. Until some standards are developed for evaluating these judgments, the judgments themselves are likely to be biased and unreliable. This does not mean that they lack truth-value, for some of them are plainly mistaken. But calling some of them "mistaken" expresses an earned entitlement, according to the pragmatist, only in relation to the incipient metapractice.[56]

Here again we see Stout's Hegelian historicism without metaphysics. He is waiting for unbiased meta-standards to be developed historically, standards that the meta-judges can then use. But on what grounds are these meta-standards to be defined and justified in the first place? If there is no universal ground, then Stout can identify no legitimacy for these standards other than the fact that they are declared and used by the meta-judges themselves. Notice, for instance, his multiple appeals

---

56. Ibid., 264, 265.

to "earned entitlement." He suggests that at the meta-level, one can call a community-specific standard "mistaken" but only by appealing to the earned entitlement of a meta-judge in the midst of the metapractice. As we saw earlier, the claim to entitlement does not offer any independent reasons for accepting something to be true or morally valid. Instead, it grants permission or status to a claim—in this case, the status of the meta-judges and their declared standard. Once the posited standard is granted, one can then assess whether meta-judges are making inferential judgments to which they are entitled, i.e., whether they are logically consistent in drawing inferences from the givenness of their underlying standard. But there is no independent way to evaluate the validity of the meta-standard employed by the meta-judges themselves. Stout may insist that later history might come along and judge earlier standards to be deficient. But since there is no standard independent of this new judgment, the process would simply repeat the appeal to meta-judges all over again.

From a different angle, one might say that the nub of Stout's pragmatic moral theory is that it waits for moral standards to become commonplaces in history, and those standards have no deeper ground than the fact that have become widely accepted.[57] Prior to gaining such currency, this theory can only appeal to authoritative judges to legitimate such standards. Stout asserts that his theory is fully grounded in concrete reality, but I would venture to say that his theory "floats" untethered to anything deeper than the passing judgments of history. He appeals only to human practices as the ground of ethics and, as he himself partially concedes to Jackson, such an appeal can never make sense if one takes the theistic claim with full seriousness.[58]

---

57. For this reason, one might be tempted to call Stout's moral theory, in a strict literal sense, an *ethic of platitudes* because it waits for and appeals to the commonplaces of history as the ground of moral norms. But since the term "platitude" also carries the connotation of something insignificant, it would not do full justice either to ethics or to Stout's thoughtful and substantive attempt to think about the moral life. Nevertheless, I think his ethics and appeal to history without metaphysics fail to provide a sufficient ground for the validity of moral claims.

58. My critique of Stout's pragmatic moral theory is not meant to deny either the pragmatic insight, namely, that how we understand the world ought to make some practical difference, or the fact that metaphysical claims have pragmatic implications and consequences. Rather, my point is only to insist that such claims must ultimately be metaphysically justified and not merely justified by appeal to pragmatic consequences or human practices. In short, one needs to be a "metaphysical pragmatist" rather than

Since I began this chapter with a critique of strong historicism, let me conclude by making more explicit how Stout's thought exemplifies this same set of problems. The basic difficulty, again, is that either strong historicism must tacitly introduce some universal, metaphysical element or else it ends up succumbing to relativism. This is the case because insofar as strong historicism argues that all rationality is finally tradition-specific, it ends up taking a part (a tradition) to define the whole and, thus, ends up merely with the relativism of parts. In Stout's case, this occurs because anything he might wish to say about universal moral obligations must be defined, according to his lights, from within social practices that are in *all* respects creatures of a specific historical tradition, i.e., he seeks to ground claims about the whole by appealing to what is unique to a part. Alternatively, if he says nothing about universal moral obligations, then he is the relativist that he denies being. Thus, given his stated view, he is stuck with either an implicit relativism (of trying to justify the whole in terms of the part) or an explicit relativism (not making any universal claims at all). Take, for example, his central distinction between "truth" and "justification." His "modest pragmatism" does not want to abandon the notion of truth, and thus succumb to relativism, but neither does it say much about what truth is. His modest pragmatism is "minimalist" when it comes to defining truth; in particular, he emphasizes its "cautionary use." When we use the word "true," he suggests, we are cautiously and humbly reminding others and ourselves that some of our current justified beliefs (those to which we are entitled) may turn out to be false. But is this distinction between "truth" and "justification," one might ask, itself universally true or is it merely the product of some specific tradition? Stout recognizes the troubling issue here: "Does not my emphasis on social practices require me in the end to view truth [merely] as a matter of communal agreement?" He answers as follows:

> There is indeed a sense in which our use of the term "true" rests on agreement within a social practice. But the agreement that matters in this context is not agreement specifying *which* substantive ethical claims are true, as if the community as a whole

---

an "empirical pragmatist" or a "neopragmatist." This illuminating distinction is made by Gamwell in a discussion in which he contrasts what he calls Iris Murdoch's Platonic or metaphysical pragmatism with the empirical pragmatism of Dewey and the neopragmatism of Rorty. See Gamwell, "On the Loss of Theism," 179–83.

could decide such things by fiat. It is rather a practical agreement that we exhibit when we use the terms "true" and "justified" differently. *What we have agreed to do, in effect, is to treat truth in practice as something that cannot be settled simply by communal agreement. It is this underlying social agreement . . . that gives the term "true" its nonrelative status* [italics added in these last two lines].[59]

This is a curious answer to a critical question. In effect, Stout says that we have decided by social agreement not to treat truth as merely the product of social agreement—"truth" is declared nonrelative based on a communal agreement that is itself relative. We see here again the problem of Stout's Hegelian historicism without metaphysics; he has nowhere to turn finally except to the particularity of authorities or communal agreement. He keeps insisting, of course, that the definition of valid moral norms is not merely the product of social agreement. As he states, "It is very important to see that in endorsing the view that norms are creatures of social practices, I am not endorsing a reduction of truth or objectivity to what some community takes to be true or objective. Our socially instituted conceptual norms do not in fact permit such a reduction."[60] Notice even here, however, he ends up having to appeal to socially instituted norms as a last-ditch effort to try to ward off relativism. But given the fact that one community or tradition may adopt a cautionary use of truth (truth ≠ justification), there is nothing pragmatically or rationally necessary on Stout's account for other communities to do likewise. Hence, another tradition may end up with a communal agreement defining truth simply as social consensus (truth = justification). In each of these cases, the definition of truth is relative to the tradition that defines it. Thus, in the end, Stout's distinction between "truth" and "justification" is itself relative to a tradition. And if this fundamental distinction is itself relative, then so too is Stout's notion of moral validity that presupposes it.[61]

This same set of issues shows up in Stout's defense of democracy. Over against the new traditionalists, Stout wants to champion democ-

---

59. Stout, *Democracy and Tradition*, 251, 253, 276, 276–77.
60. Ibid., 277.
61. My discussion here of Stout's distinction between "truth" and "justification" is informed by Gamwell, "Comment on Jeffrey Stout," 8–9; and by Gamwell, "Metaphysics of Democracy," 19.

racy—and its affirmations of equality, pluralism, public discourse, etc.—as a morally significant form of social and political life. Yet, in the end, his defense simply appeals to democracy as another particular tradition set over against the particular tradition(s) envisioned by the new traditionalists. "Democracy," Stout says, "*is* a tradition." Among those who subscribe to this tradition, "it inculcates certain habits of reasoning, certain attitudes toward ... authority ..., and love for certain goods and virtues, ..." For those of us within this tradition, "we are committed to the legitimacy of constitutional democracy under circumstances like ours and to reasoning with one another about political questions in a way that perfects and honors our democratic norms." But there is nothing here approaching the idea of democracy as a universal moral imperative. As Stout plainly states, "I am not claiming that democracy is the essence of modernity" or an essential requirement for human community as such. Instead,

> I am trying [merely] to articulate a form of [democratic] pluralism ... without fudging on its own premises.... I see this pluralism primarily as an existing feature of the [current] political culture, not as a philosophical doctrine needing to be imposed on [the culture]. Our political culture is already pluralistic in the relevant sense. What I have tried to supply is a philosophical statement of what this [given] pluralism involves.[62]

Again, the emphasis here is on the givenness of particularity; on the givenness of a tradition and its political culture. I will have occasion to say more about Stout's view of democracy in my chapter on Hauerwas, but for now I simply want to note that, on his account, democracy is finally relative to the community and tradition that presupposes it. As in the case of truth, there is no rational or universal necessity for a society or tradition to adopt a democratic way of life.

Summary

In this chapter I have sought to offer a further critical response to the diagnostic and prescriptive accounts offered by my three interlocutors. In their different ways, MacIntyre, Hauerwas, and Stout all contend that theology must ultimately rely on and appeal to the particularity of tradition to regain its voice in the broader culture. As strong historicists,

---

62. Stout, *Democracy and Tradition*, 3, 2, 289, 296–97.

they rule out any appeal to common or universal reasons. But such positions, I have argued, must either presuppose metaphysics, which they explicitly deny, or end up with some form of relativism. Theology can only be true to its central claims about the reality and necessity of God when it explicitly affirms and defends such claims as the metaphysical claims that they indeed are. As I will seek to show in Part Two, modern theology has largely lost its authentic voice because it has abandoned or left unsubstantiated the metaphysical dimensions of its own claims. Only a theology that seeks to assert and defend such claims within the context of modernity's formal commitments can hope to change the social location and influence of theology in the twenty-first century.

PART TWO

A Typological Analysis
A Study of Six Theological Approaches

4

Defining the Terms of Analysis

IN PART ONE, I ARGUED THAT THE WIDESPREAD DENIAL OF METAPHYSics in modern thought lies at the root of why theology has been marginalized in public discourse. Here in Part Two, I will specifically examine how the aversion to metaphysics has affected theology and theological ethics. To accomplish this, I will develop a typology that identifies six different theological approaches, as illustrated by six different modern or contemporary theologians. In particular, I will examine how each of them addresses the question of metaphysics in relation to his or her own theology and theological ethics. But in order to develop this typology, I must first identify the terms of analysis.

Defining the Typological Categories

As we saw earlier in our discussions of MacIntyre, Hauerwas, and Stout, understanding the plight of theology in the modern world is tied in some way to the question of Enlightenment reason. In order to figure out what has gone wrong, one must understand how various theological approaches either embrace or reject the modern understanding of reason, either in part or in whole. To be sure, I have suggested that the key issue centers on how these different approaches handle the metaphysical claims of theology; yet how one approaches these claims is certainly related to one's understanding of rationality. To unbundle this cluster of issues, I will offer a four-fold set of categories that I have developed from the work of Franklin Gamwell.[1]

In his 1990 book *The Divine Good: Modern Moral Theory and the Necessity of God*, Gamwell analyzes the general contours of modern

---

1. I first introduced this set of categories in Meyer, "On Keeping Theological Ethics Theological," 28–30.

moral thought in terms of what he calls the "modern commitment" and the "dominant consensus." In referring to the "modern commitment," Gamwell observes that one of the defining characteristics of the modern age has been the "increasing affirmation of autonomy." By this he means the ongoing formal commitment to justifying our various claims ultimately by appeal to reason and common experience rather than by appeal to authority, such as the authority of a book, person, institution, or tradition. This modern project may also be described, as I discussed in my introduction, as a commitment to *formal* autonomy or secularity, which refers, again, to the modern attempt to foster independent judgment by encouraging individuals to use their own reason in the context of communal life and discourse. This dedication to formal autonomy or secularity need not and should not mean a denigration of tradition or a disrespect for the achievements of the past, but it does mean that whatever a tradition claims to be true is not made true or shown to be true simply because it claims it.[2] Hence, the claims of tradition must finally be validated by appeal to reason and common experience and not by appeal to authority as such. Even a strong proponent of tradition like Gadamer appears to recognize this when he admits that "what the authority says . . . can, in principle, be discovered to be true."[3] Or as Glenn Tinder states in his review of George Marsden's notion of Christian scholarship:

> We must address one another on the basis of reason. Christians have no business asserting that something is true because God says that it is. They must support whatever positions they take with evidence and reasons that non-Christians can rationally weigh.[4]

Another way of describing the modern commitment, Gamwell suggests, is in terms of human fallibility. All human understandings involve

---

2. Gamwell, *Divine Good*, 3; see 3–14 for a discussion of Gamwell's terms.

3. Gadamer, *Truth and Method*, 280. Gadamer, however, does not appear to be consistent on this point; on the next page he writes: "tradition has a justification that lies beyond rational grounding" (281).

4. Tinder, "Exercising a Christian Intellect," 627. Like Gadamer, Tinder, too, does not seem to be consistent on this point. Later he says that Christian scholars will unavoidably have to appeal to special revelation at some point (see 628–29). These inconsistencies suggest to me that both Gadamer and Tinder also accept the modern denial of metaphysics and, thus, ultimately do not think that public reasons can be given. Instead, some appeal to the authority of tradition or revelation must be made.

interpretation, and all interpretations are "subject to possible distortion" and error. Hence, "a claim is never valid simply because someone or some group says that it is. In this sense," Gamwell continues, "any claim is open to question, and, therefore, no particular expression or tradition or institution can be authoritative in the heteronomous sense, no matter how pervasive adherence to it has been or how long it has endured."[5]

In order to use Gamwell's notion of the "modern commitment" for analyzing theology, I will break it down into two sub-components, which I will call respectively the *commitment to intelligibility* and the *commitment to credibility*. By "intelligibility" I mean a commitment to try to make our claims understandable and plausible to others. By "credibility" I mean a commitment to try to make our claims rationally convincing to others. There is a subtle but important difference between merely a commitment to making a claim plausible, and the more demanding commitment to making it convincing. According to the *OED*, "plausible" denotes a statement or argument that seems reasonable or probable at first blush; one that has the "appearance . . . of truth, reasonableness, or worth; [one that is] apparently acceptable or trustworthy (but often with implication of mere appearance)." In contrast, the word "convince" denotes a more systematic effort "to satisfy or persuade by argument or evidence." This distinction suggests that a commitment to making a claim convincing entails a more intentional, detailed, rigorous, and sustained effort to offer a rational defense of that claim than does merely a commitment to plausibility.[6]

---

5. Gamwell, *Divine Good*, 4.

6. *Compact Edition of the Oxford English Dictionary* (complete text), 1971 ed., s.v. "plausible," "convince," and "credible." In setting forth this distinction, I recognize that the terms "convince" and "credible" might also carry some other connotations that are more problematical. For instance, the *OED* also defines "convince" in terms of overcoming, overpowering, vanquishing, conquering; "to cause (a person) to admit, as established to his satisfaction, that which is advanced in argument." These definitions suggest the troubling legacy of what I earlier called the discursive error in Western thought, the entrenched assumption that sound arguments force or compel others to assent to them. Alternatively, what I have in mind is a commitment to offering quality reasons to others that invite, not coerce, their assent. This seems to be implied in the above definition when it speaks of offering reasons to others that are "established to his [or her] satisfaction." In other words, the listener freely makes up his or her own mind about whether the evidence or argument is satisfactorily established. Hence, I judge that one can be committed to offering reasons to others that they can find rationally convincing without seeking to coerce or vanquish them.

Unfortunately, there is no fluid noun-form of the verb "to convince" other than the rarely used term "convincement." It would be rather awkward to speak of a "com-

What Gamwell means by the "modern commitment" is a commitment to both intelligibility and credibility, since making something credible presupposes making it intelligible and plausible. Nevertheless, it is useful to make such a distinction because it provides a diagnostic nuance that helps us to understand what has happened in modern and contemporary theology. For, as I will seek to show in subsequent chapters, many theologians have, if at all, only partially embraced the modern commitment, i.e., they have attempted to make their claims publicly intelligible without fully committing to making them publicly credible. As I will also seek to show, the reason why many of them either avoid or eventually abandon the commitment to credibility is because they accept the modern assumption that metaphysical claims cannot be made rationally convincing. This brings us to Gamwell's second thematic phrase: the "dominant consensus."

In speaking of the "dominant consensus," Gamwell refers to the widespread view in modern philosophy that believes ethics can be properly understood independently of theism. Whatever differences there may be among modern philosophers, Gamwell observes, nearly all of them accept the autonomy of ethics from religion. He attributes this dominant consensus primarily to the influence of Kant. In spite of Kant's attempt to offer an argument that makes the existence of God a necessary postulate of practical reason, his lasting legacy has been his fundamental view that the ground of morality is independent of theism. What lies behind this view, Gamwell notes, is Kant's most enduring influence, namely, his denial that there can be any theoretical knowledge of reality as such, including any metaphysical knowledge of God.[7] In order to make effective use of Gamwell's notion of the "dominant consensus,"

---

mitment to convincement," so instead I speak of a "commitment to credibility." The term "credibility," however, floats a bit ambiguously between "plausible" and "convince." According to the *OED*, "credible" indicates, on the one hand, "capable of being believed" and indicates, on the other hand, "deserving credit" or belief. These two definitions mark off a spectrum between first-blush plausibility, on one end, and deserving assent based on more sustained evidence and argument, on the other. In using the term "credibility," I want to emphasize this latter connotation: a commitment to making one's claims rationally convincing. In sum, the English language appears to lack a fully pristine term to describe a sustained commitment to offering reasons to others that invite their rational assent without carrying any connotation of coercion. Nevertheless, it is precisely such a non-coercive view of argument that I have in mind when I speak of a commitment to credibility.

7. Gamwell, *Divine Good*, 8–9.

I will again break it down into two sub-components, which I will call respectively the *consensus on the autonomy of ethics* and the *consensus on the absence of metaphysics*. By "absence of metaphysics," I mean that modern thought after Kant has been decidedly postmetaphysical, i.e., it has been widely held that one can make rational and coherent sense of the world apart from metaphysics.[8] Gamwell's insight is to recognize how pervasive acceptance of these two positions (autonomy of ethics and absence of metaphysics) has been in modern philosophy and to recognize how the former is ultimately dependent on the latter. Put simply, Kant's Second Critique presupposes his First. If dedication to intelligibility and credibility reflect the formal commitments of modernity, then the dominant consensus concerning the autonomy of ethics and the absence of metaphysics reflects the substantive conclusions of modernity; the former points to modernity's embrace of formal autonomy and secularity while the latter signifies its gravitation toward substantive autonomy and secularism.

By unpacking Gamwell's notions of the modern commitment and the dominant consensus, I have identified four analytical categories that are valuable tools for diagnosing and mapping the condition of modern theology and theological ethics. In order to gain a clearer understanding of what has happened, one must discern how theologians have responded to (1) the commitment to intelligibility, (2) the commitment to credibility, (3) the dominant consensus concerning the autonomy of ethics, and (4) the dominant consensus concerning the absence of metaphysics. In offering these categories, however, I recognize that I face a dual challenge. On the one hand, I must formulate them in a relatively straightforward and non-prejudicial manner that makes them widely usable and acceptable. In short, they must be sufficiently inclusive to enable each theologian to recognize how he or she fits into them. On the other hand, these categories cannot become so broadly defined as to lose their analytical insight. Keeping these challenges in mind, I would presume, for instance, that MacIntyre would say that he is committed

8. Somewhat analogous to MacIntyre's distinction between active and passive atheism, one might say that the postmetaphysical character of modernity has both a more active side: an *aversion* to metaphysics (an intentional opposition to or avoidance of metaphysics), and a more passive side: a taken for granted acceptance of the *absence* of metaphysics. Though I use this latter term to define the overarching character of the postmetaphysical consensus, I will use both terms (aversion and absence) in my analysis and use them basically interchangeably.

to making theological claims rationally credible in an indirect manner through comparative competition among incommensurable traditions. In fact, he would insist that this is the only way to show the credibility of such claims. In contrast, when I think of a commitment to credibility, I think of reasoning directly in common with others (what I earlier called "common criticism"), which requires that we seek to make our claims mutually intelligible and credible. As I will show, some contemporary theologians follow MacIntyre in affirming only an indirect form of rational credibility; others are partially committed to making their claims directly credible, but they eventually abandon that commitment at some point; still others fully embrace a direct commitment to credibility; and yet still others reject a commitment to credibility in either a direct or indirect form. Given this range of views, I will define a "commitment to credibility" as a commitment to making theological claims rationally convincing in either a direct or indirect manner.

Likewise, when it comes to metaphysics, there is some range of perspectives on the theological landscape. Many theologians, for example, implicitly or explicitly accept the absence of metaphysics in modern thought, and thus leave the metaphysical claims of theology unsubstantiated and embedded in the background of theological discussion. Others, however, bring the question of metaphysics to the fore but, at the same time, do not believe that such claims can be shown to be rationally credible. And yet still others bring metaphysical claims to the foreground and do so in a manner that seeks to make such claims rationally and publicly convincing. As becomes evident here, one needs to be mindful of two distinct uses of the term "metaphysics." In other words, because I am breaking out modernity's formal commitments from its substantive conclusions, I am analytically separating the question of metaphysics from the question of whether it is rationally credible. From the perspective of modern secularism, for instance, these two issues are considered one and the same—the reason why metaphysics is absent from contemporary thought is because metaphysics is not considered to be credible. But since I am seeking to discern how various theologians respond both to the formal and substantive elements of modernity, I will distinguish these two questions. So from one angle, I will ask: does the theologian accept the absence of metaphysics or, on the contrary, does he or she believe that metaphysical claims should be brought to the fore of theological discussion? That is, does he or she systematically explicate the character of reality as such and, in so doing, take up the question of God as a metaphysical question? Then from another angle, I will ask: does the theologian seek to show that metaphysics is rationally credible? Thus, with this distinction in place, I will define "metaphysics" to refer to the explicit and systematic attempt to understand and articulate the character of reality as such. Relatedly, I will take the word "ontology" to be basically synonymous with "metaphysics" insofar as both ontology and metaphysics seek to explicate the character of being or reality as such. To be sure, one can develop a metaphysic of becoming rather than an ontology or metaphysic of being; but in either case, one is seeking systematically to depict the ultimate character of reality, which is my main analytical concern. With these prefatory remarks now in place, let me set forth the four categories in the following schematic manner:

Four Analytical Categories

Modern Commitment
1. Commitment to Intelligibility
2. Commitment to Credibility

Dominant Consensus
3. Autonomy of Ethics
4. Absence of Metaphysics

Commitment to Intelligibility (I)	Commitment to Credibility (C)	Autonomy of Ethics (AE)	Absence of Metaphysics (AM)
Is the theologian committed in some way to making theological claims *intelligible and plausible* to those in the academy and the wider public as well as to those in the church?	Is the theologian committed to making theological claims *rationally convincing* (in either a direct or indirect manner) to those in the academy and the wider public as well as to those in the church?	Does the theologian accept the dominant modern assumption about the *autonomy of ethics*—that ethics can be coherently conceived and understood apart from the question of God?	Does the theologian accept the dominant, post-metaphysical character of modern thought and thus *accept the absence of metaphysics*?

I will seek to analyze and understand how each theologian answers these four questions. Since each question must finally be answered either affirmatively or negatively, the answers will ultimately identify and distinguish different approaches in modern and contemporary theology. These different answers can be schematically summarized as follows:

Categorizing Responses to The Four Questions

Modern Commitment:
I = intelligibility
C = credibility

Dominant Consensus:
AE = autonomy of ethics
AM = absence of metaphysics

A theologian will ultimately respond either affirmatively (+) or negatively (-) to each of these four questions and categories:
I+ = accepts the commitment to intelligibility
I- = rejects the commitment to intelligibility

C+ = accepts the commitment to credibility
C- = rejects the commitment to credibility

AE+ = accepts the dominant consensus concerning the autonomy of ethics
AE- = rejects the autonomy of ethics: asserts that ethics must ultimately be understood in relation to the divine

AM+ = accepts the dominant consensus concerning the absence of metaphysics
AM- = rejects the dominant consensus concerning the absence of metaphysics and thus reasserts the centrality and importance of metaphysics for theology

---

Given that there are four different categories, and given that there are basically two possible responses to each of them, it is soon evident that there are sixteen different logical combinations. Not all of these combinations, however, are meaningful possibilities. For example, it makes no sense to say that a theologian is committed to making claims rationally convincing to others (C+) and yet, at the same time, that he or she is not committed to making such claims intelligible (I-); for, again, to be committed to credibility is already implicitly to be committed to intelligibility. Likewise, it does not make sense to say that a theologian is committed to making theological claims rationally convincing (C+), rejects the absence of metaphysics (AM-), and yet, at the same time, accepts the modern autonomy of ethics (AE+). For if one metaphysically asserts that God is the source and end of all things, and furthermore affirms that this claim can be made rationally credible, then it does not make sense to say that the moral life could be properly conceived apart from such a divine ground and telos.

Thus, as I survey the different logical combinations, I judge that there are basically six "live" options in modern or contemporary theology. By describing them as "live," I do not mean to suggest that all six are equally viable. On the contrary, I will seek to make a case for the superiority of one of them, the one that seeks to make the metaphysical claims of theology publicly credible. Rather, by describing them as "live," I mean simply that they are living approaches that have been vigorously pursued and thoughtfully articulated by different theologians in modern or contemporary thought. These six options (as well as the contradictory and nonviable combinations) can be schematically identified as follows:[9]

Mapping The Theological Alternatives

	AE+AM+	AE-AM+	AE+AM-	AE-AM-
I-C-	************	I-C-AE-AM+	************	************
I-C+	************	************	************	************
I+C-	I+C-AE+AM+	I+C-AE-AM+	************	I+C-AE-AM-
I+C+	************	+C+AE-AM+	************	I+C+AE-AM-

---

9. I am indebted to my colleagues Jeff Bay (statistics) and Drew Crain (biology) for helping me to formulate a schematic representation of the different logical combinations.

As one can see, the formal commitments to intelligibility (I) and credibility (C) are listed on the left-vertical axis.[10] As one moves from the top (I-C-) to the bottom (I+C+), one increasingly embraces a commitment to make theological claims intelligible and credible in some manner. Modernity's substantive conclusions regarding the autonomy of ethics (AE) and the absence of metaphysics (AM) are listed across the top on the horizontal axis. As one moves from left (AE+AM+) to right (AE-AM-), one increasingly rejects the dominant substantive conclusions of modernity. Hence, those combinations found on the left half of the

---

10. Let me say more here about the contradictory and nonviable combinations. As suggested above, all the alternatives set forth in row two across (I-C+) are contradictory insofar as a commitment to credibility presupposes a commitment to intelligibility, which is here explicitly denied. Similarly, all of the alternatives found in column three down (AE+AM-) represent a nonviable set of options for theology insofar as it concomitantly endorses the autonomy of ethics and affirms the necessity of metaphysics. This combination translates into a systematic endorsement of a nontheistic ethic and metaphysics, such as offered by Iris Murdoch (I would describe her philosophy as I+C+AE+AM-). In short, I cannot see how a *theologian* would want to affirm metaphysics and, at the same time, affirm the autonomy of ethics; because the former seeks to show how God is the source and end of all things, including the moral life, whereas the latter denies this necessary connection. With these two group of options off the table, it leaves three specific combinations to address: (I-C-AE+AM+)—this combination poses the odd and unlikely position of being fully modern in substantive conclusions (AE+AM+) while rejecting modernity's formal commitments (I-C-). Why would a theologian accept the modern autonomy of ethics and, at the same, insist that theology reject any commitment to intelligibility or credibility? Even Hauerwas's theology, as we will see, rejects the autonomy of ethics. At best, this combination would represent some hermetically sealed theology—one that neither critiques the substantive positions of modernity nor adopts its formal commitments. Alternatively, (I+C+AE+AM+) represents a secularistic modern position. What would it mean for a theologian to be fully committed to making theological claims rationally intelligible and credible and yet, at the same time, accept the autonomy of ethics and the absence of metaphysics? How would they rationally redeem the metaphysical claims of theology while, at the same time, denying the metaphysical enterprise? Moreover, this theologian would also be trying to credibly argue that God is the source and end of all things, including the moral life, and, yet, concomitantly affirm that ethics is autonomous from theism. In short, this combination does not seem to yield a viable theological alternative. Finally, (I-C-AE-AM-) represents a full rejection of both modernity's substantive conclusions and its formal commitments. In effect, this combination involves the assertion of a theistic metaphysics and, at the same time, a rejection of any attempt to make such a metaphysic either intelligible or credible. But as I will show, even Milbank's radical orthodoxy embraces some degree of public intelligibility in order to critique modern secularity and secularism by means of retrieving a premodern ontology. In sum, it seems difficult, if not impossible, to explicate a systematic metaphysics or ontology without some commitment to making it at least partly intelligible.

chart, which, in fact, is where we see four of the six options, are still under the influence of modernity's prevailing substantive assumptions. By contrast, those approaches listed on the far right-hand side are those that most directly challenge modernity's dominant consensus. Though the reader will understand each of these six types more clearly after having seen them exemplified in the thought of a specific theologian, let me offer here a skeletal description of each:

I+C-AE+AM+: This approach, one might say, is the most modern in the sense that it embodies the prevailing assumptions of modern thought in regard to religion and the wider culture. It is committed to making theological claims intelligible, but it does not think that such claims can ultimately be made rationally convincing. Even though it affirms a theological understanding of the moral life, it is circumspect about the limits of such theological claims. Hence, it accepts the modern autonomy of ethics and thereby accepts the validity of a secularistic or non-theistic ethic. Perhaps needless to say, it also accepts the absence of metaphysics and thus leaves the metaphysical claims of theology muted in the background, unredeemed and unsubstantiated.

I+C-AE-AM+: This option is also committed to making theological claims intelligible to the wider public. But unlike the first type, this one rejects the modern assumption that ethics can be coherently understood apart from theology or the question of God. Yet, because this approach also accepts the absence of metaphysics, it, too, ultimately abandons a commitment to credibility at some point, thus leaving the metaphysical claims of theology submerged in the background.

I-C-AE-AM+: This approach rejects the notion that theology should be committed to making its claims either publicly intelligible or credible, rejects the modern claim for the autonomy of ethics but, at the same time, accepts the absence of metaphysics. Thus, once again, the metaphysical claims of theology are left undeveloped and unsubstantiated.

I+C+AE-AM+: This type is committed to both intelligibility and credibility in an indirect form, rejects the modern autonomy of ethics, but like the three previous approaches, accepts the absence of metaphysics and thus leaves the metaphysical claims of theology embedded in the background. Hence, this approach attempts to make theological claims rationally credible in an indirect manner, but not by seeking to make the metaphysical claims of theology convincing in a direct way.

I+C-AE-AM-: If the first type is the most modern, then this approach is in some ways the most anti-modern. It rejects the absence of metaphysics by reasserting the necessity and centrality of a theological metaphysics or ontology. It likewise rejects any notion of an autonomous or secularistic ethic. It does so by at least partially embracing a commitment to intelligibility—seeking to challenge and engage other views in the academy and wider culture. At the same time, however, it sharply rejects any commitment to making theological or metaphysical claims rationally convincing. Hence, one has here the reassertion of metaphysics without a commitment to making such claims publicly credible.

I+C+AE-AM-: This last approach is anti-modern in regard to modernity's substantive conclusions while being fully modern in terms of its formal commitments. That is to say, it sharply challenges the modern consensus concerning the absence of metaphysics by asserting the centrality and necessity of a theistic metaphysics for understanding all of reality, including the moral life. Hence, it likewise unequivocally challenges the modern autonomy of ethics by arguing that no ethic can be finally coherent apart from an implicit or explicit affirmation of the divine reality. Yet, unlike the previous type, this approach embraces both the modern commitment to intelligibility and credibility, thus seeking to make theological and metaphysical claims publicly understandable and convincing.

I will later argue that this last type represents the most coherent and fruitful approach for theology because it explicitly seeks to articulate and defend theology's metaphysical claims about the reality and necessity of God, and it seeks to show how no aspect of existence, including the moral life, can ultimately be coherently understood apart from the divine. At the same time, this approach seeks to communicate and defend such claims in a manner that respects the formal autonomy and integrity of each person—by offering reasons to others that invite their understanding and assent while recognizing and respecting their capacity for individual judgment made in the context of conversation and community. This approach affirms the true gains of the Enlightenment (affirming formal autonomy and democracy over heteronomy and authoritarianism) while squarely rejecting its errors (the denial of metaphysics, the autonomy of ethics, and the drift toward secularism). If the error of modern liberalism has been its attempt to privatize religion, and if, conversely, the error of religious conservatism has been its attempt to impose religion on public life by basing its religious claims ultimately on appeals to authority, then this last approach avoids both of these errors by encouraging religious voices to participate in public life, but it requires them, like all participants, to seek to offer convincing reasons to others for their theological and metaphysical claims.

Outlining the Typology

Whenever one offers or encounters a theological typology, especially one that pertains to theology and public life, one cannot help but recall H. Richard Niebuhr's *Christ and Culture*. Without presuming parity between my typology and Niebuhr's classic, let me offer three points of comparison for the sake of clarifying my methodological approach.

First, as already indicated, I will, unlike Niebuhr, explicitly identify which of my six types that I judge to offer the most promising path for theology. Whereas Niebuhr left his endorsement of one of his five types merely implicit (his implicit endorsement of "Christ as the Transformer of Culture"), I will explicitly make a case for one of my types (I+C+AE-AM-) as offering the most adequate alternative. Some critics accuse Niebuhr of "rigging" his typology and then leaving his normative conclusions implicit—as if his study were merely a neutral sociological description.[11] Let me say openly that the development of my typology emerged gradually from my hypothesis that the absence of metaphysics in modern thought has been a primary cause for theology's marginalization in the academy and wider culture. Consequently, I have sought to understand how different theologians handle the metaphysical claims of theology and, relatedly, how they view the relationship between theology and rationality, i.e., whether they think theological claims can and ought to be made publicly intelligible and credible. My development of four analytical categories and six typological approaches emerged gradually from my attempt to map and critically assess this terrain.

Second, given the fact that I have four analytical categories (I, C, AE, AM) compared to Niebuhr's two (Christianity and culture), my typology unfortunately does not lend itself to obvious or felicitous names

---

11. In summarizing Hauerwas's and Willimon's criticism of Niebuhr in *Resident Aliens*, William Werpehowski uses this term to describe their criticism of Niebuhr's *Christ and Culture*. See Werpehowski, *American Protestant Ethics and the Legacy of H. Richard Niebuhr*, 107.

for its different types. Whereas Niebuhr has memorable chapter titles, such as "Christ Against Culture," "Christ Above Culture," "The Christ of Culture," etc., I have merely a list of alternative combinations that is more reminiscent of Morse code than poetry! My attempt to overcome this deficiency is related to my final point of comparison.

Third, unlike Niebuhr, whose various types each focus on a cluster of different Christian thinkers throughout history, I will focus instead on a single, different modern or contemporary theologian for each of my of six types. The six theologians that I will study are: James Gustafson, Reinhold Niebuhr, Stanley Hauerwas, Jean Porter, John Milbank, and Franklin Gamwell. As indicated, my six types represent different "live" options in theology—options that have been vigorously pursued by important modern or contemporary theologians. In choosing these six thinkers, I recognize that I could have selected others (Karl Barth, H. Richard Niebuhr, and Schubert Ogden come to mind), but these six vividly illustrate the different types and, apart from Niebuhr and the recently retired Gustafson, are current scholars seeking to influence the future course of theology and its stance toward public life. Needless to say, both Niebuhr and Gustafson are major theological figures in twentieth-century thought, and each continues to exert a profound influence on contemporary theology as well. Indeed, Gustafson continues to write and publish into the twenty-first century. Likewise, Hauerwas and Milbank are undoubtedly two of the most prominent and influential theologians today. Though Stout rightly labels them both as new traditionalists, there are some important differences between them that are revealed by my typology. Finally, though Porter and Gamwell are perhaps less well known than the other four, the work of each represents an important theological alternative—both in terms of my typology and in terms of contemporary thought in general.

Given the lack of obvious titles for my six types, I will initially describe each one using a short phrase that seeks to summarize the approach of my selected theologian. Within the context of each chapter, I will explain in due course why that phrase fittingly describes that theologian's particular approach. In brief, I will entitle and order my chapters in the following manner:

- *An Accountable Theology: The Approach of James Gustafson*
- *A Pragmatic Theology: The Approach of Reinhold Niebuhr*
- *A Witness Theology: The Approach of Stanley Hauerwas*
- *A Tradition-Engaged Theology: The Approach of Jean Porter*
- *A Radical-Orthodox Theology: The Approach of John Milbank*
- *A Transcendental-Process Theology: The Approach of Franklin Gamwell*

I will begin with Gustafson's "Accountable Theology" because his work, among the six alternatives, most embodies and reflects the prevailing assumptions of modern thought in regard to religion and the wider culture. From there, I will move on to Reinhold Niebuhr's "Pragmatic Theology," which also embraces some modernist elements but, unlike Gustafson, seeks to offer a sharper critique of culture and a more robust defense of Christian theism. I will then proceed into the anti-modernist neighborhood of new traditionalism, examining in succession the views of Hauerwas, Porter, and Milbank. Though Stout does not explicitly identify Porter as one of the new traditionalists, her "Tradition-Engaged Theology" takes its bearings explicitly and substantially from the work of MacIntyre. One can thus fairly and initially assume that she shares at least some of the new traditionalists' outlook. But, again, let me emphasize that there are also important differences between Hauerwas, Porter, and Milbank, which my analysis will seek to show. Finally, I conclude with the work of Gamwell and his "Transcendental-Process Theology." Gamwell's work embodies both an embrace and a critique of modernist elements—a combination that I judge to offer the most promising path for theology. Along with these brief descriptions, let me return to the schematic map in order to preview how I will analyze and typologize these six thinkers in the coming chapters:

Mapping The Theological Alternatives

	AE+AM+	AE-AM+	AE+AM-	AE-AM-
I-C-	************	Hauerwas's Witness Theology	************	************
I-C+	************	************	************	************
I+C-	Gustafson's Accountable Theology	Niebuhr's Pragmatic Theology	************	Milbank's Radical-Orthodox Theology
I+C+	************	Porter's Tradition-Engaged Theology	************	Gamwell's Transcendental-Process Theology

I will begin each chapter by offering a theological portrait of the selected theologian. The aim of the portrait is to describe some of his or her central views in a clear and recognizable manner. I neither intend nor presume that my portraits are exhaustive, either thematically or chronologically. Rather, like a portrait in profile, I aim to capture a realistic likeness that outlines some of their major themes without presuming to capture the fullness of their work.[12] In order to accomplish this, I will "fly close to the ground," drawing frequently on their own writings, in order to supply the reader with ample evidence to support the accuracy of my account. Having set forth the theologian's views in his or her own terms, I will then proceed in each chapter to offer a typological analysis using my four categories. I will seek to identify and describe

---

12. Since most of these theologians continue to write, I have made an effort to stay abreast of their current scholarship. However, since my aim is typological rather than chronological, I will not seek to show how their thought has developed over time up to the present (sometimes I will note changes over time, but this is not my systematic intent). Rather, my goal is to offer a thematic portrait of each theologian (one that illustrates a different alternative on the theological landscape) that is, on the whole, faithful to that theologian's own work and viewpoint.

how each theologian ultimately answers my four questions pertaining to I, C, AE, and AM. In different chapters, I will address these four categories in varying order, depending on what seems most fitting for each case. Having laid the groundwork in the portrait, my goal is to offer analysis that is evident, fair, and accurate. I will conclude each chapter with a critical assessment followed by a brief summary. In my assessment, I will offer an evaluation of each approach in terms of its handling of metaphysics and the claims of theology in public discourse.

Finally, let me note in advance that my portraits and chapters become longer as I proceed through the six types. There are multiple reasons for this. First, it is fair to say that the views of Gustafson, Niebuhr, and Hauerwas are all well-known and thus do not require as much detailed elaboration in my portraits. By contrast, the works of Porter, Milbank, and Gamwell, which I address in the later chapters, require more explication because their views are either less well-known or less well understood. Second, Porter, Milbank, and Gamwell are more explicitly philosophical and/or historical in developing their theological outlooks. Therefore, my portraits of their respective views require greater background and explanation. Third, with each additional chapter, I seek to construct a comparative conversation with the previous thinkers; thus the conversation grows more extensive as I proceed. And fourth, the subject of metaphysics, which is my central focus, is more explicitly and extensively addressed by the last few thinkers in my typology. Hence, I will give additional close attention to their views.

5

An Accountable Theology
The Approach of James Gustafson

Theological Portrait

JAMES GUSTAFSON'S SIGNIFICANT CONTRIBUTION TO THEOLOGY AND theological ethics over the past half-century is widely recognized. His approach is most succinctly captured in his 1981 Ryerson Lecture at the University of Chicago, entitled "Say Something Theological!" This important lecture was given during the same year that the first volume of his two-volume magnum opus, *Ethics from a Theocentric Perspective* (hereafter *Ethics*), was released. For many years this lecture was not widely available, but thankfully it has now been published in a collection of Gustafson's essays. Gustafson himself describes this lecture, addressed to his colleagues across all disciplines at the University of Chicago, as the most concise articulation of his theology.[1] I will use this lecture to provide a framework for my theological portrait, but I will also draw on his other major writings, especially his two-volume work, to sharpen and clarify my account.[2]

He begins the lecture by describing a friendly professional encounter with an eminent secular biologist who once put his arm around Gustafson's "shoulder and said, 'Gustafson, say something theological!' I had the presence of mind," Gustafson recalls, "to say, 'God.'" Gustafson proceeds to unpack this singular and powerful answer by briefly identifying some common perceptions of theology in the academy, and then

---

1. For Gustafson's comment about the importance of the Ryerson Lecture, see "Response to Critics," 185.

2. I offered an extended analysis of Gustafson's theology and ethics in a 1997 article that I will draw upon at various points in this chapter. See Meyer, "Ethics, Theism and Metaphysics."

how each theologian ultimately answers my four questions pertaining to I, C, AE, and AM. In different chapters, I will address these four categories in varying order, depending on what seems most fitting for each case. Having laid the groundwork in the portrait, my goal is to offer analysis that is evident, fair, and accurate. I will conclude each chapter with a critical assessment followed by a brief summary. In my assessment, I will offer an evaluation of each approach in terms of its handling of metaphysics and the claims of theology in public discourse.

Finally, let me note in advance that my portraits and chapters become longer as I proceed through the six types. There are multiple reasons for this. First, it is fair to say that the views of Gustafson, Niebuhr, and Hauerwas are all well-known and thus do not require as much detailed elaboration in my portraits. By contrast, the works of Porter, Milbank, and Gamwell, which I address in the later chapters, require more explication because their views are either less well-known or less well understood. Second, Porter, Milbank, and Gamwell are more explicitly philosophical and/or historical in developing their theological outlooks. Therefore, my portraits of their respective views require greater background and explanation. Third, with each additional chapter, I seek to construct a comparative conversation with the previous thinkers; thus the conversation grows more extensive as I proceed. And fourth, the subject of metaphysics, which is my central focus, is more explicitly and extensively addressed by the last few thinkers in my typology. Hence, I will give additional close attention to their views.

5

An Accountable Theology
The Approach of James Gustafson

Theological Portrait

JAMES GUSTAFSON'S SIGNIFICANT CONTRIBUTION TO THEOLOGY AND theological ethics over the past half-century is widely recognized. His approach is most succinctly captured in his 1981 Ryerson Lecture at the University of Chicago, entitled "Say Something Theological!" This important lecture was given during the same year that the first volume of his two-volume magnum opus, *Ethics from a Theocentric Perspective* (hereafter *Ethics*), was released. For many years this lecture was not widely available, but thankfully it has now been published in a collection of Gustafson's essays. Gustafson himself describes this lecture, addressed to his colleagues across all disciplines at the University of Chicago, as the most concise articulation of his theology.[1] I will use this lecture to provide a framework for my theological portrait, but I will also draw on his other major writings, especially his two-volume work, to sharpen and clarify my account.[2]

He begins the lecture by describing a friendly professional encounter with an eminent secular biologist who once put his arm around Gustafson's "shoulder and said, 'Gustafson, say something theological!' I had the presence of mind," Gustafson recalls, "to say, 'God.'" Gustafson proceeds to unpack this singular and powerful answer by briefly identifying some common perceptions of theology in the academy, and then

---

1. For Gustafson's comment about the importance of the Ryerson Lecture, see "Response to Critics," 185.

2. I offered an extended analysis of Gustafson's theology and ethics in a 1997 article that I will draw upon at various points in this chapter. See Meyer, "Ethics, Theism and Metaphysics."

by exploring the nature of theology itself. Within the academy, he notes, theological claims are often viewed as being "too soft" or subjective to deserve a respectful place in a serious community of inquiry. Relatedly, many tend to see theology as still reliant on appeals to authority rather than reason as the primary means of justifying its claims. Along this line, others are perhaps worried that theology might try to reclaim its medieval centrality and impose some form of authoritarian hegemony. In order to respond to these perceptions and concerns, Gustafson identifies and examines three aspects or dimensions of theology. "To say something theological," he contends, is (1) "to say something religious," (2) "to say something about how things really and ultimately are," and (3) "to say something ethical."[3] I will examine each of these in turn.

"Say Something Religious"

The religious aspect of theology, according to Gustafson, is grounded in the human affections and in the context of a religious tradition. Following in the legacy of John Calvin, Jonathan Edwards, Friedrich Schleiermacher and others, he emphasizes the affective dimension of human experience, especially the experience of piety. By "piety," Gustafson does not mean an overt religiosity or a visible emotion but rather a deep and settled disposition toward life and the world. This disposition is characterized by "a profound sense of dependence" and by an attitude of respect, gratitude, and devotion toward what is given in the world. This stance also includes a sense of recognition of and remorse for human failings as well as a sense of hope for future possibilities. Echoing Schleiermacher, Gustafson suggests that piety is "evoked by human experiences of dependence on powers we do not create and cannot fully master." In other words, "piety is not self-stimulated; [rather] it is a response to the powers, objective to ourselves, that bring life into being and sustain it, that bear down upon us, and threaten us."[4]

How one construes these objective powers is determined by how one defines the object of piety. Neither affectivity nor piety per se makes one religious, but rather how one construes the object of piety. For those who view these powers as indicative of a divine presence and reality, piety is religious or theistic in character. Such persons see an Ultimate

---

3. Gustafson, "Say Something Theological," 85–86, 86, 90, 95.
4. Ibid., 88, 87.

Power behind the powers that affect our lives. Alternatively, for those who interpret these powers as simply the manifestations and limitations of nature itself, piety is naturalistic or secularistic in character.[5] Thus, again, the key question is how does one construe the object that evokes the human response of piety? From a religious or theistic perspective, the source of evocation is understood ultimately to be God; this is where theology enters the conversation.

To borrow a fitting phrase from Brian Gerrish, one might say that Gustafson conceives of "theology within the limits of piety alone." As Gustafson himself puts it, "Theology has its deepest significance within the context of piety, and in the context of a historic religious tradition." Put even more succinctly, the task of "theology is reflection on the object of piety."[6] In these two lines, Gustafson highlights what he takes to be theology's triadic base: God as the object of piety, the human experience of piety itself, and an ongoing community of interpreters who construe this experience in religious or theistic terms. By operating out of a religious context, theology makes use of ideas and themes inherited from the biblical and Christian traditions. To be sure, like all interpreters, theologians make choices and selections from among the elements within these traditions—one emphasizes certain themes and texts more than others. Let me illustrate in reference to christology.

"Every effort to formulate a coherent Christology," says Gustafson in *Ethics*, "is selective of the biblical materials, and is determined in part by the issues that theologians and the churches face in particular times and places." In Gustafson's case, his selectivity is informed by the centrality of piety: "Jesus incarnates theocentric piety and fidelity." The gospel depictions of Jesus "clearly testify to . . . a vision of what perfect fidelity to God's governance requires. They powerfully show what human life, in fidelity to God and in openness to his empowering, can and ought to be—a life of courage and love grounded in an object of piety and fidelity that transcends the immediate objects of experience." For Gustafson, Christ reveals or represents not so much the character of God per se, since he thinks the divine nature is mostly inscrutable, but

5. See Gustafson, *Ethics*, 1:196, 33 for his use of the terms "basic piety" and "natural piety."

6. The phrase from Gerrish comes from the title of one of his essays: "Theology within the Limits of Piety Alone: Schleiermacher and Calvin's Notions of God." I am indebted to a footnote in Capetz, *God: A Brief History* for pointing me to this phrase and source; see 180 n. 31, 179 n. 11. Gustafson, "Say Something Theological," 86, 87.

rather the ideal of piety lived out in human life. Consequently, his theology is christonormative more in the sense that Christ defines the normative human response to the powers that bear down upon us than that He defines the normative nature of God as such—though Gustafson does make some nod in this direction as well. "Through the gospel accounts of [Jesus'] life and ministry," he remarks, "we can see and know something of the powers that bear down upon us and sustain us, and of the piety and the manner of life that are appropriate to them."[7]

In addition to selectively drawing upon biblical and theological traditions, Gustafson maintains that theology must also be open to criticizing and revising these traditions in light of new understandings and knowledge gained from the sciences. For instance, he believes that the Christian tradition has never fully come to terms with the implications of the Copernican revolution in science. Along this line, he approvingly quotes Ernst Troeltsch:

> "We obviously cannot lock out the consequences of a Copernican system. . . . In view of the uniformity of the entire universe opened up by spectral analysis, the geocentric and anthropocentric views of things must vanish. Man has to adapt himself to no longer being able to establish a physical centre of the universe. . . . At a certain point we [humans] emerged from the [cosmic] development, [and] at a certain point we will disappear again. More science does not say. As the beginning was without us, so will the end also be without us. Transferred to religion, this in sight means: the end is not that of the Apocalypse."[8]

According to Gustafson, Troeltsch rightly recognized that the anthropocentric suppositions of a pre-Copernican worldview have never been adequately challenged and displaced within Christianity itself. For a long time after Copernicus, Gustafson observes, persistent "anthropocentricism [even] kept scientists from seeing and understanding the significance of data. A break in the focus of concentration was required; if man is the measure (and not only the measurer) of all things, it is difficult to assess accurately the place of the human species in the long temporal scheme of things, and in the intricate web of the interdepen-

---

7. Gustafson, *Ethics*, 1:275, 276.

8. Ibid., 1:97–98. Gustafson cites Troeltsch, *Glaubenslehre*, 64, translated and quoted by B. A. Gerrish in "Ernst Troeltsch and the Possibility of a Historical Theology," in *Ernst Troeltsch and the Future of Theology*, ed. John Powell Clayton (Cambridge: Cambridge University Press, 1976) 117.

dence of things."⁹ Science eventually did break the anthropocentric spell, but Christianity still has not. This prime task awaits theology.

By tying theology to the religious notion of piety rather than to the more common notion of faith, Gustafson believes that theology is more true to religious experience and is better able to converse with other disciplines. The term "faith" carries too many unwanted connotations, e.g., it is too often associated with a presumption of a "divine beneficence [that] guarantees human fulfillment." Likewise, faith is often "contrasted with reason" because it is defined as a set of beliefs that is based on a "deposit of revelation" that is off limits to critical scrutiny. Gustafson finds these various assumptions to be untrue to the realities of experience, untrue to the integrity and authenticity of the religious life, and unhelpful in conversation with others in the academy and the wider culture. In contrast, religious piety, properly understood, connotes a spiritual stance toward the world that also recognizes human vulnerabilities and frailties. Furthermore, the notion of piety is more "open to learning" from other disciplines about the "powers that order life" and it "invite[s] rational justification."¹⁰

For Gustafson, the type of rational justification that theology and piety invite might best be described as secondary or indirect rather than primary or direct: he does not think that claims about the reality of God can be rationally justified in a logically necessary or straightforward manner. As he succinctly states in volume one of *Ethics*, "Without [religious] piety it is relatively meaningless to make a case for the existence or presence of God."¹¹ Nonetheless, he thinks that religious piety's construal of the world is still a defensible one—one for which "rational activity can provide backing and warrants." In short, he holds that the disposition and suppositions of religious piety are not "unreasonable."¹² But in what sense are they reasonable? Gustafson's answer becomes more clear when we turn to the second dimension of theology.

---

9. Gustafson, *Ethics*, 1:99.
10. Gustafson, "Say Something Theological," 87.
11. Gustafson, *Ethics*, 1:164.
12. Gustafson, "Say Something Theological," 87.

"Say Something About How Things Really and Ultimately Are"

If the first aspect of theology has to do primarily with the affective dimension of human experience, the second aspect focuses on the cognitive. Specifically, theology not only reflects on the experience of religious piety, but it also makes truth claims, such as anthropological claims about human experience, cosmological claims about the world, and metaphysical claims about the nature of ultimate reality. Gustafson, however, quickly downplays or backpedals from this cognitive task. "This aspect of the theological enterprise," he declares, "is always the most troublesome. Historically, theologians have often said too much with too great certainty about how things really and ultimately are."[13] On the one side, the problem stems from overstatement, from claiming to know more than we really know about God and the divine purpose in history. On the other side, the problem stems from overconfidence, from attaching too much certainty to our claims to knowledge. Gustafson suspects that theology has too often invoked some form of epistemological privilege for its claims. This presumption of privilege, which appeals either to special revelation or to some form of rational certitude, leads to dogmatism.

What is needed instead, he believes, is an attitude of intellectual humility. Fortunately, he states, this attitude has been found at various points in Christian history:

> Throughout the Western theological tradition there have always been those wise persons who have felt obliged to say as much as they could and dared to say on the basis of rational reflection on nature and experience or on the basis of the accounts given in the biblical materials, or a combination of the two. Then they have properly and candidly admitted the final inadequacy of human words about God, and warn themselves and others about the presumptuousness of theology while defending its necessity.[14]

Gustafson's ambivalence about the cognitive aspect of theology is captured here when he warns of the "presumptuousness of theology while [at the same time] defending its necessity." This necessity arises from

---

13. Ibid., 91.
14. Ibid.

the fact that theology inevitably makes truth claims, including metaphysical claims about the reality of God. As he says at one point, "some evidences for the reality of God need to be adduced if only to avoid the charge that God is purely a projection of the human imagination."[15] Therefore, if the root experience of piety is indeed induced by powers beyond ourselves and ultimately by a divine Power that originates and sustains the world, then Gustafson himself recognizes that "a theologian must say what he or she can about those powers and propose a way of construing the world in their light."[16]

The key word here is *construing*; drawing on the work of Julian Hartt, Gustafson describes theology as "a way of construing the world."[17] According to Hartt, "a construing belief" is "more *a believing* than it is the finished product commonly suggested by *belief*." For example, "belief in God is a construing belief" and entails "a declaration of intention both to 'see' all things belonging to God and actually so to construe them." This declaration to see the world as related to a divine reality involves "a process of [making or] running out inferences, not from some axioms in the mind but from the 'dispositions of the heart.'"[18] Thus, for both Hartt and Gustafson, a construing belief is more an act or process of believing than it is a full-fledged cognitive claim. One declares, from the standpoint of one's "dispositions of the heart," one's intention to perceive and relate to the world in a particular way—as belonging and relating to God—and then one makes inferences from that standpoint. Hence, from the perspective of religious piety, Gustafson proclaims that "the patterns of interdependence of things on each other" are construed "in theological terms [as] the patterns of the divine governance of all things."[19] Gustafson implies that the cognitive aspect of theology is

---

15. Gustafson, *Ethics*, 1:195.
16. Gustafson, "Say Something Theological," 91.
17. Gustafson, *Ethics*, 1:140, 158.
18. Hartt, "Encounter and Inference in our Awareness of God," 49, 51, 52, 53. I discuss Hartt's influence on Gustafson in Meyer, "Ethics, Theism and Metaphysics," 160–61.
19. Gustafson, "Say Something Theological," 95. Hartt and Gustafson's notion of a construing belief and the drawing out of inferences from them does seem to bear some resemblance to Stout's notion of a "faith claim" in a broad sense (in the sense of a final vocabulary) from which one then draws inferences. The construing belief and the faith claim cannot themselves be rationally assessed, but the inferences that are drawn out from them can be. See my discussion of Stout in chapter 1.

ultimately more of a practical task of confession than it is a theoretical claim of knowledge. This is what makes theological claims "soft" in comparison to the claims of the natural sciences.[20]

Yet, Gustafson by no means intends to leave theology as merely confessional. "The confessional dimension of theology," says William Werpehowski in describing Gustafson's view, "must not overrun the universal intent with which it speaks."[21] For Gustafson, this means that the task of the theologian is to systematically construe the world through the prism of religious or theocentric piety. One does this by drawing on, critically appropriating, and revising the best elements of the theological tradition "in light of contemporary knowledge and experience." Hence, "the theologian's interpretation of the powers [that bear down on and sustain us] needs to be informed by, and cannot be incongruous with, the most reliable knowledge we have from other investigations of how some things really and ultimately are."[22] Summarily stated, theology must stay current with recent knowledge gained from the natural and social sciences and must give an accounting of itself that is in harmony with what can be learned from these other sources. An *accountable* theologian, unlike a *confessional* theologian, seeks to provide some limited rational authorization or accounting for his or her religious construal of the world. But unlike an *apologetical* theologian, an *accountable* theologian does not try to provide a full-fledged metaphysical or rational justification for his or her claims. For such an undertaking, Gustafson believes, inevitably leads back to the problems of overstatement and overconfidence that have historically plagued the cognitive dimension of theology.

In his 2004 book *An Examined Faith*, Gustafson offers a three-fold typology to describe different ways that theology can relate to other disciplines, such as the natural sciences. On one end of the spectrum, theologians can simply "reject" the insights of other disciplines by claiming that theology is basically "incommensurable" with them. On the other end, theologians can completely "absorb" outside insights to the point where such views completely "determine" theological interpretations of "actions, events, texts and other phenomena." In between these two extremes, theologians can find a middle position by "accommodating" the

20. Gustafson, *Ethics*, 1:195.
21. Werpehowski, *American Protestant Ethics*, 137.
22. Gustafson, "Say Something Theological," 91, 92.

insights of other disciplines without allowing them to fully determine theological interpretations.[23] It is this "accommodating" approach that Gustafson himself favors—one that is similar to the "accountable" theologian that I just described. Thus, an *accountable* theology both accommodates itself to outside insights and seeks to give a public accounting of itself that incorporates those insights into its theological construal of the world.

"Say Something Ethical"

Along with making truth claims about reality, theology also inevitably makes ethical claims about human behavior and responsibility in the world. Put simply, theology necessarily leads to ethics. But the reverse, Gustafson asserts, is not the case: ethics neither requires nor implies theology. He makes this point emphatically in numerous writings and does so on both empirical and conceptual grounds. Beginning with the empirical question, Gustafson contends that plain observation indicates that one does not need to be religious in order to perform genuine moral actions. As he makes clear in his Ryerson Lecture, he is "not proposing that in order to be moral one must be religious. This would simply be false, empirically." For anecdotal evidence, Gustafson might point to the beginning chapter of his 1975 book *Can Ethics Be Christian?* There he begins by recounting the story of a secular colleague who, in Gustafson's presence, admirably helped out a drunken sailor in a New York City bar in the 1950s. Such everyday actions, Gustafson concludes, are indicative of the fact that secular persons both can and do frequently perform good moral deeds.[24]

When one turns to the more interesting and difficult conceptual question, one finds Gustafson asserting a similar line. One neither needs to make theistic affirmations nor draw upon theological categories, he submits, in order to think coherently about ethics. For instance, in "Say Something Theological!" he declares:

---

23. Gustafson, *Examined Faith*, 6–7.

24. Gustafson, "Say Something Theological," 95. See chapters 1 and 4 in Gustafson, *Can Ethics Be Christian?* For possible counter-evidence, one might point to a 2002 National Opinion Research Council study that suggests that religious attendees perform, on average, more altruistic acts per year than non-religious persons. For a brief discussion of this study, see Marty, "Do-Gooders." For a similar study pertaining to charitable giving, see Marty "Tipping the Plate."

> Nor am I proposing that in order to have a coherent and defensible ethical theory one must have a theology. The very distinguished recent works of two of our colleagues in philosophy, Alan Donagan and Alan Gewirth, certainly demonstrate that cogent moral theories can be developed without theological foundations.[25]

This viewpoint is echoed in volume two of *Ethics* when he writes: "Theological ethics, if done with any effort to be comprehensive and coherent, cannot avoid being philosophical. Moral philosophy, however, does not necessarily have to be theological and, indeed, it seldom is in the modern world."[26] In this statement, Gustafson not only offers the empirical observation that most modern moral philosophy has presumed the autonomy of ethics, but he also puts forth once again the conceptual claim that moral philosophy need not be theological or theistic at all. This claim is formulated most concisely and sharply in *Can Ethics Be Christian?* when he states: "A secular ontology can serve as well as God to satisfy the quest for the necessary conditions of morality."[27]

But from the perspective of religious piety, of course, the moral life is construed through a very different prism. How Gustafson juxtaposes the differences between religious and non-religious perspectives will be addressed in the next section. For now, it is important to outline how he defines the moral life in theological terms. He begins by contending that "human activity must be set in a broader and more complex context of relationships than most Western ethics, religious or non-religious, usually interprets it. Man must be seen as a participant in a larger whole." This larger whole is defined theocentrically. From a theocentric perspective, then, the theological task "is to perceive and conceive what finite human beings can of the ultimate power and the powers that bring life into being, sustain it, and ultimately destine it." From this vantage point, the "ethical task is [then] to discern what these powers are enabling and requiring us to be and to do." Gustafson puts it more crisply when he states that the theological task is to perceive "the patterns of divine governance of all things" and the ethical imperative, based on this theological vision, is "to relate ourselves and all things in

25. Gustafson, "Say Something Theological," 95.
26. Gustafson, *Ethics*, 2:97.
27. Gustafson, *Can Ethics Be Christian?* 86.

a manner appropriate to their relations to God."[28] It is in relation to this overarching imperative that more specific moral judgments must then be made.

Gustafson uses this theocentric focus to challenge and counterbalance the deeply embedded anthropocentric tendencies in Christian theology and Western culture. "[W]hile no modern theologian defends a Ptolemaic view of the universe on scientific grounds," he observes, "most theologians continue to support a geocentric and anthropocentric interpretation of the purposes of the Deity."[29] Specifically, what he finds most problematic is the unquestioned presumption that the divine purpose is always concerned with and supportive of human desires and interests. Drawing on the Reformed tradition, Gustafson puts it starkly:

> God does not exist solely to secure the interests and purposes of man; God does not exist to glorify man. The place of man within the governance of God must be reconsidered. . . .
> . . . We are human, and God is God. There is no guarantee that the ends of the power which controls the destiny of the world are the ends we perceive to fulfill our human good. Again: God is the source, but not the guarantor of the human good. The chief end of God is not to glorify man. It may be that the chief end of man is to honor God by seeing the place of man in the whole of creation, and by conducting ourselves accordingly.[30]

In seeking to discern our place in the divine economy and to relate to all things accordingly, Gustafson rejects any presumption of moral certitude, either in the form of a clear-cut teleology or through any other means. "We see through a glass darkly," he insists. Thus, "we can no longer be certain about the end, or purpose, of man and of the whole of the creation. . . . [T]here is no pre-established harmony of ends and purposes into which our cultural and moral activities can be fitted with precision." This is not to say that all is permitted or that all things are in flux, but it does mean that ethical discernment must always be pursued within "the conditions of finitude." Hence, as we seek to discern the divine governance and seek to relate to others and to the world in a manner appropriate to their relations to God, "there is no avoidance of

---

28. Gustafson, "Say Something Theological," 95, 97.
29. Ibid., 93.
30. Ibid., 94, 97.

risk and possible harm." Therefore, in the end, we can only do our best to seek to understand and respond to what "the divine governance [is] enabling and requiring us to be and to do."[31]

In sum, an accountable theology, as exemplified by Gustafson, seeks to engage in conversation with the broader culture and the diverse voices of the academy. It does so by drawing on the best insights of contemporary knowledge, especially from the sciences, and by integrating those insights into a theological construal and articulation of the world. Such a construal seeks to offer a defensible accounting of its position, but it does not ultimately seek to rationally validate its central claim about the reality of God.

Typological Analysis

Commitment to Intelligibility (I+)

It is clear that, in my typological categories, Gustafson is committed to trying to make theology intelligible and plausible to the academy and the broader culture. Indeed, his Ryerson Lecture embodies this commitment. Though Gustafson is certainly respectful of and deeply knowledgeable about the Christian theological tradition, his use and articulation of the tradition is not slavish. Because he seeks to express a theological understanding in a way that outsiders might comprehend and find plausible, he uses the theological tradition in a discriminating manner. For instance, his use of the term "piety" rather than "faith" illustrates how he draws on the tradition, yet casts it in a new and intelligible light. By retrieving the largely forgotten notion of piety rather than relying on the familiar and culturally-laden term "faith," Gustafson is able to reintroduce the theological enterprise and a theocentric perspective to outsiders in a fresh way that they can understand. They can understand it because the notion of piety ties theology into the more accessible language of the human affections.

Gustafson's commitment to making theology plausible to outsiders is embedded in his attempt to set forth an *accountable* theology—one that seeks to navigate between a purely confessional theology, on the one hand, and a fully apologetical theology, on the other. In short, Gustafson wants to be able to offer some reasons for why a theocentric construal

---

31 Ibid., 97, 96, 97.

of the world might be seen as reasonable. As he remarks in *Ethics*, "the intelligibility of the [religious tradition or any] particular can be made clearer and to some more persuasive by demonstrating that its insights and truths refer to the experiences of many if not all persons and that its justifications can be made clear in nonesoteric language." But, again, for Gustafson, the public or nonesoteric reasons come largely from the sciences and not from theology itself. Theology makes its claims plausible or reasonable not by offering a natural theology or metaphysical justification for its claims about the reality of God; rather, it does so by incorporating the insights of the sciences into religious piety's own self-understanding and expression. Gustafson makes this point as follows:

> While I believe it is not possible to construct ... a purely "natural theology" . . . in the sense that the existence of the power and powers of God is proven apart from religious affectivity, *scientific descriptions and explanations can correct and alter some traditional religious claims*, and the realities to which they [the scientific explanations] refer can be indicators of matters which inform *and make plausible certain theological affirmations* [italics added].[32]

In affirming this commitment to plausibility and intelligibility, Gustafson takes his cue from Troeltsch. "'The idea of God,'" Gustafson approvingly quotes Troeltsch, "'is ... not directly accessible in any other way than by religious belief. Yet, it asserts a substantial content which must stand in harmony with the other forms of scientific knowledge and also be in some way indicated by these.'" Troeltsch's insight, Gustafson believes, is found in his recognition that claims about God presuppose the perspective of religious piety and, thus, cannot be rationally justified as such. But Troeltsch also recognizes that theology cannot simply leave it at that; theological claims cannot be out of step with what we learn elsewhere. "The substantial content of theology," Gustafson concludes, "if it is not in perfect harmony with scientific knowledge, cannot be in sharp incongruity with it, and what we say about God must be congruent in some way with what we know about human experience and its objects through the sciences."[33] Before moving on to an examination of

---

32. Gustafson, *Ethics*, 1:151, 251.

33. Ibid., 251–52. Gustafson cites Troeltsch, "Religion and the Science of Religion," in *Ernst Troeltsch: Writings on Theology and Religion*, ed. Robert Morgan and Michael Pye (Atlanta: John Knox Press, 1977) 117.

Gustafson's commitment to credibility, it is helpful first to turn to his view of the autonomy of ethics and to his perception of the metaphysical enterprise.

Autonomy of Ethics (AE+)

As one studies the works of Gustafson, one comes to the conclusion that he stands in agreement with the modern dominant consensus concerning the autonomy of ethics. As I indicated in my portrait, he explicitly states on multiple occasions that a coherent ethic does not require a theistic understanding. As he declares, "A secular ontology can serve as well as God to satisfy the quest for the necessary conditions of morality." Yet, as I also noted, he is certainly committed to developing and articulating a theocentric ethic. "For theological ethics," he holds, "the first task in order of importance is to establish convictions about God and God's relations to the world. . . . What the theologian writes about ethics must reasonably follow from these convictions." So how does one make sense of these differing and apparently contradictory claims that Gustafson makes?[34]

The key is found in a legacy going back to Kant's bifurcation between theoretical and practical standpoints or between phenomenal and noumenal realms. Gustafson, too, operates with an underlying split into two perspectives that he believes cannot ultimately be reconciled or integrated. To understand this bifurcation, it is helpful to note its presence in the work of Gustafson's teacher, H. R. Niebuhr, and in the thinking of Schleiermacher, to whom both Gustafson and Niebuhr are indebted. For his part, Niebuhr distinguishes between the perspectives of "inner" and "outer" history. "Outer" history refers to history as it is objectively seen or interpreted from the perspective of an outside or external observer; "inner" history refers to history as it is subjectively experienced and interpreted by those participants within a particular community, such as a religious community. The claims of inner history cannot be publicly validated like the claims of outer history. Hence, inner history, Niebuhr states, "can only be confessed by the [religious] community, and in this sense it is esoteric." One must accept the standpoint or adopt the inner

---

34. Gustafson, *Can Ethics Be Christian?* 86; Gustafson, *Ethics*, 2:98. I offer an extended answer in Meyer, "Ethics, Theism and Metaphysics," 154–60. Here I will simply summarize the main points.

perspective of the members of a community to "verify their visions."[35] Niebuhr epitomizes this split into two perspectives, and its implications for theology, when he approvingly quotes Schleiermacher:

> The strange question whether the same statement can be true in philosophy and untrue in theology, or vice versa, can no longer arise for the reason that the statement as it occurs in the one can find no place in the other and, alike as they may sound, their difference must always be presupposed.[36]

By contrast, this bifurcation approach is directly at odds with a unified view, such as that offered by the seventeenth-century Cambridge Platonist Benjamin Whichcote. In language that is almost directly opposite of that used here by Schleiermacher, Whichcote is quoted as saying that "'there is nothing true in divinity which is false in philosophy, or the contrary.'"[37]

But Gustafson, like Niebuhr, takes his cue from Schleiermacher rather than from Whichcote. Hence, Gustafson is not troubled by the fact that, on the one hand, he claims that God is unnecessary for ethics, while, on the other hand, he asserts that a theocentric perspective is needed for properly understanding the world and for normatively assessing and guiding human activity. Put simply, ethics can be coherently understood philosophically without reference to God; but from the perspective of theology and religious piety, the moral life must be

---

35. Niebuhr, *Meaning of Revelation*, see 44–54; quotations come from 53, 54.

36. Ibid., 19. Unfortunately, Niebuhr does not cite the source of this quote from Schleiermacher.

37. Whichcote quoted in Hedley, "Should Divinity Overcome Metaphysics?" 298. Hedley cites Brooke F. Wescott, *Religious Thought in the West* (London: Macmillan, 1891) 394. To illustrate this contrast further, let me return to Ogden. In *Point of Christology*, Ogden draws upon Niebuhr's distinction between "inner" and "outer" history in order to distinguish between the existential meaning of an event and a strictly historical account of the event itself. However, Ogden ultimately affirms and makes use of this distinction within a unified or one-world view, like Whichcote's, not in terms of the bifurcation approach of H. Richard or Schleiermacher. The key difference, to anticipate my discussion in the next section, is that Ogden thinks that the metaphysical claims of theology can be rationally or philosophically justified. Hence, the meaning of events revealed in Jesus as the Christ can be rationally expressed and justified in a manner that makes philosophical sense. Thus, what is true in divinity is also true in philosophy, and vice versa. As Ogden puts it, "because any claim about God by its very nature implies a metaphysical claim, I have expressly insisted on the need for a transcendental metaphysics in order to confirm the truth of a christology of liberation." Ogden, *Point of Christology*, 56–57, 146.

understood theocentrically. As in Schleiermacher and Niebuhr, the two sets of claims are not adjudicated and the two perspectives are not reconciled. Rather, it is assumed that "their difference must always be presupposed." To be sure, Gustafson seeks to integrate philosophical and scientific knowledge into theology. He does not, however, insist that philosophy and science must adopt the claims of theology, and this is evidenced by his acceptance of the autonomy of ethics. Thus, at one point he simply concludes that a theocentric perspective "probably evokes, better than it explains."[38]

So, overall, why does Gustafson accept the autonomy of ethics? First, given his firm commitment to intelligibility and dialogue within the academy, he would rather accept the dominant consensus concerning the autonomy of ethics than to isolate theology into a corner by insisting on the need for a theocentric ethic. Second, he believes that piety and affectivity lie at the heart of theology and the religious life, and these fundamental experiential elements must ultimately be experienced rather than argued for. Third, Gustafson thinks that theology's claims about the reality of God cannot, in the end, be rationally justified. These claims must finally be confessed and personally experienced rather than rationally validated as such. This third element leads us to a discussion of the metaphysical enterprise.

Absence of Metaphysics (AM+)

Though Gustafson believes that theology can offer some warrants or backing for a religious construal of the world, he does not believe that theology can directly justify its claims about the reality of God. This conclusion stems in part from his acceptance of the Kantian denial of metaphysics and contributes, in part, to his ambivalence about the cognitive dimension of theology. On the one hand, Gustafson recognizes that theology inevitably makes metaphysical claims about the reality of God. As he himself admits, "it is hard to think of God without being metaphysical, covertly and implicitly if not openly and explicitly."[39] Yet, on the other hand, he ultimately backs away from or downplays these metaphysical claims. In a description of modern Protestant ethics that applies equally well to his own view, he writes:

38. Gustafson, *Sense of the Divine*, 46.
39. Gustafson, *Ethics*, 1:63–64.

> Modern Protestant ethics have operated explicitly or implicitly from philosophical presuppositions which are basically Kantian in historical origin.... If [after Kant] one could *not* have clear and certain knowledge of God by reason, there were only certain possibilities left for theology.[40]

For Gustafson, the only genuine possibility left for theology after Kant is to turn to the language of construal. To be sure, the substance of Gustafson's theocentric ethic is very different from Kant's own moral theory. As Gustafson remarks, "The theocentric perspective that I have developed yields a very unKantian ethics." Yet, in spite of this ethical difference, Gustafson still operates with Kantian assumptions at a deeper philosophical level when it comes to questions of metaphysics; like Kant, he too believes that metaphysical claims cannot be rationally validated or justified. Hence, Gustafson confesses and construes—rather than argues for—the divine reality as the supreme One behind the many forces at work in the world. As he puts it:

> Since I am not convinced that one can argue from a wide range of particular experiences to a logically necessary conclusion that a powerful Other—a monotheistic God—exists, [my theology] does not take this turn [toward theistic argument]. Rather it shows descriptively how, given affectivity and the ways in which it is engendered not only by common experience but also by participation in a religious tradition, the religious tradition provides warrants and symbols for moving from particular experiences to the experience of responding to an ultimate power.[41]

The aim here is to provide a rational accounting of and warrant for religious piety, but not to foreground or rationally justify metaphysical claims about the reality of God. As Byron Bangert observes, Gustafson "consistently ... demurs from ... metaphysics."[42]

As we have seen, Gustafson's aversion to metaphysics is due in part to the fact that he equates the metaphysical enterprise with theology's problematic tendencies of overstatement and overconfidence. I will examine his specific complaints about metaphysics below. But for now, let us simply note that if theology tends to claim to know too much about God or to know with too much certainty, then any attempt to

---

40. Gustafson, *Protestant and Roman Catholic Ethics*, 61, 64.
41. Gustafson, *Ethics*, 2:121; Gustafson, *Ethics*, 1:196.
42. Bangert, *Consenting to God and Nature*, 47.

foreground metaphysics, he believes, will contribute to the problem. Instead, it is better to leave theology's metaphysical claims quietly in the background, where they can affectively evoke rather than rationally explain. As Gustafson declares at one point: "The 'experiential confirmation' [of theology's assertions] is sufficiently relative to particular communities and persons not to warrant such a universal claim."[43]

Commitment to Credibility (C-)

Having outlined Gustafson's view in terms of the first three criteria, we are now in a position to analyze his approach to the fourth, credibility. It is evident that, in spite of his dedicated commitment to making theology intelligible and plausible to the academy and other publics, Gustafson is not ultimately committed to making theology rationally convincing to these broader audiences. Put simply, he does not think that one can succeed at this endeavor nor should one even try. For, again, without the prior presence of religious piety, he believes that "it is relatively meaningless to make a case for the existence or presence of God."[44]

As has been shown, Gustafson's accountable theology certainly seeks to engage in conversation with the broader culture and the diverse voices of the academy. It does so by drawing on the best insights of contemporary knowledge, especially from the sciences, and by integrating these insights into a theological construal and articulation of the world. Yet the relationship is predominantly one-way insofar as theology accepts and integrates the truth claims of other disciplines while, in return, it offers a confessional construal through a theocentric prism. Gustafson thinks this is the best that theology can do because he, too, like many in the academy and broader culture, thinks that theological claims are "soft" in comparison to the claims of the sciences. "[T]he 'truth claims' that a theologian can make," announces Gustafson, "are 'soft' in comparison to those that natural scientists can make according to their procedures of confirmation." Given this softness, "it is clear that theological reflection is not in a position to provide the same kind of evidences in support of its theories as are genetics or physics. Progress in theology is not possible in the same way that progress in the natural sciences is." To be sure, religious persons believe in the reality of God,

---

43. Gustafson, *Can Ethics Be Christian?* 165.
44. Gustafson, *Ethics*, 1:164.

but that reality, Gustafson submits, cannot be rationally confirmed or validated. "Whether that 'object' [God] is 'real' in the same sense that phenomena are," he remarks, "is a theological question; but surely it has reality in the perception of the person whose affectivity is evoked."[45] Notice that he identifies the question about the reality of God here as a theological question and not also as a philosophical one. This suggests again his underlying acceptance of the Kantian denial of metaphysics and his belief that the question about the divine reality is one that can be experientially confessed but not rationally validated as such. At the end of the day, therefore, his rational justification is partial and incomplete.

Critical Assessment

When Gustafson says "God" in response to a request to say something theological, he offers the quintessential answer. For God is properly the central focus of theological inquiry as well as the defining center of human existence. Indeed, Gustafson's theocentric critique of the persisting anthropocentric tendency in theology is a valuable contribution to contemporary theological ethics. Moreover, his commitment to intelligibility and conversation in the academy and broader public is commendable. However, what is finally lacking in Gustafson's theocentric ethic is adequate attention to the truth claims about God that necessarily flow from the comprehensive character of theistic convictions.[46] "Statements about God," as Robin Lovin aptly describes,

> are not simply expressions of emotion or acts of personal commitment. Theological claims have cognitive content. They may be true or false. True statements about God are true because they accurately represent a reality independent of the concepts, theories, and evidence we have pertaining to that reality.[47]

As noted earlier, Gustafson himself recognizes that "some evidences for the reality of God need to be adduced if only to avoid the charge that God is purely a projection of the human imagination."[48] Yet, in the end, his bifurcated or accountable approach does not offer an

---

45. Ibid., 195, 31, 120.

46. I outlined some of these following criticisms in Meyer, "Ethics, Theism and Metaphysics," 166–73.

47. Lovin, *Reinhold Niebuhr and Christian Realism*, 20.

48. Gustafson, *Ethics*, 1:195.

adequate defense of the reality of God or an adequate justification for why the world should be understood theocentrically rather than secularistically. Instead, it only provides a rational backing for the affective response of religious piety but not for its defining theological object or center (God).

For example, he argues that "the religious sense of dependence upon powers beyond ourselves is supported by many of the data and theories of many sciences." But he follows this immediately by saying that "in non-religious terms, this [sense of dependence] simply indicates that human life is a part of nature, and dependent upon the processes of nature."[49] In other words, for those who do not confess the reality of God, this sense of dependence can be coherently understood in naturalistic or secularistic terms. Hence, Gustafson states elsewhere that he has "no serious quarrels with . . . agnostics or declared atheists" who share this basic sense of dependence but interpret it in a thoroughgoing secularistic manner. "I cannot persuasively argue," he declares, "that their [affective and moral] stances [toward nature] entail the acknowledgment of God or gods, nor do I wish even to try." This leads back to his conclusion that a theocentric perspective "probably evokes, better than it explains."[50]

It is evident by now that Gustafson's lack of full commitment to the credibility of theocentric claims means that he ends up having much to say about the human sense of dependence but little to say about the reality of God. As Gordon Kaufman rightly observes, "what is missing throughout Gustafson's [theology] is an adequate justification for moving beyond talk of nature or the world to talk about God." And because he fails to provide this crucial step, he "does not present adequate grounds for his foundational claim that ethics should be conceived theocentrically rather than naturalistically." Or again, as Stout puts it, "Gustafson does not make clear why we shouldn't view . . . secular piety . . . as the natural successor to theocentric piety."[51] The underlying problem with Gustafson's approach, I contend, is that he dismisses the possibility of a metaphysical justification of theistic convictions, which leads him then to offer only a partial commitment to credibility. I am persuaded that

---

49. Ibid., 260.
50. Gustafson, *Sense of the Divine*, 46, 46–47, 46.
51. Kaufman, "How is *God* to be Understood in a Theocentric Ethics?" 23–24; Stout, *Ethics After Babel*, 182.

his theocentric ethic would be made stronger and more convincing if it were formulated in terms of a process metaphysics. Let me outline three reasons to support this claim.

First, Gustafson himself sees some important congruities between process thought and his own view. For instance, he recognizes that both approaches seek to provide a view of reality that perceives process and development in history and nature. Both view God, in some important way, as objective to us and the world. Both insist that God must be related to the natural world as well as to the realm of human action—and that God is affected by the consequences of these realms. And, finally, both seek to redirect attention away from anthropocentricism to theocentricism.[52]

Second, Gustafson admits that "it is hard to think of God without being metaphysical, covertly and implicitly if not openly and explicitly."[53] This is a crucial point. To speak of God, as theistic piety must do, necessarily entails making some metaphysical claims about the nature of reality as such. At this key juncture, however, Gustafson's position falters because he dismisses the possibility of justifying these claims. Hence, he leaves the metaphysical claims of theology buried in the background, undefended and unsubstantiated. In contrast, as I argued in chapter 2, process thought can offer a neoclassical alternative to the classical theism that Kant rightly rejected and, thereby, can explicitly address the metaphysical question of God and God's relation to the world, including God's relation to the moral life.

And third, process thought would enable Gustafson to abandon his bifurcated approach and thus enable him to explicate his theocentric outlook in the form of a coherent and unified "one-world thinking."[54] Of course, Gustafson has reservations about "one-world thinking" and its exemplification in metaphysics, and I will attend to his criticisms shortly. But he clearly recognizes that theistic convictions demand the

---

52. Gustafson, *Ethics*, 1:56–62. I recognize that in spite of some congruities with a process understanding of God, Gustafson also retains some classical elements in his view through his adherence to the Reformed or Calvinist tradition. In order to formulate his theocentric ethic in process terms, therefore, one would have to partly revise his doctrine of God. Also, Bangert suggests that Gustafson has become even more hesitant about the metaphysical aspects of process thought; see Bangert, *Consenting to God and Nature*, 47 n. 11.

53. Gustafson, *Ethics*, 1:63–64.

54. This phrase comes from H. Richard Niebuhr's *Meaning of Revelation*, 60–61.

attempt to conceive and explicate the whole of existence in relation to God; this is what a theocentric construal offers. However, his bifurcated approach forces him ultimately to either ignore or set aside the divine totality in the context of public discourse. For Gustafson, this is done by affirming the autonomy of ethics. Alternatively, by adopting a process form of one-world thinking, he could abandon his bifurcated approach, which undercuts his claim for theocentricism by concomitantly affirming the possibility of a coherent secularistic moral theory.

Gustafson relegates the metaphysical enterprise to the margins of theology because he believes that: (1) cognitive claims about God necessarily entail some claim of epistemological privilege, (2) a metaphysical justification of theism necessarily overlooks the importance of piety, (3) metaphysics is too abstract to illuminate the particularities of experience and, thus, is of little or no value, and (4) metaphysics and a realistic epistemology necessarily presuppose a correspondence theory of truth, which has become problematical to defend. In regard to all four of these concerns, I think Gustafson is either ultimately mistaken or has drawn the wrong conclusion from them.

His first concern, that cognitive claims about God necessarily entail some claim of epistemological privilege, overlooks the possibility that metaphysical realism can be joined with epistemological fallibilism. For instance, as Audi declares in his response to Gustafson's ethics, "I see no reason to give up realism as an *ontological* view if it is conjoined with an *epistemological* fallibilism."[55] One can make metaphysical claims about the nature of reality while also acknowledging that one's claims are indeed fallible. This was the point of my four-fold distinction in chapter 2 clarifying the four aspects of claims to knowledge (focus of content, modal status of content, form of epistemic justification, and subjective form of justification). Claims about the reality of God, like all other claims, are validated on the basis of reasons offered, not on the basis of some asserted or presumed authority or privilege; thus theologians, like everyone else, should always avoid claims of epistemological privilege. To be sure, Gustafson is right to recognize that theology, as well as philosophy, have historically been haunted by overstatement in the form of claims of epistemological certainty. But, again, as I argued earlier, such claims are neither necessitated nor warranted by the metaphysical

---

55. Audi, "Theology, Science, and Ethics in Gustafson's Theocentric Ethics," 179; see also 181.

enterprise itself. Theology should acknowledge its epistemological fallibilism but not refrain from its essential cognitive task of making and seeking to defend claims about the nature and reality of God and what difference the divine reality makes for ethics.

In his Ryerson Lecture, Gustafson takes some steps in this direction but makes a wrong turn before he gets to this conclusion. In recognizing the tendency of overstatement in theology and in calling for a more humble approach, Gustafson asks:

> Can it not be the case in theology, as in other investigations, that one conscientiously and critically says something about how things really and ultimately are within the constraints of our time and place in culture and history, and yet with the awareness that new interpretations will follow?[56]

If Gustafson is asking here whether one can recognize and affirm the fallibility and potential revisability of all theological and metaphysical claims, then the answer is an unequivocal yes. The *act* of making a claim is always done within some historical and cultural context. But that does not mean that the *scope or content* of the claim is necessarily restricted merely to that context. Indeed, though the act of making a claim about the reality and necessity of God is always done within some particular setting, the scope and content of such a claim purports to be universally valid and not merely particular. Hence, what is called for is a fallibilistic metaphysics that distinguishes between the universal content of a metaphysical claim, the necessary (non-contingent) modal status of such a claim, and the fallibilistic subjective form of our knowledge in relation to all such claims. But rather than pursuing such a fallibilistic metaphysics as part of a defense of theistic claims, Gustafson instead embraces Hartt's confessional language of construal. Combined with his commitment to intelligibility, this confessional stance leads Gustafson to accept the autonomy of ethics, which in turn enervates his claims for the need for a theocentric ethic.

Gustafson's second and perhaps overriding concern is that metaphysics necessarily devalues the importance of piety and its sense of dependence. This outlook implies that there is an inevitable trade-off between reason and piety. But this assumption, I submit, rests on a misunderstanding of the proper relation between the two. Gustafson is

---

56. Gustafson, "Say Something Theological," 91–92.

certainly right to hold that piety (or faith understood as a basic trust in the meaningfulness of existence) occurs prior to rational reflection. The task of rational reflection, however, is not to make piety redundant but, rather, to make it fully explicit and fully reflective, thereby clarifying the basic existential character of human life. The reflective task, therefore, is to distinguish rationally between true and false representations of piety and its sense of dependence and, thus, to distinguish between authentic and inauthentic piety. As Gustafson himself recognizes, "Religious affections can be altered, indeed 'corrected,' by testing the adequacy of the beliefs that inform and express them."[57] In short, Gustafson wrongly assumes that metaphysics devalues piety and, consequently, he wrongly abandons the type of rational testing that metaphysics provides for assessing the adequacy of claims that express and inform our affectivity.

Gustafson's third criticism is that "metaphysics is necessarily abstract" and, therefore

> its illumination of "the whole" sheds little light on the particulars of human life in the world. It has the strength of turning religion from preoccupations with benefits for human beings; in this sense it is highly theocentric. But its level of generalization goes beyond what I find to be very illuminating.[58]

Gustafson is indeed correct to note that metaphysics is necessarily abstract, but he overlooks two valuable implications of its generality. On the one hand, he underestimates the usefulness of metaphysical concepts as instruments for understanding "concrete matters of fact and practical affairs." A good metaphysics can provide imaginative insight into understanding differences between particulars that are not immediately apparent to direct observation. For instance, this is Whitehead's basic criticism of Baconian induction, namely, that discovery requires "imaginative rationalization" and not just observation looking for difference.[59] Or, to use an example from American politics, metaphysical insight may help us to understand more clearly the underlying philosophical assumptions that different perspectives bring to practical issues, such as in the debate over social security reform. While the relation between metaphysics and specific policy proposals is surely complex, a meta-

---

57. Gustafson, *Ethics*, 1:201. My formulation of this point and criticism of Gustafson is informed by Ogden's theology. See Ogden, *On Theology*, 72–73.

58. Gustafson, *Ethics*, 1:61.

59. Martin, "On the Language of Theology," 44; Whitehead, *Process and Reality*, 5.

physic of external relations (which sees all of reality, including human beings, as at root separate individual entities whose relations to others are merely external), if it implicitly or explicitly informs one's political judgment, might well lead one to favor some form of privatization of social security. By contrast, a metaphysic of internal relations (viewing all of reality as internally as well as externally related), might lead one to support a policy that takes human interconnectivity to be a central premise—thus seeking to secure the future of all citizens, not just the security of oneself or one's family.

On the other hand, Gustafson overlooks the fact that metaphysics, precisely because of its level of abstraction and generality, expresses the important fact that each individual or particular must contribute to the divine "whole" in some way. There are no self-contained particulars capable of being fully understood apart from an interpretation of the systematic whole.[60] Thus, metaphysics can make a rational case for why all concrete or particular realities must be understood ultimately in relation to a theocentric whole, which is exactly what Gustafson's position fails to do.

Fourth, and finally, Gustafson alleges that recent developments in the history and philosophy of science lead to "a radical qualification of the correspondence theory of truth which the metaphysical enterprise seems . . . necessarily to presuppose."[61] In order to assess Gustafson's statement here one needs to ask whether he is referring to a correspondence theory of *validity* or to a correspondence theory of *validation*. In brief, a correspondence theory of validity means that valid claims are made valid or true by virtue of reality—by the way things really are—and not by our conscious thoughts or interpretations of things, except insofar as the claims are about our conscious thoughts and interpretations. In other words, a correspondence theory of validity is a realist theory of truth; a realist theory contends that the conditions necessary and sufficient to make a claim true or valid are "independent of the conscious thoughts or explicit interpretations of humans."[62]

---

60. Pannenberg, *Metaphysics and the Idea of God*, 149; see also Whitehead, *Process and Reality*, 14.

61. Gustafson, *Ethics*, 1:258.

62. Gamwell, "Moral Realism and Religion," 477. My discussion here is informed by Gamwell's distinctions and definitions, see 476–78.

In Gustafson's own terms, realism implies that "experience occurs in relation and response to realities objective to persons, and not to mere figments of human imagination, projections of human feelings, or self-generated moments of significance."[63] By suggesting that human experience occurs in relation to "realities objective to persons," Gustafson implies that these realities exist independently of human thoughts, interpretations, and experience. Hence, the necessary and sufficient conditions (validity conditions) that must be fulfilled in order for claims about these realities to be valid or true are likewise independent of human consciousness. It is evident, therefore, that Gustafson himself accepts a correspondence theory of validity, so this cannot be the real object of his criticism. In contrast, however, a correspondence theory of validation contends that one can validate, redeem, or justify the truth of a given claim "by comparison with some experience of reality that is independent of our explicit interpretations."[64] Gustafson rightly rejects this correspondence theory of validation, for one can never validate any claim apart from explicit interpretations that entail providing reasons, evidence, and arguments in support of one's claim. In essence, *what* is validated is independent of a human community of inquiry, but *how* or *that* it is validated always occurs within such a community.[65] With this important distinction in place, it is clear that Gustafson's fourth criticism or concern is not as problematic for metaphysics as he assumes. The metaphysical enterprise does presuppose a realist or correspondence theory of validity, which Gustafson himself appears to accept, but it need not and should not presuppose a correspondence theory of validation.

Summary (I+C-AE+AM+)

Gustafson's accountable theology epitomizes multiple modern assumptions and tendencies. He embraces the formal commitment to intelligi-

---

63. Gustafson, *Ethics*, 1:200.

64. Gamwell, "Moral Realism and Religion," 478.

65. What I have in mind is an "open" community of inquiry, along the lines envisioned by Peirce. Peirce speaks of the community of inquiry as being "without definite limits," i.e., as open to all who seek to test claims by the standards of reason and common experience; it is not narrowly defined in terms of a specific tradition, as MacIntyre envisions it. Peirce, "Some Consequences of Four Incapacities," 69. See my discussion of Peirce and MacIntyre on this point in footnote 43 in my concluding chapter.

bility and accepts the substantive consensus concerning the autonomy of ethics and the absence of metaphysics. Thus, at the same time that he espouses a valuable theocentric critique of anthropocentricism and a thoughtful theocentric analysis of the world, he undercuts his gains by claiming that a naturalistic or secularistic ontology can serve as well as God for making sense of the world and the moral life. Gustafson's bifurcated approach illustrates the modern Kantian separation of reality into two contrasting perspectives that cannot be theoretically or cognitively reconciled. Finally, his approach epitomizes the modern aversion to metaphysics even though he acknowledges that theology inevitably makes metaphysical claims. This leads him to downplay such claims and to back away from the modern commitment to credibility when it comes to offering a convincing case for claims about the reality of God. Summarily speaking, Gustafson's accountable theology illustrates both some of the best and worst tendencies of modernity. At its best, it illustrates a spirit of formal autonomy and fallibilism that seeks to learn from others as well as to think independently. It puts forth theistic convictions with a "grace of self-doubt" that fosters public conversation rather than with a dogmatic certitude that stifles such interchange.[66] But, at its worst, Gustafson's approach embodies the modern tendency to marginalize theological claims by viewing them as rationally "soft" in comparison to the claims of the sciences and other disciplines. By accepting the absence of metaphysics, Gustafson has no way to redeem the central claim of theocentricism—the claim about the reality of God—and, thus, he simply leaves it hanging out there as a confessional construal; one that seeks to gain plausibility by taking account of the sciences but one that remains, nevertheless, superfluous for those who do not share this confessional outlook. Hence, claims about the centrality of God are for those who construe the world through the prism of religious piety. For everyone else, a secularistic ontology will do.

---

66. Again, this apt phrase comes from the subtitle of Gustafson's *An Examined Faith: The Grace of Self-Doubt*.

6

A Pragmatic Theology
The Approach of Reinhold Niebuhr

Theological Portrait

IF JAMES GUSTAFSON OFFERS A "SOFT SELL" VERSION OF A THEO-CENTRIC ethic, then Reinhold Niebuhr goes for the "hard sell." Indeed, the man who graced the cover of *Time* magazine in 1948 as "America's Theologian" was arguably the most influential twentieth-century American voice in making a public case for the need for theology. Along with his apologetic influence, however, Niebuhr's thought also ironically engendered the phenomenon known as "Atheists for Reinhold Niebuhr."[1] In the midst of his theological "hard sell," how is it possible that Niebuhr's thought still enabled some interpreters to think they could separate his ethics and politics from his principal theistic claims? I will answer this question in my analysis and assessment, but let me begin by offering a portrait of Niebuhr's approach. Drawing on his classic two-volume work, *The Nature and Destiny of Man* (hereafter *Nature and Destiny*), and other important sources like *Faith and History*, I will seek to illuminate some of his central theological themes and arguments.

Human Nature and the Problem of Meaning

A good starting point with Niebuhr is his attempt to articulate a biblical or Christian anthropology. As Langdon Gilkey observes, Niebuhr and

---

1. The *Time* magazine cover from March 8, 1948 can be seen in the middle photo section of Fox, *Reinhold Niebuhr*. Fox's discussion of the *Time* cover can be found a few pages later on 233–34 and his discussion of "Atheists for Reinhold Niebuhr" can be found on 246, 225.

many of his generation assumed that a common set of themes defines a unified or normative biblical outlook.² In regard to human nature, Niebuhr often contrasts this biblical perspective with a Greek or classical understanding of human existence. Unlike this classical view, which has left a legacy of dualistic thinking in the West, Niebuhr contends that a proper Christian anthropology conceives of human existence in terms of "a unity of body and soul" rather than as a separate soul entrapped in a physical body. Relatedly, a biblical conception also holds that human beings are fully created in regard to both body and spirit and not, as in the classical view, conceived as an immortal soul placed in a mortal body. What distinguishes humans from other creatures, Niebuhr argues, is not merely our ability to reason, as Aristotle and the Greeks tended to presume. Rather, it is our capacity for self-transcendence that distinguishes us from the rest of nature, and it is this capacity that identifies us with the *imago dei*. Human beings are "made in the image of God," Niebuhr states, which means that

> the human spirit has the special capacity of standing continually outside itself in terms of indefinite regression. Consciousness is a capacity for surveying the world and determining action from a governing centre. Self-consciousness represents a further degree of transcendence in which the self makes itself its own object in such a way that the ego is finally always subject and not object. The rational capacity of surveying the world, of forming general concepts and analysing the order of the world is thus but one aspect of what Christianity knows as "spirit."³

By insisting on the unity of body and soul, what Niebuhr really wants to emphasize is that humans exist at the juncture of and in the tension between nature and spirit. We are creatures, yet made in the image of God. We are limited, yet we have an indefinite capacity for self-transcendence that enables us endlessly to push against limits.⁴ We are dependent, yet we have a creative capacity that fosters independence. We are part of the evolutionary process, yet we have the capacity to "rise above" that process and to survey and understand the past as well as to

---

2. Gilkey, *On Niebuhr*, 223–24.

3. Niebuhr, *Nature and Destiny*, 1:13–14.

4. Daniel Malotky insightfully notes that Niebuhr describes this capacity as "indefinite" rather than "infinite." This means, says Malotky, that "our freedom does not abolish nature's limits or [completely] free the self from particularity." See Malotky, "Reinhold Niebuhr's Paradox," 106.

envision and anticipate the future. In short, Niebuhr thinks that human existence is most profoundly understood in terms of a juncture between "horizontal" and "vertical" axes. The error of naturalism or secularism is to emphasize the horizontal axis of nature without adequate attention to the vertical dimensions of spirit. By contrast, the error of mysticism or idealism is to focus on the vertical capacities of spirit without adequately grounding them in the horizontal axis of nature. Only by recognizing that both poles are essential can one begin to grasp the full breadth and depth of the human endeavor.

This breadth and depth, Niebuhr continues, is revealed in the human capacity to choose. Not only does our capacity for self-transcendence enable us to choose among alternative possibilities in life, but, even more profoundly, it forces us to choose our total end or comprehensive telos for life as a whole. Niebuhr expresses this dual-capacity as follows:

> Man is self-determining not only in the sense that he transcends natural process in such a way as to be able to choose between various alternatives presented to him by the processes of nature but also in the sense that he transcends himself in such a way that he must choose his total end. In this task of self-determination he is confronted with endless potentialities and he can set no limit to what he ought to be, short of the character of ultimate reality. Yet this same man is a creature whose life is definitely limited by nature and he is unable to choose anything beyond the bounds set by the creation in which he stands.[5]

This passage nicely illustrates the tension between nature and spirit. On the one hand, the human capacity for self-transcendence forces humans to be free, i.e., requires them to make choices, including, implicitly or explicitly, a choice of some comprehensive telos or underlying source of meaning. Given our indefinite capacity for self-transcendence, Niebuhr reasons, this choice of an ultimate source of meaning cannot adequately be identified or defined "short of the character of ultimate reality." On the other hand, humans are also embedded in nature and thus can only make choices from within the limits of history. Thus humans exist in a tension between ultimate reality and history; between freedom and finitude. If the ultimate telos or source of meaning is "stated in purely historical terms," remarks Niebuhr, "[it] will embody some contingency

---

5. Niebuhr, *Nature and Destiny* 1:162–63.

of nature and history and [thereby] set a false limit for the human spirit." On the flip side, however, given our situatedness within history, acting in accord with the character of ultimate reality is itself an "impossible possibility."[6] We will return to address this tension more fully, but for now it is important simply to note that it is at this intersection between nature and spirit that Niebuhr draws a triangular connection between the quintessential human problem of meaning, the fundamental problem of sin, and the need for Christian faith as the answer to each of these related problems. Before attending to his explicit arguments for the need for Christian theism, let us first focus on his understanding of the problem of sin.

The Problem of Human Sin

Given that human beings exist at the juncture of nature and spirit and have the capacity for self-transcendence, Niebuhr reckons that humans can and do inevitably seek to escape the tension of their "both-and" condition. This act of escape can occur in either direction. Humans can, on the one hand, seek to deny their freedom and responsibility of spirit by trying to lose themselves in their bodily nature and existence. Niebuhr calls this the "sin of sensuality." "Sensuality," he says, "represents an effort to escape from the freedom and the infinite possibilities of spirit by becoming lost in the detailed processes, activities and interests of existence."[7] On the other hand, humans can seek to deny their finitude through the hubris of spirit. This powerful tendency is what Niebuhr labels the "sin of pride." "Sin is occasioned," he states, "precisely by the fact that man refuses to admit his 'creatureliness' and to acknowledge himself as merely a member of a total unity of life. He pretends to be more than he is." This pretension and refusal overestimates the importance of the human self—in both individual and collective form—in relation to God and in relation to other selves and groups. Because Niebuhr believes that sin is finally rooted in the misuse of freedom (spirit) rather than in the limits of finitude (nature), he ultimately views the sin of sensuality as itself a misguided act of freedom and spirit, and hence, he

---

6. Ibid., 163–64; Niebuhr, *Interpretation of Christian Ethics*, 36.

7. Niebuhr, *Nature and Destiny*, 1:185. Given Niebuhr's wide-ranging and inclusive definition, some feminists have persuasively argued that Niebuhr's point is more aptly described as the "sin of hiding" rather than merely as the "sin of sensuality." See Dunfee, "Sin of Hiding" and Plaskow, *Sex, Sin, and Grace*.

ultimately subsumes it under the sin of pride. "Man contradicts himself within the terms of his true essence," Niebuhr remarks. "His essence is free self-determination. His sin is the wrong use of his freedom and its consequent destruction."[8] This act of self-destruction can occur either by *overestimating the self*, by engaging in the self-contradictory act of trying to deny one's finitude and creatureliness, or by seeking to *lose the self*, by engaging in the self-contradictory act of trying to lose one's spiritual freedom and responsibility in bodily or cultural forms.

As Niebuhr famously and paradoxically remarks, the self-contradictory act of sin is "inevitable though not necessary." Drawing on Kierkegaard's notion of anxiety, Niebuhr believes that humans cannot respond creatively to the dizziness of freedom, which is produced by the tension between nature and spirit, without falling into some form of self-contradiction. As he sees it,

> man, being both free and bound, both limited and limitless is anxious. Anxiety is the inevitable concomitant of the paradox of freedom and finiteness in which man is involved. Anxiety is the internal precondition of sin. . . . [But] it must not be identified with sin because there is always the ideal possibility that faith would purge anxiety of the tendency toward sinful self-assertion. The ideal possibility is that faith in the ultimate security of God's love would overcome all immediate insecurities of nature and history.[9]

This ideal possibility of faith requires both a proper answer to the problem of meaning and a life existentially grounded in and guided by that answer. The question that elicits such an answer returns us again to the problem of meaning and to the need for Christian theism.

To anticipate, Niebuhr contends that only the God revealed in Jesus as the Christ can provide an adequate comprehensive telos or source of meaning for human life and action. All action, including moral action, is ultimately informed by some underlying supposition of meaning or center of value. In Niebuhr's words, "Action which has become emancipated from nature's necessities remains incoherent until it has found a final anchor and source of coherence in a total realm of meaning."[10]

---

8. Niebuhr, *Nature and Destiny*, 1:16.

9. Niebuhr, *Nature and Destiny*, 1:150, 182–83. See Gilkey, *On Niebuhr*, chap. 6 for a helpful analysis of Niebuhr's view of anxiety in relation to sin.

10. Niebuhr, "Religion and Action," 44.

This total realm of meaning is fully captured only in a divine reality disclosed in Jesus as the Christ. This answer, Niebuhr insists, is supra-rational in character and can thus only be expressed symbolically or mythically, not literally. Nevertheless, he argues that one can still offer a limited rational defense of it through both negative and positive forms of validation. I will address each of these in turn and the specifics of his Christian answer in between.

The Negative Validation

Niebuhr's negative apologetic attempts rationally to disclose that the alternatives to Christian theism fail to provide an adequate ground of meaning for human existence. "The Christian Gospel," he writes, "is negatively validated by the evidence that [various] forms of worldly wisdom . . . give an inadequate view of the total human situation." Their inadequacy issues from the fact that they do not truly understand the full dimensions of the human spirit. Our capacity for self-transcendence, Niebuhr observes, indicates the "essential homelessness of the human spirit." And this homelessness "is the ground of all religion; for the self which stands outside itself and the world cannot find the meaning of life in itself or the world."[11]

Later in volume one of *Nature and Destiny*, Niebuhr unpacks and develops this argument as follows:

> Implicit in the human situation of freedom and in man's capacity to transcend himself and his world is his inability to construct a world of meaning without finding a source and key to the structure of meaning which transcends the world beyond his own capacity to transcend it. The problem of meaning, which is the basic problem of religion, . . . is not solved without the introduction of a principle of meaning which transcends the world of meaning to be interpreted.[12]

Only a transcendent source or center of meaning, Niebuhr reasons, can provide an adequate framework in relation to which one can make sense of "the essential homelessness of the human spirit." If any lesser principle is used, then the system of meaning will remain incoherent, i.e., it will not be able to account adequately for all aspects of existence,

---

11. Niebuhr, *Faith and History*, 164; Niebuhr, *Nature and Destiny*, 1:14.
12. Niebuhr, *Nature and Destiny*, 1:164.

especially the human capacity for self-transcendence. This tendency to define meaning in relation to some non-transcendent source manifests itself in the sin of idolatry. As Niebuhr writes:

> If some vitality of existence, or even some subordinate principle of coherence is used as the principle of meaning, man is involved in idolatry. He lifts some finite and contingent element of existence into the eminence of the divine. He uses something which itself requires explanation as the ultimate principle of coherence and meaning.[13]

Idolatry, then, is the attempt to construct a world of meaning around a source or center that is "short of the character of ultimate reality." The most obvious forms of this, Niebuhr observes, occur when "the world of meaning is organized around a centre of natural or historical vitality, such as the life of a tribe or nation, which is patently contingent and not ultimate."[14] Writing in the late 1930s and early 1940s, Niebuhr clearly has in mind the dangers of German and Italian fascism.

Yet more subtle and covert forms of idolatry occur, he maintains, when either nature or reason is regarded as the ultimate principle of meaning. "If the effort is made to comprehend the meaning of the world through the principle of natural causation alone," Niebuhr states, "the world is conceived in terms of a mechanistic coherence which has no place for the freedom which reveals itself in human consciousness." Even though reason offers a "somewhat higher" principle of meaning than nature, it, too, leads to incoherence and idolatry. "Every effort to identify meaning with rationality," he contends,

> implies the deification of reason. That such an identification represents idolatry and that the laws of reason and logic are incapable of fully comprehending the total meaning of the world, is attested by the fact that life and history are full of contradictions which cannot be resolved in terms of rational principles. Furthermore, a mind which transcends itself cannot legitimately make itself the ultimate principle of interpretation by which it explains the relation of mind to the world.[15]

In brief, both nature and reason fail to make sense of some aspect of existence. Nature, understood in terms of mechanistic causation, fails

13. Ibid., 164–65.
14. Ibid., 163, 165.
15. Ibid., 165.

to account adequately for the capacities of human freedom and self-transcendence. Likewise, reason fails to account for the antinomies of history and fails to offer a sufficient vantage point from which to make sense of the human capacity for reason itself. Consequently, neither nature nor reason can serve as an adequate source of meaning for understanding the totality of the world. "The fact of self-transcendence," Niebuhr concludes, "leads inevitably to the search for a God who transcends the world."[16]

The search for transcendence, however, does not guarantee that one will identify the proper center of value. A transcendent principle that fails to place significant and lasting value on the particularities of history leads to the opposite form of error, namely, to what Niebuhr calls "mysticism." The insight of mysticism is to recognize the need for a transcendent source of meaning; it is this insight that naturalism or secularism lacks. Nevertheless, mysticism offers an inadequate center of value precisely because it "leads to an undifferentiated ultimate reality, [and thus] it is bound to regard particularity, including individuality, as essentially evil." Hence, Niebuhr posits that "all mystic philosophies ultimately lose the very individuality . . . [that is essential to meaning] because they sink finite particularity in[to] a distinctionless divine ground of existence."[17]

A genuine source of meaning must therefore avoid the pitfalls of both idolatry and mysticism. Only the God of Christian faith, Niebuhr submits, offers an answer that can safely navigate between these perennial dangers: "God [understood] as will and personality, [as found] in concepts of Christian faith, is thus the only possible presupposition of self-consciousness. But faith in God as will and personality depends upon faith in His power to reveal Himself." The need for such self-disclosure, Niebuhr asserts, means that the answer to the problem of meaning can finally only be identified through revealed religion or special revelation. This is the case, in his judgment, because "from the standpoint of human thought," God as the "unconditioned ground of existence . . . can be defined only negatively," not in any direct or positive terms. In other words, that God exists or that God is necessary, can be indicated by general revelation, but "the character and purpose of God" can only be known through the special revelation of prophetic

16. Ibid.
17. Ibid., 14, 15.

religion.[18] Thus, the value and contribution of natural religion or general revelation—of an inchoate intuition of God in all experience that is brought to conscious reflection—is that it provides a basis in common human experience for exposing the rational incoherence of alternative answers, such as offered by naturalism and mysticism, and it points to the need for special revelation. Niebuhr summarizes this "one-two revelatory punch" as follows:

> The conviction that man stands too completely outside of both nature and reason to understand himself in terms of either without misunderstanding himself, belongs to general revelation in the sense that any astute analysis of the human situation must lead to it. But if man lacks a further [or special] revelation of the divine he will also misunderstand himself when he seeks to escape the conditions of nature and reason. He will end by seeking [mystical] absorption in a divine reality that is at once all and nothing.[19]

In essence, Niebuhr suggests that general revelation without special revelation leads either to the error of mysticism or idolatry. Conversely, he suggests elsewhere that special revelation without general revelation leads to the error of an idolatrous literalism and/or an unconversant obscurantism. I will address this latter scenario in more detail later, but for now, against both of these sets of errors, Niebuhr believes that profound Christian insight requires the incorporation of both general and special revelation. He has this "both-and" approach in mind, for instance, when he states: "Though the religious faith through which God is apprehended cannot be in contradiction to reason ... yet, ... religious faith cannot be simply subordinated to reason [either]."[20] In short, the Christian answer is not and cannot be irrational (contrary to reason), but it is ultimately suprarational (above reason).

The Christian Answer to the Problem of Meaning

Human life and action, according to Niebuhr, including moral action, can only be coherently understood in relation to the suprarational norm of Jesus as the Christ. For only Christ, as the paradoxical "God-man,"

18. Ibid., 15, 14, 127. For a helpful discussion of Niebuhr's view of general vs. special revelation, see Gilkey, *On Niebuhr*, 70–71.
19. Niebuhr, *Nature and Destiny*, 1:15.
20. Ibid., 165.

concomitantly reveals the true nature of both divinity and humanity. In regard to divinity, Christ reveals God to be both eternal and temporal, powerful and powerless. In regard to humanity, Christ reveals humans to be creatures who transcend nature and history to the point of self-conscious relation to divinity, yet they are always situated in nature and history and thus should not be equated with divinity. As Gilkey insightfully observes, Niebuhr understands the dual-nature of Christ in revelatory not ontological terms.[21] Niebuhr articulates this as follows:

> In Christian faith the place of Christ as both the revelation of the character of God and of the essential nature of man (the "second Adam") does justice to the fact that man can find his true norm only in the character of God but is nevertheless a creature who cannot and must not aspire to be God. The God who is his norm is God as He is revealed in [the particularities] of human history, that is, in Christ. Christ is at once an historical character and more than an historical character. His life transcends the possibilities of history but it remains relevant to all historical striving, for all historical goals can [coherently] be expressed only in supra-historical terms.[22]

Once again Niebuhr asserts here that humans can find their true source of meaning and their true norm of action only in the character of God, which is defined by a selfless or sacrificial love. But this norm of divine love is only revealed in the particular life and narrative of Christ. As the "second Adam," Christ reveals the proper human response to existing at the juncture of nature and spirit, which is selfless love. But "the perfect love of the life of Christ ends on the Cross, after having existed in history. It is therefore supra-historical not in the sense of setting up a non-historical eternity as the goal of human life; but in the sense that the love which it embodies" is a love that "cannot justify itself in history." From the standpoint of history, Niebuhr reasons, only an ethic of mutual love and justice can be vindicated because only these norms seek the needed reciprocity and balance of power that competing human interests require. As Niebuhr reports, "All claims within the general field of interests must be proportionately satisfied and related to each other harmoniously." These proximate norms of mutual love and justice are, nevertheless, always related to and haunted by the vertical critique

---

21. Gilkey, *On Niebuhr*, 179.
22. Niebuhr, *Nature and Destiny*, 1:163.

of the "supra-historical" norm of selfless love. Hence, the love of Christ offers a norm that is an "impossible possibility," one transcendent —yet still related—to history.[23]

Having articulated the Christian answer to the problem of meaning, Niebuhr concludes that "every facet of the Christian revelation . . . points to the impossibility of man fulfilling the true meaning of his life and reveals sin to be primarily derived from his abortive efforts to do so." Yet, the Christian gospel not only discloses "the true meaning of life," but it also provides the resources "made available to fulfill that meaning."[24] Niebuhr finds these means of empowerment in the resources of divine mercy and grace, which make possible existential assent to the Christian answer to the problem of meaning. That is to say, in the face of the inevitability of sin—of inevitably orienting our lives around false sources of meaning, these resources make possible existential transformation in terms "of inner repentance and inner trust" in God's forgiving mercy and sustaining grace.[25]

But this transformation does not consist of some triumphal form of sanctification. On the contrary, transformation for Niebuhr consists of continually turning to and submitting oneself to the mercy of God. Relative improvements in individual and collective behavior may occur, to the extent that persons recognize and rely on this divine mercy and grace and insofar as societies strive to embody approximate forms of justice, but they always remain open and vulnerable to further forms of temptation and idolatry. Consequently, existential transformation remains for Niebuhr more of an ongoing hope than a realized fact. This outlook, he proposes, does not undermine moral action but instead makes it possible by protecting against the perennial dangers of self-righteous pride and presumption:

> To understand that the Christ in us is not a possession but a hope, that perfection is not a reality but an intention; that such peace as we know in this life is never purely the peace of achievement but [rather] the serenity of being "completely known and all forgiven"; all this does not destroy moral ardour or responsibility. On the contrary it is the only way of preventing premature completions of life, or arresting the new and more terrible pride

23. Ibid., 1:164, 2:68, 69; Niebuhr, *Interpretation of Christian Ethics*, 36.
24. Niebuhr, *Nature and Destiny*, 2:98.
25. Gilkey, *On Niebuhr*, 175.

which may find its roots in the soil of humility, and of saving the Christian life from the intolerable pretension of saints who have forgotten that they are sinners.[26]

Before proceeding to the final part of my portrait, let me summarize the emerging picture to this point. Thus far we have seen Niebuhr define the human situation in terms of the problem of meaning and define the human predicament of sin in terms of our anxious and misguided attempts to supply our own answers to this problem. The only truly adequate answer is found in a God who is both transcendent and related to the world. Reason can offer a negative validation of this answer to the extent that it can show the rational incoherence of alternative responses. The answer itself, however, is suprarational because it depends on an act of faith, namely, accepting the paradoxical revelation of God and man found in Jesus as the Christ. This act of faith is rooted in an existential act of repentance, opening oneself to the divine mercy and grace. In *Faith and History*, Niebuhr expresses this point as follows:

> In proceeding to an exposition of the Christian interpretation of life and history . . . *it is necessary to disavow the purpose of proving the Christian interpretation rationally compelling*, in the sense that such a comparison could *rationally force* modern man to accept the Christian faith. The Christian interpretation of life and history is rooted in a faith prompted by repentance. *It will not be convincing* except to the soul which has [already accepted the paradoxical vision of faith through mercy and grace]. There is therefore no simple Christian "philosophy of history" which could be set against a modern or classical one in such a way as to *prove* its superior profundity through rational comparison. *Yet it may be possible to prove its relevance rationally*, even as it has been possible [through the negative validation] to make a rational analysis of the limits of a theory of history's rational intelligibility [italics added].[27]

Niebuhr appears here to presume what I earlier called the discursive error: he presumes that rational arguments are supposed to compel or force assent, and he concludes that Christian faith cannot meet this standard (I will return to this in my assessment). Hence, he seeks instead to prove *ex post facto* the rational relevance of the Christian outlook.

---

26. Niebuhr, *Nature and Destiny*, 2:125–26.
27. Niebuhr, *Faith and History*, 101.

This goal defines his positive validation, which is where his theology and ethic become explicitly pragmatic.

The Positive Validation

Niebuhr describes the positive validation of Christian faith as follows:

> While the negative proof of the Christian truth can not be transmuted into a positive one, which would compel conviction on purely rational grounds, there is nevertheless a positive apologetic task. It consists in correlating the truth apprehended by faith and repentance, to truths about life and history, gained generally in experience. Such a correlation validates the truth of faith insofar as it proves it to be a source and center of an interpretation of life, more adequate than alternative interpretations, because it comprehends all of life's antinomies and contradictions into a system of meaning and is conducive to a renewal of life.[28]

Once the suprarational Christian perspective is accepted on the basis of faith and repentance, Niebuhr reasons, it proves to offer the most effective interpretive lens for making sense of human life and history. The key task here is to correlate the Christian interpretation of life with knowledge gained from other disciplines and with the realities of common human experience. Such a correlation, he contends, will prove that Christian faith provides a more adequate principle of interpretation than other alternatives because it is able to incorporate all of the antinomies and contradictions of history into a coherent system of meaning. It is crucial to note that Niebuhr's use of the term "adequate" here is informed by a Jamesian form of pragmatism.

Though Niebuhr does not often explicitly acknowledge his indebtedness to William James, various scholars have nonetheless rightly pointed out James's significant influence on Niebuhr. This influence goes all the way back to Niebuhr's BD thesis at Yale in 1914, which focused on James and the validity of religious knowledge. Perhaps Niebuhr's most direct acknowledgment comes in a letter to a friend: "I stand in the William James tradition. He was both an empiricist and a religious man, and his faith was both the consequence and the presupposition of his pragmatism."[29] What is critical for us to recognize is that Niebuhr,

---

28. Ibid., 165.

29. This quotation is cited in Bingham, *Courage to Change*, 224. I'm indebted to Hauerwas for drawing my attention to this passage, *With the Grain of the Universe*, 97.

following James, thinks that the truth claims of Christian faith can be validated by their practical consequences and usefulness. "If theological ideas prove to have a value for concrete life," James remarks, "they will be true, for pragmatism, in the sense of being good for so much."[30] Niebuhr basically concurs. If the suprarational perspective of Christian theism works effectively as an interpretive tool and guide for understanding human affairs, then its truth claims are positively validated. Many of Niebuhr's books and writings are meant precisely to show the pragmatic superiority of a Christian understanding of life, history, and politics. For instance, in *An Interpretation of Christian Ethics*, Niebuhr describes his anti-pacifistic analysis of violence as "wholly pragmatic."[31] To be sure, one should not simply equate Niebuhr and James's respective approaches. As Henry Samuel Levinson observes,

> Niebuhr doesn't fit or follow James at the latter's theologically least realistic and most pragmatic. Nowhere does Niebuhr "reduce" the truth of his Christian theological and moral realism to a confession that God or Christ are figures whose reality is simply a function of "what we need and can use," the way James at his most pragmatic had pictured any warrantable theological doctrine.[32]

Even though there are indeed some differences between Niebuhr and James, it is still the case, nevertheless, that Niebuhr's theology and ethic can be accurately described as pragmatic insofar as he turns to a Jamesian form of pragmatism to try to offer some validation of the suprarational Christian answer to the ultimate problem of meaning.

Along with Hauerwas, Lovin also discusses James's influence on Niebuhr: see his "Reinhold Niebuhr in Contemporary Scholarship," 497–500. Both Lovin and Hauerwas offer useful references to important biographies and studies on Niebuhr.

30. James, "What Pragmatism Means," 154. Original italics/emphasis deleted.

31. Niebuhr, *Interpretation of Christian Ethics*, 119. I am indebted to Malotky for drawing my attention to this passage: see his "Reinhold Niebuhr's Paradox," 110. For another example of Niebuhr's work that seeks to show the pragmatic superiority of a Christian understanding of politics, see Niebuhr, *Christian Realism and Political Problems*.

32. Levinson, "Let Us Be Saints," 226–27.

Typological Analysis

Commitment to Intelligibility (I+)

In his early book *Does Civilization Need Religion?* Niebuhr asserts that "religion must be able to impress the modern world with the essential plausibility and scientific respectability of its fundamental affirmations." This statement nicely articulates his lifelong commitment to making the gospel intelligible in modern terms. The method he employs to do this is most succinctly captured in his famous remark that one should take the Bible "seriously but not literally."[33] This critical distinction is premised on his view that biblical language is primarily symbolic or mythical in nature. For instance, in his essay "The Truth in Myths," Niebuhr distinguishes between "primitive" and "permanent" forms of myth. "Primitive myth" refers to those parts of the Bible "derived from pre-scientific thought, which [do] not understand the causal relations in the natural and historical world, [and thus] must naturally be sacrificed in a scientific age."[34] Simply put, there is no supernaturalism in Niebuhr. Hence, the Bible should not be read literally as a scientific or historical description. In this sense, the task of demythologizing must be pursued in order to make the Christian Gospel intelligible and plausible in the modern context. Levinson offers a vivid example:

> When pressed by [the philosopher] Norman Kemp Smith, Niebuhr's host at Edinburgh for his 1939 Gifford Lecture, for giving aid and comfort to fundamentalists by defending the doctrine of bodily resurrection, Niebuhr said, "I must have expressed myself badly . . . for I have not the slightest interest in the empty tomb or physical resurrection but only in resurrection as a concept [expressing] the idea that the fulfillment of life does not mean the negation and destruction of historical reality (which is a union of body-soul, freedom-necessity, time-eternity) but the completion of this unity."[35]

---

33. Niebuhr, *Does Civilization Need Religion?* 16; Niebuhr, *Nature and Destiny*, 2:50. In regard to the first quote, I'm indebted to Daniel Rice for drawing my attention to it: *Reinhold Niebuhr and John Dewey*, 99.

34. Niebuhr, "Truth in Myths," 118.

35. Levinson, "Let Us be Saints," 230. Levinson cites William Clebsch, *American Religious Thought* (Chicago: University of Chicago Press, 1973) 181 as the source of this exchange.

As this illustration suggests, however, Niebuhr also equally holds that demythologizing must not be pursued *tout court*. For along with primitive myths, the Bible also contains "permanent" myths that deal "with aspects of reality which are supra-scientific rather than pre-scientific. Modernistic religion has been so thin on the whole," Niebuhr adds, "because it did not understand this distinction and thus sacrificed what is abiding with what is primitive in religious myth." He has in mind here central Christian symbols, such as resurrection, creation, redemption, parousia, and last judgment, which he believes offer true thematic insight into the meaning and nature of existence. All these themes point in their own way to the essential but paradoxical Christian answer to the problem of meaning, to the God who is both related to yet transcendent to history. As Niebuhr describes it, these symbols point to "the Biblical idea of an eternity involved in, and yet transcending, the temporal." Therefore, "the ultimate problem of myth is always the problem of God." One sees here the implicit legacy of classical theism in Niebuhr's thought; eternity is taken to be the ultimate or primary category. The idea of unchanging eternity being involved in the succession and change of time is paradoxical. In the conclusion of *Nature and Destiny*, Niebuhr formulates the paradox as follows: "Eternity stands over time on the one hand and at the end of time on the other."[36] In other words, eternity (God) stands nontemporally *above* time as the ultimate ground and aim (telos) of all that exists within time, and this same eternity (God) stands *within* time as its end or conclusion *(finis)*. Thus for Niebuhr, given this paradox, the problem of God can only be answered suprationally and can only be expressed mythically or symbolically. Permanent biblical myths should be taken seriously, as symbolic expressions of the true meaning of history and the deeper dimensions of existence, but they should not be taken literally as historical descriptions of events.

Niebuhr's distinction between these two types of myth returns us to a discussion of his understanding of the relationship between general and special revelation. The error of biblical literalism, of failing to demythologize the pre-scientific worldview of primitive myth, is one persistent form of the error of asserting that the Gospel can only be known by special revelation. Yet, another form of this error is found in the Christomonism of Barth. Like Niebuhr, Barth appears to be willing to demythologize the scientific pretensions of primitive myth and

---

36. Niebuhr, "Truth in Myths," 119, 131; Niebuhr, *Nature and Destiny*, 2:290, 299.

biblical literalism. For example, during his visit to America in the 1960s, Barth took questions from a group of religious leaders meeting in his honor. Among them was the evangelical theologian Carl Henry. Henry rose, introduced himself as founding editor of *Christianity Today*, and asked Barth whether he believed in the literal bodily resurrection of Christ. Without missing a beat Barth replied, "Did you say Christianity *Today* or Christianity *Yesterday!*"[37] Hunsinger suggests, nonetheless, that Barth's position is somewhat more complex than Niebuhr's insofar as Barth preferred the language of "saga" or "legend" rather than "myth." "By regarding the biblical narratives as legendary witnesses," recounts Hunsinger,

> Barth . . . construed the mode of narration in essentially "post-critical" terms. The results of modern historical criticism were neither simply accepted nor simply rejected. Rather, even at their most compelling, they were conceived as essentially external to the theological task, for the subject matter of theology was, by definition, categorically beyond their reach. For example, traditional dogmas such as . . . the resurrection of Jesus from the dead were, in the nature of the case, beyond the competence of historical-critical method. Narratives about . . . the empty tomb were, as historical criticism had helped us to see, presented unmistakably in the form of imaginative and legendary depictions. But if such narratives were not to be taken as "factual reports," neither were they to be construed as "mythological pictures." "Myth" was an appropriate category only for narratives in which the subject matter purports to be universally and conceptually accessible. The biblical narratives, however, as Barth . . . read them, were not about ideas or universals . . . but about unique and unrepeatable events.[38]

Hunsinger's description here helps to clarify the central difference between Barth and Niebuhr. While neither of them is a biblical literalist, their alternatives to literalism are quite different. Niebuhr interprets central biblical narratives, such as resurrection, as permanent myths or symbols that convey universal ideas and truths about human experience and ultimate reality. These truths are conceptually accessible and intelligible to the wider public to the extent that one recognizes them

---

37. Carl Henry told me this story during a lunch conversation I had with him in Washington, DC in the summer of 1987. It also appeared in an online obituary article in memory of Henry, *Christianity Today*, www.christianitytoday.com, December 8, 2003.

38. Hunsinger, *How to Read Karl Barth*, 47.

as universal symbols rather than as pre-scientific claims. Barth likewise accepts that these stories are not historical accounts, but he maintains that the biblical narratives must nevertheless be read as "unique and unrepeatable events"—events pertaining to the central event of Jesus Christ. Hence, for Barth, the emphasis always remains on particularity, on special revelation only. There is no general revelation; thus biblical narratives cannot be made accessible or intelligible in relation to wider realms of knowledge. But, for Niebuhr, this Christomonistic particularity is just as problematic as biblical literalism. For whenever "the effort is made to guard the truth of faith and to prevent its absorption into a general system of knowledge by insisting that Christian truth . . . has no relation to any truth otherwise known," Niebuhr holds, one condemns the Gospel to "cultural obscurantism." Thus, on the one hand, the cultural obscurantism of literalism is that it denies and contradicts "the obvious truths about life and history, discovered by modern scientific disciplines." On the other hand, the obscurantism of Barth's Christomonism is that it makes the truth of faith "completely irrelevant to the truths discovered by the social, political, psychological, and historical sciences."[39]

Of course, just as Niebuhr rejects a theology that relies only on special revelation, he likewise rejects one that relies only on general revelation. As noted earlier, he believes that the truth of Christian faith is ultimately suprarational and thus requires symbolic or mythical expression. Hence, he judges that a fully rational Christian theism, one devoid of the paradox of permanent myth, commits the error of presuming that the truth claims of faith can be directly correlated to a general system of knowledge and can be directly and rationally validated by this correlation. But having said this, it is essential to recognize that Niebuhr's insistence on myth is always pursued in a manner that remains committed to public intelligibility and relevance. In other words, like Gustafson, Niebuhr wants to make sure that theology, including its use of Christian symbols, is conversant with the language of the academy and the broader public. "Ideally there should be a constant commerce," Niebuhr remarks,

---

39. Niebuhr, *Faith and History*, 166–67. Though Niebuhr does not explicitly address Barth in this passage, he does criticize his approach in other places. See *Faith and History*, 194 n. 33; *Nature and Destiny* 1:158 n. 14, and 2:66–67 n. 16.

between the specific truths, revealed by the various historical disciplines and the final truth about man and history as known from the standpoint of the Christian faith. In such a commerce the Christian truth is enriched by the specific insights which are contributed by every discipline of culture. But it also enriches the total culture and saves it from idolatrous aberrations.[40]

Like Gustafson, Niebuhr embraces the "constant commerce" of conversation between theology and other disciplines and the enrichment that theology obtains from them. But where Gustafson and Niebuhr differ is evident in the final sentence: to a much stronger degree than Gustafson, Niebuhr argues that Christian truth "enriches the total culture and saves it from idolatrous aberrations." It is this insistence that makes Niebuhr's apologetic approach a hard sell compared to Gustafson's soft sell, and it is this affirmation that leads us to a discussion of the autonomy of ethics.

Autonomy of Ethics (AE-)

Niebuhr's fundamental claim is that human life and history cannot be coherently understood apart from God. This central claim also implies that ethics and the moral life cannot be properly understood apart from the divine. Thus, unlike Gustafson, Niebuhr rejects the modern dominant consensus regarding the autonomy of ethics by maintaining that any coherent ethic must be theocentric. However, this unequivocal stance is not always starkly explicit in Niebuhr's thought. One reason for this is the way that he approaches ethics. Questions of human choice and action, either individual or collective, are always tied to the question of meaning or value. For instance, in *An Interpretation of Christian Ethics*, Niebuhr asserts that a "moral life is possible at all only in a meaningful existence. Obligation can be felt only to some system of coherence and some ordering [center of value]."[41] Given this connection, the question of ethics depends ultimately on finding a coherent source of meaning, which, for Niebuhr, requires Christian theism—thus ethics must be theistic. To be sure, one often needs to "connect the dots" between his discussions of moral norms and his underlying normative claims about meaning and value, but this connection is certainly implied, if

---

40. Niebuhr, *Faith and History*, 167. For Niebuhr's discussion of the error of rational theism, see 165.

41. Niebuhr, *Interpretation of Christian Ethics*, 63.

not always clearly drawn. One occasion where he more visibly draws the connection is when he states: "The [moral] law of [human] nature is love, a harmonious relation of life to life in obedience to the divine centre and source of [all] life."[42]

The other reason why Niebuhr's claim that ethics must be theistic is not always self-evident is due to the way that his stance on the questions of metaphysics and credibility affects his commitment to public intelligibility. This important interrelationship will become apparent as I proceed, but for now let me draw attention to an illuminating passage from Lovin. Niebuhr, he notes, "does not always speak explicitly of God." For example,

> Larry Rasmussen observes that Reinhold Niebuhr "was at his very best in his ability to render a theological interpretation of events for a wider audience, as a basis for common action. But precisely because of the audience's diverse beliefs, Niebuhr often cast his case in ways which left his Christian presuppositions and convictions unspoken." Both friends and critics have sometimes assumed that this means that [Niebuhr's theology] is superfluous, a pious footnote to an analysis that can be accepted or rejected on its own terms [apart from his theistic claims].[43]

This passage suggests that Niebuhr's commitment to intelligibility sometimes led him to shy away from theistic language in the broader academy and general public, which led others, in turn, to conclude that his theology was ultimately superfluous to his ethic. One would be right to reject this conclusion, but one would also be right to recognize a problem here in Niebuhr's approach. Given his commitment to intelligibility and given his belief that theistic claims are suprarational, it is not at all surprising that an ambiguity arises over how "theological" his public theology really is. The key issue lying behind this ambiguity is Niebuhr's view of the metaphysical enterprise, to which I now turn.

---

42. Niebuhr, *Nature and Destiny* 1:16. I am indebted to Lovin's work for enabling me to see and contextualize this passage in this way: see Lovin, *Reinhold Niebuhr and Christian Realism*, 21 n. 34.

43. Lovin, *Reinhold Niebuhr and Christian Realism*, 33. Lovin cites Rasmussen, "Reinhold Niebuhr Public Theologian," *Cross Currents* 38 (Summer 1988) 201.

Absence of Metaphysics (AM+)

Like Gustafson, Niebuhr recognizes the metaphysical dimension of theological claims about the reality of God. In fact, the early Niebuhr said that "the metaphysical problem of religion cannot be depreciated." In regard to this metaphysical dimension, Niebuhr holds that insofar as one must inevitably choose some "total end" or ultimate source of meaning, one "can set no limit to what [one] ought to be, short of the character of ultimate reality." Describing the character of ultimate reality is of course the task of metaphysics, and for Niebuhr, as we have seen, God is at the center of ultimate reality. Hence, to choose a "total end" short of the metaphysical telos, short of God, is to choose an inadequate source of meaning. Moreover, like Gustafson, Niebuhr is a "theological realist": he believes that "true statements about God are true because they accurately represent a reality independent of the concepts, theories, and evidence we have pertaining to that reality." God is not a human construct projected in order to fulfill practical human needs. Thus, in these two senses, Niebuhr recognizes that questions and claims about the reality of God are metaphysical matters. Gilkey confirms this point when he remarks that Niebuhr "recognized the importance of 'ontology' . . . (or 'metaphysical presuppositions')."[44]

Yet, in the end, like Gustafson, Niebuhr ultimately shares the modern aversion to metaphysics. As Gilkey emphatically states, "Niebuhr was characteristically wary of [metaphysical] speculation. . . . [A]ny theological affirmations he wished to make were essentially related to and validated in experience, though their forms . . . were given by revelation. In this he shows his empiricist, even his Schleiermachian, heritage."[45] This heritage, I would add, follows in the footsteps of those who accept the absence of metaphysics. Niebuhr, like Schleiermacher, Gustafson, and many others, accepts the Kantian and Humean consensus that denies that metaphysical claims can be rationally redeemed. Niebuhr's wariness about metaphysics is evidenced, for example, in his belief that the capacity for self-transcendence means that the ultimate source of meaning must be beyond the reach of reason:

---

44. Niebuhr, *Does Civilization Need Religion?* 16; Niebuhr, *Nature and Destiny*, 1:163. The description of theological realism comes from Lovin, *Reinhold Niebuhr and Christian Realism*, 20. Gilkey, *On Niebuhr*, 245.

45. Gilkey, *On Niebuhr*, 214.

> The rational faculty by which [man] orders and interprets his experience . . . is itself a part of the finite world which man must seek to understand. *The only principle for the comprehension of the whole . . . is therefore inevitably beyond his comprehension.* Man is thus in the position of being unable to comprehend himself in his full stature of freedom without a principle of comprehension which is beyond his comprehension [italics added].[46]

Niebuhr makes two distinct claims here with a presumptive leap in between. In the first sentence, he recognizes that our rational faculty is part of the whole of reality to be understood and interpreted. In the second and third sentences, he then concludes that the whole of reality is therefore inevitably beyond our comprehension. This leap from premise to conclusion reveals Niebuhr's rejection of the metaphysical enterprise. Instead of affirming that our rational faculty can grasp at least some necessary characteristics of the whole of which it is a part, Niebuhr instead concludes that the whole must be totally beyond our comprehension. But why must one conclude this? Why must the recognition of our situatedness as parts within a whole lead to the conclusion that the whole itself is rationally incomprehensible? As Daniel Malotky observes in assessing Niebuhr's view,

> There is nothing about our finite condition that precludes our ability to know a universal truth. Our articulation of that truth will surely bear the marks of our particularity. It will be the product of a particular time, place and culture; but this does not necessarily mean that it is not true, or that it is somehow less true. As finite beings, we are unable to know everything. [But] [w]e are not shielded from knowledge [of reality] *per se*.[47]

Niebuhr's conclusion (that we are shielded from rational comprehension of the whole) is necessary only if one has already presumed that metaphysical knowledge is impossible. In part, he is led to this conclusion because he overlooks the distinction between the two meanings of the "whole" that I discussed in chapter 3, i.e., between the whole as generic characteristics necessarily found in each and every part, and the whole as all-inclusive totality. Absent this distinction, to know the whole could only mean to know it in its entirety; and for Niebuhr—going back to the primacy of eternity—the whole is the completely eternal God

---

46. Niebuhr, *Nature and Destiny*, 1:125.
47. Malotky, "Reinhold Niebuhr's Paradox," 116.

who paradoxically includes time. Thus, given Niebuhr's assumptions, the whole cannot be rationally known.

Niebuhr's subscription to the modern rejection of metaphysics is even more pronounced in his essay "Mystery and Meaning," found in *Pious and Secular America*. There, he asserts that the meaning of existence does "not quite cohere rationally" and that it is "surrounded by a penumbra of mystery, which is not penetrated by reason." He then explicitly affirms "Kant's distinction between the noumenal and phenomenal world" as exemplifying a proper "rational modesty," one "which realize[s] the penumbra of mystery and the limits of discursive reason in penetrating the penumbra." Whatever differences Niebuhr has with Kant, he accepts Kant's noumenal-phenomenal bifurcation between freedom and causality and he shares Kant's rejection of speculative metaphysics. In this same essay, for instance, Niebuhr asserts that "the freedom of man does not fit into any system of metaphysics," and he implores modern thinkers to "cease to speculate about unanswerable metaphysical problems." For "men will seek for a metaphysical validation of [faith's claims about meaning and God] in vain." Only by abandoning such efforts and by accepting the suprarational mystery of Christian faith can one begin to recognize that "the idea of a suffering and . . . merciful God is a clue to the meaning of existence." Though Niebuhr continues to proclaim the reality of God and seeks to partially validate this proclamation through pragmatic means, he believes that the underlying metaphysical claims about the reality of God cannot be validated as such. Thus, "the 'existence' of God," he says, sounding much like Gustafson, "is assumed rather than [rationally] affirmed."[48] In effect, the divine reality remains for Niebuhr a suprarational mystery, and it is this embrace of mystery and this rejection of metaphysics that finally brings Niebuhr's commitment to credibility to a halt.

Commitment to Credibility (C-)

Though Niebuhr goes further than Gustafson in seeking to rationally justify the claims of theology, he, too, eventually abandons the commit-

---

48. Reinhold Niebuhr, "Mystery and Meaning," 123, 124, 128, 136, 134, 136, 135. Even though there is an essay with this same title in Brown, *Essential Reinhold Niebuhr*, 237–49, it is *not* the same essay. Evidently Niebuhr published variant essays or sermons using the same title but having different content. See Brown's Acknowledgments, viii–ix.

ment to credibility. For instance, in his negative validation, he rationally attempts to disclose the incoherence of alternative sources of meaning to that offered by Christian theism. As he puts it, "a limited rational validation of the truth of the Gospel is possible ... by exploring the limits of historic forms of wisdom and virtue." In response to these limits, he argues that only a God who is both transcendent to and yet related to history can serve as a genuine center of value and meaning. However, when it comes time positively to validate this claim, Niebuhr declares that this answer is paradoxical or suprarational in nature. Thus, one must first accept it on the basis of faith; but once it is accepted, he submits, this divine center of meaning proves pragmatically to offer the most effective lens for coherently interpreting life and history. "Positively," he writes, "[the Gospel] is validated when the truth of faith is correlated with all truths which may be known by scientific and philosophical disciplines and proves itself a [superior] resource for coordinating them into a deeper and wider system of coherence."[49]

As is evident here, Niebuhr uses different evaluative standards to assess theistic and non-theistic positions. Though he uses rational argument to demonstrate the inadequacies of alternative sources of meaning, when it comes to the Christian answer, he claims that it is beyond reason and must be accepted as such. In fact, at one point he bluntly states that "the ultrarational pinnacles of Christian truth [are those] embodying paradox and contradiction and straining at the limits of rationality."[50] But after "sending reason on holiday," Niebuhr then seeks to recall it in the form of pragmatic argument in order to offer a partial positive validation. One might say that Niebuhr's theological approach employs a "simple" or "uncritical" correlation model in the sense that he never fully compares Christian theism and its alternatives on the same footing.[51] The alternatives are rationally shown to be incoherent, whereas the Christian position is considered suprarational in its essence and thus must be accepted on such grounds. Christian faith is thereby proclaimed to offer a *suprarational* coherence to make sense

---

49. Niebuhr, *Faith and History*, 152.

50. Niebuhr, "Coherence, Incoherence, and Christian Faith," 224.

51. David Tracy compares a simple or uncritical correlation model with his own "revised critical correlation model," in which theology and culture are both assessed in terms of publicly available criteria, which provide "mutual illuminations and corrections." See Tracy, *Blessed Rage for Order*, 32–34, 45–46.

of the world whereas the alternatives are judged to be *rationally* incoherent. This "switch in the tracks"—between his negative and positive validations—marks the place where reason goes on holiday for Niebuhr and where his commitment to credibility ends. To be sure, his pragmatic positive validation seeks to offer a limited *ex post facto* argument, but the fundamental claim about the reality of God is always finally assumed rather than defended.

In my judgment, it is because Niebuhr ultimately assumes the reality of God rather than argues for it that the phenomenon of "Atheists for Reinhold Niebuhr" makes historical sense. Because Niebuhr himself emphasized the pragmatic utility of theological concepts without defending their metaphysical validity, he opened the door for non-religious intellectuals and policy-makers to believe that they could adopt and digest his ethical diagnoses about human nature and social problems without swallowing his underlying suprarational theistic claims. They could accept, in other words, Niebuhr's conception of justice and mutuality (along with his realism) as norms for historical action, but they could not accept that these were dependent on a "higher norm" of sacrificial love or the character of ultimate reality, and this is due to the fact that Niebuhr's ethic became suprarational precisely at the point where he introduced theism. In sum, as Daniel Rice observes, Niebuhr believed that "an adequate ethics was more important for religion than an adequate metaphysics."[52] But this imbalance, I would suggest, ultimately led some to discount the centrality of theism for his ethics and politics.

Critical Assessment

Among Niebuhr's many strengths is his insight that Christian symbols, especially the cross, point to an understanding of God and history that is contrary to common expectation. These symbols reveal that "the idea of a suffering and ... merciful God is a clue to the meaning of existence."[53] For Niebuhr, this clue finds history's ultimate source of meaning in an eternal God who paradoxically includes time. This inclusive or "both-and" approach (eternity includes time) not only runs contrary to the

---

52. Rice, *Reinhold Niebuhr and John Dewey*, 99. Rice attributes the phrase "Atheists for Reinhold Niebuhr" to Morton White and discusses it on 217.

53. Niebuhr, "Mystery and Meaning," 136.

"either-or" assumptions of mysticism (time swallowed up in eternity) and secularism (time without eternity), but it also runs against much of traditional Christian thinking and practice, which give customary nod to these symbols at appropriate times of the year but do not take them with full seriousness in terms of revealing the true nature of divinity or the meaning of history. Challenging this tendency, Niebuhr rightly discerns that the love of God, as disclosed in the cross, is a genuine and full-fledged expression of the character of God and of God's relation to the world.

Although Niebuhr's intuition points in the right direction, his insight is finally clouded and partly dissipated by the fact that his conception of the relation of eternity and time is ultimately controlled by a classical understanding of God, and it appears that Niebuhr never fully or systematically questioned this inherited understanding. To be sure, he is insistent, against mysticism, that time and the world are ultimately meaningful. However, as noted, he holds that eternity is the primary or inclusive category—eternity includes time. This means, as Hartshorne suggests, that "the category of temporality . . . [is still finally] extrinsic to God, inexpressible in terms of the divine nature."[54] That is to say, God is thought to be eternally complete, notwithstanding that God includes time. If one takes eternity to be the inclusive category, as Niebuhr does, then one encounters the following basic problem: eternity by definition does not change; time is change; thus how can eternity include time? It is this rational tension, this paradox, that forces Niebuhr to assert that the answer to the problem of meaning can only be understood suprarationally and that Christian symbols can only be understood as permanent myths, not in rationally coherent terms. Furthermore, it is because his underlying conception of God is classical in this sense that Niebuhr agrees with Kant about the impossibility of metaphysical knowledge; and it is this conception that prevents Niebuhr from articulating the nature of God metaphysically. Given this underlying view, which takes God-talk finally to be suprarational, Niebuhr abandons his commitment to credibility at a critical juncture, and thus ultimately assumes the reality of God rather than defends it. This abandonment undermines the

---

54. Hartshorne and Reese, *Philosophers Speak of God*, 21. For the sake of brevity and, more importantly, since it states explicitly in the Preface (ix) that Hartshorne was the sole author of the Introduction, from which this quotation (and one below) comes, I will, with due respect to Reese, attribute this passage in the text only to Hartshorne.

connection between his theology and ethics. His attempt to put forth an adequate ethic, which he believes must be theocentric, is weakened by his own inattention to developing an adequate metaphysics. Again, this is the case because the claim about the reality and necessity of God is finally a metaphysical claim and not merely a pragmatic one. Hence, his attempt to make theological claims intelligible and relevant without making them fully credible ends up enabling others to disconnect his core theological convictions from his ethical insights. This disconnection, moreover, short-circuits his ethical insights to the extent that it cuts off the meaning of human action from its divine center of value.

My central criticism is that Niebuhr finally lacks a clear and credible expression of how time is related to eternity. This is evident in the fact that, in spite of his commitment to social action, he fails to clearly articulate why people should be committed to making the world a better place. On the one hand, he unequivocally rejects cynical despair and an attitude of disengagement from the affairs of the world. On the other hand, he emphatically dismisses a liberal optimism that believes it can progressively and permanently improve human affairs—thus embodying the kingdom of God on earth. So what third alternative does he offer? Gilkey suggests that Niebuhr "sought to reestablish the liberal concern for creative action in the world on a more realistic and . . . more solid . . . classical Christian basis. . . . If the kingdom [of God] really cannot be built in Detroit or New York," Gilkey asks, "why persist in seeking to make these cities better? Or why endanger or even sacrifice oneself for such a hopeless endeavor?" Niebuhr's answer is found in his discussion of the Christian symbol of the resurrection at the end of history:

> The idea of the resurrection implies that the historical elaborations of the richness of creation, in all their variety, will participate in the consummation of history. *It gives the struggles in which men engaged to preserve civilizations, and to fulfill goodness in history, abiding significance and does not relegate them to a meaningless flux, of which there will be no echo in eternity* (italics added).[55]

As we know, Niebuhr does not take the Christian symbols literally. So how or in what way do our actions "echo in eternity" and thus entail "abiding significance"? Niebuhr does not explain, for this claim is part of the larger suprarational Christian answer. All he can say is that these

55. Gilkey, *On Niebuhr*, 23; Niebuhr, *Nature and Destiny*, 2:312.

symbols "are even more difficult to understand when they seek to express the Biblical idea of an eternity involved in, and yet transcending, the temporal."[56] This, of course, simply brings us back to the problem of his underlying classical conception of God.

Gilkey tries to help clarify Niebuhr's position when he writes that

> creaturely life provides the basic foundation for all that is creative and meaningful in our existence: the joys of existence—sensual, bodily, aesthetic—our love for one another, our dependence on family and community, our ingenuity and faithfulness, our artistic and intellectual creativity, and the significant vocations that give point to our efforts. These 'goods' are not the whole, nor are any of them of ultimate significance; however, despite its fragmentary and insignificant character, our very finitude can be apprehended as contributing not only to our own brief joys and those of others, but also to a whole, to a plan and a purpose, transcendent to our understanding but available to each of us by faith.[57]

In one sense, Gilkey does help here by suggesting that human actions have lasting significance because they contribute to a greater whole of which they are a part. But what is the nature of this whole, and how do our actions contribute to it? Gilkey does not elaborate. Moreover, Gilkey appears to cloud matters when he suggests, contrary to what Niebuhr seems to be saying, that earthly goods and achievements do not have any ultimate significance. Where Gilkey is certainly true to Niebuhr, though, is in coming back to the claim that the whole to which we contribute is part of "a plan and a purpose, transcendent to our understanding but available to each of us [only] by faith." In other words, we cannot say how our actions are meaningful because such an answer is again suprarational. Instead, we can only affirm the hope that our actions are meaningful from a standpoint of faith. But this is exactly the problem with Niebuhr's position; it is inarticulate, and thus unconvincing, at the critical juncture of explaining the relationship between time and eternity. Given his lack of explanation, one wonders at times whether Niebuhr's answer boils down merely to a sense of Christian duty, i.e., to a deontological command to love the neighbor without regard for its effects in the world. Yet, such a non-teleological outlook runs so contrary

---

56. Niebuhr, *Nature and Destiny*, 2:290.
57. Gilkey, *On Niebuhr*, 84.

to his fundamental connection between meaning, aims, and action that it is both unsatisfactory and unconvincing. In short, for a man so committed to action, Niebuhr ultimately lacks clear and articulate reasons why we should act in the world. Hence, what we find here again is his insight being derailed by his underlying classical conception of God and his insistence on the need for permanent myths and suprarational expression.

In part, what Niebuhr fails to see is that the element of insight or truth contained in permanent myths must be articulated, at some point, in nonmythical terms. This conclusion follows necessarily from his own admission that myths cannot be taken literally. For, as Ogden observes, "to claim that a given mythical assertion is true, although not literally so, is to commit oneself to state the meaning of the assertion at some point in other, nonmythical terms."[58] It is the fulfillment of this commitment that Niebuhr thinks he can avoid. But if myths cannot be taken literally, they must be interpreted, and this interpretation can only be formulated nonmythically; otherwise one has failed to advance clarity or understanding. For Niebuhr to acknowledge the necessity of nonmythical formulation does not force him to abandon myth altogether, but it does force him to recognize that a process of demythologizing must occur at some point if religious claims are to be rationally defended or justified. As Ogden states, "the purpose of demythologizing . . . is not to *eliminate* mythology but to *interpret* it."[59]

Because the origins of the Christian revelation are historically particular, Niebuhr believes that "there is no experience which points irrefutably to the particular divine ground and end of history which Christian faith discerns in Christ and the Cross."[60] Hence, he alleges that

---

58. Ogden, *Reality of God*, 108. My discussion in this paragraph and in the next paragraph is drawn from my doctoral dissertation: Meyer, "Relation of Theism to Ethics," 137–39.

59. Ogden, *Point of Christology*, 11. If myth can and needs to be interpreted in rational or nonmythical terms, then one might ask why not eliminate myth altogether? Ogden offers a helpful answer when he distinguishes between "mythical assertions" and "mythical utterances." The former make cognitive claims that assert something to be true, which requires rational interpretation. The latter refers to other uses of mythical language, such as "to express, to evoke, to enjoin, etc." In short, myth can still serve a valuable evocative role, e.g., in worship and liturgy, even though such language needs philosophical interpretation and translation when it comes to systematic theology. See Ogden, *Reality of God*, 118 n. 21.

60. Niebuhr, *Nature and Destiny*, 96–97.

the particular insights of Christian theism cannot be expressed apart from myth and cannot be known independently of faith. But again, as Ogden argues,

> even if belongs to religion by its very nature to advance... special claims [claims that arise out of a particular history], the fact that it presents them as generally applicable and, in some cases, universally valid means that there have to be at least some reasons correspondingly general or universal for accepting them, if their acceptance is to be at all rationally motivated.[61]

Ogden's basic point is that a fundamental distinction exists between making a claim and justifying or validating it. The fact that a claim is made in or through a particular event, such as the Christ event, does not mean that the claim can be justified by appeal to that event. Similarly, as Bonjour notes, there is an important difference between how one acquires a concept and how one justifies it. The scope, breadth, or pretension of a claim, not its source or origin, determines to what a rational justification must appeal. Niebuhr himself tacitly agrees to this demand insofar as he (1) offers general reasons in his negative validation to show the incoherence of alternative sources of meaning, (2) insists that "there is no possibility of elaborating a realm of meaning without engaging the rational faculty," and (3) claims that the ultimate principle of meaning (the God of Christian faith) cannot be in contradiction to the subordinate principle of meaning (rational coherence).[62]

What Niebuhr's position needs, therefore, is a clear and credible articulation that coherently relates God and the world. Such a task ultimately requires a commitment to the metaphysical enterprise and not merely to suprarational expression in the form of permanent myth. The insights of Niebuhr's theology fit well with and would be strengthened by process metaphysics. In fact, I am tempted to say that Niebuhr's theology cries out for development along these lines. Just as Levinson observes that James's pragmatism "lurched towards a process panentheism," so, too, does Niebuhr's theology.[63] For example, Niebuhr's

---

61. Ogden, *On Theology*, 84.
62. Niebuhr, "Religion and Action," 45 and *Nature and Destiny*, 1:165–66.
63. Levinson, "Let Us Be Saints," 223. James's lecture on "Pragmatism and Religion" is one good example of where he seems to be implicitly searching for a process panentheism as an alternative to both classical theism and secularistic naturalism. See James, *Pragmatism*, 131–44, esp. 142–43.

assertion that the ultimate source of meaning can only be found in a God who is both transcendent to and immanent in history clearly points in the direction of a dipolar theism as developed by Whitehead and especially Hartshorne. Such a dipolar conception would enable Niebuhr to rationally and coherently express his insight about how God relates to the world without resorting to the cul-de-sac of suprarational paradox, which derails any effort to make Christian theism publicly credible. Within a dipolar conception, both time and eternity are affirmed, but time is understood as the primary or concrete metaphysical category; eternity is understood as an abstract characteristic—abstracted from time. Thus, temporality is understood to be intrinsic to God's own nature. God can coherently include time because succession and change are part of the very fabric of the divine life itself. The factor of temporality, Hartshorne remarks, "is our [rational] safeguard" when it comes to understanding God and the world, for it "opens the door of escape from the paradoxes of a supreme reality which yet cannot intelligibly contain the totality of existence."[64] Moreover, as we saw in chapter 2, such a dipolar conception offers an opportunity to develop a credible case for the necessary existence of God, a point that Niebuhr's position lacks. Likewise, Niebuhr's insight—that human action is not relegated to a meaningless flux but rather has abiding significance—is ably conceptualized in process thought in terms of how all things affect and contribute to the divine life, what Whitehead calls "the consequent nature of God."[65]

It is noteworthy both that Niebuhr was at least partly familiar with the works of Hartshorne and Whitehead and that he viewed them in relatively high regard. According to Niebuhr,

> Professor Charles Hartshorne's *The Vision of God* gives a profound analysis of this problem [of the divine nature] and presents the thesis that God's perfection must be defined primarily in terms of His ... "self-surpassing" character rather than in the traditional concepts of omnipotence, if the Christian doctrine of His ability to enter into loving relationship with suffering men is to have any meaning.[66]

---

64. Hartshorne and Reese, *Philosophers Speak of God*, 22.
65. Whitehead, *Process and Reality*, 345.
66. Niebuhr, *Nature and Destiny*, 2:71 n. 1.

Similarly, in "Mystery and Meaning," Niebuhr describes Whitehead as "the most searching philosopher of the sciences in modern life." Nevertheless, in spite of his praise for Hartshorne and Whitehead and their insights into the nature of God and world, insights that fit well with many of his own theological intuitions, Niebuhr does not follow their lead and seek to develop a metaphysical theism. This is due again to his underlying classical conception of God and his prior acceptance of the Kantian denial of metaphysics. This prior stance not only inhibits him from pursuing a metaphysical path, but at times it also muddies his reading of these metaphysical thinkers. For instance, Niebuhr claims that in *"Process and Reality*, [Whitehead] discerns the limits of rationality and posits a 'primordial God,' a kind of [unknowable] X to symbolize the realm of mystery." This realm of mystery, of course, is what Niebuhr seeks to affirm about the nature of God because he presumes that our understanding of the divine must be suprarational or paradoxical. Hence, later in the essay, Niebuhr claims that "the Christ revelation . . . illumines the [mystery of God because] . . . it substitutes for the unknown X of the primordial god [of Whitehead], the conception of a divine source and end of all historical meanings and purposes."[67]

Niebuhr here mistakenly reads Whitehead as an ally who concurs with him that knowledge of God is beyond reason. Hence, he interprets Whitehead's notion of the primordial nature of God as a signifier marking the unknowable realm of permanent mystery. But this is not what Whitehead means at all. On the contrary, for Whitehead, "God is not to be treated as an exception to all metaphysical principles, invoked [as a mystery] to save their collapse. [Rather,] He is their chief exemplification." In other words, the task of metaphysics is to seek to understand and elaborate the metaphysical principles of reality, including God as the all-inclusive entity who is the source and end of all things. Moreover, it is because of Whitehead's appreciation for empiricism that he claims "it is a contradiction in terms to assume that some explanatory fact can float into the actual world out of nonentity"; thus, "everything must be somewhere." It is because of this insistence that everything, including possibilities, must be somewhere, that Whitehead envisions the primordial nature of God as the source and "bank" of all possibilities. "[T]he general potentiality of the universe," Whitehead remarks, "must be somewhere" and that somewhere is in God. So for Whitehead, the

---

67. Niebuhr, "Mystery and Meaning," 125, 134.

primordial nature of God is not, as Niebuhr presumes, a symbol to indicate the suprarational nature of the divine mystery. Rather, it is an attempt to rationally conceptualize the divine nature in terms that cohere with the metaphysical generalities and the facts of experience. Whitehead by no means believes that we can exhaustively describe the divine nature, for metaphysics is always an asymptotic and fallible enterprise, not an act of complete possession. Nevertheless, "there is no first principle [including God] which is in itself unknowable, not to be captured by a flash of insight."[68]

My contention that Niebuhr's profound insights would be better developed and defended in terms of process metaphysics would, of course, engender its own response from Niebuhr. I can imagine that he might offer at least three possible objections to my claim. First, he might point back to James and argue that the value of pragmatism is precisely that it bypasses metaphysical questions, thus making them moot. As James writes:

> The pragmatic method is primarily a method of settling metaphysical disputes that otherwise might be interminable.... The pragmatic method [tries to do this by] interpret[ing] each notion [or claim] by tracing its respective practical consequences. What difference would it practically make to any one if this notion rather than that notion were true? If no practical difference ... can be traced, then the alternatives mean practically the same thing, and all dispute is idle. Whenever a dispute is serious, we ought to be able to show some practical difference that must follow from one side or the other's being right.[69]

Following James, Niebuhr might submit that what really matters are the practical implications of any claim, including metaphysical ones, and thus it is more important for theology to attend to these pragmatic consequences than to metaphysical questions about the reality of God. For without practical difference, all debate is idle.

Niebuhr and James are correct to hold that genuinely different ideas must make some difference in practice. From this insight, however, they draw a false conclusion—that metaphysical questions do not need to be directly addressed. The pragmatic method, James proceeds to say, is "the attitude of looking away from first things, principles, 'categories,'

---

68. Whitehead, *Process and Reality*, 343, 46, 4.
69. James, "What Pragmatism Means," 142.

supposed necessities; and [instead] looking towards last things, fruits, consequences, facts."[70] This attempt to bypass metaphysical questions by focusing only on practical consequences indicates two things. First, it indicates an implicit if not explicit acceptance of the modern consensus that believes that metaphysical questions are not directly redeemable. James implies this when he suggests that metaphysical disputes are interminable. Second, it reveals a serious confusion about the relationship between truth and effect. Just because an idea has some noticeable practical effect does not mean that it is true; that was Feuerbach's whole point about the idea of God. The idea of the divine may indeed have a profound practical effect on human beings, but whether that idea stems merely from a collective human projection or whether it stems from a metaphysical reality independent of human nature is a question that can only be answered metaphysically, not pragmatically. In short, pragmatism without metaphysics fails to respond adequately to Feuerbach's critique.

The fact that Niebuhr fails to attend directly to the question of the reality of God is the subject of a recent debate between Hauerwas and Lovin. Hauerwas claims that Niebuhr's pragmatism, following in the footsteps of Jamesian empiricism, undermines his talk about the reality of God. "It appears that for Niebuhr," Hauerwas surmises, "God is nothing more than the name of our need to believe that life has an ultimate unity that transcends the world's chaos and makes possible what order we can achieve in this life." In reply, Lovin points to Gilkey's reading of Niebuhr to reiterate that Niebuhr is a theological realist and not some closet-Feuerbachian in pragmatic garb, as Hauerwas implies. "Gilkey adopts a realistic interpretation of Niebuhr's theology," Lovin observes, "that puts him at odds with Hauerwas's empiricist reading of Niebuhr."[71] Lovin then points to a key passage from Gilkey's account; Gilkey writes:

> Essential to [Niebuhr's view], of course, is the reality of God. Niebuhr does not to my knowledge discuss this point; he assumes it. In Niebuhr's theology, God cannot be a projection, a human ideal shone outward onto the cosmos, an ideal made transcendent by the creativity of human self-transcendence

---

70. Ibid., 146, original italics deleted.

71. Hauerwas, *With the Grain of the Universe*, 131. Lovin's comparison of Hauerwas and Gilkey is found in Lovin, "Reinhold Niebuhr in Contemporary Scholarship," 501.

> (though many of his statements in his early writings seemed to imply this view).
>
> Such a [projected] deity would for the mature Niebuhr be the creation of ordinary and all-too-common human idolatry, [and thus not the real God of Christian faith]. . . . Like both Luther and Calvin, Niebuhr characteristically avoided ontological language; but . . . beyond the . . . (mythical) symbols about God which he used the most, lay the ontological assumption that God represents ultimate reality, or properly put, that God is Being itself.[72]

This passage from Gilkey reveals three important factors. First, Niebuhr is trying to be a theological realist; the term "God" is not just the name of our need. Second, Niebuhr makes implicit ontological or metaphysical claims about the reality of God, which underlie his use of Christian symbols. But, third, Niebuhr does not seek to justify these claims; rather, he simply assumes their validity. So in terms of the current debate, I would say that Hauerwas and Lovin are each partly correct. Hauerwas is right to recognize that Niebuhr's talk about the reality of God is undermined and, at the same time, Lovin and Gilkey are right to view Niebuhr as trying to be a theological realist.

In contradistinction to all of them, however, I would argue that the real problem is that Niebuhr's theological realism is undermined because, following James, he tries to substitute the question of practical consequences for the question of metaphysical validity. This substitution can never work because pragmatic effects are, by definition, particular and contingent, and therefore they cannot validate metaphysical claims, which are universal and necessary.[73] One can never defend the *universal reality of God* merely by pointing to the practical consequences of *our particular believing* in that purported reality. Again, this is not to say that metaphysical understandings do not have pragmatic effects. But to truly judge which effects are good or "are profitable to our lives," as James puts it, requires an understanding of the whole of reality and not

---

72. Gilkey, *On Niebuhr*, 188–89; Lovin, "Reinhold Niebuhr in Contemporary Scholarship," 501.

73. The reality of God is a claim that purports to hold for all possible states of affairs—is completely non-restrictive—whereas pragmatic effects hold only for some states of affairs, and thus they are partly restrictive. This goes back to the confusion that Niebuhr inherits from James.

merely a vision of a part.[74] For defining the good in terms of the part is precisely the kind of duplicitous or idolatrous self-understanding that Niebuhr warns against. The irony here is that Niebuhr's intuitions point again in the right direction, toward the need for knowledge of the whole. Because he accepts the absence of metaphysics, however, he instead follows James's pragmatism in order to try to justify his suprarational theism. What is needed instead is a metaphysical pragmatism, one that evaluates pragmatic effects in relation to a metaphysical whole, rather than an empirical pragmatism, which James offers and Niebuhr mistakenly accepts. In sum, Hauerwas is right to recognize that Niebuhr's adoption of James's empirical pragmatism is problematic for Niebuhr's theology. But neither Hauerwas, Lovin, nor Gilkey recognizes that what is truly called for is a metaphysical pragmatism.

In reply to this, Niebuhr's second criticism might assert, akin to Gustafson, that metaphysics cannot account for the particularities of history, especially for it contradictions, paradoxes, and unexpected cul-de-sacs. "That . . . the laws of reason and logic are incapable of fully comprehending the total meaning of the world," Niebuhr claims, "is attested by the fact that life and history are full of contradictions which cannot be resolved in terms of rational principles."[75] Niebuhr is correct that reason or metaphysics cannot account for all the particularities within the whole of reality. As Hegel rightly observes, "Reason itself requires us to recognize that contingency [and] contradiction . . . have a sphere and a right of their own, restricted though it be, and it is irrational to strive to resolve and rectify contradictions within that sphere."[76] The point of reason or metaphysics, in other words, is not to identify the particular details of history but rather to seek to understand the generic characteristics of the whole of reality, to which all the contingent parts are necessarily related. What Niebuhr insightfully discerns is that the meaning of history requires a divine reality that is both transcendent to and yet intimately related to the contingencies of history. But what he does not adequately articulate is how God relates to history—how time and eternity are conceptually related such that the contingency of history is related to the necessity of the whole. The point of a metaphysical justification of the divine reality is not to ignore or lose the

---

74. James, "What Pragmatism Means," 155.
75. Niebuhr, *Nature and Destiny*, 1:165.
76. Hegel, *Philosophy of Right*, 137.

contingencies of history but rather to make sense of them in relation to a meaningful and coherent whole, which is what Niebuhr intends but fails finally to provide.

His third and final criticism goes back to his assumptions about the function and purpose of arguments. If such a rational or metaphysical validation of theism were possible, asserts Niebuhr, it "would compel conviction on purely rational grounds." "[But] there is no force of reason," he maintains, "which moves [one] from despair to hope or transmutes remorse into repentance. Ultimately the acceptance of the truth of the Gospel is a gift of grace which stands beyond [reason]."[77] Here again Niebuhr is partly right in what he says but wrong in his underlying assumption. He is correct to hold that arguments cannot *compel* existential or cognitive assent; this was my chief point in identifying and rejecting the discursive error. But Niebuhr is guilty of this error when he presumes that compelling assent is in fact the underlying function of arguments. In making this assumption, he once again appears to follow in the footsteps of James.

In "The Will to Believe" James offers a brilliant discussion of the various psychological and existential influences that affect how individuals receive and process arguments and reasons. "Evidently, then" he concludes, "our non-intellectual nature does influence our convictions. There are passional tendencies and volitions which run before and others which come after belief.... The state of things is evidently far from simple; and pure insight and logic, whatever they might do ideally, are not the only things that really do produce our creeds." In spite of his insight here, James appears to assume that rational arguments are ideally supposed to compel or coerce assent. He begins his remarks, for instance, by saying: "I have brought with me tonight ... an essay in justification of faith, a defense of our right to adopt a believing attitude in religious matters, in spite of the fact that our merely logical intellect may not have been coerced." The implied assumption here seems to be that logical or rational arguments are supposed to coerce. And because such coercive arguments cannot be given in the area of religion, James reasons, we then have a "right to adopt a believing attitude in religious matters." This either/or formulation between coercive argument (in some matters) and the right to believe (in other matters) is suggested when he states his thesis: "The thesis I defend is ... this:

---

77. Niebuhr, *Faith and History*, 165.

Our passional nature not only lawfully may, but must, decide an option between propositions, whenever it is a genuine option that cannot by its nature be decided on intellectual grounds" (original italics removed).[78] Again, what seems to be at work here is the assumption that intellectual grounds operate along coercive lines—valid arguments compel assent. And where such coercion does not hold sway, we must decide on passional not rational grounds.

Niebuhr follows James both in assuming that rational arguments are supposed to compel assent and in concluding that such coercion cannot occur in the area of religious faith. They are certainly correct in the latter but wrong in the former. Where they go wrong is in assuming that the function of arguments is to compel assent and thus to directly establish conviction or existential faith. Again, the purpose of arguments is not to directly establish a condition or create a commitment but rather to defend the validity claims that one makes in speech and public discourse. Hence, the point of a positive or metaphysical validation of theism is not to compel the establishment of religious faith, but rather to defend the truth claims that one makes about the reality of God. Niebuhr is certainly right that "there is no force of reason" compelling one from existential despair to hope. But we still have an obligation to give the best reasons possible, including metaphysical ones, precisely because we make public claims about what is true and good for human existence. Such reasons invite the assent of others at both cognitive and existential levels. Hence, even though such arguments do not compel conviction, they may have, and hopefully do have, an indirect or luring effect that gradually influences our world and the persons living in it. In sum, by misconceiving the function of arguments, Niebuhr prematurely dismisses the need for a metaphysical validation of theology's central claims about the reality and necessity of God.

Summary (I+C-AE-AM+)

There is no doubt that Niebuhr's pragmatic approach was partly successful in giving theology a public voice in the middle of the twentieth century. His commitment to intelligibility made Christian symbols a powerful vehicle for analyzing and critiquing human nature and society. In spite of his rejection of the autonomy of ethics and his

---

78. James, "Will to Believe," 94–95, 88, 95.

insistence that human life and action can only be properly understood in relation to a theistic source of meaning, however, Niebuhr's denial of the metaphysical enterprise left his fundamental claim about the reality of God perpetually unsupported. He tried to cover this base in a pragmatic fashion by arguing that once one accepts the suprarational assumption of the Christian understanding of God, one can then offer a more adequate view of history and politics. But such an *ex post facto* assertion merely begs the question rather than adequately validating the claims of faith. Hence, even though Niebuhr went further than Gustafson in seeking to offer a credible defense of theology's claims, he, too, abandoned the commitment to credibility at some point. The cultural phenomenon of "Atheists for Reinhold Niebuhr" attests to the fact that others perceived a breach in his thought between his theistic and ethical or political claims. Though Niebuhr certainly did not intend this breach, it nevertheless indicates a genuine weakness in his approach. This weakness stems ultimately from his lack of a metaphysical validation of his central claim about the reality and necessity of God.

7

A Witness Theology

The Approach of Stanley Hauerwas

Theological Portrait

IF JAMES GUSTAFSON OFFERS A SOFT SELL AND REINHOLD NIEBUHR A hard sell, then Stanley Hauerwas rejects "selling" theology altogether. The enterprise of directly promoting theology in the public marketplace of ideas, culture, and politics, Hauerwas thinks, is a dangerous and misguided endeavor. For more than a quarter-century, he has argued that Christian theology must wake from its slumber, resist the seductive temptation of the public marketplace, and find an alternative way to express the meaning and truth of the Gospel. Throughout his prolific career, Hauerwas has made a significant contribution to theology and the church by attempting to articulate and build a case for such an alternative. Though the defining themes of his approach surface in nearly all of his works, his overall vision is perhaps most crisply articulated in his 1989 book *Resident Aliens: Life in the Christian Colony*, which he co-authored with William Willimon. This book has been one of the most widely read theological works in recent decades, especially among clergy. With due respect to Willimon, I will use *Resident Aliens* to provide a skeletal framework for my theological portrait of Hauerwas. I will also draw from his other numerous texts, ranging from his 1975 book *Character and the Christian Life* to his 1983 *The Peaceable Kingdom* to his 2001 Gifford Lectures *With the Grain of the Universe*, to flesh out the nuanced details of his thought.

The Constantinian Legacy and the Modern American Church

"Sometime between 1960 and 1980, an old, inadequately conceived world ended, and a fresh, new world began." *Resident Aliens* begins with this provocative claim. The old world is the world of the Constantinian legacy, an age-old attempt to integrate Christ and culture into a synergistic whole. Though this legacy dates back to the fourth century, Hauerwas is most interested in its modern American manifestation—the assumption that the gospel can be "adapted and domesticated" in such a way as to "fit American values into a loosely Christian framework," thereby making theology and the church "culturally significant."[1]

This endeavor stems in part, Hauerwas believes, from the aims of the Enlightenment. "The project of theology since the Enlightenment, which has consumed our best theologians, has been [to ask] 'How do we make the gospel credible to the modern world?'" By seeking to make the gospel at least partly credible, theologians from Schleiermacher to Niebuhr to Gustafson have presumed that "Christian thought must be translated in order to become intelligible to modern people." This "theology of translation assumes that there is some kernel of *real* Christianity, some abstract essence that can be preserved even while changing [or translating or discarding] some of the old Near Eastern labels [or primitive stories]."[2] This strategy of demythologization and translation has been pursued in the hopes of making theology and faith relevant to the larger culture and body politic. "Our best [theological] minds," Hauerwas states, have been

> enlisted in the Constantinian enterprise of making the faith credible to the powers-that-be so that Christians might now have a share in those powers. After all, we would never be culturally significant if we Christians talked a language unintelligible to the [body politic]. Apologetics is based on the political assumption that Christians somehow have a stake in transforming our ecclesial claims into intellectual assumptions that will enable us to be faithful to Christ while still participating in the political structures of a world that does not yet know Christ.[3]

In the American context, of course, these political structures are shaped by a vision of modern democracy. Consequently, theology has

---

1. Hauerwas, *Resident Aliens*, 15, 17.
2. Ibid., 19, 20, 21.
3. Ibid., 22.

been under the assumption that "the American church's primary social task is to underwrite American democracy" and its value of individual freedom. But the underlying fissures in this Constantinian dream of a Christianized America began to become undeniably clear, Hauerwas alleges, sometime between 1960 and 1980. For instance, as Sunday blue laws gave way even in the Southern Bible Belt to consumer shopping and capitalist money-making, the illusion and pretense of "Christendom America" was shattered. "All sorts of Christians are [now] waking up and realizing that it is no longer 'our world'—if it ever was. . . . [Before,] Christians could deceive themselves into thinking that we were in charge, that we had made a difference, that we had created a Christian culture."[4] But that time has passed, Hauerwas proclaims, and rightly so. For this passing is not a loss to lament but rather a valuable opportunity for theology to recognize the deep inadequacies of the Constantinian vision and for the church to pursue its true calling.

Hauerwas's Alternative Vision of Theology and the Church

By pursuing the modern goals of intelligibility and credibility as part of a strategy of cultural apologetics, the theology of translation gravely distorted the gospel and domesticated it in relation to modern culture. "By the very act of our modern theological attempts at translation," Hauerwas remarks, "we have unconsciously distorted the gospel and transformed it into something it never claimed to be—ideas abstracted from Jesus [and the ecclesial community]." For instance, Gustafson's attempt to translate the gospel into the language of piety and human affections or Niebuhr's attempt to translate it into the language of meaning and human action are, according to Hauerwas, misguided attempts at abstracting theological insights from the Christian tradition and generalizing them into publicly accessible categories. Their fundamental mistake, in other words, is trying to transform particular "ecclesial claims into [generally accessible] intellectual assumptions." From Hauerwas's vantage point, this is completely backward. Instead of trying to translate "Jesus into modern categories," the real task is "to translate the world to him." Or as he says elsewhere, "theology's task is not to make God intelligible to 'modern man,' . . . but rather to make ourselves intelligible to God. The appropriately phrased theological question is never 'Does

---

4. Ibid., 32, 16, 17.

God exist?' but [rather] 'Do we exist?'" It is evident here that Hauerwas rejects any attempt to make God intelligible apart from the particularity of the church. In fact, he goes so far as to suggest that even our own existence is unknowable apart from the particularity of the ecclesial community and its biblical narrative. It follows that "the theologian's job is not to make the gospel credible to the modern world, but *to make the world credible to the gospel.*"[5]

What Hauerwas has in mind with these pithy formulations is to keep the Christian message, as embodied in the church, pure and distinctive and thus to allow it to criticize culture rather than to allow culture to set the parameters for the church. Nowhere is this more visible than in his critique of liberal democracy, which he deems to be radically non-teleological, anti-tradition, and essentially anti-community. "Our society is a vast supermarket of desire in which each of us is encouraged to stand alone and go out and get what the world owes us." This liberal project, he argues,

> was an adventure that held the seeds of its own destruction within itself, within its attenuated definition of human nature and its inadequate vision of human destiny. What we got was not self-freedom but self-centeredness, loneliness, superficiality, and harried consumerism. Free is not how many of our citizens feel—with our overstocked medicine cabinets, burglar alarms, vast ghettos, and drug culture. . . . [In short,] the adventure went sour.[6]

The only way for theology to combat this sour vision is for it to reclaim its true mission. Instead of following Schleiermacher down the accommodationist road of trying to make the gospel intelligible to the modern world, theology needs to take its bearings from Karl Barth: "Barth knew that the [real] theological problem was the creation of a new and better church." Instead of trying to get culture to *think* differently about the world by offering it an intelligible gospel, "Barth hoped that, by the time one had plodded through his *Church Dogmatics*, one would *be* different."[7] If anyone had any doubts about Hauerwas's admiration for Barth, these were completely erased in his Gifford Lectures, where he champions Barth as the supreme theologian of the twentieth

---

5. Ibid., 21, 22, 24; Hauerwas, "Truth About God," 18.
6. Hauerwas, *Resident Aliens*, 77, 50.
7. Ibid., 23–24.

century. Where Hauerwas and Barth completely concur is in their insistence on special revelation only. "The church is constituted by the proclamation of the gospel" and this gospel is one that cannot be translated into publicly accessible categories. In essence, the gospel of Jesus Christ is its own foundation and hermeneutic. But where they differ, according to Hauerwas, is that Barth finally "cannot acknowledge... that the community called the church is constitutive of the gospel proclamation" itself. In Hauerwas's judgment, Barth's view of sanctification is not sufficiently developed or sanguine enough. Even though Hauerwas states that "Barth has a fairly developed account of Christian sanctification," he thinks that Barth's "understanding of our faith in Jesus Christ [nevertheless] ... falls short." Hauerwas approvingly cites Joseph Mangina to sum up his difference with Barth on this matter:

> Again Mangina puts it well when he says that an adequate account of the role of the Spirit in faith not only involves "the glad acceptance of the church's preaching, but acceptance of the church itself as the binding medium in which faith takes place. The medium [of the church] is, if not the message, the [sole] condition of possibility of grasping the message in its truth."[8]

Cast in broad strokes, Hauerwas's strong and abiding presumption that the church can and ought to be a sanctified people reflects his own Methodist roots, the influence of John Howard Yoder and the Anabaptist tradition, and his indebtedness to MacIntyre and the neo-Aristotelian view of virtue and community.[9] More narrowly defined, Hauerwas's trust in the church "as the binding medium in which faith takes place" clearly runs throughout his many works. For instance, at the end of his first book, *Character and the Christian Life*, he concludes by stating that "the task of Christian ethics is to help keep the grammar of the language of faith pure so that we [the church] may claim not only to speak the truth but also to embody that truth in our lives."[10] Later, in *The Peaceable Kingdom*, he puts it even more strongly:

---

8. Hauerwas, *With the Grain*, 145. Hauerwas cites Mangina, "Bearing the Marks of Jesus: The Church in the Economy of Salvation in Barth and Hauerwas," *Scottish Journal of Theology* 52 (1999) 294–95.

9. Stout offers a valuable historical sketch of how these three influences have shaped Hauerwas's thinking; see *Democracy and Tradition*, 140–61.

10. Hauerwas, *Character and the Christian Life*, 233.

> By virtue of the distinctive narrative that forms their community, Christians are distinct from the world. They are required to be nothing less than a sanctified people of peace who can live the life of the forgiven. Their sanctification is not meant to sustain the judgment that they are "better" than non-Christians, but rather that they are charged to be faithful to God's calling of them as foretaste of the kingdom. In this sense sanctification is a life of service and sacrifice that the world cannot account for on its own grounds.[11]

As "a sanctified people of peace," the goal of the church is to offer the world an example of a radically different polis; the means by which this can be achieved is found only within the distinctive narrative that shapes the Christian community. I will address this narrative element first, and then return to the larger goal and social vision.

The Centrality of Narrative

For Hauerwas, theology and ethics are inherently and inextricably tied to narrative. He takes his direction here in part from Iris Murdoch's Platonic connection between vision and action, namely, that we can only act in a world that we see.[12] With this in mind, Hauerwas states that

> the primary task of Christian ethics involves an attempt to help us see. For we can only act within the world we can see and we can only see the world rightly by being trained to see. We do not come to see just by looking, but [rather] by disciplined skills developed through initiation into a narrative.[13]

Echoing MacIntyre as well as Murdoch here, Hauerwas alleges that a clear vision of reality requires training under tutelage in order to develop the necessary skills and virtues to see. One cannot see "just by looking," just by using one's own autonomous resources. This is the fatal error of our modern democratic culture; it wrongly presumes that "no master [or authority] is necessary for us to become moral, for [it mistakenly believes that] being moral is a condition that does not require initiation or training." In contrast, Hauerwas argues, one needs to learn to see just as if one were learning to lay brick. "To lay brick you must be

---

11. Hauerwas, *Peaceable Kingdom*, 60.
12. See Murdoch, *Sovereignty of Good*, 37.
13. Hauerwas, "Demands of a Truthful Story," 66. I'm indebted to Kallenberg for pointing me to this text; see his "Strange New World in the Church," 200.

initiated into the craft of bricklaying by a master craftsman." Likewise, clear moral and theological vision requires analogous training. To my knowledge, Hauerwas does not specify who the master craftsmen are when it comes to Christian vision. Presumably, it is those persons in the church who are trained and authoritative interpreters of the biblical story. But whoever they may be, Hauerwas believes that "the inability of Protestant [and Roman Catholic] churches in America to maintain any sense of authority over the lives of their members is one of the most compelling signs" that American churches have lost sight of the important role of authority and training in the Christian life.[14]

If clear vision requires skills developed under authoritative tutelage, it also requires that these skills be developed in relation to a formative narrative. Hauerwas claims that story is the only appropriate way to talk about God, or at least the Christian understanding of God. "My contention," he states, "is that the narrative mode is neither incidental nor accidental to Christian belief. There is no more fundamental way to talk of God than in a story." He takes the genre of gospel, one might say, to be paradigmatic for all Christian God-talk. And it is this biblical story that is determinative for our understanding of God and world. To return to Murdoch, it is the biblical story that shapes our vision and, hence, that defines our perception of reality. In this sense, Hauerwas asserts, "the narrative character of our knowledge of God, the self, and the world is a reality-making claim."[15] Put simply, we live in a world we see and we see through the lens of the stories that we tell ourselves. "By telling these stories," he writes,

> we come to see the significance and coherence of our lives as a gift, as something not of our own heroic creation, but as something that must be told to us, something we would not have known without the community of faith. The little story I call my life is given cosmic, eternal significance as it is caught up within God's larger account of history.[16]

Like Niebuhr, Hauerwas thinks that human life finds its genuine cosmic meaning only in relation to the God disclosed in Christian faith. Yet, unlike Niebuhr, Hauerwas does not believe that this meaning can

---

14. Hauerwas, *After Christendom?* 102, 88.
15. Hauerwas, *Peaceable Kingdom*, 25.
16. Hauerwas, *Resident Aliens*, 55.

be articulated or understood in any way apart from the particularities of the Christian community. Whereas Niebuhr sees this meaning embodied in the symbols of permanent myth, symbols that can be unpacked and articulated in a broader discourse of human action and community, Hauerwas declares that this meaning is only available in and through a community-dependent narrative. This meaningful story is "something that must be told to us" within the context of the church, for it is something that cannot be "known without [or apart from] the community of faith." This strong insistence on narrative is tied to Hauerwas's understanding of Christian social ethics.

Christian Social Ethics: The Witness of an Alternative Polis

Hauerwas begins his 1981 book *A Community of Character: Toward a Constructive Christian Social Ethic* by discussing a "A Story-Formed Community" and by identifying "Ten Theses Toward the Reform of Christian Social Ethics." At the top of his list is the claim that "the social significance of the Gospel requires the recognition of the narrative structure of Christian convictions for the life of the church." This triangular relation between narrative, social ethics, and the life of the church, Hauerwas believes, separates his position from the predominant tendencies in modern theology. "The first task of Christian social ethics," he proclaims, " is not to make the 'world' better or more just, but [rather] to help Christian people form their [own] community consistent with their conviction that the story of Christ is a truthful account of our existence."[17]

He puts this even more baldly in *Resident Aliens* when he states that Christianity is not a matter of offering the world a new or better understanding; this assumption is the persistent mistake of Niebuhr and Gustafson, among many others. Rather,

> Christianity is an invitation to be part of an alien people who make a difference because they see something that cannot otherwise be seen without Christ. . . . The challenge is not the intellectual one [of right thinking] but the political one [of right living]—the creation of a new people who [identify with and are shaped by the narrative of] Christ.[18]

---

17. Hauerwas, *Community of Character*, 9 (italics removed), 10.
18. Hauerwas, *Resident Aliens*, 24.

Instead of developing an external social ethic using Christ as the transformer of the broader culture, Hauerwas develops an internal social ethic centered around Christ as the formative influence of a distinctive community. Again, he looks to Barth as paving the way: "In Barth we rediscovered the New Testament assertion that the purpose of theological endeavor is not to describe the world in terms that make sense [to the broader public], but rather to change lives, to be re-formed in light of the . . . gospel." This can be accomplished only "through conversion" into a community. Hence, "we cannot understand the world until we are transformed into persons who can use the language of faith to describe the world right[ly]." For instance, instead of using sin as a broader interpretive category like Niebuhr (for whom it has been said that the Christian doctrine of original sin is empirically verifiable every time one picks up a newspaper), Hauerwas contends that "we must be taught that we sin."[19] For Hauerwas, sin is only an ecclesiological category, not an anthropological one.

Rather than developing Christian social ethics around the typologies of H. Richard Niebuhr's *Christ and Culture*, which Hauerwas thinks are misguided in their accommodationist tendencies, Hauerwas looks instead to John Howard Yoder for a more fruitful set of categories. As Hauerwas recounts, Yoder distinguishes between an *"activist* church," a *"conversionist* church," and a *"confessing* church." Epitomized by the Social Gospel Movement, the "activist" church focuses its attention and energies on transforming the broader society and the body politic through direct engagement between the gospel and culture. The "conversionist" church focuses on individuals and their personal conversion through acceptance of Christ as their Lord and Savior, an approach embodied in most forms of modern evangelicalism. The strength of the former approach is that it rightly views the gospel in its full social dimensions, but its Achilles heel is that it too easily accommodates itself to the underlying assumptions and ethos of modern liberalism. The strength of the latter approach is that it is less tempted by the notion that "tinkering with the structures of society will counter the effects of human sin." Yet, given its overly individualistic understanding of faith and the gospel, "it has no alternative social ethic or social structure of its

---

19. Ibid., 28.

own to offer the world." Hence, it sacrifices "the political claims of Jesus" and instead "degenerate[s] into a religiously glorified conservatism."[20]

In contradistinction to these two predominant forms of church, the "confessing" church seeks to offer "a radical alternative." It defines its chief task not in terms of "the personal transformation of individual hearts or the modification of society" but rather in the formation of "an alternative *polis,* a countercultural social structure called the church." Like the conversionist church, it insists on the need for personal transformation, "but it depicts [this] conversion as a long process of being baptismally engrafted into a new people" and community. Like the activist church, it seeks to influence the world, but it does so not by means of direct participation in the prevailing structures of power. Rather, it does so more indirectly "by being the church, that is, by being something the world is not and can never be, lacking the gift of faith and vision, which is ours in Christ." The confessing church seeks to offer the world a collective witness to a different vision and mode of life—one formed by the narrative of the gospel and by the traditions, practices, and sacraments of the church. The confessing church "knows that its most credible form of witness (and the most 'effective' thing it can do for the world) is the actual creation of a living, breathing, visible community of faith."[21]

By being an alternative polis, the church functions as a "colony" in the larger society. Hauerwas plays off of both senses of this term. On the one hand, the church is an "island" or outpost of one culture in the midst of another; thus theology must keep the grammar of faith pure in order to maintain the distinctive life and vision of the Christian colony. On the other hand, the church is also a "beachhead," an outpost for incursion and peaceful insurgency against the prevailing power structures. "Our biblical story," Hauerwas announces, "demands an offensive rather than defensive posture of the church. . . . Jesus Christ is the supreme act of divine intrusion into the world's settled arrangements. . . . The message that sustains the colony is not for itself but for the whole world—the colony having significance only as God's means for saving the whole world."[22]

---

20. Ibid., 44, 45. Hauerwas cites Yoder, "A People in the World: Theological Interpretation," in *The Concept of the Believer's Church,* ed. James Leo Garrett, Jr. (Scottsdale, PA: Herald, 1969) 252–83.

21. Hauerwas, *Resident Aliens,* 45, 46, 47.

22. Ibid., 12, 51.

Defining Characteristics of a Proper Approach to Christian Ethics

In order for the church to be a distinctive community bearing witness to a unique form of life, it must pursue its own ethic and not try to adopt the prevailing modes of modern philosophy or liberal culture. In seeking to articulate such a view, Hauerwas identifies at least seven key characteristics of an authentic Christian ethic.

First, it must be *teleological*. Following in the tradition of Aristotle, Hauerwas insists that "ethics is a function of the *telos*, the end. It makes all the difference in the world how one regards the end of the world, 'end' ... in the sense of the purpose, the goal, the result."[23] For Hauerwas, the telos of life is to be part of the people of God as it participates in and proceeds on an eschatological journey of God's redemptive activity in and through Jesus Christ. There is no natural human telos; only the supernatural telos revealed in and through the Christian narrative.

Second, to effectively pursue any telos, one must cultivate the appropriate *virtues* or habits of excellence. To be on a journey following Christ requires the proper formation of character to sustain and energize one along the way. Presumably Hauerwas would endorse the traditional Christian virtues of faith, hope, and love. Yet, given his ecclesiology, he gives these a "revolutionary" slant. That is, in order to be part of an alien people functioning as a beachhead in a larger society, one must downplay "bourgeois virtues [such] as tolerance, open-mindedness, and inclusiveness" and instead emphasize virtues such as "honesty and confrontation." For instance, when Christians discuss sex, what they must "make clear is that sexual passion (the good gifts of God's creation) is now subservient to the demanding business of maintaining a revolutionary community in a world that often uses sex as a means of momentarily anesthetizing or distracting people from the basic vacuity of their lives."[24]

Third, the proper telos can only be pursued and the proper virtues can only be cultivated within *community*. Hauerwas offers a Christian version of communitarianism set against the individualistic outlook of political liberalism. In contrast to the liberal tendency of defining the self independently of communal attachments, Hauerwas asks:

---

23. Ibid., 61–62.
24. Ibid., 61, 62, 63.

> Yet, what if our true selves are made from the materials of our communal life? Where is there some "self" which has not been communally created? By cutting back our attachments and commitments, the self shrinks rather than grows. So an important gift the church gives us is a far richer range of options, commitments, duties, and troubles than we would have if left to our own devices.[25]

Applied to the life of faith, Hauerwas submits that Christianity is not principally about a personal relationship with God, as if such a relationship could take place outside of community. On the contrary, there is no life of faith or virtue apart from the church. Cast in contemporary parlance, Hauerwas rejects the popular distinction between spirituality and religion; there is no spirituality or faith outside a religious community. Learning to be Christian or learning to be moral is like learning a language: one does it "by being initiated into a community of language, by observing your elders, by imitating them. . . . So the church can do nothing more 'ethical' than to expose us to significant examples of Christian living" in the context of the faith community.[26]

Fourth, "we must get our *vision* right before we can get our actions right" (italics added). As noted earlier, Hauerwas agrees with Murdoch's Platonic emphasis on moral vision. Our actions are shaped by our vision and perceptions of reality and value. Both Gustafson and Niebuhr would largely agree with this claim. For them, Christian faith offers a theocentric vision disclosed in the life of Jesus as the Christ, but this vision can also be expressed, to some extent, in broader categories, such as piety or meaning. For Hauerwas and Barth, on the other hand, Christian faith offers a Christocentric vision that is only accessible and intelligible in the form of the Christian narrative. For them, there can be no talk of the reality of God apart from the story of Jesus as the Christ. "Our God," says Hauerwas, "is the God who is specifically, concretely revealed to us in Jesus, a God we would not have known if left to our own devices."[27]

Fifth, the Christian vision can therefore only be expressed and accessed in the form of *story*. Since I have already offered ample detail of Hauerwas's insistence on the centrality and necessity of narrative, I will proceed to the next point.

25. Ibid., 65.
26. Ibid., 97.
27. Ibid., 102, 75.

Sixth, Christian ethics is based on and must be focused on the *particularity* of the Church's story of Jesus and what it means to follow him. In an essay contrasting his position with Gustafson's (and by implication with Niebuhr's as well), Hauerwas declares that he remains stuck with only the particularity of the Christian story as being decisive, because he believes the resurrection was a unique event that defines and changes all previous and subsequent history:

> [I]t seems clear to me that I remain stuck with the problem of history [and particularity] . . . because I remain stuck with the claim that through Jesus' resurrection God decisively changed our history. Therefore, I believe we must continue to begin with the "particular," with the historical, not because there is no other place to begin, but because that is where God begins.[28]

At first blush, it appears that Hauerwas might be equivocating here when he implies that one could begin apart from the particular. That is, on one reading, he seems to suggest that particularity is merely one option among others that God just happened to choose. Yet, the whole thrust of his emphasis on narrative indicates that particularity is the one and only way to access knowledge of reality. Hence, I take him to mean here that particularity is the only correct starting point for knowing God and reality—all other starting points lead astray. Given this need for particularity, outsiders can and should be invited to join the Christian community and its commitment to being shaped and guided by the biblical narrative. But, again, there is no way to express the meaning or truth of this narrative apart from the life of the church.

Seventh, Christian ethics can only be made credible by the *witness* of the church, not by offering reasons or arguments. "The Christian claim," states Hauerwas,

> is that life is better lived in the church because the church, according to our story, just happens to be *true*. The church is the only community formed around the truth, which is Jesus Christ, who is the way, the truth, and the life. Only on the basis of his

---

28. Hauerwas, *Wilderness Wanderings*, 79. Though it is not explicitly clear, I presume that Hauerwas follows Barth here in viewing the resurrection in terms of legend or saga rather than as a literal historical account. That is, like Barth, Hauerwas wants to emphasize that the resurrection is to be understood in postcritical terms (see my discussion of Barth and Niebuhr on this point in my typological analysis in the previous chapter). In short, Hauerwas is not a biblical literalist, but nonetheless he wants to insist on the unique particularity and necessity of the Christian narrative and its central events.

> story, which reveals to us who we are and what has happened in the world, is true community possible.[29]

Following MacIntyre, Hauerwas contends that the reasoning behind all claims (including the Christian claim) is community- and tradition-dependent. "Christian ethics," declares Hauerwas,

> like any ethics, are "tradition dependent." That is, they make sense, not because the principles they espouse make sense in the abstract, as perfectly rational behavior, which ought to sound reasonable to any intelligible person. [Rather,] Christian ethics only makes sense from the point of view of what we believe has happened in the life, death, and resurrection of Jesus of Nazareth.... Tradition [in the Christian context] is a complex, lively argument about what happened in Jesus that has been carried on, across the generations, by a concrete body of people called the church.[30]

Putting these two passages together, one ends up with a Christian truth claim that is intelligible and credible only from the vantage point of those within the Christian community. This would seem to lead to the problematic assertion that Christianity is true simply because Christians believe it to be so. Hauerwas, however, does not simply leave it there. Yet, unlike Porter, whom we will discuss in the next chapter, Hauerwas does not follow MacIntyre down the road of indirect comparative rationality. Instead, he looks to the life of the church to serve as a visible witness testifying to the truth of the gospel. "[A]ny Christian ethical position is made credible," Hauerwas asserts, only "by the church." What he has in mind here is amplified elsewhere when he approvingly quotes a Roman Catholic Cardinal named Suhard: "To be a witness does not consist in engaging in propaganda nor even in stirring people up, but in being a living mystery. It means to live in such a way that one's life would not make sense if God did not exist." The uniqueness of the Christian way of life makes God credible, Hauerwas postulates, because the reality of God is the only plausible explanation for such odd behavior. This is Hauerwas's version of Tertullian: "It is . . . to be believed because it is absurd."[31]

29. Hauerwas, *Resident Aliens*, 77.
30. Ibid., 71–72.
31. Hauerwas, *Resident Aliens*, 70; Hauerwas, "Truth about God," 18. Hauerwas cites Cardinal Suhard from *Growth and Decline* (Notre Dame: Fides, 1951). For a brief discussion of Tertullian, see Latourette, *History of Christianity*, vol. 1, 84.

Though it is not obvious at first, Hauerwas appears here to draw on some implicit form of pragmatism: Christian claims are validated only by their effectiveness in creating a distinctive community. Terrence Reynolds describes Hauerwas's position this way: "Ultimately, the Christian story will prove itself advantageous to liberal society when the community of faith is set apart by its performance as a 'community of virtue.'"[32] Hauerwas would likely resist the notion that he wants the church to "prove itself advantageous to liberal society." If anything, he wants to undo liberal society, not benefit it. Yet, he clearly does not want to be sectarian and he clearly does want the church to find a proper medium by which to show the contemporary world what it means to be church. Only by seeing the otherness of the church, he contends, can the world initially begin to see any degree of value or credibility in the gospel. And it is precisely by providing this alternative community of virtue, Reynolds reasons, that Hauerwas's conception of church proves its practical worth to liberal culture.

Hauerwas's implicit pragmatism can be further illustrated by comparing it with Niebuhr's explicit pragmatism. Whereas Niebuhr seeks to offer pragmatic *arguments* on behalf of the Christian interpretation of events, Hauerwas seeks to offer a communal *witness* that is pragmatically verified. This contrast is exemplified by their different understandings of the Sermon on the Mount. Niebuhr interprets the Sermon as an expression of the ultimate possibility and moral norm of human life, namely sacrificial love. Yet, within history, an ethic of sacrificial love inevitably results in the cross. The Sermon is thus not a programmatic ethic to be illustrated or embodied as such; rather, it is an "impossible possibility" hovering over human social relations as an ever-present vertical critique. According to Niebuhr, once this interpretative lens is adopted, with its vertical critique, it pragmatically offers the most effective and clear-sighted understanding of the possibilities and realities of human action. In contrast, Hauerwas views the Sermon as a specific programmatic directive to the church:

> The Sermon, like the rest of scripture, is addressed neither to isolated individuals nor to the wider world. Rather, here are words for the [Christian] colony, a prefiguration of the kinds of

---

32. Reynolds, "Conversation Worth Having," 400. Reynolds cites Hauerwas, *Christian Existence Today* (Durham, NC: Labyrinth Press, 1988) 7. See also Paul Lauritzen, "Is 'Narrative' Really a Panacea?" 335.

community in which the reign of God will shine in all its glory. So there is nothing private in the demands of the Sermon. *It is very public, very political, very social in that it depicts the public form by which the colony shall witness to the world* that God really is busy redeeming humanity, reconciling the world to himself in Christ [italics added].[33]

The church shall live by the higher standard of the Sermon, Hauerwas posits, embodying a pacifist ethic of peace and nonviolence in the very fabric of its collective life. This embodiment and collective witness will offer practical validation of the church's proclamation of the God of Jesus Christ. To clarify, this practical validation is not defined in terms of worldly effectiveness but rather in terms of Christian faithfulness. Hauerwas is under no illusion that pacifism directly and successfully gets others to be less violent. Rather, a pacifist Christian community embodies the distinctive calling of the church, which bears witness to God's way in the world. In sum, Hauerwas believes that the pragmatic validation of the church's distinctive witness is the only form of validation available for theological claims.

Typological Analysis

Commitment to Intelligibility (I-)

Hauerwas appears to be quite explicit in rejecting a commitment to intelligibility. As I discussed in chapter 1 and here again in my theological portrait, he unequivocally rejects the modern commitment to making theological claims understandable and plausible to the academy and wider public. Indeed, he thinks modern theology's fatal error, as illustrated by Gustafson, Niebuhr, and many others, is embodied precisely in this attempt to formulate and articulate the gospel in publicly accessible categories. As he puts it, "By the very act of our modern theological attempts at translation, we have unconsciously distorted the gospel and transformed it into something it never claimed to be—ideas abstracted from Jesus rather than Jesus with his people [i.e., church]."[34] To be sure, Hauerwas draws on a range of philosophical sources, such as Aristotle and Murdoch, to inform his own perspective, but in spite of his ability to incorporate other vocabularies into his own, he repeatedly warns that

33. Hauerwas, *Resident Aliens*, 92.
34. Ibid., 21.

theology should not seek to make its own ideas intelligible and plausible to the wider public; neither theology nor the church has a genuine stake in such an endeavor.

Autonomy of Ethics (AE-)

Though he occasionally appears to suggest otherwise, Hauerwas believes that ethics must be theological. One occasion for uncertainty stems from a passage in "On Keeping Theological Ethics Theological." There he writes:

> For the assumption that there is a strong interdependence between religion and morality is but the remains of the now lost hegemony of Christianity over Western culture. That many still persist in assuming religion is essential to motivate us to do the good is an indication, however, that no satisfactory alternative has been found to replace Christianity, as worldview and cult, in sustaining the *ethos* of our civilization.[35]

This passage has long puzzled me, largely due to his use of the word "but" in the second line. It seems to suggest "merely" or "simply," as if the connection between religion and morality were merely a remnant of the Christian past but not an authentic connection for the Christian present or future. This notion however clearly goes against the grain of the Hauerwasian corpus, which defines ethics within the context of theology. Hence, his meaning here must have some other or more subtle intent, even if it is awkwardly formulated. For if he is simply trying to say that modern intellectual culture no longer presumes a strong connection between religion and morality, whereas popular culture still does, then he has expressed himself poorly. Thus, I presume that he is trying to say something more than this.[36]

---

35. Hauerwas, "On Keeping Theological Ethics Theological," 23. Rist offers a somewhat similar, though less confusing, assessment. See Rist, *Real Ethics*, 2.

36. One possible reading of this passage is to focus on certain words. For instance, his use of the term "religion" rather than "faith" might imply some modern notion of Schleiermachian piety, which Hauerwas clearly rejects in favor of his own narrative understanding of faith. This word substitution would then imply that there is a strong interdependence between faith and morality but not between religion and morality. Alternatively, perhaps the key term is his use of the word "hegemony," indicating the Constantinian synthesis that he unequivocally rejects. Clearly, Hauerwas is not interested in using Christianity to sustain the ethos of our modern civilization. Or, thirdly, perhaps the clue is found in his use of the word "motivate," which conjures up images of

The most promising reading involves a systematic analysis of the passage as a whole. The passage describes an assumption and relates that assumption to two different historical contexts:

- *Assumption* = religion and ethics are *interdependent* and thus religion is essential to motivate us to do good
- *Lost historical past* = the *hegemony* of Christianity over Western culture
- *Current historical context* = persistent attempt to *sustain* our cultural ethos

The passage suggests that the assumption of interdependence has come down to us from a now lost historical past, namely, the hegemony of Christianity over culture. Nevertheless, the persistence of this assumption in our post-Constantinian context indicates that no alternative to Christianity has been found to sustain our cultural ethos. Now, it is clear that Hauerwas:

- closely identifies the attempt to sustain the wider cultural ethos with the Constantinian legacy
- thinks modern theology has wrongly connected the assumption of interdependence to sustaining the broader culture
- affirms interdependence while rejecting both the Constantinian legacy and the attempt to sustain culture

Therefore, the mistake and confusion, he implies, comes in continually tying interdependence to the act of sustaining the culture, which is a theological hangover from the Constantinian legacy. Hauerwas wants theology to kick the habit and to allow interdependence to stand alone simply on its own narrative legs. The true interdependence between religion and morality can occur only when persons are shaped by the Christian story—thus true moral motivation and the true moral telos can only be identified and inculcated through formation in the church.

Kantian nonteleological understandings of ethics as opposed to Hauerwas's Christian neo-Aristotelian teleology. Yet, whatever plausibility any of these various connotations or implied substitutions might have, these word games seem overly subtle and unnecessarily coy. Hence, I presume Hauerwas's meaning is still to be found by another means.

Put simply, true morality is found only in true religion, which is found only in the Christian colony. Thus, as he once again asserts,

> The Christian claim is that life is better lived in the church because the church, according to our story, just happens to be *true*. The church is the only community formed around the truth, which is Jesus Christ, who is the way, the truth, and the life. Only on the basis of his story . . . is true community [or ethics] possible.[37]

This same necessary connection between theology, ethics, and the church is affirmed by Hauerwas in his Gifford Lectures, where he agrees with Pope John Paul II's view "that a church confronted by a culture of death cannot afford to entertain a distinction between faith and morality." Similarly, he claims elsewhere that "any attempt to divorce God and morality, theology and ethics, is a mistake."[38] In sum, Hauerwas rejects the modern autonomy of ethics and affirms that ethics must be theological.

Absence of Metaphysics (AM+)

By insisting that knowledge of God is possible only through the distinctive Christian story that shapes the life of the church, Hauerwas seeks to redirect the focus of theology away from God and toward the church. The problem with centering Christian ethics on claims about the reality of God, he contends, is that it makes theology look like "some kind of primitive metaphysics, that one must then try to analyze for their moral implications. To force Christian moral reflection into such a pattern," he concludes, "is to make it appear but another philosophical account of the moral life."[39] By this, Hauerwas does not mean that modern philosophical ethics have been grounded in metaphysics; he clearly knows Kant's legacy of seeking to ground ethics independently of metaphysical claims about the nature of reality. Rather, he means that any philosophical attempt to validate claims about the reality of God ends up dismissing the particularity of christology and witness. "My reticence about metaphysics," he says in an essay on Murdoch, "is a correlate of my attempt to resist reductionistic accounts of theological

37. Ibid., 77.
38. Hauerwas, *With the Grain*, 229; Hauerwas, "Truth About God," 38.
39. Hauerwas, "On Keeping Theological Ethics Theological," 42.

claims so common in modern theology."⁴⁰ By "reductionistic," he means any attempt to rationally validate the claims of theology rather than appeal to or rely on their sheer historical particularity. In *A Community of Character*, he makes this point as follows:

> But the appropriate form of [Christ's] universality is lost if metaphysical and anthropological theories are made to substitute for the necessary witnessing of Christian lives and communities to the significance of his story. Witness presupposes and claims universality, but in a manner that makes clear that the universal can be claimed only through learning the particular form of discipleship required by this particular man.⁴¹

This statement reaffirms his attempt to base the universality and validation of Christian truth claims on their historical particularity and embodiment. Hence, he concludes that "religious convictions, at least Christian convictions, are not primitive worldviews that must be given more sophisticated metaphysical or literal expression before they can be tested for their truth. Rather the [implicit metaphysical] claims they make about the way things are involve convictions about the way *we* should be if we are to be *able* to see truthfully the way things are."⁴² Hauerwas marginalizes the metaphysical enterprise in favor of the ecclesiastical task of communal witness. Stated more precisely, he extracts moral imperatives of discipleship out of implicit metaphysical claims about reality and then makes those practical imperatives, and the witness they entail, the prerequisite for and the validation of the implicit metaphysical claims themselves.

Since the Gifford Lectures are devoted to natural theology, it is not surprising that Hauerwas uses his own Gifford Lectures to attend to the subject of metaphysics more explicitly than he has in the past. Nevertheless, in analyzing and championing Barth's theology in these lectures, Hauerwas continues to share Barth's suspicion of natural theology and philosophical metaphysics. "Barth's deepest worry about natural theology," Hauerwas remarks, "was what kind of God it 'proved.' From Barth's perspective, you cannot begin by asking if God exists or if God can be known [by reason] because any god that is the answer to such

---

40. Hauerwas, "Murdochian Muddles," 193–94 n. 8.
41. Hauerwas, *Community of Character*, 41.
42. Ibid., 90.

questions cannot [be the God revealed in Jesus Christ]."[43] Furthermore, in opposition to philosophy and natural theology, Hauerwas shares Barth's starting point of the revealed Word and shares his rejection of any attempt to rationally validate it. Quoting Barth, Hauerwas writes:

> "Theology claims to say more than philosophy can say. It claims to offer and to be human knowledge that rests upon a recognition of divine revelation. Yet theology can in no way make the truth of its claim directly visible, to say nothing of making it verifiable, simply because theology can never be and offer itself as anything other than human knowledge." In *Church Dogmatics* I/1, [Barth] puts the matter as forcefully as it can be put: "The Word of God . . . is not susceptible of any proof, not even . . . by the faith present in the Church."[44]

This last sentence reveals Barth's less sanguine view of the potential validating witness of the church. In spite of this, Hauerwas goes on to argue that he and Barth share a common emphasis on the centrality of witness—even if Barth, in Hauerwas's judgment, does not always give an adequate account of it. Overall, Hauerwas asserts that Barth sought to overturn the whole tradition of rational metaphysics and to offer, in its place, a theological metaphysics grounded in revelation not reason. "The fourteen volumes of the *Church Dogmatics*," Hauerwas claims, "represent Barth's attempt to overturn epistemology and to overcome metaphysics." At the center of this endeavor is Barth's concept of the *analogia fidei* (analogy of faith) and his effort to use this concept to replace the traditional philosophical notion of an analogy of being (*analogia entis*). "Barth's development of the *analogia fidei*," Hauerwas contends,

> was not an attempt to develop a theory or method of analogy based on prior metaphysical claims but an attempt to display the metaphysical claims intrinsic to theological speech. From Barth's perspective, metaphysics is not a subject matter peculiar to itself. Rather, we speak, and in speaking we discover that we

---

43. Hauerwas, *With the Grain*, 163 n. 49. Hauerwas cites Barth, *Church Dogmatics* II/1:6. In an unpublished paper that I wrote for a graduate seminar on Barth's theology taught by Langdon Gilkey, I argued that there remains an implicit underlying Kantian bifurcation in Barth's later theology. This reflects, in part, Barth's own acceptance of Kant's denial of a rational metaphysics. Meyer, "Kantian Remnant."

44. Hauerwas, *With the Grain*, 193 n. 44. Hauerwas cites Barth, "Fate and Idea in Theology," 27–28 and *Church Dogmatics* I/1:300.

are caught up, together with that about which we speak, in an endeavor that must be described as "metaphysical."⁴⁵

Hauerwas apparently means that Barth seeks explicitly to "display" the metaphysical claims of theology, but that these claims are only accessible from within the particularity of the Christian narrative. They are neither philosophically accessible nor validated by common reason. In this sense, theological metaphysics represents an "overcoming" of philosophical or rational metaphysics. From here, Hauerwas proceeds to draw a parallel between Barth's formulation and the recent work of John Milbank and the Radical Orthodoxy Movement. "What it means to speak of metaphysics in these [theological] terms," suggests Hauerwas, "is illuminated by John Milbank's argument that 'only theology overcomes metaphysics.' Of course, Milbank does not mean to deny that theological speech is inherently metaphysical; rather, like Barth, he insists that a theological metaphysics cannot pretend to be more determinative than God," i.e., it can only be grounded in divine revelation, not in reason.⁴⁶

Hauerwas's apparent endorsement here of the development of an explicit theological metaphysics represents something of a departure from his previous thinking. For as he wryly declares in his 1996 essay on Murdoch, "I am normally willing to expose my own metaphysical and ontological claims only under severe duress." In fact this new nod toward metaphysics, as Hauerwas himself recognizes, points more in the direction of Milbank than it does to Hauerwas himself. In terms of my category (AM), this new nod toward theological metaphysics represents a different alternative than the witness ethic that Hauerwas has consistently articulated over the years. This is not to deny that Hauerwas has always recognized that theology implicitly makes metaphysical claims. "Obviously," he says, "Christian conviction entails metaphysical claims—such as all that is is finite—but one does not first get metaphysics straight and then go to theology. Rather, metaphysical claims are best exhibited . . . as embedded in our behaviors, not as the [conceptual] 'background' of our behaviors."⁴⁷ To anticipate a later chapter,

45. Hauerwas, *With the Grain*, 190, 189.
46. Ibid., 189.
47. Hauerwas, "Murdochian Muddles," 193, and 193 n. 8. For an analysis of Hauerwas's discussion of Barth's theological metaphysics, see Roger Gustavsson, "Hauerwas's *With the Grain of the Universe* and the Barthian Outlook," 75f.

this statement succinctly points to the difference between Hauerwas and Milbank. Hauerwas, more akin to Gustafson and Niebuhr, leaves metaphysics implicit and embedded in the practices and narratives of the church whereas Milbank explicitly seeks to re-center metaphysics and ontology in the foreground of theological discussion. Perhaps Hauerwas's Gifford Lectures represent something of a metaphysical "coming out party" for him, but only time and his future writings will tell. In the meantime, his view continues to illustrate a theological approach that subordinates and subsumes metaphysics to the ecclesial task of witness. Thus, I will defer analysis of the notion of theological metaphysics until my discussion of Milbank.

Commitment to Credibility (C-)

Like the attempt to make the Gospel intelligible, Hauerwas thinks it a grave mistake to try to make theological claims rationally convincing to the academy or to the broader public. In fact, as he dryly puts it, "I have, of course, been spending my life trying to make Christianity hard to be 'generally believed.'"[48] The modern commitment to credibility, he reasons, issues from a misguided political aim of trying to be *directly* influential in culture and politics. This aim leads theology down the disastrous road of trying to articulate and justify its claims apart from the particularity of its own narrative and tradition. Furthermore, not only is this commitment to credibility misguided, it is also morally dangerous. In Hauerwas's words:

> An ethic claiming to be "rational" and universally valid for all thinking people everywhere is incipiently demonic because it has no means of explaining why there are still people who disagree with its prescriptions of behavior, except that these people must be "irrational" and, therefore (since "rationality" is said to be our most important human characteristic), subhuman.[49]

Implicit here is Hauerwas's assumption, similar to that found in Niebuhr, that rationally valid arguments are inherently coercive or compelling. Thus, in light of this assumption, disagreement can only be characterized as stubbornly irrational and subhuman—as willfully resisting that which demands assent. This use of coercive means and

48. Hauerwas, "Murdochian Muddles," 197.
49. Hauerwas, *Resident Aliens*, 101.

this denigration of others are demonic and inappropriate to the gospel; hence, only some form of witness can verify the claims of theology, not rational arguments. Brad Kallenberg, in discussing Yoder's influence on Hauerwas, points to this same underlying set of assumptions in Hauerwas's thinking:

> In the second place, "witness" is the only mode for displaying the truth of Christian convictions that isn't self-defeating. The gospel tells the story of God's self-emptying in the incarnation of Jesus, [which means that any coercive means of proclaiming the gospel is contrary to the nature of God revealed in Christ].... Granted, we hanker after ways to compel assent. And surely natural theology has been co-opted as one such [coercive] strategy by well intentioned apologists. But as John Howard Yoder has argued, part of the validity of the good news is the very rejectability of the news; if hearers are coerced to believe "news," then it is no longer news but propaganda. Thus, Hauerwas's claim that the "truth of Christian convictions can only be known through witnesses" is his acknowledgment of the fact that what Christians call revelation came as good *news,* [i.e., came in a noncoercive manner and must be proclaimed in such a manner].[50]

We can see here again that Hauerwas's rejection of the commitment to rational credibility is partly premised on his assumption that all attempts to provide rationally convincing reasons are inescapably coercive, and thus contrary to the spirit and content of the Gospel. Alternatively, his insistence on the necessity of witness as the only form of validation is due in part to this same assumption. As a result, in *After Christendom* he asks, "how can we communicate the gospel without explicitly or implicitly underwriting patterns of domination and violence antithetical to the Kingdom brought by Christ?"[51] His answer, again, is only through the means of communal witness.

But not only is a commitment to rational credibility dangerous because it is coercive, it is also problematic because it makes witness redundant. Just as Gustafson fears that a rational validation will make piety unnecessary, Hauerwas fears that it will make the church and its

---

50. Kallenberg, "Strange New World in the Church," 204. Kallenberg cites *With the Grain*, 211.

51. Hauerwas, *After Christendom?* 152.

witness superfluous. "If the gospel were a truth that could be known in general [through reason]," Hauerwas reflects,

> then there would be no necessity of witness. All that would be necessary would be to confirm people in what they already know. If the gospel were about general human experience that is unavoidable, then there would be no necessity of being confronted by anyone as odd as a Christian. But because the story we tell of God is the story of the life and death of Jesus of Nazareth, then the only way to know that story is through witness.[52]

By denying that the good news of the gospel pertains to a "general human experience that is unavoidable," Hauerwas implies one of two things. On one reading, it implies that the God of Christian theology is not in fact a God related to all persons and things, but only a God related to some. Accordingly, such a God cannot be known in general or cannot be known as an unavoidable part of human experience because such a God relates only to part of reality, not to all of it. Thus, in this case, a partial God can only be known through the particularity of a witness from that part of reality that knows God. But this view is so contrary to the Christian story itself, so contrary to the Christian affirmation of a universal God, that I doubt that this is Hauerwas's implied meaning. Alternatively, and presumptively, Hauerwas implies here that the universal God—who is related to all persons and things—is a God that we cannot recognize as an inescapable part of our own experience unless and until we are confronted by the particularity of the Christian witness and story. That is, the God who is related to all and is an unavoidable part of human experience is hidden from *human* experience—there is no way to be aware of God's presence—without the particularity of the Christian witness and story. But to make this claim is to say that Hauerwas accepts the modern denial of a rational validation of metaphysical claims. The truth claim about a universal God related to all is not a claim that can "be known in general" through reason. Rather, it is a claim that can only be known through the witness of a particular community informed and shaped by a special revelation.

As I noted at the end of my portrait, Hauerwas seems to appeal to some implicit form of pragmatism when he asserts that Christian claims are made credible only through the distinctive witness of the church. So perhaps one might argue that Hauerwas does, at the end of

52. Ibid., 149.

the day, implicitly affirm at least a partial commitment to credibility in the form of a pragmatic witness. Yet, if outsiders, *qua* outsiders, can discern something intelligible and credible in the distinctive witness of the church, then presumably the gospel must indeed speak to general human experience in some way after all. Differently put, outsiders must be able to recognize and articulate at least some general or public reasons for what they find persuasive or attractive in the life of the Christian community. But it is precisely this possibility of articulating public reasons—reasons independent of the Christian tradition—that Hauerwas rejects. According to him, there are no such reasons that can be given. Hence, even his appeal to the witness of the church, as the sole means of making the gospel credible, seems to lead him down a path that he is reluctant to take.

Critical Assessment

There is little doubt that one of Hauerwas's major contributions to contemporary theology has been his clear and consistent attempt to reclaim an important role for the church, a defining focus that has given an energizing boost to many church professionals. For instance, I recall the time I introduced Hauerwas's theology to a friend who is a pastor, by pointing him to *Resident Aliens*. Reading that book transformed his vision of ministry and the church. Similarly, Stout points to Hauerwas's significant intellectual influence in contemporary seminaries and divinity schools, though Stout of course is concerned about that influence.[53] In short, Hauerwas has clearly had a profound impact on contemporary theology and ministry.

In spite of this contribution, however, Hauerwas's theological vision wrongly collapses a critical distinction between *establishing* faith and *defending* its claims. For him, there is no defense of faith other than to point to its establishment. Yet, this collapse engenders not only conceptual confusion but also the potential danger of an implicit hubris within the church. This collapse is perhaps best illustrated by Hauerwas's controversial claim, which he recognizes that even Barth does not fully share, that "the church is constitutive of the gospel proclamation." Instead of saying that the church is a community explicitly committed to proclaiming the gospel, Hauerwas makes the church itself the

---

53. Stout, *Democracy and Tradition*, 75.

binding medium of the gospel; the medium is the message, not merely the messenger. Or if Hauerwas would hesitate to go quite this far, then he would at least agree with Mangina's description that the church is the sole "'condition of possibility of grasping the [gospel] message in its truth.'"[54] Hence, the primary purpose of the church is epistemological or theoretical as well as existential or practical. In fact, Hauerwas would contend that the latter function is dependent on the former; one can only be existentially transformed in faith by looking through the epistemological lens of the church.

By making the church constitutive of the gospel, Hauerwas runs the danger of fostering hubris and idolatry, on the one hand, and the danger of conceptual confusion and irrelevance on the other. Regarding the former, I can think of nothing more potentially idolatrous than to suggest that the collective human witness of the church constitutes or establishes the reality of God as revealed in Jesus as the Christ. One might argue, as Ogden does, that it is problematical enough to define the reality of God in terms of a constitutive christology.[55] It is even more problematical, however, to posit a constitutive ecclesiology. In spite of whatever faithful intentions may be present in such a constitutive church, I am persuaded by Reinhold Niebuhr that a collective body (religious or otherwise) has an exponential proclivity to succumb to and to manifest the sin of pride—and to do so blindly. As Niebuhr powerfully states, "The self-deception of the righteous, whether godly or godless, is the chief engine of evil in the world."[56] If Hauerwas thinks a pacifist church formed by the Christian story is immune from such proclivities, then he underestimates the power of sin, as conveyed both within the biblical narrative and history itself. Whatever critical role the church plays in the world, it must always remember the insight of the "Protestant principle," namely, that a finite or particular witness must point beyond itself rather than to itself. By insisting on the constitutive role of the church, Hauerwas seems dangerously to ignore this insight.[57]

54. Hauerwas, *With the Grain*, 145.

55. Ogden, *Is There Only One True Religion*, 84f.

56. Niebuhr, *Pious and Secular America*, 144. See also Niebuhr, *Moral Man and Immoral Society*.

57. For a discussion of the "Protestant principle," see Tillich, *Dynamics of Faith*, 29. Now some might argue that a constitutive christology necessarily implies a constitutive ecclesiology and thus that there is no real difference, say, between Niebuhr and Hauerwas *on this point*. But it does seem to me that Hauerwas is making a stronger

In reply, Hauerwas would reject the notion that sin or idolatry can be defined or identified apart from the life of the church. "[O]nly a community that has properly learned . . . to recognize . . . what constitutes idolatry," he maintains, is in a position to declare its presence. Thereby only the church can call a penalty on itself; only the church can say when the church is guilty of idolatry. But it is precisely the danger of self-blindness, especially among the righteous, that Niebuhr rightly warns against. Hauerwas is willing to admit "that [just because] God has given to the church the gift of the Spirit does not insure that the church rightly obeys and embodies the commandments. [But] [w]hat the gift of the Spirit [does] insure," he contends, "is that the church is a politics [or community] that will surely be appropriately judged if it fails to live true to God." But by whom will the church be appropriately judged and when? Only by God at the end of time? By Christians within the church today? But Hauerwas has already rejected the understanding of sin offered by Niebuhr and the notion of the Protestant principle offered by Tillich.[58] He rejects any Christian voice that claims that a constitutive understanding of the church is, by definition, already dangerously crossing the line. Indeed, he asserts that only a constitutive church can define idolatry. Hence, his line of reasoning, I submit, begs the question.

Relatedly, he resists the notion that the church can point beyond itself because such a notion implies that one can articulate and defend the gospel in non-ecclesial terms. And because he rejects this implication, he saddles the full epistemological and theoretical weight of theology's truth claims onto the back of the church's witness. But such a move commits a category mistake. It is one thing to grant the church the important practical and existential functions of providing meaningful narratives and role-models in the cultivation of virtue. It is another thing, however, to say that the meaningful stories and changed lives make the church's cognitive or theoretical claims true. In his review essay of Hauerwas's *With the Grain of the Universe*, Levinson makes

---

ecclesiological claim than Niebuhr (and others) by contending that the church is constitutive of the gospel. For Hauerwas, there is no message without the community (church): church>gospel message. Alternatively, Niebuhr gives priority to the message; the church is in service of the message, not the other way around: gospel message>church.

58. Hauerwas, "Truth about God," 36–37, 38. For his critique of Niebuhr and Tillich see 37 n. 44.

this same basic point. To acknowledge the formative power of biblical narrative, Levinson observes,

> is by no means to transform a meaningful story into a true one, much less a Divinely or Truly true one.
> ... [R]elations between meaning and practice are one thing and the truth of this or that claim is another, and we can grant practical authority to [mythical] stories that we know are riddled with make-believe, without trying to find some sleight of mind that transforms make-believe into historical or metaphysical truth.[59]

Likewise, Roger Gustavsson offers a similar assessment of Hauerwas's logic: "One might well ask," remarks Gustavsson, "Has Hauerwas attended to the obvious objection that a manner of belief and confession, however admirable a way of life ostensibly deriving from it, can readily be an illusion?" He concludes that Hauerwas recognizes the issue, but he is unpersuaded by Hauerwas's reasoning. "The dubious proposition" here, Gustavsson notes, is "that it cannot be the case that there are witnesses and there is not the One to whom the witnesses witness." But this "proposition is surely false," he adds. For clearly "it is possible that there are 'witnesses' and yet there is no God."[60]

Audi offers us further help here in identifying Hauerwas's category mistake. "If I am not justified in a premise belief," says Audi, "then the subjective point of view constituted by my beliefs contains . . . no good reason for my holding the belief based on it. I may think the belief is justified, but such thinking does not make it so, nor by itself does it give me a good reason for the further belief that is based on the first one."[61] Hauerwas tries to substitute the "subjective point of view" constituted by one's premise belief for a justification of that underlying belief. This substitution lies behind his contention that narrative and community are the sources for reality-making claims. Again, as he states, "the narrative character of our knowledge of God, the self, and the world is a reality-making claim that the world and our existence in it are God's creations."[62] The premise belief here is the claim about the reality of

---

59. Levinson, "Let Us Be Saints," 231.

60. Gustavsson, "Hauerwas's *With the Grain of the Universe*," 65, 66; for his full analysis, see 64–68.

61. Audi, *Architecture of Reason*, 36.

62. Hauerwas, *Peaceable Kingdom*, 25. Hauerwas would have been more accurate to speak of "reality-influencing" rather than "reality-making" claims. Narrative and com-

God. The subjective point of view that holds this belief is formed through its participation in the Christian narrative and community. But, as Audi helps us to see, the underlying claim about the reality of God is not justified by appeal to the Christian subjective outlook, which itself is formed by this constitutive belief. The Christian may believe in the reality of God, but such an outlook is not justified simply because it is a belief attained through formation in the community. Rather, the premise belief itself needs to be justified independently of any appeal to the subjective framework that is constituted by it. And because this premise belief is metaphysical in character—a claim about the reality of God—it requires metaphysical justification.

As we saw earlier, Hauerwas acknowledges that "Christian conviction entails metaphysical claims." Yet, he contends that "metaphysical claims are best exhibited . . . as embedded in our behaviors, not as the [conceptual] 'background' of our behaviors."[63] This emphasis on embeddedness over background, however, is precisely the type of confused substitution noted above. To always leave theology's metaphysical claims embedded in the practices and narratives of the community, and to deny that these claims either need to be or can be exhibited as the necessary background for these practices, is evidence once again of Hauerwas's attempt to substitute subjective outlook for justification of the underlying premise belief. On the contrary, this premise belief must be made explicit and defended at some point, for metaphysics provides the necessary background of all human claims and actions. "Whatever is found in 'practice,'" observes Whitehead, "must lie within the scope of the metaphysical description. . . . Metaphysics is nothing but the description of the generalities which apply to all the details of practice." Even ordinary statements like "'there is beef for dinner today,' and 'Socrates is mortal'" imply a metaphysical background and make implicit metaphysical claims. Hence, "every proposition proposing a fact," Whitehead concludes, "must, in its complete analysis, propose the general character of the universe required for that fact. There are no self-sustained facts,

---

munity may influence our vision of reality, but such a vision may indeed be wide of the mark. Such a vision does not "make" reality, rather it influences the way that we see it. As Murdoch would say, the way that we see things may be mired in "fantasy" and "false consolations" rather than entailing true perception of reality. See Murdoch, *Sovereignty of Good*, 59.

63. Hauerwas, "Murdochian Muddles," 193–94 n. 8.

floating in nonentity."⁶⁴ The underlying claim that theologians want to make, including Hauerwas, is that the facts of life and experience are grounded in a divine reality at the center of it all. But this metaphysical claim, at some point, requires its own justification and no appeal to the narratives, practices, or subjective outlook of the church can substitute for this task.

Moreover, Hauerwas's appeal to the subjective outlook of the church, and to the "reality-making" claims that are based on this outlook, plays right into the hands of Feuerbach and other masters of suspicion. That is to say, by focusing fundamentally on the church rather than on defending claims about the reality of God, Hauerwas leaves theology more open than ever to assertions that all God-talk is ultimately merely a form of human projection. Indeed, even Hauerwas at times has glimpsed this danger. For instance, as a result of a conversation with Nigel Biggar at Oxford some years ago, Hauerwas has come to at least partly recognize the danger of focusing theology on the church rather than on God:

> As we were walking together Nigel observed, rather astutely, that for all my insistence that Christian ethics be Christian, . . . God was nonetheless curiously missing from my work.
>
> My response to Nigel's remark was, of course, defensive and I proceeded to show why he had to be wrong. But afterwards, the more I thought about it, the more it occurred to me that he might be right. In spite of everything I was trying to do to sustain the integrity of Christian speech, . . . when all is said and done I may have done nothing more than reproduce Durkheim [or Feuerbach], albeit with an ecclesiological twist.⁶⁵

In this revealing passage, we see Hauerwas confronted with the cost and danger of his own ecclesiastically-constituted gospel. In an extended footnote at the end of this passage, Hauerwas adds: "I mention Durkheim because he, along with Feuerbach, provided such a compelling account of the social and moral significance of 'religion' . . . . grounded in real human needs." The problem, Hauerwas concludes, is "that much of modern Christian theology tries to justify theological claims on grounds not unlike that provided by Durkheim and Feuerbach in spite of the fact that the latter [two] understood their accounts in no way entailed

---

64. Whitehead, *Process and Reality*, 13, 11.
65. Hauerwas, "Truth About God," 17.

that God—at least the God Christians have traditionally worshipped—exists."[66] Though it is certainly true that Hauerwas does not justify his theological claims by appealing to the fulfillment of human needs, he himself however does no better job in defending claims about the reality of God than these other theologians. Instead of appealing to anthropological reasons, he appeals to ecclesiological grounds. But neither anthropology nor ecclesiology can suffice, however, precisely because the claim about the reality of God is finally a metaphysical claim.

This is why Hauerwas's insistence on a strict appeal to particularity, both in terms of the particularity of the biblical revelation and the witness of the church, finally fails to make good sense. The particularity of a witness, however genuinely sincere and authentic it may be in relation to its own sources and traditions, cannot by itself validate the claims that the witnessing community makes about the nature of reality. To be sure, it may lend some plausibility to those claims, but it does not adequately justify them. This is why Lessing's famous remark still rings true today, namely, that "'the accidental truths of history can never become the proof of the necessary truths of reason.' If religious truth is genuine," notes Alasdair Heron explicating Lessing's maxim, then "surely it must be so eternally and universally." Heron amplifies further by pointing to Fichte, whom he quotes as saying that "'the metaphysical only, and not the historical, can give us blessedness.'"[67] As we saw in previous chapters, both Bonjour and Ogden recognize this important difference between the historical and metaphysical. Bonjour does so by distinguishing between concept acquisition and justification, and Ogden does so by distinguishing between the origin of a claim and its justification. Again, as Ogden well observes, "even if it belongs to religion by its very nature to advance such special [or historically particular] claims, the fact that it presents them as generally applicable and, in some cases, universally valid means that there have to be at least some reasons correspondingly general or universal for accepting them, if their acceptance is to be at all rationally motivated."[68]

Drawing on MacIntyre's notion of a proleptic knowledge of first principles, Hauerwas would respond by claiming that I am confusing

---

66. Ibid., 17–18 n. 3.

67. Heron, *Century of Protestant Theology*, 20. The quotes from Lessing and Fichte are from Heron.

68. Bonjour, *In Defense of Pure Reason*, 9–10; Ogden, *On Theology*, 84.

"the retrospective character of all human knowledge, including our natural knowledge of God, with the specific, gracious, and historically contingent avenues through which that knowledge is given." That is, in attempting to respond to Nigel Biggar's observation and criticism, Hauerwas holds that God cannot be known, defined, or evaluated by any means apart from what God defines and declares in the particularity of his revealed Word. Hence, notions of justice or good cannot be metaphysically co-eternal with God, as Plato suggested, but rather must be defined ultimately by divine fiat and made known only by the Word of God itself. Thus quoting MacIntyre, Hauerwas suggests that to invoke "'a standard of truth or goodness, established independently of our knowledge of God's revealed Word and will, is and must be an appeal to something external to that Word and will.' [But] [t]his means that 'if something external to the Word of God were necessary to establish that Word as good, then it too would be greater than the Word of God,' which of course is theologically unacceptable."[69]

There is an ambiguity here in the word "external" that needs clarification. It is one thing to say that good is defined in relation to God, it is another to say that good is defined only by the revealed Word and will of God. The former implies that "good" is an evaluative concept that can be metaphysically defined in relation to the ultimate character of reality. Alternatively, Hauerwas implies that "good" is a notion defined by divine choice that can only be known through divine revelation. If he were to assert that "good" is not defined merely by divine fiat, then his insistence that it can only be ultimately known by the particularity of divine revelation would nevertheless still make it just as logically contingent as fiat itself. Hauerwas rejects any metaphysical knowledge of the good, since he assumes that any such knowledge presupposes some notion of the good that is an eternal standard completely external to God. He is willing to say that evaluative concepts may be used in an "analogical and historically ordered way. It is at least logically possible, therefore, that divine claims might be evaluated by standards acquired and elaborated independent of [revealed] knowledge of God, but it does not follow that God is thereby judged by a standard external to God." What Hauerwas seems to mean here is that the evaluative standard is indeed ultimately one defined and known only through the revealed

---

69. Hauerwas, "Truth about God," 37, 35. Hauerwas cites MacIntyre, "Which God Ought We to Obey and Why?" *Faith and Philosophy* 3 (October 1986): 366.

Word and will of God. But human knowledge is both a proleptic and retrospective affair. We proleptically and unwittingly draw upon the revealed Word in our preliminary stages of knowledge. However, we can only truly understand looking backward that it was indeed the Word of God all along that was the source of our knowledge of the good. Hence, quoting MacIntyre again, he says that once we progress beyond the initial stages of our knowledge,

> we discover . . . that the standard by which we judged God is itself a work of God, and that the judgments which we made earlier were made in obedience to the divine commands, even although we did not and could not have recognized this at that earlier stage. God, it turns out, cannot be truly judged of by something external to his Word.[70]

So what MacIntyre and Hauerwas call "natural knowledge of God" is really only revealed knowledge anticipated proleptically. Once again, it boils down to appealing to the contingency and particularity of a witness. Indeed, as Hauerwas states, "our natural knowledge of God cannot be divorced from a way of life which the church embodies."[71] Hauerwas accuses his critics of confusing the retrospective character of human knowledge with the contingent manner in which that knowledge is given. But in my judgment, there is no confusion precisely because both sides of the equation are equally contingent. He makes knowledge of God logically contingent by making it depend on the nature of the church's witness; once again it is an appeal to the particularity of ecclesiology over the necessity of metaphysics.

By maintaining that an appeal to a metaphysical evaluative standard is theologically unacceptable, Hauerwas presumes that there are only two logical alternatives available. If one accepts a metaphysical Platonism, he reasons, then one defines the good as an eternal Form external to God, which is theologically unacceptable. In contrast, he concludes that one must accept a contingent evaluative standard made and revealed by God. But process metaphysics points to a third possibility that overcomes the deficiencies of these other two positions. From a process perspective, Plato's insight was to recognize the need for a metaphysical evaluative standard; his mistake was to define this standard as

---

70. Hauerwas, "Truth about God," 35, 36. Hauerwas cites MacIntyre, "Which God Ought We," 370.

71. Hauerwas, "Truth about God," 37.

an Idea or Form that is external to God. Alternatively, Hauerwas's insight is to recognize that the evaluative standard cannot be external to God; his mistake, however, is to define this standard as merely a contingent creation of God—"the standard by which we judged God is itself a work of God." But, as Plato rightly recognized, this view makes the statement "God is good" a meaningless tautology: good is whatever God says it is by his Word and will. For if the standard by which we evaluate God is merely a contingent product of God, then our praise for God is hollow and redundant. Yet, process thought, with its dipolar panentheism, points to a third possibility; this possibility affirms an eternal standard within God. To anticipate a later chapter, Gamwell, for instance, rejects a conception of good or perfection defined either in terms of mere contingency or in terms of a free-floating eternal Form. Against these alternatives, he argues that "perfection identifies an individual that is universal or coextensive with all other reality and, therefore, not simply one contingent thing among others and this individual includes an Idea of the Good as its own essential or constitutive purpose."[72] In this process conception, God is the cosmic individual internally related to all, whose own nature includes the metaphysical evaluative standard as its own constitutive purpose. Hence, the evaluative standard is neither external to God (in agreement with Hauerwas) nor merely a contingent product of God (in agreement with Plato). It is this kind of conceptual reconciliation that process metaphysics offers for advancing theology's truth claims. If, finally, Hauerwas were to hold that this reconciliation still leaves the evaluative standard external to the revealed Word of God, then he is merely reasserting once again his own denial of a rational metaphysics in favor of the particularity of an ecclesiological witness.

As noted earlier, part of Hauerwas's rejection of rational metaphysics arises from his presumption that all rational arguments are inherently coercive in nature, which is contrary to the gospel. But in making this assumption, Hauerwas, like Niebuhr, is guilty of the discursive error. Arguments do not work like a "laser" that compels assent. Instead, they offer reasons as invitations for agreement—reasons that can be rejected or accepted at both the cognitive and existential levels. To be sure, sound reasons and good arguments reveal the costs for not accepting the invitation of a given claim or line of reasoning, but such a disclosure does not force the listener to accept the argument. A "rea-

72. Gamwell, "On the Loss of Theism," 185.

sonable" person, Audi suggests, is willing to offer reasons for their own claims and, likewise, is willing to listen to the reasons offered by others.[73] Such an attitude implies neither a passive submission to the claims of others nor a dictatorial attempt to compel others to one's point of view. Instead, it indicates a disposition of openness—both in speaking to and listening to others—that is quite consistent with the gospel. In fact, one might say, to borrow a phrase from Tillich, that "such openness is what religion calls 'grace.'"[74]

My criticisms of Hauerwas to this point have focused on his failure to adequately defend theology's truth claims, especially its underlying metaphysical claims. This failure stems, I have suggested, from his collapsing the distinction between *establishing* faith and *defending* its claims. Let me now offer some comment on his approach to the establishment side of the equation. In basic agreement with MacIntyre, Hauerwas appears to include at least two key related ingredients in the establishment of faith and morality, namely, *training* and *authority*. In considering these elements, it is instructive to begin by returning to Murdoch in order to set forth a comparison with Hauerwas.

In *The Sovereignty of Good*, Murdoch writes:

> Knowledge of a value concept is something to be understood . . . in depth, and not in terms of switching on to some given impersonal network. Moreover, if morality is essentially connected with change and progress, we cannot be as democratic about it as some philosophers would like to think. We do not simply, through being rational and knowing ordinary language, "know" the meaning of all necessary moral words. We may have to learn the meaning. . . .[75]

There is considerable agreement here between Murdoch and Hauerwas concerning the need for change, progress, and training in order to understand the depth of a moral value or religious concept. I would concur that modernity has tended to lose sight of this preparatory role of formation and development in the blossoming of human rational capacities. This oversight may in fact go back to Descartes's egalitarian observation that "the power of . . . distinguishing truth from error, which is properly what is called good sense or reason, is by nature equal in all

---

73. Audi, *Architecture of Reason*, 151.
74. Tillich, *Dynamics of Faith*, 109.
75. Murdoch, *Sovereignty of Good*, 29.

men." The ambiguity here resides in Descartes's reference to "power." Is the power an *equal potential capacity* or an *equal realized actuality*? Presumably it is the former, which implies a likely need for some type of cultivation or fostering to realize its full potential. We all may need some assistance in coming to fully recognize and rationally express even the most fundamental elements of our experience, including experience of the divine. Nonetheless, Descartes's affirmation of equal potential in all persons points to an important fact about the nature of justification. This is why Bonjour's helpful distinction between concept acquisition and justification becomes crucial again. How one acquires a full or in-depth understanding of moral or religious concepts may indeed be important, but it cannot substitute for a justification of the validity of moral or religious claims themselves. Put simply, the *how* of acquisition can never serve as the *why* of validation. For instance, Bonjour acknowledges that experience or training may be needed to achieve full understanding and acquisition of a concept. But *"once it is understood,"* its rational justification cannot appeal to that acquisition process to justify its validity.[76]

As a rejoinder, Hauerwas might say that a justification cannot fully succeed if the listener does not understand a given concept. This of course is true in terms of how an argument is *received* by the listener. Consequently, the person making a claim must be fully committed to making the claim as intelligible and as credible as possible. Likewise, the one hearing the claim may need his or her own form of existential transformation in order to fully digest the depth and meaning of the claim, as well as to grant his or her cognitive or existential assent to it. One may need to wake from the slumber of bad faith in order to be receptive to the invitation of good reasons. But my point is that the training process, whatever it may entail, cannot itself serve as justificatory grounds for the claim. It cannot provide the model for how a sound justification should be *offered*. This goes back to my contention that the *raison d' être* of arguments is rooted in the responsibility of making a claim, and not in the response of others per se. In sum, a quality justification does not appeal to the authority of an acquisition process as grounds for the validity of a claim.

---

76. Descartes, "Discourse on Method," 30; Bonjour, *In Defense of Pure Reason*, 9–10.

It is interesting to note that this is where Murdoch and Hauerwas begin to diverge. Hauerwas, like MacIntyre, turns his attention to community and to the authority of masters within the community. For Hauerwas, the authority of this communal acquisition process serves as the source of validation for any proposed theological or moral claims. Murdoch instead looks to the transformative power of good art and to a path of Platonic inwardness. Picking up with the passage above, Murdoch continues:

> We may have to learn the meaning; and since we are human historical individuals the movement of understanding is onward into increasing privacy, in the direction of the ideal limit, and not back towards a genesis in the rulings of an impersonal public language.
>
> None of what I am saying here is particularly new: similar things have been said by philosophers from Plato onward; and appear as commonplaces of the Christian ethic, whose centre is an individual.[77]

For Murdoch, the rational capacities needed for metaphysical insight must be awakened and sharpened by an individual inwardness and autonomous process of clearer discernment of "the ideal limit" always already present, not by an outer appeal to some communal authority. The crucial difference here arises from the fact that Murdoch affirms that the Idea of the Good—as the "ideal limit"—is always something we already vaguely know in our deepest experience of reality, whereas Hauerwas denies that we have any such omnipresent exposure to God or Good. She affirms the metaphysical enterprise whereas he does not. To be sure, she insists that one must overcome the self's fantasies and preoccupations in order to fully grasp, absorb, and accept metaphysical reasons and insights about reality. But the validity of those metaphysical reasons is not justified by appeal to those preparatory practices. Alternatively, for Hauerwas, the God revealed in Jesus Christ cannot be known or validated apart from the preparatory practices of the church and its witness. Gamwell, in citing his basic agreement with Murdoch on this point, rightly suggests that "successful proofs for the divine existence are not meant to create an experience of God where one is not already present and, in that sense, [are not meant] to argue us into religious faith. On the contrary, their purpose is critically to clarify the

---

77. Murdoch, *Sovereignty of Good*, 29.

inescapable relation to perfection that [already] constitutes our every thought and action."[78]

This quotation from Gamwell helps us to sort out once again the distinction between defending or justifying the claims of faith, and the existential establishment of faith as the center of our lives. Hauerwas fears that the rational attempt to do the former nullifies the role of the church in trying to do the latter; hence, he denies the former in order to ensure the role of the church in the latter. But Hauerwas's fear and response are misplaced. The point of theistic arguments is to offer common grounds for validating claims about the reality and centrality of God as the source and end of all things. By no means do such arguments replace the cultivating role of the church in fanning such faith at the center of our individual and collective lives. In fact, one might say that the function of such arguments is to identify and reaffirm the *content* of proper desire whereas the role of the church is to cultivate and expand the *strength* of that desire. Hence, Hauerwas is wrong when he claims that there would be no need for the church or its witness if "the gospel were about general human experience that is unavoidable."[79] The reality of God is unavoidable, but the nature and strength of our response to it is completely variable. This distinction between reason's role in public justification and the church's role in personal and communal transformation can be further elucidated by turning our attention to the meaning of authority.

In his study of modern medicine and the professions, sociologist Paul Starr closely examines the nature of authority. Starr makes a distinction between our *dependence* on professionals and the *legitimacy* of that dependence. As he observes,

> what makes dependence on the professions so distinctive today is that their interpretations often govern our understanding of the world and our own experience. To most of us, this power seems legitimate: When professionals claim to be authoritative about the nature of reality, whether it is the structure of the atom, the ego, or the universe, we generally defer to their judgment.[80]

78. Gamwell, "On the Loss of Theism," 187–88.

79. Hauerwas, *After Christendom?* 149. My distinction between the content and strength of desire is informed by Audi, *Architecture of Reason*, 147.

80. Starr, *Social Transformation of American Medicine*, 4.

But why do we defer to their judgment? In answering this question, Starr offers a helpful distinction between two types of authority: "social" and "cultural." Social authority refers to the power to issue commands or statements that others will accept based strictly on the status of the one issuing the commands or statements. A baseball umpire provides a good example of this. The home-plate umpire issues action commands and statements about reality, e.g., declarations of balls and strikes, that are accepted based strictly on the role and status of the umpire. In short, the umpire's power is coercive—it compels compliance.[81] In contrast, however, the power of professionals is persuasive in nature. The physician must persuade or convince patients to take a prescribed medicine; he or she cannot compel them to do so. This type of persuasive power is at the root of "cultural authority." Such authority "refers to the probability that particular definitions of reality and judgments of meaning and value will prevail as valid and true" based on the potential reasons that could be given to back up such claims. We defer to professionals' judgments because we believe that they could, if asked, offer us convincing reasons that we could (with sufficient time and effort) understand and accept. As Starr notes, "even in surrendering private judgment, one may still believe that the words of authority can be persuasively elaborated." Indeed, we defer to their cultural authority because we view it as "a shortcut to where reason is presumed to lead." Likewise, Starr observes, "the reserve strength of professional authority . . . consists primarily of persuasion. For it is almost always to argument, rather than coercion, that independent professionals turn when their [cultural] authority fails."[82]

Starr's analysis and distinctions offer us useful tools for assessing Hauerwas's understanding of authority. As noted earlier, Hauerwas, like MacIntyre, claims that moral and theological vision requires initiation into a craft under the authority of a master craftsman. What I take both of them to mean finally is that the student or apprentice must accept the claims of the master as true based on the master's own authority. MacIntyre seems to have this in mind when he speaks of the apprentice

---

81. Of course, the modern use of center-field cameras, instant replay, and "k-zone" graphics provide the viewing public with independent means of evaluating the judgments of the umpire. This capacity enables viewers to challenge the umpire's claims, which are based on social authority, with publicly accessible evidence.

82. Starr, *Social Transformation of American Medicine*, 13, 10, 11.

following the rules of the master.[83] Cast into Starr's terminology, both Hauerwas and MacIntyre appeal to the *social authority* of the master. The student is dependent on the master because the legitimacy of the master's claims is based finally on the master's own role and status—a claim is accepted as true because the master says it is true. Thus, like an umpire, the master craftsman declares reality and others accept it. This is simply another implication of Hauerwas's endorsement of the notion of "reality-making" claims. In spite of his rejection of rational arguments as being allegedly coercive, it seems to me that Hauerwas himself implicitly accepts the coercive power of the master craftsman in the form of the master's social authority.

In reply, Hauerwas might argue that I have misunderstood—that the nature of the master's authority in the church is not really like the coercive power of an umpire. He might say that the student accepts the truth claims of the master only because the student does not yet have an in-depth understanding of the relevant concepts needed to understand theological arguments and their metaphysical implications. But the key question, I would ask, is whether the student's deference to authority is merely "a shortcut to where reason is presumed to lead" or whether it is finally a substitution for reason itself? The former would imply that rational justification can indeed be offered for theological and metaphysical claims independently of the authority of tradition, and that the student is simply forgoing or postponing the exacting process of rational engagement needed to understand. If this is what Hauerwas has in mind, then he is affirming the notion of cultural authority rather than social authority. But in this case, the legitimacy of the master's claims can be rationally validated independently of the master's status or role. In this case, the master's claims are not true simply because he or she utters them but because good reasons can be offered independently to "whoever has ears to hear" them. Hauerwas, however, cannot finally affirm cultural authority over social authority precisely because the former presupposes the need for and the possibility of a rational justification of all claims, including theology's metaphysical claims, which is what Hauerwas explicitly denies. Hence, at the end of the day, he must implicitly appeal to the social authority of the master interpreters of the Christian story. Their authority is implicitly coercive insofar as their

---

83. See, for instance, MacIntyre, *TRV*, 130.

claims are taken to be self-validating, i.e., they ultimately appeal to their own status or authority as the validating grounds for their claims.

In contrast, by making a case for the need for rational metaphysics as part of the justification of theological claims, I do not deny the role of authority in moral or theological formation. I would contend that the proper form of authority for such formation is to be found in cultural, not social, authority. To borrow and adapt Niebuhr's famous phrase, authoritative persons and texts should be taken seriously but not blindly. One should take them seriously as sources of formative wisdom, but not accept them blindly or uncritically as self-validating sources of truth and insight. Their claims can be and need to be rationally justified *de jure* if not always *de facto*. For instance, Whitehead strikes the right balance when speaking of the relationship between history (tradition), authority, and reason:

> The appeal to history [or tradition] is the appeal to summits of attainment beyond any immediate clarity in our own individual existence. It is an appeal to authority. The appeal to reason [however] is the appeal to that ultimate judge, universal and yet individual to each, to which all authority must bow. History has authority so far, and exactly so far, as it admits of some measure of rational interpretation.[84]

Because humans are fallible creatures with vague and partial rather than clear and complete understandings of reality, one must be willing to draw upon the wisdom of tradition. But precisely for those same reasons, one must be willing, when needed, to subject the claims of authority to critical scrutiny. The establishment of faith may indeed include the formative influence of authoritative stories and communal role models, but these valuable resources should never be placed beyond the bounds of critical reflection.

Let me conclude by offering further comment on Hauerwas's reliance on narrative and his implicit pragmatism, and also on his critique of modern democracy and its liberal conception of freedom. Beginning with the former set of issues, I want to recount what I take to be Paul Lauritzen's cogent criticism of Hauerwas's appeal to narrative.[85] By comparing Hauerwas's use of narrative with that of Johannes Metz, Lauritzen

---

84. Whitehead, *Adventures of Ideas*, 162. See also Gamwell, *Divine Good*, 5.

85. I first recounted Lauritzen's criticism in Meyer, "On Keeping Theological Ethics Theological," 40–41.

observes that they both affirm "the narrative structure of Christianity" and they "both agree that the truthfulness of the Christian story is to be measured by its practical consequences." Where they sharply differ, he notes, is in the Christian story that each tells and in the practical consequences each believes should follow from that story. Appealing to narrative does not help to adjudicate this difference; for the category of narrative is insufficient to resolve conflicts among different versions of the Christian story and the differing ethical understandings that flow from them. This insufficiency, Lauritzen states, "highlights a fundamental problem for anyone assigning narrative a central place in theology and ethics: when we have endorsed a preference for story over explanation and argument, what do we do when our stories conflict?" Appealing to pragmatic consequences or to the distinctiveness of the community does not help because the key question is, which consequences should count? The answer to this question must go beyond a simple appeal to narrative or consequences. As Lauritzen points out, "There is no substantive moral view entailed merely by appeal to the general category of narrative." "The root problem," he insightfully concludes, remains the question "of truth" about theological claims and convictions—a truth that can only be clarified and validated beyond an appeal to narrative.[86]

Regarding modern democracy and its conception of freedom, Hauerwas criticizes it for its rejection of or resistance to authority, tradition, virtue, teleology, and even community. By contrast, he contends that genuine community, or at least genuine Christian community, requires the cultivation of virtues in pursuit of a tradition-dependent telos under the authoritative tutelage of a master of that tradition. Hauerwas correctly recognizes that something has gone sour in the modern democratic adventure. Moreover, he is right to recognize that modernity's radical anti-teleology is problematic. What is needed, however, is not the positing of some tradition-dependent telos, as Hauerwas espouses;

---

86. Lauritzen, "Is 'Narrative' Really a Panacea?" 336, 338, 339. See also Reynolds, "Conversation Worth Having," 408. One might add to Lauritzen's observations by noting that the problem with relying only on narrative also pertains to the question of what counts as appropriate or normative Christian faith. A dispute among differing Christian interpretations, each appealing to differing narratives, cannot be resolved simply by appealing to narrative. What is required is a normative criterion by which to interpret and evaluate the narratives themselves. Thus, as Ogden rightly points out, there are two distinct criteria for measuring theological adequacy, criteria that narrative alone cannot supply: *appropriateness* and *credibility* or truth. See Ogden, *Point of Christology*, 4.

rather, what is needed is the rational pursuit of and public discourse about a metaphysical telos. A comparison between Stout and Hauerwas is instructive here.

In *Democracy and Tradition* Stout champions a democratic understanding of virtue, going back to Whitman and Emerson, to counter the new traditionalism of Hauerwas, MacIntyre, and Milbank. Whereas the new traditionalists hold that the cultivation of virtue requires an appeal to what I have called social authority, Stout usually points instead to cultural authority. As he describes it, democratic virtue "trumpets self-reliance and holds docility in contempt. It encourages individuals to stand up, think for themselves, and demand recognition of their rights." Such democratic virtue, he continues, is quite compatible with some degree of respect for authority and tradition, and with a disposition of piety. With regard to the former, he states that "all discursive practices involve authority and deference to some extent." The key, however, is that deference is limited. At any moment, "any claim may be questioned if a relevant reason for doubting it can be produced." Hence, democratic virtue values the wisdom of tradition, but it is willing to question any claim at any juncture along the way. In regard to the relation between democracy and piety, Stout defines piety akin to Gustafson: "For piety, in the sense at issue here, is virtuous acknowledgment of dependence on the sources of one's existence and progress through life." Hence:

> When traditionalists conclude that democracy is antithetical to piety itself, they must be assuming that piety consists essentially in deference toward the hierarchical powers that be. But from a democratic point of view, the only piety worth praising as a virtue is that which concerns itself with *just* or *fitting* acknowledgment of the sources of our existence and progress through life.[87]

It is evident here that Stout at least partly affirms, against Hauerwas, modernity's emphasis on formal autonomy over heteronomy and thinks that such formal autonomy is compatible with a genuine disposition of piety toward the ultimate source and meaning of existence. Yet, like Hauerwas, as well as Gustafson and to a lesser extent Niebuhr, Stout does not think that reason can finally discern whether the object of piety ought to be understood theistically or naturalistically. As Stout remarks:

87. Stout, *Democracy and Tradition*, 25, 212, 213, 30.

> Naturalists and supernaturalists describe the ultimate source of existence differently; accordingly they acknowledge their dependence on it in different ways. No one knows how to resolve such differences of doctrine and religious practice once and for all by rational means.[88]

Stout's last statement here is ambiguous depending on whether one places the accent on "once and for all" or "by rational means." Clearly, by acknowledging the fallibility of all human reasoning and understanding, I have maintained all along that no claims can be closed off to further discussion or decided "once and for all." Claims to certainty, infallibility, and incorrigibility are beyond the pale. But I suspect that Stout's real emphasis here focuses on the claim that "no one knows how to resolve such differences . . . by rational means." That is, he, too, like Hauerwas, accepts the modern aversion to metaphysics and thus downplays the metaphysical task of seeking to resolve such differences by rational means. Hence, he continues to espouse ethics without metaphysics.

So in sum, I would concur with Stout's affirmation of formal autonomy and the democratic virtues of open-mindedness, tolerance, and inclusiveness in opposition to Hauerwas's rejection or downplaying of such characteristics. But I would argue against each of them that piety requires the rational pursuit of a metaphysical telos, and not merely the positing of a tradition-dependent one (Hauerwas) or the pragmatic expression of differing teleological views that are by nature unresolvable (Stout). Differently stated, Stout's simple dichotomy between naturalism and supernaturalism overlooks a third alternative, namely, a nonsupernaturalistic metaphysical theism—what Griffin calls "reenchantment without supernaturalism."[89] Public reflection on such a third alternative, especially in the context of the academy, can begin to reintroduce serious discussion about teleology and piety within the context of a modern commitment to formal autonomy. Such reflection does not detract from the role of the church in fostering piety in the lives of Christians. Rather, it enables the church to draw out connections between the life of faith and the life of citizenship without compromising either one.

---

88. Ibid., 34.
89. Griffin, *Reenchantment without Supernaturalism.*

Summary (I-C-AE-AM+)

In his article "The Truth about God," which I have cited at various points in this chapter, Hauerwas rejects the multifarious "attempts by theologians in modernity to 'do' ethics from the 'bottom up.'" By "bottom up," he means attempts by theologians to make their claims intelligible and credible to others in terms of reason and common experience. Such efforts, he contends, have "amounted to nothing less than an apologetic strategy which is bound to fail." This judgment again confirms Hauerwas's rejection of the modern commitments to intelligibility and credibility. Such efforts, he believes, emanate from a misguided and failed strategy. At the same time, however, he asserts that "morality is not only inadequate but unintelligible without reference to God." Here he clearly rejects the modern notion that ethics can be autonomous. In fact, all efforts to make theological claims intelligible and credible, he alleges, "run aground precisely because they conform to modernity's presumption that God is, at best, something 'added on' to the moral life. Hence, the challenge most central to modern theology is: how can we show that God matters without such a display appearing as a form of special pleading?" Hauerwas's answer, of course, is found in the witness of the church. "The truth," he concludes, "is finally known in the showing."[90]

Hauerwas correctly recognizes that most modern efforts to connect God and ethics have run aground. The reason for this, however, is precisely because most modern theologians, including Hauerwas, have mistakenly accepted the absence of metaphysics. Hauerwas thinks that one can show the necessity of God—"that God matters"—by pointing to the empirical witness of the church. But I have sought to argue that an empirical witness, by itself, can never suffice to justify the central underlying claim about the reality and necessity of God. To point first and foremost to the church, rather than to God, is always going to involve a form of special pleading. Hauerwas might reply that my call for philosophical metaphysics itself begs the question, since, according to him, Christian theology can only be internal, self-description. But my point is that this assertion—that theology can only be Christian self-description—*implies* an assertion about all human experience, namely, that it does not include an awareness of God. This means either

---

90. Hauerwas, "Truth about God," 23, 33, 23.

that human experience as such has no common content *or* that it has common content but awareness of God is not included. But in either case, the implied assertion here is *philosophical*, in the sense that appeal to common human experience and reason should be able to validate this implication. In sum, theology will never cast off the Feuerbachian shadow as long as it continues to shy away from rationally asserting and defending its central metaphysical claims.

A Tradition-Engaged Theology
The Approach of Jean Porter

Theological Portrait

DRAWING ON MACINTYRE'S DIAGNOSIS OF MODERN MORAL PHILOSOphy in *After Virtue*, Jean Porter contends that the basic problem in contemporary Christian ethics is its underlying and pervasive fragmentation. Whether it is Roman Catholic moral theologians or Protestant theologians and ethicists, Porter argues that "today's Christian ethicists have seized on fragments of what was once a unified moral tradition as the basis for their interpretations of Christian ethics." By seeking to build on such fragments rather than on a more unified theory, thinkers like Gustafson, Niebuhr, and Hauerwas not only fail to solve the problem, but they also contribute to its continued disorder and incoherence. The only way forward, Porter maintains, is to critically appropriate a unified tradition from the past and to update and apply its insights to contemporary moral problems. Indeed, the whole trajectory of Porter's work is one of constructive reclamation: she seeks through a critical lens to reclaim insights from the medieval tradition, especially Aquinas, as a way forward for theology today. This reclamation project is most concisely and directly articulated in *The Recovery of Virtue: The Relevance of Aquinas for Christian Ethics* (1990). This volume sets forth the basic intellectual agenda that defines the thematic direction for many of her later works, such as *Moral Action and Christian Ethics* (1995), *Natural and Divine Law: Reclaiming Tradition for Christian Ethics* (1999), and *Nature as Reason: A Thomistic Theory of the Natural Law* (2005). Given its programmatic nature, I will use *The Recovery of Virtue* as the focus of my theological portrait; I will draw on her other books and articles to fill in important details along the way.[1]

Surveying the Fragments of Contemporary Christian Ethics

Porter begins *The Recovery of Virtue* by surveying and critiquing major alternatives in contemporary Catholic and Protestant moral thought. On the Catholic side, she discusses the Post-Vatican II debate between those who advocate the neo-natural law theory of Germain Grisez and John Finnis, which asserts "that there are some determinate kinds of actions that are never morally justified," and those, like Richard McCormick, who advocate "proportionalism," which contends that "one must always act in such a way as to bring about the greatest possible balance of goods over evils, even if that means acting against some premoral good." Yet, lacking a more unified and in-depth outlook, Porter contends, this debate leaves moral theology at an impasse.[2] On the Protestant side, Porter discusses the work of Gene Outka along with the theologies of Gustafson and Hauerwas.[3] Since Gustafson and Hauerwas are central to my study, I will focus on her critique of them. Though she does not address Reinhold Niebuhr in this context, she does offer some analysis

---

1. The above quote comes from Porter, *Recovery of Virtue*, 15. I once asked Porter in an informal conversation whether she sees her overarching arguments in *The Recovery of Virtue* and in *Natural and Divine Law* as being continuous. She replied that she does in fact see them as being on the same trajectory of thought (conversation at the Annual Meeting of the Society of Christian Ethics, Pittsburgh, PA, January 2003). On my reading, this same general trajectory is carried forward in *Nature as Reason* as well. Some might suggest that in her most recent thought Porter is more circumspect about her use of pragmatism in relation to her appropriation of the medieval natural law tradition. I take her recent view to offer a nuanced clarification rather than a wholesale rejection of her previous position. I will return to this below in n. 72.

2. On the one hand, says Porter, "the proportionalist critique of the Grisez/Finnis reinterpretation of the natural law is well-taken. It is hardly self-evident that we can never act against the basic goods, even to prevent an even greater destruction of these goods." On the other hand, "at least one of Grisez's criticisms of proportionalism is equally well-founded: Without a convincing standard of commensuration for comparing premoral goods and evils, a program for moral assessment that depends on commensurating them is meaningless." Porter, *Recovery of Virtue*, 14, 20, 21. For her full summary, see 14–15, 17–21.

3. In regard to Outka, she discusses his analysis of the different views of agape in the Christian tradition and especially his emphasis on equal regard as the most appropriate interpretation of agape. However, Porter contends that Outka, lacking a more definite and unified moral theory, is unable to offer an adequate account of what equality or equal regard concretely mean. Porter, *Recovery of Virtue*, 21–24.

of his views in *Natural and Divine Law*; thus I will add that into the mix here as well.

Porter sums up Gustafson's project as *"the return to nature."*[4] By this she seems to mean two things. First, Gustafson claims that theology must incorporate the insights of the natural sciences in order to be intelligible and in order to be faithful to the reality of God and God's world. Second, his theocentric ethic seeks to order and construe human life more broadly in the wider context of nature, thereby counteracting the narrow vision of anthropocentricism. Porter notes that some critics, such as Hauerwas, have accused Gustafson's theocentricism of failing to be adequately Christian. Though she accepts this general line of criticism, she does not pursue it; instead, she focuses her critique on Gustafson's central moral norm. After careful study, she says that she is "still uncertain as to what it means, concretely, to relate to all things in a manner appropriate to their relationships to God. How, out of all the possible construals of the complex form of ordering in the world, are we to pick out which ones are normative, even with the help of piety?"[5] Gustafson, she alleges, never adequately answers this question. He does seek to redirect theological ethics away from individualism toward greater attention to "the good of the community or the species," and "this turn from individualism is certainly significant." However, she argues that

> it is difficult to see how it is theocentric, even when theocentricism is viewed on Gustafson's own terms. The human good, now construed as the good of the community, or of the human race as a whole, is still at the center of moral concern. Gustafson might answer that the turn from individualism is only one part of his moral program, which becomes theocentric when it is placed in the context of a still wider commitment to relate to all things in a manner appropriate to their relations to God. But that only brings us back to the fundamental, and unanswered question: What, concretely, does that mean, over and above a general policy of giving priority to the well-being of human communities over that of individuals?[6]

---

4. Porter, *Recovery of Virtue*, 24.
5. Ibid., 27.
6. Ibid.

Hence, Porter contends that Gustafson's theology lacks adequate resources to provide a coherent and concrete account of the moral life.

Hauerwas's approach, as she describes it, is one *"in search of the virtuous community."* In summarizing his outlook, she notes his emphasis on the particularity of the Christian narrative and witness, and his rejection of what I have called the modern commitment to intelligibility. Unlike the Catholic and Protestant thinkers named above, who all affirm in their own way that theology must "meet wider standards of reasonableness and plausibility," she points out that Hauerwas offers "an uncompromising denial of that claim."[7] This denial, she observes, has of course led some to call Hauerwas's theology "antirational or sectarian." For instance, "as Gustafson says, Hauerwas's God is 'the tribal God of a minority of the earth's population' and his ethics therefore forfeits any relevance to a wider society." But from Porter's perspective, Hauerwas can answer this charge by responding "that such criticisms reflect a wrongheaded attachment to the Enlightenment's ideal of a universal morality."[8] Instead, she thinks other criticisms are more germane.[9]

Chief among these, she contends that Hauerwas is never clear about what he means when he claims that the Christian story is a "truthful narrative." At times, he "seems to imply that the truthfulness of a narrative can be evaluated only in terms internal to the way of life that it fosters." But if this is what he means, then we have no legitimate grounds or reasons "to prefer the Christian narrative, except [simply] that it is ours." At other times, he seems to suggest that the Christian narrative is "true in the sense of somehow conveying the actual character of reality. But if that is what he means," continues Porter, "then it

---

7. Ibid., 28.

8. Ibid., 30. Porter cites Gustafson, "The Sectarian Temptation: Reflections on Theology, the Church and the University," *Proceedings of the Catholic Theological Society of America* 40 (1985) 92.

9. Outka offers one of these criticisms: he has uncovered an underlying tension in Hauerwas's thought between his commitment to the community and his commitment to the individual. On the one hand, Hauerwas insists that the community's key authoritative narratives are central to the formation of individual identity. On the other hand, he contends "that each individual must become a self-determining person of character." Porter claims that "Hauerwas accepts this criticism and admits that he does not know how to resolve it." Yet, she also notes that he hopes that this tension "would be resolved in practice as one attempts to live out a narrative with fidelity." Porter, *Recovery of Virtue*, 30; she cites Outka, "Character, Vision and Narrative," *Religious Studies Review* 6 (1989) 111–14.

would seem to follow that, potentially at least, there are standards for evaluating Christian ethics that are not purely internal to the Christian tradition."[10] In short, either Hauerwas is a relativist who undermines Christian truth claims, or else he must affirm some external standard in order to support Christianity's claims about God and the moral life. This line of criticism is particularly telling because it hints at Porter's own commitments to intelligibility and credibility, which Hauerwas rejects, and it reveals where she and Hauerwas part company in regard to MacIntyre's tradition-constituted rationality. Whereas Porter, as I will show, follows MacIntyre in pursuit of a means by which the claims of different traditions can be indirectly rationally assessed, Hauerwas does not. Instead, he rests all his theological claims on the back of the church's distinctive witness to the world. Porter ends by suggesting that Hauerwas does not even leave us with any criteria to "adjudicate among conflicting interpretations of the central Christian story within the Christian community" itself, as illustrated by the conflict between pacifist and non-pacifist positions. Hauerwas's lack of external criteria by which narratives and their forms of life can be evaluated, Porter concludes, leaves us "with no hope of real conversation even with other sorts of Christians, much less with the world."[11]

In a chapter on "Social Ethics" in *Natural and Divine Law*, Porter outlines the similarities and differences between Niebuhr and the natural law tradition. The key similarity, she purports, is found in the fact that both of them are world-affirming while concomitantly recognizing the ambiguities of the world—including the church. In reference to Niebuhr, Porter points to his "gloss" on the serenity prayer as an illustration of his world-acceptance: "Reinhold Niebuhr prays for the willingness to take, 'as Christ did, the world as it is, not as I would have it.' This [formulation]," suggests Porter, "is a concise expression of a fundamental Christian attitude." Likewise, she claims that the scholastic natural law tradition offers us rich resources for making sense of the ambiguities of communal life: "The scholastics recognize that the fundamental institutions of their society are problematic, yet they are also prepared to accept them as necessary conditions for the attainment of social goods. In this way, they provide a theological framework for affirming the limited

---

10. Porter, *Recovery of Virtue*, 30–31. She cites Hauerwas, *Community of Character*, 97.

11. Porter, *Recovery of Virtue*, 31.

but real goodness of human societies, while also keeping open possibilities for social critique and reform." Porter admires this bifocal capacity of affirmation and realism in both Niebuhr and the scholastics. "In their awareness of the inevitable ambiguities of social life," she observes, "and their willingness to embrace it nonetheless, the scholastics are surprisingly similar to Reinhold Niebuhr."[12]

If a common virtue is found in their shared bifocal capacity, then important differences arise in terms of what each of them sees through their own bifocal lens. To explicate this difference, Porter contrasts the scholastic social ethic with Niebuhr's Christian realism by comparing how each of them envisions the relationship between nature and grace or world and gospel. For Niebuhr, as she recounts, the divine love revealed in Christ "is a purely self-sacrificial love, which by its very nature cannot be given social embodiment." This formulation of the Christian moral ideal as an "impossible possibility," she suggests, leads Niebuhr to draw a sharp line between grace and nature and between gospel and world: "Niebuhr gives as much weight to the uniqueness of Christ, the discontinuity between the ideal of humanity that [Christ] reveals and our own expectations [or potential for realizing that possibility], as do Yoder, Hauerwas, and Milbank." What Porter apparently means here is that whereas Yoder, Hauerwas, and Milbank sharply juxtapose the nonviolence of the Christian community with the world, Niebuhr likewise sharply juxtaposes the Christian moral ideal with the actual possibilities of human communities. She of course immediately points out that Niebuhr draws very different practical conclusions from this contrast than they do. Given his world-affirmation, Niebuhr holds that Christian love obliges us "to work for justice and peace, insofar as these can be secured through the 'balance of competing wills and interests' intrinsic to all human institutions." Yet, one should never forget that this worthwhile worldly endeavor is still "not consonant with the ideal of Christian love as revealed in the cross of Christ." This tension between justice and the ideal of sacrificial love points to the inevitable tragedy that Niebuhr thinks endemic to the human enterprise. Hence, there is no process of reconciling nature and grace in this world. For, on the one hand, we must "assume our responsibilities in human society," while, on

---

12. Porter, *Natural and Divine Law*, 289, 290.

A Tradition-Engaged Theology 347

the other, we can only trust "in the mercy of God [to] finally overcome" the corruption of sin that inevitably taints our efforts.[13]

In contrast to Niebuhr's sharp discontinuity between nature and grace, Porter thinks the medieval natural law tradition offers a more credible alternative in the form of a dialectical reconciliation between them. To illustrate this more promising path, Porter compares Niebuhr's interpretation of the biblical command to "turn the other cheek" with the interpretation offered by the thirteenth-century scholastic William of Auxerre. For Niebuhr, "Jesus's command represents an impossible ideal"—the ideal of sacrificial love. For William, alternatively, the command represents a "real, practical imperative that can readily be understood and put into practice once the scope of the command has been delineated." According to Porter, the key here is that William engages in an act of dialectal reflection in order to find a way to affirm both grace (scripture) and nature (human possibility). Unlike Hauerwas's witness ethic, which seeks to form an alternative community based on a literal embodiment of such biblical commands and virtues, and unlike Niebuhr's Christian realism, which designates such commands as helpful reminders but only in the form of impossible ideals, William's dialectical maneuvering is intended to affirm both biblical commands and the natural or general possibilities of human community. He does this by "delineating" or narrowing the scope of such commands in relation to a particular context and in relation to the overall theological tradition. In a passage that Porter quotes at length, William writes:

> Indications are those [precepts] which are given for a particular time and oblige conditionally, so that the opposite may licitly be done on account of some consideration which may emerge. For example, according to the law of nature it is legitimate to resist force by force, since vengeance derives from the natural law, as Cicero says in the first book of the *Rhetoric*. However, our Lord commands the opposite to the apostles, saying, "He who strikes you on the cheek, give him the other one, and he who would take your tunic, give him your cloak as well," so that in that time and place they should so offer themselves, in order that through their unaccustomed mildness men and women might be drawn to God.[14]

---

13. Ibid., 290, 291.

14. Ibid., 292, 291. Porter cites William of Auxerre, *Summa Aurea, Liber Quartus* III. 18, 1 (Paris: Centre National de la Recherche Scientifique, 1985, c. 1220).

Porter acknowledges that Niebuhr, Hauerwas, and others might describe such casuistical reasoning "as a shocking dilution of the gospel." Yet she thinks, on the contrary, that William illustrates a valuable way forward for contemporary theological ethics. "In this passage, what William offers is not a dilution of Scripture but an interpretation through which the meaning of a particular imperative is discerned in the light of its likely purpose, seen in the context of one's overall theological commitments." Moreover, what William offers is an instructive example of how the scholastic tradition affirmed both natural law and scripture, affirmed both natural human possibilities and the norms of the Christian tradition. "Most fundamentally," Porter remarks,

> William here expresses the fundamental scholastic view that human nature reflects the goodness and wisdom of its Creator. This view gives rise to the presupposition that if there is an apparent conflict between the natural law and the gospel, it is possible to reconcile them dialectically. That is what William does. In the process, he does limit the scope of the evangelical prescription, but he does not relegate it to an impossible ideal that cannot be fulfilled in history. Yet he also leaves room for the expression of fundamental human tendencies toward self-protection and the vindication of justice, even within a Christian community.[15]

It is this ability to take both nature and theological tradition seriously that Porter thinks is lacking in contemporary Christian ethics: Gustafson takes nature seriously but cannot adequately or concretely make sense of it in theological terms; Hauerwas takes the tradition seriously but lacks any public criteria or resources, such as human nature, for evaluating its claims; and Niebuhr accepts and affirms the world but ultimately relegates scriptural norms to the mere status of impossible ideals. Arguing against these fragmentary approaches, Porter asserts that "we must strive to bring together our understanding of Scripture [and tradition] and our own nature through a dialectical process of mutual interpretation that harmonizes the two while respecting the integrity of each, as far as we can do so. This process," she continues, "will also involve an element of reflectively shaping our nature to bring it into accordance with our best theological insights, through community formation and the education of children and converts."[16] Here, in anticipa-

---

15. Porter, *Recovery of Virtue*, 291, 292.
16. Ibid., 293.

tory form, we have all the ingredients of Porter's theological recipe: an emphasis on moral formation within the context of a particular community; an attempt to offer an intelligible and credible theological ethic by means of a dialectical reconciliation of nature and tradition; and an attempt to constructively reclaim the scholastic natural law tradition as the guiding vehicle by which all this can be accomplished. Porter seeks to accomplish the successful integration of these elements in *The Recovery of Virtue*, to which I now return.

Porter concludes her introduction there by noting that her survey of the contemporary theological scene is intended to reveal its fragmentary and, thus, unsatisfactory character. "But," she asks, "is there an alternative? What would a moral theory that incorporates the central concepts of contemporary Christian ethics into a unified theory look like?" She answers that, taken together, the *Prima Secundae* and the *Secunda Secundae* of Aquinas's *Summa Theologiae* (hereafter ST) offer precisely what is needed. Aquinas's approach is invaluable because it "is grounded in a theory of the human good that gives content to the fundamental norms of love of neighbor and nonmaleficence and [because it] provides criteria by which to evaluate the goodness both of actions and states of character." This theory then leads Aquinas to "a particular account of what it is for a community to be good, that is, a just community in which the equality of all persons in certain fundamental respects is preserved. At the same time," she adds, "his theory of the human good is itself grounded in a general theory of goodness, which rests upon a particular theory of nature." Before explicating the meaning and relevance of these systematic elements for today, Porter notes that she has limited the scope of her study to a reconstruction of the philosophical components of the ST rather than focusing on its "more properly theological components." The reason for this, she claims, is that "the aspect of Aquinas's moral thought that is most illuminating to contemporary Christian ethics is his conception of the natural end, or good, of the human person, seen in relation to his theory of goodness in general."[17] I will focus my attention on her development of these two concepts, beginning with her account of Aquinas's general theory of goodness and then moving systematically toward her discussion of the natural human good.

17. Ibid., 31–32. For the sake of clarity and brevity, I will not include Porter's textual references to ST unless she is specifically quoting a passage from it.

Aquinas's General Theory of Goodness

Aquinas's moral theory focuses on the human person acting in the world with "an intellectual apprehension of the good." The obvious question then is what defines the good or "what is meant by acting for the good? The whole of Aquinas's theory of morality," suggests Porter, "may be taken as an extended answer to that question." For Aquinas, the human good cannot be identified apart from "a general theory of goodness," one that distinguishes between merely apparent goods and real or authentic ones. This comprehensive conception of goodness, moreover, is grounded in his "general metaphysical theory." Given modernity's anti-metaphysical proclivities, Porter notes that many interpreters are embarrassed by the central role that metaphysics plays in Aquinas's moral thought. Some try to overlook this by "assuming that [he] presupposes our sharp dichotomy between ontological and linguistic analyses." Others try to read him as holding a modern transcendental view along the lines of Kant, namely, that notions such as "being, goodness, unity and truth are mere concepts in some modern sense, that is, . . . expressions [merely] of the way in which we [humans] apprehend or order reality." But such efforts at avoidance, Porter contends, are misreadings of Aquinas. His general theory of goodness is rooted in his ontology and metaphysics; his view is unabashedly one of metaphysical realism. Keeping this in mind, she thinks one can still use the term "transcendental"—in its more medieval sense—to describe his theory: "To say that goodness is a transcendental is to say that it is a concept of such ubiquity and generality that it can be applied to anything whatever, in any category of real existence." Clearly the sense here is one of metaphysical ubiquity, not one of limit or restriction in the Kantian sense. The reason for this emphasis, remarks Porter, is that for Aquinas "the concept of goodness can be applied to anything whatever, insofar as it exists in some way. . . . That is, *goodness* is convertible with *being*; it can be asserted whenever, in whatever way, and to whatever degree existence can be asserted of something."[18]

Porter recognizes that the convertibility between goodness and being might suggest that the two may be used interchangeably. But this conclusion, she argues, would involve a misreading. For Aquinas, on her

---

18. Porter, *Recovery of Virtue*, 34, 35, 36, 37. For a brief helpful discussion of "transcendentals," see Ogden, "Theology Without Metaphysics?" 150–51.

account, goodness has two distinct but related meanings: "In its most proper sense, 'goodness' applies to *perfected* being, to whatever is, insofar as it is what it ought to be." Therefore, "to be good without qualification is to be perfect, that is, to exist in the fullest degree of actuality possible to a creature of this given kind." In another or underlying sense, however, "'goodness' can be applied to anything whatever, insofar as it exists, since to exist at all is to be in act and therefore to possess some degree of perfection." One can clearly see here Aquinas's inheritance and affirmation of the Western metaphysical notion of a chain of being: to exist at all, even in a minimal degree, is a relative good; by contrast, evil is defined in terms of a "deficiency," in terms of a lack of being. Because evil is always "parasitical upon good in this way, nothing that exists can be wholly evil."[19]

In further explicating Aquinas's understanding of goodness, Porter suggests that each existing entity has an interrelated three-fold good. First, there is the good of self-preservation. In nature, "the tendency of every creature to maintain itself in existence indicates that for every creature, its [own] existence is a good." Second, there is the specific good or perfection of each type or form of creature: "[S]ince no creature exists at all except insofar as it instantiates some determinate kind of nature, however imperfectly, it follows that perfection in accordance with its own nature is the primary good that all creatures necessarily desire and seek." And third, each entity is also oriented to a wider set of goods beyond its own preservation and beyond the perfection of its own form; this wider set of goods involves the goods of community. Porter later elaborates on these, but first she turns our attention back to a deeper understanding of Aquinas's connection between goodness and being.[20]

For anything to exist at all, it must exist as some type of thing. This critical connection between existence and form, states Porter, "is a necessity in the order of existence, but at the same time it is manifested by a parallel necessity in the order of knowledge: Unless we can identify at least in a general way what kind of thing something is, we would not be able to recognize it as an individual existing creature at all." Aquinas's metaphysics, in other words, draws a three-fold epistemological connection between knowledge of existence, knowledge of form, and knowledge of goodness. To know *that something is* is to know at least

19. Porter, *Recovery of Virtue*, 37.
20. Ibid., 38.

to some degree *what it is* and to know what it is is to know to some extent *what is good for it*. There is no Humean gap here between "is" and "ought" or Weberian gap between "facts" and "values." For Aquinas, to know that something exists is to know, however minimally or implicitly, what its good is. Porter acknowledges that

> this claim may seem implausible at first. Surely we can recognize that this lump of something *is* a something, without knowing *what* kind of something it is? We can indeed but only within very narrow limits. That is, we can perceive that something exists without knowing *exactly* what it is, or what it *truly* is. Even so, unless we have at least a plausible general idea of what it is that we are perceiving, we cannot perceive that there is something there at all. An existence that is finite and yet not qualified in any way is inconceivable and *therefore* not perceivable. And so, we must have some idea that what is before us is, let us say, a solid object, somewhat resembling a stone, in order to recognize that here is something, we don't know what, that we might examine further.[21]

We garner knowledge about what something is in part by observing its interaction with its environment. For Aquinas, "whenever anything exercises efficient causality, it communicates something of its intelligible being by introducing a new quality, or a new ordering, into the configuration of events surrounding it."[22] The ink of a pen, for example, "communicates something of its intelligible being" onto the environment of the paper. This communicative effect is also evident in living beings: they seek not only "to thrive as individuals, in accordance with the ideal of their species," but also "to communicate that specific ideal to new creatures by reproducing themselves."[23]

Given his affirmation of a chain of being and his emphasis on each being's causative influence, Porter suggests that there is a "a natural hierarchy of being" in Aquinas's thought: "[A]s we move through the gradations of creatures, from stones to the highest forms of animal life, we see an increase in the scope and power of causality." But "for Aquinas, God, as Creator, is wholly outside this hierarchy."[24] Porter does not

21. Ibid., 39.
22. Ibid., 40, 41.
23. Ibid., 42.
24. Ibid.

offer comment here on Aquinas's doctrine of God, yet it is worth noting its implicit classical assumption. Unlike Whitehead or Hartshorne, who argue that God is *not* an exception to the metaphysical categories that apply to the world, Aquinas displays here the classical theistic assumption that treats God as an exception to those categories, namely, as one "wholly outside" the world and the chain of being.

Having explicated these elements of Aquinas's general theory, Porter returns to the claim that each entity affirms a wider set of goods beyond its own self-preservation and beyond its realization of its own ideal form. To be sure, she says, these latter goods are primary for Aquinas, especially the good of instantiating the "specific perfection" of one's own species. But "in a secondary sense, creatures may be said to be [also] directed to a wider good." This may be said in two senses. First, "lower kinds of creatures exist for the sake of the higher kinds of creatures (although it does not seem that we [humans] exist for the sake of the angels)." Reciprocally, the good of lower creatures is apparently also "promoted through the activities of creatures of higher kinds." And second, "all creatures are oriented toward the good of the universe as a whole." Porter nicely integrates these two points when she writes: "Aquinas's universe is a web of creatures bound together by relationships of mutual benefit, in which each is oriented to the good of some others, and all together, in their ordered interrelationships, are ordered to the good of the whole."[25]

Like other creatures, human beings are also oriented to these wider goods; these include specifically the common good of one's community. While acknowledging this emphasis on the common good, Porter claims that Aquinas shares two modern concerns, at least in an anticipatory way: an emphasis on the value and dignity of each individual, and an affirmation of human equality. Since a human being is rational, "she enjoys an individual and distinctive existence in the highest way possible to a creature. For this reason, the good of an individual person cannot simply be subordinated to any wider good in the way that individual goods of lesser creatures can be." This premise lies at the root of Aquinas's understanding of justice. Likewise, Porter emphasizes Aquinas's tacit if not explicit affirmation of human equality: "He does not assert a hierarchy of being *within* the human species (or any other

---

25. Ibid., 49, 50.

species), in virtue of which some have authority to dominate others."[26] With these two caveats in place, Porter is then more comfortable with acknowledging his emphasis on the common good. In brief, she suggests that the true common good, embodied in a just community, promotes the individual flourishing of its members. Conversely, true individual flourishing occurs in the context of community and includes commitment to the common good. Similarly, true self-love contributes to the good of community and genuine love of community includes proper self-love.[27]

Can Aquinas's General Theory of Goodness Be Defended Today?

After having set forth Aquinas's general theory of goodness and its relation to his underlying metaphysics, Porter then puts on her critical lens to assess whether his theory holds any contemporary credibility. In brief, she thinks that his theory can be made credible today, but how she goes about doing this is essential for properly understanding her approach. The primary challenge to the contemporary relevance of Aquinas, Porter maintains, is posed by the "incommensurability thesis," a thesis she accepts in some form. By incommensurability, she means that human perceptions of experience and the world are structured by culturally-specific or tradition-specific "classificatory schemes." "Moreover," she claims,

> there is no way to show that one scheme is simply wrong, without presupposing the foundational beliefs of another scheme. That is, there is no neutral standpoint from which to evaluate different schemes, on the basis of which we could decide which one offers the correct classification of things in the world. In that sense, the rival schemes are incommensurable.[28]

Porter implies here that there are no a priori or rationally necessary claims about reality. Rather, all such claims are logically contingent—based on some empirically given cultural scheme. In reference to Aquinas, this means that the morphology of forms that structures his analysis of being and the world is grounded in his own culturally

26. Ibid., 50, 42.
27. Ibid., 51.
28. Ibid., 54.

specific scheme, and not in reality itself. This issue of incommensurability points to an important difference between Aquinas and Porter. Whereas he puts forth direct metaphysical claims about the nature of reality as such, and believes that reason and experience offer a common basis upon which to directly adjudicate such claims, Porter does not believe that reason and experience can, even in theory, directly validate such claims. "Hence, it would appear," she remarks, "that the specific kinds that are so important to Aquinas are grounded in the particular conceptual scheme that he brings to things, and not in the nature of things themselves. At the very least," she concludes, "the burden of proof is on Aquinas (or more precisely, his present-day defenders) to prove otherwise."[29]

If I understand Porter correctly, she wants to take up this burden in order to try to show how one can affirm some form of incommensurability and still affirm a form of realism that avoids relativism. The key, she suggests, lies in how one defines incommensurability. Among those who subscribe to this thesis there are at least two distinct trajectories of interpretation. One path, illustrated by Hauerwas, concludes that the specific schemes or narratives of a community cannot be rationally evaluated by any external criteria. Hence, he emphasizes the internal life and witness of a community as the sole possible source of validation. Porter emphatically rejects this relativistic approach. Alternatively, she declares that a more promising version is found in MacIntyre's attempt to delineate an indirect form of validation among different and competing traditions. With this avenue in sight, Porter argues that one can accept the incommensurability thesis without undermining "Aquinas's argument for the intrinsic intelligibility of things, in accordance with their various ways of instantiating specific kinds."[30] To explain how these can both be affirmed, she begins by analyzing the nature of incommensurability in greater detail and then by outlining MacIntyre's notion of tradition-constituted rationality.

Contrary to what one might expect, she asserts that "genuine incommensurability" presupposes rather than excludes "a generally agreed upon body of knowledge of species of creatures." This is the case, she

29. Ibid.
30. Ibid., 54. Porter's endorsement of MacIntyre is most explicit at 192 n. 31: "The version of this [incommensurability] thesis that I accept is developed by . . . MacIntyre in his *Whose Justice?*, 349–88."

submits, because incommensurability cannot go all the way down. "In order for two interpretations of a thing to be genuinely incommensurable, they must refer to the same thing, and the proponents of the different views must recognize it to be the same thing." This implicit shared recognition points back to Aquinas's connection between knowledge of existence and knowledge of form. If persons with different interpretive schemes identify the existence of a single disputed object, then "they must share a common classificatory scheme at some [underlying] level, however basic. Incommensurability still remains," Porter alleges, "but it enters in at the more advanced level of reflection at which people begin to develop interpretive and explanatory theories about things." What Porter seems to be saying here is (a) that we share a common reality at a fundamental level, (b) that human understanding of this reality is one at this deep level, but (c) interpretations immediately become culturally specific and diverse as one rises to the surface of explicit articulation and understanding. "If this argument is sound," states Porter, "it shows that Aquinas's claim that the creatures of the world are divided into intelligible specific kinds is consistent with the incommensurability thesis."[31] It follows from this, she concludes, that neither his general theory of goodness nor his theory of morality are invalidated by this modern proposition.

Given her own apparent affirmation of an underlying intelligibility, Porter acknowledges that it would be tempting to claim that Aquinas's view "escapes the constraints of incommensurability altogether, that is, that it can be shown to be universally valid even to those who do not accept its starting points." But this temptation, she believes, must be resisted. She again acknowledges, however, that Aquinas himself neither shares her doubts nor subscribes to the incommensurability thesis. Indeed, he "thought that at least the central tenets of morality are knowable to all." But on this important point, she holds, Aquinas and others are mistaken. Nothing in her preceding argument "serves to establish that Aquinas's theory of morality would be rationally compelling to anyone, operating from within any conceptual scheme whatever. To the contrary, there is good reason to believe that it would not be [rationally compelling]." In addition to being dependent on his general theory of goodness, his theory of morality also "presupposes the whole structure of his philosophical and theological beliefs." Given these

31. Porter, *Recovery of Virtue*, 55, 56.

theistic and philosophical presuppositions, Aquinas's moral theory would not be "compelling to someone whose starting points" were different. However, this admission, Porter adds, does not mean that we are back to the relativistic conclusion that "Aquinas's moral theory is 'only true for us,' or . . . that it is irrelevant or [inherently] unconvincing to those who do not share his starting points."[32] It is at this juncture, in seeking to find a middle way between relativism and universalism, that Porter explicitly turns to MacIntyre for help.

The common error of these two poles is that each holds "an untenable view of rational discourse as [being] necessarily perspective-free. [MacIntyre rightly] argues to the contrary that both rationality and truth are embedded in tradition-constituted inquiry, in such a way that this inquiry is capable of both self-assessment and genuine critique by others." Applied to Aquinas, this means that anyone who recommends his moral theory to others who hold a different set of underlying assumptions will need "to find some starting point from within those others' own tradition." Only from the perspective of their own *internal* basis can Aquinas's moral theory possibly be rendered plausible to them. We cannot be sure, admits Porter, that such an empirical point of contact can be found. "But I believe," she declares, "that both Aquinas' theology and the central tenets of Christianity give us reason to hope that such a starting point could always be found, sooner or later." In other words, Porter, like Aquinas and Christianity as a whole, affirms a common universe in relation to a single God. But unlike Aquinas, Porter denies both the possibility of a common or universal metaphysics and the possibility of translating or directly validating such metaphysical claims. She therefore hopes that there will be some contingent point of contact between incommensurable traditions. Once this point of contact is found, she reasons, then one can begin the arduous but hopeful path of each tradition assessing its own strength and validity in terms of how effectively its conceptual and practical resources are able to resolve both its own internal problems and the problems of the other tradition (in comparison with the resources offered by the other tradition). By means of this indirect comparison—a comparison that is always indirect because it is always mediated through a tradition's own internal assumptions—Porter believes a natural law theory, such as offered by Aquinas, can purport to offer an understanding of human

32. Ibid., 56, 56–57.

existence that is universal in scope while simultaneously recognizing its own tradition-specific ground. "[I]f MacIntyre's theory of rationality is correct," concludes Porter, then such natural law attempts "are not self-deluded in proposing their theories as possible candidates for a description of The Way Things Really Are. Admittedly, there is no guarantee that they will be able to prove their theories to all challengers, *even if* they are in fact correct." But neither does the fact that it is developed from within a specific tradition "necessarily invalidate its claim to truth. Of course, Aquinas himself would not have defended his theory of the natural law in this way," Porter adds, "but I believe that it could [and must] now be defended in this way."[33]

The Hierarchy of Being

In seeking to critically retrieve and defend Aquinas's general theory of goodness in an indirect, MacIntyrean way, Porter recognizes that she still must explain how notions such as a hierarchy of being are credible today. Aquinas views the world "as an ordering from lower to higher, or lesser to greater" in the chain of being. It is only in this way, she notes, that "he can view the universe itself as an ordered and hence unified whole." But why should the universe be viewed in this manner at all? For his part, Aquinas thought that an orderly world was the work of a creator God and that the existence of this creator God can be proved "from the orderliness of the universe. As I read him," Porter comments, "all five of his well-known proofs for the existence of God are variants of a proof from the reality of order in the universe." At this juncture, it is worth noting another point of divergence between Aquinas and Porter. As she herself suggests, Aquinas's theistic proofs seek to make direct metaphysical claims about the reality of God and the order of the universe. By contrast, given her acceptance of the incommensurability thesis and MacIntyre's tradition-constituted rationality, Porter is hesitant or reluctant to foreground such theistic proofs or metaphysical claims in her own constructive expression. To be sure, she does say in *Nature as Reason* that she accepts the "long-standing and officially sanctioned [Catholic] view" that "the existence of God can . . . be established through rational reflection." But to the best of my knowledge, she never really highlights or foregrounds theistic arguments in her own work.

---

33. Ibid., 57.

Instead, such claims remain primarily in the background—embedded in the tradition, but not front and center as they are for Aquinas himself. Thus, instead of aggressively defending his theistic proofs or offering a variant theistic argument of her own, she simply notes that "the existence of a creator God and the claim that the universe is itself a unified whole mutually imply one another in the framework of Aquinas's thought." What Porter is willing to explicitly recommend is that the concept of a holistic universe does have some merit on pragmatic grounds. As she states, it "has proved to be fruitful for further efforts to investigate the nature of our world, since it is one of the presuppositions of modern science."[34]

One of the most valuable contemporary benefits of Aquinas's hierarchy of being, Porter claims, is its "challenge, and perhaps [even] corrective, to Gustafson's theocentric ethic." Unlike Gustafson, who cannot ultimately articulate what it means to relate to all things as they relate to God, "Aquinas does have a persuasive theory of the way in which creatures are ordered to God and one another, and it is precisely that theory that provides the basis for what Gustafson would call Aquinas's anthropocentricism." Instead of criticizing anthropocentricism, as Gustafson does, Porter embraces Aquinas's version of it. She does so for two reasons. First, his version places us in a chain of being in which we are higher in importance than the creatures below us, and below the angels above us and, of course, below the God who stands above and beyond the chain itself. According to Porter, this chain mitigates some of the idolatrous tendencies that Gustafson rightly fears while, at the same time, offering us some of the broader vision that he recommends. For Aquinas, "the good of the universe as a whole is greater than the good of any particular creature, however exalted. [Hence, he] takes the supreme goodness of the universe as a whole very seriously."[35]

---

34. Ibid., 58, 59; Porter, *Nature as Reason*, 328, 86–87. I recognize that there is a contemporary debate within Thomistic studies about whether Aquinas thought that he was, in fact, putting forth theistic arguments accessible on the basis of reason as such or whether, alternatively, he saw his "proofs" as premised on theistic assumptions that presupposed the prior acceptance of the Christian tradition. I am not prepared to enter this debate here. But it does seem to me that Porter describes Aquinas's view as if she thinks he is trying to make straightforward theistic arguments. Because she accepts the modern incommensurability thesis, and he does not, she cannot follow him in this direction.

35. Porter, *Recovery of Virtue*, 61.

Yet, second, Aquinas (unlike Gustafson) "holds that concern for human well-being is [still] central to the moral life." In fact, "he asserts that a proper love of oneself should take precedence over love of the neighbor, and we are obliged to love those who are more closely connected to us more than strangers." The basic insight that Aquinas offers us, Porter argues, is a way to take our own natural inclinations seriously and to see how those natural inclinations fit into the divine ordering of the world. In spite of his talk of taking nature seriously, Porter believes that Gustafson fails finally to do so (likewise with Niebuhr and Hauerwas). In contrast, Aquinas takes both the part and the whole seriously because he integrates a "macro-ordering of all creatures into an array of species" with a micro-ordering of the individual "toward the attainment of [its] own proper good and the exercise of [its] own proper causality." With this macro-micro integrative framework in place, we can recognize "that our own existence, as individuals or as a species, is not the greatest created good," while also affirming that it is right (because in accordance with the divine ordering) "for us to be concerned first of all with our own well-being, rather than with the good of the universe as a whole. The good of the universe is God's proper concern," not ours. Though "we are obliged to conform our wills to God's [will] formally, God is not so unreasonable," Porter suggests, "as to expect us always to will concretely what he wills [universally] in his capacity as the governor of the whole universe."[36]

Distinguishing the Natural and Supernatural Ends

In order to discuss the human good in detail, Porter makes one important final segue by examining Aquinas's distinction between the natural and supernatural ends of human life. Porter's account of the human good presupposes that Aquinas takes the natural telos to be "the proximate [or guiding] norm of the moral life." She acknowledges that this is not obvious, since Aquinas "also clearly holds that the true ultimate perfection of the human person is not natural, but supernatural in character." This true ultimate perfection is realized only in our beatific vision of the divine. Nevertheless, this aim "is totally beyond" our natural capacities and can only, at best, be anticipated in this life through the bestowal of divine grace in the form of "a supernatural transformation

36. Ibid., 61, 62.

of our capacities for knowledge and love." Its full realization is attained only in the life hereafter.[37]

Porter recognizes that there are various possible ways to interpret Aquinas's view of these two ends. One possibility holds that the supernatural completely trumps the natural, thus leaving humans with only one telos, "the direct vision of God." Another view claims that Aquinas leaves us with no unified or coherent aim at all. On this account, humans have "natural inclinations to finite ends, but these are directed to a plurality of goods, and not to a unified state of perfection that would count as a true end." Yet, different still, a third reading argues that Aquinas leaves us with two completely separate ends, one natural and the other supernatural. But Porter rejects all three of these options. Instead, concurring with Kevin Staley's interpretation of Aquinas, she argues "that the human person is actually directed toward only one end, which is attained in a twofold manner, natural and supernatural." The one and only telos is God, but this aim is attained "in radically different ways." In the form of natural happiness or fulfillment, "the human creature attains God in the same manner as any other creature does, that is, by created participation in God's goodness, but in supernatural happiness, she attains God as he is in himself, and not merely as the principle of her created existence."[38] It is evident here that the mode of natural happiness is achieved by the human creature, as it is for all creatures, by fulfilling its own distinct perfection as defined by its own specific nature or form. Put simply, one attains God in this life by being truly human. By contrast, the mode of supernatural fulfillment is largely beyond our capability and responsibility in this life. Hence, in an almost Niebuhrian way, Porter implies that the supernatural end is an impossible possibility in regard to this life.

Even more than Niebuhr, though, who still makes moral use of the ultimate perfection of the cross as a transcendent vertical critique of the human condition, Porter largely sets aside the supernatural telos in regard to moral theory. "[O]n Aquinas's own premises," she states,

> the natural and supernatural ends of human life cannot function in precisely the same way in moral reflection. The supernatural end of human life as such cannot be the subject of direct knowledge for creatures such as ourselves, since it consists in direct

---

37. Ibid., 63.
38. Ibid., 63, 65. Porter cites Staley, "Happiness," 215–34.

union with *the God who is utterly inaccessible to our conceptual knowledge. For this reason, it cannot directly serve as the goal by which we evaluate our actions, since we cannot orient our practical reason by a goal that we cannot conceive* [italics added].[39]

Porter's assumption here about the impossibility of our rational or theoretical knowledge of God's nature is critical. As noted earlier, she gestures in the direction of affirming that the existence of God can be rationally shown. Yet, by itself, such an acknowledgment is merely an empty place-holder. What is truly needed, she suggests elsewhere, is special revelation: "Scripture reveals God's existence in and through revealing God's identity, God's stance and character in relation to us." That is, revelation "provides definite content for what would otherwise be [merely] a series of placeholders for whatever we take to be ultimate in given categories of explanation—in Aquinas's lapidary words, whatever it is 'that all call God' (ST I 2.3). As such, revelation . . . indicates the proper significance of God's existence for us."[40] Hence, a God who is "utterly inaccessible to our conceptual knowledge" apart from revelation, Porter holds, "cannot orient our practical reason" or serve as a meaningful moral telos. To be sure, she does suggest that "we can know something about the moral content . . . of the life of grace." Otherwise, we would have no way of talking about the theological virtues of faith, hope, and love. Nonetheless, similar to Hauerwas, she maintains that this "knowledge is based [only] on our observation of graced lives, interpreted in the light of" a tradition. Unlike Hauerwas, however, Porter is unwilling to leave moral theory merely with the empirical witness of "graced lives." In contrast, she thinks a publicly accessible moral norm is rooted in our human nature. Given the inaccessibility of the supernatural aim, Porter therefore focuses her attention squarely on the natural end, which becomes the relevant and "proximate norm of morality."[41] God is still the one and only end, according to Porter, but it is interesting to note how God functions in this context. If conceptual knowledge of God's nature is impossible, then God as the aim of human life is, at best, pushed into the background—functioning as a theistic inference

39. Porter, *Recovery of Virtue*, 66. Porter cites David Burrell as influencing her thinking her; Burrell, *Aquinas: God and Action* (Notre Dame, IN: University of Notre Dame Press, 1979) 12–77.

40. Porter, *Nature as Reason*, 328.

41. Porter, *Recovery of Virtue*, 66, 67.

or hypothesis beyond the horizons of our direct experience of nature and the world. Put simply, God as telos functions as a background assumption rather than as a direct and relevant moral norm; this becomes evident when we turn to Porter's account of the human good.

The Human Good

Because Porter is convinced that the guiding moral norm is found in natural rather than supernatural fulfillment, and because she believes this natural fulfillment is defined by the ideal specific to the human creature, she seeks to reconstruct Aquinas's own answer to the question: "In what does our natural perfection consist?" Interestingly, she states that Aquinas himself never directly answers this question; he addresses it only in passing. When he does make reference to it, he simply "repeats Aristotle's view that our highest natural happiness consists in contemplation." But this answer, Porter concludes, is not true to the fullness of Aquinas's own account. On deeper inspection, "it becomes apparent that the ideal, as he [truly] sees it, would be a life that strikes an appropriate balance between activity and contemplation in accordance with the temperament of the individual."[42] This emphasis on a balance of goods is central to Porter's reconstructive account. To get there, she begins with Aquinas's description of what is distinctive about human nature.

According to Aquinas, humans distinctively possess a capacity for reason and a capacity to choose in light of our reasoned understanding. Like all creatures, we have a natural inclination toward our own specific good. Yet, unlike subrational creatures, such as Porter's pet parakeet, we have the freedom to ignore or even to act contrary to our own natural bent. This is due to the fact that our capacity for freedom is tied to our ability to understand and reason; the distinctively human good is one that can only be discerned with understanding— one that can only be recognized through reason and intellect. Unlike the parakeet, which moves toward its own specific good "by natural instinct," Porter notes that

> mature humans are free to choose this or that (seemingly) good thing, whether it is helpful and appropriate to them or not. Negatively, [Aquinas] says that the human will is not

42. Ibid., 67.

determined to any particular good or class of goods *(except God, who is not directly present to us in this life anyway)*. Positively, he says that the human person (in contrast to a subrational animal) chooses among the array of seeming goods on the basis of a rational apprehension of what is truly good for human beings, on the basis of which she determines (correctly or not) which seeming particular goods are truly such [italics added].[43]

Though the human will is "determined" toward "God" in some vague or general sense, this determination is not sufficiently strong to guide human choice toward its own true good. It is noteworthy that Porter makes the reference to God here merely parenthetical—indicating that God "is not directly present to us in this life anyway." One can rationally infer the existence of God beyond the world from God's effects within the world, but there is no direct presence or intuition of God within the realm of experience. This points again to Aquinas's classical theistic assumption that the essence or character of God is absent from the realm of experience. Thus the God who is meant to be the one true telos of life is, at the end of the day, a God who "is not directly present to us in this life anyway." Given this absence, the human intellect is left to "a rational apprehension of what is truly good" among a host of lesser goods. To be sure, a happy or fulfilled human life involves rationally habituated freedom directed toward the true human good; a misguided life is one spent in pursuit of apparent goods that do not in fact contribute to genuine human perfection. In order to identify what the true human good is, Porter proceeds to examine two central claims in Aquinas.

First, like Aristotle, he asserts that every human action is oriented, either directly or indirectly, toward one overarching aim: happiness. It is this one supreme good that "the agent believes will perfect him as a human being." One might call this the shared subjective aim—the goal that all persons seek in and through all of their various activities. Second, Aquinas then proceeds to postulate that "there is in fact one end, and only one, in which human happiness truly can be found." If the first claim focuses on a shared subjective aim, then the second alleges that there is only one objective telos or authentic content that can serve as the true source of happiness. Though these two affirmations are combined into one theory in Aquinas, Porter argues that they are in fact

43. Ibid., 71.

"independent claims."[44] It is hard enough to make a convincing case for the first one, she submits, but the second one is even more challenging.

In regard to the first claim, she quotes Aquinas's statement that "'it is necessary that all things which a person desires, he desires on account of a final end' (ST I–II.1.6)." She interprets Aquinas here to be offering an ideal account of human behavior rather than an empirical description. "Let me say at once," Porter declares, "that if Aquinas does indeed claim that each person *always* directs *all* her actions and activities toward some one goal or ideal [such as happiness], then I do not see how that claim could be defended." Such comprehensive or consistent intentionality, she reckons, seems more "fanatical than saintly." Quoting John Rawls approvingly, she says: "'Surely it is contrary to our considered judgments of value, and indeed inhuman, to be so taken with but one of these ends that we do not moderate the pursuit of it for the sake of anything else.'" With this air of moderation in mind, Porter argues that what Aquinas really offers is not an empirical description but rather "a metaphysically informed analysis of rational action, which still leaves room to admit that some behaviors which do not meet this ideal can still be said to be rational, and hence true human actions, albeit in a derivative sense." She has in mind here the notion that we can respond to apparent goods, such as ice cream cones, in a reflexive and unreflective way. Such responses are similar to what one would find in subrational animals; hence, they do not measure up to the full human ideal, since it is defined by "the exercise of discursive rationality in thought and action." These derivative actions can be an occasional part of a good human life, Porter suggests, but they cannot become the norm: "[I]ndividuals who live their lives on the basis of pursuing what appeals [to them] from moment to moment do not lead notably successful lives, even on their own terms." In the end, she concludes, "this weaker claim"—that he is offering an ideal account of human action rather than an empirical description—"is all that Aquinas needs as the foundation of his moral theory."[45]

Porter finds Aquinas's second claim even more problematic. As noted, he posits that "there is in fact one end, and only one, in which human happiness truly can be found." If human happiness can indeed only be found in one true or objective telos, then is that end a single

44. Ibid., 72.
45. Ibid., 72, 73, 77. Porter cites Rawls, *Theory of Justice*, 553.

(determinate) good, or is it an inclusive good? "It is easy to assume," admits Porter, "that Aquinas holds that the good toward which one's life is directed must be some one determinate kind of good." In this case, presumably, Aquinas would say that the true single good is God; a good life is one devoted to the love and contemplation of God. By contrast, to devote one's life to the pursuit of a lesser good, such as "riches, honor, physical pleasure, and so on," would result in a misspent life. "We can readily agree," says Porter, "that there really are people who only live for such [lesser aims,] . . . [a]nd we are likely to agree with Aquinas that this sort of life is wretched. . . . Yet, it may seem," she continues, "that our reasons for this judgment are very different from Aquinas' own. He says that these kinds of goods are the wrong goods around which to structure a life." But is this the real problem? She thinks not. This line of interpretation "is a very natural misunderstanding of Aquinas' claim," but a misunderstanding nonetheless. The real problem, Porter argues, is "that once *any* particular good is taken as the basis for one's whole life, the individual will be forced to forgo many other good things. . . . Even a life that is wholly devoted to some noble goal . . . is likely to strike us as somehow distorted and impoverished, in comparison to a life that is built around a balanced pursuit of a number of different kinds of goals." Hence, contrary to what may seem to be the case, Porter thinks Aquinas can and should be read to permit a diverse-inclusive telos rather than a singular-determinate one. "And in fact," she claims, "Aquinas does allow for the possibility that the goal of a human life might be inclusive rather than a dominant [single] end (although of course, he does not use that terminology)."[46]

This inclusive end, as the natural aim of human life, consists of an aggregate of different goods that are properly ordered. The connection between diverse goods and proper ordering is found in Aquinas's account of the natural human inclinations. "My contention," states Porter, "is that Aquinas' account of the fundamental inclinations of the human person, including his account of their proper order to one another, should indeed be taken as his theory of the natural human good." These natural inclinations, listed in ascending order of importance, are self-preservation, procreation (at least on a species level), living in society, and knowing the truth about God. A good human life, then, is one in which the goods of the natural inclinations "are pursued in an orderly

46. Porter, *Recovery of Virtue*, 77, 78.

way, with the pursuit of the lower inclinations being subordinated to the pursuit of the higher [ones]." This normative account, observes Porter, "allows for considerable flexibility in the specific goods that are pursued, as well as allowing for considerable variety in the way in which these pursuits are combined into a complete life." Yet, because the inclinations stand in a natural hierarchy to one another, there is always still an ordering principle involved. Hence, in a good human life, the lower inclinations will not be neglected, but neither will their pursuit be "conducted at the expense of the higher" ones; rather, the lower will always be subordinated to the pursuit of the higher.[47]

For instance, Porter envisions that a person will "preserve her health and well-being, but health will not be an end in itself to her. She will eat to live, . . . and live in order to participate in the life of her family and community, and to attempt to gain some insight into the highest realities." Conversely, "The individual who lives to eat, or to jog, or to dress nicely, will fail to live a naturally good human life because he subordinates the pursuit of the higher goods to the pursuit of the lower [ones], even if he does not actively do anything to cut himself off from the attainment of those [higher] goods." In regard to procreation, the person "attempting to live a naturally good human life will usually [though not necessarily] have children and raise them, but the point of raising children for her will not be to perpetuate her own family line or to pass on her genes, but to initiate those children into the wider life of their community and its constitutive traditions, and to educate them to be capable of some degree of intellectual contemplation of God." Whether the individual has children or not, she "will participate actively in the life of her community, both drawing on and attempting to contribute to its sustaining traditions, and she will [also] devote herself, to some degree at least, to the intellectual contemplation of God."[48]

This thick normative account of the natural human good raises at least three important and interrelated issues. First, as Porter observes, "It may seem that the inclination to seek the truth about God cannot play a role in natural human perfection, because it cannot be attained by means of unaided human reason but requires the theological virtues of faith, hope and charity." Yet, "Aquinas makes it clear," she remarks, "that even without the assistance of grace, the human person is capable

47. Ibid., 89, 90.
48. Ibid., 90–91.

of knowing God as the first and preeminently excellent cause of all things, and can even recognize and love God as the good toward which the universe as a whole tends (note, however, that this latter capacity has been seriously vitiated by sin)." With Aquinas's affirmation of our natural capacity for the knowledge of God in place, Porter contends that "we may infer that a naturally good human life will always include some form of intellectual reflection on the ultimate principles of reality, directed toward an ever-fuller appreciation of the first cause of all things."[49] Given her acceptance of the incommensurability thesis and her muted response to Aquinas's theistic proofs as direct or publicly accessible arguments, it is not immediately clear how Porter attempts to base her conclusion here on Aquinas's theistic argument about a divine first cause. The answer, however, is found again in her turn to MacIntyre, which leads to our second issue.

It is interesting to note that Porter, immediately after making this claim about the normative necessity of reflecting "on the ultimate principles of reality," states that "we may infer that whatever form this reflection takes for a particular individual, he will pursue his reflections in a community of others . . . , since all intellectual activities presuppose an ongoing tradition of inquiry. This may be," she speculates, "why Aquinas links the inclinations to seek the truth about God and to live in community."[50] With this statement, Porter attempts to tie all intellectual contemplation of ultimate reality to some form of tradition-constituted rationality. For those within the Christian tradition, one has convincing reasons to think that a good natural life includes reflection on the divine, since the divine is understood to be the source and end of all things. However, in order for these reasons to be potentially convincing to outsiders, one would have to engage in the indirect form of validation offered by MacIntyre's competition among different traditions. That is, unlike her description of Aquinas, which suggests a direct theistic argument for the possibility of natural knowledge of God, Porter shifts the emphasis to the communal basis and tradition-dependence of all such reasoning. Such reasoning presupposes the underlying metaphysical and theistic assumptions of the tradition (in this case that God is the first cause of all things) rather than arguing directly for them. MacIntyre describes this tradition-constituted approach in *WJWR*:

49. Ibid., 91.
50. Ibid.

> [E]very such rational tradition begins from the contingency and positivity of some set of established beliefs. . . . Hence such first principles are not self-sufficient, self-justifying epistemological principles. They may indeed be regarded as both necessary and evident, but their necessity and their evidentness will be characterizable as such only to and by those whose thought is framed by the kind of conceptual scheme from which they emerge as a key element.[51]

To be sure, Porter insists that she does not follow Hauerwas or the earlier MacIntyre of *After Virtue* down the road of proposing "the notion of narrative unity as a substitute for Aristotle's [or Aquinas's] account of the true end of human life." In other words, she wants to offer a substantive naturalistic account of the true human telos rather than simply say, as the earlier MacIntyre did, that "the good life for man is a life spent in seeking for the good life of man."[52] Nevertheless, her naturalistic account and its theistic component are ultimately based on MacIntyre's later notion of tradition-constituted rationality and its indirect form of validation.

The third issue pertains to this tradition-constituted rationality and Aquinas's distinction between what is self-evident to all and what is self-evident or known only to the wise. Porter contends that Aquinas's first principle of practical reason (that good should be done and evil should be avoided) is self-evident to all persons. In fact, this principle is the underlying ground and guide for all creaturely activity insofar as "all creatures, including us, act (in a wider sense of 'act') in order to obtain or to hold on to some good." This underlying "ontological necessity," however, is not something that all persons are consciously aware of. In other words, when Aquinas says that this principle "is known to all, he is not necessarily saying that everyone could formulate it." I take Porter to mean here that this principle is implicit in all human activity, but not explicitly recognized by all persons. Even though this general principle is implicit in all human action, Porter argues that it is too formal or generic to define the substantive nature of the human good:

---

51. MacIntyre, *WJWR*, 360.

52. Porter, *Recovery of Virtue*, 82. Porter cites MacIntyre, *After Virtue*, 219. MacIntyre now concludes that he made a mistake in *After Virtue* of "supposing an ethics independent of [Aristotle's] biology to be possible" (*Dependent Rational Animals*, x).

> It is clear that Aquinas holds the first principle of practical reason is self-evident to all, but it is not at all clear that the true nature of the human good, which alone can give this principle concrete meaning and practical force, is similarly self-evident to all. Indeed, it would seem that the true nature of the human good *cannot* be self-evident to all, since, as Aquinas often remarks, many persons are in fact mistaken about that in which true happiness consists.[53]

At this point, Porter directs attention to the natural human inclinations (discussed above) to fill out Aquinas's substantive account of the human good. Even though these natural inclinations provide "a widely held starting point for moral reflection," she remarks, "the goodness of the objects of these inclinations is not necessarily self-evident to all." This "is why the substantive meaning of the human good, which alone can give concrete content to the first principle of practical reason, is not self-evident to all, but only to the wise, who are able to develop the data of common human aspirations into a theory of the human good."[54]

By relying on the knowledge of the "wise" to discern the human good, does Porter's reading of Aquinas follow MacIntyre's emphasis on the need for authority and authoritative tutelage within the context of a tradition? In other words, must one validate truth claims about the substantive human good based on an appeal to the authority of the wise? Or, alternatively, is she simply saying that "the wise" are the ones most able to do the heavy philosophical labor to unearth the nature of the human good, but once this is completed, they can then offer intelligible and credible reasons to all persons to justify these claims? The answer to these questions is not immediately clear. On the one hand, Porter tends to underscore the ideal of equality in the medieval tradition more than MacIntyre does. For instance, in her essay on natural equality in the medieval tradition, Porter writes: "The high value on freedom, again, tended to reinforce an ideal of equality, because freedom implied a relative—although not absolute—independence from the control of religious or civil authorities." Speaking of Bonaventure and Aquinas in that essay, she suggests that "both place a high value on the virtue of obedience, but at the same time, both also value the capacities for free judgment and self-determination which they take to be fundamental

---

53. Porter, *Recovery of Virtue*, 86, 87.
54. Ibid., 89.

human qualities." Likewise, in *Natural and Divine Law*, she asserts that the scholastics "give the greatest weight, morally speaking, to those aspects of human personality that are most directly connected to rationality and freedom, even though they do not go as far in this direction as Kant was later to do."[55]

In brief, Porter's reading of the medieval tradition reveals some ambivalence between formal autonomy and heteronomy, and between free judgment and obedience to authority. Is formal autonomy ultimately limited because knowledge of the human good finally requires authoritative appeal to special revelation and/or to the effects of divine grace? What is clear is that Porter thinks that the first principle of practical reason is implicitly known by all, but that it is too formal to offer a substantive end, and thus the empirical observations and reflections of the wise are needed "to develop the data of common human aspirations into a theory of the human good." Does this line of thinking lead Porter to concur with MacIntyre that the authority of the wise is the initial basis of justification within the dialectical process of discernment? That is, must students and other apprentices within the tradition initially accept truth claims about the human good based on the authority of the master? Perhaps Porter's most direct answer to these questions is found in *Moral Action and Christian Ethics*:

> One of the most interesting things about Aquinas' discussion of obedience is that it illustrates so well his dialectical approach to moral reasoning. The general norm of equality serves to modify the norm of obedience, even as that norm [of equality] is qualified in its turn by the incorporation of a limited form of legitimate subordination.[56]

Given this dialectical reasoning, it appears in the end that Porter is willing to follow MacIntyre down the road of permitting some role of authority because she believes that Aquinas ultimately subordinates equality, in some measure, to obedience. In fact, in a journal article in which she approvingly describes and defends MacIntyre's approach, Porter states that he "begins . . . with the observation that a tradition is inescapably grounded in those particular beliefs and commitments that comprise its contingent starting points, at least some of which are

---

55. Porter, "Natural Equality," 279, 290; Porter, *Natural and Divine Law*, 142.
56. Porter, *Moral Action and Christian Ethics*, 106.

initially placed beyond question by being embodied in texts which are taken to be authoritative for the community."[57]

The Permanent Significance of Aquinas

Porter concludes her reconstructive efforts by describing what she takes to be the permanent significance of Aquinas's thought. This "permanent significance," she holds, "lies precisely in the fact that his thought contains the seeds of its own transcendence." In seeking to articulate this path of transcendence, Porter explicitly acknowledges that her "defense of the permanent significance of Aquinas' work is dependent upon MacIntyre's account of the rationality of traditions." That is, like MacIntyre, Porter champions Aquinas because he most successfully addressed "the tensions and problematics" of the Christian tradition of his day (by integrating the distinct traditions of Augustine and Aristotle), and because he offers us a valuable paradigm for successfully "addressing the tensions and problematics of the Christian tradition in our own time." However, this can only be done, Porter adds, "through expansion and development that will take us beyond the limits of Aquinas' own system (as he himself transcended both Aristotle and Augustine)."[58]

This move beyond Aquinas is required because "the incommensurability thesis poses a very serious challenge to the Christian claims for the universal truth of the central Christian beliefs" about God and the moral life. In other words, Aquinas offers "an account of the moral life which integrates the central concepts of his metaphysics into a unified account of human goodness and the virtues." But "we can no longer accept that account as it stands," argues Porter. Given the incommensurability thesis, "the universal validity of the natural law," including Aquinas's account of the universal human good, "could be established [today] only in conversation with rival traditions, and indeed there can be no guarantee that its universal validity could be established even then." In sum, the key move beyond Aquinas is to contextualize his metaphysical, theistic, and moral arguments within the framework of MacIntyre's notion of tradition-constituted rationality. This move shifts the focus away from trying to engage in direct metaphysical, theistic, or moral argument to engaging instead in the indirect comparison of rival

---

57. Porter, "Openness and Constraint," 519.
58. Porter, *Recovery of Virtue*, 172, 173.

traditions in competition with one another. Once one acknowledges that all rationality is tradition-dependent, reflects Porter, one can then recognize that "the aspiration ... to establish an account of morality that would be rationally compelling to anyone whatever must therefore be abandoned."[59]

Porter insists, however, that this move beyond Aquinas to MacIntyre does not mean,

> as Hauerwas argues, that there can be no rational grounds on which to promote and defend a Christian theory of the natural law over against rival theories of morality. As MacIntyre has shown, it is possible rationally to assess the rival claims of incommensurable traditions, and so it would be possible to defend a Christian theory of the natural law *so long as* it is understood and defended as part of a wider tradition of thought.[60]

Porter emphasizes here, once again, her tradition-engaged reading of MacIntyre as opposed to Hauerwas's singular focus on the witness and narrative of the Christian community. She also proceeds to conclude, in general agreement with Gustafson, that "an adequate Christian response to the challenges of modern science must be grounded in the doctrine of God." However, instead of concurring with Gustafson's theocentricism, Porter points instead to what she takes to be the promising resources found in Aquinas's own doctrine of God and, more importantly, found in his affirmation of the need for a "natural theology." Of course, what she has in mind here is some notion of a tradition-dependent natural theology, not a natural theology in the usual apologetic or direct sense of appealing to common reason and experience. Looking to the wider horizon beyond the scope of her book, Porter states:

> I would argue that Aquinas' theological doctrine of God implies that Christians have reasons, implicit in their own tradition, to take the project of natural theology seriously. This conclusion would be especially significant because a sort of natural theology is emerging today among scientists themselves. While the details of this natural theology may not be compatible with a Christian doctrine of God, nonetheless, it would be foolish to

---

59. Ibid., 175, 179, 175.
60. Ibid., 175.

deny that Christians can and should attempt to learn from it and to incorporate its genuine insights into Christian theology.[61]

In sum, Porter suggests that Christian natural theology should develop its positions based on reasons implicit in its own tradition while concomitantly seeking to learn from and incorporate insights from outside perspectives, such as those offered by contemporary scientists.

Typological Analysis

Commitment to Intelligibility (I+)

As evidenced by this openness to outside voices, Porter does seek to engage theology in intelligible conversation with scientists and others in the academy and the wider public. More like Gustafson and Niebuhr, and less like Hauerwas, she, too, engages in the commerce of ideas between theology and the diverse publics within the academy and society at large. For instance, in *Nature as Reason*, she engages in an extended conversation with modern biology over the question of what is required to have a truly adequate understanding of human nature, as well as other kinds of creatures, within the context of evolutionary change. Such an understanding, she argues, requires the reintroduction of the notions of formal and final cause. Likewise, the whole structure of *Moral Action and Christian Ethics* is geared toward engaging in conversation with philosophers and theologians in the academy. The argument proceeds inductively, working its way through modern and contemporary philosophical alternatives toward a critical reclamation of Aquinas's account of moral judgment and action. "It is important," says Porter, "that we be able to mount a critique of the practices and institutions of our societies, in terms that will be intelligible and persuasive" to others. Society requires "a high degree of consensus; otherwise, common life could be sustained only at the cost of an unacceptable level of coercion."[62] This consensus can only be attained through intelligible public discourse.

Yet, if Porter concurs with Niebuhr and Gustafson in seeking to make theology intelligible to those outside the church, she intends to do it in a different way. One might say that the flow of commerce between theology and other disciplines is not quite as fluid for Porter as

---

61. Ibid., 175–76.
62. Porter, *Nature as Reason*, 82f.; Porter, *Moral Action and Christian Ethics*, 85.

it is for the other two. By this I mean that she is much more intent on working within and out of a unified tradition than they are. In other words, Porter follows MacIntyre in rejecting the notion of a common human reason, whereas Niebuhr and Gustafson each presuppose such a common reason, even if they also think that theistic claims cannot be fully validated by it. For instance, both Niebuhr and Gustafson take the insights and language of science to be part of the shared knowledge and common stock of modern intellectual life. Hence, Niebuhr interprets religious language symbolically or mythically in light of this shared understanding. Likewise, even though Gustafson self-consciously works out of a tradition, he is more willing than Porter to assess and discard elements of that tradition in light of the shared common knowledge of modern science. In sum, for Niebuhr and Gustafson, the commitment to intelligibility entails more of an "open-door" policy toward the broader culture. In contrast, Hauerwas illustrates more of a "closed-door" policy—he rejects the idea, voiced by Gustafson, that "the intelligibility of the particular . . . can be made clear in nonesoteric [or nonparticularist] language."[63] In between these two poles, Porter seeks a middle way. In one article she formulates her search for this alternative by asking: "What is the proper relationship between Christian and non-Christian sources in theological ethics?" She finds that one error is committed by those who have too much of an open-door policy, thus allowing the wider academy and non-Christian sources to set the terms of intelligible discourse for theology. In this case, the theological ethicist "faces the difficulty of explaining why Christian sources should have any relevance for moral discourse at all." The other error is committed by those who have too much of a closed-door policy, thus cutting theology off from the insights of non-Christian sources and outside voices. In this case, the theological ethicist "takes distinctively Christian texts and traditions as her starting point, [but] she risks the implication that Christian morality is essentially a self-contained game with no relevance except for those who choose to play by its rules." In either of these two approaches, concludes Porter, the theological ethicist "loses the opportunity to draw on the resources, and the challenges, that both Christian and non-Christian sources for morality can offer."[64]

63. Gustafson, *Ethics from a Theocentric Perspective*, 1:151.
64. Porter, "Subversion of Virtue," 40.

Given her search for a middle way between open and closed-door approaches, one might say that her commitment to intelligibility is more like an "intercom system" through which she seeks to have conversations with the outside world from within the "walls" or context of a tradition. For instance, in the passage quoted above from *Moral Action and Christian Ethics*, Porter continues by saying that "while this sort of [intelligible] critique [of society] does not require a moral theory in the modern sense, it does seem to require an appeal to some kind of framework [or tradition] for evaluation and critique."[65] With her acceptance of the incommensurability thesis, she disavows here the idea of intelligibility based on the notion of common reason, as presupposed for instance in modern moral theory. Instead, the intelligibility to be gained must be that attained across and between different frameworks or traditions; conversations from behind the walls of different traditions require each participant to learn each other's language from within the perspective of each other's own framework. Thus, in order to make one's own claims intelligible to others, one must proceed by seeking "to find some starting point from within those others' own tradition."[66] For example, modern scientists operating out of the Enlightenment tradition will have a hard time understanding Porter's Thomistic account of human nature unless they learn the theistic and teleological assumptions that underlie her account. In brief, to render the part intelligible, one must learn the whole framework. In spite of this challenge, Porter believes that "Aquinas offers resources for rational conversation across cultures [and traditions], as well as for rational self-scrutiny on the individual and the social level." Though this approach "cannot offer us the basis for certainty that this sort of . . . comparison will be fruitful in every case, ... it is the most that we can have, and I believe," says Porter, "that it will suffice."[67]

---

65. Porter, *Moral Action and Christian Ethics*, 85.
66. Porter, *Recovery of Virtue*, 57.
67. Porter, *Moral Action and Christian Ethics*, 199. Porter cites Lee Yearley, *Mencius and Aquinas* (Albany, NY: SUNY Press, 1990) as the source of her thinking here. What she apparently means is that Aquinas's account of the virtues can be developed in such a way as to offer resources for cross-cultural conversation.

Commitment to Credibility (C+)

Porter's commitment to making theology credible as well as intelligible to the broader public comes through most clearly in her repeated criticisms of Hauerwas. As we saw earlier, her chief complaint against his stringent emphasis on particularity is that he offers no "standards for evaluating Christian ethics that are not purely internal to the Christian tradition."[68] She not only wants theology to be publicly conversant, she also wants it to be publicly assessable, at least in some manner. This requires some external or inter-traditional means of evaluating the claims coming from a tradition.

Porter argues that MacIntyre offers just the right prescription for this task: in seeking to defend theology's claims as credible, one should avoid both the errors of universalism and relativism. "But if earlier beliefs in a universal morality are no longer philosophically tenable," she asks, "then do we have any other option but to concur with Rorty's grim [relativistic] conclusions?" She concludes yes; "There is at least one other viable option, namely, the theory of rationality as tradition-guided inquiry developed in Alasdair MacIntyre's most recent works." As I have suggested, this approach asserts that the credibility of claims can be validated indirectly through the competition among different traditions. For instance, Porter concludes that rival moral frameworks "can be brought into conflict, and subject to adjudication, in and through the process of rational conflict of the wider traditions in which these moral systems are embedded." Epistemological adequacy is the criterion at work in this process of competition. In MacIntyre's words, "it is in respect of their adequacy or inadequacy in their responses to epistemological crises that traditions [either] are vindicated or fail to be vindicated."[69] In my terms, this process of validation is *indirect* insofar as the conversation and mode of adjudication always takes place from within the framework of one contingent tradition or another. That is, success is measured from within traditions and only indirectly across them. Hence, participants may "jump back and forth" over the gulf of incommensurability to the extent that they are fully bilingual, but they may never talk directly to one another, as if the gulf were not there.

---

68. Porter, *Recovery of Virtue*, 31; see also 28.
69. Porter, "Openness and Constraint," 516, 534; MacIntyre, *WJWR*, 366.

MacIntyre's appeal to adequacy leads Porter to describe him as "a late twentieth-century Thomistic/pragmatist realist." In fact, Porter accentuates this description when she argues that a pragmatic criterion must be added to or be understood as part of MacIntyre's account of the competition of traditions. As she describes it,

> a clash of traditions that engages the normative dimensions of each will not be resolved solely on the basis of the relative success of each in addressing theoretical difficulties. It will also be resolved on the basis of what might be described, roughly, as the *liveability* of each one. That is to say, in order to be successful as a normative tradition, a given tradition *must enable its proponents to respond in a practical, straightforward, and flexible way to the cultural and economic forces shaping their society*, neither leaving large areas of social life outside the realm of moral discourse nor holding up standards that simply cannot be met under the conditions that actually obtain in a particular community. Moreover, . . . I would suggest that a normative tradition that does not provide a way for the majority of the members of a community to *lead meaningful and reasonably satisfying lives* will not prove to be stable in the long run, at least once its members are presented with genuine alternatives. And if this is the case, if *practical workability is indeed one criterion by which broad normative traditions must be judged*, then a clash of traditions may well involve the proponents of each in some assessment of how well the rival tradition offers resources out of which they can *negotiate practical problems* that had heretofore seemed intractable when approached through the resources of their own tradition alone [italics added].[70]

By appealing to "liveability" or "practical workability," Porter sounds as if she is appealing to some version of modern pragmatism in which traditions are judged by how well they help us get along in the world. In fact, Porter cites Peirce as a forerunner of MacIntyre insofar as he emphasized the importance of particular communities, such as the scientific community, for "the maintenance of intellectual discourse."[71] But are the standards of liveability, workability, and flexibility defined merely internally by the different traditions themselves, or do they serve as some common measure of assessment? Is what counts as a "meaningful and reasonably satisfying" life defined only in tradition-specific

70. Porter, "Openness and Constraint," 535–36, 534.
71. Ibid., 525.

terms, or is there some common measure of value? In response to both of these questions, Porter would presumably affirm the former rather than the latter. I will return to this issue in my assessment, but for now let me simply note that Porter appears to be drawing on modern pragmatism in some manner.[72]

---

72. As I indicated above in n. 1, some might suggest that Porter is now more circumspect about her use of pragmatism. In her 2006 essay "Moral Ideals and Human Nature," she contrasts strict "naturalism" with strict or "radical forms of pragmatism" and rejects each of these polar alternatives. She writes: "A [strict] naturalistic ethic which regards moral norms as immediate expressions of a universal human nature would leave little scope for the emergence and expression of deep [and incommensurable?] differences among ways of living—but for that very reason, it would not be plausible, since on any showing deep differences do exist among different ways of life. Similarly, a [strict or radical] pragmatism which analyzes moral norms without remainder in terms of the play of social forces . . . would relegate any recurrent similarities among socially situated moralities, even the most general and pervasive, to the realm of sheer coincidence. Yet there do seem to be real and important, albeit very general, points of convergence among different moralities, and it is asking a lot of coincidence to explain them all. . . . For this reason, . . . radical forms of pragmatism are likewise not plausible." But Porter goes on to advocate "a more plausible construal of ethical naturalism and pragmatism—one which holds these two approaches together, rather than driving them apart. On this account," she says, "moral norms do reflect some elements of a universal human nature, and this accounts for the broad similarities that characterize them. Yet that nature underdetermines the norms through which it is expressed; these must be specified in and through the processes giving rise to and sustaining a particular way of life, and as such they will reflect, the local, provisional and contingent character proper to all social arrangements" (69–70). I take it that Porter still appeals here to pragmatism as a way to assess moral norms that arise within the particularity of different traditions or ways of life. Since she affirms a common human nature, she rejects a radical pragmatism that claims that all moral commonalities are merely the result of a coincidence among social practices. Put simply, she affirms some form of essentialism that a radical pragmatism would reject. Nevertheless, she still wants to draw upon pragmatism as a way to evaluate tradition-specific norms. Also, what is interesting here is whether her claim about a universal human nature is a claim stemming from the particularity of Thomistic rationality and tradition or whether it is a claim that she now sees as stemming from common human reason and experience. Presumably it is the former, given her commitment to the incommensurability thesis and MacIntyre's notion of tradition-dependent rationality. Like MacIntyre's discussion in *Dependent Rational Animals*, where he speaks about human nature in general while presupposing rather than making explicit the tradition-constituted rationality of the Thomistic tradition, I presume that Porter here is likewise taking for granted the particularity of the Thomistic tradition as the underlying source of her claims about universal human nature. In support of this reading, one detects, in the passage quoted above, a similarity to her account of the incommensurability thesis, namely, an underlying commonality that becomes incommensurable at the level of more specific interpretation. In sum, I take her current view to be a more nuanced expression of her previous work, not a significant departure from it.

Similarly, in other places, Porter's commitment to credibility sounds as if she is appealing directly to some notion of common human experience. For instance, when she argues that Aquinas's account of human activity (that all human desires and actions are directed toward one overarching aim) is an ideal rather than an empirical description, she recognizes that this interpretation still does not validate Aquinas's position as such:

> But of course, the validity of Aquinas' account of action and freedom is not secured simply by showing that it is meant as an ideal, which may never be fully instantiated. Even an ideal account of human action must necessarily have some recognizable bearing on what we actually do. Hence we must still ask whether this ideal makes sense of human behavior as we observe it. That is, . . . can we . . . see patterns or tendencies in human behavior that can be understood as directed toward this ideal? And correlatively, is this ideal plausible *as* an ideal by which we would really want to live our lives?[73]

She seems to appeal here to some notion of common experience as the test by which we assess the validity of this ideal. That is, she asks whether this ideal "makes sense of human behavior as we observe it" and whether we can detect general "patterns or tendencies in human behavior" that point toward this normative model. Finally, she also seems to appeal to a common standard of desire "by which we would really want to live our lives." Obviously the key question here is who is the "we" that is the subject of these queries? Is it the "we" of any reader, whoever he or she may be, thus implying an evaluative standard of common experience? Or is the "we" meant more narrowly, as the group of those who already identify themselves as members within the Thomistic tradition, and thus whose experience is already shaped by the lens of the Thomistic ideal? This latter rendering would seem problematic insofar as the whole point of the query is to validate the Thomistic ideal itself. Yet, alternatively, an appeal to some notion of common human experience runs against the tide of Porter's agreement with MacIntyre, namely, that there are no common grounds or standards for assessing truth claims. Again, as MacIntyre sharply puts it, "There is no standing ground, no place for enquiry, no way to engage in the practices of advancing,

---

73. Porter, *Recovery of Virtue*, 75–76.

evaluating, accepting, and rejecting reasoned argument apart from that which is provided by some particular tradition or other."[74]

Porter would likely respond to my question about the "we" by pointing to Thomas's dialectical approach. Speaking of this method in *Moral Action and Christian Ethics*, she suggests "the dialectical method of the *Summa*, with its emphasis on the balancing and weighing of arguments in an ongoing debate, enables Aquinas to invite his readers to enter as participants in a common inquiry. That is what I hope to do in what follows," remarks Porter, "in order to see what Aquinas can offer to us in the way of a more satisfactory account of moral rationality."[75] With this response in place, Porter might say that the "we" can be either outsiders or insiders, since the dialectical method invites any and all readers to participate. What is not immediately clear, however, is whether this open and direct invitation—"to enter as participants in a common inquiry"—is equivalent to or different from MacIntyre's indirect validation through competition among traditions. Given Porter's and MacIntyre's acceptance of the incommensurability thesis, it would seem that there is no such thing as common inquiry—there is only inquiry from within a tradition. To be sure, outsiders might learn the language of the particular tradition and thus participate as "dual citizens" of competing traditions. But surely this task of learning would require more than simply reading the text itself. I will return to this discussion in my assessment.

Absence of Metaphysics (AM+)

Though Porter goes further than Gustafson, Niebuhr, or Hauerwas in foregrounding some discussion of metaphysical themes, she, too, ultimately foregoes the metaphysical enterprise when it comes to the divine reality. Let me explain. In her account of Aquinas, Porter explicitly reads him as a metaphysician who grounds his moral theory in his general metaphysical theory. And insofar as she seeks to reclaim Aquinas for contemporary purposes, Porter ends up discussing and retrieving some metaphysical elements, such as Thomas's language of formal and final cause. To this extent, I would concur with one reviewer of *Nature as Reason* who observes that "Porter explicitly (and rightfully)

---

74. MacIntyre, *WJWR*, 350.
75. Porter, *Moral Action and Christian Ethics*, 91.

links metaphysics and natural law." Yet, as has become abundantly clear, Porter's critical retrieval of Aquinas is filtered through her own acceptance of the modern incommensurability thesis and her acceptance of MacIntyre's notion of tradition-constituted rationality. Both of these notions, as Porter acknowledges, are foreign to Aquinas. Hence, to borrow MacIntyre's own phrase, Porter appropriates and defends Thomas in some rather "unThomistic ways."[76]

At the heart of this "unThomism," I would suggest, is the fact that Thomas makes explicit and direct metaphysical claims, such as illustrated by his theistic proofs, whereas Porter embeds and backgrounds such claims within the context of a broader notion of tradition. In other words, Porter presumes that any attempt to formulate a direct metaphysical argument for public consumption is a non-starter, certainly at least when it comes to making a direct case for the reality and necessity of God. Now one might say that Porter is more willing to foreground metaphysical claims about nature, such as in reasserting the need for formal and final cause in understanding different species, but not so inclined when it comes to claims about the divine reality; in effect, she is more inclined toward metaphysical biology than metaphysical theology. This dichotomy, between world and God—between physics/biology and theology—in part goes back to Aquinas's own insistence that reason cannot know the divine essence. For instance, as we saw earlier, Porter denies that the supernatural end of human life can serve as a relevant moral norm precisely because it seeks direct union "with the God who is utterly inaccessible to our conceptual knowledge." She describes this inaccessibility at greater length in *Moral Action and Christian Ethics*:

> Yet, it is important to take careful note of the kind of unified account that Aquinas offers. The first principles of sacred doctrine are *sui generis*, since they consist in truths which are properly known only to God, and are revealed by God to us. There is no question of *understanding* these principles, since they reflect the mystery of God, which only God can comprehend. Correlatively, we cannot derive anything from these principles, and so we are not surprised to find Aquinas asserting that the purpose of argument in theology is to draw out the implications of revealed doctrine, to address seeming inconsistencies, and to respond to the arguments of critics of the faith. Whatever one

---

76. Jeffreys, review of *Nature as Reason*, 489. MacIntyre, *First Principles*, 2, 3.

thinks of this project, it is not the equivalent of modern philosophical foundationalism.[77]

Porter is in agreement with Aquinas that reason can know nothing about the divine essence—God's nature is a mystery beyond reason. Hence, the purpose of theology is to "draw out the implications of revealed doctrine." But Porter seems less robust than Thomas when it comes to a philosophical argument for the divine reality, and this difference is due again to her siding with MacIntyre and the incommensurability thesis. For MacIntyre, as for Porter, metaphysical claims are contingent, tradition-dependent claims that stem from a culturally and historically given classificatory scheme. There is no point in seeking to push these claims to the foreground of public discussion, for they make sense only embedded within the context of a specific tradition. Their validity, moreover, can only be shown through the indirect comparison of different traditions as a whole. Thus, even though Porter gives a nod to the Thomistic affirmation that the divine existence can be known by reason alone, she does not pursue it. In fact, she emphasizes the need for revelation to make any real sense of divinity. Thus, I think it is fair to say that Porter would not describe herself as a metaphysician, as she so describes Thomas. In her own way, as with MacIntyre, she concurs with the modern aversion to metaphysics by relegating it to the background assumptions of a tradition. As I will discuss in my assessment, Porter's aversion is due in large part to assumptions she makes about the metaphysical enterprise—assumptions that I will argue are mistaken. But before getting to that, let us turn our attention to the question of the autonomy of ethics.

Autonomy of Ethics (AE-)

On the whole, Porter rejects the modern attempt to define and justify morality independently of theism. Yet, at times, her contemporary rendering of Aquinas seems to veer in that direction in spite of her intentions. I will endeavor to articulate and explain each of these strands—both the overarching theistic one and the more autonomous undercurrent.

77. Porter, *Recovery of Virtue*, 66; Porter, *Moral Action and Christian Ethics*, 90. I'm indebted to Gamwell's essay "On Metaphysical Necessity," 4, for helping me to fully clarify the distinction between metaphysics as biology/physics and metaphysics as theology.

As we have seen, Porter is explicitly trying to reclaim Aquinas for contemporary moral thought and, like him, she identifies God as the supreme telos of human life. "Staley argues convincingly," she declares, "that for Aquinas, the human person is actually directed toward only one end, which is attained in a twofold manner, natural and supernatural. . . . Indeed, both aspects of [this one end] have the same object, that is, God." If the human person is in fact directed only toward a divine end, then any attempt to formulate a valid moral theory independently of theism would undoubtedly be inadequate. Along this line, she states in one article that "Christian theological ethics should become even more robustly and resolutely theological than it already is." Yet, along with affirming the need for a theistic ethic, she also says that the one divine end of human existence is attained "in radically different ways," namely, in the forms of natural and supernatural happiness.[78] And, as we have seen, she argues that supernatural happiness cannot serve as the viable or proximate moral norm of human action, since it is totally beyond our natural capacity to know. Consequently, ethics must focus its attention on the natural human good. It is in her account of the natural human good that Porter, at times, sounds as though she is veering toward something like an autonomous ethic.

An interesting passage in *Nature as Reason* reflects this ambiguity or ambivalence. In discussing the value of human life, she says

> it might appear that a theological justification for endorsing the value of human existence is not needed. Seen from one perspective, this is indeed true—that is, it is no part of my argument [to claim] that modern societies will collapse into nihilism or radical utilitarianism unless they adopt this theological perspective. Yet . . . it is not out of place to reflect on [theological] reasons for endorsing morality as we commonly experience it—even granting that these reasons are not logically compelling. More importantly, those of us who come to the task of moral reflection from a Christian standpoint have a stake in reflecting on our distinctive reasons for endorsing morality, even at the level of a naturalistic ethic.[79]

---

78. Porter, *Recovery of Virtue*, 65; Porter, "Christian Ethics and the Concept of Morality," 17.

79. Porter, *Nature as Reason*, 135.

Sounding rather like Gustafson here, she seems to imply that ethics need not be theological. In fact, she later affirms that a Thomistic theory of the natural law recognizes "a plurality of natural moralities." Instead of affirming that ethics must be theistic or theological, she seeks rather to articulate the distinctively Christian "reasons for endorsing morality, even at the level of a naturalistic ethic." In other words, theological reasons are distinctive or tradition-specific, not common or natural. Since Porter contends that there is no common or direct way to validate metaphysical claims, she presumes there is no common or direct way to show that ethics requires theism. And yet, if I understand her correctly, she does think that God is the true end of human existence. This same ambivalence appears again at the end of *Nature as Reason* when she discusses the doctrine of human rights. On the one hand, she argues that this doctrine stems from historical origins that are theological. However, in regard to the question of whether the validity of human rights ultimately depends on theistic affirmations, Porter offers this rather roundabout answer: "I have yet to see a persuasive philosophical argument, developed on grounds that would be compelling to all, for a doctrine of human rights, and this [failure] inclines me to the view that a theoretical defense of human rights must ultimately rest on theological grounds." So she affirms the theistic ground of human rights, albeit in a negative sense. On the other hand, however, she recognizes the widespread embrace of human rights language along secular and philosophical lines, and thus does not think it is essential to affirm the theistic ground of human rights. "[W]e have no theological stake," she adds,

> in the validity of these arguments [about whether or not human rights presuppose theism]. Our own commitment to promoting human rights does not depend on their validity, but by the same token, we Christians, as such, have no stake in claiming that a commitment to rights can *only* be defended theologically (even though many of us may be persuaded on philosophical grounds that this is in fact so).[80]

Thus, sounding a bit like Gustafson, Porter affirms, from one angle, that human rights in particular and morality in general ultimately require a theological ground. Yet, from another angle, such a ground is unnecessary.

80. Ibid., 339, 371–72.

This ambivalence stems, I think, from Porter's account of the natural human end. As noted earlier, she argues that the supreme good is an inclusive, multi-item balance among a host of different goods; no single good, whatever it is (including the divine), can serve as the defining end of human life. Instead, God is included as one item alongside others within a hierarchy of goods—albeit God ranks at the top of the hierarchy. A fulfilled or happy life thus includes items such as health, sufficient wealth, family and relationships, civic engagement, and "intellectual contemplation of God" or at least some "attempt to gain insight into the highest realities."[81] By placing God as one item alongside others within a hierarchy, Porter's account appears to be in tension with her central theistic claim, namely, that human life is directed toward only one divine end (I will return to this point in my assessment). Moreover, her description sounds at least amenable to modern autonomous formulations. In one article, for instance, Porter describes natural happiness as "a life in which the natural inclinations of the human person are all attained in a balanced, orderly way, without injury to one's fellows; imagine [for example] the life of a happily married, inoffensive professor of philosophy with a pleasant social life and a bent towards civic affairs."[82] In fact, reminiscent of the language of the early Rawls, one reviewer describes Porter's presentation of the natural human good "as an agent's consciously chosen 'life plan' ordered toward the goal of her life."[83] To be sure, Porter insists that there is a hierarchy of goods within a fulfilled life and that contemplation of the divine must be included. Nevertheless, her descriptions at times do not seem all that different from more autonomous accounts.

To further illustrate this, let me offer a brief comparison with Stout. "A life lived merely in pursuit of external goods," remarks Stout,

> is morally empty. A society of people living such lives, a society in which people did not learn the virtues of social practices, would be morally corrupt. That such people would be idolatrous, that their loves would be distributed unjustly, is a truth we need not be Augustinians [or Thomists] to recognize. A good

---

81. Porter, *Recovery of Virtue*, 90.

82. Porter, "Desire for God: Ground of the Moral Life in Aquinas," 68.

83. Harak, review of Porter's *The Recovery of Virtue*, 581. In his reference to Porter's use of "life plan," Harak cites *Recovery of Virtue*, 82.

human life is, at minimum, one oriented toward goods worthy of our love, each in proper proportion.[84]

Like Porter, Stout claims that there must be both a diversity and a hierarchy of goods within a fulfilled life. Whereas she includes Thomism as an interpretive lens and spiritual contemplation as a required practice, he dispenses with the necessity of a theistic framework. Though I suspect that Stout would be inclined to include meditation or contemplation within the basket of diverse goods, he does not see any need to define it in terms of contemplation of God. Now Porter might argue that Stout's description requires the very theism that he takes to be superfluous. Yet, for her part, she never seems to make that argument as strongly or as clearly as Stout or others of us might expect. Instead, given her acceptance of the Thomistic framework and the incommensurability thesis, she merely assumes God "as the obscure cause [and aim] of the finite creation" and, thus, as a needed component within a good life.[85] In short, what Nigel Biggar says about Hauerwas seems to apply—to some extent—also to Porter: she is relatively silent on the question of God. Consequently, her description of the good life and Stout's description do not seem as far apart as one would expect.

In their cumulative effect, these various observations suggest that Porter's description of the moral life has more of a tilt toward the autonomy of ethics than she intends. By speaking of the moral life in terms of a natural human good, by assuming the reality of God rather than explicitly arguing for it, and by describing the natural human good in terms of a balance of diverse goods, Porter's account seems to open itself to an autonomous undercurrent—one that can go a long way in defining the moral life apart from the question of God. Put simply, if "atheists for Reinhold Niebuhr" was a historical phenomenon, then one might also imagine a contemporary rendition of "secularists for Porter." Porter certainly does not intend this, but neither did Niebuhr.

Critical Assessment

Porter's valuable contribution to contemporary theology and ethics is her call for the need for a more holistic or comprehensive framework. She rightly recognizes that something has gone wrong in modern

---

84. Stout, *Ethics After Babel*, 291.
85. Porter, "Desire for God," 55.

theology, which has led to the fragmentation and marginalization of theology's voice. Yet, in my judgment, her prescription misses the mark. She tries to regain Thomistic comprehensiveness in the contemporary context by shifting the focus away from direct theistic and metaphysical claims toward a MacIntyrean notion of the rationality of traditions. Like MacIntyre, she tries to find a middle way between making direct universal claims and accepting a merely relativistic outlook. I am unpersuaded, however, that either she or MacIntyre succeeds in this endeavor. I submit that Porter, like MacIntyre, implicitly presupposes an independent universal standard when she talks about the rational superiority of one tradition over another. Moreover, her aversion to the metaphysical enterprise is due, I will argue, to her mistaken assumption that metaphysics is inherently foundationalist in a narrow or problematical sense. I will seek to support these claims with the following critical observations and comments.

Let me begin by returning to Porter's notion of liveability as a measure of traditions. She contends that "a clash of traditions" can be resolved on the basis of their "liveability."[86] By this, I take her to mean that traditions can be evaluated according to their ability to enable us to live well. But surely the notion of "living well" implies a normative or evaluative standard: Is this standard one that transcends the two traditions or, alternatively, does each of them have its own internal, tradition-specific standard, i.e., a standard that they may each purport to be universal in scope but a standard that nonetheless depends upon the authority of its own tradition as the ground of its justification? If it is the former (a standard that is universal in both scope and validity), then I can see how liveability might serve as a means of adjudication between traditions. This alternative, however, is precisely what Porter and MacIntyre explicitly deny when they assert that there are no common or universal criteria by which to assess validity claims. If it is the latter, if each tradition defines and measures liveability merely in terms of its own tradition-specific standard, then I do not see how one can adjudicate between these two standards; for one cannot appeal again to liveability to assess the validity of the underlying normative standard that is supposed to assess liveability in the first place. Hence, I do not see how Porter can avoid relativism.

86. Porter, "Openness and Constraint," 534.

Put differently, Porter says that traditions can be assessed in terms of whether they enable participants "to lead meaningful and reasonably satisfying lives."[87] But as Niebuhr shows us, the idea of a meaningful or satisfying life presupposes some ultimate center of value or source of meaning. Furthermore, as I argued earlier, these presuppositions about meaning are ultimately related to underlying metaphysical claims about the way things really are. Hence, how can one assess liveability and meaningfulness without being able to assess and adjudicate between the underlying and competing metaphysical claims? Porter tries to avoid this task by leaving the metaphysical claims embedded in the background of each tradition and by trying, instead, to adjudicate among the traditions as a whole by assessing their liveability. Yet, this move merely begs the question.

Along with liveability and meaningful lives, Porter also appeals to the related pragmatic notion of "practical workability."[88] But surely practical workability is tied to how one defines work and success, and, in turn, work and success are tied to the question of how one defines the normative standard. Thus, the practical resources of one tradition will not be "workable" or useful to members of another tradition unless there is some underlying, common evaluative standard of practicality already shared by the traditions themselves. Let me illustrate this by means of an old adage. To members of tradition H, whose only tool is a hammer, everything looks like a nail. For them, practicality is defined in terms of pounding. Alternatively, to members of tradition S, whose only tool is a saw, everything looks like a sheet of wood; for them, practicality is defined in terms of cutting. Members of tradition H see no practical value in tradition S's saw because, for H, practicality is defined solely in terms of pounding and not in terms of cutting. Conversely, members of tradition S see no practical value in tradition H's hammer because, for S, practicality is defined solely in terms of cutting and not in terms of pounding. In short, if there is no common or universal evaluative standard but, rather, only tradition-specific ones, then I do not see how practical workability can ever be used as a means to evaluate rival traditions.

Porter might answer as follows. It is likely that members of traditions H and S will each eventually develop their own internal problems

87. Ibid.
88. Ibid.

because experience will show each of them the practical limits of their current tools. Tradition H will become frustrated with its hammer-only resource because it will come to see that its creative ability is currently limited only to pounding-related activities. Likewise, tradition S will become frustrated with its saw-only resource because it, too, will come to see that its creative ability is currently limited only to cutting-related activities. Hence, each of them will have a practical incentive to learn the language and evaluative standard of each other's tradition. By learning the language and internal standard of S, members of tradition H will come to better understand their own current limits and problems and, at the same time, come to see how S's saw can enable them to expand their creative workability. Likewise, by learning the language and evaluative standard of H, members of tradition S will come to better understand their own current limits and come to see how H's hammer can enable them to expand their creative potential. In sum, Porter would claim that there is no universal evaluative standard at work here; instead, there is only the engagement and comparative rationality of distinct traditions, each one learning and practically benefiting from the evaluative standard embedded in the other tradition.

I would argue, however, that there is a major unstated assumption in this line of reasoning. The key assumption here is that experience teaches us and enables us to see limits and problems with our current practices. But experience is shot-through with evaluation from the outset. If there is no evaluative standard that transcends traditions, then I do not see how members of either tradition H or S could become dissatisfied with their respective current practices, and that is precisely because their current practices already satisfy their respective evaluative standards (pounding or cutting). On the contrary, one can only come to recognize the creative limits of one's current practice if one is already implicitly operating with a larger measure of value beyond one's tradition. Porter's key unstated assumption is that reality itself has its own built-in evaluative standard, and it is through our encounters with reality that we come to see the inadequacies and lack of creativity in our current practices and standards. Moreover, reality can challenge our current practices and standards only if one assumes that common human experience includes an understanding—implicit and prelinguistic—of reality as such. Thus reality informs experience, but reality, contrary to Weber and others, is no value-free zone. As Murdoch nicely puts it, "value, [or] valuing is not a specialized activity of the will, but an apprehension of the world, an aspect of cognition, that is everywhere." Or as Rist observes in discussing Plato, without a shared built-in evaluative standard, "any sense even of what is useful to us . . . must also be lost." [89] Hence, experience and practice are assessed in relation to the measure of value inherent in reality itself. For if there is no such metaphysical measure of value, if evaluative standards are merely tradition-specific, then I do not see how one can ever appeal to practice to assess normative standards.

Again, Porter might answer by saying that she and MacIntyre, like Aquinas, are indeed metaphysical realists, and thus they agree, in some sense, that reality has its own built-in metaphysical measure of value. The problem, she might argue, is that human perception of metaphysical first principles is always mediated or filtered through a tradition and cannot be known directly through a priori reason. This, I take it, is at least partly what she implies when she affirms both the incommensurability thesis and the notion that incommensurability does not go all the way down. That is, if persons from different traditions or classificatory schemes each identify the existence of a single disputed object, then "they must share a common classificatory scheme at some [underlying] level, however basic. Incommensurability still remains," she claims, "but it enters in at the more advanced level of reflection at which people begin to develop interpretive and explanatory theories about things."[90] What she seems to be saying here is that, in a basic or fundamental sense, we experience a common underlying reality but that difference and incommensurability come into play as soon we begin to interpret and explain that reality. And what incommensurability means is that no common standard or independent criterion exists by which we can assess these different interpretive schemes; rather, each scheme offers its own normative standard and way of looking at the world. So what we have then is an affirmation of a common underlying reality or metaphysical background coupled with diverse and incommensurable interpretations and expressions of that reality. The assumption of a common reality or metaphysical background is either an implicit or explicit belief. As a truth claim, however, it is presumably a tradition-specific claim insofar as it relies upon the metaphysical and epistemological assumptions of

89. Murdoch, *Metaphysics as a Guide to Morals*, 265; Rist, *Real Ethics*, 20.
90. Porter, *Recovery of Virtue*, 55.

an empirically and historically given tradition. To try to validate this claim, Porter would again engage in the dialectical rationality of assessing distinct traditions in terms of their liveability and in terms of their ability to deal with their own internal epistemological problems.

What seems problematic here is the ambiguous role played by the background assumption of a common reality. In order to avoid relativism, Porter insists that incommensurability does not go all the way down; thus she claims that persons of different traditions "must share a common classificatory scheme at some [underlying] level, however basic." *But how does she know this?* If this claim is made merely from within her own tradition or classificatory scheme, then she begs the question and it would seem that incommensurability does in fact go all the way down. Alternatively, if there is some underlying common recognition and knowledge of reality at a basic level, then the claim of incommensurability at a higher level appears to be unnecessary, misleading, and false. Otherwise stated, her distinction between a common classificatory scheme at a basic level and incommensurable understandings at a higher level makes no sense unless the implied belief in a common underlying knowledge of reality is indeed universally valid. For if this implicit belief is itself merely tradition-specific, then the distinction collapses and incommensurability does in fact go all the way down. Hence, we again see the insight of Davidson: "Different points of view make sense, but only if there is a common co-ordinate system on which to plot them; yet the existence of a common system belies the claim of dramatic incomparability."[91]

This same tension in Porter's thought can be seen when we turn to the distinction between truth and warranted assertibility. She concurs with MacIntyre and others in claiming that there is a difference between *truth* and *warranted assertibility*. "The concept of truth," says MacIntyre, "is timeless. To claim that some thesis is true is not only to claim for all possible times and places that it cannot be shown to fail to correspond to reality in the sense [that there can be no dissonance between the thesis and reality as it is understood or experienced,] but also that the mind which expresses its thought in that thesis is in fact adequate to its object." Porter amplifies MacIntyre's notion of truth when she says that "if his theory is indeed valid, [then] he has opened up the possibility that at least some of our claims about moral matters might turn out to

---

91. Davidson, "On the Very Idea of a Conceptual Scheme," 184.

be true in the strong sense of being adequate to a reality that is independent of our judgments about it."[92] In contrast to the timeless quality of truth, warranted assertibility is fluid since it pertains to our historically situated interpretations of reality that are shaped by and filtered through our various classificatory schemes and current traditions. An assertion is warranted when it meets with the best standards achieved thus far within a tradition or through the dialectical engagement between traditions. Nevertheless, the potential gap between reality and classificatory scheme, between truth and warranted assertibility, always remains. MacIntyre implies this gap when he claims "that false beliefs and false judgments represent a failure of the mind [its classificatory scheme], not of its objects [reality]. It is mind which stands in need of correction. Those realities which mind encounters reveal themselves as they are."[93] In sum, Porter endorses MacIntyre's distinction between truth and warranted assertibility because she, too, wants to affirm both (a) a common reality behind or independent of our conceptual and moral judgments, and (b) that our knowledge and expression of reality are always tradition-dependent.

What puzzles me about MacIntyre's (and Porter's) distinction between truth and warranted assertibility is how could one, given his view, ever endorse anyone making truth claims? If in making a truth claim one must "claim for all possible times and places that it cannot be shown to fail to correspond to reality," then by MacIntyre's own tradition-dependent lights, one ought never to make such a bold claim. As he himself states, "Every tradition, whether it recognizes the fact or not, confronts the possibility that at some future time it will fall into a state of epistemological crisis," i.e., its claims will be shown by experience to fail to correspond to reality. Once this happens, a "particular tradition's claims to truth can . . . no longer be sustained."[94] Given this ever-present possibility, why doesn't MacIntyre call for the abandonment of making truth claims altogether and submit, instead, that one can merely make claims of warranted assertibility? He wants to maintain the distinction,

92. MacIntyre, *WJWR*, 363; Porter, "Openness and Constraint," 531. Porter makes a distinction between how MacIntyre's theory applies to science and how it applies to morality. She suggests that scientific claims are more directly accessible to comparative assessment whereas moral claims can only be addressed indirectly through the comparative assessment of their overall, wider traditions. See 531–34.

93. MacIntyre, *WJWR*, 357.

94. Ibid., 364.

I judge, because he is trying to affirm some form of metaphysical realism and trying to avoid the charge of relativism. At one point, he tries to navigate this intellectual channel by putting it this way:

> Doctrines, theses, and arguments all have to be understood in terms of historical context [i.e., as tradition-specific]. It does not ... follow that claims to timeless truth are not being made [by these arguments]. It is rather that such claims are being made for doctrines whose formulation is itself time-bound and that the concept of timelessness [i.e., truth,] is itself a concept with a history, one which in certain types of context is not at all the same concept that it is in others.[95]

MacIntyre's attempt at navigation here, however, runs aground precisely because it collapses his own distinction between truth and warranted assertibility. Above, he said that the concept of truth is timeless. Yet here he asserts that it has its own distinct history, which would imply that the concept of truth is itself merely warrantedly assertible. Perhaps one might claim that MacIntyre is making a nuanced distinction here between truth and timelessness, namely, that the concept of truth is timeless but the concept of timelessness is not timeless. But such a distinction seems at best very odd and at worst simply incoherent. Furthermore, MacIntyre's own usage seems to deny such a distinction.

Commenting on this same passage and tension in MacIntyre, Gamwell offers the following observation: "MacIntyre . . . insists that 'claims to timeless truth' can be made from within a tradition because 'the concept of timelessness is itself a concept with a history, one which in certain types of context is not at all the same concept that it is in others.' But this implies," remarks Gamwell, "that the distinction between warranted assertibility and truth is itself only warrantedly assertible—when in fact the distinction does not make sense unless it is true." Gamwell's incisive point here is that MacIntyre's own distinction makes no sense unless there is indeed a notion of truth or rationality that is not merely tradition-dependent. Otherwise, you merely have warranted assertibility on both sides of the supposed distinction. As Gamwell concludes,

> the claim to truth is meaningless absent universal standards of rational assessment. We may say, then, that [MacIntyre's] notion of "truth" is either purely formal [and empty] or equivalent to

95. Ibid., 9.

> warranted assertibility—and the insistence upon tradition-constituted inquiry has not withstood the relativist challenge. The basic point, I believe, is that thought about one's tradition of inquiry transcends, at least in some respects, that tradition, so that one cannot argue about the character of tradition-constituted inquiry without presupposing universal rational standards. Were it the case that one's thought is tradition-constituted in MacIntyre's sense, one could never know that it is.[96]

Gamwell's last point here hints once again at the unexpected similarity between MacIntyre and Kant. That is to say, MacIntyre's distinction between truth and warranted assertibility is a historicized version of Kant's distinction between noumena and phenomena; in both cases, they are seeking to affirm some ultimate truth or reality and, at the same time, strictly limit what humans can know about it. Just as Whitehead and Hegel pointed out against Kant, so, too, Gamwell argues against MacIntyre that if such supposed limits of human reasoning were in fact genuine, then one could not even know that they are there. In the end, both Kant's and MacIntyre's distinctions are exercises in false modesty.[97]

For her part, Porter tries to come to MacIntyre's defense by suggesting that all we need in order to make use of his notion of truth is some reasonable confidence in our claims. MacIntyre, she writes,

> does not show, and does not intend to show, any way by which we can be *certain* that a particular claim does in fact attain reality [i.e., is true]. Nonetheless, he does claim that the ideal of truth as adequation to reality has application to our actual investigations and reflections, in that *we can be reasonably confident* under some circumstances that our judgments really do attain the reality toward which they are directed.... That is, to the extent that an individual's intellectual tradition has successfully resolved internal difficulties and has responded to the challenges of rival traditions, *he can be confident* that that tradition offers a framework within which his mind can attain a real adequation to the reality toward which it is directed [italics added].[98]

---

96. Gamwell, *Divine Good*, 80–81 n. 6.

97. See Whitehead, *Process and Reality*, 4 n. 1; and see section 10 of Hegel's Introduction to *The Encyclopedia of the Philosophical Sciences in Outline*, 53–54.

98 Porter, "Openness and Constraint," 531.

If reasonable confidence is all that one needs to make truth claims, then let me ask two questions. First, by defining the standard of truth in terms of our reasonable confidence or in terms of our ability to win the current dialectical engagement between traditions, is not Porter herself implicitly collapsing MacIntyre's distinction between truth and warranted assertibility? Is not her description of truth, in other words, quite close to what MacIntyre means by warranted assertibility? By MacIntyre's own understanding, warranted assertibility enables one to feel reasonably confident about one's conclusions insofar as they are the best answers given at a particular time in light of prevailing standards. How is this different from Porter's account of truth claims? I see no meaningful difference.

Second, if reasonable confidence is all that one needs to make truth claims, then why not simply abandon the notion of warranted assertibility altogether and acknowledge that all truth claims—including metaphysical ones—are fallible? Why not endorse the notion of fallibilistic metaphysics, as I did in chapter 2? Porter seems reluctant to do either of these because she is still unknowingly, to some degree, under the spell of the foundationalist quest for certainty. Notice, for instance, that her first instinct is to measure MacIntyre's view of truth against the standard of certainty. And because she explicitly does not want anything to do with foundationalism, either in terms of its quest for certainty or in terms of its pursuit of metaphysics, she seeks to maintain a distinction between truth and warranted assertibility. She assumes that to affirm a universal standard of reason one must also affirm the quest for certainty; and because she rightly does not want to pursue the latter, she wrongly denies the former by concluding that all claims are tradition-dependent.

In addition to falling under the shadow of certainty, Porter is also unwittingly under the spell of the discursive error—under the misplaced assumption that valid arguments should compel assent. This spell is revealed, for instance, when Porter discusses the incommensurability thesis and its alternative. The only alternative to affirming incommensurability, she presumes, is to affirm the notion of a universal reason that compels agreement from others. Unlike Aquinas, who "thought that at least the central tenets of morality are knowable to all," Porter contends that "nothing in [her] argument serves to establish that Aquinas's theory of morality would be rationally compelling to anyone, operating from within any conceptual scheme whatever. To the contrary," she claims, "there is good reason to believe that it would not be [rationally compelling]." And this again, according to Porter, is because Aquinas's view depends on his general theory of goodness, which in turn depends on his underlying theistic and metaphysical assumptions, which she claims are tradition-dependent. "That being the case," Porter concludes, his theory of morality "would not be necessarily compelling to someone whose [metaphysical and normative] starting points" were different from his. It is quite evident here, and from her other works, that Porter presumes that the affirmation of a universal standard of reason entails the assumption that valid arguments work like "lasers" that necessarily compel assent from all who get in their way. She rightly recognizes that arguments do not in fact work like this, but she wrongly presumes that this assumption is entailed by the affirmation of universalism itself. Hence, she mistakenly assumes that the only viable alternative is to affirm that all rationality is tradition-dependent. Once one accepts this, she maintains, then one can recognize that "the aspiration ... to establish an account of morality that would be rationally compelling to anyone whatever must therefore be abandoned."[99] My point is that once one abandons this false assumption about the nature of arguments, one is then free to affirm a fallibilistic universalism rather than accept Porter and MacIntyre's tradition-constituted rationality.

When Porter makes her case for tradition-constituted rationality, she maintains that one is "not [mistaken or] self-deluded in proposing [one's claims or] theories as possible candidates for a [valid] description of The Way Things Really Are. Admittedly," she adds, "there is no guarantee that [one] will be able to prove [one's] theories to all challengers, *even if* they are in fact correct."[100] My contention is that this description applies equally well to a priori metaphysical claims and to all claims that affirm a universal standard of rationality. Why does Porter not recognize this? Because she assumes that there are only two possible alternatives: either one affirms universal standards of rational assessment, based on the assumption that valid arguments compel assent, or one denies such universal standards and holds instead that all standards are

---

99. Porter, *Recovery of Virtue*, 56, 175. For other examples of Porter referring to the rationally compelling nature of arguments, see *Nature as Reason*, 24, 29, 134, 150, 318, 326, 338, 340, 359, 363, 371, 372, 378.

100. Porter, *Recovery of Virtue*, 57.

merely tradition-specific, based on the assumption that even valid arguments do not compel our agreement. There are, however, two distinct and separable issues here: the question of universal standards, and the question of whether valid arguments compel assent. Why does Porter not recognize this distinction? Because she conflates what I have called (in chapter 2) the "form of epistemic justification" and the "subjective form of knowledge." Just because one makes a claim that appeals to an a priori or universal form of justification does not mean that one is claiming it to be epistemologically certain (without the possibility of error) or that it will compel assent from all hearers. As Porter rightly discerns, a valid claim cannot guarantee its own validation precisely because the process of validating a claim requires not only the offering of good reasons but also the willing assent of the listener; and the former cannot guarantee the latter. Again, in the apt words of Rawls, "philosophy cannot coerce our considered convictions any more than the principles of logic can."[101] Hence, to claim that a moral or metaphysical theory is both valid and potentially knowable to all does not mean that such a theory can guarantee its acceptance by others. Furthermore, one does not seek to give a priori reasons on the assumption that such reasons will compel assent. Rather, one gives such reasons precisely because one is trying to make claims about the necessary characteristics of reality, and only such reasons are finally adequate or appropriate to that task. In short, all forms of reason and rationality are fallible and subject to the possibility of revision. Hence, I am inclined to conclude that if Porter freed herself from her underlying mistaken suppositions about the nature of a priori and universal claims, then she would be in a position to rethink her embrace of the incommensurability thesis and her aversion to metaphysics.[102]

101. Rawls, *Political Liberalism*, 45.

102. In discussing the relationship between truth, expression, and criticism, Whitehead offers a helpful analysis for how one might understand this fallibilistic metaphysics. "A dogma," observes Whitehead, whether in philosophy, science, or religion, "is the precise enunciation of a general truth, divested so far as possible from particular exemplification." But "it is not the case," he adds, "that our apprehension of a general truth is dependent upon its accurate verbal expression. For it would follow that we could never be dissatisfied with the verbal expression of something that we had never apprehended." So what we have here, Whitehead suggests, is the critical distinction between our *apprehension* of reality and its general characteristics, which we glean from the width of experience, and our accurate verbal, linguistic, or dogmatic *expression* of those truths about reality. If our apprehension through experience were not

Movement toward this new vantage point would also be advanced if Porter cast a more critical eye upon Aquinas's doctrine of God. On the one hand, she accepts Aquinas's doctrine as it stands. For instance, she thinks his view offers richer resources than Gustafson's understanding of God. Yet, on the other hand, she implicitly resists some aspects of Aquinas's view, resistance that reveals itself in her discussion of the inclusive nature of the supreme telos. As we saw earlier, Porter acknowledges that her "inclusivist" reading of Aquinas goes against the grain of the text; at best, she concludes that he allows for such an inclusivist reading, but she admits that this reading goes against the obvious or surface meaning of the text. For Aquinas, the plain moral task is to iden-

---

indeed prior to accurate linguistic expression, we could never be dissatisfied with our expression—we could never feel that our words fail to do justice to the truth we seek to express. "But this consciousness of failure to express our accurate meaning," Whitehead notes, "must have haunted most of us." He points to the history of mathematics for illustrations. The general truths that Pythagoras or Euclid accurately expressed were the same general truths that the Egyptians had vaguely anticipated or understood "for more than thirty generations." Likewise, "the notion of irrational number had been used in mathematics for over two thousand years before it received accurate definition in the last quarter of the nineteenth century." In short, we know more of the character of reality "than we can accurately express in words." Hence, "a one-sided formulation may be true, but may have the effect of a lie by its distortion of emphasis." Given this fallible nature of our linguistic expression, "a dogma—in the sense of a precise statement—can never be final" and, thus, should never be viewed as infallible, indubitable, incorrigible, or certain. And this is just as true of religious or metaphysical claims as it is true of all other claims. When one seeks to express a metaphysical truth, one is seeking to express those aspects of reality that are necessary, and thus present to all possible experience. But one's linguistic or dogmatic expression of this necessary truth is itself always fallible—it draws upon the linguistic stock available in one's own time and place. This is not to say, however, that there is no common reality, no necessary aspects of reality, or no universal standards. Rather, it is to say that our dogmatic formulation is always a situated attempt to express that which is universal and necessary—that which transcends our situation. To presume that our formulation should compel assent from others is to succumb to "an ill-balanced zeal for the propagation of [our own] dogma." It displays, in other words, "a strain of indifference to the fact that others may require a proportion of formulation different from that suitable for ourselves." For, on the one hand, "perhaps our pet dogmas require correction: they may even be wrong." On the other hand, our "dogma may be true in the sense that it expresses such interrelations of the subject matter as are expressible within the set of ideas employed. But if the same dogma be used intolerantly so as to check the employment of other modes of analyzing the subject matter, then, for all of its truth, it will [still] be doing the work of a falsehood." In sum, Whitehead concludes that "progress in truth . . . is mainly a progress in the framing of concepts, in discarding artificial abstractions or partial metaphors, and in evolving notions which strike more deeply into the root of reality." Whitehead, *Religion in the Making*, 126, 126–27, 127, 130, 128, 131.

tify and pursue the right good in life, the one that is truly supreme, and not to be misdirected by the many lesser goods. Alternatively, Porter argues that the real problem is defined not in terms of wrong versus right but rather in terms of one versus many: any life devoted to a single end or good, whatever it is, including God, is a misguided one. "Even a life that is wholly devoted to some noble goal," she remarks, "is likely to strike us as somehow distorted and impoverished, in comparison to a life that is built around a balanced pursuit of a number of different kinds of goals."[103] Hence, a genuinely good life is one devoted to the pursuit of a balanced plurality of diverse ends. My hunch here is that, in resisting the singular identity of the good, Porter is unwittingly resisting Aquinas's classical understanding of God. In order to unpack this hypothesis, let me offer the following observations.

Porter openly rejects the notion that the supreme telos can be an end that is unrelated to the diverse aspects and goods of human life. In *Moral Action and Christian Ethics*, she nicely elucidates this point in a discussion of human integrity. "What characterizes the person of integrity," she observes,

> is her consistent willingness to construe her own good *in the context of some greater good (or goods)*, which she values more than she values her own personal satisfactions, precisely because *her participation in this wider good bestows meaning and purpose on her life*. The person who attains integrity does [so through] ... a new construal of her own good, which is *now seen in relation to a larger good*. Because she sees her own good in this way, the person of integrity will not tolerate compromises, on her part or on the part of others, which would tend to undermine *that good* or to alienate her from it.
>
> Moreover, because a wider good is also, potentially, a shared good, the person of integrity is open to the participation of others in this good.... In other words, [this good is] *a transpersonal good* [italics added].[104]

Two things are striking about this illuminating passage. First, it suggests that a life devoted to a single comprehensive good is at the heart of integrity; defining our own good in relation to a greater good is what it means to live in an integrated way. Second, this single comprehensive good must be completely wide, inclusive, and "transpersonal" and, thus,

103. Porter, *Recovery of Virtue*, 78.
104. Porter, *Moral Action and Christian Ethics*, 194.

able to bestow "meaning and purpose on [the totality of] life." What is significant here is that Porter is not averse to defining the supreme good as a single good, if it is properly conceived.

Yet, when she turns to Aquinas's understanding of God, she does not find divinity defined in such an integrated manner—defined in a way that is internally related to the totality of the world. Instead, she finds something more akin to what she describes in *Natural and Divine Law* as "the classical Christian doctrine, [namely, that] God is a complete and self-sufficient being, 'without any shadow of variation or change.'"[105] Such a self-sufficient and totally unchanging God, Porter implicitly reasons, cannot serve as an adequate end for a life of integrity precisely because such a conception of divinity offers no direct or internal relation to the diverse goods of life. Porter, however, never explicitly challenges Aquinas's doctrine of God on this point. Instead, she argues that the supreme good must be defined as a balanced set of diverse goals, with God included as one among the many. Of course the danger here is that God becomes one good among others rather than the true telos of life. Thus, Porter becomes caught between her allegiance to Aquinas's doctrine of God and her insight about the meaning of integrity. What she is implicitly looking for is a conception of divinity that is internally related to the diverse and particular goods of the world. Such a conception, I would argue, is more adequately found in the dipolar theism offered by Hartshorne and Whitehead. Hence, Porter could make better sense of her theism and her understanding of a transpersonal good inclusive of all others—of unity-in-diversity—by shifting from Aquinas's classical metaphysics to a neoclassical or process metaphysics. In fact, she implicitly hints at this kind of shift in the closing words of *Nature as Reason*. There, sounding a bit like Niebuhr, she remarks that "the doctrine of final judgment promises us that God will at least not relegate our efforts to meaninglessness, or look upon them with indifference—they will be assessed in the light of God's own wisdom and love, and whatever is good in them will be preserved." What Porter seeks here is an internal relation between God and the world, specifically, that the world echoes everlastingly in God. That is, given her insight about integrity, Porter is rightly looking for an understanding of divinity internally related to and affected by the world. Hence, our efforts and our lives matter to God and are preserved everlastingly in the divine life. Porter could make explicit

---

105. Porter, *Natural and Divine Law*, 290.

sense of this insight by shifting to a process understanding of God. Of course, given her ties to the scholastic tradition, she would explicitly resist such a suggestion; at one point she openly rejects process theism because it does not endorse the classical theistic assumption—held by the Scholastics—that God is wholly transcendent to the world in all respects.[106] But only by making this shift, I contend, can she be true to her insight about the nature of integrity.

Such a fundamental shift would also enable her to rethink her bifurcation within the first principle of practical reason. As we saw earlier, she thinks this first principle (to seek good and avoid evil) is self-evident to all, but it is too abstract or formal to identify the true substantive human good. "It is clear," she states, "that Aquinas holds the first principle of practical reason to be self-evident to all, but it is not at all clear that the true nature of the human good . . . is similarly self-evident to all."[107] This distinction ultimately derives from Aquinas's claim that the divine existence is knowable to reason, but the divine nature can only be known through special revelation. To claim that God exists, yet without knowing what God is, leaves one with an inadequate principle for identifying the overarching telos of human existence. Following through with this division, Porter argues that the substantive human good can only be known by the wise. Let me offer two critical responses.

If the first principle of practical reason is truly self-evident to all, then presumably it must be known and justified a priori. Does not the following stand to reason: that which is self-evident to all, is at least implicitly known to all, and that which is implicitly known to all, is known prior to any particular experience? The answer, I judge, is yes. Hence, to say that the first principle of practical reason is self-evident to all is to suggest that it is an a priori principle. Porter would presumably resist this description; concurring with Aquinas that "all our knowledge originates from sense" (ST, I.1.9). Yet Porter's own description indicates that this principle is neither learned through the senses nor presumably can it be denied without contradiction, which is a tell-tale sign of an a priori principle. "This [logical] necessity," remarks Porter, "is grounded in the wider ontological necessity that all creatures, including us, act . . . in order to obtain or to hold on to some good."[108] Given Porter's

---

106. Porter, *Nature as Reason*, 400, 83–84.

107. Porter, *Recovery of Virtue*, 87.

108. Ibid., 86. It seems to me that, at times, even Aquinas comes close to offering an a priori form of argument, such as his "third way" for proving the existence of God

claim that the first principle of practical reason is self-evident to all, and given my argument above that a priori claims need not and ought not entail presumptions of certainty or guarantees of successful validation, she should be open to the idea that the first principle of practical reason is known and justified a priori.

Porter supports her (and Aquinas's) bifurcation between this formal first principle and the substantive content of the human telos by pointing to the diverse and mistaken views of the human good among various persons. Because many people are mistaken about the true meaning of the human good, she reasons, then the substantive end cannot possibly be known to all and thus cannot be an a priori principle. But this line of reasoning entails its own mistakes. To unearth this, let me retrace Porter's steps. She begins, promisingly enough, by formulating the right question: "How can Aquinas say that all persons seek the specifically human good, by a kind of metaphysical necessity, when elsewhere he claims that most persons spend their lives in pursuit of a sham happiness?" The obvious answer is that "for most of us, our natural inclination toward the good fails to operate correctly." The reason for this, she contends, issues from our mistaken understanding of the good. The natural inclination will not operate correctly "if we are mistaken about that in which true human perfection consists, since we, unlike subrational creatures, can only direct ourselves toward our specific perfection on the basis of an intellectual apprehension of what that perfection would be."[109]

The disconnect in this line of reasoning occurs between the affirmation of a natural inclination toward the good and our understanding of it. What is denied in between, by Porter and Aquinas, is the possibility that humans have an *implicit* apprehension of the substantive end. This denial means that the natural inclination toward the good is inherently "blind" insofar as it comes without any built-in knowledge of the substantive telos. Hence, knowledge of this aim is utterly dependent on and defined exclusively in terms of our *explicit* "apprehension of what that perfection would be." But does this view offer an adequate account of the good or of the failure of the natural human inclination? Does it

---

"from possibility and necessity" (ST, I.2.3). Without going into detail here, there are some interesting parallels between Aquinas's third proof and Kant's "ontological" argument in *TOPB*.

109. Porter, *Recovery of Virtue*, 86.

make sense, in other words, to affirm that humans have a natural inclination toward the good, but have no built-in knowledge of it? I contend not. As Niebuhr teaches us, the human fault lies not in our ignorance or utter lack of awareness of the true good but, rather, in our internal self-contradiction: "Man contradicts himself within the terms of his true essence," Niebuhr rightly observes.[110] This means that humans are at cross purposes insofar as their implicit existential decision (their implicit choice of an ultimate telos) is at odds with their underlying, implicit knowledge of the true good.[111]

In reply, Porter might contend that I am overlooking an important passage, quoted earlier: "Aquinas makes it clear," she observes, "that even without the assistance of grace, the human person is capable of knowing God as the first . . . cause of all things, and can even recognize and love God as the good toward which the universe as a whole tends (note, however, that this latter capacity has been seriously vitiated by sin)."[112] Such a statement, she might argue, indicates that the natural human inclination toward the good is not "blind." But this passage itself raises further problems. First, notice that it says that humans "can [potentially] . . . recognize . . . God as the good." It does not indicate that they necessarily do have this recognition, however implicit. To suggest that they *can* recognize it is only to note that they could potentially garner the relevant knowledge. In this case the "blind" inclination happens to hit on the right target; yet the inclination remains naturally contingent or blind insofar as there is still no necessary or built-in knowledge of the proper end. Second, the effect of sin in this case simply makes this contingent endeavor more difficult, if not impossible. Sin is defined here as an external or added impediment rather than as an internal indictment, that is, as an internal contradiction between one's implicit existential decision and one's underlying apprehension of the true telos. In sum, does sin keep us from knowing God altogether or, alternatively, is it rather a self-deceptive stance that seeks to deny what it always already implicitly knows? I judge that it is the latter.

110. Niebuhr, *Nature and Destiny*, 1:16.

111. The relation between implicit and explicit understandings is complex: We might affirm a true explicit understanding of our telos and have deceived ourselves about the aim that we in fact chose implicitly; we might affirm a false explicit self-understanding, for various reasons, and still have implicitly chosen authentically; or both implicit and explicit self-understandings may be false.

112. Porter, *Recovery of Virtue*, 91.

As indicated, what lies at the root of Porter's bifurcation in the practical principle is her acceptance of Thomas's bifurcation between our knowledge of the divine existence and the divine nature. To affirm a formal practical principle that is self-evident to all but is inadequate to point us toward our true substantive end parallels Aquinas's claim that we can rationally discern the existence of God as first cause, but we cannot know what God is in God's own nature. In both of these cases, Porter and Aquinas cast the crucial substantive question out of the realm of common reason and into the realm of authoritative traditions. In fact, insofar as Porter accepts the incommensurability thesis and MacIntyre's notion of tradition-constituted rationality, and thus shies away from making direct metaphysical or theistic arguments even for the divine existence, one might say that she travels down this path even further than Aquinas himself. Summarily stated, then, her argument about how the substantive human good cannot be known to all is another indication of her aversion to metaphysics.

Summary (I+C+AE-AM+)

Porter tries to advance contemporary Christian theology and ethics by reclaiming a holistic framework supplied by the medieval scholastics, specifically, Aquinas. Such an endeavor, she claims, overcomes the fragmentation of contemporary thought by supplying a coherent and full-fledged normative and metaphysical background for theological reflection. By turning to the past, Porter does not intend to cut off conversation with contemporary voices outside the Christian tradition. On the contrary, she is committed to making theological claims intelligible and credible to a wider public audience. Yet, given her acceptance of the modern incommensurability thesis and MacIntyre's notion of tradition-constituted rationality, Porter goes about these endeavors in a very particular way. She is committed to making theology intelligible, but only by speaking from within and out of the Thomistic tradition. Each tradition can learn the languages of other traditions and conceptual schemes; by this (bilingual) means intelligibility can be pursued (not by presuming some notion of a common rationality). Likewise, a commitment to credibility can only be fulfilled indirectly, through the comparative rational engagement of different traditions and their conceptual schemes; there are no common or universal standards of rational assessment. Because of these assumptions, Porter is averse to the metaphysical enterprise and thus reluctant to foreground metaphysical claims and arguments about the reality and necessity of God. Such claims, she believes, including Thomas's theistic proofs, make sense only within the context of the tradition as a whole. Hence, such claims are better left embedded within the tradition. There is no point in trying directly to prove the reality and necessity of God, since there are no common or universal reasons to validate such claims. The God-hypothesis can only gain credibility indirectly, by showing the comparative rationality of the Thomistic tradition as a whole. Given her adherence to the Thomistic tradition, it seems clear that Porter wants to reject the modern autonomy of ethics. This intent notwithstanding, I noted that there seems to be an undercurrent in her thought that, at times, unwittingly pulls toward the autonomy of ethics. Though Porter's attempt to reclaim a more systematic framework for theology is laudable, I have argued that her MacIntyrean approach to this endeavor is problematic. Like MacIntyre, she seeks a middle course between universalism and relativism. But her effort, I contend, cannot avoid relativism without implicitly affirming a universal standard of evaluation. Indeed, I submit that her insights about integrity and the multiplicity of goods within a fulfilled life makes the most sense within the context of a process metaphysical understanding of God.

9

A Radical-Orthodox Theology

The Approach of John Milbank

Theological Portrait

IF JEAN PORTER SEEKS TO RETRIEVE THE PAST IN ORDER TO SOLIDIFY modern Christian ethics, then John Milbank's turn to the past may be described as a bombshell meant to shatter all modern disciplines, including theology, and to catapult modernity into a postmodern future by radically retrieving and reasserting the premodern metaphysical vision of Neoplatonic Christian orthodoxy. More radically than Porter and more philosophically than Hauerwas, Milbank—and the movement of "Radical Orthodoxy" that he has helped to engender—seeks to unhinge theology from its modern setting and to rehang it within a patristic and medieval frame. His aim, he vows, is not a nostalgic grasping for an idealized past but, rather, a radical critique of secularity in order to save modernity in a new postmodern form. To accomplish this, he has vigorously sought to rouse theology from its modern and secular slumbers. In the words of Lois Malcolm, "Milbank jolts mainstream theology out of complacency, forcefully suggesting that it has been neither robustly Christian nor rigorously intellectual in its engagement with modernity." Yet, as Douglas Hedley reminds us, central to this engagement with modernity and to "Milbank's project is the retrieval of premodernity with postmodern tools."[1]

As one might guess, this critical interweaving of postmodern, premodern, and modern sources gets rather complicated. To describe Milbank's work as "dense" is an understatement. In fact, I recall one

---

1. See Milbank, "Programme of Radical Orthodoxy," 45; Malcolm, "Radical, orthodox," 1079; Hedley, "Should Divinity Overcome Metaphysics?" 289.

leading scholar handing me a copy of Milbank's first major book, *Theology and Social Theory: Beyond Secular Reason* (1990), and saying something to the effect of: "Here, see if you can make heads or tails of this!" Since then, Milbank has published other equally demanding works, such as *The Word Made Strange: Theology, Language, Culture* (1997) and *Being Reconciled: Ontology and Pardon* (2003).[2] Nonetheless, with continued effort, "the clouds begin to lift" and one comes to see central, repeated themes in Milbank's writings. Hence, in casting my portrait, I will draw on these three books as well as on his other essays and collaborative works.

A Fundamental Critique of Modernity

Like a starburst, Milbank's *Theology and Social Theory* served as an explosive catalyst to crystallize "Radical Orthodoxy" as a new theological movement. Led by Milbank, Radical Orthodoxy (hereafter RO) coalesced among a group of British theologians at Cambridge University. Though most of them subsequently left Cambridge, RO has continued to have a significant impact on trans-Atlantic theology in the early twenty-first century. At the heart of their project is a fundamental critique of modern secularity, not just secularism. This critique, they contend, also requires a restructuring of modern theology—one that radically diverts it from its modern trajectory and turns it around in order to critique modernity itself and to reestablish theology on patristic and medieval footings. Contrary to Gustafson, Milbank thinks that modern theology has been too humble and too accountable to modern thought and science. As Malcolm observes,

> Milbank's intent is to overcome what he calls the "pathos" of modern theology, a pathos that lies in its [false] humility. Modern theology, he argues, has felt it must conform to secular standards of scientific "objectivity." But with the advent of the postmodern critique of reason—and the recognition that all thought is situated in specific cultural and linguistic systems—theology has an opportunity to reclaim its own premises. . . . Theology can therefore embrace its historically conditioned nature without negating its claim to speak of transcendent reality.

---

2. As this book goes to press, Milbank's new book *Proposing Theology* has not yet been released.

Theology can ground its claims in terms of its own language of belief.

In calling theology to reclaim its voice as a "master discourse," Milbank systematically uncovers how the concept of the "secular" emerged. Rather than show how theology makes sense in light of secular philosophy, he aims to show how secular philosophy is a countertheology or an inadequate offshoot of Christian theology.[3]

This attempt to disrobe and reveal the "secular" is one of the central aims of *Theology and Social Theory*. Like Niebuhr, Milbank seeks to offer a sharp negative apologetic. Yet, whereas Niebuhr in a modern spirit seeks to show the rational incoherence of secularistic alternatives to a theistic source of meaning, Milbank pursues a postmodern path that seeks to outnarrate secularity by showing its historical roots in theology itself. By suggesting that all worldviews are rooted in some form of myth *(mythos)* or narrative, including modern liberalism and nihilism, Milbank seeks to offer an alternative myth in the form of orthodox Christianity. In pursuing this aim, his targeted audience is clearly the wider academy, not just the church. As he announces:

This book is addressed both to social theorists and to theologians. To social theorists I shall attempt to disclose the possibility of a sceptical demolition of modern, secular social theory from a [Christian] perspective.... I will try to demonstrate that all the most important governing assumptions of [modern social] theory are bound up with the modification or rejection of orthodox Christian positions. These fundamental intellectual shifts are, I shall argue, no more rationally 'justifiable' than the Christian positions themselves.

The book can, therefore, be read as an exercise in sceptical relativism. If my Christian perspective is persuasive, then this should be a persuasion intrinsic to the Christian *logos* itself, not [to] the apologetic mediation of a universal human reason.[4]

This attempt to collapse modern social theory back into theological terrain is the gist of Milbank's negative apologetic. Once he does this, his positive strategy is to seek to enable the rhetorical or nonrational persuasiveness of orthodox Christianity to outshine and lure the hearts

---

3. Malcolm, "Radical, orthodox," 1074.
4. Milbank, *Theology and Social Theory*, 1.

and minds of readers with the aesthetic luminosity of its alternative vision.

But before pursuing these moves, Milbank sets forth his critical diagnosis of modern theology:

> The pathos of modern theology is its false humility. For theology, this must be a fatal disease, because once theology surrenders its claim to be a metadiscourse, it cannot any longer articulate the word of the creator God, but is bound to turn into the oracular voice of some finite idol, such as historical scholarship, humanist psychology, or transcendental philosophy. If theology no longer seeks to position, qualify or criticize other discourses, then it is inevitable that these discourses will position theology: for the necessity of an ultimate organizing logic ... cannot be wished away.[5]

This passage encapsulates Milbank's muscular agenda. He believes that modern theology has lost its bold voice because it has lost its ability to offer an understanding of reality as a whole, one that ultimately relates all other disciplines within a comprehensive framework. Reminiscent of Hegel, Milbank asserts that "the necessity of an ultimate organizing logic ... cannot be wished away." (I will later discuss Milbank's similarities to and differences with Hegel). It is this need for an explicit comprehensive ontological or metaphysical vision—one that provides an ultimate organizing logic for reality as a whole—that modern theology has fatally lost due to its false humility. Only the reclamation of such a vision, Milbank asserts, will enable theology to regain its authentic voice. Along this line, James K. A. Smith observes that "one of the most refreshing aspects of RO is its unabashed and shameless affirmation of the project of metaphysics, despite all the supposedly postmodern talk of 'the end of metaphysics.' ... Indeed, how could we ever theorize without a metaphysics—an understanding of the nature of being and reality?" The predominate modern tendency to construct theology without offering a developed and explicit metaphysics, remarks Smith, is due to a confusion between "a particular *direction* metaphysics has taken with the *structure* of metaphysical reflection as such."[6] In brief, one might say that Milbank rejects the direction of metaphysics after 1300 CE; in its place, he seeks to reclaim the content and insights of an earlier ontologi-

---

5. Ibid.
6. Smith, *Introducing Radical Orthodoxy*, 186, 186 n. 3.

cal endeavor. I will fill in important details as we proceed, for at times Milbank sounds as though he, too, rejects metaphysics outright. Yet, as Smith correctly notes, what Milbank really objects to is a particular approach to metaphysics, not to metaphysics as such.

A brief comparison with Porter is instructive at this early juncture. Whereas she, following MacIntyre, seeks to reclaim theology's coherence by leaving its metaphysical or ontological claims embedded in the background of the tradition, Milbank, in his critique of modernity, seeks to boldly reassert such claims to the forefront of theology. To be sure, he does so using the language of particularity and tradition, but he does so nonetheless. Porter shies away from such claims because, like MacIntyre, she still seeks to pursue some form of indirect rational validation of all tradition-constituted claims; and the underlying metaphysical claims of a tradition, she believes, only make sense deeply embedded within the context and presuppositions of that tradition. Hence, such claims must remain muted in the background, awaiting the dialectical, comparative engagement of differing traditions as a whole. By contrast, Milbank believes that such metaphysical quietism is precisely what has led to the marginalization of theology. Instead, he seeks to assert and foreground the ontological while, at the same time, resisting any attempt to positively or rationally validate such claims. It is this combination of an assertive ontology in a rhetorical or nonrational mode that is one of the distinctive marks of Milbank's theology. In order to fully unveil his approach, we must now turn to his critique of the secular.

The Negative Apologetic: A Critique of the Secular

At the start of chapter one in *Theology and Social Theory*, Milbank begins with the following words:

> Once there was no "secular." And the secular was not latent, waiting to fill more space with the steam of the "purely human," when the pressure of the sacred was relaxed. Instead there was the single community of Christendom, with its dual aspects of *sacerdotium* and *regnum*. The *saeculum*, in the medieval era, was not a space, a domain, but a time—the interval between fall and *eschaton* where coercive justice, private property and impaired natural reason must make shift to cope with the unredeemed effects of sinful humanity.

> [Hence,] [t]he secular as a domain had to be instituted or *imagined*, both in theory and practice.[7]

Here are the two central claims of Milbank's negative apologetic. First, there was no such thing as a secular public square in the medieval world where differing claims could be asserted and adjudicated by a common public reason. There was no such thing as secular space outside the purview of the authority of the church, for the secular was defined not as a space but rather as an ecclesial and eschatological time between the fall and the eschaton. Second, therefore, the predominant modern notion of secular space independent of sacred authority was an invention—and a badly misguided one at that. It is this invented notion of a secular domain that has defined modern philosophy, politics, and social theory, and has poisoned almost all of modern theology as well. As a result, reason became defined independently of revelation, nature became defined apart from grace, philosophy became defined independently of theology, and freedom became defined apart from teleology. So how did this misguided invention come about? The answer, Milbank argues, lies in late medieval theology itself.

Similar to MacIntyre, Milbank defines the fateful turning point after Aquinas, around the beginning of the fourteenth century. According to Milbank, the chief culprit is Duns Scotus and his late-medieval nominalist voluntarism and his insistence on the use of univocal language in reference to God.[8] Summarily speaking, by defining divine omnipotence in terms of an unfettered divine will and fiat, Scotus's nominalism created a gulf between God's declared will or ordained power *(potentia ordinata)* and God's absolute will or infinite power to do whatever God desires *(potentia absoluta)*. The former is factually and contingently known through revelation while the latter "is absolutely unknowable for theology and knowable only formally, for *logic*." One of the effects of this nominalist chasm, Milbank maintains, is that

> the Trinity loses its significance as a prime location for discussing will and understanding in God and [for discussing] the

---

7. Milbank, *Theology and Social Theory*, 9.

8. MacIntyre also identifies Scotus as one of the chief suspects, though he does not seem to single out or emphasize Scotus quite much as Milbank. For MacIntyre's account of Scotus, see *TRV*, 152–56. More recently, Milbank has been willing to concede "a certain *recognition* of the rational power of the arguments of Duns Scotus" (Milbank, "Preface to the Second Edition," xxv).

relationship of God to the world. No longer is the world participatorily enfolded within the divine expressive *logos*, but instead a bare divine unity starkly confronts the other distinct unities which he has ordained.⁹

Furthermore, what this chasm begins to do, Milbank and his RO colleagues state elsewhere, is to "prise apart" ontology from theology:

> [T]his prising apart was itself governed by ironically "pious" motives: it arose because God was now regarded as a supreme, untrammeled individual Will rather than that *esse ipsum* [Being itself] in which mere existences come to share. Hence, [Scotus's and Ockham's] ... "pious" conjecture that God might so dispose things that what *appears* to humans has no connection to the truly real itself opens the space for the emergence of the modern "epistemological" focus. Without formally surrendering the circumstances in which they were nearly always doing theology and *not* philosophy [in a modern autonomous sense] ... , the later medieval theologians nonetheless managed to construct the theological preconditions for the modern autonomy of philosophy and secular practice.¹⁰

The nominalist proclivity for emphasizing an "untrammeled individual [divine] Will," Milbank and company suggest, led to the presumed fissure between appearance and reality that fueled the modern epistemological project. This theological move, in other words, created the conditions for the emerging illusion that philosophy is a discipline autonomous from theology. Adding even more fuel to the fire, however, was Scotus's insistence on the use of univocal language.

When we use words and language to speak of God (such as "love," "justice," and "existence"), are we using these terms in the same sense that we use them in reference to human experience (univocal)? Alternatively, are we using them in a completely different and thus totally unrelated sense (equivocal)? Or, thirdly, are we using them in a way that is similar yet different (analogical)? Scotus was convinced that in order to avoid falling into sheer equivocation, theology must be able to make at least some univocal statements about God.¹¹ But this insistence on univocity, Milbank contends, had the fateful effect of implying that one could

---

9. Milbank, *Theology and Social Theory*, 14.

10. Milbank, et al., "Introduction—Suspending the Material," 5–6.

11. For a concise, lucid discussion of Scotus's univocity, see Cross, *Duns Scotus*, 33–39.

understand being or existence independently of God; by trying to identify a conceptual point of contact "from below," Scotus suggested that being can be known on its own terms and, thus, independently of the divine transcendence. This outlook had at least four disastrous consequences. First, it lost the qualitative difference between finite being and Infinite Being; this had a leveling effect that elevated the finite and lowered the transcendent. For Scotus, Milbank remarks, "being ... possessed the same simple meaning of existence when applied to either [the finite or infinite]. 'Exists,' in the sentence God 'exists,' has therefore the same fundamental meaning (at both a logical and metaphysical level) as in the sentence, 'this woman exists.'"[12] Second, this univocal leveling also implied that created being could be coherently understood independently of its ontological dependence on and participation in the divine Creator. "Scotus's shift away from a metaphysics of participation to an ontology predicated on the univocity of being," remarks Smith in his introduction to RO, "rent the cords of suspension that hooked the immanent to the transcendent, the material to the more than material. The result ... was modernity's 'flattened' ontology."[13]

Third, this shift signaled a paradigm change in ontology, namely, a shift away from "Aquinas's theological metaphysics" to "Scotus's autonomous metaphysics."[14] I will later unpack the former but, for now, it is important to emphasize the paradigm shift itself. For it is this modern "autonomous metaphysics" that Milbank rejects and seeks to overcome when he declares that "Only Theology Overcomes Metaphysics." What Milbank resists is "Scotus's claim that there can be an independent science of finite being."[15] In other words, what he rejects is a post-Scotist understanding of metaphysics—one that attempts to define the nature of being independently of and prior to the question of divinity. Fourth, Scotus's univocity not only sought to create an autonomous sphere for a rational metaphysics, but it also disconnected revelation from a proper understanding of being itself. As Milbank and company put it,

> revelation is now something positive in addition to reason, precisely because a rational metaphysics, claiming to comprehend

12. Milbank, *Theology and Social Theory*, 302–3.
13. Smith, *Introducing Radical Orthodoxy*, 93.
14. Ibid., 93, 97.
15. Milbank, "Only Theology Can Overcome Metaphysics," chap. 2 in *Word Made Strange*, 36–51, 47.

being without primary reference to God, frames all discourse, including the theological. Ironically, revealed truth becomes something ineffably arbitrary, precisely because this is the only way it can be construed by an already intrinsically godless reason.[16]

What is crucial to recognize here in these third and fourth elements is that Milbank is implicitly rejecting two distinct forms of autonomy, which I have called respectively "substantive" and "formal." By the former, I mean again that Milbank rejects the notion that one can understand being or reality independently of the divine. By the latter, I mean that he rejects the notion that one can rationally discern or adjudicate any truth claim, including claims about God, being, or social science, apart from the resources and authority of revelation. For his part, Milbank assumes that these two forms of autonomy necessarily go together, so much so that he likely would not even distinguish between them. For instance, he approvingly proclaims that "traditional theology never entertained a 'metaphysics' or 'ontology' in autonomy from a discourse illuminated by God."[17] According to him, pre-Scotist theology rightly affirmed a theistic metaphysics (not an autonomous metaphysics) that was grounded in revelation or divine illumination (not in autonomous reason). That is, for traditional theology, reason was embedded in revelation and thus truth was only discerned in relation to revelation. But now, after the errors of substantive and formal autonomy, "revelation is . . . [seen as] something positive in addition to reason, precisely because a rational [autonomous] metaphysics . . . frames all discourse, including the theological." In short, he believes that the distinctions between general and special revelation and between reason and revelation are the misguided results of the twin errors of autonomy. The consequence is that "revealed truth becomes something ineffably arbitrary, precisely because this is the only way it can be construed by an already intrinsically [autonomous and] godless reason."

With these four deleterious consequences in place, Milbank sums up the legacy of Scotus:

---

16. Milbank, et al., *Radical Orthodoxy*, 5.
17. Milbank, *Word Made Strange*, 2.

> Roughly speaking this story goes as follows. An ontology entirely prior to theology and unaffected by an orientation to revelation, which emerged in early modernity, depended upon the post-Scotist notion that one can univocally grasp Being as indifferent to infinite and finite. This allowed one to think of infinite Being as simply *a* being, which either exists or does not exist, in the same fashion as any finite creature. . . . And once God had ceased to surmount, through consummate transcendence, this perfective scale [of being] and is instead regarded as a mere supreme item, he soon gets thought of as first cause in univocally the same sense as later finite causes, and then eventually as self-caused, as the supreme self-determining will laying down arbitrary laws and so forth, as with Descartes. . . . Thus the very first pure [modern] metaphysics, free of an extra-rational practice of erotic ascent (as with Plato), or of the reception of sacramental grace (as with Christianity)—in other words the first pure ontology delivered by reason alone which emerged in the early seventeenth century—was *already* better . . . expressed as a fundamental epistemology.[18]

Modernity's flattened ontology, Milbank here surmises, loses sight of God's distinctive and necessary existence because it comes to treat "infinite Being as simply *a* being, which either exists or does not exist, in the same fashion as any finite creature." He blames this loss on Scotus's univocity as much as on his nominalism. This downward spiral then inexorably pushes modernity into its preoccupation with epistemology. In contrast, the only way to truly discern the proper nature of ontology and divinity, he suggests, is to ground one's discernment in "an extra-rational practice," such as found in "the reception of sacramental grace" in the church. This focus on "extra-rational practice" will later be central in Milbank's exposition of his theological metaphysics. But for now let us finish his critique of modernity.

One might suppose that Kant's critique of metaphysics is precisely the remedy needed to halt Scotus's pursuit of a misguided metaphysics. But Milbank thinks that "Kant only completes" the misguided legacy of Scotus, he does not abandon it. Hence, "Radical Orthodoxy does not situate itself in a post-Kantian intellectual space." Kant rightly recognizes "the *finititude* of our knowledge," Milbank contends, but he couples this with "the false idea that we can once and for all specify the bounds of possible knowledge for finite minds." Embedded in this misguided

---

18. Milbank, "Programme of Radical Orthodoxy," 38–39.

attempt to define the limits of reason, Milbank alleges, is Scotus's legacy of univocal reason:

> For Kant, the finite being of appearances is pre-determined by the possibilities given in the framework of our mediated knowing of this being, while the Infinite Being of real, . . . noumenal, existence, is predetermined through the purest self-realising possibility of . . . reason as such; and as rational beings we can univocally grasp this possibility. . . . Kant *perfects* metaphysical dogmatism because his limiting of the import of the phenomenal is only attained by a safeguarding of the noumenal against the phenomenal. . . . What is refused here is not groundless extrapolation from the phenomenal, but rather (without grounds) any notion of attributive analogy or participation, that is to say any real kinship between the visible and the invisible worlds.[19]

Kant is charged here with two related errors. First, his phenomenal-noumenal distinction wrongly implies that "we can univocally grasp" the difference between appearances (finite being) and reality as such (Infinite Being). Second, based on this distinction, Kant wrongly tries to identify and safeguard a self-contained phenomenal realm that denies "any real kinship between the visible and invisible worlds." As Milbank says elsewhere, Kant "disliked the fractal incursion of the infinite into the finite."[20] In short, by pursuing the path of univocity instead of analogy, of separation instead of participation, Kant perfects the misguided notions of secular space and autonomous reason.

In rejecting Kant's philosophy, Milbank reveals his ambivalent relationship to Hegel, which he sums up in a chapter in *Theology and Social Theory* entitled: "For and Against Hegel." On the one hand, Milbank, like Hegel, rejects the false humility of Kant's attempt to identify the limits of reason. "Hegel [rightly] rejects Kant's ban on constitutive metaphysics," Milbank remarks, "because . . . it is not possible to make universal statements about knowing . . . in isolation from statements about universal being."[21] In effect, he concurs with Hegel in stressing the need for an explicit substantive metaphysics. For instance, in *The Word Made Strange*, he declares that "one can see the continued *inevitability* of metaphysics, and the continuing significance of Hegel's argument

19. Ibid., 38, 39.
20. Milbank, "Invocation of Clio," 17.
21. Chapter 6 in *Theology and Social Theory* is entitled: "For and Against Hegel," 147–76; 153.

that the enlightenment claim to 'end' constitutive metaphysics is itself the result of ideological maneuverings to guarantee the self-sufficiency of a liberal 'civil society.'" Yet, on the other hand, Milbank rejects Hegel's rationalist attempt to delineate a substantive metaphysics. "This insight of Hegel's [about the need for a constitutive metaphysics]," continues Milbank, "is perfectly separable from the form of his own metaphysics as a rationalist determinism, a form in fact traceable to his failure to *emancipate* himself from the Kantian-Fichtean stress on history as the rational coming to be of freedom."[22] Hegel's mistake is that he tries to articulate a genuinely theistic metaphysics within the parameters of modern secularity. In other words, he rightly rejects the substantive autonomy of Scotus, but he wrongly tries to do so within the formal autonomy of Kant ("the rational coming to be of freedom"). Otherwise stated, if Kant made the mistake of trying to bracket out the infinite from the self-contained realm of the finite or phenomenal, Hegel made the converse mistake of trying to rationally grasp the infinite from the side of the finite. On the contrary, a true metaphysics cannot be discerned apart from revelation, asserts Milbank, which requires once again the extra-rational practice found in the sacraments of the church.

If the errors of modern philosophy are summed up in the twin forms of autonomy, their fateful consequence for political theory was to accept and ingrain violence into the modern worldview at a deep ontological level. This is the basic thesis of much of *Theology and Social Theory*. Using a postmodern "'archeological' approach," Milbank seeks to demonstrate, through a long, dense, and winding discussion of modern thought, "the questionability of the assumptions upon which secular social theory rests." These assumptions are questionable, he contends, because "'scientific' social theories are [really] themselves theologies or antitheologies in disguise." For instance, Hobbes stands in the tradition of the misguided theology of medieval "nominalism-voluntarism" whereas Machiavelli represents a form of antitheology in his reclamation of pagan virtue. In Hobbes we have "heresy on the one hand" and in Machiavelli we have "the half-return of paganism on the other." What they share in common, nevertheless, and upon which much of modern social theory depends, is a deep-seated ontological assumption that identifies violence and conflict at the heart of reality itself. Hence,

---

22. Milbank, *Word Made Strange*, 27–28.

in either case [Hobbes or Machiavelli], it seems that, from the outset, the "science of conflict" is not merely one branch of social science but rather that the "scientific" approach seeks "to know" power and conflict as ontologically fundamental. It follows that if Christianity seeks to "find a place for" secular reason, it may be perversely compromising with what, on its own terms, is either deviancy or falsehood.[23]

As part of the invention of the secular, this incorporation of violence into the fabric of modern social theory likewise had its roots in the corrosive effects of late medieval theology, namely, in the reinterpretation of the meaning of Adam's dominion over nature. "For the *factum* (the made) to become identified with the secular," Milbank claims, "it was necessary that Adam's *dominium* be redefined as power, property, active right, and absolute sovereignty, and that Adam's personhood be collapsed into this redefined mastery that is uniquely 'his own.'" In contrast, in traditional medieval thought ranging from the ancients to Aquinas, *dominium* was interpreted not as dominance over external matters but, rather, as self-mastery or "self-government" in the sense of a "rational mastery of [one's own] passions." What was critical here was a teleology that gave purpose and direction to power. Hence, self-government was ultimately equated with self-mastery, which meant that the self was free to serve its true end. But with the rise of nominalism, teleology disappears and *dominium* begins to take on the form of naked, direction-less, absolute power. From this perspective, the *factum* or created order is seen as

> rooted in an individualistic account of the will, oblivious to questions of its providential purpose in the hands of God, it has difficulty in understanding any "collective making," or genuinely social process. To keep notions of the state free from any suggestions of a collective essence or a generally recognized *telos*, it must be considered on the individualist model of *dominium*.[24]

From this vantage point, the created world and human society serve no intrinsic purpose. Rather, they are objects to be directed by arbitrary power. In fact, self-government itself comes to mean little more than arbitrary power serving the self-interests and aims of individuals. Again, since there is no teleological order, these interests and aims are rooted

---

23. Milbank, *Theology and Social Theory*, 3, 13, 23.
24. Ibid., 12, 13.

merely in preference and preservation. The consequence of this trajectory is that even the ideals of modern political thought, such as freedom and equality, become distorted. "The problem ... with the modern 'release' of these ideals," says Milbank elsewhere, "is that in gradually losing their theological and teleological ground, [they became] distorted. ... Freedom becomes freedom without point, freedom for futility; equality, without a basis in the common good ... degenerates into a treatment of all people formally as the same—a treatment that both disguises and constitutes actual brutal disparities."[25]

In sum, if modern secularity is rooted in a misguided metaphysics, which, in turn, spawned a misguided trajectory for political theory, then what is needed is an alternative approach to metaphysics and politics. It is precisely this combination that Milbank seeks to offer in setting forth a positive alternative in the form of a counter-ontology and a counter-polis. Yet, in order to lay the groundwork for these substantive visions, I must first outline some of Milbank's key underlying assumptions.

Toward a Counter-Ontology using Postmodern Tools

At the outset, I suggested that Milbank seeks to retrieve a premodern ontology using postmodern tools.[26] As we have seen, one of these tools is his historicist approach. "Philosophy," he urges, "must be historicist." That is, it must seek to offer a genetic account that tries to show the contingent origins of all human ideas. It then tries to outnarrate alternative views (by showing unexpected or forgotten historical origins and connections) rather than trying to out-argue them in some a priori or rationalist sense. For the latter attempt, as illustrated by Kant's "apriorism," "is always a conservative attempt to deny radical historicity." Alternatively, Milbank proposes, the historicist "kind [of] tracking back is. . . . [a] matter of discovering how contemporary thought is rooted in certain decisions that it has forgotten were ever made. Most significant here, in my view, are the instances where modern philosophy is grounded in certain forgotten *theological* decisions that doom it to pursue a

---

25. Milbank, "Programme of Radical Orthodoxy," 45.

26. It should be noted that Milbank and RO are also critical of postmodernism. Given the limits of space, I have omitted this critique here. In brief, RO critiques the underlying nihilism of postmodernism. For a concise summary, see Smith, *Introducing Radical Orthodoxy*, 43f.

certain style of anonymous theology in the guise of philosophy."[27] As we have seen, these ill-fated theological decisions began with Scotus and his legacy. Along with historicism, Milbank employs at least two other postmodern tools or tendencies, namely, the blurring of reason and revelation, and the priority of rhetoric over reason. If historicism is the proper instrument for retrieving a premodern counter-ontology, then Milbank believes that these latter two elements are the proper tools for interpreting and defending such an ontology. To show how these tools fit into his work, we must return to our larger discussion of modernity and metaphysics.

The way to overcome the errors of modernity, Milbank holds, is by overcoming its metaphysics; and since the modern approach to metaphysics is rooted in the nominalism and univocity of Scotus, the way forward is found by returning to a premodern ontology characterized by realism and analogy. In *Theology and Social Theory*, this counter-ontology is developed principally in terms of the Neoplatonism of Augustine and the Church Fathers. In his later books, *The Word Made Strange* and *Being Reconciled*, Milbank shifts the emphasis slightly more toward Aquinas's theological metaphysics. From among these various sources in the tradition, Milbank seeks to identify an integrated or shared ontological vision—one stretching from Augustine to Aquinas. He sees Augustine and Aquinas in basic harmony, for it is the Augustinian-strand of Thomas that he emphasizes, not the Aristotelian one. Moreover, the common lens through which he views the tradition is one crafted by Henri de Lubac (1896–1991) and *la nouvelle théologie*. I will later outline this ontological vision but let us begin by examining the influence of de Lubac.

"Radical Orthodoxy," declares Milbank, "considers that Henri de Lubac was a greater theological revolutionary than Karl Barth, because in questioning a hierarchical duality of grace and nature as discrete stages, he transcended, unlike Barth, the shared background of all modern theology." Though some critics like Hedley charge that Milbank's theology is really just "a reaffirmation of Barthianism," Milbank himself goes to some lengths to distinguish RO from Barth.[28] In his judgment,

---

27. Milbank, "Invocation of Clio," 5, 21, 9.

28. Milbank, "Programme of Radical Orthodoxy," 35; Hedley, "Should Divinity Overcome Metaphysics?" 274.

Barth is still too much under the spell of Kant and neo-orthodoxy is still too accommodating to modernity:

> In this fashion, Barth tends to embrace the post-Enlightenment notion of [a] fixed ascertainable limit to human reason, and also, at times, the idea of a valid secular autonomy within those limits. The assertion of pure faith, pure unanticipated revelation over against reason, is the counterpart of an acceptance of an entirely secure but limited human reason, sovereign within its own terms of reference. By contrast, Radical Orthodoxy, re-invoking premodern positions . . . , does not consider there to be any secure reason without reference to our remote and uncertain vision of the divine—an anticipation of the beatific vision granted by grace, which in a fallen world must take the shape of a figurative anticipation of the incarnate logos, or else . . . a commentary on the textual and sacramental relics of that incarnation. For this outlook, faith is not alien to reason, but simply its intensification.[29]

It is from de Lubac that Milbank gets the idea of faith as an integral intensifier of reason rather than as an independent revelatory source. Just as Barth and neo-orthodoxy embody the Protestant mistake of separating faith and reason, so, too, according to de Lubac, did Catholic neo-Scholasticism make the mistake of separating the supernatural and the natural. In both cases, revelation and grace become gratuitous additions—something separate and ultimately alien from the realm of pure nature and reason. As one commentator puts it, by seeking to elevate the transcendence of revelation and grace, they unintentionally "cut the divine off from the human, as if God were not the creator of both nature and grace." Instead of separating the two or seeking to naturalize the supernatural, de Lubac went the other way and pressed that theology must supernaturalize the natural, i.e., must view the natural from the start as infused with the presence of divine grace.[30]

It is in light of de Lubac's supernaturalizing the natural that Milbank sees faith and reason as integrally related. In fact, he sees them as so interrelated that they are blurred. "The radical implication of de Lubac's work," he states, "is that, for Aquinas and the preceding tradition, faith and reason are not essentially distinct, since both are but differing

---

29. Milbank, "Programme of Radical Orthodoxy," 34.

30. Livingston, et al., "Henri de Lubac and the *Nouvelle Théologie*," in *Modern Christian Thought*, vol. 2, 202f., see esp. 203.

degrees of participation in the mind of God."³¹ Milbank explicates this central claim as follows:

> And just as both reason and faith are framed by the participation of our being and knowing in the divine being and intellection, so also they are both—reason as much as faith—framed by eschatology. For reason to think at all, it must somehow already know what it seeks to know: reason, to be reason, must therefore also be faith, and in articulating this view in different ways Augustine, Anselm, and Aquinas are all conscious that at the heart of their Christian articulation of grace and revelation they are nonetheless radicalising and resolving the specifically Platonic view that reason, to be reason, in some fashion knows before it knows.³²

Similar to MacIntyre, Milbank emphasizes here the proleptic nature of reason, namely, that reason "must somehow already know what it seeks to know." Yet, unlike MacIntyre, who is closer to the neo-Scholastics, Milbank seeks to blur the secular and the eschatological, the philosophical and the theological. For Milbank, reason is always cast in light of the *Logos* made flesh, in light of the second person of the Trinity. Hence, there is no philosophical reasoning, even within traditions, that is not already imbued with the theological *Logos*. But this also has inverse implications as well. For "if reason is already Christological, then inversely, faith, until the eschaton, remains dispersed in all the different discourses of human reason. To speak about God it must speak about something else; indeed its speaking about God really is only the difference it makes to speaking about something else." So, on the one hand, Milbank claims that all reasoning makes "reference to our remote and uncertain vision of the divine." Yet, on the other, he seems to suggest that we cannot speak about God directly, for "to speak about God [one] must speak about something else [other than God]." Given his extended discussion of God in various places, I take it that what he means here is that "in a fallen world," where we have lost our clear and distinct knowledge of the divine, our knowledge of God "must take the shape of a . . . commentary on the textual and sacramental relics" of the incarnate logos.³³ Our talk of God, in other words, draws on the theological tradi-

---

31. Milbank, "Programme of Radical Orthodoxy," 35.
32. Ibid.
33. Ibid., 34. See also Milbank, *Being Reconciled*, 9.

tions and liturgical practices of the church. Again, in pursuing this position, he rejects any positivism of revelation akin to Barth as well as any notion of an independent philosophical reason. In classical Anglican fashion, Milbank is looking for a "both-and" approach—both revelation and reason intrinsically blurred. Interestingly, in seeking to articulate this epistemological blurring, he implies that the whole point of speaking of God at all is found in the difference it makes for speaking about other subjects. Presumably this difference has theoretical, pragmatic, and/or existential implications.

This blurring tendency is also evident when comparing Porter and Milbank. Even though Porter claims that Thomas ultimately affirms only one telos, she holds that this one end is attained in radically distinct ways. Thus, she clearly demarcates the natural from the supernatural and largely sets aside the latter when talking about the natural human end. In contrast, it is precisely this clear demarcation and segregation of the supernatural that Milbank rejects. "In the case of Aquinas, for reason to be reason," he writes,

> it must aspire to the complete knowledge of the beatific vision, yet such aspiration, as exceeding finite nature, must somehow receive some dim glimpse of that vision in advance if it is to recognize it even as a possibility. Reason ascending, therefore, is an inchoate and relatively non-discursive anticipation of the final end, and in consequence reason ascending is already grace descending.[34]

At first blush, this position sounds similar to Porter. The ultimate end exceeds finite nature and "reason ascending" is only "an inchoate and relatively non-discursive anticipation of the final end." But whereas Porter then demarcates natural and supernatural, Milbank wants to affirm the infusion of grace and the supernatural down into all forms of reasoning—"reason ascending is already grace descending." In short, he opts for a blurred fusion rather than a clear demarcation. If the first key to Milbank's approach is rooted in this blurring of reason and revelation, then the second key is found in his preference for communal witness and rhetoric over reason.

In the final chapter of *Theology and Social Theory*, after eleven chapters of historicist analysis and critique of modern social theory,

---

34. Milbank, "Programme of Radical Orthodoxy," 35. Porter explicitly rejects this tendency to blur nature and grace. See Porter, *Nature as Reason*, 383f.

Milbank sets forth an alternative metanarrative, namely, what he calls "Theology as a Social Science." As he reflects:

> Theology has frequently sought to borrow from elsewhere a fundamental account of society or history, and then to see what theological insights will cohere with it. But it has been shown [in this book] that no such fundamental account, in the sense of something neutral, rational and universal, is really available. It is theology itself that will have to provide its own account of the final causes at work in human history, on the basis of its own particular, and historically specific faith.[35]

In rejecting any correlational approach to theology or any notion of common reason or even any indirect form of validation (a la MacIntyre and Porter), Milbank echoes Hauerwas in emphasizing the historical particularity of the Christian interpretation of the world. Indeed, sounding like Hauerwas, Milbank asserts that "there can only be a distinguishable Christian social theory because there is also a distinguishable Christian mode of action, a definite practice.... The theory, therefore, is first and foremost an *ecclesiology.*" It is only out of this ecclesiology that one can offer a sociology or an ontology. More precisely, a social theory is rooted in a metaphysical vision of reality as a whole and this vision, in turn, is grounded in the practices and traditions of the church. Hence, "the task of such a theology is not apologetic, nor even argument. Rather, it is to tell again the Christian *mythos*, pronounce again the Christian *logos*, and call again for Christian *praxis* in a manner that restores their freshness and originality. It must articulate Christian difference in such a fashion as to make it strange [to the assumptions and outlook of modern secular culture]."[36] This different Christian mythos is universal in its scope and vision, but it is particular in its accessibility and source of validation. As Milbank describes it in *Being Reconciled*, there is a

> need for at least some modicum of universal attachment, universal *mythos*. But here ... transcendence offers a thought of the universal not as something clearly grasped, spatially fixed and operable, but rather as something eternally present yet not fully accessible. This universal is instead only available as diversely mediated by local pathways, as Augustine already divined....
> But inversely, it is only by virtue of a local ecstatic opening to

---

35. Milbank, *Theology and Social Theory*, 380.
36. Ibid., 380, 381.

this universal that one has giving, or community, or sacred locality at all.[37]

The universal or divine is always present in our lives and world, Milbank suggests, but it is not "something clearly grasped" or "fully accessible." Rather, it is only available as it is "mediated by local pathways," that is, by the particular witness and community of the church. Yet, the possibility of genuine *ecclesia* (of genuine giving and community) is itself only possible "by virtue of a local ecstatic opening to this universal," i.e., insofar as the church is open and receptive to the ever-present possibility of the divine.

The fundamental difference that the Christian mythos makes is expressed most fully in terms of ontology. For "it is only at the ontological level," notes Milbank, "where theology articulates (always provisionally) the framework of reference implicit in the Christian story and action, that this 'total' difference is fully clarified, along with its ineradicable ties to non-provable belief." By emphasizing that ontology is grounded in story and "non-provable belief," Milbank illustrates what he calls "metanarrative realism." By this, I take him to mean that the act of offering a metaphysical vision of reality as a whole is grounded in story or narrative rather than philosophical reason. Such an approach, he reiterates, appeals to rhetoric rather than reason:

> Christianity does not claim that the Good and the True are self-evident to objective reason, or dialectical argument. On the contrary, it from the first took the side of rhetoric against philosophy and contended that the Good and the True are those things of which we "have a persuasion" *pistis*, or "faith." We need the stories of Jesus for salvation, rather than just a speculative notion of the good, because only the attraction exercised by a particular set of words and images causes us to acknowledge the good and to have an idea of the ultimate *telos*. *Testimony* is here offered to the Good, in a witnessing that also participates in it.[38]

As I will later develop, Milbank's preference for rhetoric over reason stems from his conception of what reason involves and from his vision of what the church is called to bear witness to. Hence, in order to explicate a Christian ontology, one must abandon "all scholastic attempts to graft faith onto a universal base of reason." Instead, theological meta-

---

37. Milbank, *Being Reconciled*, 173.
38. Milbank, *Theology and Social Theory*, 381, 382, 398.

physics rightly turns "to the Church Fathers, and indeed goes beyond them, seeking to elaborate a Christian *logos*, or a reason that bears the marks of the incarnation and pentecost."[39] By pointing us to the Church Fathers and the incarnation, Milbank puts us in a position to now outline his counter-ontology.

A Counter-Ontology: Recovering a Metaphysics of Participation

Taken as a whole, Milbank's ontological vision can aptly be described as a *panentheism of plenitude*. By this, I mean that the world and all things exist within God but nothing affects or changes God. Rather, all things emerge out of the plenitude of divine Being and only exist insofar as they participate within the divine. Outside of and apart from God, there is simply nothing at all. Hence, the notion of an independent secular space apart from the divine is literally impossible. In setting forth this vision, Milbank seeks to offer a theological realism based on analogy to counter the dominance of nominalism and univocity, which led to the misguided notion of an autonomous philosophy. In some ways, Milbank's panentheistic vision departs from classical theism's sharp distinction between God and world. Yet, insofar as he still takes eternity to be the inclusive category and insofar as he continues to suggest that the divine nature is impassible, I will argue that his vision remains allied with classical theism. It is precisely because of this combination of deviation and continuity, one might say, that he and his cohort describe their position as "Radical Orthodoxy."[40] To unpack this combination, let me begin with his discussion of time and eternity and unity and difference.

Like Niebuhr, Milbank takes eternity to be the primary or inclusive category—eternity includes time. But whereas Niebuhr suggests that this paradoxical relationship can only be hinted at through mythical or symbolic expression, Milbank states it directly and then seeks

---

39. Ibid., 381.

40. Smith appears to reject the label "panentheism" as a description of RO. Yet, he clearly recognizes that RO "sees *all* as participating in the divine." It is in this literal (all-in-God) sense that I describe Milbank's position as panentheistic. As I will argue, I also think there are some traditional or classical elements in his doctrine of God. See Smith, *Introducing Radical Orthodoxy*, 189, 191 n. 17.

to elaborate it in a full-fledged ontological conception.[41] For instance, in *Being Reconciled* he speaks of "the economy of the participation of time in eternity."[42] Likewise, in *Theology and Social Theory* he states that "the created world of time participates in the God who differentiates; indeed, it *is* this differentiation insofar as it is finitely 'explicated' [or unfolded], rather than infinitely 'complicated' [or folded together]." Presumably, the "it" here refers to the created world, but where God ends and where the world begins cannot be sharply distinguished. For just as Milbank suggests that the world is this differentiation finitely unfolded, he also says that "God is the infinite series of differences, and what he knows is the infinity of differences." So just as God is "the reality which includes and encompasses in his *comprehensio* every difference, [so, too,] God is also the God who differentiates." Put simply, God is both creator and creation insofar as all creation exists within the divine itself. Otherwise stated, God is "an infinite differentiation that is also a harmony." What this means is that, "as Dionysius the Areopagite realized, God is superabundant Being, and not a Plotinian unity beyond Being and difference."[43] Milbank is making clear here that his version of Neoplatonic participation is not participation in the sense of emanation from the One who is "beyond Being and difference," as found in Plotinus. Rather, for Milbank, participation involves and requires the One who participates in Being and difference. To borrow a phrase from H. Richard Niebuhr, one might say that God is not the "One beyond the many," but rather God is the One containing and differentiating the many.[44]

Yet, just as Milbank affirms this close connection between God and world, he also seeks to maintain some difference. For "as Dionysius also saw, [God is] a power within Being which is more than Being, an internally creative power." In other words, God is a creative superabundance that is more than the unfolded differentiation that emerges from within the divine itself. This is Milbank's way of trying to differentiate

---

41. I recognize that Milbank offers a sharp critique of Niebuhr in his chapter entitled: "The Poverty of Niebuhrianism," in *Word Made Strange*, 233–51. Yet, apart from their many real differences, I think there are some illuminating structural similarities between their respective theological approaches.

42. Milbank, *Being Reconciled*, 40.

43. Milbank, *Theology and Social Theory*, 424, 423, 427.

44. H. Richard Niebuhr, *Radical Monotheism and Western Culture*, 32.

his panentheism from pantheism. However, at the same time that he sets forth his panentheism, he also attempts to straddle more classical affirmations, such as the notion that God is pure act. "As infinite power which is unimpeded," he contends,

> nothing in God can be unrealized, so that it would appear that God is *actus purus*, yet it must be equally the case that no actualization, even an infinite one, exhausts God's power, for this would render it finite after all. The pre-Thomist intimation in Dionysius of a kind of surplus to actuality in God is therefore correct, but one needs to state clearly that no priority can be given to either pure *actus* or pure *virtus*. Infinite realized act and infinite unrealized power mysteriously coincide in God, and it must be this that supports the circular "life," that is more than *stasis*, of the Trinity.[45]

Instead of clearly stating that there is unrealized potential and possibility in God, Milbank asserts on the contrary that "nothing in God can be unrealized." Yet, at the same time that he points toward the traditional formulation of God as pure act, he also wants to maintain that there is "a kind of surplus to actuality in God," i.e., that there is some differential between divine actualization and divine possibility and power. But, again, instead of coming out on one side or the other, he tries to straddle both sides by claiming that "infinite realized act and infinite unrealized power mysteriously coincide in God."

Neither God nor the created world of time and difference that participates in Him are a substance. There is "no underlying matter, and no discrete and inviolable 'things,'" claims Milbank. Rather,

> one can only think of the elements of creation as inherently interconnected "qualities" which combine and re-combine in all sorts of ways (Basil, Gregory of Nyssa) and as "seeds" or "monads" (Eriugena) or numerical ratios (Augustine) which participate in the divine creative power/act, and themselves continuously propagate *ex nihilo*, in the sense of continuously reproviding their own "matter" (as Eriugena affirms) through time. There are no "things" (as Augustine sees in *De Musica*) but only tensional *ratios* which in their "intense" state, do not pre-contain all that they later unfold, but have an "incorporeal" power for expansion. Creation is therefore not a finished product in space, but is continuously generated *ex nihilo* in time.

---

45. Milbank, *Theology and Social Theory*, 423.

> To sustain this process, the monads, seeds or ratios also self-generate, but in this they do not "assist" God, who supplies all power and all being, but rather participate in God. For if God is an internally creative power-act, then he can only be participated in by creatures who do not embody an infinite coincidence of act and power, but a finite oscillation between the two, yet are themselves thereby radically creative and differentiating.[46]

In unpacking this rich and dense passage, one can offer several observations. First, it appears that Milbank rejects any notion of God or reality as substance let alone any materialist metaphysic. Instead, he excavates the tradition, looking for an alternative way to conceptualize reality, and unearths metaphors such as "qualities," "seeds," monads," or "tensional ratios." Indeed, this mathematical or musical notion of tensional ratios calls to mind both ancient views, such as found in Pythagoras and Plato, and contemporary ones, such as offered by string theory. Put simply, the world is ultimately more like the relation between musical notes, Milbank suggests, than it is like a receptacle of matter or things. Second, the created order contains an element of novelty, for the tensional ratios "do not pre-contain all that they later unfold," but rather "have an 'incorporeal' power for expansion." Hence, creation is not a fixed order or "finished product" extended once and for all in space but rather "is continuously generated *ex nihilo* in time." What he means here by *ex nihilo* is a bit puzzling. Does he mean that each new moment is generated literally from nothing? But what about the influence of the past moment, the influence of the previous note or tensional ratio? Do Milbank's monads have "closed windows," receiving no internal influence at all from the past and, thus, each one arising *de novo*? Unless he is presuming some form of Leibnizian pre-established harmony, such a world would presumably show little or no continuity let alone any resemblance of cause and effect. Of course, if he were assuming a Leibnizian-like notion of pre-established harmony, then there would be no genuine novelty, since all was foreordained from the beginning. Perhaps what he has in mind is simply that the past note, monad, or quality does not fully define the new one. Hence, the cause does not fully determine the effect, thereby leaving room for creative novelty.

---

46. Ibid., 424–25. Like Hegel, Milbank wants to insist that ultimate reality is more like spirit than substance. For a brief discussion of Hegel's view, see Capetz, *God: A Brief History*, 123–24.

But, third, what is also then unclear is the source or relation of creativity between God and these monads. On the one hand, Milbank affirms that "the monads, seeds or ratios . . . self-generate," and that, as finite creatures, they themselves are also "radically creative and differentiating." On the other hand, he maintains that "they do not 'assist' God" in their self-generating or creative endeavor because it is God "who supplies all power and all being." So is Milbank trying to say that the monads only "participate in God" and do not, in any sense, co-create with God? Or, alternatively, is he saying that God is the ultimate source and ground of all creative possibilities and that the finite creative achievements of the world always depend on and take place within God?

Milbank seems to lean toward this latter view in the next paragraph where he, interestingly, contrasts this rich Patristic ontology "(intimated by Eriugena)" with the scholastic views of Aquinas and Scotus, whom, he claims, both mistakenly follow Augustine here. Aquinas and Scotus denied that creatures could be co-creators with God for two reasons. First, following Aristotle, "they [wrongly] thought of making as merely a modification of existing forms, [and] not as the inauguration of radically new 'types' of thing[s]." Second, "they [wrongly] supposed that co-creation implied an 'assistance' to God in the act of creation, whereas, of course, for Christianity only God is commensurate with the bringing about of Being from nothing, in the absolute sense of a 'first' creation, [which is] impossible for creatures." Aquinas and Scotus came to this mistaken conclusion about creaturely assistance to the divine, Milbank reasons,

> because they did not conceive God as internally creative, . . . and therefore failed to see that a creature is *not* primarily something which is, but primarily something which is creative. Seeds *do* cause creatures to be, human beings *do* cause houses, bridges, novels to be, for where are these in nature? . . . It is only the infinity of Being, and a new being without precursors, that creatures do not make. Yet in creating things, creatures do not assist God, for *all* this power/act of a finite creation is created by God.[47]

The mistake of Aquinas and Scotus, Milbank apparently suggests, is that they were wrongly tied to a static ontology of being instead of a dynamic one of becoming; God is the infinite well-spring of creative possibilities, but finite creatures are the actual occasions for the divine creativity to

47. Milbank, *Theology and Social Theory*, 425.

be realized. However, one should note again that Milbank quickly qualifies the creative context of finite things by insisting that they "do not assist God, for *all* this power/act of a finite creation is created by God." By emphasizing creaturely dependence on the divine and by appearing to shy away from any hint of autonomy, Milbank is quite willing to blur the line between infinite and finite, between God and world.

However, when he offers accounts of divine unity and knowledge, Milbank seems to leave room for some sense of creaturely autonomy. God's unity is not a bare simplicity that metaphysically stands over against the diversity of the world. On the contrary, "Unity, in this Christian outlook, ceases to be anything hypostatically real in contrast to difference, and becomes instead only the 'subjective' apprehension of a harmony displayed in the order of the differences, a desire at work in their midst, although 'proceeding' beyond them (as the Holy Spirit)." Unity, Milbank suggests here, is achieved only in the divine subjectivity apprehending and harmonizing the diversity of difference within the world. Drawing again on Dionysius, he describes this harmony or unity as a "transcendental peace which 'overflows in a surplus of its peaceful fecundity' and 'preserving [all things] in their distinctness yet linking them together.'" This notion of divine order, as a process of achieving unity in diversity, must be understood diachronically, not synchronically. In contrast to a static synchronism of divine Being, Milbank claims that "the infinity of God, his never exhausted 'surplus', means that the context for development is always open to revision by the development. The unity, harmony and beauty of the emanation of difference cannot, in consequence, be anticipated in advance, even for God himself." Milbank appears here to reject any traditional notion of divine omniscience—of divine foreknowledge of the future. "As Eriugena realized," declares Milbank, "God's knowledge is not 'before' but *in* the infinity of generation, and this knowledge can only be . . . , as Dionysius says, 'limited', if it is the infinite happening of the new in harmony with what 'precedes' it."[48] In this context, one gets the sense that the "development" of the world has a degree of creative autonomy that keeps the divine infinity "always open to revision" and this means, in turn, that the concrete choices and actualities of the world are unknowable, even to God, until they in fact occur. However, as noted earlier, eternity includes time and is ultimately unchanged by it. Thus, presumably one can also say for Milbank that the

48. Ibid., 428.

specific choices and actualities of the world are eternally known by God. In fact, as we saw above, Milbank says that "God is the infinite series of differences, and what he knows is the infinity of differences."[49] If God *is* the infinite series of particularities, and if God is eternal, then these differences are known eternally as enfolded—but known concretely as unfolded in time. If one asks how eternity can be becoming, Milbank's answer apparently is that "becoming" is an analogical, not a literal, term (I will address this appeal to analogy in my critical assessment).

This appeal to analogy shows up in other ways as well. For instance, Milbank at times seems to imply that creative autonomy adds something novel to the divine experience, something that God values. "For the trinitarian God," he writes,

> does not . . . stand in an indifferent relation to what he creates. God's love for what he creates implies that the creation is generated within a harmonious order intrinsic to God's own being. And only by means of this conception, this admission of some analogous exchange of predicates between God and finitude, can one conceive of an absolute that is *itself* difference, inclusive of all difference.[50]

If one were to understand this exchange of predicates literally or univocally, it would suggest that the finite contributes some creative actuality to the divine experience, which was not actualized before. Moreover, this contribution to the divine experience would be valued or loved by God. In this case, Milbank would be rejecting the traditional notion of divine impassibility—the notion that nothing adds to God's experience; that God does not feel what the world feels. But by appealing to analogy, Milbank seems to want to straddle both sides of the equation—God loves or values what creation gives, yet nothing adds genuine novelty to the divine experience. From another vantage point, this straddling seems to point back to the pantheistic blurring of God and world. On this account, the exchange of predicates signals a commingling of God and world to such an extent that nothing adds to God because all is already God, through and through. It is this reading that seems to be suggested when one turns to Milbank's discussion of incarnation and atonement in *Being Reconciled*.

49. Ibid., 423.
50. Ibid., 429.

There, in developing what he takes to be Aquinas's position, Milbank rejects any notion of incarnation as a "negative" act in the sense of being a means of redress to God to atone for sin and to reconcile the world to God. There is no debt or substitution to be paid for sin, Milbank holds, because God never incurred any loss or change due to sin. Such "negative" views of atonement and incarnation certainly had some pre-Scotist roots, such as in Anselm, but Milbank again judges that "Scotus's Christology" and "ontotheology" contributed to this misguided understanding. In contrast, "Aquinas's Christology" and his theological metaphysics, or "theology . . . in excess of metaphysics," offer a "positive" conception of the "divine-human commencement of forgiveness." Given his realist stand over against nominalism, Milbank further contends that this positive conception must issue in intra-human forgiveness; for divine forgiveness without human forgiveness is "surely . . . no more than nominal."[51] To see how Milbank gets from sin to forgiveness, let us begin with what he describes as the "three absolute impossibilities," namely, the impossibilities of creation, fall, and redemption.

"First of all, there is the impossibility that anything else should exist outside of God, who is replete Being. For this to be possible, God must have gone outside of himself, and yet there is no exterior to God, no sum which might add to his amount." Here we see a clear expression of Milbank's panentheism—there is nothing outside of God, hence all is within God. Moreover, he contends that Aquinas holds this same panentheistic view. "[F]or Aquinas, the creation is not really outside of God."[52] Yet, Milbank also appears here to endorse some traditional version of divine immutability. God "is replete Being," therefore, "no sum . . . might add to his amount." If all is in God and nothing is added, then what is created? This is the first "impossibility." Second is the "impossibility of sin, namely that creatures enjoying to their appropriate degree the absolute, . . . might discover an illusory 'of themselves' wherewith to reject the absolute in the name of something lesser." In agreement with Augustine's notion of sin as privation, Milbank understands sin as "loss," that is, as "the desire of something less." But how did humans ever come to desire the less over the superabundant more? This is why "the first sin that imagined [or contemplated] sin does appear to be a surd." And third is the "impossibility of redemption." Since sin "cuts finite

---

51. Milbank, *Being Reconciled*, 64, 60.
52. Ibid., 62–63, 66.

being off from (infinite) reality, [it] would appear to be without redress, even by that [infinite] reality."[53] If creation involves the impossibility of creating something distinct from God when there can be nothing outside of God, then, in parallel fashion, Milbank apparently surmises that even God could not reconnect that which in fact cuts itself off from the divine. Nevertheless, the Christian story, he submits, does precisely that. In sum, the Christian story seeks to address and overcome these three distinct but interrelated impossibilities.

To shed light on these matters, especially in terms of understanding redemption, Milbank turns to Aquinas:

> For Aquinas, it is possible that God, according to his *potentia absoluta*, might have forgiven us without the incarnation of the Logos. . . . Thomas assures us [in other words] that God had no need to be appeased in order to become reconciled to us and that instead, in himself, he always and eternally was reconciled to us. One can express this in the terms that . . . God does not need to forgive since he goes on giving. For Aquinas, therefore, the Incarnation does not bring about this reconciliation for God, but rather mediates this reconciliation to us, making it effective for us and in us, so ensuring that we, too, are reconciled.[54]

There are at least three important points to note here. First, Milbank contends that Thomas shares his view that God was and is eternally reconciled to the world. Put simply, there was never a breach from God's vantage point. Hence, the divine gift of giving never needed to forgive, because it was never offended or interrupted. It is, in part, his twin affirmations of divine impassibility and divine plenitude that informs Milbank's thinking here. For instance, he says that

> a human sovereign power in some measure suffers what those it represents suffer, but not so God, who is perfectly in act, beyond all suffering. Thus God is so disconnected from all victimage, so impervious to offence, that it seems that he has nothing to forgive. Indeed, . . . Julian of Norwich roundly declared that God does not forgive, since he cannot be offended, but only continues to give, despite our rejection of his gift.[55]

---

53. Ibid., 63.
54. Ibid., 64–65.
55. Ibid., 60.

Second, in his description of Aquinas, notice how Milbank interprets the function of incarnation. For Thomas, the incarnation does not bring about reconciliation but rather is an effective means for mediating it to us. Milbank's use of the term "mediate" here carries two important connotations. On the one hand, it connotes that the incarnation re-presents to us the eternal gift of giving—it does not constitute it. That is to say, it does not launch anything new on the part of God, rather, it discloses to us what was and always is the case, namely, the plenitude of the divine nature. And because the incarnation does that, it serves as an effective means for eliciting in us a response to the divine gift, thereby fostering reconciliation on our part. Milbank reiterates this point by stressing that Aquinas "argues that the actual means of incarnation and atonement adopted for our salvation, while not absolutely necessitated, were nonetheless . . . fitting, suitable for this purpose."[56] They were suitable rather than necessary because they fittingly represent God's nature. On the other hand, "mediate" connotes here Milbank's rejection of any notion of formal autonomy. The divine nature or existence cannot be known apart from the particularity of the incarnation; hence, the reality and grace of the divine plenitude cannot be known apart from the Christian story. So ontologically, the incarnation is not necessary, but epistemologically, it—or some other form of divine revelation—is required for us to know and respond to the divine good.

Third, given his earlier criticisms of Scotus's distinction between God's declared will *(potentia ordinata)* and God's absolute will *(potentia absoluta)*, he is a bit skittish here of possible nominalist interpretations of Aquinas. As Milbank reads him, the incarnation for Thomas lies somewhere in between logical necessity and nominalist contingency. "A certain pleasing *logos* is exhibited here beyond merely capricious arrangement," Milbank remarks, "and yet God is not bound to this order in the same way that he is bound to conclude that $a = a$ and is not *not a*." Notably, Milbank describes Thomas's reference to God's *potentia absoluta* as a "counterfactual invocation," that is, as "an essentially abstract, logical moment, designed to indicate where God is not . . . ineluctably constrained." Such an invocation, he stresses, does not carry any later connotation of absolute caprice—of an ultimate divine whim. In fact,

---

56. Ibid., 65. Again, I borrow the useful distinction between "re-presenting" and "constituting" from Ogden; see my discussion of Ogden in chapter 3.

Milbank's unease with this invocation and the distinction it implies is further evident when he concludes that

> for Aquinas, *all* that God actually does belongs to his *potentia ordinata,* which is not an order of caprice, but itself reflects the eternal divine sense of justice and appropriateness. Therefore, Aquinas's God is "compelled" not only by the absolute exigencies of logical possibility, but also by something one may dub "actual necessity," or the agreeable that appears in the harmonious proportions of an infinite actual order. This is then reflected in the divine economy.[57]

In his realism and resistance to the caprice of nominalism, Milbank's introduces here a distinction between the absolute necessity of logic and the "actual necessity" of the agreeable. Given the representative function of the incarnation, he seems to reason that one can only re-present the true nature of the divine giving within a certain range: plenitude can only be disclosed through some form of boundless giving. In *Theology and Social Theory*, he points toward this "actual necessity" when he asks if "God's 'ultimate' word, expressed in Christ, [is] . . . indissociable from his very being and identical with deity itself? . . . Disconcerting as it may appear," he answers, one must come to recognize "the 'finality' of God's appearance in a life involving suffering and violent death, and [one must recognize] also that in a certain sense God 'has to' be like this, and has not just 'incidentally' chosen this path."[58]

Again in *Being Reconciled*, Milbank proclaims that "it is appropriate that God should draw near to humanity in this most radical and unexpected fashion, because God as infinite and replete cannot be rivaled, and therefore can give himself entirely—even his own divine nature." Milbank points here to one of the defining characteristics of divinity, namely, its unrivaled status. Yet precisely because of this unrivaled status, he suggests that only God can give in such an unrivaled manner as to surpass even God's self. "Here Aquinas is exploiting to the full the mystery of the first theological impossibility, that of Creation. Just because there is no outside to God, God can most freely . . . exceed himself."[59] The tension, which Milbank calls "mystery," is fully revealed

---

57. Milbank, *Being Reconciled*, 65. For a helpful discussion of this distinction, see Oakley, "Absolute and Ordained Power of God."

58. Milbank, *Theology and Social Theory*, 384.

59. Milbank, *Being Reconciled*, 65–66.

in these two sets of affirmations. On the one hand, in traditional or classical fashion, Milbank describes God's being as "replete," which means that nothing can be added. On the other hand, in a more radical reading of the tradition, he talks about the divine unsurpassability in terms of its infinite ability to surpass or "exceed" itself. Only God can surpass God, Milbank concludes, because there is nothing outside of God and nothing that can rival God. But if the self-exceeding is not adding anything new, since the divine is replete, then is the self-exceeding merely again the unfolding of the divine in a Spinozan or Hegelian sense?

Milbank points toward Hegel (and perhaps also the Neoplatonic notion of *theosis*) by emphasizing that the incarnation involves the aim and process of the deification of the finite. "[I]n the Incarnation," he writes, "[God] causes a human creature not just to receive as finite the infinite in due measure, but actually to be . . . God himself, as 'appropriated' to that persona which is the *Logos*. This is not so much a new gift of God to humanity, [but rather] as a making of a human nature also to be the means of absolute uninterrupted [divine] giving." For God to be "all in all," Milbank observes, implies that the diving giving must become embodied and actualized in the human. Likewise, he reads Thomas in this same fashion. In fact, at one point he refers to it as a cautious "'Hegelian' Thomism." In this Hegelian Thomism, as Milbank reports,

> The Incarnation stands higher than deification for Aquinas's understanding, not because it realizes a higher finite goal for the Creation, but because here God's own infinite *telos* in himself has become also the realization (**though incomprehensibly with no real addition to God, and no "real relation" of God to it**, as Thomas puts it) of this particular human nature *in atomo*. This is the case for Aquinas in the *Tertia Pars*, because he recognizes only one *esse* in Christ, which is the divine *esse* itself. For this reason, God gains nothing in glory through the Incarnation, since he gains only himself, which is no gain [emphasis added].[60]

This Hegelian Thomism not only involves the telos of divine self-realization within the world in and through Christ, but in it we also see again the orthodox affirmation of impassibility and the traditional

---

60. Ibid., 67, 71, 69. Milbank points to Michel Corbin as the source of this reading and phrase "Hegelian Thomism." He cites Corbin, *L' Inoui de Dieu: Six Etudes Christologiques* (Paris: Desclée de Brouwer, 1979). For a brief discussion of the notion of *theosis*, see Capetz, *God: A Brief History*, 72.

denial of any "real" or internal relation between God and world. Milbank can only describe this combination as incomprehensible.

In subsequent pages, he reiterates the tension of this incomprehensibility. "One must deliberately refrain," he submits, "from any actual ascription of 'event' as involving change to God: this would be incompatible with his aseity. Nevertheless, the implication of the Chalcedonian doctrine appears to be that God is not only infinite *esse,* outside time, but also the subject of this particular series of events in time." Likewise,

> for Aquinas this [incarnational] event, this arrival, involves nothing new for God: it is not a real relation for him. Thus the human nature of Christ belongs integrally to the *Logos* and its being is only the being of the *Logos,* and yet, to its human attribute, the *Logos,* is not really related. This seems highly strange, yet it is really an outcome of the same old impossibility of something being outside God when there is no outside of God. God for Aquinas is not really related to the Creation, and yet the Creation is real, and really participates in him.[61]

Here again we see traditional characterizations of divinity, such as the denials of any change or real relations, coupled with more radical affirmations of God's participation in time (as the subject of changing events). What is clear here is that, for Milbank, the relations between God and world are only a one-way street. God is not really or internally related to the creation, but the creation is fully related to God in the sense of participating in and depending on the divine. One of the points of difference between Hegel and Milbank is precisely over this question of real or internal relations. In the incarnation, Milbank concludes, "we have seen that the recognition of God as the provider of forgiveness . . . entails that the infinite always was, if certainly not (as for Hegel) really related to the finite, nonetheless eminently fused with it at a certain incomprehensible point of identity." Hegel was willing to grant that God was really related to the finite, Milbank is not. Instead, he insists on the "incomprehensible point of identity," one that can only be told through story, not through a rationally coherent or justified metaphysics. "This need to tell even [the story] of God, since he is also in himself a telling, arises from the mysterious and incomprehensible paradox that God is as originally forgiving (or rather the giver of forgiving) as he is

---

61. Milbank, *Being Reconciled,* 71, 73.

giving."[62] The task of telling this particular story, with its paradoxical counter-ontology and its universal significance, is the defining task of the counter-polis, which is the church.

A Counter-Polis: The Church in the World

At the root of Milbank's theology is a three-way connection between ontology, peace, and the church. "If there is truth," he declares,

> then it is ontological—the fact that there are essences (however complex); the fact that there is a true way for things to be and a way things eternally are. Only in that case does it follow that things may be ultimately compatible with each other, as mere shifting perspectives need not be. If there is truth, then it must apply universally, and the truth of one thing must be compatible with the truth of all other things. But this is peace.[63]

Peace is the condition of ontological truth, which, in turn, is the condition of mutual compatibility and harmonious relations among diverse entities. Hence, one of the central claims of *Theology and Social Theory* is that a true Christian metanarrative must retrieve a vision of history akin to Augustine's *City of God*.[64] For if peace is the tranquility of order, then the peace of the City of God must be fundamentally juxtaposed with the earthly city, which is "the city of violence." As noted earlier, Milbank reads modern social theory—starting with Hobbes and Machiavelli—as accepting conflict as an ontological given. Hence, as "an *altera civitas*," the *Civitas Dei* must have "no logical or causal connection with the city of violence." But, again, this Christian vision of an ultimately peaceful, ontological, and social mode of being is rooted in myth and narrative, not in a rationally justified metaphysics. As Milbank puts it, "the ontological priority of peace over conflict . . . is [a principle] firmly anchored in a narrative, a practice, and a dogmatic faith, not in universal reason."[65]

In giving priority to narrative and rhetoric over reason, Milbank believes that rational arguments, at least in the modern sense of argu-

---

62. Ibid., 74.

63. Ibid., 106.

64. Indeed, James Wetzel describes Milbank's *Theology and Social Theory* "as a postmodern *City of God*." See Wetzel, "Splendid Vices and Secular Virtues," 271.

65. Milbank, *Theology and Social Theory*, 389, 390.

is no salvation. Hauerwas affirms this because, outside the gathered church, there is no community that embodies the virtues and social practices of the God revealed in Jesus Christ. Alternatively, Milbank affirms this because "there is no grace not mediated by the Church (it being understood that the Church, like grace, is everywhere)."[68] Here, one finds a universal church as opposed to a gathered community of "resident aliens." Yet, in another context, Milbank sounds like Hauerwas when he emphasizes the distinctive and even exemplary witness of the church:

> In this fashion a gigantic claim to be able to read, criticize, [and] say what is going on in other human societies, is absolutely integral to **the Christian Church, which itself claims to exhibit the exemplary form of human community**. For theology to surrender this claim, to allow that other discourses—"the social sciences"—carry out yet more fundamental readings, would therefore amount to a denial of theological truth. The *logic* of Christianity involves the claim that the "interruption" of history by Christ and his bride, the Church, is the most fundamental of events, interpreting all other events. And it is *most especially* a social event, able to interpret other social formations, **because it compares them with its own new social practice** [emphasis added].[69]

We see here a strong emphasis on the distinctive witness and social practice of the church, which is centered on peace. The church must not surrender its metanarrative or critical perspective on all forms of discourse, for such surrender would amount "to a denial of theological truth."[70] For Christ and the Church, Milbank urges, are the fundamental events in history—the interrupting and normative events that interpret all other events. As we saw in our last section, the advent of Christ and the Church do not change or affect God, but they do fundamentally alter human history itself.

Milbank rejects those readings of Augustine that "play down [his] explicit identification of the visible, institutional Church with the 'city of God on pilgrimage through this world." Though Milbank acknowledges that Augustine stressed "that many true members of the city of God

---

68. Milbank, *Being Reconciled*, 138.
69. Milbank, *Theology and Social Theory*, 387, 388.
70. Ibid., 388.

ments that do not presuppose grace and revelation as givens, are ultimately coercive in nature. That is, he takes for granted the notion that rational arguments seek to compel assent. And to "compel" is to constrain, force, or oblige; to bring about or evoke by force. Such overt or subtle forms of coercion, needless to say, are antithetical to the Christian vision of peace. Hence, Milbank concludes that Christianity must be committed to the path of rhetoric, not reason. And this rhetorical path to the Good leads to

> the following implication: only [rhetorical] persuasion of the truth can be nonviolent, but truth is only available through persuasion. Therefore truth, and non-violence, have to be recognized simultaneously in that by which we are persuaded. Without attachment to a particular [narrative or rhetorical] persuasion—which we can never *prove* to be either true, or non-violent—we would have no real means to discriminate peace and truth from their opposites.[66]

Milbank is engaged in his own subtle form of syllogistic reasoning here: truth cannot be arrived at by force or coercion; rational argument involves coercion; therefore, truth must be pursued in a nonrational manner, i.e., by means of prior attachment to the rhetoric of a nonviolent narrative. Without such a prior commitment and perspective, he reasons, "we would have no real means to discriminate peace and truth from their opposites." But "an abstract attachment to non-violence," Milbank adds, is "not enough—we need to practice this as a skill, and to learn its idiom. The idiom is built up in the Bible, and reaches its consummation in Jesus and the emergence of the Church."[67] Put simply, the task of the church is to teach, embody, and bear witness to the underlying ontological truth of divine peace.

At times, Milbank sounds very similar to Hauerwas in his ecclesiastical emphasis. Yet, whereas Hauerwas's ecclesiology is influenced by the Mennonite and Anabaptist lens of Yoder, Milbank's is filtered through the Catholic prism of Augustine. This difference is revealed in how each of them interprets the distinctiveness of the church. Whereas Hauerwas emphasizes the distinctive virtues of the gathered community, Milbank emphasizes the sacramental signs of the universal church. For instance, each of them affirms the traditional claim that outside the church, there

66. Ibid., 398.
67. Ibid.

lie outside the bounds of the institutional Church, just as many of the baptized are not true members," he insists that "this does not mean that [Augustine] regards institutional adherence as a secondary and incidental matter." On the contrary, Milbank goes so far as to argue that "the Church itself, as the realized heavenly city, is the *telos* of the salvific process." Again, as we saw earlier, the point of incarnation and redemption is not to change anything in God but, rather, to mediate God's plenitude in and to the world. The church itself, Milbank believes, is the locus of this mediation. This locus ought to be measured and assessed diachronically, not synchronically or spatially. That is, on Milbank's reading of Augustine, "the Church is . . . measured more by endurance through time than by extension through space." By this I take him to mean that the church is true to its calling when it exemplifies enduring witness, not when it simply attains numerical size or geographical dominance. But again, following Augustine rather than Hauerwas, Milbank suggests that this faithful and distinctive witness is not marked so much by virtue as it is by the administering of the sacraments. "What matters is not the cultivation of excellence in the heroic present, which cyclically appears and disappears, but rather the ever-renewed transmission of the signs of love and the bringing to birth of new members from the womb of baptism." In fact, Milbank goes to some lengths to play down the church's pursuit of virtue:

> The goal of the *ecclesia,* the city of God, is not collective glory, as if the city itself were a hero, any more than it is the production of heroic individuals. Instead, it really has no *telos* properly speaking, but continuously *is* the differential sequence which has the goal beyond goal of generating new relationships, which themselves situate and define "persons."[71]

We see here the ecclesiastical import of Milbank's panentheism of plenitude. Because God is replete and impassible, the church has no aim to achieve because it, like the world, has no contribution to make to the divine life. Instead, the church is the fountain of divine peace and plenitude flowing into the world—it is the differential sequence that generates new relationships of peace that situate human beings.

---

71. Ibid., 402, 403, 405.

"How does it help," Milbank proceeds to ask, "to imagine a state of total peace, when we are locked in a world of deep-seated conflict which it would be folly to deny or evade? It helps," he answers,

> because it allows us to unthink the necessity of violence, and [it] exposes the manner in which the assumption of . . . an always prior violence helps to preserve violence in motion. But it helps more, because it indicates that there is a way to act in a violent world which assumes the ontological priority of non-violence, and this way is called "forgiveness of sins."[72]

At first blush this reply sounds more like Niebuhr than Hauerwas, though with a sharper ontological edge than either of them. That is to say, like Niebuhr, Milbank contends that the Christian interpretation of life offers us a different way of thinking about the world because it offers us a fundamentally different ontological vision, i.e., it "allows us to unthink" the dominant assumptions of culture. Whereas Hauerwas wants the church *to be different*, Milbank here initially emphasizes that Christianity enables us *to think differently*. Yet, in the second line, Milbank moves toward Hauerwas by emphasizing that Christianity also indicates a different way of acting in a violent world—a way that assumes the ontological priority of peace and is found in the forgiveness of sins. Though Hauerwas also certainly emphasizes the importance of forgiveness, he is more inclined than Milbank to emphasize the possibility of sanctification and thus to emphasize the distinctive virtues of the Christian community. In contrast, following Augustine, Milbank puts more emphasis on the forgiveness mediated through the sacraments rather than on the embodied virtues of the Christian community per se. "Augustine asserts that, for us, the approach to divine perfection cannot be by any achieved excellence of virtue, but only through forgiveness. This does not," Milbank concludes, "imply a protestant resignation to sinfulness." What it does imply is that given the persistence of sin, "there is only one way to respond to [sin] which would not itself be sinful and domineering, and that is to anticipate heaven, and act as if . . . sin was not there, by offering reconciliation." In short, either the church enacts the vision of the heavenly city as a forgiving community or it contributes to the violence of the world.[73]

72 Ibid., 411.
73. Ibid., 411, 433–34.

Milbank admits, nonetheless, that things are not quite so dichotomous on the ground. On the one hand, as noted, he eschews rational justification in part because he presumes that rational arguments are inherently coercive, and thus contribute to the condition of sin and violence; hence, he espouses the priority of rhetoric over reason. On the other hand, however, his willingness to follow Augustine's ecclesiology also leads him to accept some aspects of Augustine's "bare-knuckled" realism, which perhaps leads to some tensions within Milbank's own position. For Augustine, he reports,

> the division coercion/non-coercion was the important criterion in separating the political from the ecclesial. It is true that Augustine increasingly saw the necessity for the Church as well as the *imperium* to use coercive methods, and that he distinguishes the two . . . according to the purpose that coercion has in mind. However, the purpose of ecclesial coercion is peace, and this can only in the long-term be attained by non-coercive persuasion, because the free consent of will is necessary to this goal. Augustine admits, correctly in my view, the need for some measure of coercion in some circumstances, because freedom . . . itself is not the goal, and sometimes people can be temporarily blind and will only be prevented from permanent self-damage when they are forced into some course of action, or prevented from another. Such coercive action remains in itself dangerous, . . . but this risk is offset by the possibility that the recipient can later come to understand and retrospectively consent to the means taken. Such action may not be "peaceable," yet can still be "redeemed" by retrospective acceptance, and so contribute to the final goal of peace.[74]

In this revealing passage, Milbank explicitly accepts ecclesial forms of coercion as necessary means for pursuing the goal of peace or non-coercion. Whereas Hauerwas thinks that peace is a virtue that must be illustrated in the life and actions of the Christian community, Milbank views peace as an ultimate goal to be pursued, which may require some coercion along the way. Indeed, while Hauerwas, Porter, and MacIntyre all affirm the need for authority, Milbank explicitly acknowledges that this appeal to authority entails some form of coercion. What distinguishes worldly coercion from justified Christian coercion, Milbank suggests, is their differing ultimate goals. Worldly coercion seeks peace

---

74. Ibid., 418.

as, at best, a mere balance of power and, at worst, as self-assertion and domination in the guise of peace. In contrast, Christian coercion pursues the goal of true ontological peace and uses coercion as a heuristic device in pursuit of this noble end.

In *Being Reconciled*, Milbank makes the point even more sharply by comparing religious violence with modern liberalism and democracy. Speaking of the religious use of violence in the past, Milbank contends that sometimes the church "*should* have done just this: it was a matter of proper self-belief. The liberal enlightenment also pursued a vision of universal peace and also defended it coercively." The critical difference between them, he argues, is that liberalism accepts violence and conflict as endemic to reality itself and pursues freedom without purpose. In contrast, religious "violence enacted in the name of a substantive *telos* can more plausibly pose as essentially educational, as a self-denying coercive ordinance. The real point here," he continues,

> is, that although Christianity . . . certainly requires in the end *free consent* to the truth, it does not fetishize this freedom merely as a correct mode of approach; truth is what most matters, and moreover a *collective* commitment to the truth, since truth itself is the shareable and harmonious. Thus in certain circumstances, the young, the deluded, those relatively lacking in vision require to be coerced as gently as possible. Anyone professing to be shocked by this is, I submit, naively unreflective about what in reality he already accepts (for example in the secular schooling of the young) and is thinking in over-individualistic and over-voluntaristic terms that are ontologically impossible.[75]

Even Milbank recognizes that readers might be "shocked" by what he says here, namely, because he justifies religious violence and coercion as proper steps to bring about "a *collective* commitment to the truth." Free consent to the truth is the ultimate goal, he proclaims, but freedom itself is not the goal. This is the "fetishizing" mistake of liberalism. On the contrary, truth is what counts and a collective affirmation of it is the real aim. To draw again on Augustinian terms, Milbank is willing to coercively impose intellectual assent in the hope that such coercion will eventually bring about real assent or existential faith on the part of each individual and the collective whole. This discussion clearly indicates that Milbank, at least explicitly, does not believe in rational persuasion

---

75. Milbank, *Being Reconciled*, 38.

or modern liberal notions of discourse, such as respecting and protecting the autonomy and free consent of each human person. If one needs to use coercive means to help others to see the truth, then so be it. There appears to be an underlying irony or paradox in Milbank's comparison between Christianity and liberalism. On the one hand, he claims that liberalism accepts violence and coercion at a deep ontological level but eschews them at the epistemological level in the name of protecting freedom and autonomy. On the other hand, he claims that Christianity rejects violence and coercion at the ontological level but accepts them at the epistemological level in pursuit of attaining a collective affirmation of the deeper ontological truth.

Milbank identifies "the young" and "the deluded" as those in need of gentle coercion. Even liberalism, he suspects, is willing to acknowledge its own subtle forms of coercion in educating the young and caring for the mentally ill. Yet, the real heart of Milbank's position is his further claim that "those relatively lacking in vision require to be coerced as gently as possible." Who decides who is lacking in vision and who decides what constitutes a lack of vision? Furthermore, who decides what defines gentle coercion, especially if religious violence is sometimes appropriate? Milbank looks to the ecclesial authority of the Bishop as the final arbiter of such questions. In agreement with Jean-Luc Marion, Milbank states that "the Bishop is the true theologian." Such a view is perceived as pernicious or "authoritarian," Milbank submits, only "under an erroneous understanding of the relationship of the Bishop to the Eucharist, to the word of God and to his *cathedra*, which is at once his teaching office and also literally the place where he sits and presides, usually a city of long-standing."[76] Instead, if one recovers a proper medieval "triadic" view, one which properly interrelates (1) the eucharist and sacraments, (2) the church and ecclesial authority, and (3) scripture, then the embracing of the Bishop's authority is not so authoritarian as it sounds to modern ears. In Milbank's words, we ought to recognize that the

> high mediaeval model offers us a much better understanding of the relation of the Bishop to teaching and so to theological reflection. Theology is answerable to the Bishop as the occupant of the *cathedra* and as President at the Eucharist. But this

---

76. Ibid., 123. Milbank cites Marion, *God Without Being*, trans. Thomas A Carlson (Chicago: University of Chicago Press, 1991) 139–61.

> means that the theologian is primarily answerable, not so much to a Church hierarchy in its synchronic spatiality—this is all too modern—but rather to a hierarchical, educative *manuductio* of the faith down the ages. Equally he is answerable to a specific locality, ... such that his sense of perpetuating a history must be combined with his sense of ... mapping a geography.[77]

Milbank argues here that we must recover a diachronic notion of authority, one that conceives of authority as the proper reenactment of the past, rather than viewing it as some form of contemporary imposition. By handing down to us the living tradition of the past, Milbank reasons, the Bishop embodies and offers us an educative guide to the true faith. But along with being a conduit to the past, Milbank admits that the Bishop is also a contemporary voice—one holding office in a current locality. In short, it is still the current Bishop who decides what counts as clear vision or good reasons. Hence, as Milbank himself puts it, "theology, therefore, is answerable to reason precisely in so far as it is answerable to the Church."[78]

Milbank envisions this form of ecclesial authority as ultimately an historical approximation of "divine democracy." In contrast to modern liberal conceptions, which he views as all forms of a *modus vivendi* overlaying a deeper ontological acceptance of violence, true or divine democracy involves hierarchy and authority in the service of a greater ontological truth. Based on his Anglo-Catholic reading of the tradition, Milbank conceives of a conciliar rather than a papal model of episcopal authority. Drawing on Nicholas of Cusa and Augustine, Milbank argues that "from the *highest* perspective, all that is created is equal.... Since the true ontological character of the Church, following Augustine, is peace and harmony, which for Cusa is extended into *discors concordia*, the first ruling principle within the Church is consensus. Not of course ... majority rule, but absolute consensus." So, on one level of a conciliar model, a democratic consensus of equality is envisioned. Yet, on another level, such a model concomitantly affirms the necessity of hierarchical authority. Milbank describes this tension in relation to divine democracy:

> So the principle of hierarchical ascension guards truth against democracy, but the more ascension is enacted, the more also

77. Milbank, *Being Reconciled*, 124, 126.
78. Ibid., 133.

> democracy is implemented in the truth. It is not that democracy is a compromise for here and now: it is rather that it can only finally arrive in the perfection of *concordantia* as deification. To eternalize democracy, and maintain its link with excellence rather than the mutual concessions of baseness, deification as the doctrine of the offer of equality with God is required.[79]

This passage reveals Milbank at his most Platonic or Neoplatonic; he juxtaposes the excellence of an eternalized democracy with the baseness and mutual concessions of a compromised democracy for the here and now. There is no Niebuhrian call here for democracy as a necessary means for the pursuit of relative justice within history. On the contrary, only through the recognition and acceptance of the church's hierarchical authority, Milbank posits, can the world glimpse the true "divine democracy" of perfect concord. The more we pursue modern liberal and equalitarian aims, the more we move away from true democracy. Conversely, the more we embrace a properly understood ecclesial authority, the more we approach a true understanding of democracy. The authority of the church is a prerequisite because the church itself is the embodiment of "deification" in the world. This goes back to Milbank's Hegelian Thomism; the church does not have a telos, rather it is the telos—the church is the fountain of divine plenitude and peace flowing into the world. This is one illustration of how Milbank thinks that his postmodern reclamation of a medieval past is meant to save modernity—in this case, saving democracy.

Citing Nicholas of Cusa's apocalyptic and eschatological vision of the twenty-first century—writing in 1433, he "gave the world 600 more years"—Milbank conjectures that Cusa "anticipated in a sense both globalization and the end of Christendom. Yet this disastrous era is also for him precisely the time in which a conciliar and democratic ideal that will truly reflect the Trinity can at last be achieved on earth. Disaster will make us see more truly." In sum, Milbank darkly yet hopefully concludes that a bleak outlook for the twenty-first century "can be a time of meaningful realization of deified democracy."[80]

---

79. Ibid., 128, 132.
80. Ibid., 133.

Typological Analysis

Commitment to Intelligibility (I+)

As a professor of philosophical theology, Milbank and his version of RO are committed to intelligibility, at least in a partial sense. That is, given his commitment to offering a negative critique of modern thought, he is committed to making a case that can be understood by others in the academy and the wider society. This is apparent from the opening words of *Theology and Social Theory* when he declares: "This book is addressed both to social theorists and to theologians. To social theorists I shall attempt to disclose the possibility of a sceptical demolition of modern, secular social theory." In the preface to the second edition of this work, Milbank echoes this point. Looking back, he reflects that this work was written "out of the conviction that a theological vision alone could challenge the emerging hegemony of neo-liberalism. . . . I sought to show [a broad academic audience] why . . . a Catholic Christian account of reality might be entertained as the most finally persuasive one."[81] It is evident from these two passages that Milbank wants RO's perspective and critique to be heard and understood by an audience beyond as well as within the church. In order to do this, he recognizes that he must offer an intelligible and plausible critique. As he states elsewhere, RO does not "oppose all apologetic[s]. Indeed, . . . it tends to start with some non-specifically Christian category such as peace, gift, liturgy, motion, beauty, or whatever—and then argue that only Christian thought and practice safeguards the purity of this category. . . . [T]here is no sheerly Christian language which will not be somewhat understood by non-Christians."[82] In pursuing and formulating this negative apologetic, Milbank is not averse to adopting postmodern language and tools, such as those found in historicist and deconstructionist strategies. For instance, in critiquing the modern affirmations of self-possession and self-government in relation to eudaimonia, luck, and the moral life, Milbank writes: "I now want to show (drawing freely on [Robert] Spaemann, Derrida, and Bernard Williams) how both notions are subject to inner dialectical collapse (or deconstruction), in a fashion that concerns pre-

---

81. Milbank, *Theology and Social Theory*, 1; Milbank, "Preface to the Second Edition," xi.

82. Milbank, "Programme of Radical Orthodoxy," 37.

cisely their attempts to manage and control 'fortune.'"[83] Smith concurs with this assessment when he says, "methodologically, RO finds its voice [of critique] in the discourses of contemporary continental thought. ... [It is especially] articulated in the language of—and in response to—the critical insights of contemporary critical theory haling from the Continent."[84]

Yet, when it comes to articulating his constructive theological vision, Milbank's commitment to intelligibility begins to wane or at least becomes much more ambiguous. That is, like Niebuhr, Milbank appears to treat his negative critique and his positive theological vision in different ways. In the case of Niebuhr, this is done in terms of differing commitments to credibility; with Milbank, we see it in terms of his differing commitments to intelligibility. This difference or ambiguity surfaces in his discussion of premodern theological sources, which of course is where he turns for his positive theological vision. "[T]he Fathers and early-to high-Scholastics," he claims, "made little sharp division between exposition of the faith upon the basis of its own suprarational assumptions, and discursive developments of this faith that are to a degree [intelligible and] convincing even to those outside faith's circle. Thus I, [again], do not apologise for residual apologetics."[85] Milbank distinguishes here the internal suprarational bases of Christian faith and some discursive expositions of this faith "that are to a degree" intelligible and potentially convincing "to those outside faith's circle." On my reading, this distinction describes the different ways that Milbank articulates his negative critique and his positive theological expression. Put simply, he is much more reluctant to adopt non-Christian language to express his theological vision than he is in critiquing the errors and failures of modernity. For instance, unlike Niebuhr, who is willing to forge a modern distinction between primitive and permanent myth in order to analyze and express the character of Christian faith, Milbank is unwilling to use any such cultural category to make theology understandable to those outside the church. Indeed, as he declares in *The Word Made Strange*, "any 'contemporary garb' for Christian truth is of course the most puerile form of betrayal."[86] Such attempts to articu-

83. Milbank, *Being Reconciled*, 142.
84. Smith, *Introducing Radical Orthodoxy*, 68.
85. Milbank, "Programme of Radical Orthodoxy," 37.
86. Milbank, *Word Made Strange*, 1.

late Christian claims in contemporary categories are a form of betrayal because they do not recognize the fundamental error and illusion of modern secularity. Put simply, modernity itself is based on its own misguided theological assumptions going back to Scotus; there is no terminology that is not ultimately theological in some form, Milbank reasons. This is what modernity lost sight of and this is the error of all attempts to translate the gospel into more accessible terms.

For his part, Milbank is seeking to find a third alternative between a modernist commitment to intelligibility, such as found in Gustafson and Niebuhr, and a strong rejection of intelligibility (theology as an internal discourse only), as found in Hauerwas and Barth. Yet, Milbank's third alternative is also different from Porter's approach as well. This difference arises, I judge, from the fact that Milbank's reading of the Christian tradition is shaped by the supernaturalizing lens of de Lubac while Porter's is not. In other words, given this supernaturalizing lens, Milbank's reading of Augustine, Aquinas, and others does not lend itself to intelligibility to those outside the church—to those who do not start off with presuppositions of supernatural grace and revelation. In contrast, even though Porter works intentionally from within the Thomistic tradition, she thinks that theology ought to have at least a semi-open door policy toward outside voices—a policy that can at least partly learn from and draw on non-theological sources. Yet, when it comes to speaking theologically, Milbank comes closer to Hauerwas and Barth in adopting a more closed-door stance. He does so, again, because he believes that any attempt to translate the gospel into nontheological terms participates in the fundamental error and illusion of modern secularity. Hence, Christianity can only express its comprehensive metaphysical vision (and its metacritique of all disciplines) from within its own grace-filled or revelatory framework. Smith sums up RO's hard-line resistance to a broader intelligibility as follows:

> RO is advocating a distinctly theological engagement with the world—and the academy that investigates this world—undergirded by the belief that the way to engage the contemporary world is not by trying to demonstrate a correlation between the gospel and cultural values but rather *by letting the gospel confront these (apostate) values*. . . . Because of this conviction, RO has (in)famously eschewed "dialogue" with secular disciplines. Unlike correlationist strategies that defer the "truth" of the natural sphere to secular sciences . . . , *RO claims that there is not a*

> single aspect of human existence or creation that can be properly understood or described apart from the insights of revelation. ... Therefore, Radical Orthodoxy defers to no experts and engages in no dialogues because it does not recognize other valid points of view outside the theological [italics added].[87]

Commitment to Credibility (C-)

This closed-door approach obviously has implications for the question of trying to make theological claims credible. If one does not seek to make theology's positive claims more broadly intelligible, then neither is one committed to making them more broadly convincing. And this is certainly the case with Milbank. In *Being Reconciled* he explicitly addresses this issue in the form of a question:

> A contemporary way of putting this question would be to ask, should theology owe its primary allegiance to academic standards or to the Church community? Should it be ... primarily a "public discourse" answerable to the critical norms and liberal values of free society in the West, or should it be [answerable to] the faith of the Church seeking understanding, according to a logic indissociable from this faith?[88]

Before answering this question, Milbank considers and dismisses attempts to find "a compromise" between these two alternatives. On the one hand, these attempts at compromise rightly recognize that "the [modernist] notion of a contextless reason, without presuppositions and affective practical commitments, is a fiction ... [and therefore that] ... a well-established community and tradition may undertake to articulate its own implicit reasonings." Yet, on the other, in order to avoid theology being relativistic and "merely self-regarding," such attempts try to "subject [theology] to critical reflections coming from external sources." Though Milbank does not specifically mention MacIntyre here, he is implicitly criticizing his approach, along with other "semi-Hegelian solutions." As we have seen, MacIntyre and Porter seek to pursue an indirect form of rational validation through the dialectical

---

87 Smith, *Introducing Radical Orthodoxy*, 69–70. Smith cites "Radical Orthodoxy: Twenty-four Theses," thesis 5 as the source behind this description. In response to my query, Smith indicated that this was an unpublished document that circulated around Cambridge in the mid-1990s; email, 10/2/07.

88. Milbank, *Being Reconciled*, 109.

engagement of different traditions. Hence, they are willing to subject theology's claims indirectly to external sources through the dialectical process of comparative engagement. But such an effort, Milbank claims, "leaves us in no better plight.... The idea that a tradition will edge towards the universal through the outworking of contradiction [or dialectical engagement], ... is itself contradictory." Such efforts to forge a compromise, he argues, fail because one cannot finally overcome the "ineliminably subjective" givenness of a tradition. "One remains [ultimately] inside a tradition."[89]

Milbank's implicit criticism of MacIntyre here is made explicit in *Theology and Social Theory*. There, in chapter eleven, he offers an extended critique of MacIntyre's pursuit of rational dialectics. "[I]n contrast to most critiques of MacIntyre," opines Milbank, "I do not find him *sufficiently* relativistic or historicist.... There is for me no method, no mode of argument that charts us smoothly past the Scylla of [rationalist] foundationalism and the Charybdis of [relativistic] difference." MacIntyre's error, in other words, is that he still trying to pursue rational dialectics in order to avoid relativism rather than accepting the non-rational and relativistic mode of rhetoric; but such a rational justification cannot be offered. "A solution is only really possible," proclaims Milbank, "in terms of a tradition like Christianity, which starkly links particular to universal by conceiving its relationship to transcendence in a rhetorical fashion." This *logos* of rhetoric gives "pride of place to opinion *(doxa)*, testimony *(marturia)*, and persuasion *(pistis)*" rather than to reason and argument. Sounding like Hauerwas here, Milbank claims that "we can [only] *persuade* people—for reasons of 'literary taste'—that Christianity offers a much better story." MacIntyre's mistake is that he is not "content to leave the matter at this point of saying that one might embrace by 'faith' a particular ethos because of its persuasive power of attraction, while at the same time maintaining the universal rightness for humanity of this way of life. Instead, [he] is still interested in a mode of dialectical validation for narrative preference." As we have seen, MacIntyre thinks that through the comparative engagement of traditions one can have good dialectical reasons for recognizing the superiority of one tradition and, thus, good reasons for abandoning another. But Milbank contends that such an encounter is ultimately "a clash of rhetorics," and "'rhetorical victories'" are based only on the

---

89. Ibid., 109–10.

appeal of narratives and not on an appeal to some supposed superior rationality. Put simply, story "really *is* the [only] argument for the tradition (a perilous argument indeed, which may not prove persuasive at all)." "Hence, there is a *questionableness* about every switch of tradition, which escapes [MacIntyre's] dialectical adjudication. What triumphs is simply the persuasive power of a new narrative."[90]

Overall, it is clear that for Milbank "the universal mythos" of the Christian ontological vision is and must remain "an alternative *logos* to the *logos* of reason." In part, what drives him away from even MacIntyre's indirect approach to rational credibility is Milbank's total rejection of the substantive conclusions of modernity and his insistence on the need for the comprehensive metaphysical vision of Christianity. And because he assumes that any mode of formal autonomy presupposes substantive autonomy, he rejects all forms of seeking to make theology rationally credible. "Theology, therefore, is answerable to reason precisely [and only] in so far as it is answerable to the Church." The divine plenitude, which is the source of all things, can only be recognized and known through the revelation and practices of the Church. As Milbank puts it at one point, "the esoteric aspect [of the Church] is mystical theology, which is theology pure and simple; theology as experience and discourse that is [only] possible through reception of the Eucharist."[91]

Absence of Metaphysics (AM-)

For all of his resistance to a commitment to credibility and for all of his mixed- commitment to intelligibility, there is no doubt that Milbank is one of the few modern or contemporary theologians who rejects the absence of metaphysics by seeking to bring theology's ontological and metaphysical claims back to center stage. Though there were "Atheists for Reinhold Niebuhr," and though perhaps one can imagine "Secularists for Porter," one cannot fathom the notion of "Atheists for Milbank." This is because, unlike Gustafson, Niebuhr, Hauerwas, or Porter, Milbank seeks to re-center theology around its fundamental metaphysical claims about the reality and necessity of God. In saying this, one must again distinguish between what Milbank considers to be the misguided approach to metaphysics, which has dominated

90. Milbank, *Theology and Social Theory*, 327–28, 329, 328, 330, 339, 347, 346.
91. Milbank, *Being Reconciled*, 170, 133, 108.

since the late-medieval legacy of Scotus, and the proper Christian Neoplatonic approach, which he seeks to reclaim from the Patristic tradition stretching from Augustine to Aquinas. But once this clarification is made clear, then one can see that what lies at the heart of Milbank's theology is an attempt to reconnect the world and all knowledge to its ontological ground in God. "If there is truth," Milbank declares, "then it is ontological." One of the great mistakes of the late medieval period was the attempt "to purge theology itself of an essential metaphysical detour through a cosmic vision of the participatory reflection of the divine essence in the cosmos." By moving away from a metaphysics of participation, theology lost the essential connection of all things to God. Moreover, this misguided move also pulled the doctrine of God away from its biblical roots. "[T]he metaphysical cosmology of the high Middle Ages was thoroughly informed by, and transformed through, the Biblical legacy. When this metaphysics was lost, with the nominalists, it was not on the basis of a rediscovery of a Biblical God"—on the contrary, it led to a loss of this God.[92]

In essence, an authentic and vibrant Christian theology, Milbank concludes, can only be recovered when it reasserts the centrality of a proper metaphysics. For too long, theology has been mute because it failed to recognize this. After first falling under the wrong metaphysics, it then allowed itself to fall under the spell of Kant and others who maintained that all metaphysical claims, including those of theology, must be left backstage—beyond the scope of reason and serious attention. But this fateful move only contributed to the dominance of secularism—to a world without ultimate depth or meaning. "For several centuries now," observes Milbank and his RO colleagues, "secularism has been defining and constructing the world. It is a world in which the theological is either discredited or turned into a harmless leisure-time activity of private commitment."[93] To make theology a serious discipline again, it must recover its metaphysical voice. To be sure, Milbank does not seek to rationally justify these metaphysical claims. As is clear, he thinks they can only be rhetorically persuasive, not rationally convincing. And in this limited sense, putting aside for a moment their vast differences, one could perhaps say that Milbank agrees with Kant on this specific

---

92. Ibid., 106, 116, 119. Milbank comfortably uses the terms "metaphysics" and "ontology" to describe his own view in the "Preface to the Second Edition," xvi.

93. Milbank, et al., "Suspending the Material," 1.

point, namely, that metaphysical claims cannot be rationally justified. Of course, from Milbank's perspective, Kant says this from his mistaken attempt to safeguard the limits of a secular reason whereas Milbank is trying to undermine such a reason altogether.

In fact, in his more recent writings, Milbank now suggests that true reason is and can be only grounded in a theistic ontology of peace. In response to critics, he now holds that theological and ontological claims are not "'merely' persuasive." In granting this, he says,

> I do not, however, need "criteria" for persuasion, else it would not be truth that persuades. Since truth is also the good and good is also peace and harmony, it is the latter which persuade. Whom would they not persuade? If they are not so persuaded, then speech (the *logos*) falls silent.
>
> But, my critics will protest, here it is a matter of being persuaded of *their ultimate reality*. And do I not seem always to say that one *may* equally opt for [choosing] the ultimacy of [a different metanarrative] . . . ?
>
> Here I feel I can now go a little bit further. To opt for truth and peace is also to opt *for reason*—for the ultimate reality of reason. If peace is the ultimate reality, then reason sinks its roots into being; it goes all the way down. Reason allows that the world we inhabit is to a degree real . . . since it shares in the real-of-itself. It reveals that all the actuality of this world and all its potentialities . . . are given "to be" by an infinite actuality of "to be." And this provides a genuine ontological difference between what "is" of itself [God] and what merely exists as granted a contingent being from this ultimate source.
>
> Since reason goes all the way down in this way, our reasoning is not epiphenomenal. . . .
>
> . . . [Yet,] [b]etween the ultimate ontological truth of reason and unreason, only persuasion can [still] choose. But only the persuasion of the ultimate truth of reason is rational—all the way down.
>
> So the historical lure of love [embodied in the Church] is also the permanent witness of the understanding.[94]

Here we see Milbank in a combined Platonic and particularist mode. The lure of the Good or the true "Sun" does not need any reasons or criteria to justify it: either one understands it, and therefore one does not need any further reasons, or one does not understand it, and there

---

94. Milbank, "Invocation of Clio," 41, 42.

is nothing else to say. That is, either one is attracted by the lure of peace and harmony or one is not and, if not, there are no justificatory reasons that could foster this receptivity. But if one chooses peace, Milbank holds, one is also choosing truth and reason—a reason that is ontologically grounded in being itself. One is on the side of reason if one has made the proper choice in relation to being. Yet, this reason can only be chosen in response to and exemplified in the rhetorical practices and witness of a particular form of life, namely, the Church. So the recovery of theology's metaphysical voice is ultimately dependent on the particularist and historical witness of the Church and, only subsequently or secondarily, on reason itself.

Autonomy of Ethics (AE-)

Given his wholesale rejection of autonomy, it should come as no surprise that Milbank rejects the modern attempt to define the moral good independently of the question of God. In contrast to Gustafson's nod toward the possibility of a secularistic ethic, and in contrast to Porter's partial drift in this direction, for Milbank there is no ambiguity when it comes to the autonomy of ethics. A nontheistic ethic is just as illusory as the notion of a secular space or public square. To put it "in Kierkegaardian terms," says Milbank, "the Good is only possible beyond the ethical, in the religious realm." For Milbank, this religious realm must ultimately be articulated in ontological or metaphysical terms. Every attempt to define the moral or good independently of being itself, which is the divine plenitude, ends up with merely a fictional ethic. For instance, a merely "willed good" in the Kantian sense "has only an 'ironic' fictional status—and in the end no one acts in the name of a fiction. This is one crucial reason," continues Milbank, "why there cannot really be a *secular* [moral] theory: secularity will not see being as such as good and so will have to identify the Good in terms other than the full presence of the actual." Returning to what he said above about reason and being, Milbank suggests here that the secular, in its attempt to define the ethical apart from God, ultimately chooses unreason because it does not recognize being as such as the true ground of the moral good.[95]

On the one hand, all attempts to pursue an autonomous ethic are misguided for the reasons just noted. Yet, if I understand Milbank cor-

---

95. Milbank, *Being Reconciled*, 138, 16.

rectly, he also thinks that all such attempts are also implicitly operating in terrain already informed by the theological tradition. "[N]o natural beatitude [or ethic] will be concluded to," submits Milbank,

> save under the promptings of an explicit orientation to the supernatural.... What I mean by this is that all the traces of "wisdom" on which philosophy might build in our modern world do not stand simply "outside" Christian tradition, as far as this tradition is concerned. All ethical topics, for example, are marked by the passage of the gospel through the world, and even when philosophy appeals to the Greeks, it appeals to a legacy which is taken up, in part and in places, within the New Testament itself, and thereby is now a constituent element of Christianity.[96]

If Christianity has already covered this terrain in some form and if the moral good cannot be properly identified apart from being itself, then "no secularization of Christian ethics . . . is [genuinely] possible" in either form or content.[97] Hence, an adequate ethic must be Christian, insists Milbank, and it must contain at least three key elements.

First, it must offer a genuine "hope that [true] community is possible, that people and objects can analogically blend [harmoniously] beyond identity or difference, though we can never prove such a possibility *a priori* or *a posteriori*. We can only receive instances that we judge to constitute such blending and seek, in hope, to perpetuate them." The hopeful pursuit of such community requires love or charity, which "is neither simply eudaemonistic nor 'other-regarding.'" Instead, it is an "ecstatic" love, one that "passes *through* death" based on a trust that, in our participation in God, death does not have the last word. Such trust engenders a "self-less" love that is not "egoistic or [merely] self-sacrificial." In short, it is a love that seeks the good of the whole, which is inclusive of the self but not defined by the self.[98]

Second, an adequate ethic must recognize "a universal tragic condition" without ontologizing this condition. To ontologize this condition is to undermine the good of being itself by rendering conflict and violence as metaphysical givens, thus, implicitly making them normative. This was the mistake of Hegel and the rest of modern thought, contends Milbank. In this case, ethics is defined only reactively—only as a

96. Ibid., 118.
97. Ibid., 148.
98. Ibid., 148, 149.

"first-aid" response to this ontological conflict. Instead, "one needs the myth of the Fall in order to think a genuine Good, which to be non-reactive can only be an original plenitude." Reminiscent of Kierkegaard and Niebuhr, Milbank argues that the Fall must not be defined principally as the "doing of something bad" but rather as a fundamental *"refusal...* [to give] with joyful uncertainty in faith" and trust. "Here the Fall is not an act, but rather a first mistrusting of the joyfully confident 'risk' and uncertainty constitutive of the field of action" itself.[99]

Third, and finally, an adequate ethic requires the "hope for resurrection." In any secularistic ethic, which accepts the finality of tragedy and loss, "there *cannot* be any [truly] ethical, not even in any degree." This is the case, reasons Milbank, because in such a view, "death, [and] the experience of loss, contaminates our wills; this leads in turn to more barriers, more wars, more loss. Loss is ineradicable, and so we tend to assume that ethics is a sort of maximum possible minimization of loss." In contrast, only an ethic grounded in a hope where nothing is ultimately lost can engender the proper disposition of the will to foster action that breaks the cycle of violence and conflict. "Hence hope, hope that it may be given to me in the next moment to act well, is inseparable from hope that there may be universal acting-well, and at last a non-futile mourning; to be ethical therefore is to believe in the Resurrection, and somehow to participate in it. And outside this belief and participation there is, quite simply, no 'ethical' whatsoever."[100]

Critical Assessment

What makes Milbank's thought so refreshing and valuable is its retrieval of the metaphysical question to the forefront of the theological stage. For much of modern and contemporary theology, as we have seen illustrated in Gustafson, Niebuhr, Hauerwas, and Porter, this question has remained "recessive, sinking into an unexpressed background." The importance of this question, nevertheless, has always remained lurking behind the scenes, "giving a tonality to all that happens."[101] Milbank's insight is to recognize that truth is ultimately ontological and, therefore,

---

99 Ibid., 149, 150.

100. Ibid., 150, 148.

101. I am borrowing these descriptive phrases from Whitehead's apt account of how past ideas remain related to current modes of thought. Whitehead, *Essays in Science and Philosophy*, 24.

that theology cannot recover its authentic voice until it explicitly reasserts and develops its central metaphysical claims. For instance, he recognizes that most modern theologians, including Barth, have remained under the spell of Kant, which has cut theology off from its metaphysical roots. Furthermore, he recognizes that theology must challenge the substantive autonomy of modernity, which implies that the world can be coherently understood apart from the metaphysical question of God. Indeed, part of his insight is to recognize the need for theology to affirm some version of panentheism. To assert or imply that the world is metaphysically outside of God, as classical theism has tended to do, always leaves the door open for a materialist and secularistic metaphysic. In the history of philosophy, thinkers like Berkeley, Hegel, and others have recognized this and have sought, in their own ways, to counteract it. Milbank and RO have to sought join this effort by retrieving a premodern ontology stretching from Augustine to Aquinas. Yet, for all of Milbank's insights, I have serious reservations about the formulation of his metaphysical vision and about his attempt to assert this vision in the name of rhetoric over reason. I will address each of these in turn.

I have described Milbank's metaphysics as a "panentheism of plenitude." This description is meant to capture both the more radical modes of his thought as well as the more traditional elements. At times, in his more panentheistic moments, Milbank takes positions that are akin to the panentheism of Whitehead and Hartshorne. This is the case, for example, when he eschews a metaphysics of substance in favor of an organic monadology, or when he denies divine foreknowledge, or when he affirms novelty in the world. This resemblance is also evident when he affirms an unactualized potential or surplus in God, or when he affirms the self-surpassing nature of divinity, or when he describes the unity of the world in terms of God's subjective apprehension of the totality of diverse things. Moreover, even his christology at times offers interesting parallels with process thinkers like Ogden, such as when Milbank asserts that the incarnation mediates or re-presents to us what has always been true of God rather than being a new and constitutive change in God's relation to the world. In a similar vein, Milbank holds that the life of suffering revealed in Christ re-presents to us the true nature of God's love rather than being merely an incidental or nominalistic means chosen by the divine. Yet, at other times, Milbank hits more traditional or classical notes with equal or greater vigor. That is, just as he affirms time and temporal sequence, he holds to eternity as the inclusive category; just as he affirms unactualized potential in God, he maintains that God is pure act; just as he alleges that the world exists within God, he claims that God is not internally related to the world; just as he affirms that the world involves change and difference, he insists that nothing ever adds to God; just as he affirms creative novelty in the world, he asserts divine impassibility. Summarily put, God is replete Being, according to Milbank, therefore nothing ever adds to the divine sum.

Taken as a whole, I judge that Milbank's metaphysical and theistic formulations are at best unstable, and at worst incoherent. As we have seen, even he at times describes his position as incomprehensible and mysterious. He does not see this as a problem, however, precisely because he entrusts his position to rhetoric rather than reason. His underlying error, it seems to me, is his total disavowal of any form of autonomy. In the name of reaffirming theology and denying secularism, he runs his panentheism aground on the rocks of pantheism and runs his rhetoric of peace aground on the rocks of coercive authority.

It is clear that Milbank wants to reject any form of substantive autonomy, that is, any reality existing independently of God. Nevertheless, what he cannot clearly explain or adequately express is how the finite actualities are in themselves creative. As I noted in my portrait, he is at best ambiguous when it comes to articulating this. On the one hand, he asserts that the finite monads "self-generate" and "do not pre-contain all that they later unfold." Yet, in the same breath, he maintains that "they do not 'assist' God" in their self-generating or creative endeavor because God "supplies all power and all being." His answer to this ambiguity is to say that they "participate in God. For if God is an internally creative power-act, then he can only be participated in by creatures who do not embody an infinite coincidence of act and power, but a finite oscillation between the two, yet are themselves thereby radically creative and differentiating."[102] But if they are indeed "radically creative," then they must assist God in the sense of being at least co-creators of novelty in the world; they must add something new to the world and to the divine experience.

Milbank sets up something of a straw man here when he holds that God "can only be participated in by creatures who do not embody an infinite coincidence of act and power." Of course creatures do not have

102. Milbank, *Theology and Social Theory*, 425.

this infinite combination. The real question is, does it make sense to say that God has an infinite coincidence of power and act? In other words, is Milbank asserting here the traditional notion of divine omnipotence? His affirmation of *creatio ex nihilo*, when describing the finite monads, seems to suggest this. If so, then he will have a difficult time articulating how creatures are in fact genuinely creative. Creativity requires some degree of power and autonomy. For instance, in process thought, creativity, power, and autonomy—in some measure—are necessary metaphysical characteristics of any possible world. All actual entities or monads exhibit these in some degree, not just God. Hence, though the many are necessarily related to the divine One (denying substantive autonomy in the sense of a world apart from God), the many—as well as the One—necessarily exhibit these metaphysical traits (granting some degree of subjective autonomy to all actualities). Milbank's language of participation lacks this type of distinction and, thus, tends to blur the distinction between God and finite actualities. This blurring is evident, for example, when he describes both God and world in terms of the process of differentiation, and when he describes God as internally creative—and then describes creatures in terms of that creativity itself.

Because Milbank's panentheism is afraid to grant genuine creative autonomy to the world, his view, in spite of his intentions, tends toward some variation of Spinoza's pantheism. Smith echoes this same assessment when he notes that RO exhibits "a tendency to emphasize the creature's participation in the divine to the extent that it seems the divine does everything. While seeking to undo the regnant secular concept of an autonomous nature," Smith asks, "does RO's participatory framework risk sliding toward an alternative model that does not grant any independence to the creation?" My answer is yes. Milbank's ambivalent attraction to Hegel might partly explain this tendency. As Robert Hartman observes, in paraphrasing Ernst Cassirer, Hegel divinizes history as Spinoza divinized nature. And just as Spinoza's infinite modes are manifestations of the One substance, Milbank's unfolding monads seem to be manifestations or modes of the divine One. The creation is nothing more or other than the unfolding of the Creator.[103]

---

103. Smith, *Introducing Radical Orthodoxy*, 204. Hartman's observations are found in his "Editor's Introduction" to Hegel's, *Reason in History*, xxi. He cites Ernst Cassirer, *The Myth of the State* (New Haven: Yale University Press, 1946), 262. Whitehead contends that "the gap in [Spinoza's] system is the arbitrary introduction of the 'modes.'" Whitehead, *Process and Reality*, 7.

In response, Milbank might argue that I am misreading him because I have not taken to heart his insistence on need for analogical language. To say that the world participates in God is to say that there is a close connection between the two (in the form of a creaturely dependence on the divine) but one should not, he might hold, try to understand this relationship in literal or univocal terms. The whole point of analogy, he might insist, is to forever maintain the difference between God and world at the same time that one seeks to bring them into some connection. For instance, in a passage quoted earlier, Milbank says that it is "only by means of . . . some analogous exchange of predicates between God and finitude [that one can] conceive of an absolute that is *itself* difference, inclusive of all difference."[104] I focused my attention on the "exchange of predicates" whereas he might say that I should have instead focused on the qualifier "analogous." In this case, there is no literal exchange or intercourse between God and world. Such an exchange would compromise traditional or orthodox affirmations of divine aseity, immutability, and repleteness. Instead, the language of analogy points to similarity between God and world without implying that they literally share characteristics in the same sense. With this in mind, he might say that I have been looking for too much precision or explication in terms of his articulation of how the finite is creative and yet adds nothing to God.

Whatever shortcomings Scotus's philosophy may have, I am persuaded that he was at least right to hold that theology must be able to make some univocal statements about God. As Richard Cross argues, Scotus did not deny analogy as such. In fact, he thought most theological statements are analogical. Yet, analogy's attempt to steer a middle course—asserting similarity yet maintaining difference—cannot succeed, Scotus rightly maintained, unless there is some point of conceptual contact that grounds or anchors the various analogies themselves. Without such an anchor, the analogies are, at best, begging the question or, at worst, simply equivocating.[105]

In rejecting this conclusion, Milbank concurs with Aquinas's insistence on analogical predication. In discussing the question of univocal language in ST I.13.5, Thomas presupposes that God is the infinite and all-determining first cause of the world. And because the finite effect is

---

104. Milbank, *Theology and Social Theory*, 429.
105. Cross, *Duns Scotus*, 33–39.

always less than the infinite cause, our knowledge of the worldly effect offers only a partial or ambiguous knowledge of the divine cause. Given this ambiguity, Aquinas argues that knowledge of God cannot be univocal but only analogical. For instance, qualities or perfections that we know in a diverse and scattered way from our experience in the world, are, by contrast, united in God's very essence and existence. Thomas uses wisdom as an example. When we say that a human person is wise, we conceive of this attribute as something distinct from the person's existence, i.e., wisdom is something added onto his or her existence, not constitutive of it. In contrast, in the case of God, such an attribute or predicate is inseparable from the divine essence and existence itself. In short, what is partial and fragmented in the world is simple and unified in God. By way of ontological eminence, the qualities are perfect in God and imperfect in us. Yet, by way of epistemological order, we proceed from our experience of finite qualities in the world and then infer their unity and perfection in God's nature. Hence, given this gap between the ontological and the epistemological, between "what is signified" and "our mode of signification" (ST I.13.3), Thomas concludes that the meaning of "wise" cannot be univocal in the two cases but, rather, only analogical.

Insofar as Milbank follows Aquinas here, let me offer two related comments. First, Thomas's whole argument is premised on the classical theistic notion that God is an exception to the metaphysical categories that apply to the world; this exception is embodied in his claim that we can infer God's existence from His effects in the world, but we cannot know God's nature. As Thomas says at one point,

> from the divine effects we cannot know the divine nature as it is in itself, so as to know what it is. . . . Thus the name God signifies the divine nature, for this name was imposed to signify something existing above all things, the principle of all things, and removed from all things; for those who name God intend to signify all this.[106]

Therefore, given that God is an exception to the metaphysical categories that apply to the world, terms that apply to experience in the world cannot be applied directly or literally to God. At best, one can only draw inferential analogies and project them proportionally onto the divine

---

106. Thomas Aquinas, *Summa Theologica* I.13.8. reply 2.

nature, as illustrated in the case of wisdom. As we saw in his criticism of Scotus, Milbank maintains that even existence cannot have the same meaning when applied to God and world. Milbank fears that such univocity leads to a flattened and secularistic ontology. But the need for univocity, I judge, is first and foremost an epistemological requirement, namely, to avoid always begging the question. Analogies that stop with themselves—offering no point of univocal contact—merely invite further questions about how one knows that there really is any divine referent to correspond with the proportionate projections from human experience. This was Feuerbach's whole point. Why do we insist on projecting or adding a divine reality, which cannot be univocally known, if all that we really know are predicates from human experience? Put otherwise, how can one ever know a proportion or analogy if one does not know the separate terms independently of the supposed proportion? An insistence on analogical predication can never adequately respond to these questions. Alternatively, a panentheism that makes God the supreme exemplification of the world's metaphysical categories, rather than an exception to them, can help to articulate why there can be no world of actuality apart from the divine reality. This latter aim is precisely what Milbank is rightly trying to fulfill. Yet, this aim cannot be successfully achieved without some degree of univocity.[107]

Second, Thomas's argument against univocity is premised on the notion that the divine first cause is infinitely powerful and fully determinative of the world—the infinite cause fully determines the finite effect and is qualitatively or metaphysically different from it. Therefore, because the finite effect falls short of the infinite causal power, the effect is always inadequate for providing any univocal knowledge of the cause. In the case of Milbank, however, this line of reasoning leads back to the problem of trying to explain creaturely freedom and creativity. As I argued above, what his view lacks is a coherent explanation of how the finite creatures are genuinely creative and not simply fully caused by the divine unfolding. To insist on the language of analogy here merely begs the question, for Thomas's own argument for analogy presupposes

107. See Feuerbach, *Essence of Christianity*, esp. chap. 1. For a thorough and detailed critique of Aquinas's analogical predication, see Gamwell, "Speaking of God After Aquinas." Though my comments were originally formulated independently of Gamwell's article, I am indebted to that article for further clarifying Aquinas's distinction between "what is signified" and "our mode of signification" and for pointing me to Aquinas's passage in ST at I.13.8.

that the cause fully determines the effect. What is needed instead is a metaphysical conception that makes sense of genuine creativity and freedom and one that expresses the divine-world relationship in at least some univocal terms. For, in the end, analogical arguments are parasitical upon univocal ones.[108]

Before proceeding to a discussion of Milbank's reliance on rhetoric, and its political and moral implications, let me offer some observations about his ontology of peace. Drawing on Augustine, Milbank's metaphysical vision is one of ultimate peace and harmony—one defined by the tranquility of order. Yet, for Milbank, does this mean in a strong sense that the nature of ultimate reality is such that no conflict can occur, and hence reality is pure tranquility? Or does it mean, in a weaker sense, that ultimate reality has some ontological order that enables events to coalesce in such a way as to realize the value of harmony and compatibility? In other words, it is one thing to say that ultimate reality seeks to foster the realization of those possibilities that tend toward greater harmony and mutual enrichment, while acknowledging that other possibilities will be incompatible and conflictual with each other (weaker sense). It is another thing, however, to say that ultimate reality is a condition of pure tranquility that excludes the possibility of any conflict at all (stronger sense). As I read him, Milbank seems to have the stronger sense in mind, for this is the ontological vision that he wants to advocate over against secular social theory. On occasion, such as in *Being Reconciled*, he offers a formulation that could perhaps be interpreted in a weaker sense as well. This weaker version, I will argue, offers a more promising path than does Milbank's predominant and stronger form.

The stronger version is front and center in *Theology and Social Theory*. There, Milbank sharply demarcates between the ontology of conflict and the ontology of peace; there is no commingling between the two. Augustine, he indicates, "puts peaceful reconciliation in no dialectical relationship with conflict."[109] Milbank suggests here that there is no possibility of conflict inherent in true reality; the divine reality is the tranquility of order and tranquility excludes all forms of agitation, disturbance, and conflict. To suggest otherwise is to fall into the error

---

108. I'm indebted to Emory University philosopher Jack Zupko for the insight that it is a parasitical relation.

109. Milbank, *Theology and Social Theory*, 389.

of modern social theory. But what does it mean to say that conflict and disturbance are categorically excluded from true reality? Is not potential conflict inherent in any possible world of multiple actors, options, possibilities, and goods? One thinks of Antigone having to face the conflictual choice of either burying her brother or obeying the law of the state. Or one thinks of Sartre's young Frenchman during World War II having to choose between joining the French Resistance and staying home to take care of his mother.[110] In each of these cases, there are two alternatives that are in conflict with each other. Each offers some value that is incompatible with pursuing the other possibility; both cannot be had and therefore disturbance and conflict cannot be avoided.

In response, Milbank might say that these two examples still presuppose a world of violence (Antigone's brothers at war with each other over Thebes, and the German occupation of France) and that if one removes the violence, then the dilemmas melt away. Yet, my point is still made, if less vividly, by more mundane examples. Gamwell argues, for instance, that there is an inevitable choice and tension for any individual between breadth and depth in pursuing the divine good in the world. As Gamwell observes:

> Maximizing the opportunities for some and maximizing the number for whom opportunities are created involve two different variables.... Were each individual always to choose in terms of her or his maximal contribution to the widest number of others, the emancipation of each and thus our common humanity would be greatly impoverished, because the actor's distinctiveness [or depth] would be sacrificed to the width of effect....
>
> ... [Pursuit of the divine telos in the world] does not eliminate such dilemmas precisely because it is both self-widening and self-localizing. But these situations, given that neither alternative is finally prescribed by that telos, do not imply that the comprehensive good is in conflict with itself. On the contrary, the proper conclusion is that the alternatives involved are equally good.[111]

Gamwell's point is that there are multiple alternatives that "are equally good" in terms of value, yet these alternatives are mutually incompatible. To borrow language from economics, Gamwell is pointing out that

---

110. Sartre, *Existentialism and Humanism*, 35. I am indebted to Gamwell, *Democracy on Purpose*, 289 for pointing to the relevance of this Sartre illustration.

111. Gamwell, *Democracy on Purpose*, 288, 289.

any possible world, and hence the divine good itself, will involve opportunity costs (to pursue alternative A is to forego alternative B and so on), and these opportunity costs entail some inevitable degree of tension, conflict, and loss in terms of unrealized possibilities. "In its essence," adds Whitehead, "realization is limitation, exclusion. But [God as the] ultimate fact includes in [his] appetitive vision all possibilities of order, possibilities at once incompatible and unlimited with a fecundity beyond imagination." What is crucial here is the realization that there is no coherent notion of a maximal possible good—no coherent notion of a static, fully tranquil order without some tension, conflict, and unrealized possibility. Just as the notions "'greatest possible number'" and "highest infinity" make no coherent sense, so, too, does the notion of highest possible good or fully tranquil order fail to make sense.[112] Yet, it is precisely this assumption that seems to underlie Milbank's Augustinian vision of ultimate reality devoid of any possible conflict.

In some ways, Milbank tries to have it both ways. On the one hand, he affirms this static vision of a tranquility of fully actualized order while, on the other, he affirms a dynamic divinity always unfolding new possibilities and actualities in the world. This Janus-like attempt is embodied in his statement that "infinite realized act and infinite unrealized [potential] mysteriously coincide in God."[113] To claim that a dynamic unfolding could occur without any tension, conflict, or unrealized possibilities is not credible; to call it a "mystery" merely begs the question. Hence, I am persuaded that Milbank needs a "weaker," and thus more persuasive, formulation of his ontology of peace.

Such a formulation is hinted at in *Being Reconciled*. There, Milbank says:

> If there is truth, then it is ontological ... ; the fact that there is a true way for things to be and a way things eternally are. Only in that case does it follow that things may be ultimately compatible with each other.... If there is truth, then it must apply universally, and the truth of one thing must be compatible with the truth of all other things. But this is peace.[114]

---

112. Whitehead, *Essays in Science and Philosophy*, 89; see Hartshorne, *Omnipotence and Other Theological Mistakes*, 7 for a critique of the notion of highest possible number or good.

113. Milbank, *Theology and Social Theory*, 423.

114. Milbank, *Being Reconciled*, 106.

If one reads this in the strong sense, then one again finds a static notion of tranquil order. There is a single true and eternal way for things to be and because of this, "the truth of one thing must be compatible with the truth of all other things." In this case, there is perfect peace because there cannot be any incompatibility. Yet, here again one wonders about any genuine freedom or creativity on the part of the world if there is only one true way for things to be. The dynamism and creativity of creatures do not have much place here.

But, alternatively, if one reads this passage in a weaker sense, then it casts a different light. If Milbank means that any possible world requires some eternal characteristics and metaphysical order, then I would certainly agree. Moreover, it is only as a result of such order that the particularities of the world may ultimately be compatible with each other. That is, to be realized at all, value and creativity require a background order; without such order, there is merely chaos or fleeting perspectives. Furthermore, the truth of this metaphysical order must apply universally and the truth of one actuality must be compatible with the truth of all other actualities.[115] The key here, which Milbank does not offer, is to specify that the truth of all actualities—but not necessarily all possibilities—must be compatible with each other to some extent. Whatever goods or facts are realized must be compatible with the metaphysical order of reality and, in that sense, they are compatible with each other. The truth of Mary sitting at Jesus's feet and the truth of Martha serving the guests are compatible with each other, yet each of them cannot simultaneously actualize both goods. In contrast, the notion of a "squared-circle" is impossible in any world. Likewise, as Milbank also admits, the notion of divine foreknowledge—of God knowing the future as actual and not as a set of possibilities—is not compatible with the truth of any genuine notion of future possibility and freedom. But the defining feature of this "weaker" reading is that it does not presume that all tension and conflict are whisked away from this metaphysical order. On the contrary, the divine order creates conditions for value to be realized, but there is a multiplicity of possible values and not all of them are compossible with each other. It is this combination of metaphysical order coupled with potential conflict among incompossible goods and alternatives that Gamwell had in mind

---

115. This brief discussion of metaphysical order is informed by Hartshorne or Whitehead, but unfortunately I have lost track of my specific source here.

when he said that this situation does "not imply that the comprehensive good is in conflict with itself. On the contrary, the proper conclusion is that the alternatives involved are equally good."[116] In other words, the metaphysical order and the divine good do not permit only one set of possibilities and, because of this, there is always the possibility of tension and conflict. Put simply, the kingdom of God must be conceived as a dynamic telos, not as a static harmony.

One of Milbank's defining themes is the priority of myth and rhetoric over reason and argument. The true universal ontology, he claims, can only be communicated through and grounded in the particularity of the Christian story. That is, following de Lubac, he claims that reason and revelation are inherently blurred. But why should we accept these claims? On what grounds are we asked to accept them? Milbank cannot simply offer reasons to justify these claims, for doing so would performatively contradict the content of his own stated position. Instead, he must implicitly or explicitly appeal to the authority of tradition and/or to the rhetorical attraction of his own proffered vision. Moreover, since reason and revelation are supposedly blurred, then one cannot separate out where reason ends and revelation begins. Hence, one must be prepared to accept the authority of tradition—and its interpretation of revelation—from the outset. In response to this, let me offer five sets of critical comments.

First, at times Milbank appeals more straightforwardly to reason and is less relativistic than his own stated position suggests. For instance, insofar as he seeks to offer a historical reconstruction that outnarrates alternative views, is he not indeed offering historical *reasons* to justify the validity of his interpretation of the past? What does it mean to "outnarrate" other views other than to offer more convincing historical reasons—reasons that invite the reader to rethink the past? An argument from history is still an argument that appeals to reason—one that does not appeal to revelation, rhetorical persuasion, or the authority of tradition. In short, insofar as Milbank takes history and historical arguments seriously, then he is more of a closet-rationalist and modernist than he admits.

Second, his preference for rhetoric over reason issues partly from his presumption that rational arguments are inherently coercive insofar as they seek to compel assent. Only rhetorical persuasion can be non-

---

116. Gamwell, *Democracy on Purpose*, 289.

violent, he insists. But as I have repeatedly argued, this presumption is mistaken. Properly conceived, rational arguments do not compel assent but, rather, invite agreement. To offer reasons to others is to offer them intellectual and cognitive grounds that invite them to accept one's claims as valid or true.[117] Summarily speaking, then, there is nothing antithetical between the invitation of reason and the Christian affirmation of peace. Hence, Milbank cannot convincingly claim that rhetoric is more fitting than reason.

Third, Milbank might proceed to claim that the Christian story and other rhetorical and liturgical practices are pragmatically more effective for engendering existential assent and transformation than are rational arguments as such. "We need the stories of Jesus for salvation," he contends, "rather than just a speculative notion of the good, because only the attraction exercised by a particular set of words and images causes us to acknowledge the good and to have an idea of the ultimate *telos*."[118] It may indeed be true that the particular stories and practices of the tradition are existentially powerful and transformative. I agree with this. However, precisely because of their emotional and existential power, their validity claims need to be assessed on more dispassionate grounds. "Religion requires a metaphysical backing," Whitehead astutely observes,

> for its authority is endangered by the intensity of the emotions which it generates. Such emotions are evidence of some vivid experience; but they are a very poor guarantee for its correct interpretation.
>
> Thus dispassionate criticism of religious belief is beyond all things necessary. The foundations of dogma must be laid in a rational metaphysics which criticises meanings, and endeavors to express the most general concepts adequate for the all-inclusive universe.[119]

---

117. A classic example of this, it seems to me, comes at the beginning of Plato's *Republic* when Socrates suggests to Polemarchus that reasoned persuasion is the alternative to coercion (Bk. I, 327c-328). In response, Milbank might submit that the persuasion that Socrates speaks of is the persuasion of rhetoric rather than the persuasion of rational dialectic. But such a claim itself, I would want to argue, requires its own rational defense—and not merely a further appeal to rhetoric.

118. Milbank, *Theology and Social Theory*, 398.

119. Whitehead, *Religion in the Making*, 83.

Milbank certainly recognizes the importance of metaphysics for religion, but he does not subscribe to the need for a rational metaphysics. Instead, he appeals to the stories, practices, and authorities of the church to ground his metaphysics, which, in turn, is meant to ground the truth of these particularities in a more inclusive vision. But if we are never offered independent reasons for accepting the truth of this larger vision, then how do we discriminate between properly directed and misdirected rhetoric or between proper and improper responses to that rhetoric? Surely the debate between Plato and the Sophists was largely over the question of whether rhetoric required independent backing and assessment. In brief, Milbank shortchanges the importance of his own reaffirmation of metaphysics by appealing to a rhetorical metaphysics rather than a rational one.

Fourth, I suggested earlier that Milbank agrees with Kant and the modern dominant consensus insofar as Milbank agrees that metaphysical claims and claims about an ultimate or metaphysical telos are tradition-specific. That is to say, any such claims cannot be known or validated by common reason but, rather, require the narrative of a particular tradition. Milbank illustrates this in the passage above when he suggests that we can only "have an idea of the ultimate *telos*" based on the "particular set of words and images" stemming from "the stories of Jesus." Otherwise put, he suggests that all humans have a dim awareness of the divine prior to any particular experience; this is due to the fact that all things participate in and have their being within God. Yet, rather than describing this awareness in terms of a rational or a priori knowledge, he describes it in terms of a proleptic anticipation that can only be known in and through the particularities of the Christian faith. In a critical passage noted earlier, he states:

> For reason to think at all, it must somehow already know what it seeks to know: reason, to be reason, must therefore also be faith, and in articulating this view in different ways Augustine, Anselm, and Aquinas are all conscious that at the heart of their Christian articulation of grace and revelation they are nonetheless radicalising and resolving the specifically Platonic view that reason, to be reason, in some fashion knows before it knows.[120]

Milbank starts off here by suggesting that reason has a prior knowledge or awareness, which he calls "faith." Now one way of conceptualizing

120. Milbank, "Programme of Radical Orthodoxy," 35.

this prior knowledge, as I outlined in Part One, is to define "faith" as an existential disposition of trust in the meaningfulness of existence, which all persons implicitly presuppose insofar as they take their lives and actions to be valuable and worthwhile. Such a view would suggest that "faith seeking understanding" means that one seeks rationally and cognitively to make sense of one's prior faith, i.e., to make sense of one's fundamental trust in life's lasting value and meaningfulness. Such a position would contend, moreover, that this trust ultimately presupposes the reality of God and that rational knowledge of the divine is possible apart from the particularity of religious or Christian narrative. Hence, on my account, faith is prior to reason, as Milbank suggests, but this faith—and its theistic ground—can be rationally articulated and justified apart from appeal to the particularities of the Christian story. The particularity of this story may indeed be existentially valuable and powerful, but it itself is not constitutive of faith or knowledge of God as such. In short, reason has prior knowledge, which it can articulate and handle on its own. In sum, this view rejects substantive autonomy but does so by affirming formal autonomy.[121]

In contrast, Milbank assumes that in order to reject substantive autonomy, one must also reject formal autonomy. Hence, he has a very different understanding of faith and reason in mind. For him, reason has a prior awareness but this awareness cannot be accessed except through the specific revelation of God in Christ. Hence, "faith seeking understanding" means an attempt to understand all things in light of a prior acceptance of the particularities of the Christian narrative. In fact, he suggests that, insofar as reason is dependent on faith, and faith is dependent on grace and revelation, reason itself is dependent on the particularity of the Christian tradition. *All* reasoning, therefore, is ultimately *Christian* reasoning insofar as the Son, the divine Logos, is the revelatory Word that illuminates the world. This is what Milbank means when he describes his account as "radicalising and resolving the . . . Platonic view." It is radicalizing Plato's view by making it Christian-dependent and Christian-specific.

Yet, on what grounds should we find this radicalizing approach convincing? On what grounds should we accept the claim that reason's

---

121. The view that I articulate here is my attempt to paraphrase and loosely summarize what I take to be Ogden's understanding of faith and its relation to reason. See, for instance, *Point of Christology*.

prior knowledge can only be understood in terms of a proleptic anticipation of the Christian story and not in terms of a natural knowledge of God available to human existence as such? Why should we accept that ultimate reality has a structure that cannot be known apart from the particularities of the Christian revelation? Milbank's claims here all stand in need of their own justification. To say, as he does, that these questions can only be decided on the basis of rhetorical persuasion and the witness of the Church and its sacraments is to again beg the question. What is it that is inviting my free assent to these fundamental propositions? According to him, it cannot be reason, since this is a choice itself about whether to choose reason (the true reason made available only through the particular revelation of the divine Logos). As he puts it, "between the ultimate ontological truth of reason and unreason, only [rhetorical] persuasion can choose."[122] But a choice that is beyond reason is either an arbitrary choice, which Milbank presumably would not want to say, or a choice that we are to accept finally in deference to the authority of others. Hence, at best, Milbank's new traditionalism begs the question; at worst, it is a reassertion of authority and heteronomy.

Fifth, Milbank admits that truth must be arrived at freely, but he is not averse to using coercion as a means of getting there. To insist on free assent as a strict norm, he contends, is to "fetishize" freedom above truth. Rather, a collective affirmation of truth is the ultimate goal and for those who need some help in recognizing this truth, ecclesial authorities ought rightly to use some coercive methods. This is clearly Milbank's most anti-modern stance, and undoubtedly the most troubling. In response, he claims that it is not troubling if one recovers a proper medieval view of ecclesiastical authority tied into the sacraments and scripture. Yet, on my reading, it is still in sharp tension with two of modernity's central affirmations, namely, an affirmation of human equality in terms of potentially discerning truth from error, and an unwavering recognition of human fallibility and the potential error of all human claims.

When Descartes said that "the power of judging aright and distinguishing truth from error . . . is by nature equal in all men," I take it that he was affirming an equality of human capacity, not an equality of actuality.[123] That is, he affirmed that all humans have the capacity to discern truth,

---

122. Milbank, "Invocation of Clio," 42.
123. Descartes, "Discourse on Method," 39.

but all do not develop it or apply it with equal effectiveness. Hence, modernity does leave room open for compulsory education of the young, to help them develop and apply their innate capacity. Does this mean that all adults exercise a discriminating capacity to distinguish truth from error? Obviously not. But does this then justify Milbank's affirmation of coercion to help them "see the light?" I think not. Here is where Milbank's ontological difficulty of articulating the creative autonomy of creatures has clear practical implications. Milbank is less concerned with respecting the autonomy of finite individuals precisely because, in the end, he is less clear about the genuine individuality of the many than he is about their participation in the ontological One. His panentheism of plenitude slides toward a pantheistic monism. And in such a monism, the One takes clear priority over the many. In contrast, the modern emphasis on discourse takes the plurality and autonomy of the many to be central. And because of this respect for plurality, modernity rightly emphasizes the importance of offering reasons and arguments to each individual as invitations and lures of assent. Milbank might be partly right in suggesting that modern thought "fetishizes" freedom. But it does so, not in what it affirms but rather in what it denies. That is, modernity's error is not in respecting the many, but rather in losing sight of the One. Its error is not in placing great weight on respecting the autonomous judgment of human individuals but, rather, in largely denying the metaphysical enterprise and, thus, separating freedom from a metaphysical telos. In contrast, Milbank's error is in failing to appreciate the many in the name of reclaiming the One. By rejecting the modern commitment to rational discourse, Milbank is willing to reaffirm medieval coercion in the name of reclaiming an ontological vision.

The danger of Milbank's formulation is that it does not take seriously enough the perennial possibility of human fallibility. By opting for a conciliar rather than a papal model of ecclesial authority, Milbank might argue that he does take fallibility seriously. To his credit, at least in his more recent writings, he does now emphasize the potential fallibility and revisability of all human answers. As he indicates,

> We possess only a remote, mediated access to the eternal, and our intimations must be ceaselessly revised. Hence, our account of eternal truth, unless we are sadly deluded idolaters, must responsibly include an account of how we arrived at some truth, or rather of how some truth arrived at us—and of how at first

and later, and perhaps still today, we misapprehended even this bare modicum. Our weak truths are indeed doubly contingent: something permanent is only disclosed in a passing advent, and this advent itself is only perceived by us through our signifying, symbolic, and verbal response.... All these apprehensions are contained therefore by human language, which is itself of long and particular origin.... All human terms, including abstract ones, retain some residue of their cultural genesis, which means ultimately that even philosophical language deploys the resources of cultural myth making.... Hence, even without recourse to deliberate mythic supplementation, the philosophic *logos* is merely the refinement of myth, since it can only re-work the prior speculative efforts of culture as such.

To propose a vision, therefore, must mean to re-propose an inherited vision and simultaneously to refine this vision by retracing its epiphany and the ways in which this epiphany has been authentically repeated or else has become distorted.... For us, in the present, ... *traditio* is itself the only epiphany, which is not, however, to deny its vertical ecstasy.[124]

In this richly dense passage we see Milbank affirm human fallibility and, yet, ultimately turn to the authority of tradition. He begins in an almost modernist spirit by emphasizing the fallibility and potential revisability of all claims, including especially those about eternity and ultimate reality. Only "deluded idolaters" would deny this. Moreover, he contends that we must always offer an account of how we arrived at our truth claims. This sounds like a call for some form of justification or validation. However, I suspect that he has a more genetic approach in mind rather than an explicitly rational one. Nonetheless, as I argued earlier, any genetic attempt to provide an historical account is at least implicitly a rational argument insofar as one offers historical reasons both to support one's historical reconstruction and to outnarrate alternative interpretations. It is at this juncture in the passage, however, that Milbank begins to move toward a traditionalist outlook. Our fallible and partial grasp of eternal truths, he continues, is only perceived through symbol and language. And since language is always historically and culturally particular, all human terms, including philosophical ones, retain some cultural particularity. Given this reality, Milbank jumps to the conclusion that even philosophy "is merely the refinement of myth." Therefore, since philosophy itself is only about reexpressing and refining cultur-

124. Milbank, "Invocation of Clio," 7.

ally-given myths, philosophy is ultimately tradition-dependent, i.e., it is horizontally conditioned. This does not deny, he insists, "its vertical ecstasy" or disclosive function in relation to the eternal.

The key assumption here is Milbank's claim that "something permanent is only . . . perceived by us through our signifying, symbolic, and verbal response." In short, he reduces metaphysics to its linguistic expression. All we perceive, according to him, is our symbolic response. Once this is granted, it is merely a short step to reducing philosophy to cultural myth and to making it strictly dependent on tradition. In contrast, as I argued in chapter 2, there is a critical difference between propositions and their linguistic expression. What we perceive or prehend of reality is a propositional content prior to and independent of our linguistic expression of that content. Simply put, there is a crucial difference between *what* we prehend and *how* we articulate or express it. Language, to be sure, is culturally and historically particular. That is why Whitehead argues that philosophy must always stretch language in new ways to seek to make it more adequate for expressing the reality and propositional content we prehend. The aim of philosophy, therefore, is to seek to use reason and innovative linguistic expression to gain greater adequacy in our understanding and expression of reality. In contrast, Milbank collapses this distinction between content and expression and thus reduces all that we perceive merely to "our signifying, symbolic and verbal response." But once he makes this move, how can he still maintain that tradition vertically reveals something about the eternal? He has no grounds, it seems to me, for this affirmation. On the contrary, his affirmation here must presuppose some distinction between propositions and their linguistic expression. And once this distinction is implied or granted, philosophy is no longer reduced merely to myth and the reformulation of tradition. Philosophy can add novelty to the world and make progress in human understanding insofar as it stretches our complacent formulations and presumptions about time and eternity.

An equally important question raised by Milbank's passage goes back to the issue of ecclesial authority and coercion. Given his acceptance here of the fallibility and potential revisability of all claims, how does he justify elsewhere the use of coercion by ecclesial authorities to make people see the truth about reality? He suggests that any squeamishness about this is a result of fetishizing freedom. But I would argue that an aversion to coercion is due precisely to the possibility of error in all human claims, including those of the church and the bishop. Given that power tends to blind us to our own fallibility, it is especially those in positions of power that need to be reminded of and humbled by this reality. Milbank tries to mollify our concern by suggesting that a proper understanding of medieval authority makes the use of coercion less authoritarian. Moreover, he thinks that a collective affirmation of and consensus about the truth is more important than how one gets to it. Yet, most modernists and I remain unconvinced. A consensus must be achieved and not ascribed. That is, free assent can only be achieved or reached through the testing and invitation of reasons offered, not through an ascription imposed by authority and tradition. Habermas, for example, makes this point quite starkly in light of the historical realities of Nazism and the Holocaust. Tradition presupposes, he notes, a "questionless continuity" that draws its

> sustenance from trust. "Tradition" means just that we carry something forward as unproblematic which others began before us. . . . I believe exactly this basis of trust was destroyed at the threshold of the gas chambers. . . . Since then a conscious life is no longer possible without mistrust for continuities that assert themselves without question and also want to draw their validity out of their questionlessness.[125]

Clearly Milbank does not want to condone atrocities done in the name of God, authority, or tradition, let alone those done in name of any nation-state. Nevertheless, he is too cavalier when it comes to the use of ecclesial coercion in the name of the True and the Good. This cavalier spirit is equally evident in his dismissal of modern democracy.

He dismisses modern democracy as a mere *modus vivendi* tainted, allegedly, by its underlying ontological acceptance of violence and conflict. Over against this, he espouses divine democracy, which requires the hierarchy and authority of ecclesial tradition. It is only by means of this reassertion of traditional authority, he holds, that one can conceptualize and pursue a true consensus and a common love, where God is all in all. Yet, akin to Habermas's concerns about tradition, Stout draws on Walt Whitman to echo similar concerns about Milbank and the new traditionalists' rejection of modern democracy. As noted earlier, Stout is

---

125. Habermas, "Ethics, Politics and History," 434–35.

leery of the docility implicit in the reverence for authority; in contrast, modern democracy rejects docility in favor of self-reliance.[126]

If Milbank truly accepts the fallibility and potential revisability of all claims, then he, too, should agree with Stout in rejecting the docility fostered by authority; he, too, should affirm the self-reliance and autonomous thinking that modern democratic ideals espouse. But as we have seen, Milbank is less interested in individual affirmation than in collective consent. Concern about the individual, he alleges, smacks of the fetishizing tendencies of modern liberalism. In response, Stout wants to know if Milbank is willing finally to authorize Christian participation in the secular and democratic sphere in order to pursue relative justice. "The practical issue," says Stout,

> is whether Christians, for their own theological reasons, may join hands with others in the struggle for justice—and do so without holding their noses in the presence of their comrades. If Milbank thinks they may, then he is implicitly granting the legitimacy of what I am calling a secularized political sphere, and his conclusions are much less radical than they are made to seem. If he thinks they mustn't, then he has little to offer besides nostalgia, utopian fantasy, and withdrawal into a strongly bounded enclave. In that event, he would owe his readers reasons for avoiding the conclusion that his theology has restricted divine sovereignty and inhibited charity toward the non-Christian other.[127]

I suspect that Milbank would be somewhat ambivalent in his response to Stout. On the one hand, he would encourage Christians to struggle for justice, but he would strongly deny Stout's contention that this amounts to an implicit endorsement of "a secularized political sphere." On the contrary, he would reassert that the secular is a time or "interval between fall and eschaton," not a neutral public square. In this eschatological interim, defined in relation to God, relative or "coercive justice, private property and impaired natural reason must make shift," says

---

126. Stout, *Democracy and Tradition*, 25. I realize that Stout, unlike Habermas, is espousing democracy as itself a tradition. Yet, what they have in common here is the modern affirmation—embodied in the ideals of democracy itself—that all individuals should think for themselves and not simply defer to the authority and thinking of others. Of course, I also noted in chapter 3 how Stout's ethics without metaphysics ends up sliding toward authority since it has no other ultimate evaluative standard upon which to draw.

127. Ibid., 105.

Milbank, "to cope with the unredeemed effects of sinful humanity."[128] There is a reluctant endorsement here for pursuing earthly justice, one in which Milbank is indeed "holding his nose."

Yet, I suspect that Milbank's lack of a strong endorsement for affirming political democracy or pursuing earthly justice has deeper roots than Stout recognizes. Whereas Stout affirms democracy and ethics without metaphysics, Milbank affirms metaphysics without an ultimate telos for human action. Because no action in the world ultimately affects or contributes to God, there are no goals or creative actions in the world that have any lasting value. Hence, pursuing relative justice is, at best, an act of restraining sin, not a creative achievement in any ultimate sense. Milbank sums up this outlook when he declares that the Church has no telos; instead, the Church is the telos in the sense that it is the visible locus of God's unfolding in the world. Since relative achievements have no lasting impact on the divine life, it is only ultimate conditions, like divine democracy, that carry much weight for Milbank. In the end, if history is about a divine unfolding in the midst of finitude rather than about the creative use or misuse of finite freedom in relation to the divine, then subjects like earthly justice and political democracy just seem insignificant. But Milbank wrongly devalues these endeavors because he ultimately devalues freedom, and he devalues freedom because he cannot metaphysically make sense of creaturely autonomy. His panentheism once again ends up as a pantheism of plenitude. In sum, Milbank's cavalier and misguided attitude toward political democracy, freedom, and justice stem from his lack of an ontological appreciation for the many in relation to the One, and from his lack of an epistemological appreciation of his own recognition of human fallibility.

Summary (I+C-AE-AM-)

As Lois Malcolm suggested at the outset, Milbank's Radical Orthodoxy does indeed jolt mainstream theology out of its complacency with the currents of modernity. At the heart of this endeavor, I propose, is Milbank's attempt to reassert the central importance of metaphysics. Only by making clear how all of reality is related to the divine, can one make a strong case for showing how ethics, politics, and all other aspects of life are connected to the question of God. Though Milbank seeks to

---

128. Milbank, *Theology and Social Theory*, 9.

make this case in at least a partially intelligible and perhaps even plausible manner, he clearly refuses any commitment to rational credibility. Such a commitment, he presumes, is indicative of the modern error of secular reason. But the error of modernity, I have consistently argued, is found not in its formal commitment to secularity but rather in its substantive conclusions, which pull it toward secularism. Milbank's valuable contribution issues from his attempt to re-center theology around ontology and metaphysics. The multiple shortcomings of his effort, however, stem from his rejection of the modern commitment to formal autonomy and from his panentheism of plenitude, which is still plagued by the problems of classical theism. Such a metaphysical vision, in short, does not finally make room for creaturely autonomy and creativity, and thus fails to recognize how the world genuinely contributes value to the divine life.

10

A Transcendental-Process Theology
The Approach of Franklin Gamwell

Theological Portrait

IF JOHN "MILBANK'S PROJECT IS THE RETRIEVAL OF PREMODERNITY with postmodern tools," then Franklin Gamwell's endeavor is the completion of modernity with modern tools that have not been sufficiently or properly utilized.[1] For more than a quarter-century, Gamwell's modern project has involved the attempt to publicly reconnect theology, ethics, and politics by way of reason. Commenting on Gamwell's efforts, David Tracy observes that this enterprise is necessary because "the question of ethics today (including, even more surprisingly, a good deal of theological ethics) seems strangely silent on the need to argue over the nature and reality of God and what difference the divine reality makes for ethics."[2] Gamwell sets out to break this silence by seeking to show why ethics and politics cannot ultimately be understood apart from the question of God. In fact, beginning with his 1973 doctoral dissertation on Reinhold Niebuhr, Gamwell's venture can aptly be described as an attempt to restructure and complete the public theology pursued by Niebuhr himself.[3] Yet, whereas Niebuhr's public theology ultimately relied on the suprarational language of myth and symbol, Gamwell turns to Whitehead and Hartshorne's modern process metaphysics and to Ogden's theology in order to rationally conceptualize and validate theology's public truth claims.

---

1. Hedley, "Should Divinity Overcome Metaphysics?" 289.
2. Tracy, Foreword to Gamwell's, *Divine Good*, ix.
3. Gamwell, "Theism and Political Theory Beyond Reinhold Niebuhr."

Gamwell's endeavor is perhaps best summed up in two passages from his book *Democracy on Purpose: Justice and the Reality of God* (2000). There, at the beginning of his introduction, he writes: "Morality and politics depend on a purpose in the nature of things. I seek here to redeem this assertion and to articulate the moral and political principles it implies." How he goes about redeeming this assertion is, in part, revealed at the beginning of chapter one, where he quotes the opening words of Calvin's *Institutes*:

> "Our Wisdom, in so far as it ought to be deemed true and solid wisdom, consists almost entirely of two parts: the knowledge of God and of ourselves. But as these are connected together by many ties, it is not easy to determine which of the two precedes, and gives birth to the other." If these famous opening sentences in Calvin's *Institutes of the Christian Religion* assert that knowing ourselves depends on knowing God, they also suggest that we can know God if we truly understand ourselves.... Does human life necessarily include an understanding of God?[4]

Gamwell proceeds to argue yes in response to this central question. So, on the one hand, he contends that morality and politics ultimately depend on a theistic metaphysical telos while, on the other, he argues that we implicitly always know this telos because the transcendental conditions of human understanding always include some understanding of God. I will seek to explicate these two central claims and related aspects of Gamwell's thought. I will do so by drawing principally on his two major books, which deal respectively with moral and political theory, namely, *The Divine Good* and *Democracy on Purpose*. I will draw on his other works, such as *Beyond Preference* (1984) and *Politics as a Christian Vocation* (2005) to fill in the various details of my overall portrait.

Reexamining Moral Theory: Aristotle, Kant, and Beyond

In modern philosophical ethics, it has been widely held that Aristotle and Kant represent two basic and incompatible approaches for thinking about the moral life: either one pursues some version of Kant's deontological approach or one follows Aristotle's teleological path (or some utilitarian variation thereof), but one can never integrate the two, or so it is generally assumed. Yet, beginning with a set of course lectures

---

4. Gamwell, *Democracy on Purpose*, 1, 13.

delivered at the University of Chicago in 1987, Gamwell set out to challenge this deep-seated assumption. In a course on the "Foundations of Ethics," co-taught with Paul Ricoeur and David Tracy, Gamwell argued that not only *can* Aristotle and Kant be coherently integrated, they *must* be in order for moral theory to advance. It was this set of lectures that formed the basis for *The Divine Good*.[5]

There, in a chapter devoted to Aristotle and Kant, Gamwell demonstrates that certain elements of their respective approaches can be coherently synthesized because they differ on two fundamental questions, not just one. Moreover, he contends that "each thinker has the better of the contrast in one of these two respects." The first contrast pertains to the question of whether "moral action is identified by desire," that is, by the desire to realize some purpose or telos in a future state of affairs. The second pertains to the question of whether "the ground of moral claims is an a priori principle." On Gamwell's reading, Aristotle answers yes to the first question and implicitly no to the second; conversely, Kant answers no to the first and yes to the second. Hence, Aristotle's approach may be described as a non-a priori or empirical teleology whereas Kant's may be called an a priori non-teleology. Each of them, Gamwell concludes, is right in what he affirms and wrong in what he denies: Aristotle (contra Kant) is correct to affirm that moral action is identified by desire for some telos, and Kant (contra Aristotle) is correct to affirm that the ground of moral claims is an a priori principle.[6]

In regard to the first contrast, Gamwell concurs with Aristotle's view in the *Nichomachean Ethics* that "'intellect itself . . . moves nothing.' (1139a36)." Hence, "good action cannot be identified independently of desire. This is not to say that good action is identified only by desire, as if reason were irrelevant." On the contrary, good action must be "in accord with a rational rule or principle." But the decisive point, Gamwell maintains, is "that the part reason plays in good action is inseparable from desire. For desire is the principle of motion in living beings, so that, with respect to action, reason can only give a rule to or guide and direct something else." In brief, reason deals with abstract forms and universals that are "devoid of particular reference to past or future" whereas desire

---

5. In his foreword to *Divine Good*, Tracy notes how the book originated from the course, ix, x.

6. Gamwell, *Divine Good*, chapter 2: "Teleology and Nonteleology: Aristotle and Kant," 19–60, 19.

is "the appetition for . . . some future state of affairs or characteristic of existence, and can 'move' the agent because this attachment affirms that the possibility should be realized." Desire implies a telos and, conversely, "a telos of human activity implies desire." Therefore, moral action is fueled by the desire to realize some future state of affairs in accordance with a rational rule or principle. Aristotle views happiness or fulfillment (*eudaimonia*) as the overarching telos that defines a good human life, namely, one of virtuous activity over a complete lifetime. As we will see shortly, Gamwell parts company with Aristotle when it comes to defining the overarching telos. But for now, the relevant point is that they both agree that reason plays a crucial supporting role but not an initiatory one. More precisely, they agree that "reason is involved in good action in two ways." First, in a general way, reason is critical "in the formation or education of desire." But, second, once a virtuous disposition is formed, it still requires the practical deliberation *(phronesis)* needed to "move from the general to the particular or from the end to the means." It is this practical wisdom that enables one to perform "the right action at the right time." Given Gamwell's concurrence with Aristotle that desire is central to moral action, there yet remains the following question: "How is the rational rule . . . by which desire is properly formed to be identified, such that one could know which states of character are good and which among alternative actions are morally prescribed?"[7] It is this question that leads to the second point of contrast.

For Aristotle, this question is answered by looking to the example of the virtuous person; one knows what constitutes good action by looking at a good role model. But what counts as a good role model is based on an empirically given starting-point, and only from there does it proceed to define what is morally good. Hence, in describing Aristotle's view, Gamwell denotes that

> one must generalize from certain people or actions already . . . accepted as examples of the good precisely because human action as such does not presuppose a moral principle. Accordingly, one cannot argue that these people or actions are good, that is, one may deny this claim without self-contradiction, and this is what it means to say that the "starting point" [for Aristotle] is the [presumed] "fact" that they have moral worth.[8]

---

7. Gamwell, *Divine Good*, 20, 21, 25.
8. Ibid., 27.

Gamwell's key point here is that, for Aristotle, "human action as such does not presuppose a moral principle." Thus, his ethic is based on the prior acceptance of an empirically given starting-point (such as what counts as virtue in ancient Athens), not on a rational or a priori ground. In reply, some might argue that Aristotle views happiness as the moral principle implied by human action as such. But Gamwell notes that a life of complete virtue for Aristotle consists merely of an aggregation of acts in pursuit of different and particular ends, for instance, "the defense of the polis or assistance to those in need," ends that are not themselves part of a more inclusive aim. Thus, for Aristotle,

> good action as such has no inclusive telos except a complete life in pursuit of particular states of affairs that are good. Were the rational rule by which virtuous activity is distinguished an a priori principle, then each of the particular . . . tele that diverse activities pursue would be instances of some general or inclusive state of affairs. This follows because an a priori condition is implied . . . by human action as such. Hence, the integrating telos of the good life could be identified in some manner other than a complete life in accord with virtue.[9]

Cast in terms of our earlier discussion of Porter, Gamwell suggests here that Aristotle's supreme good is a multi-item list of particular ends that do not themselves participate in or point to a more inclusive end. In short, happiness and virtue consist of doing a lot of different and independent activities well; the sum is merely the aggregate of the parts.[10]

---

9. Ibid.

10. If some might contend that Aristotle views happiness as the moral principle implied by human action as such, others might purport that theoretical contemplation is the moral end implied by all human action. This account, which draws on Book X of the *Ethics*, contends that Aristotle envisions happiness as a life in accord with the highest or best virtue, which Book X identifies as theoretical contemplation. Gamwell summarizes this view as follows: "Since 'the activity of God, which surpasses all others in blessedness, must be contemplative,' Aristotle argues, 'of human activities, . . . , that which is most akin to this must be most of the nature of happiness' (1178b21–23)." If this is what Aristotle has in mind, Gamwell reasons, then the moral mean for all persons and activities must be defined in relation to maximizing opportunities for contemplation. But, like Porter, Gamwell argues that this reading does not square with the rest of the *Ethics*. On the contrary, Books I–IX emphasize the value and virtue of various activities within the polis. Hence, "what seems apparent in the *Ethics* as a whole," he concludes, is "that Aristotle affirms different kinds of good activity which are independent of each other in the sense that there is no one kind of excellence in relation to which all of the others can be specified. Differing kinds of happy lives, then, involve differing compositions of these kinds of good activity" (Gamwell, *Divine Good*, 28, 29).

In response to Aristotle's empirical starting-point, Kant declares that this approach begs the question. "For Kant," as Gamwell reports,

> a circularity in Aristotle's argument displays its failure: Aristotle begs the question when he defines virtue by assuming that he already knows who the virtuous people are. "Nor could anything be more fatal to morality," Kant writes, "than that we should wish to derive it from examples. For every example of it that is set before me must first itself be tested by principles of morality, [to see] whether it is worthy to serve as an original example, that is, as a pattern, but by no means can it authoritatively furnish the conception of morality."[11]

In contrast to basing ethics on a given example, Gamwell agrees with Kant that morality must be based on an a priori principle. Kant's great insight, Gamwell avers, is his recognition that practical reason prescribes an a priori moral law. That is, when Kant famously seeks to identify that "which is good without qualification," what he is really doing is attempting to define the underlying "distinction between all moral and immoral choices and thereby [to identify] moral worth as such."[12] Kant's wisdom is to recognize that practical reason prescribes that we ought to choose in accordance with the truth about the fundamental condition of human freedom, whatever that condition may turn out to be. Let me unpack this critical point into four sub-components.

First, Kant "begins with the claim that humans are free because they are rational." To illustrate, Gamwell quotes Kant: "'The will is nothing but practical reason'; humans have the 'faculty of determining their causality through the conception of a rule.'" This means, Gamwell suggests, that practical reason "is the capacity to think about or understand one's action, . . . and this capacity allows humans to choose." The import of this is that "an understanding or exercise of reason cannot be solely the product of prior or external causes but is always [implicitly or explicitly] chosen." Second, "Kant then seeks to show that practical reason implies that human choice is obligated by an a priori principle. Since action is determined by concepts or understandings, he argues, 'the *will* is a kind of causality belonging to living beings insofar as they are rational,' and causality without a law 'would be an absurdity.'" Put simply,

---

11. Gamwell, *Divine Good*, 42. Gamwell cites Kant, *Fundamental Principles of the Metaphysic of Morals* (Indianapolis: Bobbs-Merrill, 1949) 26.

12. Gamwell, *Divine Good*, 30–31.

causality implies explanation, and the explanation of freedom implies some law, rule, or principle. But, third, "the law of the 'free will' must be 'of a peculiar kind,' namely, 'the property of the will to be a law to itself.'" In other words, it must be "a law of obligation presupposed in freedom as such." And, fourth, to speak of that which is presupposed in freedom as such is to speak of its fundamental or a priori condition. Hence, the crucial question is, what is the "a priori condition of human choice"?[13]

At first blush, it would appear that there are two equal possibilities: either human freedom comes with some built-in moral law to guide and assess choices or it does not. For instance, the "amoralist" view, as illustrated by Weber, denies that freedom comes with a built-in moral law. To be sure, Weber would affirm that reason can play a valuable instrumental role in identifying means and consequences in the moral life, but reason itself cannot identify which values, goods, or choices one ultimately ought to seek. Hence, all moral choices are, to use Kant's term, hypothetical, that is, contingent on some prior commitment. *If* one is committed to health, *then* reason can identify the most effective means for obtaining it; but Weber would deny that one has a categorical or unconditional obligation to seek health or any other alternative. Against this interpretation, some might allege that Weber is open to the possibility that there may be a built-in moral law, but reason simply cannot identify what it is; instead, humans require some particular revelation, charismatic individual, or personal insight to glean its identity. But this assertion merely repeats the point that for Weber and amoralism, all moral claims are hypothetical. *If* one accepts or commits oneself to a particular revelation or charismatic insight, *then* one has reasons to follow its moral prescriptions; but there is no binding obligation to accept the revelation or insight itself. Hence, according to amoralism, the choice among moral values is ultimately rationally arbitrary.[14]

---

13. Ibid., 35, 36. Gamwell cites Kant, *Fundamental Principles*, 49, 63; and Kant, *Critique of Practical Reason* (Indianapolis: Bobbs-Merrill, 1956) 32.

14. For Gamwell's discussion of Weber and amoralism, see *Divine Good*, 9–10, 35–38. It should also be noted that since Aristotle bases ethics on the empirical role model, his ethic, too, is ultimately hypothetical rather than categorical. *If* one accepts the given example or role model as definitive of moral worth, *then* one ought to define and measure virtue accordingly. But, as noted above, Gamwell contends that Aristotle "cannot argue that these people or actions are good, that is, one may deny this claim without self-contradiction, and this is what it means to say that the 'starting point' [for Aristotle] is the [presumed] 'fact' that they have moral worth" (*Divine Good*, 27).

Significantly, Gamwell argues that Kant's insight is to recognize that even amoralism itself implies a moral law, which renders the amoralist position self-contradictory. Therefore, there is in fact only one genuine possibility, namely, that human freedom must come with some built-in moral law. Gamwell makes this point as follows:

> Were it the case that practical reason prescribes only hypothetically, so that amoralism is true, then *this* condition of human freedom would have to be implied by human choice as such, [for] the absence of a moral law could only be itself a priori. But it is, Kant claims, self-contradictory to assert that amoralism is an a priori condition of human choice, because any a priori condition obliges the will to choose accordingly. If it is said that there is no law of obligation by virtue of which one should distinguish among the possible ends of human action, so that all choice among ends is rationally arbitrary, this cannot mean that such choices are prerational but [only] that practical reason implies the [following] a priori law: *Always choose among ends arbitrarily*. In other words, a moral law is implied by the claim that amoralism is an a priori condition of human choice, so that the claim refutes itself [italics added].[15]

Gamwell recognizes the potential objection that this argument commits "something like a category mistake." If there is no built-in moral standard to evaluate ends, this objection maintains, then "we cannot be obligated to choose ends arbitrarily, because there is no alternative to doing so." But Gamwell indicates that there is indeed an alternative. If the truth of human freedom is as the amoralist describes it, then "one might fail to accept this truth." That is to say, "one might choose one's ends in the mistaken belief that there *is* a moral distinction among them; one might choose one's purposes in the mistaken belief that one is morally bound to pursue happiness or obey the will of God or in some other way to distinguish among the possible ends of action." In fact, of course, "most humans throughout most of the relevant human history have chosen in the belief that some ends in distinction from others are morally required and, therefore, have failed to obey the imperative: Choose ends arbitrarily." Gamwell's point here, again, is that acts of human reasoning and understanding are always at least partly chosen. Thus, the question is, does one choose one's understanding in

---

15. Gamwell, *Divine Good*, 36.

accordance with the true condition of freedom or, on the contrary, does one choose in defiance of that truth? In sum, Gamwell concludes that

> it does make sense to say that any claim regarding the a priori condition of human choice, including [the amoralist claim], implies an obligation to choose accordingly. It implies the obligation to make all of one's choices without deception or illusion about the will's a priori character. Given that practical reason must have some a priori condition, this condition [itself] is a law of its causality, so that rational causality without a law "would be an absurdity."[16]

Thus far, Gamwell has agreed with Aristotle that desire and teleology are central to moral action, and he has agreed with Kant that morality presupposes an a priori moral principle. What is needed, therefore, is an a priori teleology. Yet, for his part, Kant believes that morality cannot be based on teleology precisely because he assumes that all such attempts, as illustrated by Aristotle, end up begging the question. "For Kant," as Gamwell remarks, "Aristotle is bound to this illicit approach to moral theory *because* Aristotle identifies moral virtue with rational desire. No object of desire can be a priori, so that any teleological ethic must wish to derive morality from examples. In truth, the moral law must [instead] be radically nonteleological." The key here is that Kant presumes that no object of desire can be a priori and, therefore, he concludes that the a priori moral law can only be nonteleological. If an a priori telos could be rationally identified, Kant reasons, then it would be a necessary or metaphysical condition of reality as such and the moral law would then indeed be based on it; the a priori condition of human freedom would then be defined by its implicit or built-in desire for this metaphysical telos. To deny such a telos would be self-contradictory because the very act of human choice would always presuppose it. But Kant, of course, denies that metaphysical knowledge of reality as such is possible; therefore he denies the possibility of any a priori telos. As Gamwell observes, "the success of Kant's argument against the moral relevance of desire and for the purely formal [or nonteleological] character of the moral law depends upon the truth of his claim that all existential statements are empirical or rationally contingent." Summarily speaking, "the radical nonteleology of Kant's ethic, implying as it does that all existential statements are rationally contingent, expresses the coherence between

16. Ibid.

his *Critique of Practical Reason* and his *Critique of Pure Reason*. The ground of moral claims is purely formal or independent of all ends or tele because metaphysics is impossible."[17] Before taking up the question of metaphysics directly, let us examine Gamwell's critique of Kant's non-teleological ethic.

Since Kant believes that the moral law must be a priori, and since he contends that no metaphysical or a priori telos can be rationally identified, he concludes that the moral law must be grounded only in a good will. A good will is identified not by the ends it seeks but only by the form or purity of its act of willing. More precisely, a good will is one whose actions arise from a reverence for the moral law and whose proposed actions or maxims conform to what the moral law requires. What the moral law requires, Kant famously suggests, can be identified through the categorical imperative—expressed in either of his two primary formulations: first, "*act only on that maxim through which you can at the same time will that it should become a universal law,*" or, second, "*act in such a way that you always treat humanity, whether in your own person or in the person of any other, never simply as a means, but always at the same time as an end [in itself].*"[18] Overall, Gamwell agrees with Hegel "that Kant's putative moral law is in truth empty and, therefore, not a ground for any moral claims at all." By this, Gamwell means that Kant's theory, in spite of his intention, "does not provide the ground in accord with which one can distinguish between moral and immoral choices or actions."[19] Gamwell seeks to substantiate this judgment by assessing these two forms of the categorical imperative.

With regard to the first, Gamwell argues that Kant unwittingly conflates two different kinds of tests here. In other words, the first formulation does not in fact assess the *morality* of maxims, as Kant believes, but rather assesses the *formal nature* of what can or cannot be a maxim at all. Whatever apparent success Kant's examples have, such as testing whether making a false promise is morally permitted, is based on a conflation built into the test itself. This conflation is due to the fact that Kant has forgotten the truth of his own famous aphorism: "ought implies can." Maxims should be formulated explicitly in terms of what one *can* do or *can* control, and what one can control is the *attempt* to

17. Ibid., 42, 44.
18. Kant, *Groundwork of the Metaphysic of Morals*, 88, 96.
19. Gamwell, *Divine Good*, 56.

do an action, not the presumed or actual *outcome*. What this means, Gamwell argues, is that Kant should be testing maxims in regard to what one can attempt to do, not in terms of the implications or results of one's actions.

To illustrate this critical distinction, Gamwell borrows an example from the work of Jonathan Harrison, namely, the maxim: "Always to enter an open door first."[20] Initially, it might appear that this example validates Kant's position—showing how Kant's test rejects this proposed maxim. As Gamwell notes, "clearly one cannot consistently will that this maxim should become a universal law, because, when more than one person is involved, everyone cannot be the first person through an open door." Hence, "one might conclude that Kant's purely formal [or non-teleological] imperative does indeed provide in this admittedly trivial case a distinction between moral and immoral maxims." But such a conclusion, Gamwell posits, is both premature and mistaken. This is the case because the proper formulation of the maxim should read: "Always to *try* to enter an open door first" or *"insofar as possible*, always to enter an open door first." This latter formulation is the proper expression of a genuine maxim because if "ought implies can," then a genuine maxim should refer only to what one *can* do or what one *can* control, which in this case is to *try* to enter an open door first. In contrast, the initial formulation implicitly refers to an outcome or result, namely, entering an open door *first*. But once one recognizes how maxims should be properly formulated, it becomes clear that Kant's test is empty when it comes to assessing the morality or immorality of actions, for there is nothing logically contradictory about "*trying* to enter an open door first." "Notwithstanding the confusion that would obtain," says Gamwell, "everyone could [consistently] try to be the first person through an open door, as the cry of 'fire' in a crowded theatre is likely to confirm."[21]

When one returns to Kant's own examples, the same point becomes evident. For instance, in the case of borrowing money without the intent to repay, Gamwell cites Kant's proposed maxim: "'When in difficulty, to promise whatever one pleases, with the purpose of not keeping the promise.'" As is known, Kant concludes that one cannot

---

20. Ibid., 57. Gamwell cites Harrison, "Kant's Examples of the First Formulation of the Categorical Imperative," in *Kant, Foundations of the Metaphysics of Morals: Text and Critical Essays*, ed. Robert Paul Wolff (Indianapolis: Bobbs-Merrill, 1969) 213.

21. Gamwell, *Divine Good*, 57.

consistently will that this maxim should become a universal law because "'the promise itself would become impossible, . . . , since no one would consider that anything was promised to him, but would ridicule all such statements as vain pretenses.'" But "what follows from Kant's argument," Gamwell maintains, "is not a moral conclusion but [rather] a formal criticism of the maxim [itself]." What Kant shows, in other words, is that a complete or successful promise involves two or more parties (one making the promise and one or more accepting it). But this means then that "whether an agent promises or not . . . is not completely within the control of the agent in question." Yet, moral questions pertain only to what is within one's control or sphere of responsibility (ought implies can). Thus, "the relevant maxim should be formulated: 'When in difficulty, to *try* to promise whatever one pleases . . .' or 'when in difficulty and *insofar as possible*, to promises whatever one pleases. . . .' But this maxim," Gamwell points out, "can be consistently willed to become a universal law, since the attempt to make a promise does not depend upon whether another person believes that something is 'promised to him.'" In sum, "a genuine maxim . . . must identify an action within the control of an agent." And once this is recognized, Kant's first formulation of the categorical imperative fails to offer any moral bite.[22]

Likewise, in regard to the second formulation, Gamwell asserts that it too "fails to introduce a distinction between moral and immoral choice or action." To be sure, when Kant insists that the moral law prescribes that one treat all persons as ends rather than merely as means, he is claiming that respect for the freedom of others and oneself is a moral obligation. Moreover, Kant agrees that to exercise freedom is to exercise choice, and to exercise choice is to choose among some possible purposes. But the problem, Gamwell contends, arises from the fact that Kant's understanding of the moral law offers no criterion by which to assess these possible purposes or states of affairs. We are to respect the freedom of others and ourselves, but what one chooses with that freedom is itself morally arbitrary insofar as the moral law does not identify which ends one ought to choose. Otherwise stated, for Kant the choice among ends is merely preferential or "private" insofar as the moral law is silent or indifferent on the question of which aims we ought to pursue. Put simply, then, why is respecting freedom a moral obligation if what one chooses with that freedom is itself morally arbi-

---

22. Ibid., 57, 58. Gamwell cites Kant, *Fundamental Principles*, 40.

trary? As Gamwell sees it, "if the unqualified goodness of a good will is independent of any [telos or] state of affairs to be pursued, one cannot affirm another's pursuit of ends as morally good and, therefore, respect for her or his freedom is meaningless."[23]

To respond, one might propose that Kant does offer a criterion by which to assess choices insofar as he holds that there is a "supreme limiting condition" to the exercise of freedom, namely, that one's choices ought also to "treat all rational beings as ends in themselves." Yet, "this reply," Gamwell argues, "simply repeats the problem":

> If a good will is independent of all states of affairs to be pursued, then it follows that all possible purposes are neither good nor bad [i.e., are morally indifferent]. But the affirmation that it is morally good for another to pursue any one of a class of possible purposes implies that they are all equally good, and this implies some telos by virtue of which *that* evaluation is justified. So far as I can see, there is no meaning to a moral affirmation of freedom if there are no morally good ends, for this is simply the affirmation of freedom independently of its exercise.[24]

Kant's position is ultimately self-contradictory, Gamwell reasons, because his denial that the moral law is teleological is at odds with his affirmation that respect for freedom is morally obligatory. To put it in Kant's own terms, his implicit claim that the exercise of freedom (the choice among possible purposes) involves only hypothetical imperatives is at odds with his explicit claim that respect for freedom is a categorical imperative. Thus, "if no [telos or] state of affairs is morally good, [then] there is no morally worthwhile freedom." To affirm the moral worth of freedom independently of any telos, Gamwell reckons, is as problematical and incoherent as affirming the "right to freedom of belief" while concomitantly denying "that any proposition is true."[25] In either case, the value of freedom is left bankrupt. In sum, Kant's categorical imperative cannot distinguish between moral and immoral actions because the only way to distinguish among actions is in terms of their purposes, and for Kant, the moral law is independent of purposes.

Based on his analysis of Aristotle and Kant, Gamwell purports that the future direction of moral theory is led not to a simple *either-or* but,

23. Gamwell, *Divine Good*, 50, 48, 50.
24. Ibid., 50.
25. Ibid., 49.

rather, to a critical *both-and*—one that moves beyond each of them. That is, given that Kant rightly affirms that practical reason prescribes that we choose an understanding of ourselves and our actions in accordance with the a priori truth of freedom, and given that Aristotle rightly recognizes that the exercise of freedom necessarily involves the choice and pursuit of some telos, then the moral law must be defined, against both Aristotle and Kant, by some a priori telos. "It follows [from this]," declares Gamwell, "that there must be some state of affairs or characteristic of existence that is implied by the affirmation of any purpose or state of affairs at all and is, therefore, rationally necessary." But to speak of a rationally necessary characteristic of existence is to speak of "metaphysics." "Thus, the contrast of Aristotle and Kant argues that the a priori character of practical reason implies . . . that morality is dependent upon metaphysics."[26] Gamwell acknowledges that this conclusion still requires a positive validation, but such a validation first requires that he lay some further groundwork.

Toward A Theistic Metaphysical Telos

In seeking to redirect moral theory toward a metaphysical and theistic teleology, Gamwell recognizes that he must confront and remove Kant's monumental "roadblock" to the metaphysical enterprise. However, he submits that this cannot be successfully done if one seeks to return to a premodern metaphysics. That is, unlike Milbank and the other new traditionalists, Gamwell rejects the quest to retrieve either a medieval theology or metaphysics; likewise, he rejects their skepticism toward democracy. On the contrary, he argues that what is needed is a modern process metaphysics and an unequivocal affirmation of democracy as the social and political manifestation of the divine telos. I will later address his discussion of democracy, but first let us turn our attention to his critique of Kant's denial of metaphysics.

At the center of Kant's famous critique of metaphysics are two related claims: (1) that there is a coherent and essential distinction between phenomena and noumena, and (2) that all positive existential statements—all statements about existence—are logically contingent. As Gamwell sees it, Kant's "rejection of the traditional metaphysical enterprise depends upon the validity" of these two claims. In regard

---

26. Ibid., 59.

to the former, Gamwell states that "for Kant, traditional metaphysics is impossible precisely because things-in-themselves or reality as such [noumena], at least may be different from things-as-they-appear [phenomena], so that things-in-themselves are in principle unknowable." This supposed unbridgeable gap between phenomena and noumena arises from Kant's second claim, which is that "no positive existential statements are logically necessary."[27] To say that no positive existential statements are necessary is, by implication, to say that completely negative existential statements are possible. What Gamwell means here by the latter, as he remarks elsewhere, is "a negation that has no positive content, the assertion of absence that is not by implication the assertion of some presence."[28] Returning to Kant, his "distinction between phenomena and noumena asserts that completely negative existential statements are logically possible; noumena are simply not-phenomena."[29] Summarily stated then, all that Kant can say about noumena, since he claims that they are unknowable, is that they are not phenomena. But Gamwell argues that such completely negative existential assertions are finally incoherent. To support this stance, he makes the following case.

To claim, as Kant does, that no positive existential statements are necessary is to claim that "nothing exits" is logically possible and, by implication, to claim that "'something exists' is not logically necessary." Hence, Kant's position implicitly asserts the following hypothesis: "'Nothing exists' and 'something exists' are both logically possible." But this joint hypothesis, Gamwell asserts, "is itself self-contradictory or logically *impossible*." In making this case, Gamwell's argument centers on the following question: What subjects can logically be connected with the verb "to exist"? That is to say, what is the *class* that contains all the logical possibilities that can be connected with existence? According to Kant's hypothesis, the class contains two basic members: "nothing" and "something." Gamwell, however, argues that this hypothesis ends up contradicting itself, and therefore that the class can only contain one member, namely, "something." In the argument below (proposition 3 and beyond), he uses "X" to refer to this class—to the class of logically possible subjects connected with the verb "to exist." To keep this clear, I will add the term "class" in brackets where appropriate. Furthermore,

27. Ibid., 158, 159.
28. Gamwell, "On the Loss of Theism," 180.
29. Gamwell, *Divine Good*, 159.

I will italicize the various propositions of the argument and add spaces between the different sections in order to demarcate its components. With these clarifications in place, Gamwell's argument reads as follows:

> *[Kant's] Hypothesis: "Nothing exists" and "something exists" are both logically possible.*
>
> 1. *"Nothing exists" is logically possible.*
>   [As stated in the] Hypothesis
> 2. *"Something exists" is not logically necessary.*
>   Implication of (1)
> 3. *"X exists"* [i.e., the class] *does not imply "something exists."*
>   Implication of (2)
>
> 4. *"Something exists" is logically possible.*
>   [As stated in the] Hypothesis
> 5. *"Something exists" implies "X exists"* [i.e., "something exists" implies the class of which it is a member].
>   Implication of (4)
> 6. *"X" is a positive concept* [i.e., the class, which includes "something," is identified by some positive or defining characteristic. For identification of the class cannot be defined in purely negative terms since affirmation cannot imply sheer negation].
>   Implication of (5)
> 7. *"X exists"* [i.e., the class] *implies "something exists."*
>   Implication of (6)
>
> 8. *"'Nothing exists' and 'something exists' are both logically possible" is logically impossible.*
>   Implication of (3) and (7).[30]

In propositions 1-3, he seeks to show that the assertion "nothing exists" leads to the conclusion that the class *does not* imply "something exists." By contrast, in steps 4-7, he seeks to demonstrate that the assertion of "something exists" leads to the conclusion that the class *does* imply "something exists." Hence, taken together, these two conclusions—(3) and (7)—contradict each other.

Gamwell recognizes that "the pivotal claim in this argument is 6." By holding that the class of existence must be "positive," he means that

---

30. Gamwell, *Divine Good*, 110–11; italics added.

there must be some definable characteristic that is shared by all members of the class. The relevant point here

> is that two members of a class must have the class characteristic in common. If, for instance, "red" and "green" are both members of the class of "color," then "red" and "green" have in common the class characteristic "being a color." Thus, if "nothing exists" and "something exists" were both logically possible, then "nothing" and "something" would have some class characteristic in common. But "nothing" and "something" can have no class characteristic in common.[31]

The reason why "nothing" and "something" can have no class characteristic in common is because they are contradictory terms and thus, by definition, cannot overlap or share any intermediary. It does no good, he continues, to suggest that what they have in common is the class of "logical possibility," for that merely begs the question. Moreover, "any given class characteristic must be either negative or positive. Hence, a class of which 'something' is a member must be something." In other words, something is not nothing and thus must be identifiable by some positive characteristic. Therefore, since "'something exists' is logically possible, . . . it is also logically necessary, and 'nothing exists' is self-contradictory."[32]

Gamwell's argument here is reminiscent of Kant's own ontological argument in *TOPB*. There, as we saw in chapter 2, Kant contends that the logical class defining "existence" cannot contain both "nothing" and "something" because this assertion annuls "possibility" itself, and therefore is self-contradictory. The upshot of this argument, according to both Kant and Gamwell, is that "something exists" is logically necessary, which means that completely negative existential statements are logically incoherent. But the obvious question, then, is to ask why does the later Kant not adhere to this conclusion? I suggested in chapter 2 that Kant only conceived of necessary existence in classical theistic terms, and this assumption never changed for him. Hence, rather than jettisoning classical theism, the later Kant instead gives up his own logical insight by relegating it from metaphysical to merely regulative status. Gamwell thinks this is Kant's fundamental mistake: instead of abandoning the logical insight, Kant should have abandoned classical

31. Ibid., 111.
32. Ibid.

theism. Having done this, he could have then recognized that his critical distinction between phenomena and noumena is ultimately incoherent because it wrongly presupposes that completely negative existential statements are possible. As Gamwell denotes,

> the class of logically necessary existential claims is the class of valid metaphysical claims. Hence, the denial of a valid metaphysical claim is self-contradictory in the sense that the denial contradicts the existential claim that it also logically implies . . . , namely, the implication that something exists.[33]

Summarily speaking then, once one recognizes that "something exists" is logically necessary, it then serves as a touchstone and criterion by which one can validate other metaphysical claims.

A Theistic Metaphysical Telos

Thus far, Gamwell has argued that ethics requires a metaphysical telos and that metaphysics, contrary to the later Kant, is a necessary and viable enterprise. What Gamwell means by a metaphysical telos is a comprehensive evaluative standard or "ideal by which alternative possible purposes may be compared, so that some are evaluated as better than others, and [that] one is morally obligated to *maximize* the good."[34] He has consistently defined this metaphysical telos in relation to a "comprehensive variable." For instance, in *Beyond Preference* he contends that "human activity entails a moral principle in accord with which human choice as such may be evaluated." In other words, human choice presupposes a moral "yardstick" by which one can compare and evaluate all possible choices and alternatives; such a yardstick entails a standard or variable applicable to all possible states of affairs. Therefore, "the variable according to which alternatives for a particular activity are correctly understood," he says, "always implies a comprehensive variable for comparing choice alternatives as such, a variable that is objective and one in terms of which all choice alternatives may be compared in all aspects."[35]

In reply, some might urge that the standard by which human choices are evaluated is not singular and comprehensive but, rather, culturally,

33. Ibid., 162.
34. Ibid., 164.
35. Gamwell, *Beyond Preference*, 69, 75.

historically, or individually pluralistic and particular. Furthermore, they might claim that only this view enables one to truly appreciate cultural and human diversity. But Gamwell argues that such diversity cannot in fact be coherently understood or properly appreciated from a relativistic outlook. "[T]here is no escaping the fact," he recounts,

> that all truth cannot be relative, because the assertion that it is so is [itself] clearly nonrelative in character. Similarly, to say that different situations of choice are correctly understood through different objective variables is to make a nonrelative assertion about the correct understanding of human choice; in other words, relativism is a nonrelative theory and, therefore, self-refuting. In order to understand that there are specifically different conditions of human choice (specific differences of culture, historical age, etc.), one must have an understanding of those differences and, therefore, a comparative variable that is nonrelative. The specific variables relative to specific conditions must themselves be specifications of, because comparable by, a nonspecific variable that is *supreme*, a variable in terms of which all human choices are properly understood.[36]

Reminiscent of Davidson, Gamwell suggests here that one cannot recognize, understand, or appreciate differences unless one implicitly understands them in reference to some more inclusive or comprehensive measure—a supreme variable in relation to which one can assess differences. The specific differences are themselves "specifications of, because comparable by, a nonspecific variable."

Having insisted on the necessity of a comprehensive, metaphysical variable, it is important to clarify that Gamwell does not mean that all differences are in fact metaphysical in nature. Indeed, as he says in the *Divine Good*, clearly "not all human inquiry is metaphysical." In fact, "most of our attempt to understand the world and ourselves as a part of it seeks to answer nonmetaphysical questions of one kind or another regarding the differences among things." But his key point, nonetheless, is that metaphysics is the attempt to understand the ultimate background conditions and supreme variable that lie behind all such differences and provide the context for them as such. In another work, he describes the relationship between metaphysics and more proximate concerns as follows: "A theory inclusive of metaphysical principles might still be [context-dependent] in the sense that discourse begins with specific issues

36. Ibid., 76.

in the ethical life of a people, and the [metaphysical] principles have practical importance only as a given discourse yields relevant disagreements incapable of resolution by considerations of lesser scope."[37] One might characterize this statement as Gamwell's version of the principle of subsidiarity: the ultimate role of metaphysics only comes explicitly into play when discourse cannot resolve conflicting claims at a more concrete level of discussion.

Along with subsidiarity, Gamwell specifies the role of metaphysics in another way as well. If I read him correctly, the comprehensive variable is *applicable* to all possibilities, but the comprehensible variable may not always identify a *relevant* moral difference among alternatives. In other words, to borrow terms from economics, what he envisions is that: (1) there are differing degrees of good measured in relation to the comprehensive variable, and (2) there are, at these differing levels of good, indifference curves among alternative possibilities in relation to the comprehensive variable. Hence, it is the comprehensive variable that ultimately compares and measures differing degrees of value or goodness, but within a given level of value, there are alternatives that are indifferent in relation to the comprehensive variable. This distinction is implied, for instance, in Gamwell's discussion of vocation in *Democracy on Purpose*. There, he suggests that as long as one is making life choices that maximize the comprehensive variable, which he defines here as "our maximal common humanity," then the choice of one's specific vocation may be morally indifferent. As he depicts it, there are

> many kinds of activity through which individuals properly pursue our maximal common humanity. The same pursuit may occur in family life and personal relationships and through participation in economic, educational, cultural, religious and other forms of social action. [Hence, within an indifference curve at a given or maximal level of value,] [t]here is no principle for the measure in which each individual's contribution should occur through one or another form except that [already] defined by our maximal common humanity itself, and there is every reason to think that individuals have alternatives in this regard that are equally good. Whether, for instance, one's vocation should focus on politics or education or art, economic production or reli-

---

37. Gamwell, *Divine Good*, 166; Gamwell, "Comment on Jeffrey Stout," 4.

gious activity, health delivery or child care, may not be a moral question for a given individual.[38]

Though I will later discuss what he means by "maximal common humanity," the point here is that not all differences are metaphysical in nature, even though metaphysics defines the comprehensive variable in relation to which all choices are ultimately evaluated.

Having argued that ethics requires a comprehensive variable, Gamwell seeks to establish that such a variable can only be coherently understood in terms of "a supreme or all-inclusive [actuality] in which all things are compared and thereby evaluated." Such an all-inclusive reality, he further contends, can only be coherently understood in theistic terms. But it is not traditional or classical theism that he has in mind. On the contrary, in order to evaluate the differences among all possibilities and concrete actualities, the comprehensive variable must be an all-inclusive reality that is supremely relative to all potential and actual states of affairs. Drawing on the dipolar theism of Hartshorne, Gamwell describes this all-inclusive reality as "the divine relativity." That is to say, divinity is defined and constituted in part "by its complete or fully adequate internal relations to all actuality and possibility, such that all other things are parts of it." Put simply, God is the all-inclusive reality in which all things exist and to which all things contribute. Moreover, in order for the divine relativity to be able to distinguish and evaluate the differences between mere future possibilities and present actualities, God must in some fundamental sense be temporal. "Given that actuality implies possibility" and given that the passage from possibility to actuality implies change, "reality without time," notes Gamwell, "is not a sensible idea." In essence, time rather than eternity is the primary or inclusive metaphysical category. "As the future becomes past, possibilities are realized and determinate reality is increased, and the all-inclusive relativity is different." Thus, given his joint affirmations of divinity as an all-inclusive actuality, on the one hand, and as participating in temporal process, on the other, Gamwell submits that "one must distinguish between the divine as an actuality or activity and the divine as an individual. An individual may be understood as a composite of activities that is serially or sequentially ordered and has genetic identity. . . . Hence, the divine must be an individual or temporally ordered series

---

38. Gamwell, *Democracy on Purpose*, 302.

of activities whose distinguishing characteristic is 'complete relativity to all actuality and possibility.'"[39] In sum, God is the comprehensive individual who experiences and assesses all things and in relation to whom all possibilities and actualities ought to be ultimately evaluated.

This version of a dipolar process theism, Gamwell argues, offers a third way that moves theism, metaphysics, and ethics forward. Up to this point, the two main options have been either a metaphysical theism based on a pre-Kantian metaphysics or a post-Kantian ethic that concludes that morality is non-metaphysical and at root non-theistic. But both of these alternatives have tended to assume that the only metaphysical option is found in some version of classical theism. Again, by "classical theism," Gamwell refers to that dominant tradition in the West in which the divine or ultimate reality "is said to be completely absolute and, therefore, completely changeless and necessary." From this perspective, the world is relative to God, but God cannot be relative to the world, i.e., divinity cannot be internally related to contingent and temporal realities. "Kant was quite correct to reject the traditional arguments or 'proofs' for the existence of this God," remarks Gamwell. "Since it implies the absence of all real differences, the notion of a completely necessary being is in truth completely negative, and one cannot argue for the existence of something that cannot be positively identified." But there is a genuine alternative, he proposes:

> My principal point is . . . that the understanding of God that I have outlined and that Hartshorne more than any other single thinker has developed stands in contrast to the classical view, so that it constitutes an alternative to both Kant's denial and the pre-Kantian formulation of metaphysics. With Hartshorne, we may call this third alternative "neoclassical theism." It asserts that the abstract . . . character of the divine individuality is the only absolute aspect of God. The . . . concrete member activities of the divine are always inclusive of a possible future as well as an actual past, so that the temporal passage is a process of never ending divine change. God is the everlasting individual. Thus, God is both the one individual to which all others are relative and the one individual relative to all others.[40]

---

39. Gamwell, *Divine Good*, 169, 170, 171. See Hartshorne, *Divine Relativity*.
40. Gamwell, *Divine Good*, 175, 176.

A Transcendental-Process Theology 505

Based on this neoclassical theism, Gamwell proceeds to define the telos inherent in the nature of reality as such. Since God is internally related to all concrete actualities and states of affairs, and since these actualities contribute to the divine life, one can say that God is directly related to and affected by the past, present, and future of the world. Since the present quickly becomes the immediate past, and the past as such cannot be changed, it is toward the future that a telos is directed. Moreover, as we saw in his discussion of Aristotle, Gamwell defines desire as "a living being's positive relation to some future possibility, the appetition for or attachment to some future state of affairs or characteristic of existence." Thus, value or creativity is defined in terms of what one contributes to the future. "[T]he telos that all human activity ought to pursue is the maximal creativity of all future activities or the future as such." But since God is indeed the comprehensive variable in relation to which all value and creativity is measured, "we are now in a position," announces Gamwell,

> to draw the principal conclusion toward which this [argument] as a whole has been directed. Since I have argued that the realization of greater or lesser good can be identified only by the concrete comparisons within the divine relativity, to call a more creative activity better means precisely that it contributes more to the supreme diversity that is unified in the activity of God. It then follows that the [metaphysical] telos can be nothing other than the maximal creativity realized in the activities of the divine existence. To pursue maximal creativity in the future as such is nothing other than to affirm the maximal future creativity of God, that is, the future as such *is* the future of God. But the creativity of God, as all creativity, is good, and we may say that the [metaphysical] telos is the divine good. In sum, the divine good identifies the moral law.[41]

The metaphysical telos that is an a priori condition of all reality, including human freedom, is the divine good. Whatever value all things have is measured ultimately in relation to what they contribute to the future as such, which is none other than the future of God. God is the one metaphysical or cosmic individual who fully experiences all things and who integrates them—through comparison and evaluation—into the one divine experience. Hence, maximal creativity in the future, as

---

41. Ibid., 21, 182.

understood as maximal unity-in-diversity, is creativity that contributes to the divine good.

Gamwell's notion here can be further illuminated by returning to a comparison with Aristotle. On Gamwell's account, Aristotle's understanding of happiness is empirical rather than metaphysical in that "happiness is not identified by the character of reality as such but rather by a good that can only be peculiar to human life. Accordingly, Aristotle's moral theory must make appeal to actions and persons that are arbitrarily assumed to be examples of the good." This view, as Gamwell sees it, has at least two negative implications. First, it lacks an all-inclusive telos—happiness ultimately consists merely of an aggregation of acts in pursuit of different ends. Second, because it lacks an all-inclusive telos, it thereby lacks "the inclusive virtue in accord with which all other [virtues] are properly ordered." By contrast, Gamwell's metaphysical notion of the divine good is an all-inclusive telos insofar as all activities, in the midst of all their diversity, contribute to this comprehensive aim. Following from this, he defines the all-inclusive virtue in terms of "'piety'" or "'reverence.'" Using these terms, he defines the comprehensive virtue as the "abiding disposition to act in accord with an attachment to the divine good. Hence, the several other virtues are properly understood as those dispositions through which desire for the divine good informs action within specific kinds of circumstances of a person's life, so that all of one's life becomes an act of piety or reverence."[42] Let me explicate each of these points by way of further contrast.

First, Gamwell's notion of an all-inclusive telos is singular in terms of its comprehensive aim (the divine good) and diverse in terms of its content (all the distinct creative activities and particular goods in the world). One will recall from our discussion of Porter that she resists Aquinas's contention that there is a single ultimate good because such a claim, she argues, is problematic at best and perverse at worst. Instead, she seeks to define the human end in terms of a natural human good that consists of a balanced assortment of diverse goods, including contemplation of God. There is diversity here, Gamwell would note, but not a single all-inclusiveness. That is, like Aristotle, Porter's notion of happiness involves an aggregate of different goods and virtues but no single comprehensive telos. Hence, Gamwell agrees with Aquinas (contra Porter) that there is indeed a single final end; alternatively, Gamwell

---

42. Ibid., 210.

concurs with Porter (contra Aquinas) that happiness involves a diversity of goods. What enables Gamwell, unlike these others, to affirm an all-inclusive telos that is both singular in nature and diverse in content is precisely his process metaphysic and his neoclassical understanding of God. In short, Gamwell's divine good integrates Thomas's monistic insight with Porter's humanistic sensibility.

Second, by describing the all-inclusive virtue in terms of "piety" or "reverence," Gamwell is using terms here that echo Schleiermacher and Gustafson, in the first instance, and Kant in the second. Yet, whatever similarities there may be, it should be noted that Gamwell's use of these terms (unlike their use) is distinctly teleological. For instance, Gamwell would not disagree with or diminish Schleiermacher or Gustafson's emphasis on the human affections or on piety as chief among them. But, for Gamwell, piety is first and foremost a disposition to pursue the metaphysical telos in all aspects of one's life. "Only insofar as all of our affections are educated in accord with piety," he suggests, are we properly directed to our true end of loving God and neighbor.[43] Moreover, given the internal relation between God and world, the Great Commandment "to love God and neighbor" does not consist of two separate commandments but rather of one integrated one. "This twofold calling," observes Gamwell in *Politics as a Christian Vocation*,

> is the Great Commandment because it is [ultimately] the only commandment, in the sense that all others are applications of it. We are called to love God in all that we do and, therefore, to lead our lives with no other purpose than to love all those who God loves, and this means to treat all as individuals who belong to God.[44]

Since all things relate to God, and since God loves the world, we are to love the neighbor and the world in the manner that God relates to them. This again is roughly similar to Gustafson but, again, Gamwell interprets this as a teleological contribution to the divine life and not merely as a duty of Reformed piety.[45]

---

43. Ibid., 211.

44. Gamwell, *Politics as a Christian Vocation*, 8.

45. To be precise, it should be noted that Gamwell has always objected to Gustafson's formulation that we should relate to all things in the manner that *they relate to God*. If "relation" means real or internal relation, then the proper formulation, Gamwell holds, is that we should relate to all things in the manner *that God relates to them*. This is the

Finally, Gamwell is open to describing the divine good in terms of the divine will. To act in accordance with the divine good is to act in accordance with the will of God. But he insists that one must recognize that "the abiding character of God's 'will' . . . is metaphysical." Hence, this means that "God cannot choose whether or not to condition maximal creativity in the future as such. On the contrary, the unchanging nature of God's successive acts of self-determination is the necessary identity of the divine." Yet, this metaphysical view does not eliminate all freedom and reduce divinity to mere necessity. "[T]here may be many ways," he states, "in which any given divine activity may unify all actuality and possibility and thereby 'pursue' maximal creativity in the future as such. In other words, there may be for any particular divine activity alternative self-determinations all of which exemplify God's [metaphysical] identity."[46] Here again one can see an economic-like distinction between levels of value and indifference curves at those levels. That is, given God's nature of perfect goodness, God must seek maximal creativity for the future as such; but how this maximal creativity is precisely actualized leaves room open for both divine and worldly freedom.

On my reading, Gamwell here implicitly critiques the medieval distinction between God's declared will *(potentia ordinata)* and God's absolute will *(potentia absoluta)*. If this distinction is meant to affirm that God originally had unfettered power and freedom, then Gamwell rejects such an affirmation. For the divine nature must always necessarily maximize the creativity of the future as such. To be sure, within this divine necessity, there remains significant room for freedom in terms of how this maximal realization is actualized. But there is no absolute or unfettered divine freedom. If it makes sense at all to speak of an "absolute divine will," then that absoluteness is defined in terms of metaphysical necessity, not in terms of nominalistic omnipotence; God's will must always be absolutely in accord with God's "abiding character."[47] Likewise, if it makes sense to speak of a "declared divine will," then that refers to the divine freedom exercised within the parameters of the divine nature; it refers to the freedom of how maximal creativity is actualized,

case because we relate to God as the all-inclusive whole whereas God relates to us as parts; thus we, too, should relate to other parts as parts—as God relates to them—not as they relate to God as all-inclusive whole.

46. Gamwell, *Divine Good*, 183.
47. Ibid.

A Transcendental-Process Theology 509

not to whether or not God could choose that end. As we saw in the last chapter, Milbank's reading of Aquinas points in this general direction. Yet, Milbank seems more hesitant than Gamwell to unequivocally identify the metaphysical necessity of the divine nature. I judge that this difference stems in part from Milbank's attempt to critically embrace the medieval tradition whereas Gamwell is intent on redirecting theology away from medievalism toward a critical embrace of a modern or neoclassical theism. Gamwell's position on this matter is perhaps best summed up in a passage in *Democracy on Purpose*:

> [T]heism has no reason to accept the view that God's will is ... arbitrary power. Because God is the metaphysical individual, the distinguishing divine character is necessarily the comprehensive purpose affirmed authentically or duplicitously by every exercise of human freedom, and "the divine will" designates a decision that is necessarily good. Accordingly, it is proper to say that an action is moral because God wills it. To be sure, it is also proper to say that God wills it because it is moral, but this could only mean that God wills it because it is consistent with God's own character.[48]

A Transcendental Argument: The Divine Good as Transcendental Telos

Just as Gamwell defines metaphysics as the rational attempt to identify the necessary characteristics of reality as such, he likewise defines transcendental arguments as the rational attempt to identify the necessary

---

48. Gamwell, *Democracy on Purpose*, 145. Again, for a helpful discussion of this medieval distinction, see Oakley, "Absolute and Ordained Power of God." Oakley distinguishes among three different interpretations. The "outrageous" version thought that God's unfettered power and freedom could act arbitrarily in any moment or context (444); the "classic" version thought that God's original or "absolute power served to affirm the freedom of God and the contingency of the entire created order of nature and grace." But, once established, "the ordained power served ... to affirm the *de facto* stability and reliability of that contingent order" (445). Oakley identifies Aquinas with this classic view. Finally, the "operationalized" version distinguishes "ordained power whereby God acts *de jure*, in accordance with the ... law he himself [contingently] established, [from] the absolute power whereby *de facto* he can [still] act apart from or against that law" (447). Oakley identifies Scotus with this operationalized view (447). But notice that the even the "classic" view of Aquinas affirms an original unfettered divine freedom that is only limited *de facto* after the decision for and creation of a wholly contingent world. For Gamwell, the freedom of God is always defined within and in accordance with the divine nature—there is never a point of change.

characteristics of human understanding as such. Unlike Kant, who rejected the former and embraced the latter, Gamwell argues that these two distinct but related enterprises are both valid endeavors. Specifically, he suggests that "valid metaphysical claims may be identified as a subclass within valid transcendental . . . claims. This relationship follows because conditions of the possibility of human understanding include conditions of the possibility of existing." That is, since human beings are part of reality, human existence must participate in and exemplify those generic and necessary characteristics of reality as such. Of course, what is necessary for distinctively human understanding is a broader category insofar as it also includes characteristics unique to human existence. But this larger category also contains within it those necessary characteristics generic to all reality, i.e., metaphysics is a subset of transcendental conditions. Hence, Gamwell contends that "any valid metaphysical claim . . . may be reformulated as a valid . . . transcendental claim." For instance, having argued that "'God exists" is a valid metaphysical claim, this assertion may now be reformulated transcendentally as "all human subjects are related to God."[49]

He further articulates this transcendental claim by suggesting that "the divine good evokes our moral commitment." This is the case because implicit within all human activity "there is always included the reality of God." In concurrence with Whitehead and Hartshorne, Gamwell holds that experience is prior to reflection; hence, "reasoning is always about a prior experience." Thus, if we can reason about human experience at all, Gamwell submits,

> then we can argue transcendentally to the existence of God *only because an experience of the divine reality is ever present*. In that experience we are related to the telos . . . by which the divine individual is identified. Thus, moral inquiry is in principle nothing other than our attempt to understand . . . *the divine telos that has already affected us*. Indeed, we enjoy the very possibility of deliberation and choice only because our appetition for the divine telos relates us to the future as such. *It is, therefore, an affection which one can never completely refuse*; its negation would be the negation of reality as such and, therefore, of oneself. *Immoral action can only be a . . . self-corrupting mode of activity, because it is the choice of a self-understanding and . . . of a telos in conflict with the attachment that precedes our choice and constitutes our*

---

49. Gamwell, *Divine Good*, 160.

freedom. Piety or reverence, then, is also the virtue of integrity. If the divine telos identifies the good to be pursued, it also evokes our attachment to itself and, in this sense, *empowers the good life* [italics added].[50]

This passage, which comes near the end of *The Divine Good*, asserts the inescapable omnipresence of the divine reality. Human life cannot be properly oriented or grounded apart from the divine good, which is an a priori condition of human experience. All attempts to deny this are self-contradictory precisely because they seek to deny "the attachment that precedes our [every] choice and constitutes our [very] freedom." Gamwell returns to and further develops this transcendental argument at the beginning of *Democracy on Purpose*. There, as noted earlier, he quotes Calvin: "If these famous opening sentences in Calvin's *Institutes of the Christian Religion* assert that knowing ourselves depends on knowing God," then "they also suggest that we can know God if we truly understand ourselves."[51] Unlike Calvin or most Calvinists, Gamwell does not believe that human sin irredeemably darkens or distorts this transcendental knowledge of God. To be sure, he recognizes and seeks to describe the fundamental human fault, but he does not believe this condition vitiates the role of rational discernment as such. Hence, he proceeds in chapter one with a detailed transcendental argument and then moves in chapter two to a discussion of human sin. I will summarize each of these in turn.

I can best delineate Gamwell's transcendental argument in terms of a series of twelve extended propositions:

(1) "Humans live with understanding." To exist with understanding means that humans have, at least some of the time, conscious awareness of the world around them. To be sure, "human beings are sometimes in a state of unconsciousness or dreamless sleep" and some humans remain in persistent vegetative or unconscious states. But most humans, at least some of the time, are consciously aware. This conscious awareness also sometimes includes self-conscious awareness.[52]

---

50. Ibid., 210–11.
51. Gamwell, *Democracy on Purpose*, 13.
52. Ibid., 17.

(2) Conscious awareness always involves two distinct but simultaneous components. These consist of: (a) the focus of our attention (what we are *explicitly* aware of). For instance, as I sit here and type on the computer, my explicit focus is centered on the screen and on my thoughts; and (b) a dim apprehension of a vast background (what we are only *implicitly* aware of). This dim background includes both our past knowledge and our vague apprehension of most elements of our present experience. For instance, as I sit here and type, I am only dimly aware of my experience of sitting on this chair. This experience remains part of the dim background until I draw it into explicit focus for the sake of this illustration. In regard to our background knowledge, what Gamwell has in mind includes what Habermas and others call a "lifeworld," that is, the vast background of implicit and "taken-for-granted" knowledge that we operate with in everyday life.[53]

(3) Human understanding and awareness are both fragmentary and fallible. By "fragmentary," Gamwell conveys that our understanding and awareness of the world are partial and certainly not exhaustive. As he puts it,

> We are by nature limited in the sense that a human activity does not understand all things in complete detail; in fact, we are in any given moment conscious of very few things in any significant measure, and the same can be said about a human life as the sum of all its moments or activities. . . . [Hence,] [w]e can say that explicit consciousness is a fragment of our fragmentary understanding.[54]

Conscious awareness, in other words, is the explicit part of our partial grasp of the whole. Given this fragmentary character, Gamwell insists that our understanding is always also fallible, i.e., susceptible to the possibility of error.

(4) Given our place in a cultural context or "lifeworld," and given its influence in shaping our vast background knowledge, human understanding is always communally and linguistically situated. "Given that learning largely depends on a communication among individuals," observes Gamwell, "we can also say that understanding is a thoroughly

---

53. Ibid., 19. Gamwell cites Habermas, *Theory of Communicative Action*, 1:335.
54. Gamwell, *Democracy on Purpose*, 19.

communal matter, and this means that language is important to distinctively human subjectivity." Because human understanding is always fragmentary, and because it is communicated among persons in society, "it is mediated by conventional or publicly fixed symbols." Hence, "the possibilities for explicit consciousness in a present human activity depend on the measure in which understandings previously given in linguistic form are now implicit," i.e., are now part of the available repertoire in a given cultural and historical context.[55]

In order to understand Gamwell correctly here, it is essential to make two critical but related distinctions. First, when he says that human understanding is *thoroughly* communal and linguistically situated, he does not mean that it is *merely* so. In other words, what we understand is indeed influenced by our context, but it is not merely our context that we are seeking to grasp; there is more there than merely our communal, historical or linguistic stock. Second, and relatedly, it is important to emphasize the distinction between *explicit* and *implicit* awareness. Our explicit awareness is always influenced by "conventional or publicly fixed symbols." We can only consciously articulate ideas or understandings of the world given the conceptual and linguistic tools available to us at a given time. So in this important sense, our linguistically constituted lifeworld certainly does influence our understanding. But our awareness also includes an implicit element, namely, our vague awareness of that dim and vast background that sets the backdrop for all our experience, including our explicit and selective conscious awareness. Included in the background is our implicit awareness of the transcendental conditions of subjectivity—those conditions of human understanding whose presence does not depend on language, history, or cultural particularity. Indeed, one definition of transcendental conditions defines them as implicit objects of understanding in all human subjects, whatever else they may or may not understand. Hence, one of the tasks of philosophy is to stretch language in new directions—to make it more resourceful for expressing a wider range of experience, especially the dim background elements. As Gamwell states,

> we will be misled if we take the features of our plain or perspicuous apprehension to define understanding [*in toto*], and the recognition that understanding may include something on which we do not explicitly focus will be important throughout

55. Ibid., 19–20.

the argument for our inescapable apprehension of a comprehensive purpose.[56]

It is these two sets of distinctions that distinguish Gamwell's position from strong historicism and related views. He believes that we are part of and in touch with a total reality and that we can make metaphysical and transcendental claims about this reality. To be sure, our claims will always be fallible and culturally situated; but the content or object of our claims can transcend this particularity and insofar as our philosophical and linguistic tools are stretched and improved, our claims will improve as well. In sum, our grasp of the whole may always be fragmentary or incomplete, but it is, nevertheless, always still a grasp of the whole.[57]

(5) Human understanding includes conscious awareness, and conscious awareness involves the capacity to distinguish or discriminate. "To be conscious of something is to be related to it in a manner that discriminates it from other things, that marks it off." To distinguish something means not only to be aware of it as a particular but also as "an instance of some universal or universals." Gamwell would agree, for instance, with Porter's reading of Aquinas when she says that "unless we can identify at least in a general way what kind of a thing something is, we would not be able to recognize it as an individual existing creature at all." Discernment of particularity, in short, requires some discrimination of a universal characteristic. "If we see or smell a yellow rose," notes Gamwell, "we see it as an instance of the universals 'yellow' and 'rose' or

---

56. Ibid., 20.

57. In a more recent, unpublished essay, Gamwell develops this point further. He says: "Understanding cannot be in all respects dependent on a lifeworld, that is, all understanding cannot be constituted by an inherited context of cultural and linguistic interpretations or by reflection on those interpretations. If the metaphysical character of beings is [implicitly] discriminated whenever anything at all is understood, then inherited interpretations themselves presuppose a discrimination of existential possibility as such. This latter understanding must be present whenever understanding occurs and thus present whether or not one has ever learned to think or speak of it in terms of the concepts and symbols of a lifeworld. . . . This is not to say that understandings can be explicit . . . without their constitution by lifeworld concepts and symbols. For this reason, it may be thoroughly appropriate to say that metaphysics . . . has a history. But this cannot be the history of Being, if that means a history of how beings as such are given. To the contrary, metaphysical necessity is given the same everywhere and always, and the history of metaphysics can only be the course toward making fully explicit an understanding of beings as such always already present and thus the conditions of all history." Gamwell, "On Metaphysical Necessity," 26–27.

smell it as an instance of the universals 'fragrant' and 'rose.' Accordingly, we discriminate or mark off not only the particular thing but also the universals that we perceive it to exemplify."[58]

(6) All discrimination involves an implicit contrast between the thing (x) and what it is not (-x), and what it is not, includes all other realities other than that thing (x). Since discrimination involves universals, moreover, this contrast also includes all future possibilities and past actualities of universals. Identification, in other words, is an act of *total* discrimination; to identify a part, we implicitly contrast it with the whole, i.e., with all other realities other than the part marked off. Hence, to identify a yellow rose, one is contrasting it not only with red rose but with all other things as well. "'Not a red rose,'" remarks Gamwell, "fails to be a contrast that discriminates a yellow rose, because a yellow rose is only one of many things that is not a red rose."[59]

What is critical here is that contrast always requires contrast with something positive, i.e., all that is not x must be something positively perceived, however dimly. "To contrast something with sheer nothing is, in truth, not to discriminate at all; that is, sheer nothing . . . provides no contrast." This line of reasoning is again roughly similar to that of the early Kant of *TOPB*: just as Kant argued there that the possibility of anything requires the necessary existence of some actuality, Gamwell argues here that discrimination of any particularity requires the necessary existence of some total background, which contrasts the part from the whole. The upshot of these arguments, Gamwell suggests, implies "that completely negative statements about realities, such as 'nothing exists' or 'there might have been nothing,' do not designate the content of a possible understanding and, therefore, are not sensible statements at all." Over against this, the later Kant attempts to posit the contrast between "phenomena" and "noumena." But since things-in-themselves cannot be known, noumena can only be identified as "not phenomena." Yet, this means that Kant is attempting to contrast phenomena simply with not-phenomena without providing any positive content by which to identify the contrast. As Gamwell sees it, this famous distinction

---

58. Gamwell, *Democracy on Purpose*, 22–23, 23; Porter, *Recovery of Virtue*, 39. In a footnote, Gamwell suggests that our dim or vague background knowledge also involves an implicit form of discrimination. See Gamwell, *Democracy on Purpose*, 23 n. 4.

59. Gamwell, *Democracy on Purpose*, 29.

"commits Kant to the notion that a completely negative object of understanding provides a contrast to positive objects of understanding as such, since, without that contrast, he could not discriminate appearances from things-in-themselves." But we may then ask: "What is the difference between a completely negative object of understanding and a putative object that is in truth no object at all?" What Gamwell has in mind in this latter case is the putative assertion of a self-contradictory notion, such as "a colorless yellow rose." "To the best of my reasoning," he concludes,

> there can be no distinction that is more than merely verbal between putative objects whose descriptions are self-contradictory and objects that are completely negative [like noumena]— because in both cases, the supposed objects are completely negative. Thus, a completely negative object cannot be discriminated or provides no contrast.[60]

To encapsulate, just as he earlier critiqued Kant's bifurcation between phenomena and noumena in the process of making his case for the possibility of metaphysics, so, too, Gamwell offers here in his transcendental argument a parallel assault upon Kant's position.

(7) Since understanding involves discrimination and discrimination involves a contrast between x and all other realities other than x, this means that any understanding at all also has a dim background knowledge of reality as a whole. Here's where Gamwell's transcendental analysis explicitly intersects with metaphysics. Again, this is a fallible and fragmentary understanding but it is, nonetheless, an understanding of reality as such. "[O]ne can discriminate any actual or possible reality from all other realities if only one has an understanding of 'reality as such'. . . ." By "reality as such," he refers to "the character common to all possible realities." To be sure, "a discrimination of any actual or possible reality . . . does not require a complete understanding of each and every other reality [in its particularity] but, rather, a consciousness [or implicit awareness] of reality as such." To borrow a phrase from Davidson, Gamwell suggests here that to know or identify any particular fact is implicitly to know and identify "the Great Fact," which always lies in the background of every foregrounded fact. As noted in proposition (2), one must distinguish between our explicit attention, which is usually "focused on representations of particular things and specific possibili-

60. Ibid., 28, 28–29.

ties," and our dim or implicit apprehension of a vast background.⁶¹ Our knowledge of reality as such lies in this dim background; yet, it is always this background that provides the context for the explicit foreground.⁶²

(8) Conscious awareness involves a discrimination of self from other parts of the whole. Having noted above our dim awareness of the background whole as well as our explicit attention on some part, Gamwell here identifies the self as a third element in the tripartite structure of awareness. Quoting Whitehead, he says "'the primitive stage of discrimination . . . is the vague grasp of reality, dissecting it into a three-fold scheme, namely, The Whole, That Other, and This-My-Self.'"⁶³ Building on his earlier discussion of Kant's notion of practical reason, Gamwell proceeds to affirm that the self is free to choose among ends and is, thus, self-determining. Even more strongly, he declares that the self is its act of decision among possibilities, and its decision is defined by its selection of a telos. "The self *is* its purpose, and to understand oneself is to be a purpose consciously." Gamwell certainly does not mean to deny the influence of other factors in shaping the self (biology, history, society, family, etc.), but *how* one responds to these factors is itself an act of freedom. Thus, succinctly put, we are our freedom and the ends pursued define our freedom and ourselves.⁶⁴

(9) In making choices or decisions, the self evaluates its alternatives. In order to evaluate, the self must have a comprehensive and objective mea-

---

61. Ibid., 31, 32. For Davidson's phrase, see *Inquiries into Truth and Interpretation*, 42.

62. Gamwell clarifies here his earlier discussion of our cultural learning and situatedness (proposition 4). "[N]othing [previously] said," he remarks, "implies that everything implicitly understood must have been previously learned. If representation [of particulars] occurs by way of [contrast], then all human subjectivity . . . includes at least an implicit awareness of reality as such, because this background is a necessary condition for any other understanding." He makes the point even more clearly in a footnote: "Although I have no doubt that the development of explicit thought about all things involves learning, the more apparent [or perspicuous] account of this learning is that it brings to explicit consciousness something of which the individual was always implicitly aware" (*Democracy on Purpose*, 32, 30 n. 12).

63. Gamwell, *Democracy on Purpose*, 33. He cites Whitehead, *Modes of Thought*, 150.

64. Gamwell, *Democracy on Purpose*, 34, 37. This identity between self and freedom—defined in terms of a trajectory of purposive activity—explains Gamwell's chapter title: "The Freedom We Ourselves Are," 13.

sure of worth by which to assess all possible alternatives. Even Hume, Gamwell observes, recognizes that evaluation involves alternatives as wholes (although Hume believes that this entails solely a movement of the heart and not an act of understanding). "'In moral deliberations,'" Gamwell quotes Hume, "'we must be acquainted beforehand with all the objects, and all their relations to each other; and from a comparison of the whole, fix our choice or approbation.'"[65] Moving beyond Hume, Gamwell argues that conscious evaluation requires a comparison of wholes and thus requires a comprehensive variable, an inclusive measure of value in relation to which all possible and actual realities can be assessed.

(10) This comprehensive variable must be part of our dim metaphysical background knowledge. Of course, this is one of the many places where Gamwell and Hume part company. "Against Hume," Gamwell states, "what follows from the inclusive character of 'worth' is that it cannot be understood as a more or less specific characteristic or universal." On the contrary, it must be understood as an "inclusive universal"—the "'universal of universals'"—and not merely as a specific or particular characteristic. "Life with understanding not only has, at least implicitly, an awareness of reality as such but also . . . evaluates specific possible ends in the terms given by this [metaphysical] awareness."[66]

(11) What we mean by the term "God" is, in part, the ultimate reality that is the source and measure of worth as such. Hence, all human understanding always has at least an implicit background knowledge of God as the measure of value—as the comprehensive yardstick in relation to which all possible choices are evaluated and in relation to which all actual and possible realities are assessed. As described earlier, God is the one cosmic or metaphysical individual who fully experiences all things and who integrates them through comparison and evaluation into the one inclusive divine experience. Hence, "we may now return to Calvin," declares Gamwell. "For Calvin, as for theists generally, the character of worth as such is defined by the character of God. If this theistic under-

---

65. Gamwell, *Democracy on Purpose*, 42. He cites Hume, *Enquiries Concerning Human Understanding and Concerning the Principle of Morals*, ed. P. H. Niddich (Oxford: Clarendon, 1975) 290.

66. Gamwell, *Democracy on Purpose*, 43, 44. The phrase "universal of universals" comes from Whitehead; Gamwell cites *Process and Reality*, 21.

standing is true, then it follows from our inescapable knowledge of the comprehensive purpose that our existence is constituted by knowledge of both ourselves and God."[67]

(12) Because the human self is free to choose—indeed the self *is* a trajectory of situated choice (prop. 8)—we must implicitly choose some understanding of ourselves in relation to reality as such. Since reality as such refers to the character common to all possible realities (prop. 7), since this character can only be found in a comprehensive and metaphysical measure of value (prop. 9 and 10), and since this comprehensive measure is what we mean in part when we employ the term "God" (prop. 11), we must therefore implicitly choose some understanding of ourselves in relation to the divine reality. This constitutive existential choice is what Gamwell calls "the exercise of original freedom":

> This means that every human activity knows both itself and God, where "God" is used to designate ultimate reality as the ground of worth. Because our subjectivity is fragmentary [prop. 3], we must decide whether to affirm God alone or also to affirm something else as the comprehensive telos in relation to which we complete ourselves.[68]

This original or fundamental choice, which is implicit in every human moment, is the choice of *either* to live and act "authentically" *or* to live and act "duplicitously." As Gamwell states: "Humans can choose to be authentic or inauthentic only because every human activity knows God. Thus, the choice to be inauthentic always . . . includes knowledge of the [theistic] comprehensive purpose and, therefore, knowledge that the chosen alternative is false." In short, "[the] decision to be inauthentic is a self-contradictory self-understanding," one that implicitly knows itself to be ultimately duplicitous.[69]

Defining Human Sin: "The Duplicity We May Choose"

If we always have some dim background awareness of God as the ground of worth, "how could any false interpretation of ourselves be

---

67. Gamwell, *Democracy on Purpose*, 57.
68. Ibid., 59.
69. Ibid., 59, 60.

tempting if we [already implicitly] know the comprehensive purpose?"[70] Gamwell seeks to answer this fundamental question by engaging in an extended and critical conversation with Niebuhr's view of sin. "[N]o thinker of the twentieth century," he proclaims, "more profoundly analyzes the original human decision for or against authenticity than does Reinhold Niebuhr." This profundity issues in part from the fact that "Niebuhr seeks to reformulate the traditional Christian doctrine of original sin in a manner that makes sense in our century because it is more adequate to 'the psychological and moral facts in human wrongdoing.'" This psychological and moral adequacy is due largely to the fact that Niebuhr rightly recognizes that sin involves self-contradiction, duplicity, and rebellion against God. Quoting Niebuhr, he states: "[S]in 'can only be understood as a self-contradiction, made possible by the fact of . . . freedom but not following necessarily from it.'" And, "duplicity is 'rebellion against God' or an 'effort to usurp the place of God.'" Gamwell concurs with Niebuhr in stressing that this duplicitous rebellion is not primarily an explicit or conscious act, but rather an unconscious and implicit one. Furthermore, he agrees with Niebuhr's focus on anxiety as a precondition of sin, and with his insistence that the failings of the past or of contemporary society, though significant, cannot exhaust an account of human fault. In short, each and every individual is confronted by temptation and the possibility of sin. With Niebuhr, Gamwell posits that "temptation occurs because something attracts the self to a duplicitous interpretation, and this is why temptation makes human freedom anxious. One knows that the tempting alternative is false, and the attraction to it is, therefore, felt as a threat to one's [true] worth."[71]

It is at this juncture, however, that Gamwell begins to find Niebuhr's view problematic. Niebuhr describes this tempting force as a "'mystery,'" which Gamwell thinks is Niebuhr's way of saying that "sin is inevitable." On Niebuhr's account, this mystery originates from "a mysterious 'defect of the will'" that leads to "'a bias toward sin,'" which in turn leads the will inevitably to choose sin. In effect, "sin posits itself." Hence, Niebuhr paradoxically asserts that sin is inevitable but not necessary. With this

70. Ibid., 95.

71. Ibid., 61, 62, 65, 78, 68. Gamwell cites Niebuhr, *Nature and Destiny*, 1:248, 17, 179; see also 180–81. Porter quotes a passage from Cicero that seems to make this same point: "God is the author, the promulgator, and the judge of this [natural] law. And he who does not observe it is a fugitive from himself and rebellious against his own nature" (Porter, *Nature as Reason*, 2; she cites Cicero, *De republica* III.XXII, 33).

distinction in place, he attempts to maintain human responsibility for sin in spite of its inevitability. On the whole, Gamwell thinks that Niebuhr resorts to the language of mystery and "paradox in order to protect his theistic understanding of duplicity" in the face of the fundamental question raised above, namely: "If every human activity knows God as the ground of worth as such, why would any human activity choose against God, that is, understand itself as if something else were God?"[72]

Gamwell proposes that this question can be better answered without resorting to the language of mystery or without claiming that sin is strictly inevitable. The basic problem, he alleges, is that Niebuhr's paradox ends up being a distinction without a difference: in spite of his insistence that temptation and sin are not the same thing, Niebuhr ends up collapsing them. Hence, he undermines the human responsibility for sin that he rightly seeks to maintain. "[I]f Niebuhr's [overall] account displays a profound insight," Gamwell contends, then

> I also believe that his [specific] solution to the radical problem [of sin] cannot be correct. If I have read him rightly, we are bound to say that *his account is conceptually impossible*. "Sin posits itself," in his sense, could only say that a human activity decides before it decides, and since the prior decision was sinful, it posits another decision prior to itself, and *the choice of a self-understanding becomes an infinite regress of duplicitous decisions*.... [I]n other words, *Niebuhr labors without success to distinguish between what is inevitable and what is necessary in human existence, so that his formula "responsibility despite inevitability" asserts the ... logical contradiction* that humans as such choose between alternatives one of which cannot be chosen. *Calling the will's defect a "mystery" does nothing to change the matter*, and his persistent reference to authentic faith as an "ideal possibility" rather than a real alternative characterizing "the situation of freedom and finiteness" *is simply an attempt to have it both ways* [italics added].[73]

Over against what he takes here to be Niebuhr's contradictory position, Gamwell seeks to remove the inconsistencies by developing a "proposal

---

72. Gamwell, *Democracy on Purpose*, 68, 101, 68, 69, 61, 62. He cites Niebuhr *Nature and Destiny* 1:181, 250, 242.

73. Gamwell, *Democracy on Purpose*, 78, 83–84. He cites Niebuhr, *Nature and Destiny*, 1:255, 182–83.

on which temptation is understood without assuming that it controls the exercise of freedom." Only by maintaining a distinction between temptation and freedom, and thus between temptation and sin, can one avoid making sin a necessity that undercuts human responsibility. The key to Gamwell's alternative is the recognition that all concrete existence is fragmentary. To illustrate, he quotes Niebuhr: "'The human imagination is too limited to see and understand the interests of the other as vividly as those of the self.' This citation," Gamwell continues, "explicates the fragmentary character of our contingent existence by specifying that the extent to which we can understand or appreciate the specific possibilities of other individuals is far more limited than the extent to which we can imagine our own future activities." Gamwell is trying to walk an intellectual tightrope here by explaining the power of temptation without claiming that sin is strictly inevitable. Because our experience is partial or fragmentary, we tend to attribute greater worth to that which we experience most concretely and intensely; and that which we tend to experience most concretely is that which is most proximate, namely, our own past, present, and future. Hence, "the pursuit of my own satisfaction in a manner contrary to the equal worth of my neighbor," observes Gamwell, "has greater persuasive power than the affirmation of equality, and I am [therefore] tempted to think that my own future is inherently more important."[74]

But the self is not only exposed to the persuasive power of the proximate. It is also always exposed to the comprehensive telos of the divine good, which implicitly relates the self to a total or inclusive measure of value. Thus, "if the greater concreteness with which I appreciate my own future tempts me to give it undue regard, then it must tempt me also to an inauthentic self-understanding." Returning to the central question, Gamwell is now in a position to offer an answer:

---

74. Gamwell, *Democracy on Purpose*, 69–70, 91–92, 92, 95. He cites Niebuhr, *Nature and Destiny*, 1:296. Schneewind describes Descartes' view in terms somewhat similar to what Gamwell means here by the temptation that results from our fragmentary understanding. "Because the soul is tied to the body the first confused loves we feel will be directed toward preserving our own body; but that is due not to the nature of love and desire [as such], but to the lack of clarity in our perceptions" (Schneewind, *Invention of Autonomy*, 192). But the key difference is that Gamwell will proceed in the next paragraph to define this confusion as a result of duplicitous choice and not merely as a result of unclear perceptions.

> How could any false interpretation of ourselves be tempting if we know the comprehensive purpose? If original freedom always includes the [background and implicit] feeling of God, ... how could some other feeling tempt one to choose immorally ... ?
>
> The answer is this: The positive sense of worth attached to the comprehensive purpose may not be significantly strong or, to say the same, our relation to God may not be accompanied by significant persuasive power. The true understanding of worth as such defines terms for evaluation that are indifferent to the measure in which we understand [and feel] possible ends concretely. Thus, a duplicitous alternative for self-understanding may be tempting because, at some level of specificity, its evaluation of our alternatives for purpose is sensed more intensely than is the possibility of an authentic self-understanding.[75]

Summarily speaking, we are tempted to sin because we usually have more intense attachments to that which is concrete and proximate in our experience than to that which is most inclusive and all-embracing. That is, we lack sufficiently developed habits and affections of piety, and therefore find it difficult to attach ourselves to the inclusive divine purpose that is always already a part of our experience; instead, our love and loyalty gets devoted to our own more narrow aims.

Gamwell derives at least two important implications from this view. First, he draws a critical distinction in terms of how one defines the universality of sin. He accepts that sin is universal in a statistical or empirical sense but not in Niebuhr's strict sense of being completely inevitable, i.e., in the sense of sin as having always posited itself prior to human choice. Sin is empirically massive but not strictly inevitable; on the contrary, the possibility of piety and the lure of the divine good are genuine if usually faint alternatives on the horizon of every human choice. They may be improbable, but they are not, in Niebuhr's sense, impossible possibilities. "In sum," Gamwell concludes,

> we can account for the consistency between our inescapable knowledge of God and our temptations to sin and, at the same time, for the pervasiveness of human fault without recourse to a mysterious defect of the will. The fragmentariness and social

---

75. Gamwell, *Democracy on Purpose*, 95.

character of human understanding are sufficient to offer a rational account of the "facts in human wrong-doing."[76]

Second, in characterizing human experience as partial and one that tends to attribute greater worth to what is proximate, Gamwell recognizes that his view might be misunderstood. This is the case because he agrees with Aquinas, Porter, and others "that we do have a special moral responsibility for individuals to whom we are closely related or associations in which we are participants." For instance, in regard to "family members, friends, or local communities," we do have a special responsibility to them because we can feel and appreciate their future needs and aims "more concretely than we can others more distant from us." The danger here, Gamwell notes, is to assume that this moral responsibility means that these proximate groups and their interests are "inherently more worthy" than the needs of distant others. The key to clarity, he implies, is found in the distinction between the *application* and the *identification* of the comprehensive purpose. "[I]t remains one thing to affirm this [local] responsibility because the comprehensive purpose is thereby specified [or applied] to our particular situation, and [it remains] something else to act in a similar way because we [mistakenly] understand the individuals and associations we can appreciate more concretely as inherently more worthy."[77] To modify an old adage, Gamwell advocates that we "act locally but always think globally." The danger occurs when we falsely identify the local as the sum of the comprehensive purpose rather than seeing it as an appropriate application of the inclusive aim to our concrete situation in the world. This characterization of local and global responsibilities leads us to a discussion of Gamwell's affirmation of democracy.

Democracy as the Political Specification of the Divine Good

In contrast to the new traditionalists who criticize modern democracy as antithetical to fostering moral virtue and Christian faith, Gamwell fundamentally affirms democracy as the necessary social and political aim for pursuing the divine good. Indeed, even more strongly than Niebuhr's pragmatic affirmation, Gamwell affirms democracy on metaphysical and teleological grounds. That is to say, whereas Niebuhr affirms democracy to a great extent for its instrumental ability to curb

---

76. Ibid., 99, 101. Gamwell cites Niebuhr, *Nature and Destiny*, 1:234.
77. Gamwell, *Democracy on Purpose*, 97.

man's inhumanity to man, Gamwell affirms it as the positive and necessary form of loving God and neighbor in the world. Likewise, Gamwell welcomes Stout's support for democracy, but he thinks that Stout's tradition-specific and nonmetaphysical attempt to explicate and defend it is ultimately inadequate.[78] Without going into lengthy detail, I will outline how democracy fits into Gamwell's theological outlook.

As noted earlier, he defines the metaphysical telos in terms of the divine good, and he sums up the divine good in terms of the two integrated aspects of the Great Commandment—to love God and neighbor is "to pursue maximal good in the future as such." He then proceeds to define "justice" as "the conditions in or through which the divine purpose is specified [or pursued in relation] to political life." In turn, he defines "politics" as the "associational process whose distinguishing purpose is to determine the activities of the state or the governing order of society." Gamwell states unequivocally that the "principles of justice [ultimately] depend on a comprehensive purpose," which is the divine good. Yet, he recognizes that this claim is at odds with the dominant presumptions of modern political theory. Therefore, rather than pursuing the question of justice as a direct application of the divine good, he instead takes an indirect path whereby he seeks to work back from discussions of justice and politics toward the question of a comprehensive purpose. In pursuing this indirect path, he identifies and follows three essential steps. First, he seeks to identify "a principle of democratic politics." Second, he attempts to show that such a "principle is contradicted by any theory on which justice is independent of a comprehensive purpose." And, third, he seeks to specify "the principle of justice implied by maximizing the divine good and argue[s] that justice so conceived is consistently democratic."[79]

STEP 1: A PRINCIPLE OF DEMOCRATIC POLITICS

In seeking to specify how the divine good relates to questions of society and politics, Gamwell begins by clarifying his conception of comprehensive teleology. Some critics argue that any comprehensive teleology is self-defeating because, by prescribing maximal pursuit of a telos, it leads to social unpredictability (pursuit of the telos trumps all other

---

78. See Niebuhr, *Children of Light and the Children of Darkness*, xiii. Gamwell's analysis of Stout is set forth in "Comment on Jeffrey Stout."

79. Gamwell, *Democracy on Purpose*, 179, 180, 181.

duties), which, in turn, undermines maximal pursuit of the telos itself. Gamwell replies that this "criticism fallaciously assumes that comprehensive teleology means 'looking at each calculation in isolation, and not taking adequate account of the effects on a society's capacity to function.'" On the contrary, what is required, he argues, is an "indirect" rather than a "direct" application "of a comprehensive purpose." If I understand him correctly, what a comprehensive purpose requires can best be described, to borrow terms from utilitarianism, as a *rule-teleology* rather than an *act-teleology*. As Gamwell remarks, "it is one thing teleologically to validate a particular action 'separately taken' [i.e., act-teleology,] and another to validate it by appeal to a system of rules that is itself validated teleologically [, i.e., rule-teleology]." The divine good, in other words, requires us to identify a system of rules and a set of social practices that foster widespread social cooperation and common decision-making and thereby "maximize the good" in the long run. These rules and practices, moreover, are authorized and validated by the comprehensive telos itself.[80]

From here Gamwell argues that "communicative respect" is the meta-ethical social practice and principle underlying all human interaction. Drawing on the communicative theory of Habermas and Apel, he contends that all validity claims imply "a specific social practice," namely, "the practice of communicative respect." To be sure, Gamwell recognizes that Habermas and Apel "are among those who doubt the credibility of comprehensive teleology." Nonetheless, he believes that they offer profound insights about the nature and implications of discourse that can and must be incorporated into a coherent teleology. With Habermas, then, what Gamwell means by "discourse" is "the specific social practice that suspends other purposes in order commonly to assess the validity of contested claims." Discourse is a particular form of what I earlier called *common criticism*, one that is devoted specifically to testing validity claims. "Whether this [discursive] practice achieves its common purpose," Gamwell adds, "depends solely on the soundness of arguments, the opportunity for criticism, and common pursuit of the truth. Accordingly, its necessary conditions include . . . equal freedom for all participants to advance and contest any claim and the arguments for it; the absence of internal coercion in the form of strategic activity . . . ; and the absence of external coercion that might influence the accep-

---

80. Ibid., 185. The critic that Gamwell cites here is Brian Barry, *Justice as Impartiality* (Oxford: Clarendon, 1995) 219.

tance or contestation of claims." This social practice thus requires that we treat *all* human beings "as potential participants in moral discourse" who are bearers of "communicative rights" and who are, therefore, entitled to communicative respect.[81]

Gamwell proceeds to define communicative respect as a *"formative* principle." By this, he means "it prescribes social action that is explicitly neutral to all moral disagreement." It defines the ground rules for adjudicating disputes without taking sides within the disputes themselves; the rules themselves can be challenged, but only by further discourse, not by coercive assertion. By contrast, a *"substantive"* principle "prescribes social action that is not explicitly neutral to all moral disagreement. Thus, the distinguishing mark of a formative [principle] is its explicit neutrality to all substantive [prescriptions]," including those pertaining to conceptions of "good human association" and to the comprehensive question of the good.[82]

Having identified communicative respect as a formative principle embedded within our everyday speech and moral claims, Gamwell proceeds to link this principle inextricably to a democratic polity. As noted, the right of communicative respect means that all humans should be treated as potential participants in moral discourse. Yet, the most concrete and significant form of practical moral interchange is political discourse, which is "discourse about the governing rules or norms that define all potential action and association in society as morally permissible or impermissible, and this is discourse in its widest possible form." Hence, the right to participate in moral discourse implies the equally important right to participate in political discourse. But the equal right of all to participate in political discourse implies and requires nothing less than a democratic form of politics. "Communicative respect as a formative principle," Gamwell concludes, "prescribes a democratic political association." A democratic association, moreover, "should be constituted as a full and free political discourse. It should be full in the sense that it takes no moral principle or norm, formative or substantive, to be immune from dissent, and the discourse should be free in the sense that all individuals who are subject to the common decisions in question should have equal rights to participation." In sum, he contends

---

81. Gamwell, *Democracy on Purpose*, 196, 197, 182, 197, 201, 200. He cites Habermas, *Theory of Communicative Action*, 1:25, and Habermas, *Justification and Application*, 31.

82. Gamwell, *Democracy on Purpose*, 198–99.

that democracy is "a formative principle [that] is a presupposition of every moral claim."[83]

Step 2: Democracy and Justice Require a Comprehensive Purpose

Having outlined the formative principle of communicative respect and its democratic political implications, Gamwell argues that an adequate and coherent understanding of justice must recognize the "compound" nature of justice itself. That is, one must recognize that justice includes *both* "a formative principle or set of principles" *and* "a substantive principle or set of principles." The formative principles specify the basic procedures or ground rules that set the conditions for full and free discourse in society. Again, as formative, they are explicitly neutral among competing moral and political visions; they are the societal embodiment of the principle of communicative respect. Hence, the formative principles of justice, Gamwell adduces, require a democratic constitution that ensures genuine religious freedom and, thus, one that is explicitly neutral among all competing religious and moral conceptions of the good. But along with such formative principles, justice also requires substantive ones, for it is substantive principles that provide the necessary content for moral and political discourse. As Gamwell emphatically states:

> *democracy makes no sense in the absence of something about which citizens may engage in full and free political discourse.* The democratic discourse cannot be solely about the formative character of the discourse. This would mean that democratic politics has nothing to argue about except its own constitution, and it would be senseless to constitute a discourse for the sole purpose of constituting it.... [On the contrary, democratic] discourse is about the legislated norms by which the society will be governed. Hence, *a democratic constitution presupposes a universal substantive principle to which all activities of the state ought to conform* [italics added].[84]

On Gamwell's account, a just society must be democratic, and a democratic society must have a constitution that, on the one hand, explicitly

---

83. Ibid., 208, 209, 212, 231.
84. Ibid., 231, 229.

guarantees formative conditions of full and free political discourse and, on the other, implicitly presupposes a universal substantive principle by which the claims and counterclaims of discourse can themselves be adjudicated. There is no point in setting up a fair and free game, he reasons, unless there is a substantive way to decide the game itself. As he describes it: "Democratic discourse presupposes a substantive principle that is universal because [democratic discourse] is prescribed as a metaethical presupposition of moral claims and makes no sense in the absence of a moral principle in relation to which the validity or invalidity of moral claims is determined."[85] In brief, it is critical that one recognize that the formative and substantive principles of justice must be distinguished, but they can never be separated; justice must be understood as compound.

In staking out this compound view, Gamwell is advocating "a teleological theory of justice," that is, "a theory on which justice is inseparable from the comprehensive good." In defending this position, he critiques both "separationist" theories, which seek to establish justice independently of the good, and religious conceptions of justice that purport that theological understandings of the good are suprarational and thus cannot be validated through public discourse. Beginning with this latter view, Gamwell seeks to respond to the possible objections of "religious adherents for whom religious truth transcends the capacities of natural reason." From their perspective, "the stipulation that political decisions should be taken through full and free discourse itself denies legitimacy to the belief that ultimate reality, and therefore, human authenticity as such cannot be known or fully known without some special revelation or disclosure." What they object to, in short, is that a democratic state may "teach that politics should be by the way of reason [alone]. But if democracy is a meta-ethical presupposition of every claim to moral validity," responds Gamwell,

> then a democratic constitution stipulates only [formative] conditions that all citizens must explicitly accept in order to have a political discourse about any moral prescription, including the prescription that . . . democratic discourse is the proper constitution of a political community. Those who hold on religious grounds that knowledge of the comprehensive purpose is impossible without a special revelation are legitimate participants

---

85. Ibid., 276.

in that discourse, in the sense that they are invited to argue for any politically relevant claims they wish to make, including the claim for that understanding of religious knowledge.[86]

One can advocate or contest any claim, including questioning democracy itself or asserting that theological truth is suprarational. But whatever the claim may be, one must support the claim by offering reasons to others that are intelligible and potentially credible to all participants; for to assert that one's own claims are true but cannot be rationally justified is a form of special pleading. Such an assertion, Gamwell submits, could only be valid "if the question about human authenticity as such did not constitute a rational order of reflection, in the sense that answers to it can be validated or invalidated by argument." But to make *that* claim requires its own rational support. In effect, one cannot avoid the responsibility of rationally defending one's claim at some level of discussion. Moreover, it is precisely this widespread view in theology and culture—that theistic claims can finally only be validated by appeal to special revelation—that Gamwell seeks to counter with his case for a theistic metaphysical teleology. That is to say again, most modern religious thought is "postmetaphysical" in the sense that it denies "the possibility of [rationally or publicly] validating a conception of the comprehensive purpose."[87]

Of course, it is not only modern religious thought that tends to be postmetaphysical. It is precisely because most modern philosophy is postmetaphysical that many prominent contemporary accounts of justice, such as those offered by Rawls and Habermas, are "separationist" in nature. Because they believe that ultimate questions about the human good or about reality as such cannot be rationally or publicly adjudicated, they seek to separate the question of justice from any teleology or conception of the good. As Gamwell reports,

> recent political philosophy in the West is marked by a widespread, although hardly unanimous, agreement that valid principles of justice are nonteleological. On my reading, this common conviction expresses the yet wider consensus that Kant decisively discredited all attempts to validate metaphysical assertions and, therefore, comprehensive teleology.[88]

---

86. Ibid., 239, 236–37.
87. Ibid., 237.
88. Ibid., 265. Italics deleted.

Gamwell categorizes separationist theories of justice into two main types: "universalist," such as illustrated by Habermas's universal theory of discourse, and "nonuniversalist," such as illustrated by the later Rawls and his stipulation that a conception of justice must be political but not metaphysical. Without going into his critique of each of these two approaches, I will summarize Gamwell's criticism of separationist theories as a whole.[89]

Basically what these theories hold in common is, on the one hand, the affirmation of religious freedom and, on the other, a formulation of justice that is independent of or freestanding from any comprehensive conception of the good (religious or otherwise). But "the price of separating justice from the good," Gamwell argues, is that it ultimately "contradicts religious freedom" and, therefore, "a separationist theory of [justice or] democracy cannot [itself] be internally consistent." For instance, "if the constitution stipulates certain principles [of justice] as freestanding," then "the state makes a claim to validity for them." But the problem here is that "the assertion of such [freestanding] principles [implicitly] denies the validity of all universalist conceptions of justice and, with that denial, the [separationist] theory becomes universalist [itself]." Differently stated, religious freedom is contradicted because a religious or theistic conception of the good implies that the divine or ultimate reality is indeed the ground of all worth and, therefore, is the measure of moral evaluation and justice as such. Hence, to exercise one's religious freedom is to make a public case for the divine good as the source and end of all things, including justice. But it is precisely such a case that separationist theories seek to preclude by insisting that principles of justice are truly independent of any such comprehensive claim. The fundamental mistake of all such theories, Gamwell contends, is that they wrongly "seek to substitute [the] separation [of justice from the good] for the distinction between formative and substantive principles of justice." Instead of a separationist theory, what is truly needed is a compound theory:

> In sum, all such [separationist] theories contradict the principle of religious freedom that they intend to protect as a *sine qua non* of democratic politics. So far from separating justice from the good, democracy makes sense only if justice is dependent on

---

89. For Gamwell's detailed critique of each of these types, see *Democracy on Purpose*, 240–79.

the comprehensive good. It then follows that religious freedom prescribes nothing other than a full and free discourse among conceptions of this good, and the purpose of democratic politics is to determine the activities of the state in accord with principles derived from the comprehensive purpose.... Contrary to a widespread consensus in liberal theory, democracy implies a comprehensive purpose because it implies the compound character of justice.[90]

From this critique, it is clear that Gamwell believes that democracy necessarily presupposes that there is some true or valid comprehensive good. Like a sealed envelope containing the valid answer, the purpose of democratic discourse is to publicly reason and debate about what the envelope contains, and thus what the correct answer is. The formative principles of justice, and thereby the constitution of a democratic society, are and must forever remain explicitly neutral to all such proposed answers, including those that claim that there is no such valid answer, i.e., those that claim that the envelope is empty. As Gamwell puts it, "the state is never allowed to teach what conception of the comprehensive purpose is or is not implied by statutory law or by the social practice of democracy itself." The written laws must be explicitly neutral, but the moral vision behind them (the substantive principles of justice informing the laws) is precisely what public moral and political debate should be largely about. Again, the only stipulation is that one seeks to offer common reasons to defend one's substantive moral claims. Hence, the state has the duty to teach the formative principles of justice without reference to any view of the comprehensive good. "But this is not the teaching that justice is independent of religious conceptions; to the contrary, these [formative] principles mean that the activities of the state are properly determined through discourse about the good that is not only free but also full."[91] In short, a democratic state should be explicitly secular, not secularistic or theistic. But the citizens and the culture can and ought to engage in lively debate over the comprehensive question of the good.

By proclaiming that justice is compound, Gamwell is arguing, on the one hand, that formative principles necessarily presuppose some valid substantive principles, and, on the other, that the assertion of any

---

90. Gamwell, *Democracy on Purpose*, 239, 240, 277, 278, 277–78.
91. Ibid., 279, 278–79.

substantive principle implicitly presupposes valid formative principles. In light of this compound assertion, therefore, he rejects both the separationist tendencies of modern liberalism and the anti-democratic tendencies of the new traditionalists. "If the previous argument [of steps one and two] has been successful," he remarks, "it convicts not only all separationist theories of justice but also all teleological theories that are not consistently democratic. A conception of the comprehensive purpose is false if it does not consistently imply the conception of justice as compound."[92] Contrary to Milbank, for instance, Gamwell does not see modern democracy as an abject *modus vivendi* that is fundamentally at odds with the ultimate divine good. On the contrary, the divine good is both embodied and furthered by the expansion of democratic discourse and participation in the world. Whatever may be the failings of modern democracy, they are not due to its emphasis on rational argument and discourse. Rather, its shortcomings stem in part from the separationist tendencies among some and from the anti-rationalist tendencies among others. In sum, to affirm God as the comprehensive good is to affirm democracy within history, and to affirm democracy within history, is to imply, however implicitly or indirectly, the divine good itself.

Step 3: Democracy and the Divine Good—Spelling out the Substantive Connection

If democracy involves debate over the valid substantive principles of justice (over what is truly in the envelope), then Gamwell follows through by offering his own answer, which he calls "justice as general emancipation." Since the metaphysical telos involves pursuing the divine good, and since the divine good involves maximizing the future creativity of the world as such, one therefore needs further specification of how to maximize future creativity. Gamwell does this by first distinguishing between human and nonhuman forms of activity:

> In comparison with nonhuman worldly existence, human activities enjoy a measure of freedom or opportunity for good that is vastly extended. This is because the order of creativity in the human body makes self-understanding and complex participation in language possible. The difference is finally a difference of de-

---

92. Ibid., 282.

gree, but the degree of difference is so dramatic that Whitehead can [rightly] say "the Rubicon has been crossed."[93]

On the one hand, Gamwell agrees here with Gustafson in emphasizing a theocentric ethic that sees all of life in relation to a theistic center of value. Hence, any difference in value between human and nonhuman activity "is finally a difference of degree" and not a difference of kind. Yet, on the other hand, Gamwell, like Niebuhr, sees the human capacity for self-transcendence as being so significant that Gamwell finally concludes that a major threshold has indeed been crossed; the difference of degree becomes so sizable that it constitutes a *de facto* qualitative distinction. Gamwell seeks to express this theocentricism "with a human face" by affirming an anthropocentric tilt within the framework of a theocentric telos. As he puts it, "given the dramatic extension of opportunity that emerges with distinctively human existence, the aesthetic character of all achievement means that the creativity realized in the nonhuman order of the world is maximized when it maximizes the possibilities of [human creativity] in the long run." Now he immediately qualifies this by announcing that "this is emphatically not to say that worth is identical with human achievement, much less with the satisfaction of human wants and preferences." Nevertheless, he does conclude, contrary to or at least more readily than Gustafson, that a "coincidence" exists "between maximizing the [human good] and maximizing creativity in the future as such." Therefore, the divine good may be "reformulated: maximize creativity in the human future as such." He again seeks to qualify this by affirming a "principle of environmental respect." This principle affirms the intrinsic value of nature and postulates that, all other things equal, the divine good is maximized "when our relations to the natural habitat appreciate the nonhuman world for its own sake." But the key point, nevertheless, is that Gamwell comes to define the comprehensive purpose in terms of pursuing the human good in the long run, which he calls pursuit of "our maximal common humanity." By "our common humanity," he refers to our capacity for language and communication, which enables us to create and share community and, thus, to realize ever greater creative possibilities.[94]

---

93. Ibid., 282, 283. Gamwell cites Whitehead, *Modes of Thought*, 38.
94. Gamwell, *Democracy on Purpose*, 283, 284, 286, 287.

Having reformulated the comprehensive telos in terms of pursuing our maximal common humanity, Gamwell specifies four implications. First, our common humanity has a "self-surpassing character," which is normative. Drawing explicitly on Niebuhr, Gamwell holds that human emancipation is not merely a negative freedom from constraint but, rather, a freedom for creatively contributing to the common good. Quoting Niebuhr he says: "'The individual is related to the community . . . in such a way that the highest reaches of his individuality are dependent upon the social substance out of which they arise and they must find their end and fulfillment in the community.'" Second, "our common humanity is self-widening," that is, ever-expanding to include more human individuals; greater value is achieved whenever the interests of all humans are considered, not just some. "This feature expresses," notes Gamwell, "the universal character of the telos by which human purpose is properly directed."[95] But, third, our common humanity also includes a "self-localizing" character. That is, not only does the comprehensive good seek maximal universal breadth, it also seeks maximal individual depth. And these two aims, of course, may be in tension. "Maximizing the opportunities for some and maximizing the number for whom opportunities are created," observes Gamwell, "involves two different variables. For most of us most of the time, the fragmentariness of human experience localizes [the] possible effects" of our creative endeavors. This localizing focus, however, is not merely the result of our fragmentary existence. Indeed, Gamwell again draws attention to the important distinction between the *application* of the comprehensive aim and its *identification*. To always apply or pursue the comprehensive telos in terms of universal width would be detrimental to the divine good itself: "Were each individual always to choose in terms of her or his maximal contribution to the widest number of others, . . . our common humanity would be greatly impoverished, because the actor's [own individual potential and] distinctiveness would be sacrificed to the width of effect." Hence, as a guiding maxim for most persons, who lack significant power and global reach, Gamwell concludes that "an individual can contribute significantly to the emancipation of others only if she or he limits the number of others." In fact, he summarily states, "the human order is greater when it includes the wider realization of

---

95. Ibid., 287, 288. Gamwell cites Niebuhr, *Children of Light and Children of Darkness*, 48.

more distinctive local and immediate associations, and therefore our maximal common humanity is not only self-widening but also self-localizing."[96]

He admits that there will always be some tensions between these widening and localizing aims. Moreover, since our common humanity is the highest moral measure, and since it seeks both of these aims, there is no criterion by which to resolve this dilemma. "The conditions common to wider communities set the larger context for the creative possibilities of more local associations," he remarks, "and whether an individual's action or larger project ought to be directed to wider or more local conditions of emancipation depends on her or his situation." The choice between them, therefore, "may not be a moral one, in the sense that one alternative is better." But this moral indifference curve, Gamwell submits, does not "imply that the comprehensive purpose is in conflict with itself. On the contrary, the proper conclusion is that the alternatives involved are equally good."[97] Unlike Milbank, Gamwell believes that ultimate reality inescapably includes some degree of tension among alternative possibilities. Concreteness involves opportunity costs, therefore, even among equally good alternatives, all possibilities cannot be realized; thus, there forever remains some unrealized potential and value. In short, there is no pure tranquility of order without remainder.

The fourth implication of our common humanity is to recognize and recall the connection between all creativity and the divine good. Specifying "our common humanity" as the guiding telos, ruminates Gamwell, "may seem to be a collective noun that designates a mere multiplicity of human orders, making senseless the notion of maximizing the whole." Yet, this polyvalence lacks integration only if one forgets the critical role of the divine relativity. "[T]he telos seems senseless," he replies,

> only because one ignores the unification of all things that occurs in the divine relativity. What is, if understood solely in terms of human existence, a mere multiplicity of human orders becomes our common humanity as a whole within the divine good. The

---

96. Gamwell, *Democracy on Purpose*, 288, 289.
97. Ibid., 289.

theistic character of this teleology is the necessary and sufficient condition of its conceptual coherence.[98]

As indicated here, Gamwell thinks that an affirmation of a common world only makes coherent sense within a theistic context; but within this context, the world specifies a critical component of the divine good itself.

From here, he returns to the principles of justice and how they relate to the telos of our common humanity. The self-widening character of our common humanity grounds both the formative and substantive principles of justice and the pursuit of democracy within the comprehensive purpose itself. That is to say, pursuit of the divine good necessarily entails pursuit of the principle of communicative respect and its democratic political embodiment. As Gamwell observes, "the larger purpose of justice . . . [is] to provide the widest communal context in which individuals live valuable lives." To achieve this maximal context requires not only the formative conditions of communicative respect and democratic participation but also the substantive conditions that facilitate human flourishing. The laws of any community affect the "circumstances and resources" that, in turn, affect "the creative opportunities of all individuals in the society." He calls these contextual conditions "the general conditions of emancipation." It is these general conditions, pertaining to circumstances and resources, that are the focus of substantive justice. Drawing on Rawls's notion of primary goods, Gamwell argues that justice in pursuit of the divine purpose requires a society to "[m]aximize the general conditions of emancipation to which there is equal access" (italics removed). These general conditions involve prima-

---

98. Ibid., 290. Gamwell's view here is similar in some respects to Aquinas's argument in the *ST* for the divine unity of the world. "[T]hings that are diverse," says Aquinas, "do not agree in one order unless they are ordered thereto by some one being," which he proceeds to argue is God (ST I:11.3). Of course, the critical difference between Gamwell's neoclassical and Aquinas's classical theism is that Gamwell believes that God *internally* integrates the diversity of the world into the divine experience itself, whereas Aquinas sees God ordering the world only *externally* as a first cause. For Gamwell, the divine unity reflects the divine *composition* (the integration of the divine experience of the world); for Aquinas, the divine unity reflects the divine *simplicity* (the pure undivided nature of the divine experience) in reference to both potentiality and actuality (ST I:11.3 and I:11.1). Milbank's reading of Aquinas might suggest that there is a divine composition in the sense of a divine unfolding of the world, but this is not composition in Gamwell's sense of divine integration of creaturely creativity (of God's internal relation to the world and of creaturely contribution to the divine life).

ry goods like "health, economic provision, education, cultural context, beauty and integrity in the [environment] . . . , and the general pattern of associational life itself." Yet, because the comprehensive purpose is complex or multifaceted, Gamwell also recognizes the limits of justice and the political sphere. As he recounts,

> justice is limited because our maximal common humanity is . . . self-localizing as well as self-widening. Our common humanity would be debilitated to the point of near impotence if individuals did not assume special responsibility for their own families, enduring attachments, and local communities and associations. This is, on my accounting, [why society] . . . should be zealously protected against every attempt to expand the legal order beyond its mandate to provide and promote general conditions of emancipation.[99]

In brief, the divine good seeks a socially empowered world that fosters personal responsibility for oneself, one's family, and one's community. Though the state should always seek to promote general conditions of equality and emancipation, it should never impede the virtues of personal responsibility.

Finally, Gamwell considers whether justice as general emancipation is a meaningful possibility or an unrealistic ideal. In answering this question, he seeks to integrate Niebuhr's political realism with Dewey's democratic idealism. Niebuhr is right to affirm the need for political realism in the sense that we must always have our eyes wide open to the realities of power in the world. Hence, a "democratic constitution should be realistic in its institutionalization of the democratic decision-making process, recognizing that bargaining will often be in greater or lesser measure involved." Furthermore, both democracy and justice will be threatened if society blindly allows "the concentration of power and [naively relies] on a commitment to the common good among the powerful." Nevertheless, Gamwell maintains that this affirmation of realism should neither replace nor obscure the telos of democratic discourse itself—this was Dewey's insight and Niebuhr's oversight. "In Niebuhr's more sustained treatment of politics," observes Gamwell, "the [telos that] Dewey raised in his formulation of our maximal common humanity is lost." This occurred because Niebuhr, in advancing "an ideal of mutuality that is merely transcendent and, therefore, historically im-

---

99. Gamwell, *Divine Good*, 298 n. 2, 292, 294, 299.

possible," lost sight of the positive importance of democratic discourse in the world and, instead, sought democracy merely as an instrumental means for seeking a rough equilibration of power. Hence, by losing sight of this discursive aim within history, Niebuhr's view, in spite of its theistic source of meaning, "becomes in its own way nonteleological." In contrast,

> commitment to discourse affirms that convincing argument can have its part in determining the associational order and, therefore, that politics in significant measure can both depend on and help to evoke a general commitment to the common good. So understood, participation in discourse assumes that the possibilities of justice in this world are not exhausted by increasing the satisfaction of asserted interests more or less equally but include the pursuit of mutuality or our common humanity. Indeed, this participation assumes that the democratic process itself can be a realization of mutuality.[100]

Moreover "it is telling," Gamwell notes, "that Niebuhr's famous aphorism, 'man's capacity for justice makes democracy possible; but man's inclination to injustice makes democracy necessary,' does not explicitly assert that our capacity for justice also makes democracy necessary." Had Niebuhr fully recognized the positive aim and necessity of democracy, he would have rightly discerned that "justice is in service to our common humanity, and democratic discourse is required to realize within the political process itself the good that human life as such ought to maximize." In sum, one needs to bring a measure of realism to politics, but one must never lose sight of the aim of democratic discourse; for if discourse is "futile, so, too, is democracy."[101]

Representative Christology and Christian Expression

By this point, or perhaps much earlier, someone like Hauerwas might ask in what sense is Gamwell's view specifically Christian. I will conclude this portrait by responding to this important query. It is certainly the case that Gamwell understands himself first and foremost as a philosophical theologian rather than as a dogmatic theologian who focuses principally on Christian doctrine as such. Hence, the locus of

---

100. Ibid., 323, 324, 323, 324.
101. Ibid., 324, 325. Gamwell cites Niebuhr, *Children of Light and Children of Darkness*, xiii.

his work is often directed toward philosophical conversation partners in moral and political theory. Nevertheless, as I suggested at the outset, his project is intent on improving and completing the public theology that Niebuhr so prominently launched in the middle of the last century. Like Niebuhr, Gamwell seeks to articulate and defend the moral and political implications of Christian faith in God. Along this line, *Politics as a Christian Vocation* seeks to specify the political and democratic implications of Christian faith. Moreover, like Niebuhr, Gamwell believes that the center of this faith is found in the love of God revealed in Jesus as the Christ. Yet, if Gamwell inherits his public theology largely from Niebuhr, he inherits his systematic theology largely from Ogden. For instance, in the preface to *The Divine Good*, Gamwell states: "I take the liberty of dedicating [this] book . . . to Schubert M. Ogden, to whom, more than any other single individual, I owe my education."[102] The formative influence of this education has shaped Gamwell's understanding of Christian faith in at least three important respects.

First, taking his bearings from Ogden, Gamwell's theology is structured around a representative christology. "For Christians," Gamwell declares, "Jesus Christ re-presents explicitly the love and calling of God that humans experience everywhere. In this sense, Christian faith presents again the primal belief about reality and human authenticity all humans always share, the 'overtone implied in all experience.'"[103] For Gamwell, the reality of God, which is re-presented in Jesus Christ, is a reality that is part and parcel of any and all possible experience. General revelation—as the overtone implied in all experience—discloses that God is the source and end of all things whereas special revelation re-presents the character of this underlying reality in the life of Jesus as the Christ.

Second, building on this representative christology, Gamwell, like Ogden, believes that "faith and the way of reason" go fully hand-in-hand. "Because [Christian] faith means that God as re-presented through Jesus Christ is present to and [dimly or implicitly] understood by all humans," contends Gamwell, "Christians may without pause pledge that this faith can be redeemed through reasons authorized by common human experience." This is not to say that reason can replace

---

102. Gamwell, *Divine Good*, xiii.

103. Gamwell, *Politics as a Christian Vocation*, 75–76. He cites, Niebuhr, *Nature and Destiny*, 1:127.

the role of faith or trust, but it does assert that the claims of faith can be publicly assessed and validated by reason apart from appeals to special revelation or the Christian story. "[H]aving Christian faith is one thing," states Gamwell, "and validating the beliefs by which Christian faith is characterized is something else." As he further specifies, "To hold that argument can validate Christian belief in God's prior act of redemption is not to say that success in the argumentative practice can substitute for God's grace or is equivalent to an acceptance of it." Rather, the "'way of reason' designates solely an argumentative practice in or through which beliefs that have been contested or called into question may be validated or invalidated." Hence, he identifies "[d]iscourse as a Christian [c]ommitment" and responsibility. "To refuse [this commitment] is to deny that God is revealed to all humans in their primal decision for a self-understanding." Otherwise stated, "affirmation of God's omnipresence prescribes [a] . . . commitment [to discourse]." Thus, "Critical reflection on re-presentations of ultimate worth is the attempt to reach by argument something about ourselves that, at the deepest level of consciousness, we already know."[104] In sum, Gamwell distinguishes between our existential assent to divine love and grace and our cognitive and public responsibility to discursively validate our truth claims about the reality and character of God.

A brief comparison with Milbank is again instructive. Like Milbank, Gamwell affirms a representative christology in an *ontological* sense, i.e., the Christ event does not constitute a change in God or in God's relation to the world. But where they differ is that Gamwell, unlike Milbank, also affirms a representative christology in an *epistemological* sense. That is, for Gamwell, the truth re-presented in Christ can be validated by reason apart from special revelation, whereas for Milbank, this truth can only be known through Christian rhetoric. Hence, Milbank's christology is ontologically representative but epistemologically constitutive, whereas Gamwell's is representative on both counts.

Third, Gamwell, like Ogden, thinks that Christian claims must not only be rationally credible but also appropriately Christian. As we have seen, Gamwell and Ogden hold that the love of God re-presented in Jesus as the Christ is the normative core of the Christian proclama-

---

104. The phrase "Faith and the Way of Reason" is the title of chapter three in Gamwell's *Politics as a Christian Vocation*, 56–79. Other quotes in this paragraph come from the following pages of that work: 75, 65, 69, 76, 77, 171. For Ogden's view of faith and the way of reason, see Ogden, *On Theology*, 83.

tion; and this proclamation calls Christians and all human beings to creatively contribute to the divine life through maximizing good in the world. On Gamwell's account,

> Christian faith asserts that God as all-embracing love is the ground of all worth. The effects we have in the world would be without any worth except that the world has the significance God gives to it by receiving all of it into the everlasting divine life. In the end, the only difference we can make is the difference we make to the divine good.[105]

Here we see the interconnection between Gamwell's process panentheism and his understanding of the Christian norm of love. We are called to love all that God loves because all that we do and value in the world affects the divine life. "Loving the world *is* loving God," Gamwell remarks, "in the sense that God's love receives all the world. We are called to love our neighbors as ourselves because thereby we contribute most fully to the divine good, and that is why the second part of the Great Commandment follows without pause from the first." He contrasts the implications of this divine relativity and receptivity with the classical insistence on divine immutability and impassibility. "[T]o understand God as eternally complete," he suggests, "is finally to deny any ultimate importance to what we do or become. Whatever effect we have in the world, we cannot make a difference to something that cannot receive it." This difference, which the love of God both receives and calls forth, requires a commitment to justice in both its substantive and formative dimensions—one that promotes both general emancipation and democratic participation. Hence, "politics today is a common Christian vocation because the moral principles implied by the Christian faith prescribe, at least in our [modern] setting, democracy as a form of political rule and thus democratic citizenship as a general form of Christian witness." In a sermon reflecting on the legacy of Martin Luther King, Jr., Gamwell eloquently summarizes the connection between love and justice:

> We can no more accept God's love without a passion for justice than we can open a window without letting in the wind. Living for the beloved community is, in fact, the chance of a lifetime—

---

105. Gamwell, *Politics as a Christian Vocation*, 104. For Ogden's discussion of the twin theological criteria of adequacy, namely, credibility and appropriateness, see Ogden, *On Theology*, 4–6.

the chance given to us again and again in every present moment to receive God's abiding presence. This is why, I like to think, King evoked the arc of the moral universe, the future that waits on what we decide. And, with him, we may also have the hope—although not sure and certain—that its course, however long, bends toward justice.[106]

Typological Analysis

As noted earlier, my four-fold typology is informed by Gamwell's distinction between the modern commitment and the modern dominant consensus. Hence, it should be relatively clear where he stands in relation to my categories and, thus, I will only briefly restate his positions with some elaboration.

Commitment to Intelligibility (I+)

As evident both by his representative christology and his active engagement with philosophy, Gamwell is fully committed to making theological claims intelligible to the wider public and the academy. Indeed, a commitment to free and full public discourse, he argues, is a necessary commitment of Christian faith itself. Because the reality of God is necessarily present in all possible experience and in all possible cultural contexts, Gamwell believes the divine reality, as re-presented in Jesus Christ, can be expressed in terms beyond the Christian tradition. To be sure, translation and mutual understanding are not easily achieved, but they are potential achievements to be pursued. He recognizes that our conscious and explicit human understandings are influenced by the cultural and linguistic resources available to us, but these resources are neither fixed nor impervious to creative new possibilities and understandings. Summarily speaking, Gamwell agrees with Davidson that "translatability" is ultimately "a criterion of languagehood."[107] And, for Gamwell, this translatability is finally possible because the world is integrated and unified in and through the divine relativity.

---

106. Gamwell, *Politics as a Christian Vocation*, 103, 104, 4. The passage comes from Gamwell, "Of Time and Purpose," 38; the famous full quote from King is: "The arc of the moral universe is long, but it bends toward justice," found on 28 in the Gamwell text.

107. Davidson, "On the Very Idea of a Conceptual Scheme," 186.

Commitment to Credibility (C+)

One of Gamwell's chief criticisms of twentieth-century theology is its widespread failure to fully embrace the commitment to credibility. As he sees it,

> most theologians have resisted a full endorsement of the modern commitment. At some point in the formulation and defense of Christian convictions, each of these theologians has insisted that moral claims are redeemed by appeal to special divine revelation and, therefore, without appeal to human experience and reason as such. The conviction that valid moral claims have a divine ground, we are told, is validated by appeal to the normative Christian . . . tradition, that is, the normative witness to Jesus as the Christ. . . . [I]t is fair to say that theologians who have not at some point compromised the affirmation of [formal] autonomy in favor of an appeal to the special Christian revelation are dramatically few.[108]

Over against this tendency, Gamwell seeks to show how and why theology ought to embrace formal autonomy and its commitment to credibility. One reason this commitment is necessary, he holds, is because all claims, including theological ones, are fallible. Thus, the comprehensive conviction "that any given religious community represents [or proclaims] is itself fallible and, therefore, cannot be simply confessional in a sense inconsistent with assessment by appeal to human experience and reason as such."[109] No claim is made true or shown to be true simply because it is asserted with heartfelt conviction or religious fervor. On his account, as we have seen, a public assessment of theological claims involves both transcendental and metaphysical forms of argument.

Gamwell not only seeks to embody this commitment to credibility in his own work, but he also seeks to show that a denial of this commitment is self-contradictory. As he states:

> [A]ll resistance to the formal affirmation of autonomy is self-refuting, because it cannot avoid presupposing the modern commitment in the very act of questioning it. When one asserts that the modern affirmation is open to question, one implies that a sufficient condition for choosing this affirmation or its heteronomous alternative includes considerations or reasons other

---

108. Gamwell, *Divine Good*, 10–11.
109. Ibid., 208.

than the [mere] fact that one or another is simply asserted. But this [affirmation of reasons] is implicitly to share the [modern] commitment.[110]

It does no good to propose that the choice between the two alternatives is merely arbitrary, he submits. "For *that* claim [itself] purports to be valid," and thus it "presupposes that there is a sufficient condition for affirming it; but this is impossible if both autonomous and heteronomous appeals are arbitrary." Furthermore, nothing is gained if one claims, à la Niebuhr, "that the choice must be taken by deciding which alternative yields a more adequate interpretation of human existence. For this [claim] presupposes a procedure for assessing interpretations of the human condition, and what is at issue in the choice between autonomy and heteronomy is precisely the appeal by which any such interpretation might be redeemed." Hence, Gamwell concludes that "the only alternative to the affirmation of [formal] autonomy is an authoritarian affirmation." Yet, even to ask about the two alternatives is already implicitly to have rejected the authoritarian path. Therefore, the very "choice between autonomy and heteronomy [already] presupposes autonomy."[111]

Absence of Metaphysics (AM-)

Like Milbank, but even more unequivocally, Gamwell seeks to bring the metaphysical question back to the fore of theological and philosophical discussion. They each pursue this task because they both agree that medieval thought rightly oriented all of life in relation to what Gamwell calls "an all-inclusive context of importance," and that modernity has wrongly jettisoned this comprehensive question and framework.[112] Furthermore, they concur that the comprehensive question is ultimately metaphysical or ontological in nature; all subsidiary questions, such as those of meaning, value, and politics, ultimately and inescapably presuppose questions about the nature of reality as such. Finally, they also agree that modern theology has wrongly turned its back on the centrality of metaphysics and thereby lost its ontological depth and its public or cultural voice.

110. Ibid., 13.
111. Ibid.
112. Gamwell, *Democracy on Purpose*, 1.

Notwithstanding these points of agreement, they differ markedly in the paths they take to conceptualize, articulate, and defend a renewed metaphysical and theistic vision. Milbank seeks to recover medievalism's comprehensiveness by reclaiming an early medieval ontology whereas Gamwell seeks to reclaim it by advancing a modern process metaphysics. For instance, whereas Milbank's medieval panentheism of plenitude continues to adhere to aspects of classical theism, such as holding that eternity is the inclusive category (eternity includes time) and affirming divine impassibility, Gamwell's modern panentheism emphasizes that time is the inclusive category (time is the concrete characteristic; eternity is an abstraction from time), that God is supremely passible and relative, and that the divine experience receives and integrates all the creative contributions of the world. The world is not a divine unfolding, Gamwell maintains, rather, it is what the divine receives and enjoys. Moreover, because Milbank holds that eternity includes time, he recognizes that such a notion is rationally paradoxical; thus he eschews the modern commitment to credibility in seeking to articulate his theistic metaphysical vision—opting for rhetoric over reason. For this same reason, Milbank denies a representative christology in an epistemological sense. Alternatively, because Gamwell takes time to be the inclusive category, he develops and expresses his metaphysical theism within the terms of a commitment to credibility, and he affirms a representative christology in both an ontological and epistemological sense. In sum, Gamwell believes that theology must explicitly return to the metaphysical question, and it must do so in a manner consistent with the formal commitments of modernity.

Autonomy of Ethics (AE-)

Given the fact that Gamwell's understanding of justice draws at specific points upon the insights of thinkers like Habermas and Rawls, one might assume that "secularists for Gamwell" is a conceivable notion. But such a conjecture would involve a fundamental misunderstanding, for Gamwell emphatically seeks to show that neither justice nor morality can be coherently understood apart from theism. Indeed, he boldly and directly seeks to challenge the modern philosophical consensus that presupposes that ethics can be coherently understood apart from the question of God. What troubles him as much as this philosophical assumption is the fact that some theologians and many religious adherents "have given tacit consent to this [widespread] conviction. Theological or religious ethicists have generally pursued the moral commitments" of their religious convictions, Gamwell notes, "[b]ut they have rarely argued that religious affirmations are implied by the moral enterprise as such." As we saw earlier, Gustafson is a prime example of this insofar as he accepts the philosophical autonomy of morality while, at the same time, giving theological voice to a theocentric ethic. In contrast, as developed in his critical analysis of Kant and Aristotle, Gamwell argues "that success in modern moral theory waits upon the reassertion of theism." As he observes, "philosophical ethics subsequent to Kant has in the main sought to validate moral claims independently of theism because it has also been decidedly nonmetaphysical." What is required, therefore, is a metaphysical theism, specifically, one in the form of a process panentheism. Once metaphysics and the divine reality are properly conceived, Gamwell reasons, one can then make an unreserved and coherent philosophical case that God is indeed "the ground of any moral claim." By "ground," he "refers to that which makes a moral claim valid." Hence, "one cannot affirm or deny any moral claim without implicitly affirming [the] divine reality." Moreover, "this thesis is required by theistic belief itself. At least if one means by 'God' a being or individual that is the source and end of all things, theism includes the conviction that God alone provides the authentic telos for the human enterprise as such. . . . It follows" from this, he points out, "that adherents of theistic religions compromise the integrity of their religious belief insofar as they also believe that a secularistic morality is possible. To believe in God and also to affirm a common morality that is neither explicitly nor implicitly theistic is to embrace an inconsistent self-understanding."[113] As much as for Barth or any other theologian, ethics for Gamwell is inescapably tied to the doctrine of God. Of course, the critical difference is that Gamwell thinks the doctrine of God is one that can and must be made rationally intelligible and publicly credible.

Critical Assessment

Gamwell's signal contribution to contemporary theology is his systematic attempt to bring the question of God back to the center of moral and political theory. He does this by fully embracing modernity's formal

---

113. Gamwell, *Divine Good*, 1, 16, 2, xii.

commitments (I, C) while, at the same time, fundamentally rejecting its predominant substantive conclusions (AE, AM). Like MacIntyre, Stout, Hauerwas, and Milbank, Gamwell thinks that theology has indeed lost its authentic voice. For example, he would fully concur when Stout proclaims, in discussing Barth, that "Christianity, if it is to be true to itself, will have to make ontological claims." Yet, Gamwell parts with Stout—and the rest of them—when Stout immediately asserts that theology "cannot *defend* [these claims] in secular or philosophical terms."[114] Of the six theologians that I have examined, Gamwell is the only one who fully embraces both the metaphysical claims of theology and the modern commitments to intelligibility and credibility. On one end, Gustafson, Niebuhr, and Porter affirm these commitments up to a point while leaving theology's metaphysical claims largely recessed in the background. On the other end, Milbank seeks to strongly reassert the ontological claims of theology while at the same time emphatically rejecting any attempt to make these claims rationally credible. In between these alternatives, Gamwell seeks directly to challenge modernity's roadblock to metaphysics while concomitantly embracing modernity's formal commitments. He does this by affirming a fallibilistic understanding of metaphysics—one that recognizes the critical difference between the *content* of metaphysical claims (claims about the necessary characteristics of reality) and the *act* of making such claims (an act that is always fallible and culturally and historically situated). Given our concrete particularity, we see through a glass darkly; thus our claims to knowledge are always fragmentary and fallible. Nevertheless, we can still see through the glass to some extent; we can still catch glimpses of insight into the necessary characteristics of reality. Hence, Gamwell engages neither in the sin of epistemological hubris nor in the false humility of postmetaphysical modernity. Positively stated, it is precisely this combination of epistemological humility and metaphysical inquiry that is needed in order for theology to regain a serious hearing in the academy and the wider public. For it is only by changing the perception of the God-question in the academy, and by implication in the larger culture, that theology will begin to step meaningfully back into the public arena. To accomplish this, theology needs to be able to affirm both the centrality and necessity of God, and the modern commitments to intelligibility

---

114. Stout, *Flight from Authority*, 143.

and credibility. In my judgment, Gamwell does this more unequivocally and more effectively than other modern or contemporary theologians.

Process panentheism, with its affirmation of the divine relativity, lies at the center of Gamwell's endeavor. It is only by seriously rethinking the doctrine of God that theology can regain its authentic voice, for the question of God's relation to the world has plagued Christian theology ever since it cast its eyes upon Greek philosophy. By defining perfection in terms of immutability and impassibility, classical theism has left theology unable to attribute any ultimate significance or value to the changing world and its dynamic activities. Yet, if the modern world has sought anything, it has sought to be world-affirming. Therefore, "to understand God as eternally complete," Gamwell incisively observes, "is finally to deny any ultimate importance to what we do or become. Whatever effect we have in the world, we cannot make a difference to something that cannot receive it." How can Christian theology ever be relevant to the affairs of the world, such as in relation to questions of ethics, politics, or vocation, if the affairs of the world ultimately make no difference to the God who is the center of theological concern? "Were there nothing ultimate at stake in what we do," Gamwell adds, "then ultimately there would be nothing at stake." Hence, he rightly critiques both modernity's attempt to affirm worldly value apart from divine ultimacy and traditional theology's attempt to affirm divine ultimacy apart from worldly value. Gustafson, Niebuhr, Porter, and Hauerwas all affirm worldly value in some way, but all of them have difficulty connecting it to the divine reality. Alternatively, Milbank seeks to make this connection by viewing the world itself as part of the divine unfolding. Nevertheless, there remains a problematic ambiguity in Milbank's view as to whether there is or is not genuine creaturely autonomy and creativity. The source of this ambiguity (and the source of difficulty for most of these other theologians as well) emanates from an underlying acceptance of the classical notion of God as replete Being—where no creaturely value can add to or enrich the divine experience because God is not internally related to the world. In contrast, Gamwell fundamentally critiques and jettisons this classical notion and, instead, affirms a divine relativity that supremely relates to and incorporates the value of all things into the divine life. "The effects we have in the world," Gamwell insightfully concludes, "would be without any worth except that the world has the significance God gives to it by receiving all of it into the everlasting divine life. In the end, the only difference we can make is the difference we make to the divine good."[115]

In addition to reformulating the doctrine of God, Gamwell, drawing on Ogden, also rightly points to the critical need for rethinking christology and the implications that follow from it. In order for theology to regain its public voice, it must not only question classical theism, but it must also challenge the dominance of constitutive christology. There are at least four important theological reasons for rethinking this and related questions. First, as Milbank himself recognizes, the divine nature neither changes nor needs to be placated in the face of human fault and frailty. "Thomas assures us," declares Milbank, "that God had no need to be appeased in order to become reconciled to us and that instead, in himself, he always and eternally was reconciled to us.... For Aquinas, therefore, the Incarnation does not bring about this reconciliation for God." Likewise, Ogden, quoting Tillich, denies "that God 'is the one who must be reconciled.' Since the message of Christianity, on the contrary, is that 'God, who is eternally reconciled, wants us to be reconciled to him,' the only appropriate thing to say is that 'through the Cross' salvation 'becomes manifest.'"[116] Hence, Christ does not constitute divine reconciliation but, rather, reveals the God who is already eternally reconciled and graciously disposed to the world. This is the case because the divine love is the very essence of God and that love was, is, and always will be dispositive; Christ re-presents this disposition, he does not initiate it. Thus, the Christ-event is decisive because of what it represents, not because of what it constitutes.

Second, if one affirms this divine reality and its omnipresence, then one must affirm the divine relatedness to all things in all moments of time. The God re-presented in Jesus Christ is a God who is always present to all of reality; thus, any and all experience includes the experience of God in some measure. To suggest otherwise is to imply that God relates to parts but not to the whole of reality. Hence, Gamwell correctly states that Christian faith "means that God as re-presented through Jesus Christ is present to and [at least implicitly] understood

---

115. Gamwell, *Politics as a Christian Vocation*, 104.
116. Milbank, *Being Reconciled*, 64. Ogden, *Is There Only One True Religion*, 93. Ogden cites Tillich, *Systematic Theology*, vol. 2, 169f., 175f.

by all humans."[117] Third, the doctrine of sin, properly understood, does not deny or eradicate our universal and implicit knowledge of God. On the contrary, as Gamwell convincingly argues in his discussion of Niebuhr, our omnipresent background knowledge of God always points, however faintly, to an alternative choice that stands over against and condemns our massive tendency to choose and act duplicitously. To deny our implicit knowledge of God is to deny the ground of worth that is the measure of all value and disvalue, and the measure of all virtue and vice. But there is no sin where there is no knowledge of the divine measure; and where there is no sin, there is no putative argument based on sin to reject the claim of universal and implicit knowledge of God.

Fourth, following on these other three points, "Christians may without pause," Gamwell rightly concludes, "pledge that [the claims of] faith can be redeemed through reasons authorized by common human experience." Instead of affirming this, however, Christian theology has wrongly tended to assume that it must (in Kant's words but not with Kant's meaning) deny reason in order to make room for faith. This severed link between faith and reason, I judge, has been due in varying degrees and in interrelated ways to the dominance of classical theism and the modern denial of metaphysics, to the dominance of constitutive christology, and to understandings of sin that eliminate all natural knowledge of God. For example, notice again how Hauerwas approvingly describes Barth's suspicion of natural theology:

---

117. Gamwell, *Politics as a Christian Vocation*, 75. Hauerwas and others might interject that God is present to all, but not implicitly known by all. This rejoinder, however, is problematic on multiple fronts, but I will here only mention one. To affirm that God is present to all but not implicitly known by all leaves Christian faith with an intractable problem of evil. This is the case because if knowledge of and right relation to God are only possible through response to the explicit Christian witness, then salvation is dependent on the vagaries and contingencies of history, specifically, on access to this explicit witness. This, however, creates two categories of human beings: those who have access and those who do not. But this distinction then leaves the latter group in a "predicament" not of their own making, "without prospect of salvation. And this is the great difficulty," notes Ogden, "for it means, in effect, that the human predicament of some persons is radically different from that of others." One group is guilty of sin—of the misuse of freedom—but has access to the means of salvation; the other group is guilty but has no access. Hence, to exclude the latter group due to "a matter of fate rather than freedom" is unjust and morally capricious. If one were to suggest that all persons have implicit access to the God represented in Christ, then one grants my original point (Ogden, *Is There Only One True Religion*, 41).

> Barth's deepest worry about natural theology was what kind of God it "proved." From Barth's perspective you cannot begin by asking if God exists or if God can be known [by reason] because any god that is the answer to such questions cannot but be "the World-Ground or the World-Soul, the Supreme Good or Supreme Value," [and none of these are the God revealed in Jesus Christ].[118]

This statement merely begs the question; to assume that any God known by reason cannot be the same God known through Jesus Christ is to presume one or more of the factors listed above. Clearly, Hauerwas and Barth contend that reason cannot understand the nature of true reality, which is only accessible through the constitutive means of Jesus Christ. Likewise, as the particularity of this constitutive christology morphs into the particularity of Hauerwas's own constitutive ecclesiology, we see him assert that "the appropriate form of [Christ's] universality is lost if metaphysical and anthropological theories are made to substitute for the necessary witnessing of Christian lives and communities to the significance of his story."[119] So now, not only does Christ play a constitutive role, but so, too, does the church. In this case, however, the church becomes its own *raison d'être* and the world has no value apart from the church. For how could the world have any independent value if there is no measure of genuine value apart from the church and its constitutive witness? Hence, it is not surprising that Hauerwas finds relatively little value in democracy or other world-affirming endeavors.

Having said all this, I think Gamwell's view could use an ecclesiological "shot in the arm." His account does not spell out in sufficient detail what the role of the church is in the world; he is explicitly helpful when it comes to *defending* the claims of faith, but he is somewhat more silent when it comes to *establishing* them in the lives of individuals and communities.[120] Gamwell would agree with Hauerwas that the church is a community that is called to bear witness and to cultivate virtue. For Gamwell, this chief virtue is piety, a disposition that orients one's desires and actions toward pursuing the divine good in all things. Again,

---

118. Gamwell, *Politics as a Christian Vocation*, 75. Hauerwas, *With the Grain*, 163 n. 49. Hauerwas cites Barth, *Church Dogmatics*, 2/1:6.

119. Hauerwas, *Community of Character*, 41.

120. Though it is important to note that Gamwell has long been active in a community group in Chicago called "Protestants for the Common Good" (http://www.thecommongood.org).

this virtue has self-localizing as well as self-widening implications; to pursue the divine good means loving and caring for one's family as well as loving and worshipping God and seeking social justice. The church is that community called to bear explicit witness in the world to the love of God as re-presented in Jesus Christ. Moreover, it is explicitly called to foster those habits of mind, heart, and character that amplify our recognition of and responsiveness to the omnipresence of God and to the divine telos in our lives. If the pervasiveness of sin is found in the persuasive power of the proximate, then the role of the church is to foster the cultivation of desire and the habits of character that can reach beyond the proximate to see and respond to the all-inclusive aim of the divine good. Peirce succinctly articulates this vision when he declares that "the *raison être* of a church is to confer upon men [and women] a life broader than their narrow personalities, a life rooted in the very truth of being." In this sense of expanding and transforming our habits of character, Hauerwas correctly emphasizes sanctification as a part of the church's mission. But this emphasis should not mean that the church defines itself over against either the world or the formal commitments of modernity, for as Gamwell's position illustrates, the formation of virtue does not require the foregoing of modernity in this regard. Though Gamwell's view may lack sufficient development of an ecclesiology, it by no means precludes it. Indeed, the church is called not to be a constitutive end-in-itself, but rather to be a witness that points to and manifests the love of God in the world. In order for the church to do this, "it must," as Peirce again aptly states, "be based upon and refer to a definite and public experience."[121] Both Peirce and Gamwell rightly point toward a *public* church—one that serves and bears witness to the fact that the future of the world is the future of God.

---

121. Peirce, *Collected Papers*, vol. 6, paragraph 451. I am indebted to Raposa, *Peirce's Philosophy of Religion*, 12 for drawing my attention to these passages. In response to my analysis of his ecclesiology vis-à-vis Hauerwas and Milbank, Gamwell remarks: "Understanding the specifically religious community as having the distinctive function of mediating our relation to God through attention to explicit representations of God's original [or general] revelation seems to me precisely right. What I find problematic in Hauerwas and Milbank is the apparent absence of original revelation, so that the function of the church becomes, not only cultivating the persuasive power of an understanding we already [implicitly] have, but also [constitutively] introducing us to our true relation to God. In the end, that is, so far as I can see, a denial of theism" (email, 9/26/03).

If Gamwell's position needs further ecclesiological elaboration, it also needs further clarification in terms of how it defines the divine good. Simply stated, I wonder if he takes Gustafson's critique of anthropocentricism seriously enough. To be sure, Gamwell qualifies his equation of maximal common humanity with the divine good. He does so, in part, by specifying that the divine good and the human good are teleologically coincident rather than identical, and, in part, by offering a principle of environmental respect. Moreover, he might concur with Porter insofar as she contends that Gustafson's position ends up affirming the human good as the measure of value, in spite of appearances to the contrary. Nevertheless, I think Gustafson's position, if nothing else, serves as a valuable tonic—one that offers us an important prophetic reminder to keep a principle of environmental respect always clearly in view. Gamwell may indeed be right that the potential for human creativity is significantly greater and thus "crosses the Rubicon" compared to nonhuman forms of activity. But the collective value of the environment or nonhuman world certainly has significant worth for the divine life, and this worth should never be quickly or easily discounted. In fact, Gustafson might warn us not to be too presumptuous in doing the collective calculus. Justice and human enrichment in the global community are undoubtedly central aims in pursuing the divine telos. Nonetheless, these aims must always be held in concert with a principle of environmental respect—one that holds the human good accountable by requiring us consistently to seek to live in greater harmony with nature. In a time that appears to be marked by an acceleration of global warming, Gustafson's prophetic warning is ever the more pertinent.

Furthermore, Gamwell's intimate connection between the divine and human good runs the danger of ignoring his own insight about the nature of temptation and sin. Our perennial temptation, he correctly observes, is to attach greater worth to those possibilities that we experience more concretely than to those that we do not.[122] It is surely human value that we experience most directly and concretely; thus, we are tempted to undervalue non-human worth and experience. This notwithstanding, I do not want to disparage the pursuit of social justice or the human good. Gamwell's persisting question is: How could one specify obligations to the nonhuman world that could potentially override the pursuit of justice or human emancipation? Could such obliga-

---

122. See Gamwell, *Democracy on Purpose*, 97f.

tions or constraints, for instance, permit a violation of some persons' communicative rights? In effect, he worries that such an override would undermine a rule-teleology and undercut the pursuit of social justice. In sum, my concern is to keep us mindful of our place in the larger divine economy—thus recognizing both the importance of human justice and flourishing, and the worth of the environment and nonhuman world. For as Gustafson, Troeltsch, and modern scientists remind us, the earth will eventually disappear and so will human beings.[123] It is God who is everlasting, not us; our abiding worth is *part* of the divine good, not its totality.

Summary (I+C+AE-AM-)

Gamwell's view powerfully illustrates what it means to complete modernity by using modern tools that have not been sufficiently utilized. Modernity has been developed around a false assumption, namely, that a commitment to formal autonomy or secularity requires a denial of the metaphysical enterprise. But this assumption has cut us off from any public expression and defense of our most fundamental convictions about the meaning, nature, and worth of existence. Gamwell shows theology a way forward by directly challenging this deep-seated modern assumption. By fully embracing the modern commitments to intelligibility and credibility, and by fully developing a neoclassical theistic metaphysics, Gamwell challenges the pervasive modern assumption that ethics, politics, and culture can ultimately be coherently understood apart from the reality of God. But precisely by fully embracing the formal commitments of modernity, he exemplifies how this is done in a spirit of epistemological humility coupled with deep substantive conviction—a combination sorely lacking in much of contemporary public discourse.

---

123. In a recent study, scientists claimed that the sun will eventually vaporize the earth in about 7.59 billion years. In response, one scientist described this finding "a touch depressing" but also as "an incentive to do something about finding ways to leave our planet and colonize other areas in the galaxy" (Overbye, "Kissing the Earth Goodbye"). My response to this "incentive" is ambivalent. On the one hand, I encourage exploration and human flourishing, wherever they may lead us. On the other, part of me wants to say that, in the end, it is God who is everlasting not us; theism must ultimately be theocentric not anthropocentric.

Conclusion

The Future of Theology and the Academy

THE GUIDING AIM OF THIS INQUIRY HAS BEEN TO UNDERSTAND WHY theology has been marginalized in the modern world and, consequently, to understand what is required to change its social location in the contemporary cultural landscape. I have argued that the deep aversion to metaphysics in modern thought, including in most modern theology, lies at the center of this problematic. For if theology is a discipline that seeks to offer systematic and critical reflection on the meaning and truth of religious claims, and if religious claims at some point inevitably make metaphysical claims about the nature of reality as such, then theology cannot be a vital and vibrant voice in the cultural conversation unless it takes up the metaphysical mantle. My six-fold typological survey sought to show that only a theology that affirms modernity's formal commitments (intelligibility and credibility) while rejecting its substantive conclusions (absence of metaphysics and autonomy of ethics) can make the question of God central again in contemporary intellectual and cultural life. In brief, such a theology must offer a public theistic metaphysics while affirming the modern commitment to secularity. I specifically argued that such a combination is most successful when formulated in terms of the process thought of Whitehead and Hartshorne, as illustrated by the work of Gamwell. Such a view is most adequate because it is oriented to the future state of affairs in the world, and because it directly relates such affairs to the ultimacy of the divine integrity. Hence, such a view can give utmost significance and attention to issues of social justice, democratic politics, the global environment, and individual vocation because it understands our responsibility for and contribution to the future of the world as our indelible contribution to the future of the divine life. In sum, the integration of both faith and reason and religion and public life wait upon a process metaphysical theology.

What is required, in an overarching sense, is an intellectual change leading to a cultural change. Changing the social location of theology, changing the way that people think about the relation between religion and public life, requires an underlying intellectual change in what people presuppose about the rationality of metaphysics; it requires the conclusion that the question of God is a rational public question—one that is, in theory, susceptible to rational inquiry and consensus. Short of this intellectual change, religion will remain either largely privatized, insofar as secularity is affirmed, or culturally imposed, insofar as secularity is abandoned. Theology must be a catalyst for this intellectual change.

Stout, of course, thinks I have it backwards. As we saw in *Ethics After Babel*, he argues that a dramatic cultural change is first required in the form of a religious resurgence, not an intellectual change; only the revival of widespread religious piety, including among intellectuals, could get people to take theology seriously again. Theology cannot contribute to its own changed social location, he submits, rather it must wait for a cultural wave to wash it back into the center of public life. Yet, such a religious resurgence without an underlying intellectual change, I contend, simply leaves deep-seated assumptions about religion and metaphysics in place. For instance, the religious resurgence in much of the world today, whether in the form of Christianity, Islam, or some other tradition, continues to presume, by and large, that the question concerning the reality of God is a non-rational question whose true answer is ultimately dependent upon the particular and constitutive response provided by a unique special revelation. On the other end of the spectrum, Stout's expressive pragmatism likewise continues to presume that underlying religious and metaphysical convictions, that which constitutes one's final vocabulary, cannot be rationally validated as such. Hence, such ultimate truth claims can never, even in theory, be publicly adjudicated; at best, only their claims to entitlement can be justified and accommodated. So in Stout's view of modern democracy, people are free to express their deepest convictions while, at the same time, such convictions can never be taken fully seriously as the truth claims that they indeed are. Instead, all one can do is seek to find some common overlap on less ultimate concerns, such as on specific policy questions. Though Stout's position perhaps allows religious views more free expression than the liberal theorists he criticizes, his position is one that still marginalizes the metaphysical truth claims of religion. Such marginalization is evident, for instance, in his ethics without metaphysics, where he seeks to establish moral norms on pragmatic grounds independently of theism. From that vantage point, theistic stances are accommodated but the theistic claim that God is the universal measure of value is relegated to the realm of private belief—one that can be accommodated but not substantiated.

If, as I argue, an underlying intellectual change is needed, then such a change must occur at some point in the academy. In my introduction, I noted Loomer's observation that the fundamental failure of modern universities is their lack of intellectual integrity, that is, their lack of intellectual wholeness in the sense of relating the various disciplines and bodies of knowledge in an integrated way and thereby providing an understanding of and relation to reality as a whole. In short, a modern university is not a uni-versity but rather a multi-versity offering multivious sets of disparate forms of knowledge and expertise. To further develop this analysis of the academy and the role of theology within it, I will examine three distinct critiques. To begin, I will look at MacIntyre's distinction among what he calls the preliberal, liberal, and postliberal universities. Then, I will sketch out the neo-Calvinist critique of the modern academy as offered by Nicholas Wolterstorff and Alvin Plantinga. Finally, I will conclude by offering my own critical assessment by drawing on the works of Loomer and Ogden.

MacIntyre's Critique: Preliberal, Liberal, and Postliberal Universities

In the concluding chapter of *TRV*, MacIntyre, like Loomer, criticizes the lack of wholeness and integrity in the modern academy. In seeking to diagnose this condition, he begins by offering a distinction between what he calls the early "preliberal modern university and college," which was predominant up through the late eighteenth and early nineteenth centuries, and the later "liberal modern university," which came to dominate in the nineteenth and twentieth centuries. Unlike the liberal university, MacIntyre argues that the preliberal academy achieved a sense of intellectual wholeness in the midst of fostering rational inquiry and generating an educated public. But the chief precondition for this wholeness was "a high degree of homogeneity in fundamental belief, especially as regarded standards of rational justification." What he has in mind here is homogeneity in terms of fundamental convictions and, relatedly, in terms of rational evaluative standards. In effect, this commonality implies sharing a common tradition. This homogeneity was achieved through three factors. First, the emergence of consensus was based on scholarly inquiry itself; to be sure, such consensus was subject to the possibility of revision and change, but it was an operating consensus nonetheless. Second, "there were the enforced exclusions from the universities and colleges of points of view too much at odds with the consensus underpinning both enquiry and education." MacIntyre points to disciplinary exclusions, such as the exclusion of astrology from the study of astronomy, and to exclusions based on "the use of religious tests and prohibitions," both "formal and informal." Such religious tests were used to exclude skeptical, agnostic, and secularistic perspectives, "such as that of Hume," and were used, on the other end, to exclude "anti-intellectual" perspectives of "radical Protestant evangelicals." Third, "a counterpart to these forced exclusions was the use of preferments and promotions to ensure that upholders of the consensus," including those who sought to revise and improve it, "occupied the relevant professorial chairs" in the college and universities. "From this point of view," reflects MacIntyre, "Cleghorn was rightly preferred to Hume for the chair in moral philosophy at [the University of] Edinburgh."[1]

It is evident from MacIntyre's text that he believes, on the one hand, that preliberal universities were on the right track insofar as they achieved intellectual wholeness by way of fostering and requiring some degree of homogeneity, thereby maintaining the authority and distinctiveness of a tradition. Yet, on the other hand, he admits that policies that excluded major dissenters and only hired and promoted those who basically subscribed to the prevailing consensus "were liable to error and abuse, and to consequent injustice." This injustice was particularly pronounced when it applied to the exclusion of whole groups, "most notably Jews."[2] The rise of the modern liberal university was due in part to resisting this injustice.

The liberal university "appealed to two sets of premises," MacIntyre contends, "one true and one false." The true set pertained to resisting the

1. MacIntyre, *TRV*, 222, 223, 224.
2. Ibid., 224.

unjust tendencies of the preliberal academy—"those injustices [done] to individuals and to groups of which the preliberal university was certainly guilty." The false set pertained to the liberal university presupposing the notion of a common human reason, that is, presupposing a shared rationality that could, if freed from external constraints (religious and moral tests), produce progress in inquiry and produce "agreement among all rational persons as to what the rationally justified conclusions of such enquiry are." From this liberal standpoint, "the enforcement of prior agreement as a precondition of enquiry was simply an error, an error resulting in arbitrary constraints upon liberty of judgment." In other words, the liberal academy was unwilling to enforce the authority of tradition as the starting point for any further inquiry. Instead, subscribing to the modern commitment to secularity, it sought in theory to allow the best argument to prevail on its own merits at each point in time, however close it was or was not to the prior consensus. "The subsequent history of the liberal university," MacIntyre concludes, "has been one of increasing disarray generated in key part by this initial error [of presupposing a common rationality]." The natural sciences have been successful in advancing inquiry, he claims, precisely because they have quietly, informally, and perhaps even unwittingly had an "unstated" policy of "enforced exclusion" for those who do not subscribe to the prevailing standards. By contrast, the humanities have been a barren landscape of complete openness and tolerance defined merely by a "change of [intellectual] fashion" rather than by any "progress in enquiry." Yet, theology and morality "cannot accept the indifference presupposed by such tolerance," he submits. Thus, "[theological and moral] standpoints have to be at best exiled to the margins of the internal conversations of the liberal university." What MacIntyre apparently means here is that theological and moral convictions imply or explicitly make truth claims about ultimate reality or make claims about what is morally right or good. Such claims and convictions are, by nature, antithetical to a preferential or relativistic view of truth and morality. Hence, such theological and moral viewpoints cannot abide the interminable lack of resolution or consensus in the modern liberal arts and humanities. Given this impasse, "the liberal university can provide no remedy. And by providing no remedy it has [in effect] successfully excluded substantive moral and theological enquiry from its domain."[3]

3. Ibid., 225, 226.

As MacIntyre sums it up, the preliberal context "was a university of enforced and constrained agreements" whereas "the liberal university aspired to be a university of unconstrained agreements." What both of these models wrongly thought they could avoid was the fundamental conflict between incommensurable rationalities and traditions. The preliberal academy thought it could avoid this by means of institutionally enforced homogeneity whereas the liberal milieu thought it could avoid this by means of an open and rationally achieved consensus. As a way forward, MacIntyre proposes a third alternative in the form of a "postliberal university" as a place of "constrained disagreements." Like Milbank and Porter, MacIntyre again thinks that the way forward is found by looking backward to the medieval Thomistic tradition. "For what I have imagined," announces MacIntyre, "is . . . in some ways nothing other than a twentieth-century version of the thirteenth-century university." What is required is the "reestablishment of thirteenth-century forms, even if with twentieth-century content." At the heart of these medieval forms is the mode of "disputation"—explicit conflict and competition among competing traditions or schools of thought. Hence, what he has in mind is something like a contemporary version of the thirteenth-century University of Paris, a setting "in which Augustinians and Aristotelians each conducted their own systematic enquiries while at the same time engaging in systematic controversy."[4]

Faculty and scholars in such a postliberal academy would have to fulfill two important roles. On the one hand, each would be a partisan of a specific tradition—a "protagonist of a particular point of view." Such a role would seek both to advance inquiry within that specific tradition as well as to engage in debate and competition with rival traditions. In short, faculty would model to students the role of intellectual competitor—one engaged in the pursuit of knowledge and truth through the competition among rival and incommensurable traditions. On the other hand, each faculty member or scholar would also have to play a non-partisan role of modeling to students a respect for the openness and diversity of the intellectual forum. The modeling of such a disposition would seek "to ensure that rival voices were not illegitimately suppressed, [and would seek] to sustain the university—not as an arena of neutral objectivity, as in the liberal university, . . . —but as an arena of conflict in which the most fundamental type of moral and theological

---

4. Ibid., 230, 234, 232, 233, 232.

disagreement was accorded recognition." Significantly, MacIntyre adds that an important aspect of this second role is to "enable [students] to arrive at independent interpretive judgments, so that they can on occasion protect themselves against too facile an acceptance of—or indeed too facile a rejection of—their teachers' interpretations [of texts and traditions]." Members of different traditions should be able to agree on this aim of fostering some degree of independent judgment, MacIntyre remarks, because it is only by way of such independent reading "that rival interpreters are able to identify what it is about which they are in conflict." Relatedly, it is important to teach intellectual civility and some degree of independence in order "to ensure that the recognition of conflict and disagreement do not blind us to the importance of those large areas of agreement without which conflict and disagreement themselves would necessarily be sterile."[5]

MacIntyre recognizes that his vision of a postliberal university involves some degree of internal tension. If the university is a place of incommensurable traditions and rationalities, a place where people speak fundamentally different and untranslatable intellectual languages, then "how could the university achieve a genuinely shared conversation?" In keeping with his overall view, MacIntyre concedes that such a shared or direct conversation could not take place. Instead, what he really and finally has in mind is "a set of rival universities," each representing a different tradition:

> [T]hus the wider society would be confronted with the claims of rival universities, each advancing its own enquiries in its own terms and each securing the type of agreement necessary to ensure the progress and flourishing of its enquiries by its own set of exclusions and prohibitions, formal and informal. But then also required would be a set of institutionalized forums in which the debate between rival types of enquiry was afforded rhetorical expression.[6]

It is only through this vision of competing traditions and universities, MacIntyre thinks, that theology can reclaim its public voice. Only when theology is able to have its fundamental claims, convictions, and standards define the intellectual agenda of a specific tradition and

---

5. Ibid., 231, 232, 231.
6. Ibid., 234.

university, such as a Thomistic one, can it then speak to and challenge the larger intellectual landscape through the rivalry and competition among different traditions and institutions.

MacIntyre's retro-vision of a "medieval" postliberal university shares at least some similarities with both the modern preliberal and liberal educational environments. Like the preliberal college, rival postliberal universities, or at least the Thomistic version (and perhaps others as well), would each foster some strong degree of internal intellectual homogeneity—sharing a common tradition of intellectual convictions and standards. This is why MacIntyre is drawn to the preliberal university, because he believes that institutions need to exercise both some degree of forced exclusion and some form of preferential hiring in order to maintain the authority and integrity of a tradition. Intellectual inquiry alone is not sufficient to foster a meaningful and sufficient consensus; this is the mistaken assumption of the liberal academy. Rather, a tradition requires forms of authority that must be exercised in some constructive fashion. Yet, like the liberal university, it is clear that MacIntyre is concerned about the abuses and injustices of such practices. Furthermore, his postliberal vision, like the liberal university, affirms the virtue of an open intellectual forum, at least among traditions, and affirms some degree of intellectual autonomy among students.

MacIntyre's interesting discussion of preliberal, liberal, and postliberal institutions raises a host of questions and observations; I will simply offer four here and then return later for final evaluative comments. First, in spite of his explicit concerns about injustice, it is not immediately clear how MacIntyre can ultimately affirm the exclusionary and preferential tendencies of the preliberal university, in the name of fostering homogeneity and tradition, and, at the same time, fully separate himself from its unjust tendencies. Presumably, he would respond by saying that persons should be hired or promoted in terms of their beliefs and convictions and not in terms of their ethnic, racial, gender, or socio-economic identity. One is looking for a good fit, he might say, in terms of the intellectual, moral, and theological tradition of the institution. But what about the question of core existential, religious, and metaphysical convictions? He would likely respond by saying that exclusion on such grounds is both just and necessary. Hence, Hume was rightly passed over for the philosophy chair at Edinburgh because of his skeptical and agnostic tendencies. Likewise, he might say that Hume is not a good fit for a Thomistic university because he is a skeptic (but not because he is Scottish or white). But then is a Jew, Muslim, or atheist not a good fit for a Thomistic institution because of his or her comprehensive convictions? If MacIntyre's postliberal vision finally comes down to rival and competing universities, then presumably some important degree of homogeneity within each tradition and institution would rule the day. Hence, he would again presumably accept and seek to justify such exclusions as necessary and appropriate.

Second, from which vantage point do members of rival traditions each share an affirmation of an open pluralistic public square, of an open and diverse intellectual arena, in which they all equally speak and compete? Differently stated, MacIntyre asserts that scholars in any postliberal university would not only have to be intellectual partisans of their own specific tradition but also champions of open public discourse. But given MacIntyre's overall view, why should one grant him this assumption? Thinkers like Apel and Habermas argue that such respect for discourse is presupposed in the very act and structure of communication itself. But MacIntyre, as we know, explicitly rejects any such universal or transcendental grounds. Yet, without such grounds, he can only allege that it is merely a happy and lucky coincidence that rival universities and traditions would all affirm and teach their students to respect an open and diverse form of discourse. And without such respect, without such a happy and convenient coincidence, MacIntyre's notion of competition among traditions dissolves into a relativistic will to power. To be sure, he repeatedly refers to underlying areas of agreement between rival and incommensurable traditions. But, again, he is never willing to concede that such commonalities are rationally or transcendentally necessary; rather, his strong historicism can only claim that they are contingent and empirical coincidences. In short, he happily always presupposes on contingent grounds what he explicitly denies on necessary grounds.

Third, and relatedly, how would the wider public, when confronted by rival universities, ever decide or adjudicate among their conflicting claims and rational standards? Since presumably most members of the general public are not adherents of any specific tradition, do they then assess these rival claims from some independent standard? But MacIntyre always denies such independent grounds. Is the wider public then merely a mute and vulnerable bystander, waiting to be ruled by one of these competing traditions? Moreover, since the public would have no grounds to assess these claims, any ruling tradition would be, from their perspective, no more or less rational or just than any other tradition. MacIntyre is not explicitly clear on these matters. What he does say is that "a set of institutionalized forums" is needed to give expression to different perspectives and to ensure "debate between rival types of enquiry." But what is the basis or ground of these forums? Or perhaps better yet, who sponsors these forums? Are these neutral public forums, not representing any particular tradition but rather reflecting the non-aligned wider public, such as an intellectual version of the League of Women Voters? But again MacIntyre always rejects such claims of neutrality. Alternatively, does each specific tradition and university sponsor forums reflecting, and thereby tilted toward, its own intellectual predisposition? For, as indicated earlier, he holds that each tradition is committed to ensuring the advancement of its own inquiry and convictions by means of its own standards and set of exclusions. But if the playing field is always tilted toward the home team, then what does this "rigged" contest accomplish? Perhaps one might answer by saying that athletic competitions occur all the time with one team having home-field advantage. But the key difference, I would note, is that in sports all the teams share the same rules and evaluative standards, so home-field advantage does not change this underlying commensurability—whereas for MacIntyre, the home team plays by different rules and standards than does the visiting side. In sum, as I argued in chapter 3, MacIntyre's philosophy trades extensively on the underlying notion of a shared competition. But his insistence that all evaluative standards are merely tradition-specific makes any notion of a shared or coherent competition problematic.

Fourth, and again relatedly, is there finally a tension between MacIntyre's earlier emphasis on the incommensurability of traditions, which alleges that persons in one tradition only seek out, engage, and come to learn other traditions as a second first-language when they have internal difficulties within their own tradition that they unable to resolve by internal means, and his emphasis here on disputation and regular engagement between traditions in the context of institutionalized forums? It seems so. For when MacIntyre envisions a postliberal academy or set of competing academies, he seems to give not only a stronger nod toward modern notions of independent judgment and openness to diversity than he did earlier, but he also appears to envision more regular and frequent conversation and intercourse among competing traditions. For instance, one would think that regularly scheduled disputations would presuppose that each side could understand one another relatively well without having to learn a second first-language. Moreover, one would also presume that the audience and/or judges could understand both teams relatively well without necessarily being or becoming a member of either side.

The Neo-Calvinist Critique: The Need for Christian Scholarship

In his essay "What New Haven and Grand Rapids Have to Say to Each Other," Yale philosophical theologian Nicholas Wolterstorff seeks to identify and describe the key similarities and differences between the Barthian roots of "Yale theology" and the neo-Calvinist mode of thought that Wolterstorff imbibed as an undergraduate at Calvin College. What they share most in common, suggests Wolterstorff, is a rejection of modernity's insistence on translating biblical language into and assessing theological claims in non-theological idioms. That is, instead of seeking to explicate and validate theological claims in common rational or experiential terms, these two schools of thought send out a "call to *reverse the direction of conformation*." This reversal involves rejecting "the regnant self-image" of the academy, which basically means abandoning the modern notions of formal autonomy and common reason. Instead, by reversing the direction of conformation, one must allow the particularities of the Christian revelation and tradition to be the ground and guide in assessing claims. "Over and over," says Wolterstorff, "Christian thinkers in the modern world have felt a general obligation to conform their thought to the results of reputable non-theological learning and to the academy's self-image of its standards and methods. To this pattern of conformation, [these] two traditions urge the same response, namely, that the pattern of conformation be broken, that it be reversed."[7]

In more detail, Wolterstorff's characterization of the modern academy is similar to MacIntyre's description of the liberal university. As Wolterstorff writes:

---

7. Wolterstorff, "What New Haven," 255, 256, 259, 274. I'm indebted to historian Ronald Wells for bringing this essay (and book) to my attention.

> Fundamental in the regnant self-image of [modern] academic learning has been the conviction that one is to practice academic learning just qua normal adult human being—not qua American, ... not qua Christian, ... not *qua* any particularity whatsoever. We can expect that the results of learning so practiced will eventually gain consensus among all normal adult human beings knowledgeable in the discipline. When academic learning is rightly conducted, pluralism in the academy is an accidental and temporary phenomenon. Particularist learning—learning practiced not *qua* human being but *qua* some particular kind of human being—is misbegotten learning.[8]

Along with its emphasis on autonomy and commonality, the self-image of the modern academy, Wolterstorff suggests, is defined by a foundationalism that views philosophy as the ultimate discipline outlining the underlying structure of knowledge, with other disciplines then supplying specific and concrete details. I take it that he is referring here to an earlier version of the modern university, more Cartesian in nature, rather than to the disparate contemporary multiversity. In fact, he goes on to define foundationalism in terms of what he calls "classical foundationalism," specifically, a theory of knowledge that makes a fundamental distinction between "mediated" and "immediate" beliefs. "Mediated beliefs" are *probable* beliefs that must be capable of being traced back and grounded ultimately in the primacy of "immediate beliefs," which are beliefs that are known with *certainty*. Taken as a whole, neo-Calvinists argue that this "regnant self-image of the modern academy" ought to be rejected as "a piece of ideological illusion" and "self-delusion." "Academic learning is not and *could not* be an autonomous, generically human, foundationally structured enterprise whose final foundations, universal theory, and necessary conditions are developed by philosophers."[9] Instead, what is needed is an alternative account, which the neo-Calvinists gladly offer.

Drawing on the late-nineteenth-century philosophy and theology of Abraham Kuyper, Wolterstorff begins his description of this alternative with the notion of *"belief-dispositions*—dispositions which, upon being activated, produce beliefs." What he has in mind here is the notion that certain conditions or dispositions inevitably produce in us

---

8. Ibid., 259. Hauerwas offers his own account of the contemporary academy in Hauerwas, *State of the University*.

9. Wolterstorff, "What New Haven," 259, 288, 289, 259, 278.

consequent beliefs. In other words, there is a straight causal line between condition and consequence. I will develop this notion further below. But given the importance of underlying conditions for shaping one's beliefs, Wolterstorff adds that our belief-dispositions are affected by sin. In fact, "sin results in their *malformation*. And we [unavoidably] bring these malformed dispositions with us to our practice of [any] science." This malformation is particularly problematical when it comes to understanding the reality of God and the nature of reality as a whole. Quoting Kuyper, Wolterstorff remarks that sin leads to the malformation of our capacity

> "for obtaining the knowledge of God, and thus for obtaining the conception of the whole. Without the sense of God in the heart no one shall ever attain unto a knowledge of God, and without love, or . . . a holy sympathy for God, that knowledge shall never be rich in content."[10]

As Wolterstorff observes, Kuyper is pointing here to a fundamental distinction, one that is rooted in faith. On the one hand, there are those persons who through divine grace know and love God and thereby apprehend "a fundamental aspect of what reality is like as a whole." On the other hand, there are all other persons who do not have a "holy sympathy for God" in their heart and thereby lack a true apprehension of reality. For those with the disposition of grace or faith, such knowledge of the whole does not merely add to their consciousness, rather "it fundamentally alters [it] and gives [them] a new hermeneutic of reality." Hence, there are ultimately "two kinds of people: those who, by second birth and faith, have the rudiments of an accurate apprehension of the totality of things, and those who, remaining in a state of malformation, lack such apprehension."[11]

Given this fundamental bifurcation, the neo-Calvinists claim that there cannot be any universal or common human knowledge, as the modern university presupposes. Rather, there are fundamentally different hermeneutical lenses at work in the academy. Though there may be some places of overlap, each group works with and from different underlying "'control beliefs'—general convictions as to the sorts of theories acceptable to us, . . . including convictions as to how our theories

---

10. Ibid., 279, 279, 281. Wolterstorff cites Kuyper, *Principles of Sacred Theology* (Grand Rapids: Baker, 1980 reprint), 113.

11. Wolterstorff, "What New Haven," 281, 282.

must be related to our data." Hence, quoting Kuyper again, Wolterstorff adds:

> There comes a point in the dialogue between Christian thinkers and others where it proves "impossible to settle the difference of insight." At that point, "No polemics . . . can ever serve any purpose." All each party can do is explain to the other why it thinks as it does. It is important to offer such explanations. Yet they must be seen for what, at bottom, they are: "the confession of the reason why one refuses to follow the tendency of the other. . . ." It was clearly Kuyper's view that this standoff in persuasion may well leave each party entitled to its views and entitled to pursue academic learning in accord with its views. Pluralism within the academy is unavoidable in our religiously divided world.[12]

This language of entitlement in the midst of fundamental convictions that cannot be rationally resolved is reminiscent of Stout's expressive pragmatism. Once again, the underlying metaphysical and theistic claims are beyond rational adjudication; instead, each side is entitled to its control beliefs in a world of irreconcilable pluralism. The rational task is therefore delimited to expressing and explaining one's position without the possibility of convincing others of the truth of one's ultimate claims. Unlike MacIntyre even, who espouses competition among traditions as a means of indirectly adjudicating their respective claims, the view here seems to be one of irreconcilable visions that remain side by side.

In the end, Wolterstorff places some distance between himself and the neo-Calvinist outlook of his formative education. Whereas the neo-Calvinists categorically insist on reversing the direction of conformation, Wolterstorff is more ambivalent and open to the possibility of conformation coming from either direction—either from Christian particularity toward the wider culture or from the wider culture toward Christian particularity. As he puts it, "the conformation must sometimes be allowed to go in one direction and sometimes in the other." But if one is looking for a contemporary expression and defense of the neo-Calvinist position, Wolterstorff points unhesitatingly to the philosophy of Alvin Plantinga.[13]

---

12. Ibid., 289, 283. Wolterstorff cites Kuyper, *Principles of Sacred Theology*, 160, 160, 161.

13. Wolterstorff, "What New Haven," 293, 290. It is worth noting that both Plantinga and Wolterstorff attended Calvin as undergraduates, and each of them later taught there before moving on to Notre Dame and Yale respectively.

In his essay "The Twin Pillars of Christian Scholarship," Plantinga offers a Reformed perspective on why there needs to be explicitly Christian colleges and universities. Given the "basic Reformed tenet that all of life must be lived from the perspective of Christianity," Plantinga states, "our scholarly life must be so lived."[14] It is noteworthy that Plantinga defines the Reformed tenet here explicitly in terms of Christianity rather than in terms of God as such. That is to say, one might describe the Reformed tenet as the conviction that all of life and the world is related to God, and therefore that all subject matters are worthy of study. Yet, instead of this basic theistic emphasis, Plantinga stresses the particularity of the Christian tradition; the significance of this will become apparent as we proceed.

Given the comprehensive scope of the Christian outlook, Plantinga defines the twin pillars of Christian scholarship as: (1) the need to offer Christian cultural criticism, i.e., the need to offer a critical appraisal of the whole of life in the earthly city, including a critique of dominant perspectives in the academy, and (2) the need to offer Christian answers to life's various questions, answers "that take into account *all* that we know, *everything* that is relevant to the question at hand." Beginning with the first pillar, Plantinga contends that the modern Western intellectual landscape is defined by a contest among three fundamentally different worldviews: ancient naturalism, Enlightenment humanism, and Christian theism. Ancient naturalism, as illustrated by Democritus, offers an atheistic and materialistic account of the world, one that views humans as merely an insignificant part of a purposeless universe of materialistic forces. Such a view, Plantinga suggests, still has significant influence in many strands of modern science, particularly among some neo-Darwinists. Alternatively, Enlightenment humanism places humans squarely at the center. Pointing to the influence of Kant, Plantinga describes the subjectivist and constructivist implications of Kant's bifurcation between phenomena and noumena: "Here the fundamental idea—in sharp contrast to Naturalism—is that we human beings, in some deep and important way, are ourselves responsible for the structure and nature of the world; it is *we*, fundamentally, who are the architects of the universe." That is, given our inability to know reality in itself, Kant's metaphysical agnosticism pulls in the direction of giving ultimate significance to the human construction of the world. To be

---

14. Plantinga, "Twin Pillars of Christian Scholarship," 122.

sure, Kant did not explicitly draw this conclusion. "But the fundamental *thrust* of Kant's self-styled Copernican Revolution," writes Plantinga, "is that the things in the world owe their basic structure and perhaps their very existence to the noetic activity of our minds." Over against these two views, Christian theism offers a realist account of the world, one that views humans as valuable parts of God's created order. Like Kuyper, Plantinga contends that scholarship in the academy is never neutral or generic; rather, it always reflects, at some deep level, the hermeneutical assumptions of one of these competing worldviews.[15]

The second pillar of Christian scholarship adduces that one should use all relevant resources to answer life's questions, including especially those provided by the particularity of the Christian revelation and tradition. Plantinga acknowledges the role and importance of various academic disciplines; yet, he suggests that the Christian lens has the final word vis-à-vis all forms and branches of inquiry. "Take a given area of scholarship," he remarks; "should we take for granted the Christian answer to the large questions about God and creation, and then go on from that perspective to address the narrower questions of that discipline?"[16] He answers affirmatively; the Christian may properly begin from and appeal to Christian premises in any area of scholarly or scientific research. He recognizes of course that this claim requires some epistemological explanation.

In order for a belief to be counted as knowledge, continues Plantinga, it must be true and one must have warrants or grounds for it. After setting forth and rejecting three prominent conceptions of "warrant" in modern philosophy, Plantinga offers an alternative account, namely, that "a belief has warrant for a person only if his [cognitive] faculties are *working properly*, working the way they ought to work, working the way they were designed to work (working the way God designed them to work), in producing and sustaining the belief in question." Hence, "a necessary condition of warrant is that one's cognitive equipment . . . be free of cognitive malfunction." And under conditions of proper functioning, "the more firmly you believe a proposition, the more warrant it has for you; and if you believe it firmly enough, it will have enough warrant for knowledge."[17]

---

15. Ibid., 138, 124, 144, 128, 129, 132–33.
16. Ibid., 143.
17. Ibid., 146–50, 152.

Lying behind this view one can initially see at least two important similarities to Wolterstorff's discussion of Kuyper: first, there is a critical distinction between those perceptions of the world that are properly receptive and calibrated, and those that are caught in cognitive malfunction; and second, Plantinga presupposes and develops a notion similar to belief-dispositions. Given his Christian theistic perspective, he submits that God has "created us with cognitive faculties designed to enable us to achieve true beliefs with respect to a wide variety of propositions." Under the appropriate conditions, these faculties inevitably produce in us the proper belief. As he puts it, "the appropriate belief is *formed in us*; in the typical case we do not *decide* to hold or form the belief in question, but [rather] simply find ourselves with it." He concedes that we sometimes weigh the evidence, but he still denies that we ever really choose our belief or conclusion: "Even in this sort of case I still don't really *decide* anything: I simply call the relevant evidence to mind, try in some way to weigh it up, and find myself with the appropriate belief."[18] So the key, then, is to have proper or unimpaired cognitive faculties at work—properly receiving and therefore inevitably believing what is truly there.

The critical question then is what defines proper cognitive content—that which is to be received? If God is ultimately part of what is received, as Plantinga and Reformed epistemology hold, then the discussion must turn at some point to the question of the reality of God. In seeking to address this issue, Plantinga defines "reason" as being "part of our original created noetic endowment, the cognitive powers and faculties we have just by way of being human beings." Alternatively, he defines "faith" as "a special cognitive response to a special revelation on the part of God; what we believe by faith is what the Lord teaches (in Scripture and through the church) about himself and his plan for our salvation." From here, following Calvin, Plantinga points in one direction toward a general revelation and natural knowledge of God: we have a natural awareness of God *(sensus divinitatis)* made accessible by reason and common experience alone. As Plantinga describes it, "there is a natural apprehension of God, and belief in God produced by that mechanism or cognitive process . . . is produced by reason, not by faith." Yet Plantinga then immediately follows Calvin in the opposite direction, in the direction of diminishing this claim, by insisting that such "knowl-

18. Ibid., 151.

edge has been spoiled and distorted, overlaid and suppressed by sin." Given this severe cognitive malfunction, it comes as no surprise that such "natural knowledge isn't nearly sufficient for salvation." Plantinga notes that Christian scholarship is done by and from the perspective of the Christian believer. And in the case of the believer, knowledge of God "isn't a *merely* natural knowledge; it is a natural knowledge qualified and corrected by faith, absorbed by and taken up into faith. The believer accepts God's promises; she therefore knows vastly more about God than is to be had by the workings of the *Sensus Divinitatis* alone." What enables one to believe? Following Calvin again, Plantinga answers by pointing to divine grace and the workings of the Holy Spirit: "In the believer, [the natural knowledge of God] is restored, deepened, broadened by virtue of the testimony [and activity] of the Holy Spirit."[19]

As one will observe, the affirmation of the natural knowledge of God is largely vitiated here from both sides. On the one hand, the condition of sin so distorts, damages, and suppresses our rational and cognitive faculties that they exist only in a malformed state. And as Plantinga argues, cognitive faculties that malfunction cannot accurately receive or perceive reality as it truly is; they cannot form or be the source of true beliefs. On the other hand, for persons of faith, their knowledge of God is dependent upon a super-charged version of knowledge, one that is completely "absorbed by and taken up into faith." And as Plantinga defines it, faith is "a special cognitive response to a special revelation." So there appears to be little or no grounds here for achieving genuine knowledge of God through natural or rational means. To be sure, Plantinga elsewhere gives significant and critical attention to the theistic proofs, notably the ontological argument. But he concludes that such arguments, even at their best, do not establish the truth of theism, rather they simply show its "rational acceptability" by showing that theistic belief is not *"contrary to reason or irrational."*[20]

Thus, at the end of the day, Plantinga, like Kuyper, is not looking to convince others in the academy or the wider public about the truth of the reality of God. Either they see through the lens of Christian faith already, and thus need no persuasion, or they do not see with the eyes of faith, and thus are stuck with their malfunctioning cognitive equipment. Instead, Plantinga and Reformed epistemology are seeking to

19. Ibid., 153, 154, 155, 154, 155.
20. Plantinga, " Contemporary Modal Version of the Ontological Argument," 183.

make a more defensive case, namely, one that argues that Christians are epistemically entitled to their faith perspective. As Plantinga states in "The Reformed Objection to Natural Theology," belief in God is a *properly basic belief,* by which he means a belief that cannot be rationally inferred or argued for by appealing to other evidence. Put simply, one cannot and need not argue to or for the reality of God. Rather, all one can and should do is show that belief in God is reasonable—show that it is something to which one is epistemically entitled precisely because it is a basic belief. "[A] person is entirely within his epistemic rights, entirely rational, in believing in God," says Plantinga, "even if he has no argument for this belief and does not believe it on the basis of any other beliefs he holds." Along these lines, Griffin, quoting Plantinga, notes that Plantinga rejects "the idea that 'belief in God is rationally acceptable if and only if there is adequate evidence in the form of good arguments for it.'"[21] To support this view, Plantinga argues by way of analogy that just as one is entitled to believe in the reality of other minds without having direct evidence of them, so, too, is one entitled to believe in the reality of God as a basic belief without direct evidence as well. Both beliefs are equally rational—one has rational grounds for holding such beliefs even though one cannot provide direct evidence or arguments for them. Of course the question then is, what counts as a properly basic belief? Can one say that belief in "the Great Pumpkin" is also properly basic, as Plantinga famously asks? He answers no, though he proposes that what counts as properly basic "must be reached [empirically] from below rather than [rationally from] above." What is needed, he suggests, is agreement about "a relevant set of examples. But there is no reason to assume, in advance," he admits,

> that everyone will agree on the examples. The Christian will of course suppose that belief in God is entirely proper and rational; . . . . Followers of Bertrand Russell and Madaylyn Murray O'Hair may disagree; but how is that relevant? Must my criteria, or those of the Christian community, conform to their examples? Surely not. The Christian community is responsible to its set of examples, not to theirs.[22]

---

21. Plantinga, "Reformed Objection to Natural Theology," 333; Griffin, *Reenchantment without Supernaturalism,* 368; Griffin cites Plantinga, "Reformed Epistemology," in *A Companion to Philosophy of Religion,* ed. Philip L. Quinn and Charles Taliaferro (Cambridge, MA: Basil Blackwell, 1997) 384.

22. Plantinga, "Reformed Objection to Natural Theology," 338, 340.

This passage clearly reveals Reformed epistemology's defensive rather than apologetic posture. The goal is to carve out rational space, permission, and justification for the Christian theist to believe, not to rationally convince the non-theist of the truth of theism. As Griffin observes, Plantinga's overall aim "is to be able to call his belief in God *knowledge.*" And he seeks to do this by submitting "that the theist's belief in God can be seen to be reasonable even though 'the theist has no very good answer to the request that he explain his reasons for believing in the existence of God.'"[23]

In sum, the neo-Calvinist position seeks to achieve intellectual integrity in the academy by creating and maintaining an independent space for distinctively Christian scholarship, colleges, and universities. Like MacIntyre's preliberal model, the neo-Calvinist vision presupposes and seeks to foster a relatively high degree of intellectual homogeneity and consensus. In pursuit of this agreement, it uses some form of religious test and some degree of forced exclusion based on such tests. For instance, all institutions that are current members of the Council for Christian Colleges and Universities must follow its employment policy, which explicitly requires that "only persons who profess faith in Jesus Christ" may be hired "as full-time faculty and administrators." Calvin College is a member of the Council; presumably, Plantinga and Wolterstorff would point to Calvin College as at least a partial approximation of the neo-Calvinist vision.[24] What this neo-Calvinist milieu seeks to offer is a comprehensive perspective of the whole of reality as seen through the lens of Christian faith. Yet, given the power and predominance of the liberal university, especially in regard to graduate education, the challenge is to fully educate and train scholars in this Christian context. "Scholarship is an intensely social activity," concludes Plantinga. "[W]e learn our craft from our elders and mentors; but we can't learn how to do Christian scholarship from our mentors at these [liberal] universities. That is why it is of first importance that there be Christian universities, institutions where these questions do take pride

---

23. Griffin, *Reenchantment without Supernaturalism*, 368, 369. Griffin cites Plantinga, *God and Other Minds*, 2nd ed. (Ithaca: Cornell University Press, 1990; orig. edit. 1967) 268.

24. For the Council for Christian Colleges and Universities see http://www.cccu.org; and for Calvin College see http://www.calvin.edu/about/mission.htm.

of place, and where a student can think about the bearing of Christianity on her disciplines in a regular and institutionally sanctioned way."[25]

As suggested here, theology both broadly and narrowly construed has a clear and influential voice within the neo-Calvinist model; education is comprehensively shaped by the Christian theistic vision. But as suggested above, the conception of theology put forth here appears finally to be based on special revelation—on the particularity and authority of the Christian revelation—not based on general revelation or natural theology. Hence, as Wolterstorff notes in his discussion of Kuyper, this model presupposes an irreducible pluralism in the academy. Unlike even MacIntyre, who seeks ultimate consensus and resolution through competition among incommensurable traditions, there is no hope here of resolving conflicts at the level of fundamental claims and convictions. Thus there is no hope here of convincing or influencing the larger academy—of creating a new dominant consensus. Rather, the aim is to offer a distinctive vision of the world based on the unique particularity of the Christian revelation; a vision that sits uneasily side-by-side with the predominant liberal perspective in the academy. Perhaps the hope here finally is, in an almost Hauerwasian or Milbankian manner, to provide an intellectual witness to the world rather than trying directly to convince the world of the truth of the theistic vision. Yet, in the end, it appears that such a perspective remains marginalized on the sidelines of the cultural conversation—a particularist vision for a particularist community.

An Alternative Critique: The Liberal-Metaphysical Model

Instead of MacIntyre's retro-vision of a medieval university or the Neo-Calvinist version of a Christian college or university, I would argue that intellectual integrity in the academy waits upon a new pursuit of the metaphysical enterprise within the parameters of the modern commitment—what I will call the *liberal-metaphysical* model. Both MacIntyre and the Neo-Calvinists assume that the failures of the modern academy are due to the modern commitment itself, that is, to the formal character of modernity, whereas, in truth, those failures are due to the university's implicit or explicit endorsement

---

25. Plantinga, "Twin Pillars of Christian Scholarship," 161.

of modernity's substantive character, i.e., its postmetaphysical mindset. Hence, the problem with the modern liberal university is not its commitment to seeking consensus based on free rational assent apart from the authority and constraints of tradition. Rather, the problem is that the modern academy has been built on the presupposition of the Kantian dominant consensus and thus has precluded rational inquiry concerning the ultimate questions about the nature of reality as such. In a postmetaphysical world, intellectual integrity is systematically abandoned precisely because the dominant presumption is that one cannot meaningfully address questions about the whole of reality within the context of open and critical rational inquiry; thus questions about the whole go by the wayside and one is left with a dis-integrated array of disciplines, areas of knowledge, and forms of technological and instrumental manipulations. Theology must seek to be a catalyst for changing this intellectual landscape, both because it is suited for such an endeavor and because its own future is affected by it.

As I noted in my introduction, Loomer perceptively argues that the failure of modern universities is due in large part to the failure of religion. "The nature of religious faith," he states, "is such that it must of necessity seek for intellectual integrity, for one intellectual world. It must concern itself with the problem of intellectual direction." That is to say, because religion deals explicitly with the meaning and nature of reality as a whole, it ought to foster integrated human understanding. "For the nature of religion," Loomer adds, "is such that it is either fundamental, central, and basic or it is nothing. In the nature of the case, religion cannot be a peripheral concern and discipline. Yet an adequate religion must [also] not result in dogmatism or uniformity of thought." Here one sees Loomer sharing my dual concern of seeking intellectual integrity and affirming the modern commitment to free, open, and critical inquiry. Though he does not spell it out here, what he seeks to encourage, I judge, is a theological voice that fosters intellectual integrity by asserting and redeeming its related existential and metaphysical claims about the meaning and nature of reality as a whole. The danger and consequence of prolonged narrow specialization in the modern university, he observes, "is the atrophy of a sensitive awareness to the fundamental and pervasive features of everyday life." To epitomize, what the modern academy offers is compartmentalized knowledge, not integrated wisdom. "Wisdom is the result of a penetrating analysis of the obvious, of common everyday experience. Whitehead has said that it takes a very unusual mind to elucidate the obvious." Going back to our discussion in chapter 2, what Whitehead means by elucidating the obvious is to discern and distinguish between the conspicuous and changing elements of experience and the inconspicuous and unchanging elements that necessarily form the background of every experience. The task of metaphysics is to express and critically reflect on the latter. "The great themes of life," continues Loomer, "are the themes that deal with the basic and foundational character of day-by-day existence. The great religions and great philosophies are those which disclose the greatness and profound resources to be found within [ordinary] occurrences." By contrast, the specialization of the modern university "has a tendency to become blind to these features and resources" of everyday experience.[26] In sum, Loomer is implicitly looking for theology and philosophy to speak with a metaphysical voice, one that can reclaim wisdom through critical reflection on the comprehensive questions about the meaning and nature of existence. Whereas Loomer points to this need, Ogden speaks to it directly.

In his essay "Theology in the University," Ogden addresses the question of whether theology properly belongs "in the liberal arts curriculum of the university." To answer this, he distinguishes between two forms of theology and two types of educational institutions. The former distinction pertains to one between *philosophical theology* and specifically *Christian theology*, and the latter refers to one between non-religious colleges and universities (including presumably state and public ones) and explicitly Christian or church-related colleges and universities. Overall, Ogden argues that philosophical theology ought to be an important curricular component in *all* liberal arts institutions, both public and private, whereas explicitly Christian theology properly belongs only in church-related colleges and universities. "Philosophical theology ... must have a place in the liberal arts curriculum" of all institutions, declares Ogden.[27]

---

26. Loomer, "Religion and the Mind of the University," 167, 166, 149, 156.

27. Ogden, "Theology in the University," 128, 129. In this essay, Ogden also discusses religious studies and its relation to philosophical and Christian theology. For my purposes here, I will put that discussion aside and focus strictly on his discussion of the roles of philosophical and Christian theology in the academy.

What he means by philosophical theology is "the type of theological reflection constituted by human existence as such," namely, open, rational, and critical reflection on the meaning and truth of claims about the ultimate nature of existence and reality.[28] In another essay in the same volume, Ogden spells out "The Task of Philosophical Theology" in more detail. There he argues that the underlying task of philosophy is to offer a "fully reflective understanding of the basic existential faith that is constitutive of human existence." In order to pursue this substantive aim, philosophy must address metaphysical questions about the ultimate nature of reality, existential questions about the meaning of existence, linguistic questions about the grammar and language used to express these metaphysical and existential understandings, and historical questions about how other thinkers and cultures have answered these various questions in the past. Yet, chief among these distinct and related assignments is "philosophy's central task of metaphysics." The history of philosophy has rightly recognized metaphysics as the "noncompressible core of philosophy" because it is the metaphysical enterprise that seeks to understand "the completely general [or universal] features of reality" whereas the various sub-areas of philosophy deal with some contributory part, such as language, history, nature, religion, ethics, or politics. Metaphysical inquiry, in short, "involves the most basic and comprehensive questions that can occur to the human mind."[29]

"The task of philosophical theology," continues Ogden, "is integral to philosophy's central task as metaphysics." That is, because religions implicitly or explicitly make universal claims about the meaning and nature of reality as a whole, philosophical theology is charged with the task of critically examining the meaning and validity of these metaphysical and existential claims. In the case of theistic religions, these claims of ultimacy revolve around the question of the reality of God. Since humans are always culturally and historically situated, Ogden recognizes that their basic existential faith and related metaphysical claims are always expressed in terms of some particular cultural form—either religious or otherwise. Yet, the point again is that such particular forms and traditions still make universal claims that require, at a philosophical level, rational analysis and assessment. Hence, the proper role of philosophical theology in any liberal arts curriculum—pursued either from

28. Ibid., 126.
29. Ogden, "Task of Philosophical Theology," 67, 73 (italics removed), 76, 76, 77.

the angle of philosophy or religious studies or both—is to understand and critically assess various historic, cross-cultural, and contemporary answers to these fundamental existential and metaphysical questions. For the liberal arts to ignore or bracket such questions is to ignore the integrative and comprehensive dimension of human understanding. The liberal arts cannot serve as the arts of freedom or as the arts of authentic existence if these ultimate questions are left unexamined. Thus, "There is no doubt in my mind," concludes Ogden, "that constructive *philosophical* theology does indeed have a place in the liberal arts curriculum...."[30]

Since religious traditions implicitly or explicitly make metaphysical claims about the nature of reality as such, they presuppose the task of philosophical theology at some underlying level. In the case of Christianity, this means that Christian theology "presupposes philosophy" in the "form of philosophical theology or theistic metaphysics." The task of Christian theology is to critically reflect on the meaning and truth of the distinctive Christian witness. And because the Christian kerygma implicitly or explicitly makes metaphysical claims about the reality of God and existential claims about authentic existence, the charge of Christian theology is to rationally express and validate such claims. To complete this assignment, Christian theology must, at some point, draw upon philosophical and metaphysical forms of inquiry. This is "why Christian theology is necessarily dependent on an integral theistic metaphysics," says Ogden. "For how can the venture of faith be reflectively confirmed, or theology's assertions rationally justified, except on the basis of just such a metaphysics? To reply, as has often been done, that faith and theology do not need rational justification is either to ignore faith's own claim to be true or else to admit, in effect, that its claim is empty and not to be taken seriously."[31]

More specifically, the task of Christian theology is to fully reflect on the meaning and truth of the Christian claim that the nature of God and authentic human existence are decisively re-presented in Jesus as the Christ. Such theology is properly included in the curriculum of a church-related college or university. But since the truth of the Christian claim presupposes and requires the enterprise of philosophical theology, Ogden notes that "Christian theology's standards of reflection are

30. Ibid. 78 (italics removed), 85; Ogden, "Theology in the University," 130.
31. Ogden, "Task of Philosophical Theology," 88, 90.

no different in principle from those of . . . any other field of study . . . in the liberal arts." His point is that the truth claims of Christian theology should be held to the same critical standards of reason and common experience that all other disciplines are held to, and thus should not be given special dispensation based on the authority of tradition or revelation. From this perspective then, the study of

> Christian theology . . . requires neither special qualifications of its students in the way of prior adherence to the Christian religion, nor special criteria for its claims in the way of criteria of truth sufficiently based only in specifically Christian experience. On the contrary, all that it asks of its students is that they be able and willing to ask the universally human questions about the meaning and structure of ultimate reality, to which all Christian thinking and speaking in one way or another gives answers.[32]

One does not need to be Christian in order to study Christian theology, Ogden reflects, nor does such study appeal to special criteria based only in Christian experience. Having said this, he recognizes that Christian theology will perhaps hold most interest and importance for those who explicitly profess Christian faith. Since Christians have existentially staked their lives on the Christian answer to life's fundamental questions about the meaning and nature of existence, it is Christians who most need to gain literacy about and critical reflection on the historic Christian witness.[33]

In sum, Christian theology presupposes and requires philosophical theology, but philosophical theology does not presuppose Christian theology. Hence, in regard to the curricular question, Ogden envisions philosophical theology as a necessary and proper requirement of any quality liberal arts curriculum in any public or private institution. All liberally educated persons should critically reflect on life's basic existential and metaphysical questions and on various historic answers given to such questions. Within the context of a church-related college or university, Ogden envisions both philosophical theology and Christian theology being proper elements of the liberal arts curriculum. In this context, these two curricular components mutually enrich one another by offering students a deeper and critical understanding of explicitly Christian answers to life's fundamental questions as well as offering

32. Ogden, "Theology in the University," 130, 130–31.
33. Ibid., 131.

them philosophical reflection on these matters. For students who hold Christian convictions, such an environment gives them an opportunity to fully and critically reflect on their Christian understanding of faith. For students who hold different religious convictions or profess a secularistic outlook, such an opportunity gives them some exposure to and clarity about the Christian tradition and, at the same time, gives them a chance to reflect thoughtfully and critically both on the Christian answers and on their own answers and traditions.

As one can see, Ogden seeks to complete the modern academy by emphasizing the need for metaphysical reflection within the context of modernity's formal commitments. Such a model offers, I submit, the most promising way of regaining intellectual integrity in the academy because it affirms modernity's strength (formal autonomy) while, at the same time, critically addressing its substantive failure (its postmetaphysical character). In fact, I would propose that the ideal college or university would have one or more professorships in *metaphysics and the human & natural sciences*. Such positions would seek to foster inquiry and critical reflection across all disciplines by examining the underlying metaphysical and existential assumptions that drive our guiding conceptions of reality in the natural sciences, mathematics, social sciences, humanities, and the arts. From art to architecture, from business to biology, from ethics to education, from math to medicine, and from politics to physics, all forms of human understanding presuppose some set of fundamental assumptions about the ultimate character of reality and our existential place within it. For example, as Gadamer rightly notes, one cannot finally make sense of the concept of "health" without addressing questions about reality as a whole. Indeed, as he astutely observes, modern culture invents phrases like "quality of life" in order to try to fill the void created by a postmetaphysical mindset that precludes such questions.[34] Hence, a truly integrated educational experience would expose students to questions of metaphysics and

---

34. See Gadamer, *Enigma of Health*, 56, 115, 104. I do not mean to suggest that Gadamer himself fully pursues the metaphysical implications of the notion of health, but he points out that classical thinkers like Plato did. As Gadamer states: "Plato says at one point that it is impossible to heal the body without knowing something about the soul, indeed without knowing something about the nature of the 'whole'. The term 'whole' here is not intended as a methodological catchword. It refers, rather, to the unity of being itself" (115). I develop these points further in my review of Gadamer's *Enigma of Health*.

philosophical theology in a variety of places across the curriculum. Unlike the medieval academy, the aim here is neither to appeal to the authority of church or tradition at some point in order to limit inquiry within the various disciplines nor to impose some philosophical or theological conception from above. Rather, the aim is to foster open and critical discussion, with the hope of achieving a gradual consensus over the long run about fundamental questions concerning the nature of ultimate reality and the human enterprise within it. As Whitehead summarily states: "You cannot shelter theology from science, or science from theology; nor can you shelter either of them from metaphysics, or metaphysics from either of them. There is no short cut to truth."[35]

For instance, the current debate over whether to teach evolution and/or intelligent design in schools is a debate that calls out for a deeper philosophical conversation. Though advocates of intelligent design are right to seek coherent integration between the theistic question and our understanding of the evolutionary process, they go about it the wrong way insofar as they conceive of the divine-world relationship in traditional or supernaturalistic terms, presuppose or hint at any form of creationism (including any presumed inevitability of human evolution), and implicitly appeal to the authority of scripture or tradition as grounds for justifying their claims. On the other side, defenders of evolution are right to affirm the critical standards of modern science, to be leery of any form of creationism, and to insist that this debate should not be taking place in high school science classrooms. Yet, at the same time, anyone who thinks that science does not always operate with underlying philosophical assumptions or thinks that such assumptions are immune from legitimate scrutiny is someone who is at odds with the spirit of modern inquiry itself. For whether the concept of "natural selection" is by itself the most adequate explanation for evolutionary change is a question worthy of critical discussion and inquiry, including philosophical inquiry. Whitehead, for instance, argues convincingly that it is not finally an adequate explanation when one takes into account the full facts of experience. The underlying urge in all of nature, he notes, is not merely a singular truncated urge to survive, but rather "a three-fold urge: to live, to live well, [and] to live better. In fact," he adds, "the art of life is *first* to be alive, *secondly* to be alive in a satisfactory way, and *thirdly*

---

35. Whitehead, *Religion in the Making*, 79.

to acquire an increase in satisfaction."[36] Such an account of evolutionary change overcomes the reductionistic tendencies of Darwinian or neo-Darwinian thought by offering a more comprehensive understanding of existence.[37] Whitehead's account, in other words, is informed by his larger metaphysical conception whereas the Darwinian explanation simply takes for granted the modern denial of metaphysics and teleology, which excludes precisely the kind of reflection that enables Whitehead to make sense of the creative urge within nature itself. It is this urge that gives rise to conscious awareness of value, purpose, and beauty within human life, and human life is undoubtedly part of and reflective of the evolutionary process itself. Yes, the simpler explanation is to be preferred; but as Peirce learned from Galileo, simpler does not mean reductionistic or merely logically simpler. Rather, it means simpler in the sense of taking into account the full palate of experience and then offering the most adequate and integrative explanation.[38] Again, there is no shortcut to truth; this undeniable fact applies both to our arduous efforts and to the full adequacy of our explanations.

Like MacIntyre's pursuit of a postliberal university, I recognize that my liberal-metaphysical model is an ideal to be pursued over time, since it is far from the norm in the current context. For the foreseeable future, I suspect that a few church-related colleges and universities, and also a few secular or non-religious institutions, that embrace something remotely approximating the liberal-metaphysical view will need to be the standard-bearers for this hope and ideal. This initial step is itself a major challenge given the dominant aversion to metaphysics in the academy and in theology. Hence, select theological and philosophical voices will need to seek to influence both their scholarly colleagues (near and far) and the curricular structures within their institutions. Then over time, if they are successful in slowing, halting, or reversing the tide of postmetaphysical thinking, such curricular changes might perhaps also begin to take root in a wider range of private colleges and

36. Whitehead, *Function of Reason*, 8 (enumeration omitted); see 3–34 for his critique of natural selection within the context of his discussion of the function of reason. See also his discussion in *Science and the Modern World*, 107–12. For a neo-Darwinian perspective, see Coyne, "Seeing and Believing."

37. For example, some neo-Darwinists suggest that art stems merely from underlying evolutionary aims of sexual reproduction and survivability. See Angier, "Dance of Evolution."

38. See Peirce, "Neglected Argument for the Reality of God," 372–73.

universities; and, from there, such a change might also begin to occur in public institutions as well. Such a fundamental change, again, would mean pursuing intellectual integrity by addressing questions of philosophical theology and metaphysics in all forms of quality liberal arts education. Then, over an extended period, as educated men and women moved out into the world of the wider public, having critically engaged existential and metaphysical questions as part of their integrative liberal education, they would bring a different view of theology to bear in public life. In sum, over a long period of time, a tipping-point might be reached, one that changes the social location of theology, moving it from the periphery toward the center of culture.

Comparative Reflections on the Three Models

Needless to say, the liberal-metaphysical model is quite different from that which is proposed by either MacIntyre or the neo-Calvinists. Both MacIntyre and the neo-Calvinists think that the error of the modern liberal university lies in its commitment to reasoning in common, its commitment to secularity, its commitment to achieving open, free, and unconstrained agreements. In rejecting the liberal university, they each argue in their respective ways for more narrowly defined intellectual communities, communities held together by the bonds of authority and homogeneity. Only such tightly bound communities, they presume, can provide intellectual integrity and give theology an adequate voice. In contradistinction to these views, the liberal-metaphysical model criticizes the modern academy on different grounds. The error of liberalism lies not in its commitment to secularity but rather in its banishment of metaphysics from the modern intellectual landscape. What is needed is the completion of the modern project by reintroducing the metaphysical enterprise into the flow of intellectual discourse and into the structure of liberal arts education; it is by this avenue that theology can regain its public voice. As noted, such a process will likely require the contribution of church-related colleges and universities along the way. But to make clear, such institutions are conceived here very differently than they are in either MacIntyre's Thomistic university or the neo-Calvinist Christian college. Unlike these latter two approaches, the liberal-metaphysical model envisions church-related institutions that fully embrace modernity's formal commitments while, at the same time, rigorously engaging questions of both philosophical and Christian theology within their studies of the liberal arts. To be sure, such church-related institutions must identify with the Christian tradition in some specific or denominational manner, and they must seek some degree of Christian identity among their faculty and staff in order to maintain a meaningful and living connection. Nevertheless, such institutions have an openness to diversity that tilts them much closer to the liberal university than it does to the enforced homogeneity of the other two models. In sum, these liberal-metaphysical, church-related institutions seek to contribute in a direct way to the gradual formation of a larger intellectual and cultural consensus regarding metaphysical and religious questions.

A comparative discussion of these three models doubtlessly raises a host of issues worthy of critical engagement. I will seek to give further attention to at least some of them here, namely, to those surrounding the issues of consensus, sin, natural theology, and the formation of beliefs. To begin, let me turn to another passage in Ogden that is directly pertinent to a discussion of these matters.

In the midst of explaining how theology presupposes philosophy and how philosophical theology is distinct from specifically Christian theology, Ogden states:

> Because theology and philosophy by their very natures finally lay claim to the same basic ground, . . . in short, serve an identical truth—their material conclusions must be in the last analysis mutually confirming if either is to sustain its essential claim. This does not mean, of course, that their complete mutual confirmation must be actually realized, either now or at some time in the future. The essentially historical character of reflection, not to mention such other constants of the human equation as finitude and sin, hardly permits this as a real possibility. We simply have to reckon with the indefinite continuation of our present more or less irreducible pluralism of philosophical and theological positions. But in doing so, we have no reason whatever to set aside the ideal that philosophy and theology alike establish as governing their relationship—even though we have the best of reasons for suspecting all claims to have already realized this ideal.[39]

---

39. Ogden, "Task of Philosophical Theology," 88.

Unlike what we saw in Gustafson, and his inheritance from Schleiermacher and H. Richard Niebuhr, Ogden rightly notes that what is true in philosophy and what is true in theology should be one and the same; truth is one because we live finally in one world. So the ideal is that the substantive conclusions of philosophy and theology should be mutually confirming. Yet, Ogden recognizes that "their complete mutual confirmation" has not in fact occurred and, he adds, there is no reason to expect such complete confirmation at any time in the future. In fact, actualization of this ideal appears to be forever hindered by the realities of historical situatedness and sin. Instead, we simply have to come to terms with the "indefinite continuation of our present more or less irreducible pluralism of philosophical and theological positions." If one were to pause at this juncture, Ogden might appear to be in the same camp as the neo-Calvinists—contending that the reality of sin forever precludes consensus, thereby leaving us with irreducible pluralism. But Ogden does not leave it there; even in accepting this present pluralistic reality, he maintains that we have no reason to set aside the ideal. If I understand him correctly, this is because the ideal is presupposed in our very act of making claims itself. That is, in basic agreement with Habermas and Apel, Ogden contends that what it means for philosophy or theology to set forth a truth claim or other claim to validity necessarily entails the presupposition of seeking to offer to others mutually confirming reasons—reasons that could lead to a consensus. Hence, in this sense, Ogden states that we already "have the best of reasons for suspecting all claims to have already realized this ideal." So the ideal is not fully achieved on a macro-scale within history, but it is inescapably presupposed at the micro-level in every act of making a claim. This is why he affirms the liberal ideal of rationally achieved consensus at the same time that he acknowledges its historical limitations.

Though I share Ogden's general outlook, I am somewhat more sanguine than his words suggest here about the possibility of at least approximating a wider historical consensus over the long run. Gradual but significant changes in intellectual assumptions, assumptions that filter down through the structure of liberal arts education, can measurably change the intellectual landscape and the social location of theology. Hume once remarked that "the genius of philosophy, if carefully cultivated by several [persons], must gradually diffuse itself throughout the whole society, and bestow a [corrective influence] on every art and calling."[40] Though I am of course seeking to counter the anti-metaphysical legacy of Hume's own philosophy, he accurately discerns the subtle but powerful influence of philosophical assumptions in shaping and changing the cultural landscape. Yet, at the same time, I recognize the constraining realities of history and sin. To affirm this combination, of pursuing the ideal while at the same time recognizing its constraining limitations, requires specific conclusions about natural theology, sin, and the formation of beliefs. As we saw, neo-Calvinists like Plantinga affirm natural theology in principle but basically deny it in practice. This is because they believe that sin so distorts and diminishes our natural capacity as to preclude it from serving as the basis for a meaningful conversation or consensus about the question of God. Furthermore, Plantinga contends that we find ourselves holding beliefs, we do not choose them at any level. Hence, for those who have been touched by divine grace, they find themselves holding true beliefs about God and the whole of reality relatively free from the distorting effects of sin; they see the world through the lens of a Christian hermeneutic. For all others, they find themselves with beliefs filtered through a distorted lens. In contrast, we saw Gamwell take Calvin's affirmation of natural theology in a very different direction. This natural knowledge is inhibited by our sin and fragmentary condition, acknowledges Gamwell, but it is not totally suppressed; meaningful conversation about natural theology can occur. A key difference between Gamwell and Plantinga is that Gamwell affirms that we ultimately choose, at a deep level, our understandings

---

40. Hume, "An Enquiry Concerning Human Understanding," 311. Kant argued that traditional metaphysical arguments coming out of the medieval schools had no public influence (see Preface to 2nd ed., *Critique of Pure Reason*, sect. xxxii). Kant is correct that metaphysical and theistic arguments are more complex and abstract than the average person can easily understand. Nevertheless, I would argue that the overarching attitude toward metaphysics and theistic arguments taught in colleges and universities seeps into the larger culture through the effects of higher education on its students. For instance, most members of the public have never read or heard of Kant. Nevertheless, his influence in shaping a postmetaphysical culture is pervasive. Whether or not most men and women recognize or understand this pervasive outlook, they take it for granted that religion is a matter of "faith not reason." I would contend that, over time, to change this view within the academy would likewise have widespread cultural effects. As Whitehead puts it, "the mentality of an epoch springs from the view of the world which is, in fact, dominant in the educated sections of the communit[y] . . . Philosophy works slowly. Thoughts lie dormant for ages; and then, almost suddenly as it were, mankind finds that they have embodied themselves in institutions" (*Science and the Modern World*, vii, viii).

of ourselves and the world. No human understanding is simply given; rather, there is always some degree of choice at an underlying level, most fundamentally at the level of choosing our constitutive self-understanding. Hence, as we saw in his discussion of Niebuhr, Gamwell argues that sin is never strictly inevitable. Our functioning capacity to respond to the ever-present divine reality in every moment of experience may be weak, it may be hindered by our persistent tendency to choose a duplicitous self-understanding, but it is never null and void. Thus, the act of putting forth reasons and arguments from natural theology is not a futile activity. Rather, it is an act of invitation to others, inviting them cognitively, affectively, and existentially to begin to see and respond to the world differently. Consensus and agreement may or may not in fact be achieved, but the hope for such agreement is rooted in the very act of discourse itself.

For the reasons outlined in chapter 2, I find Gamwell's account of human understanding convincing. In reply, Plantinga would argue that experience imposes or implants beliefs into us directly. "Upon being appeared to in the familiar way," says Plantinga,

> I find myself holding the belief that there is a large tree before me; upon being asked what I had for breakfast, I reflect for a moment and then find myself with the belief that what I had was eggs on toast. In these and other cases I do not decide what to believe; I don't total up the evidence . . . and make a decision as to what seems best supported; I simply find myself believing.[41]

It is certainly true that our encounter with the world provides us with an objective inflow or datum that is a constitutive element of experience. And it is also true that we do not often go through a conscious process of evidence evaluation. But Whitehead's insight, nonetheless, was to recognize that each moment of experience contains not only an objective datum but also a subjective response: *That* the world impinges on us is undeniably true; this is the fundamental basis for any realist conception. But *how* one responds to that influx is the element of uncertainty or freedom that introduces the elements of novelty and creativity into the world. The past does not fully determine the present; the influx of the world does not fully determine one's beliefs. In most ordinary cases, such as in the appearance of a tree or eggs on toast,

---

41. Plantinga, "Twin Pillars of Christian Scholarship," 151.

we do not notice the element of subjectivity in our receptivity to the data of experience. When the stakes are low, we accept the influx of the world without hesitation and our beliefs are formed accordingly. But as illustrated by the naysayers of global warming, belief formation is not quite so straightforward when there are economic or other interests at stake. And this element of choice or subjectivity becomes even more pronounced when it comes to forming our comprehensive and constitutive beliefs about the meaning and nature of reality as a whole. It is perhaps no accident of history that achieving rational consensus on religious, metaphysical, and existential matters is the most difficult of all. Furthermore, as Gamwell aptly notes, the concept of sin only makes coherent sense if one finally maintains the element of choice in the formation of our constitutive understanding. If sin is strictly inevitable, if sin is not finally about our duplicitous choice of self-understanding, then human responsibility for sin is ultimately absolved. Given Calvin's emphasis on the total sovereignty of God, leading eventually to the Calvinist doctrine of double-predestination, it is perhaps no mere coincidence that a neo-Calvinist like Plantinga emphasizes our lack of choice in the formation of our beliefs. Yet, I am persuaded that such a view fails finally to make adequate sense of experience.

For his part, MacIntyre would draw our attention back to a discussion of the liberal university and its inability to pursue, let alone achieve, consensus about matters theological. He contends that theology cannot abide such a climate; thus he encourages it to abandon the modern project in favor of a return to medieval tradition and authority. Such a medieval model can achieve theological consensus within the parameters of a bounded community and tradition, he argues, one in which rational standards for inquiry can be defined and enforced. MacIntyre is indeed correct that the liberal university is unable to pursue consensus about theological claims; he is also right to point out that theology cannot be true to itself and, at the same time, accept relativistic or preferentialist views concerning the nature of the good or reality as such. Yet, I would submit once again that the problem with the liberal academy is not its formal commitment to achieving an open and rational consensus but, rather, its dominant substantive assumption—filtering from scholars down through the curricular structure into society at large—that such a consensus could never possibly be achieved around metaphysical questions. Hence, the lack of consensus in the modern university has not been merely *de facto* but rather *de jure* in the sense of precluding any meaningful pursuit of these matters. If this dominant substantive assumption were to be reconsidered, however, then the modern academy would take on a very different climate and tone, one that could seriously pursue relevant metaphysical and theological questions while still affirming a formal commitment to secularity. Under such conditions, modern institutions like Harvard would have no reason to balk at the prospect of engaging students in critical reflection about reason and faith in its core curriculum.

But could this metaphysical enterprise even be pursued, MacIntyre might ask, without prior agreement concerning the appropriate rational standards? If there is no consensus at this level, can one ever hope to achieve consensus regarding metaphysical conclusions? MacIntyre correctly holds that the inquiry would have to work toward some agreement about rational standards, determining on what grounds metaphysical claims are to be assessed, but this process itself would need to be part of the inquiry and debate. Such standards are neither imposed from above nor in advance; rather, any consensus about these matters must be achieved, not ascribed. For example, as discussed in chapter 2, Whitehead proposes four criteria for testing metaphysical schemes (coherent, logical, applicable, and adequate). This four-fold proposal would itself need to be assessed. But I would think that the initial and overarching standards would simply be those in accordance with the general standards of discourse, such as the principle of non-contradiction. Thus, for instance, Gamwell's claim that Kant's position falls into self-contradiction should be assessed accordingly.

But can theology accept and abide, MacIntyre might continue, "the indefinite continuation of our present more or less irreducible pluralism," as Ogden describes it? MacIntyre's answer is no; his strategy is therefore to retreat into the more hospitable confines of one's own tradition, preparing to fight another day via the indirect competition among traditions. I agree that theology cannot accept irreducible pluralism as the final theoretical word, if one means by this accepting a fundamental inability to adjudicate among competing metaphysical and theological claims. I do not think that Ogden himself would finally subscribe to this view either. In fact, the tone of his 1963 book *The Reality of God* is one that clearly seeks to change the intellectual and cultural climate concerning the understanding of God and the social location of theology.

In that work, he unequivocally seeks and demands "a new Christian theism," one that can coherently affirm both the reality of God and modern secularity.[42] Perhaps one might conjecture that Ogden has become more pessimistic over time, abandoning his earlier hope of working toward a new consensus and coming instead to accept an irreducible pluralism as the inescapable human condition. Yet, I do not think he has taken such a turn. Rather, in the extended passage above, his operative point is that we have no reason to expect a *complete* mutual confirmation between philosophy and theology; no reason to expect a *total or perfect* consensus. This recognition, however, precludes neither working toward *greater* mutual confirmation nor seeking to foster a *growing* consensus over the long run within the formal commitments of modernity. Since the ideal of achieving mutual consensus is presupposed in the very act of making a claim itself, one should not abandon the pursuit of its actualization in the face of indefinite setbacks. So, with Ogden, I would assert that theology can weather the indefinite condition of irreducible pluralism in practice if, at the same time, it denies it in principle and continues to work explicitly toward building a new consensus. What is interesting about MacIntyre is that he is so averse to the condition of prolonged pluralism. On the one hand, he is willing to accept the idea that validating the truth claims and superiority of a particular tradition will take an indefinitely long time, via the indirect and ongoing competition among traditions. Yet, on the other hand, he simultaneously insists that theological voices must speak from within the confines of a distinct and authoritative tradition—a condition closer to homogeneity than pluralism. In short, he concludes that theology cannot truly speak its mind and stay afloat in the middle of the open and pluralistic waters of modernity. But I would argue again that this conclusion stems from his underlying acceptance of the modern aversion to metaphysics. Given this assumption, coupled with his affirmation of theistic convictions, MacIntyre sees no other course of action for theology except to retreat from the open waters of modern secularity into the backwaters of tradition-dependent inquiry.[43]

42. Ogden, *Reality of God*, 52.
43. As we saw earlier, Porter suggests that MacIntyre shares some noteworthy similarities with Peirce. Yet, whatever similarities they may or may not share, it seems to me that Peirce finally affirms the openness of modern discourse much more than does MacIntyre. "The real," says Peirce, "is that which, sooner or later, information and reasoning would finally result in, and which is therefore independent of the vagaries of me

Let me add one important observation before closing. Christian theology's commitment to a university within the parameters of modern secularity is due, finally, to the critical recognition that Christianity may not be true. If the truth sets us free, then a commitment to truth requires a commitment to wherever truth may lead us. In Ogden's terms, this recognition draws on the key theological distinction between "appropriateness" (determining what is appropriate to Christian faith) and "credibility" (determining whether Christian faith is publicly true or credible).[44] Thus any public consensus that one seeks to achieve in the long run—regarding the question of God or human existence—may or may not turn out to be in concert with (or appropriate to) Christian faith. In other words, the reason for insisting on a university constituted by the modern commitment is the same reason for insisting on a body politic constituted by religious freedom, namely, that truth can be critically discerned only by way of argument.

Final Reflections

At the end of the day, MacIntyre might suggest that what I have really offered over these many pages is mostly a narrative about what has gone

---

and you. Thus, the very origin of the conception of reality shows that this conception essentially involves the notion of a COMMUNITY *without definite limits*, and capable of a definite increase of knowledge" (italics added). Peirce, "Some Consequences of Four Incapacities," 69. MacIntyre clearly emphasizes the first and third elements here, namely, that knowledge of reality is achieved within community and that such a community is capable of a definite increase of knowledge. I, however, want to point to the second element, which holds that this community is without definite limits. This is where Peirce swims out into the open waters of modern inquiry rather than opting for the defined limits of tradition-dependent inquiry. MacIntyre would admit that this community is without limits over time (diachronic), but he insists that it is narrowly limited at any given point in time (synchronic). In contrast, I would suggest that Peirce means without definite limits in both senses. To be sure, the process of inquiry and the process of validating one's claims do take place within a community. Yet, the key point is that it is a community without narrow limits. Peirce's community of inquiry is open to all who seek to test claims by the standards of reason and common experience; it is not narrowly defined in terms of a specific tradition. And yes, it must be a community capable of increasing knowledge. But, as I have argued, such an increase can take place within an open community or liberal university if all the relevant questions, i.e., metaphysical and theological, are deemed susceptible to rational inquiry and consensus. Peirce recognizes that consensus in such an open community may be indefinitely postponed, thus leading to a present condition of irreducible pluralism. Yet, it is a *de facto* pluralism, not a *de jure* one. See also Peirce, "How to Make Our Ideas Clear," 133.

44. See Ogden, *Point of Christology*, 4.

wrong in modern theology. What I have really been up to, he might say, is an attempt to outnarrate other accounts in explaining the marginalization of modern theology. In some ways, this is true; I have sought to offer a more convincing account of what has gone wrong in modern and contemporary theology and what it must do to change course. Yet, in offering a metaphysical reading of the situation, I have never lost sight of the fact that metaphysical claims and remedies can never be strictly validated by narrative as such. On the contrary, metaphysical claims require corresponding forms of validation, including especially those that are a priori. Hence, I have sought to offer and analyze philosophical and theological arguments along the way to support my thesis. As noted at the outset, the case that I make here points beyond itself to the need for the difficult but essential work of metaphysical inquiry itself.

If I am mistaken about the viability of the metaphysical enterprise, if it is indeed a dead-end that leads nowhere, then I am persuaded that the world of the twenty-first century will continue to be stuck in ongoing public conflict between secularistic tendencies and religiously authoritarian forces. Neither side can abide the implications of the other: persons of religious faith cannot abide the privatization or neglect of religious convictions in seeking truth about reality or in seeking to influence the affairs of the world; alternatively, persons who affirm the autonomy of modern secularity cannot abide public policies and broad cultural influences that are grounded finally in appeals to the authority of special revelation and tradition. In short, reason and faith will continue to be viewed as antithetical alternatives, like astronomy and astrology. Non-metaphysical proposals to remedy this situation, such as those offered by MacIntyre, Hauerwas, and Stout, fail in the end precisely because they do not adequately address the underlying metaphysical claims made by religions themselves. For to assert the reality of God is finally to make a metaphysical claim, one that demands and deserves direct and sustained intellectual and existential attention.

Yet, if I am correct, if a reconsideration of the metaphysical enterprise can indeed break through the modern roadblock and lead to a new appreciation and understanding of metaphysics, then the possibility of integrating reason and faith is a possibility that could turn culture away from the current, intractable, zero-sum conflict between the voices of secularism and religion. This is by no means to say that everyone will hold the same ultimate convictions or view them in the same way. But it does suggest that central religious claims, such as claims about the reality of God, would no longer be widely viewed as rationally irredeemable and incurably heteronomous. On the contrary, meaningful rational inquiry could and would need to occur concerning such claims and liberal arts education could and would need to incorporate such inquiry. To catalyze such a change, I have argued that theology must take up its metaphysical mantle and seek to make its own metaphysical claims intelligible and credible to the academy, church, and wider public. For again, as Loomer rightly notes, "we shall not have better universities until we have better theology, and . . . we shall not have better theology until we have better universities." And likewise, "we shall not have better universities until we have better churches, and . . . we shall not have better churches until we have better universities."[45] In sum, only by seeking personal integrity (of mind, body, and spirit) and social integrity (of religion and public life) can we live holistically and authentically in relation to the ultimate integrity of the divine reality.

---

45. Loomer, "Religion and the Mind of the University," 168.

Bibliography

Albanese, Catherine L. "Introduction: Awash in a Sea of Metaphysics." *Journal of the American Academy of Religion* 75 (2007) 582–88.
Angier, Natalie. "The Dance of Evolution, Or How Art Got its Start." *New York Times*, Science Section, November 27, 2007.
Apel, Karl-Otto. "The Communication Community as the Transcendental Presupposition for the Social Sciences." In *Towards a Transformation of Philosophy*. Translated by Glyn Adey and David Frisby. London: Routledge & Kegan Paul, 1980.
Aquinas, Thomas. *The Summa Theologica*, vol. 1. Translated by Fathers of the English Dominican Province, revised by Daniel J. Sullivan. University of Chicago Great Books Series. Chicago: Encyclopaedia Britannica, 1952.
Audi, Robert. *The Architecture of Reason: The Structure and Substance of Rationality*. Oxford: Oxford University Press, 2001.
———. "Theology, Science, and Ethics in Gustafson's Theocentric Ethics." In *James M. Gustafson's Theocentric Ethics: Interpretations and Assessments*, edited by Harlan R. Beckley and Charles M. Swezey, 159–85. Macon, GA: Mercer University Press, 1988.
Bangert, Byron. *Consenting to God and Nature: Toward a Theocentric, Naturalistic, Theological Ethics*. Princeton Theological Monograph Series 55. Eugene, OR: Pickwick, 2006.
Barth, Karl. *Church Dogmatics*. 14 volumes. Translated by G.W. Bromiley. Edited by G. W. Bromiley and T. F. Torrance. Edinburgh: T. & T. Clark, 1975.
Bellantoni, Lisa. *Moral Progress: A Process Critique of MacIntyre*. Albany: State University of New York Press, 2000.
Bernstein, Richard J. *Beyond Objectivism and Relativism: Science, Hermeneutics, and Praxis*. Philadelphia: University of Pennsylvania Press, 1985.
Bingham, June. *Courage to Change: An Introduction to the Life and Thought of Reinhold Niebuhr*. New York: Scribners, 1961. Reprint, University Press of America, 1992.
Bonjour, Laurence. *In Defense of Pure Reason: A Rationalist Account of A Priori Justification*. Cambridge Studies in Philosophy. Cambridge: Cambridge University Press, 1998.
Breitenberg, E. Harold, Jr. "To Tell the Truth: Will the Real Public Theology Please Stand Up? *Journal of the Society of Christian Ethics* 23.2 (2003) 55–96.
Brandom, Robert. *Articulating Reasons: An Introduction to Inferentialism*. Cambridge, MA: Harvard University Press, 2000.
———. *Making it Explicit: Reasoning, Representing, and Discursive Commitment*. Cambridge, MA: Harvard University Press, 1994.

Brown, Robert McAfee, editor. *The Essential Reinhold Niebuhr: Selected Essays and Addresses*. Edited and introduced by Robert McAfee Brown. New Haven: Yale University Press, 1986.

Capetz, Paul E. *God: A Brief History*. Minneapolis: Fortress, 2003.

Cavell, Stanley. *The Claim of Reason*. Oxford: Oxford University Press, 1979.

Caygill, Howard. *A Kant Dictionary*. Oxford: Blackwell, 1995.

Clayton, Philip. *The Problem of God in Modern Thought*. Grand Rapids: Eerdmans, 2000.

Colapietro, Vincent. "Introduction to Charles Sanders Peirce." In *Pragmatism and Classical American Philosophy: Essential Readings and Interpretive Essays*, 2nd ed., edited by John J. Stuhr, 43–54. Oxford: Oxford University Press, 2000.

Copleston, Frederick. *A History of Philosophy*. Vol. 2, *Medieval Philosophy*. New York: Doubleday, 1993.

Coupland, Douglas. *Life After God*. New York: Simon & Schuster, 1994.

Coyne, Jerry A. "Seeing and Believing." *The New Republic*, February 4, 2009.

Cross, Richard. *Duns Scotus*. Great Medieval Thinkers Series. Oxford: Oxford University Press, 1999.

Davidson, Donald. "A Coherence Theory of Truth and Knowledge." In *Truth and Interpretation: Perspectives on the Philosophy of Donald Davidson*, edited by Ernest LePore, 307–19. Oxford: Basil Blackwell, 1986.

———. *Inquiries into Truth and Interpretation*. Oxford: Clarendon, 1984.

———. "On the Very Idea of a Conceptual Scheme." Chap. 13 in *Inquiries into Truth and Interpretation*. Oxford: Clarendon Press, 1984.

Descartes, René. *A Discourse on Method*. In *The Rationalists*, translated by John Veitch, 35–96. New York: Anchor, 1974.

———. *Meditations on the First Philosophy*. In *The Rationalists*, translated by John Veitch, 97–175. New York: Anchor, 1974.

Dewey, John. *A Common Faith*. New Haven: Yale University Press, 1934.

———. *The Quest for Certainty: A Study of the Relation of Knowledge and Action*. The Gifford Lectures 1929. Capricorn Books edition. New York: Putnam, 1960.

Dunfee, Susan. "The Sin of Hiding: A Feminist Critique of Reinhold Niebuhr's Account of the Sin of Pride." *Soundings* 65 (1982) 316–27.

Feuerbach, Ludwig. *The Essence of Christianity*. Translated by George Eliot. New York: Harper Torchbooks, 1957.

Fish, Stanley. "Liberalism and Secularism: One and the Same." Op-ed. *New York Times*, September 2, 2007. http://fish.blogs.nytimes.com/2007/09/02.

Fox, Richard Wightman. *Reinhold Niebuhr: A Biography*. New York: Pantheon, 1985.

Freud, Sigmund. *The Future of an Illusion*. Translated and edited by James Strachey. New York: Norton, 1961.

Fuller, Thomas. "Europe Debates Whether to Admit God Union." *New York Times*, February 5, 2003.

Gadamer, Hans-Georg. *The Enigma of Health: The Art of Healing in a Scientific Age*. Translated by Jason Geiger and Nicholas Walker. Stanford: Stanford University Press, 1996.

———. *Truth and Method*. 2nd rev. ed. Translated and revised by Joel Weinsheimer and Donald G. Marshall. New York: Continuum, 1997.

Gaddis, John Lewis. *The Landscape of History: How Historians Map the Past*. Oxford: Oxford University Press, 2002.

Gamwell, Franklin I. *Beyond Preference: Liberal Theories of Independent Associations.* Chicago: University of Chicago Press, 1984.

———. "Comment on Jeffrey Stout, *Democracy and Tradition*." Paper presented at the University of Chicago, February 2005.

———. *Democracy on Purpose: Justice and the Reality of God.* Washington, DC: Georgetown University Press, 2000.

———. *The Divine Good: Modern Moral Theory and the Necessity of God.* Foreword by David Tracy. San Francisco: HarperCollins, 1990.

———. "The Metaphysics of Democracy." Unpublished paper, 2008.

———. "Moral Realism and Religion." *Journal of Religion* 73 (1993) 475–95.

———. "Of Time and Purpose." *Criterion*: University of Chicago Divinity School 43.2 (2004) 28–31 and 38.

———. "On Metaphysical Necessity." Unpublished paper, 2005.

———. "On the Loss of Theism." In *Iris Murdoch and the Search for Human Goodness*, edited by Maria Antonaccio and William Schweiker, 171–89. Chicago: University of Chicago Press, 1996.

———. "Speaking of God After Aquinas." *Journal of Religion* 81 (2001) 185–210.

———. *Politics as a Christian Vocation: Faith and Democracy Today.* Cambridge: Cambridge University Press, 2005.

———. "Theism and Political Theory Beyond Reinhold Niebuhr." PhD diss., University of Chicago, 1973.

Garber, Daniel. "Religion and Science, Faith and Reason: Some Pascalian Reflections." *Criterion*: University of Chicago Divinity School 41.1 (2002) 2–9, 36–38.

Geertz, Clifford. *The Interpretations of Culture.* New York: Basic, 1973.

Gerrish, Brian A. "Theology within the Limits of Piety Alone: Schleiermacher and Calvin's Notions of God." In *The Old Protestantism and the New: Essays on the Reformation Heritage*, 196–207. Edinburgh: T. & T. Clark, 1982.

Gibson, Lydialyle Gibson. "Mirrored Emotion." *University of Chicago Magazine* 98.4 (2006) 34–39.

Gilkey, Langdon. *On Niebuhr: A Theological Study.* Chicago: University of Chicago Press, 2001.

Graham, Gordon. "MacIntyre on History and Philosophy." In *Alasdair MacIntyre*, edited by Mark C. Murphy, 10–37. Cambridge: Cambridge University Press, 2003.

Greggs, Tom. "Bringing Barth's Critique of Religion to the Inter-faith Table." *Journal of Religion* 88 (2008) 75–94.

Griffin, David Ray. *Reenchantment without Supernaturalism: A Process Philosophy of Religion.* Ithaca, NY: Cornell University Press, 2001.

Gustafson, James M. *Can Ethics Be Christian?* Chicago: University of Chicago Press, 1975.

———. *Ethics from a Theocentric Perspective.* 2 vols. Chicago: University of Chicago Press, 1981–84.

———. *An Examined Faith: The Grace of Self-Doubt.* Minneapolis: Fortress, 2004.

———. *Protestant and Roman Catholic Ethics: Prospects for Rapprochement.* Chicago: University of Chicago Press, 1978.

———. "Response to Critics." *Journal of Religious Ethics* 13 (1985) 185–209.

———. "Say Something Theological!" In *Moral Discernment in the Christian Life: Essays in Theological Ethics*, 85–97. Edited and with an introduction by Theo A.

Boer and Paul E. Capetz. Louisville: Westminster John Knox, 2007. Originally presented as the Nora and Edward Ryerson Lecture at the University of Chicago, April 28, 1981. The University of Chicago printed limited copies of the lecture.

———. *A Sense of the Divine: The Natural Environment from a Theocentric Perspective.* Cleveland: Pilgrim, 1994.

Gustavsson, Roger. "Hauerwas's *With the Grain of the Universe* and the Barthian Outlook: A Few Observations." *Journal of Religious Ethics* 35 (2007) 25–86.

Habermas, Jürgen. "Ethics, Politics and History: An Interview with Jürgen Habermas." Conducted by Jean-Marc Ferry. Translated by Stephen K. White. *Philosophy and Social Criticism* 14 (1988) 433–39.

———. *Justification and Application: Remarks on Discourse Ethics.* Translated by Ciaran P. Cronin. Cambridge, MA: MIT Press, 1993.

———. *The Theory of Communicative Action.* 2 vols. Translated by Thomas McCarthy. Boston: Beacon, 1984–1987.

Harak, G. Simon. Review of *The Recovery of Virtue*, by Jean Porter. *Theological Studies* 52 (1991) 581–82.

Hartshorne, Charles. *Anselm's Discovery: A Re-Examination of the Ontological Proof for God's Existence.* La Salle, IL: Open Court, 1965.

———. *Aquinas to Whitehead: Seven Centuries of Metaphysics.* The Aquinas Lectures 1976. Milwaukee: Marquette University Publications, 1976.

———. *Creative Synthesis and Philosophic Method.* La Salle, IL: Open Court, 1970.

———. *The Divine Relativity: A Social Conception of God.* New Haven: Yale University Press, 1948.

———. *Insights and Oversights of Great Thinkers: An Evaluation of Western Philosophy.* Albany: State University of New York Press, 1983.

———. *A Natural Theology for Our Time.* La Salle, IL: Open Court, 1967.

———. *Omnipotence and Other Theological Mistakes.* Albany: State University of New York, 1984.

———. *Whitehead's Philosophy: Selected Essays, 1935–1970.* Lincoln, NE: University of Nebraska Press, 1972.

———. *The Zero Fallacy: And Other Essays in Neoclassical Philosophy.* Edited by Mohammad Valady. La Salle, IL: Open Court, 1997.

Hartshorne, Charles, and William L. Reese. *Philosophers Speak of God.* Chicago: University of Chicago Press, 1953. Reprinted, University of Chicago/Midway, 1976.

Hartt, Julian N. "Encounter and Inference in our Awareness of God." In *The God Experience: Essays in Hope*, edited by Joseph P. Whelan, SJ. New York: Newman, 1971.

Hauerwas, Stanley. *After Christendom? How the Church is to Behave if Freedom, Justice, and a Christian Nation Are Bad Ideas.* Nashville: Abingdon, 1991.

———. *Character and the Christian Life: A Study in Theological Ethics.* San Antonio: Trinity University Press, 1975.

———. "Christian Ethics in America (and the JRE): A Report on a Book I Will Not Write." *Journal of Religious Ethics* 25 (1998) 57–76.

———. *A Community of Character: Toward a Constructive Christian Social Ethic.* Notre Dame: University of Notre Dame Press, 1981.

———. "The Demands of a Truthful Story: Ethics and the Pastoral Task." *Chicago Studies* 21 (1982) 59–71.

---. "Murdochian Muddles: Can We Get Through Them if God Does Not Exist?" In *Iris Murdoch and the Search for Human Goodness*, edited by Maria Antonaccio and William Schweiker, 190–208. Chicago: University of Chicago Press, 1996.

---. "On Keeping Theological Ethics Theological." Chap. 2 in *Against the Nations: War and Survival in a Liberal Society*. Notre Dame, IN: University of Notre Dame Press, 1992. Originally published in *Revisions: Changing Perspectives in Moral Philosophy*, edited by Stanley Hauerwas and Alasdair MacIntyre, 16–42. Notre Dame, IN: University of Notre Dame Press, 1983.

---. *The Peaceable Kingdom: A Primer in Christian Ethics*. Notre Dame, IN: University of Notre Dame Press, 1983.

---. *The State of the University: Academic Knowledges and the Knowledge of God*. Oxford: Blackwell, 2007.

---. "The Truth About God: The Decalogue as Condition for Truthful Speech." *Neue Zeitschrift für Systematische Theologie und Religionsphilosophie* 40 (1998) 17–39.

---. *Wilderness Wanderings: Probing Twentieth-Century Theology and Philosophy*. Boulder, CO: Westview, 1997.

---. "Will the Real Sectarian Stand Up?" *Theology Today* 44 (1987) 87–94.

---. *With the Grain of the Universe: The Church's Witness and Natural Theology*. The Gifford Lectures, University of St. Andrews, 2001. Grand Rapids: Brazos, 2001.

Hauerwas, Stanley, and William H. Willimon. *Resident Aliens: Life in the Christian Colony*. Nashville: Abingdon, 1989.

Hedley, Douglas. "Should Divinity Overcome Metaphysics? Reflections on John Milbank's Theology Beyond Secular Reason and Confessions of a Cambridge Platonist." *Journal of Religion* 80 (2000) 271–98.

Hegel, G. W. F. Introduction to *The Encyclopedia of the Philosophical Sciences in Outline*. In *Nineteenth-Century Philosophy*, edited by Forrest E. Baird and Walter Kaufman, 48–58. Philosophical Classics, 3rd ed., vol. 4. Upper Saddle, NJ: Prentice Hall, 2003.

---. *On Art, Religion, Philosophy: Introductory Lectures to the Realm of Absolute Spirit*. Edited and with an introduction by J. Glenn Gray. New York: Harper & Row, 1970.

---. *The Philosophy of Right*. Translated by T. M. Knox. Oxford: Clarendon, 1952. Reprinted 1967.

---. *Reason in History: A General Introduction to the Study of History*. Translated and with an introduction by Robert S. Hartman. Indianapolis: Bobbs-Merrill, 1953. Reprinted 1983.

Herdt, Jennifer. "Alasdair MacIntyre's 'Rationality of Traditions' and Tradition-Transcendental Standards of Justification." *Journal of Religion* 78 (1998) 524–36.

Heron, Alasdair I. C. *A Century of Protestant Theology*. Philadelphia: Westminster, 1980.

Hibbs, Thomas. *Aquinas, Ethics, and Philosophy of Religion: Metaphysics and Practice*. Bloomington, IN: Indiana University Press, 2007.

Hösle, Vittorio. "The Idea of a Rationalistic Philosophy of Religion and its Challenges." *Jahrbuch für Religionsphilosophie* 6 (2007) 159–81.

———. *Objective Idealism, Ethics and Politics*. Notre Dame, IN: University of Notre Dame Press, 1998.

Hume, David. *Dialogues Concerning Natural Religion*. Edited with an introduction and notes by Martin Bell. London: Penguin, 1990.

———. *An Enquiry Concerning Human Understanding*. In *The Empiricists*, 307–430. New York: Anchor, 1974.

———. *A Treatise of Human Nature*. Abridged and edited by John P. Wright, Robert Stecker, and Gary Fuller. London: Everyman, 2003.

Hunsinger, George. *Disruptive Grace: Studies in the Theology of Karl Barth*. Grand Rapids: Eerdmans, 2000.

———. *How to Read Karl Barth: The Shape of His Theology*. Oxford: Oxford University Press, 1991.

Jacoby, Susan. "One Nation, Under Secularism." Op-ed. *New York Times*, January 8, 2004.

James, William. *Pragmatism*. Cambridge, MA: Harvard University Press, 1975.

———. "The Types of Philosophic Thinking." In *Pragmatism and Classical American Philosophy: Essential Readings and Interpretive Essays*, 2nd ed., edited by John J. Stuhr, 151–61. Oxford: Oxford University Press, 2000.

———. "What Pragmatism Means." In *Essays in Pragmatism*. Edited with an introduction by Alburey Castell, 141–58. New York: Hafner, 1948.

———. "The Will to Believe." In *Essays in Pragmatism*. Edited with an introduction by Alburey Castell, 88–109. New York: Hafner, 1948.

Jeffreys, Derek S. Review of *Nature as Reason: A Thomistic Theory of Natural Law*, by Jean Porter. *Journal of Religion* 86 (2006) 487–89.

Kallenberg, Brad J. "The Strange New World in the Church: A Review Essay of *With the Grain of the Universe* by Stanley Hauerwas." *Journal of Religious Ethics* 32 (2004) 197–217.

Kant, Immanuel. *Critique of Pure Reason*. Unabridged edition. Translated by Norman Kemp Smith. New York: St. Martin's, 1965.

———. *Groundwork of the Metaphysics of Morals*. Translated and analyzed by H. J. Paton. New York: Harper & Row, 1964.

———. *Lectures on Philosophical Theology*. Translated by Allen W. Wood and Gertrude M. Clark with an introduction and notes by Allen W. Wood. Ithaca, NY: Cornell University Press, 1978.

———. *The One Possible Basis for a Demonstration of the Existence of God*. Translated and with an introduction by Gordon Treash. New York: Abaris, 1979. Reprinted by the University of Nebraska Press, 1994.

———. "What is Enlightenment?" In *On History*. Edited with an introduction by Lewis White Beck. Translated by Lewis White Beck, Robert E. Anchor, and Emil L. Fackenheim, 3–10. New York: Macmillan, 1963.

Kaufman, Gordon D. "How is *God* to be Understood in a Theocentric Ethics?" In *James M. Gustafson's Theocentric Ethics: Interpretations and Assessments*, edited by Harlan R. Beckley and Charles M. Swezey, 13–37. Macon, GA: Mercer University Press, 1988.

Knight, John Allan. "Why Not Davidson: Neopragmatism in Religion and the Coherence of Alternative Conceptual Schemes." *Journal of Religion* 88 (2008) 159–89.

Kolata, Gina. "Lactic Acid is Not Muscles' Foe, It's Fuel." *New York Times*, Science Section, May 16, 2006.

Körner, Stephan. *Kant*. New Haven: Yale University Press, 1982.

Kuhn, Thomas S. *The Structure of Scientific Revolutions*. 2nd ed. Chicago: University of Chicago Press. 1970.

Leclerc, Ivor. *Whitehead's Metaphysics: An Introductory Exposition*. Atlantic Highlands, NJ: Humanities, 1958.

Latourette, Kenneth Scott. *A History of Christianity*, vol. 1, *Beginnings to 1500*. New York: Harper & Row, 1953.

Lauritzen, Paul. "Is 'Narrative' Really a Panacea? The Use of 'Narrative' in the Work of Metz and Hauerwas." *Journal of Religion* 67 (1987) 322–39.

Leibniz, G. W. F. *Discourse on Metaphysics*. In *The Rationalists*, 409–53. New York: Anchor, 1974.

———. *The Monadology*. In *The Rationalists*, 455–71. New York: Anchor, 1974.

Levinson, Henry Samuel. "Let Us Be Saints If We Can: A Reflection on Stanley Hauerwas's *With the Grain of the Universe*." *Journal of Religious Ethics* 32 (2004) 219–34.

Livingston, James C., Francis Schüssler Fiorenza with Sarah Coakley and James H. Evans, Jr. *Modern Christian Thought*. 2 vols. 2nd ed. Upper Saddle River, NJ: Prentice Hall, 1997–2000.

Loomer, Bernard M. "Religion and the Mind of the University." In *Liberal Learning and Religion*, edit. by Amos N. Wilder, 147–68. New York: Harper & Brothers, 1951.

Lott, Micah. "Reasonably Traditional: Self-Contradiction and Self-Reference in Alasdair MacIntyre's Account of Tradition-Based Rationality." *Journal of Religious Ethics* 30 (2002) 315–39.

Lovin, Robin. *Reinhold Niebuhr and Christian Realism*. Cambridge: Cambridge University Press, 1995.

———. "Reinhold Niebuhr in Contemporary Scholarship: A Review Essay." *Journal of Religious Ethics* 31 (2003) 489–505.

MacIntyre, Alasdair. *After Virtue: A Study in Moral Theory*. 2nd ed. London: Duckworth, 1985.

———. "Atheism and Morals." In *The Religious Significance of Atheism*, by Alasdair MacIntyre and Paul Ricoeur, 31–55. New York: Columbia University Press, 1969.

———. *Dependent Rational Animals: Why Human Beings Need the Virtues*. Chicago: Open Court, 1999.

———. *Difficulties in Christian Belief*. Naperville, IL: SCM, 1959.

———. "The Fate of Theism." In *The Religious Significance of Atheism*, by Alasdair MacIntyre and Paul Ricoeur, 3–29. New York: Columbia University Press, 1969.

———. *First Principles, Final Ends and Contemporary Philosophical Issues*. Milwaukee: Marquette University Press, 1990.

———. *Three Rival Versions of Moral Enquiry: Encyclopaedia, Geneaology, and Tradition*. The Gifford Lectures, University of Edinburgh, 1988. Notre Dame, IN: University of Notre Dame Press, 1990.

———. *Whose Justice? Which Rationality?* Notre Dame, IN: University of Notre Dame Press, 1988.

Malcolm, Lois. "Radical, orthodox." *Christian Century*, October 25, 2000.

Malotky, Daniel James. "Reinhold Niebuhr's Paradox: Groundwork for Social Responsibility." *Journal of Religious Ethics* 31 (2003) 101–23.

Martin, R. M. "On the Language of Theology: Hartshorne and Quine." Chap. 3 in *Existence and Actuality: Conversations with Charles Hartshorne*. Edited by John B. Cobb, Jr. and Franklin I. Gamwell. Chicago: University of Chicago Press, 1984.

Marty, Martin E. "Do-Gooders." *Sightings*. September 22, 2003. http://www.sightings@listhost.uchicago.edu.

———. "Tipping the Plate." *Sightings*. November 17, 2003. http://www.sightings@listhost.uchicago.edu.

McCarthy, Eugene J., and Keith C. Burris. "The Singular Piety of Politics." Op-ed. *New York Times*, August 31, 2000.

McGrath, Alister E., editor. *The Christian Theology Reader*. 3rd ed. Oxford: Blackwell, 2007.

Meacham, Jon. "The God Debate." *Newsweek*. April 9, 2007.

Menand, Louis. *The Metaphysical Club*. New York: Farrar, Straus & Giroux, 2001.

Meyer, William J. "Ethics, Theism, and Metaphysics: An Analysis of the Theocentric Ethics of James Gustafson." *International Journal for Philosophy of Religion* 41 (1997) 149–78. Due to some printing errors, see also the later corrections in Corrigenda, *International Journal for Philosophy of Religion* 42 (1998) 196.

———. "On Keeping Theological Ethics Theological: An Alternative to Hauerwas's Diagnosis and Prescription." *Annual of the Society of Christian Ethics* 19 (1999) 21–45.

———. "The Kantian Remnant: An Analysis of the Remaining Kantian Element in Barth's Theology." Unpublished paper, University of Chicago, Spring 1988.

———. "The Relation of Theism to Ethics: A Comparison of the Views of Reinhold Niebuhr and Jürgen Habermas." PhD diss., University of Chicago, 1992.

———. Review of *The Enigma of Health: The Art of Healing in a Scientific Age*, by Hans-Georg Gadamer. *Nature Medicine* 2 (1996) 1043–44.

———. Review of *Is There Only One True Religion or Are There Many?* by Schubert M. Ogden and *A World Theology: The Central Spiritual Reality of Humankind*, by N. Ross Reat and Edmund F. Perry. *Religion* 29 (1999) 188–91.

Milbank, John. *Being Reconciled: Ontology and Pardon*. London: Routledge, 2003.

———. "The Invocation of Clio: A Response." *Journal of Religious Ethics* 33 (2005) 3–44.

———. "Preface to the Second Edition: Between Liberalism and Positivism." *Theology and Social Theory: Beyond Secular Reason*. 2nd edition. Oxford: Blackwell, 2006.

———. "The Programme of Radical Orthodoxy." In *Radical Orthodoxy? A Catholic Enquiry*, edited by Laurence Paul Hemming, 33–45. Burlington, VT: Ashgate, 2000.

———. *Theology and Social Theory: Beyond Secular Reason*. Oxford: Blackwell, 1990.

———. *The Word Made Strange: Theology, Language, Culture*. Oxford: Blackwell, 1997.

Milbank, John, Graham Ward, and Catherine Pickstock. "Suspending the Material: The Turn of Radical Orthodoxy." Introduction to *Radical Orthodoxy: A New*

Theology. Edited by John Milbank, Catherine Pickstock, and Graham Ward. London: Routledge, 1999.

Miller, Lisa. "BeliefWatch: Ivy League." *Newsweek*, January 22, 2007.

Mother Teresa. *Come be my Light: The Private Writings of the Saint of Calcutta*. Edited with an introduction by Brian Kolodiejchuk, M.C. New York: Doubleday. 2007.

Murdoch, Iris. *Metaphysics as a Guide to Morals*. New York: Penguin, 1993.

———. *The Sovereignty of Good*. London: Routledge, 1970. Reprinted, 1989.

Niebuhr, H. Richard. *Christ and Culture*. New York: Harper, 1951.

———. *The Meaning of Revelation*. New York: Macmillan, 1941; Macmillan's paperback edition, 1960.

———. *Radical Monotheism and Western Culture: With Supplementary Essays*. New York: Harper & Row, 1943.

Niebuhr, Reinhold. *The Children of Light and the Children of Darkness: A Vindication of Democracy and a Critique of its Traditional Defense*. New York: Scribner's, 1960.

———. *Christian Realism and Political Problems*. New York: Scribner's, 1953.

———. "Coherence, Incoherence, and Christian Faith." In *The Essential Reinhold Niebuhr: Selected Essays and Addresses*, edited and introduced by Robert McAfee Brown, 218–36. New Haven: Yale University Press, 1986.

———. *Does Civilization Need Religion?* New York: Macmillan, 1927.

———. *Faith and History: A Comparison of Christian and Modern Views of History*. New York: Charles Scribner's Sons, 1949. Reprinted Scribner/Macmillan Hudson River edition, 1987.

———. *An Interpretation of Christian Ethics*. New York: Harper & Row, 1935; Seabury paperback edition, 1979.

———. *Moral Man and Immoral Society: A Study in Ethics and Politics*. New York: Scribner's, 1932.

———. "Mystery and Meaning." Chap. 9 in *Pious and Secular America*. New York: Scribner's, 1958. Reprinted, Fairfield, NJ: Kelley, 1977.

———. *The Nature and Destiny of Man*. 2 vols. New York: Scribner's, 1941–43. Reprinted 1964.

———. "Religion and Action." In *Science and Man*, edited by Ruth Nanda Anshen, 44–64. New York: Harcourt, 1942.

———. "The Truth in Myths." In *The Nature of Religious Experience*, edited by J. S. Bixler, R. L. Calhoun, and Reinhold Niebuhr, 117–35. New York: Harper, 1937.

Oakley, Francis. "The Absolute and Ordained Power of God in Sixteenth-and Seventeenth-Century Theology." *Journal of the History of Ideas* 59 (1998) 437–61.

Ogden, Schubert M. *Christ Without Myth: A Study Based on the Theology of Rudolf Bultmann*. New York: Harper & Row, 1961. Reprint Dallas: Southern Methodist University Press, 1991.

———. *Is There Only One True Religion or Are There Many?* Dallas: Southern Methodist University Press, 1992.

———. *On Theology*. San Francisco: Harper & Row, 1986.

———. *The Point of Christology*. San Francisco: Harper & Row, 1982.

———. *The Reality of God: And Other Essays*. New York: Harper & Row, 1963. Reprint, Dallas: Southern Methodist University Press, 1992.

———. "The Task of Philosophical Theology." Chap. 4 in *On Theology*. San Francisco: Harper & Row, 1982.

———. "Theology in the University." Chap. 7 in *On Theology*. San Francisco: Harper & Row, 1982.

———. "Theology Without Metaphysics?" Chap. 6 in *Religion and the End of Metaphysics*, edited by Dewi Z. Phillips and Mario von der Ruhr. Claremont Studies in the Philosophy of Religion, Conference 2006. Tübingen: Mohr Siebeck, 2006.

Overbye, Dennis. "Kissing the Earth Goodbye in About 7.59 Billion Years." Science Section, *New York Times*, March 11, 2008.

Pannenberg, Wolfhart. *An Introduction to Systematic Theology*. Grand Rapids: Eerdmans, 1991.

———. *Metaphysics and the Idea of God*. Translated by Philip Clayton. Grand Rapids: Eerdmans, 1990.

Peirce, Charles S. *Collected Papers of Charles Sanders Peirce*. Vol. 6, *Scientific Metaphysics*. Edited by Charles Hartshorne and Paul Weiss. Cambridge, MA: Harvard University Press, 1935.

———. "The Fixation of Belief." In *Charles S. Peirce: Selected Writings*, edited with an introduction and notes by Philip P. Wiener, 91–112. New York: Dover, 1966.

———. "A Neglected Argument for the Reality of God." In *Charles S. Peirce: Selected Writings*, edited with an introduction and notes by Philip P. Wiener, 358–79. New York: Dover, 1966.

———. "How to Make Our Ideas Clear." In *Charles S. Peirce: Selected Writings*, edited with an introduction and notes by Philip P. Wiener, 113–36. New York: Dover, 1966.

———. "Some Consequences of Four Incapacities." In *Charles S. Peirce: Selected Writings*, edited with an introduction and notes by Philip P. Wiener, 39–72. New York: Dover, 1966.

Perry, Edmund F. See entry below for Reat, N. Ross, and Edmund F. Perry.

Plantinga, Alvin. "A Contemporary Modal Version of the Ontological Argument." In *Philosophy of Religion: Selected Readings*, 2nd ed., edited by Michael Peterson, William Hasker, Bruce Reichenbach, and David Basinger, 170–83. Oxford: Oxford University Press, 2001.

———. "The Reformed Objection to Natural Theology." In *Philosophy of Religion: Selected Readings*, 2nd ed., edited by Michael Peterson, William Hasker, Bruce Reichenbach, and David Basinger, 329–41. Oxford: Oxford University Press, 2001.

———. "The Twin Pillars of Christian Scholarship." In *Seeking Understanding: The Stob Lectures, 1986–1998*, Calvin College and Calvin Theological Seminary, 117–61. Grand Rapids: Eerdmans, 2001.

Plaskow, Judith. *Sex, Sin, and Grace: Women's Experience and the Theologies of Reinhold Niebuhr and Paul Tillich*. Lanham, MD: University Press of America, 1980.

Popper, Karl. *The Logic of Scientific Discovery*. London: Routledge Classics, 2002. Original German ed. 1935, and 1st English ed. 1959.

Porter, Jean. "Christian Ethics and the Concept of Morality: A Historical Inquiry." *Journal of the Society of Christian Ethics* 26.2 (2006) 3–21.

———. "Desire for God: Ground of the Moral Life in Aquinas." *Theological Studies* 47 (1986) 48–68.

———. *Moral Action and Christian Ethics*. New Studies in Christian Ethics. Cambridge: Cambridge University Press, 1995. First paperback edition, 1999.

———. "Moral Ideals and Human Nature." In *Universalism vs. Relativism: Making Moral Judgments in a Changing, Pluralistic, and Threatening World*, edited by Don Browning, 59–78. Lanham, MD: Rowman & Littlefield, 2006.

———. *Natural and Divine Law: Reclaiming Tradition for Christian Ethics*. Foreword by Nicholas Wolterstorff. St. Paul University Series in Ethics. Grand Rapids: Eerdmans, 1999.

———. "Natural Equality: Freedom, Authority and Obedience in Two Medieval Thinkers." *The Annual of the Society of Christian Ethics* 21 (2001) 275–99.

———. *Nature as Reason: A Thomistic Theory of the Natural Law*. Grand Rapids: Eerdmans, 2005.

———. "Openness and Constraint: Moral Reflection as Tradition-guided Inquiry in Alasdair MacIntyre's Recent Works." *Journal of Religion* 73 (1993) 514–36.

———. *The Recovery of Virtue: The Relevance of Aquinas for Christian Ethics*. Louisville, KY: Westminster John Knox, 1990.

———. "The Subversion of Virtue: Acquired and Infused Virtues in the *Summa theologiae*." *The Annual of the Society of Christian Ethics* (1992) 19–41.

Prothero, Stephen. *Religious Literacy: What Every American Needs to Know—and Doesn't*. New York: HarperOne, 2007.

———. "Worshipping in Ignorance." *Chronicle of Higher Education*, March 16, 2007.

Raposa, Michael L. *Peirce's Philosophy of Religion*. Bloomington, IN: Indiana University Press, 1989.

Rawls, John. *Political Liberalism*. Paperback edition with a new introduction and a "reply to Habermas." New York: Columbia University Press, 1996. Original clothbound edition, 1993.

———. *A Theory of Justice*. Cambridge, MA: Harvard University Press, 1971.

Reat, N. Ross, and Edmund F. Perry. *A World Theology: The Central Spiritual Reality of Humankind*. Cambridge: Cambridge University Press, 1991.

Reynolds, Charles. "Conversations with Jeffrey Stout on *Democracy and Tradition*." *Soundings* 87:3–4 (2004) 247–57.

Reynolds, Terrence P. "A Conversation Worth Having: Hauerwas and Gustafson on Substance in Theological Ethics." *Journal of Religious Ethics* 28 (2000) 395–421.

Rice, Daniel F. *Reinhold Niebuhr and John Dewey: An American Odyssey*. Albany: State University of New York Press, 1993.

Rist, John M. *Real Ethics: Reconsidering the Foundations of Morality*. Cambridge: Cambridge University Press, 2002.

Rorty, Richard. "Religion as Conversation-stopper." Chap. 11 in *Philosophy and Social Hope*. New York: Penguin, 1999.

Rushdie, Salman. "Yes, This is About Islam." Op-ed, *New York Times*, November 2, 2001.

Sartre, Jean-Paul. *Being and Nothingness: An Essay on Phenomenological Ontology*. Translated with an introduction by Hazel E. Barnes. New York: Philosophical Library, 1956.

———. *Existentialism and Humanism*. Translated and introduced by Philip Mairet. London: Methuen, 1973.

Schilbrack, Kevin. "The Study of Religion After Davidson." *Method & Theory in the Study of Religion* 14:3–4 (2002) 334–49.

Schneewind, J. B. *The Invention of Autonomy: A History of Modern Moral Philosophy*. Cambridge: Cambridge University Press, 1998.

Smith, James K. A. *Introducing Radical Orthodoxy: Mapping a Post-Secular Theology*. Foreword by John Milbank. Grand Rapids: Baker, 2004.

Smith, Norman Kemp. *A Commentary to Kant's "Critique of Pure Reason."* 2nd ed., revised and enlarged. Atlantic Highlands, NJ: Humanities, 1992.

Staley, Kevin. "Happiness: The Natural End of Man?" *The Thomist* 53 (1989) 215–34.

Starr, Paul. *The Social Transformation of American Medicine*. New York: Basic, 1982.

Stout, Jeffrey. *Democracy and Tradition*. Princeton: Princeton University Press, 2004.

———. *Ethics After Babel: The Language of Morals and their Discontents*. Boston: Beacon, 1988.

———. *The Flight from Authority: Religion, Morality, and the Quest for Autonomy*. Notre Dame, IN: University of Notre Dame Press, 1981.

———. "Radical Interpretation and Pragmatism: Davidson, Rorty, and Brandom on Truth." In *Radical Interpretation of Religion*, edited by Nancy K. Frankenberry, 25–52. Cambridge: Cambridge University Press, 2002.

———. "The Spirit of Democracy and the Rhetoric of Excess." *Journal of Religious Ethics* 35 (2007) 3–21.

———. "The Voice of Theology in Contemporary Culture." In *Religion and America: Spirituality in a Secular Age*, edited by Mary Douglas and Steven M. Tipton, 249–61. Boston: Beacon, 1983.

Sullivan, Andrew. "Goodbye to All That." *Atlantic Monthly*, December 2007.

Taylor, Charles. *A Secular Age*. Cambridge: Harvard University Press, 2007.

Tillich, Paul. *Dynamics of Faith*. New York: Harper & Row, 1957.

———. *Systematic Theology*. 3 vols. Chicago: University of Chicago Press, 1951–63. Reprinted by SCM Press, 1978.

Tinder, Glenn. "Exercising a Christian Intellect." *Christian Century*, July 2, 1997, 626–29.

Toulmin, Stephen E. *The Uses of Argument*. Cambridge: Cambridge University Press, 1958.

Tracy, David. *Blessed Rage for Order*. New York: Seabury, 1975.

———. *The Analogical Imagination: Christian Theology and the Culture of Pluralism*. London: SCM, 1981.

———. Foreword to *The Divine Good: Modern Moral Theory and the Necessity of God*, by Franklin I. Gamwell. San Francisco: HarperCollins, 1990.

Treash, Gordon. "Introduction." In *The One Possible Basis for a Demonstration of the Existence of God*, by Immanuel Kant. Translated and introduction by Gordon Treash. New York: Abaris, 1979. Reprinted by the University of Nebraska Press, 1994.

Van Biema, David. "Mother Teresa's Crisis of Faith." *Time*, August 23, 2007.

Werpehowski, William. *American Protestant Ethics and the Legacy of H. Richard Niebuhr*. Washington, DC: Georgetown University Press, 2002.

Wetzel, James. "Splendid Vices and Secular Virtues: Variations on Milbank's Augustine." *Journal of Religious Ethics* 32 (2004) 271–300.

Whitehead, Alfred N. *Adventures of Ideas*. New York: Macmillan, 1933. 1st Free Press paperback edition. New York: Free, 1967.

———. *Essays in Science and Philosophy*. New York: Philosophical Library, 1948.

———. *The Function of Reason*. Boston: Beacon, 1958.

———. *Modes of Thought*. New York: Macmillan, 1938. 1st Free Press paperback edition. New York: Free, 1968.

———. *Process and Reality: An Essay in Cosmology*. Corrected edition. Edited by David Ray Griffin and Donald W. Sherburne. New York: Macmillan, 1978. First edition, 1929.

———. *Religion in the Making*. Lowell Lectures, 1926. Introduction by Judith A. Jones and glossary by Randall E. Auxier. New York: Fordham University Press, 1996. Originally Macmillan, 1926.

———. *Science and the Modern World*. The Lowell Lectures, 1925. New York: Free, 1925. 1st Free Press paperback edition, 1967.

———. *Symbolism: Its Meaning and Effect*. New York: MacMillan, 1927. Reprinted by Capricorn Books-Putnam's, 1959.

Wills, Garry. *Head and Heart: American Christianities*. New York: Penguin, 2007.

———. "The Day the Enlightenment Went Out." op-ed. *New York Times*. November 4, 2004.

Wolterstorff, Nicholas P. "What New Haven and Grand Rapids Have to Say to Each Other." In *Seeking Understanding: The Stob Lectures, 1986–1998*, Calvin College and Calvin Theological Seminary, 251–93. Grand Rapids: Eerdmans, 2001.

Wood, Allen W. "Translator's Introduction." In *Lectures on Philosophical Theology*, by Immanuel Kant. Translated by Allen W. Wood and Gertrude M. Clark with introduction and notes by Allen W. Wood. Ithaca, NY: Cornell University Press, 1978.

www.ingramcontent.com/pod-product-compliance
Lightning Source LLC
Chambersburg PA
CBHW052109010526
44111CB00036B/1574